Tools *for* Teaching

SECOND EDITION

Barbara Gross Davis

JOSSEY-BASS
A Wiley Imprint
www.josseybass.com

The Jossey-Bass Higher and Adult Education Series

Library of Congress Cataloging-in-Publication Data

Davis, Barbara Gross.
  Tools for teaching/Barbara Gross Davis.—2nd ed.
    p. cm.
  Includes bibliographical references and index.
  ISBN 978-0-7879-6567-9 (pbk.)
  1. College teaching—United States—Handbooks, manuals, etc.   2. Classroom management—United States—Handbooks, manuals, etc.   3. Curriculum planning—United States—Handbooks, manuals, etc.   I. Title.
  LB2331.D37   2009
  378.1'25—dc22

                                                                 2008041906

Printed in the United States of America
FIRST EDITION
PB Printing   10 9 8 7 6 5 4

CONTENTS

Tools for Teaching provides new and experienced faculty in all disciplines with practical, tested strategies for addressing all major aspects of college and university teaching, from planning a course through assigning final grades. Graduate student instructors and teaching assistants will also benefit from the foundational knowledge and research findings described in this book.

This second edition includes twelve new chapters devoted to innovations in classroom technology and current trends on American campuses. In addition, all of the chapters from the first edition have been thoroughly revised to incorporate recent research on college-level teaching and learning.

Certain assumptions about you, the reader, have guided the design and organization of this second edition:

- You teach a course that is primarily face-to-face and use technology for administrative and educational purposes.
- You want to know about specific instructional strategies that faculty members have used successfully and that researchers have found to be effective in developing students' intellectual and cognitive skills.
- You can figure things out for yourself. Once you are presented with the gist of a strategy, you can adapt it to your particular circumstances and needs—or reject it as inappropriate for you and your students.
- You are busy and have little time to read through the burgeoning literature on teaching and learning. You want to be able to quickly locate information and appropriate strategies for improving your teaching and students' learning.

Each chapter contains a brief introduction, a set of general strategies, and concise descriptions of teaching ideas, supported by research, that instructors can adapt and try out. The format lends itself to easy and efficient identification of major points and to quick reading or browsing. Each chapter can be read independently of the others, and the chapters can be read in any order.

Many of the suggestions can be readily implemented; others require planning or modifications in course design. No one instructor could possibly use even half of the ideas—nor would any instructor want to. *Tools for Teaching* is truly a toolbox from which to select and adapt those ideas that match your teaching style and the needs of your students. Indeed, one of the premises of the book is that there are no pat answers, quick fixes, or sure-fire recipes for excellent teaching and optimal learning, only endless ways to improve.

Sources of *Tools for Teaching*

The information in *Tools* comes from many sources: the research literature in higher education on teaching and learning; books published by scholars, researchers, and faculty development experts on effective educational practices; articles on pedagogy by college and university faculty; conversations with and classroom observations of faculty at the University of California, Berkeley; the Web sites of colleges and universities, especially the resources at teaching.berkeley.edu; and local and national listservs devoted to teaching.

I have made every effort to attribute each entry to a published source or to cite a reference that provides greater detail, although the source cited is not necessarily the originator of the strategy. Some tools, though, are part of general lore or reached me without attribution. If I have misinterpreted any findings or conclusions or if I failed to give appropriate credit, I hope readers will contact me so that I can make corrections in a future edition.

Though *Tools* derives from a substantial body of research and theory, the text focuses on practice. For readers who want to know more about the origin and testing of the strategies, the end-of-chapter reference lists provide starting points. Those seeking discussions of theory and philosophy, essays on good teaching, personal reflections about classroom experiences, examination of the teaching persona, case studies on college teaching, or discipline-specific perspectives on teaching will want to look elsewhere to the many excellent books on these topics. For example, see, among others, Bain's analysis (2004) of the teaching practices of nearly one hundred college and university instructors; Lang's personal week-by-week guide (2008) aimed at those embarking upon their first teaching experience; Palmer's exploration (2007) of a teacher's inner landscape and the importance of emotion and spirit in the educational process; and Kalman (2008) for teaching science and engineering, Showalter (2003) for teaching literature, or Buskist and Davis (2005) for teaching psychology.

Organization of *Tools for Teaching*

Tools is designed to be used as a reference book; it is not meant to be read cover to cover. The twelve parts represent, in a roughly chronological sequence, the principal teaching responsibilities and activities of college instructors. The table of contents, index, and internal cross-references should help you locate the material you need. The following overview may also help you decide where to begin.

Part One, "Getting Under Way," addresses planning: designing a new course or revising an existing one, creating a syllabus, preparing for the first days of class, and managing classroom conduct and decorum.

Part Two, "Responding to a Changing Student Body," offers suggestions for working with students who have disabilities, students from ethnic or cultural backgrounds different from your own, and older students returning to school. The last chapter in this part focuses on classes in which students have widely varying academic skills and abilities.

Part Three, "Discussion Strategies," provides ideas for leading a productive discussion, framing challenging questions, and encouraging student participation, both in class and online.

Part Four, "The Large-Enrollment Course," explores aspects of the lecture method: preparing and delivering effective lectures, engaging students and providing for student participation, and maintaining instructional quality with limited resources.

Part Five, "Alternatives and Supplements to Lectures and Discussion," continues the theme of student participation, looking at the advantages of group work and ways to involve students in role playing, case studies, games, virtual worlds, fieldwork, and undergraduate research. Web-based activities are highlighted in this part.

Part Six, "Enhancing Students' Learning and Motivation," provides research-based approaches to helping students become more confident, independent, and self-motivated learners. Informal ways to assess learning and the use of mobile technologies are also described.

Part Seven, "Strengthening Students' Writing and Problem-Solving Skills," describes how instructors in all departments can help students develop their writing skills—and how to do so without spending enormous amounts of time grading and marking students' papers. This part also offers strategies on designing and grading problem sets.

For many faculty members, testing and grading are among the most difficult aspects of teaching. Part Eight, "Testing and Grading," offers pointers on developing good exams, alleviating students' test anxieties, implementing various grading methods, and promoting academic honesty.

Part Nine, "Presentation Technologies," explores low-tech media (flipcharts, chalkboards), audio and video multimedia, and PowerPoint presentations.

Part Ten, "Evaluation to Improve Teaching," explains how instructors can gather and interpret information that will help them become better teachers. This part includes quick methods for getting immediate feedback from students as well as the use of video recordings, colleague observation, and self-assessment.

Part Eleven, "Teaching Outside the Classroom," offers ideas on office hours, electronic communication with students, advising undergraduates, and working with graduate students as teaching assistants.

Part Twelve, "Finishing Up," covers end-of-term activities: review sessions, student ratings, and letters of recommendation.

Suggestions for Using *Tools for Teaching*

Because each chapter is designed to be read independently, some themes are mentioned in several chapters, an overlap that I hope will not bother the careful reader. Readers will also notice that not all the suggestions are compatible: they represent a variety of strategies from which to choose. As with any new undertaking, it is best to pick one or two activities to start with and add new items to your repertoire over time.

If you are a new instructor, you may want to begin by looking at Parts One, Three, and Four ("Getting Under Way," "Discussion Strategies," and "The Large-Enrollment Course"). You could then read the chapters that seem particularly relevant to your teaching responsibilities and refer to *Tools* during the term as different challenges arise (for example, encouraging students to talk during discussion periods).

If you feel generally comfortable about your teaching but are looking for ways to inject some excitement into your courses, browse through the book and select topics that appeal to you. Or start with Part Three ("Discussion Strategies") and Part Five ("Alternatives and Supplements to Lectures and Discussion"), both of which offer ways to actively engage students.

If you already have a sense of the areas you want to improve, read the chapters that directly relate to those areas.

If you are unsure about your teaching strengths and weaknesses, read Part Ten ("Evaluation to Improve Teaching") for suggestions on how to assess your teaching. Once you have identified areas for improvement, scan the table of contents and the index for the relevant topics.

All instructors can benefit from "Informally Assessing Students' Learning" (in Part Six) and "Early Feedback to Improve Teaching and Learning" (in Part Ten), which offer suggestions for gauging students' comprehension of course material and for eliciting their opinions of the strengths and weaknesses of your teaching.

A Request

I would be most grateful for your comments on the ideas and perspectives presented in *Tools*. Let me know what you think, and please pass along the good ideas you use in your own courses (email: barbara@BarbaraGrossDavis.com).

Acknowledgments

The second edition of this book could not have been written without the contributions of a great many people, and I am deeply indebted to each of them for their assistance and encouragement.

For sharing freely their ideas about good teaching: I am especially grateful to the faculty of the University of California, Berkeley. Their lively discussions, their generosity in sharing good teaching practices, and their diverse instructional perspectives have contributed both directly and indirectly to this book. A special thanks to those who participate in the Office of Educational Development's listserv, which has been a source of many good ideas about teaching and learning.

For reviewing and commenting on draft material at various stages: I received wise suggestions, insightful comments, and constructive criticism from the following faculty members and administrators at the University of California, Berkeley: Connie Chiba, Steven Chin, Nancy Chu, Aaron S. Cohen, Kevis Goodman, Sarah J. Hawthorne, Bryan Mayberry, Michael H. O'Hare, Oliver O'Reilly, Norma Partridge-Wallace, Eva Rivas, David O. Robinson, Larry Rowe, Susan Schweik, Diane Sigman, Cara Stanley, Philip B. Stark, Kim Steinbacher, Stephen K. Tollefson, Marc Treib, and Linda von Hoene.

For providing a student perspective: Many thanks to Molly McRoberts, Sam McRoberts, Kevin Poindexter, and Sarah Firestone (current and future undergraduates) for their review of selected chapters and their "gr8" suggestions on the use of technology in teaching and learning.

For reviewing and commenting on the entire manuscript: Larry Braskamp, Gary L. Firestone, and Ole Hald provided detailed critiques of the manuscript and were invaluable resources for crucial ideas, critical concepts, and different points of view that helped shape the final text. I am grateful to them for identifying problems, challenging me to be clear and specific, and making important contributions to both the substance and tone of this book.

For project management, bibliographic, editorial, and research assistance: I would like express my deep appreciation to Jean Barker for her judicious balance of patience and persistence in the face of almost-impossible deadlines; her attentiveness always kept this project moving forward. Her superb organizational skills, proficiency in locating hundreds of resources, and impressive mastery of the intricacies of copy editing have been invaluable. I also thank Mark Rhynsburger and Samuel Case for their help in verifying citations.

For editorial assistance: I am deeply indebted to Amy Einsohn, who worked on both the first and second editions of the book, for her prodigious expertise in condensing and clarifying the text, catching infelicities of language, and providing structural transitions.

For the team at UC Berkeley: My colleagues in my immediate office deserve special accolades for their steadfast support, considerable patience, ongoing encouragement, and complete understanding. Their graciousness and good humor helped make it possible for me to complete this book, and I respect them all: Jean Barker, Debra Fong, Bryan Mayberry, Norma Partridge-Wallace, Julie Rivera, Michele Robinson, Kim Steinbacher, and Steven K. Tollefson. I also thank Christina Maslach and Gibor Basri for their support during the writing of this second edition.

For the team at Jossey-Bass: I would like recognize the expert advice and support of David Brightman, Cathy Mallon, Barbara Armentrout, and Aneesa Davenport. Their editorial and production skills ably guided the book to publication. I am also grateful to Alan Venable for his assistance as development editor in the early stages of this project: he made my work easier.

For reality checks throughout the process: Rita Berro, Karen Gross McRoberts, Molly McRoberts, Sam McRoberts, Gary L. Firestone, Larry Braskamp, Ole Hald, Hilda Kessler, David Sweet, Jean Barker, Norma Partridge-Wallace, Steven K. Tollefson, and Amy Einsohn kept me grounded, motivated, and on track.

For their help on the first edition: I would like to thank the following reviewers and research assistants who helped me with the first edition and whose contributions are intertwined with the concepts presented in this second edition: Natalie Bosworth, Larry Braskamp, Cherry Chaicharn, Frederick C. Crews, Sam Davis, Marian Diamond, W. Russell Ellis, Sally Fairfax, Debra Fong, Ole Hald, Gary Handman, Michael Hardie, Francisco Hernandez, Sheila Humphreys, Helen Johnson, Peter Kerner, Jo Keroes, Matt Kondolf, Leif Krauss, Kristin Luker, Michele Mattingly, Flora McMartin, Margarita Melville, William K. Muir, Rose Nash, John Ory, Kevin Padian, David Palumbo-Liu, McCrae Parker, David Patterson, Matthew Rabin, Vincent Resh, K. V. S. Sastry, Michael Scriven, Mary Ann Shea, Mary Deane Sorcinelli, Daniele Spellman, Richard Sutch, Marilla

Svinicki, Ronald Takaki, Stephen K. Tollefson, Jon Wergin, Joanne Wile, Jana Woodard, and Christi Zmich.

Finally, a private acknowledgment and expression of gratitude to ITG, who has been a steady rock of unconditional support, completely selfless in providing assistance above and beyond the contract. For giving me free passes on my bad days, and for helping this book reach the highest possible standard, I am deeply indebted to him.

References

Bain, K. *What the Best College Teachers Do*. Cambridge, MA: Harvard University Press, 2004.

Buskist, W. and Davis, S. F. (eds.) *Handbook of the Teaching of Psychology*. New York: Wiley-Blackwell, 2005.

Kalman, C. S. *Successful Science and Engineering Teaching: Theoretical and Learning Perspectives*. New York: Springer, 2008.

Lang,

J. M. *On Course: A Week-By-Week Guide to Your First Semester of College Teaching*. Cambridge, MA: Harvard University Press, 2008.

Palmer, P. *The Courage to Teach: Exploring the Inner Landscape of a Teacher's Life*. 10th Anniversary Edition. San Francisco: Jossey-Bass, 2007.

Showalter, E. *Teaching Literature*. London: Blackwell, 2003.

CREDITS

We gratefully acknowledge permission to use the following material:

Chapter 1, pages 9–10: Wankat, P., and Oreovicz, F. "Content Tyranny." *ASEE Prism*, 1998, *8*(2), 15. Used by permission from the American Society for Engineering Education.

Chapter 6, page 82: University of California, Berkeley, Counseling and Psychological Services. Used by permission from Associate Vice Chancellor Steve Lustig, University of California, Berkeley.

Chapter 9, pages 98–99: Tiberius, R. G. *Small Group Teaching: A Trouble-Shooting Guide*. London: Kogan Page, 1999, p. 64. Used by permission.

Chapter 13, page 129: Sprague, J., and Stuart, D. Cengage Advantage Books: *The Speaker's Handbook* (with SpeechBuilderExpress™ and InfoTrac®), 1E. © 2006 Wadsworth, a part of Cengage Learning, Inc. Reproduced by permission. www.cengage.com/permissions

Chapter 26, page 233: University of California at Berkeley Task Force. *Advancing Public Service*. Berkeley: Service Learning Research and Development Center, University of California, 2000. Used by permission from Professor Andrew Furco, formerly of the University of California, Berkeley.

Chapter 40, page 380: Listserv, University of California, Berkeley, Office of Educational Development. Used by permission from Director Stephen K. Tollefson, University of California, Berkeley.

Chapter 43, page 409: Scriven, M. "Evaluation of Students." Unpublished manuscript, University of California, Berkeley, 1974. Used by permission from the author.

Chapter 61, page 555: Swensen, E. V., and Keith-Spiegel, P. *Writing Letters of Recommendation for Students: How to Protect Yourself from Liability*. Washington, D.C.: American Psychological Association, 1991, p. 2. Used by permission from E. V. Swensen.

Barbara Gross Davis, Assistant Vice Provost for Undergraduate Education at the University of California, Berkeley, received a B.A. degree in psychology, an M.A. degree in educational psychology, and a Ph.D. degree, also in educational psychology, all from the University of California, Berkeley. Davis's main areas of interest have been program and curriculum evaluation, instructional improvement, and faculty development—all in higher education. She has conducted workshops and seminars on topics related to teaching, learning, and evaluation, and she has written about faculty evaluation, assessment, and teaching improvement.

To my mother, Rita Berro, my first and best teacher

PART I

Getting Under Way

Designing or Revising a Course

In designing or revising a course, faculty must consider what material to teach, how best to teach it, and how to ensure that students are learning what is being taught. Many instructors, hoping to impart to students everything they know about a subject, attempt to include far too much material. Indeed, one of the most difficult steps in planning a course is deciding which topics must be excluded if the whole is to be manageable. The following suggestions are designed to help you make decisions about the content of your course, the structure and sequence of activities and assignments, the identification of learning outcomes, and the selection of instructional resources.

General Strategies

Let your decisions be guided by what you want your students to accomplish. Instead of thinking about the topics you want to teach, focus on learning outcomes: What do you want your students to be able to do after they have studied the material and completed their assignments? What knowledge, skills, attitudes, and "habits of mind" do you want your students to acquire during the semester? (Sources: Diamond, 1998; Fry et al., 2003; Ramsden, 2003; Suskie, 2004)

Apply principles that will enhance students' learning and intellectual development. The most important of these principles are discussed in Chapter 29, "Helping Students Learn." For example, you will want to think about how to provide your students with opportunities for active learning and for peer interaction, how to organize and communicate the material, what constitutes a reasonable workload, and how you and your students will monitor and assess their progress. (Source: Donnelly and Fitzmaurice, 2005)

Design or revise your course with principles of universal design in mind. Universal design is based on the premise that barrier-free, inclusive design benefits everyone—those with and without disabilities—and thereby eliminates or reduces the need for assistance and accommodation (see Chapter 6, "Students with Disabilities"). In college classes, instructors can

- use a variety of instructional methods
- offer students multiple ways to demonstrate mastery
- use technology to increase accessibility
- provide options for participation and presentations
- invite students to make their needs known

Aim for alignment of course elements. *Alignment* means that learning outcomes, instructional activities, and assessments of student learning are consistent and reinforce each other. Research shows that learning is improved when there is alignment among what instructors intend to teach, what they actually teach, and what they test. (Sources: Whetten, 2007; Wulff, 2005)

Preliminary Information Gathering

When preparing to teach a course for the first time, talk with faculty who have taught it previously. Ask your colleagues for their syllabus, course Web pages, instructional resources, list of assignments and papers, and old exams. Find out about the typical problems their students had with the material and any other difficulties the instructors encountered. Student evaluations of earlier offerings will also help you identify strengths and weaknesses of previous classes. If webcasts or podcasts of the course are available, view them as well.

When preparing a brand new course, review textbooks on the topic and materials or webcasts from similar courses at other universities. Current textbooks will give you a sense of the main themes, topics, and issues your course might address. Reviewing syllabi and webcasts or podcasts will let you see how other instructors approach the topics. Syllabi for introductory courses are often available from professional associations; some universities post syllabi online (see, for example, the MIT OpenCourseWare Web site).

Think about how your course fits into your department's curriculum and sequences. Look at the syllabi for prerequisite courses and the courses for which your course serves as a prerequisite. The former will give you a sense of what your students will already know, and the latter will help you identify the knowledge and skills that your course is expected to address.

When revising a course you have taught, assemble all your old materials. You will want to look at your syllabus, textbooks and readings, handouts, exams, notes for each class session, and other instructional resources. Review the students' end-of-semester evaluations to remind yourself of the course's strengths and weaknesses. Examine your materials in light of students' comments, new developments in the field, and your own changing interests.

Consider the characteristics of your students. As you plan your course, think about your prospective students: What range of knowledge, skills, and attitudes might they bring to the course? Will they be new to the field, potential majors, majors, or nonmajors? What courses have they already completed? What preconceptions and misperceptions might they have? Will all or most of your students be just out of high school, or older and more mature? Will some be part-time students who have work or family responsibilities? Will they be living on campus or will they commute?

Identify constraints on the course. As you begin to design the course, ask yourself, How many hours are available for instruction? How many students will be enrolled? Will you have lab assistants, graduate student instructors, or readers? What sorts of technology will be available in the classroom? Will there be opportunities for fieldwork or internships? What barriers or obstacles might detract from your students' learning?

Deciding What You Want to Accomplish

Think beyond this semester. Imagine yourself overhearing a group of graduating seniors who have taken your course and are discussing why it was among the most valuable courses they had ever taken. What would they be saying about your course? Or imagine that several of your students will become local or national power brokers, or that half of them will drop out of school before graduation. What would you like the legacy of your course to be for these students? What will distinguish students who have taken this course from those who have not? (Sources: Bergquist and Phillips, 1977; Fink, 2003; Wiggins and McTighe, 2005)

Use taxonomies to help identify a range of learning outcomes. Bloom's classic *Taxonomy of Educational Objectives* (1956) outlines six levels of cognitive processing: Knowledge, Comprehension, Application, Analysis, Synthesis, and Evaluation. Although Bloom's taxonomy oversimplifies how learning occurs, and research has not supported its hierarchical structure, it provides a useful starting point for defining learning outcomes that go beyond the memorization of facts. Applying new research on learning and cognitive development to Bloom's taxonomy, Anderson and Krathwohl (2001) offer a matrix that matches four types of knowledge (Factual, Conceptual, Procedural, and Metacognitive) against each of six cognitive processes (Remember, Understand, Apply, Analyze, Evaluate, and Create). In this revised taxonomy, learning progresses from the remembering of factual knowledge to the creation of new knowledge and the ability to reflect on one's own learning.

Fink (2003) developed a taxonomy that takes into account types of learning not readily apparent in the Bloom taxonomy or revised taxonomy: leadership, interpersonal skills, ethics, tolerance, and the ability to change. He proposes six nonhierarchical categories (Foundational Knowledge, Application, Integration, Human Dimension, Caring, Learning How to Learn). Here's an example of a learning outcome from the Human Dimension: "You will be able to inform and educate others about the role of microbiology in personal and public life; for example, by educating your roommate about proper ways of cooking a hamburger."

Erickson, Peters, and Strommer (2006) have developed a framework that uses everyday language in four categories: Knowing (memory), Understanding (ability to recognize), Thinking (applying what one has learned), and Learning How to Learn. Here's an example of an outcome from Understanding: "You will be able to identify which of a list of chemical equations conform to the Law of Conservation of Mass."

Another framework (Fry et al., 2003) takes into account research on deep and surface approaches to learning (See Chapter 29, "Helping Students Learn"). The first three levels are surface approaches: Increase in Knowledge, Memorizing, and Acquisition of Procedures. The last two are deep approaches: Abstraction of Meaning and Understanding Reality. Here's an example of an outcome from Abstraction of Meaning: "You will be able to provide a causal analysis of the seminal historical events that have shaped modern British society." Still another taxonomy (called SOLO and developed by Biggs, 2003) also has five levels: Prestructural, Unistructural, Multistructural, Relational, and Extended Abstract. An example of a learning outcome from Relational is "When shown a graph of severity of asthma attacks by time of a day, you will be able to advise a patient how to cope with diurnal variation in symptoms."

Marzano's taxonomy (2001) articulates six levels of mental processing: Retrieval, Comprehension, Analysis, Knowledge Utilization, Metacognition, and Self-System Thinking. Here's an example of a learning outcome from

Metacognition: "You will be able to monitor the extent to which you are effectively carrying out the proper experiments needed to isolate a gene."

Some two dozen frameworks or taxonomies have been developed to define domains of learning, development, and cognition. For descriptions of some of these taxonomies, see Anderson and Krathwohl (2001).

Draft a list of learning outcomes. What do you expect your students to know, do, demonstrate, or produce as a result of taking the course? Writing down these learning outcomes will help you (1) clarify what you want your students to accomplish; (2) determine what will count as evidence of student achievement; and (3) select appropriate teaching methods, materials, and assignments. At the start of the semester, you can refer to these learning outcomes when introducing the course to your students, and your students can use your list to monitor their progress. (Source: Wiggins and McTighe, 2005)

Identify both content outcomes and content-neutral outcomes. Content outcomes relate to students' grasp of the subject matter: "At the end of this course, you will be able to summarize the key forces affecting the rise of China as an economic power." Content-neutral outcomes relate to cognitive skills, interpersonal skills, and other outcomes independent of a student's mastery of course content: "At the end of this course, you will have learned to work collaboratively with peers." For each outcome, think about what constitutes acceptable performance and how your students will demonstrate that they have achieved the outcome. (Source: Fuhrmann and Grasha, 1983)

When writing learning outcomes, use clear language and everyday words. Express your learning outcomes in the second person ("you"), rather than the third person ("each student" or "the students"), and in the future tense: "When shown an electrocardiogram, you will be able to identify the duration, amplitude, and morphology of the QRS complex."

Fry, Ketteridge, and Marshall (2003) and Race (2007) offer other useful tips:

- Describe the learning that will result from an activity. Instead of "You will read one journal article on trade flows," write "You will be able to apply the analysis presented in a journal article on trade flows, and predict the effects that higher commodity prices will have on the U.S. trade deficit."
- Favor precise terms (*critique, define, distinguish among, argue, identify, solve, predict*) over vague ones (*understand, know, appreciate, become familiar with*).
- Drop trivial items from your list; help students focus on the most important learning outcomes.

- Think ahead to assessment. As you draft each learning outcome, ask yourself how you will measure how well a student has achieved the outcome.
- Recognize that some educational aspirations cannot be evaluated with certainty: aesthetic appreciation or creativity, for example (Toohey, 1999).

Reduce your preliminary list of learning outcomes to a realistic set. Take into consideration the different abilities, interests, and expectations of your students and the amount of time available for class instruction. How many outcomes can your students reasonably achieve during your course? (Source: Lowman, 1995)

Anticipate students' questions about learning outcomes. Students may want to know why a particular learning outcome is being addressed or the importance of an outcome. When your students understand the short-term and long-term benefits of acquiring a particular skill or competency, they are more likely to try to achieve it. To reinforce the importance of learning outcomes, mention them throughout the course. (Source: Race, 2007)

Defining and Limiting Course Content

Review your preliminary list of topics and toss the excess baggage. Designing a course is somewhat like packing for a long trip. First, list everything that you feel might be important for students to know, just as you might pull out armloads of clothes and personal items for a trip. Then severely pare down the topics you have listed, just as you would limit yourself to whatever will fit in one or two suitcases. Research shows that including too much detail or too many topics interferes with students' efforts to learn the material. (Source: Bransford et al., 2000)

Distinguish between essential and optional material. Divide the course concepts or topics into three groups: basic material that should be mastered by every student, recommended material that should be mastered by every student who is seeking a good knowledge of the subject, and optional material that should be mastered by students with special interests and aptitudes. Course sessions and exams should focus on the basic topics. Recommended and optional topics, labeled as such for students, can be included in class sessions, supplementary materials and resources, and readings.

Draw a concept map. To help you determine which topics are most important, you can create a concept map, a chart that captures the central, major, and minor concepts and the relationships among them. To draw a concept map, follow these steps:

- Write down all the ideas that seem important in the course.
- Reduce your list by circling the ideas that are most important.
- Write each of the circled concepts on a sticky note.
- Sort the sticky notes into meaningful clusters or groups.
- Name each cluster, and write each name on a sticky note.
- Arrange the cluster names (key concepts) in a way that is meaningful to you.

   (Sources: Amundsen et al., 2004; Donald, 2002)

Emphasize the core concepts. For example, in engineering, as one professor points out, there are thousands of formulas, but all of them are variations on a small set of basic ideas or theories. In a single course, students might encounter a thousand equations. Rote memorization is futile because no one can remember that many equations. Instead, the instructor repeatedly emphasizes the fundamentals by showing students how the thousand equations are embedded in a dozen basic ones.

Focus on the "big idea." A big idea is a concept, theme, theory, issue, underlying assumption, or critical principle that gives meaning to an array of discrete facts, topics, inquiries, or issues. In different fields, examples of big ideas are the challenge of defining justice, the distinction between the letter and the spirit of the law, adaptation, and the need for communicators to focus on audience and purpose. (Source: Wiggins and McTighe, 2005)

Stress the classic issues, or the most enduring values or truths. Often the most interesting issues and themes for undergraduates are those that first attracted you to the discipline. You might also focus on the most critical skills or ideas, and drop the rest. Or give special attention to important ideas that are usually hard for students to understand. (Source: McManus, 2005)

Limit course content to five types of information. When reducing your preliminary list of topics, limit yourself to

1. key points and general themes
2. especially hard-to-understand material
3. important material that is not addressed in the readings or elsewhere

4. examples and illustrations
5. material of high interest to students
    (Source: Wankat and Oreovicz, 1998)

Include multiple perspectives and scholarship. A unit on the impact of World War II on the American economy, for example, could address the views and experiences of different ethnic and income groups. See Chapter 5, "Diversity and Inclusion in the Classroom."

Select a manageable number of course topics. Experienced instructional designers recommend four to seven topics or issues for a semester-long introductory class. For example, in an introductory biology class, the principal topics might be (1) molecules, cells, and tissues, (2) cellular communication and hormone action, (3) human reproduction, (4) stem cells and human development, (5) the physiology of organ systems, and (6) organ dysfunction and disease.

Structuring the Course

Devise a logical arrangement for the course content. Material can be arranged chronologically, by topic or category, from concrete to abstract or vice versa, from theory to application or vice versa, or by increasing level of skill or complexity. Here are some other organizing principles (Bergquist and Phillips, 1977, pp. 146–149):

Micro/macro: Begin by describing a large complex phenomenon (macro perspective) or by offering a detailed analysis of one aspect of the phenomenon (micro perspective). Establish a broad general base of knowledge and information (macro), or focus on a specific event or concern (micro).

Distal/proximal: Begin by presenting an immediate, urgent problem (proximal perspective) or by describing a phenomenon's origins, heritage, or context (distal perspective). Begin by discussing the relevance of a topic (proximal) or by presenting a historical or theoretical perspective (distal).

Phenomenon/structure: Emphasize description and analysis of unique and significant events, people, or ideas (phenomenon) or emphasize description and analysis of theories, themes, and universal applications (structure).

Stark (2000) and Toohey (1999) offer additional patterns for ordering topics:

- how ideas have evolved chronologically
- how relationships occur in the real world
- how students will use the information in social, personal, or career settings
- how major concepts and relationships are organized in the discipline
- how students develop competencies (from prerequisite to novice to expert skill sets)
- how knowledge has been created in the field

Keep in mind that a structure that seems logical and clear to you (an expert) may not be the best way for a student (a novice) to learn the material (Ramsden, 2003). From a student's point of view, it may be preferable to begin the course with a topic that will generate confidence and interest in the material. Students tend to be more motivated to work hard when they succeed at the beginning of the term and when they can relate the new material to something they already know.

Create a schedule. List all class meetings, accounting for university holidays, major religious holidays, breaks, and any college events that may preempt classes. Write in tentative topics and dates for exams. Keep in mind the rhythm of the term, and leave open at least part of the class before each exam to allow for catch-up or review. Allow extra time for complex or difficult topics. Schedule time during the middle of the semester for quick student evaluations of the course (see Chapter 52, "Early Feedback to Improve Teaching and Learning"). Also give special consideration to the first days of class (see Chapter 3, "The First Days of Class"), the meetings right before exams, and the last week of class (see Chapter 59, "The Last Days of Class"). You will want to include this schedule in your course syllabus (see Chapter 2, "The Comprehensive Course Syllabus").

Select instructional methods for each class meeting. Instead of asking, "What will I do at each session?" focus on what you want your students to be doing, thinking, or feeling. Look at your learning outcomes and identify suitable classroom activities. (Activities discussed in different sections of this book include lectures, small-group discussions, independent work, simulations, debates, case studies, role-playing, and demonstrations.) For each topic, decide how you will introduce the material, present new concepts, have students apply what they have learned, and assess whether students can put into practice what they have learned. (Source: Bligh, 2000)

Design in-class and homework assignments. See Chapter 35, "Designing Effective Writing Assignments"; Chapter 37, "Homework: Problem Sets"; Chapter 21, "Learning in Groups"; and other chapters.

Selecting Textbooks, Readings, and Course Materials

Choose textbooks and reading assignments that reflect your learning outcomes. McKeachie and Svinicki (2006) recommend that instructors select textbooks that generally match their own approach to the material. Students can be annoyed or confused if you repeatedly disagree with the text, and some will wonder why they were required to buy and read such an unsatisfactory book. To expose students to a range of perspectives, you can assign articles and shorter texts that espouse different points of view. And to help students understand that the textbook is not a final authority on a topic, you can pose occasional counterarguments and other interpretations. (Source: National Research Council, 1997)

Avoid requiring students to purchase a textbook you have authored. Although it may arguably be the best resource available, the fact that an instructor stands to benefit financially can be alienating to students, especially if the textbook is expensive, and can be seen as a real or perceived conflict of interest. If you decide to require students to purchase your textbook, consider making a contribution of the royalties to your financial aid office or other campus program or service.

Consider a range of criteria in selecting textbooks. If several textbooks are appropriate to your course, use the following criteria to select among them (adapted from Dake, 2007; Forsyth, 2003; Lowman, 1995; National Research Council, 1997; Robinson, 1994):

- content: accuracy, currency, coherence, and clarity
- scope and sequence of topics (organization of material)
- level of difficulty and interest for students (challenging but not too difficult)
- conceptual orientation and approach to the subject matter
- availability of alternative media formats for students with disabilities
- quality of writing
- pedagogical design (clear headings and subheadings, chapter previews and summaries, review questions, glossaries, and so on)
- cost (paperback instead of hardback; a less expensive book if it is of comparable quality)

- environmental impacts (use of processed chlorine-free paper; publisher's participation in green press initiatives)
- reviews by faculty who have used the textbook (published book reviews and posts on Web sites or listservs of professional associations; ratings on bookseller Web sites and the Faculty Center (www.facultycenter.net), which has information about textbooks; comments from colleagues)
- opinions of a sample of students after they take a look at the books you are considering

More detailed lists of criteria are offered by Altman, Ericksen, and Pena-Shaff (2006); Landrum and Hormel (2002): and Payne (2003).

Assign a mix of texts and articles, including some current items. Advanced courses typically include journal articles, essays, and research reports. But students in introductory courses should have an opportunity to read at least a few recent pieces.

Be mindful of the high cost of textbooks. Textbook prices increased by 6 percent a year between 1987 and 2005 (Government Accountability Office, 2005). Some campuses have started book-swapping programs and textbook rentals; others have asked faculty to think twice before switching textbooks or assigning a new edition.

You can help your students in several ways (adapted from Boyd, n.d.; listserv discussions from PsychTeacher and POD):

- Place your textbook orders early. Early orders allow your local bookstores to buy back used books from students at higher prices and keep those books for the next semester (rather than shipping the used copies to a consolidator).
- Be cost-conscious when you prepare your required reading list.
- Retain textbooks for longer periods (not immediately switching to a new edition), and use the same text for multiple courses, if possible.
- Make reading lists available, with the ISBN for books, well before the term begins so that students can do some comparison shopping.
- Adopt lower-priced alternatives: no-frill textbooks, free online textbooks (such as Wikibooks or through Creative Commons), and resources such as the Million Books Project (led by Carnegie Mellon) and the Global Text Project (electronic texts for students in the developing world).
- Avoid "bundled" books (with extras like CDs or workbooks) and custom textbooks.
- Give students advice about online shopping for textbooks. Let them know about comparison book sites to find the cheapest version of a textbook

(searching by "used textbooks"). Remind them of the cautions in purchasing books online (such as wrong editions, delays in receiving books, difficulties in making returns).

- Let students purchase an earlier and less expensive edition of the textbook or a similar cheaper textbook of their choice (but make students aware that they will be responsible for matching their chosen text with the required reading assignments).
- Indicate in your syllabus whether you will be using the text again the next time you teach the course so that students will know they can get a higher price on reselling their book.
- Donate textbooks to your campus library.

Compare the costs and benefits of electronic and paper textbooks. Electronic textbooks (e-books), sold on compact disc, are cheaper, lighter, and more environmentally friendly than paper textbooks. Because the text is online, students can conduct keyword searches, adjust the display format, and use text-to-speech software. E-books can be read on special e-book readers, computer screens, mobile phones, or PDAs.

Many e-books also include simulations, audio and video clips, links, and chat tools. One disadvantage is that students cannot sell back their e-books at the end of the term. Another is that some publishers restrict use through expiration dates, limits on the number of page views, and security features that limit use to only one computer. Research shows no difference in course grades between students who use textbooks and those who use e-books, but students complain that e-books can be inconvenient and hard to read for long stretches. (Sources: Nelson, 2008; Shepperd et al., 2008)

Consider coursepacks. Coursepacks are photocopies of copyrighted journal articles, book chapters, and other materials. Coursepacks can be the sole reading material for a class or can supplement the textbook. For advanced classes, some faculty create coursepacks in order to include new research, partial outlines of course lectures, or diagrams that students complete during class. Because coursepacks have little resale value, some instructors do what they can to contain the cost of their coursepack.

If you are preparing a coursepack, here are some tips:

- Carefully select and limit the number of items.
- Include a table of contents or an overview that provides a context for the readings; without guidance students may see only a jumble of articles.
- If appropriate, include a glossary of technical terms and concepts.
- Secure all copyright permissions before duplicating the coursepack.

A note on using copyrighted material: Under "fair use" provisions, educators can use copyrighted materials for instructional purposes, but the conventions for acceptable fair use are complicated. For help in making judgments about fair use, consult your campus librarians and your library's Web site. The Web site of the University of Minnesota Library offers a Fair Use Analysis Tool as well as scenarios of what is and is not fair use for reproducing digital photographs of works of art, audiovisual works for class presentations, electronic reserves, course packs, copies of your own articles, copies of student papers, downloads from the Web, and several other kinds of reuse. The American Library Association Web site (www.ala.org) also has helpful information about copyright issues including a slide rule for copyright advice.

Plan how to handle errors in the textbook. Despite the author's and publisher's best intentions, errors will creep into textbooks, study guides, and workbooks. Researchers report that errors can have a large negative impact on student learning. Keep a list of the errors that you identify, and encourage students to spot them as well. Send the list to the publisher's representative or author. In some cases, the publisher may make corrections and send an online version of, say, the study guide. If immediate corrections from the publisher are not possible, make the correction yourself and place it on the course Web site. If students find errors and the publisher responds, be sure to share the letter with students. (Source: National Research Council, 1997)

Prepare a set of tips for students on how to use the textbook and readings. First-year students and students in introductory courses may benefit from the following advice:

- Study the assigned reading before class.
- Take notes on key points and jot down any questions that come to mind.
- When reading an assignment, stop every half hour or so to summarize what you have read.
- Bring your questions about the readings to class.
- When you are not sure you have understood the assigned text, look at the supplemental texts to see how they present similar topics.
- For homework problems: study and review the worked-out examples before you tackle the assignment.
- Review the readings regularly throughout the term rather than cramming before the test.

(Source: Boyd, n.d.; National Research Council, 1997)

Be aware of your students' workload. Most colleges expect students to spend two to three hours on outside work for each hour in class. For full-time students taking fifteen hours a week of classes, that would mean devoting thirty to forty-five hours a week to studying, reading assignments, problem sets, projects, and papers. But in one survey (National Survey of Student Engagement, 2007), full-time students reported spending only about thirteen to fourteen hours a week preparing for their classes; many hold part-time jobs and have family or other responsibilities. You might want to discuss this topic with your students and share with them research (Stinebrickner and Stinebrickner, 2007) that shows studying an extra hour a day is estimated to have the same effect on grades as a five-point increase in ACT score. As Laurillard (2002) notes, students need realistic estimates of how much time is appropriate for them to spend on assignments, readings, and study groups.

Learning Management Systems and Collaborative and Learning Environments

Find out which system your campus is using. Most colleges and universities use either a commercial software, a homegrown application, or an open source solution for their learning and course management system. Examples of commercial software include Blackboard Learning System (which purchased WebCT in 2006), eCollege Course Management System (purchased by Pearson in 2007), Desire2Learn Learning Environment, and Angel. Examples of open source solutions (which allow users to share tools and are called "collaborative and learning environments") include Sakai (a collaboration begun by University of Michigan, MIT, Stanford, and Indiana University), and Moodle (distributed under one of the Open Source Initiative approved licenses).

Become familiar with features of your campus's system. The following kinds of tools may be available as part of your system (adapted from www.edutools.com):

- communication (discussion forums, file exchanges where students can submit papers and assignments online, e-mail, class lists, real time chat)
- productivity (calendars, announcements)
- student involvement (sites for collaboration and group work, community networking, student home pages)
- administration (authentication, authorization, integration with campus registration and enrollment systems)

- course delivery (tests and quizzes; online marking tools, online grade books, student tracking)
- content development (accessibility, document uploads such as class notes, PowerPoint presentations, course readings)

Let students know how you will be using the system. Will the system be the primary vehicle for course announcements? Should students sign up for RSS feeds? Are students required or encouraged to participate in online discussion forums? When will PowerPoint notes be posted?

Setting Course Policies

Extra-credit assignments. If you are offering extra-credit assignments, announce them in class so that all students will be aware of the option. Some faculty allow only students who are doing satisfactory work (C or higher) on the regular assignments to undertake extra-credit tasks. Here are some examples of extra-credit options:

- Offer a set number of extra-credit points for a specified activity (such as attendance at a professional conference or submission of a book review in the topic area).
- Offer extra credit for completing problems in the textbook that were not assigned as homework.
- Offer extra credit for keeping a reading journal that documents each course-related article, book, or monograph read in addition to the assigned readings. Each journal entry should include the title, author, date, and source as well as the student's comments on the piece. (Faculty typically spot-check the journals weekly and read them at the end of the term.)

Attendance. Let students know in the syllabus and on the first day of class that you expect them to come to class regularly. Do your best to make class time worthwhile—a time when real work takes place. Students are also more likely to attend if they know that exams will include items that have been discussed in class (and not mentioned in the readings). Some faculty use attendance as a factor in grading, but many do not. If you want to reward good attendance, let students know how you will determine whether they come to class. Rather than penalize absences (by subtracting points), reward perfect or near-perfect attendance (by giving bonus points); the numerical result will be the same, but students feel better about the latter. Set a good example by arriving early to class, starting and ending on time, and staying late to answer questions.

Makeup exams. For advice on offering makeup tests see Chapter 40, "Allaying Students' Anxieties about Tests."

Late work. Some faculty refuse to accept late work and give students an F on the assignment. Other faculty impose various kinds of markdown penalties. See Chapter 43, "Grading Practices."

Grading. See Chapter 43, "Grading Practices."

Classroom Behavior. See Chapter 4, "Classroom Conduct and Decorum."

References

Altman, W. S., Ericksen, K., and Pena-Shaff, J. B. "An Inclusive Process for Departmental Textbook Selection." *Teaching of Psychology*, 2006, *33*(4), 228–231.

Amundsen, C., Saroyan, A., and Donald, J. Analysis of Course Content. In A. Saroyan and C. Amundsen (Eds.), *Rethinking Teaching in Higher Education: From a Course Design Workshop to a Faculty Development Framework*. Sterling, VA: Stylus, 2004.

Anderson, L. W., and Krathwohl, D. R. (Eds.). *A Taxonomy for Learning, Teaching and Assessing: A Revision of Bloom's Taxonomy of Educational Objectives*. New York: Addison-Wesley Longman, 2001.

Bergquist, W. H., and Phillips, S. R. *A Handbook for Faculty Development*. Vol. 2. Washington, DC: Council for the Advancement of Small Colleges, 1977.

Biggs, J. *Teaching for Quality Learning at University*. (2nd ed.) New York: Open University Press/McGraw-Hill, 2003.

Bligh, D. A. *What's the Use of Lectures?* San Francisco: Jossey-Bass, 2000.

Bloom, B. S., Engelhart, M. D., Furst, E. J., Hill, W. H., and Krathwohl, D. R. (Eds.). *Taxonomy of Educational Objectives: The Classification of Educational Goals*. Handbook I: *Cognitive Domain*. New York: David McKay, 1956.

Boyd, D. R. *Using Textbooks Effectively: Getting Students to Read Them*. Association for Psychological Science, n.d. http://www.psychologicalscience.org/teaching/tips/tips_0603.cfm

Bransford, J. D., Brown, A. L., and Cocking, R. R. *How People Learn: Brain, Mind, Experience, and School*. Washington, DC: National Academy Press, 2000.

Dake, L. S. "Student Selection of the Textbook for an Introductory Physics Course." *The Physics Teacher*, Oct. 2007, *45*(7), 416–419.

Diamond, R. M. *Designing and Assessing Courses and Curricula: A Practical Guide*. (Rev. ed.) San Francisco: Jossey-Bass, 1998.

Donald, J. *Learning to Think: Disciplinary Perspectives*. San Francisco: Jossey-Bass, 2002.

Donnelly, R., and Fitzmaurice, M. *Designing Modules for Learning*. In G. O'Neill, S. Moore, and B. McMullin (Eds.), *Emerging Issues in the Practice of University Learning and Teaching*.

Dublin: All Ireland Society for Higher Education, 2005. (Released under Creative Commons License)

Erickson, B. L., Peters, C. B., and Strommer, D. W. *Teaching First-Year College Students.* San Francisco: Jossey-Bass, 2006.

Fink, L. D. *Creating Significant Learning Experiences: An Integrated Approach to Designing College Courses.* San Francisco: Jossey-Bass, 2003.

Forsyth, D. R. *The Professor's Guide to Teaching: Psychological Principles and Practices.* Washington, DC: American Psychological Association, 2003.

Fry, H., Ketteridge, S., and Marshall, S. *A Handbook for Teaching and Learning in Higher Education: Enhancing Academic Practice.* (2nd ed.) New York: RoutledgeFalmer, 2003.

Fuhrmann, B. S., and Grasha, A. F. *A Practical Handbook for College Teachers.* Boston: Little, Brown, 1983.

Government Accountability Office. *College Textbooks: Enhanced Offerings Appear to Drive Recent Price Increases,* July 2005. http://www.gao.gov/new.items/d05806.pdf

Landrum, R. E., and Hormel, L. "Textbook Selection: Balance between the Pedagogy, the Publisher and the Student." *Teaching of Psychology,* 2002, *29*(3), 245–248.

Laurillard, D. *Rethinking University Teaching: A Framework for the Effective Use of Learning Technologies.* (2nd ed.) New York: RoutledgeFalmer, 2002.

Lowman, J. *Mastering the Techniques of Teaching.* (2nd ed.) San Francisco: Jossey-Bass, 1995.

Marzano, R. J. *Designing a New Taxonomy of Educational Objectives.* Thousand Oaks, CA: Corwin Press, 2001.

McKeachie, W. J., and Svinicki, M. *McKeachie's Teaching Tips.* (12th ed.) Boston: Houghton Mifflin, 2006.

McManus, D. A. *Leaving the Lectern: Cooperative Learning and the Critical First Days of Students Working in Groups.* San Francisco: Jossey-Bass/Anker, 2005.

National Research Council. *Science Teaching Reconsidered: A Handbook.* Washington, DC: National Academies Press, 1997.

National Survey of Student Engagement. *Experiences That Matter: Enhancing Student Learning and Success.* Bloomington, IN: Center for Postsecondary Research, 2007.

Nelson, M. R. "E-Books in Higher Education.: Nearing the End of the Era of Hype?" *Educause Review,* Mar/Apr 2008, *43*(2), 40–56.

Payne, D. A. *Applied Educational Assessment.* (2nd ed.) Belmont, CA: Wadsworth/Thomson Learning, 2003.

POD Listserv: A moderated online community for instructors and administrators with interests in teaching and learning in higher education; see http://podnetwork.org. Professional and Organizational Development Network in Higher Education. *Bright Idea Network,* 1989.

PsychTeacher listserv: A moderated online community for instructors involved in teaching psychology; see teachpsych.org/news/psychteacher.php

Race, P. *The Lecturer's Toolkit.* (3rd ed.) London: Routledge, 2007.

Ramsden, P. *Learning to Teach in Higher Education.* (2nd ed.) New York: RoutledgeFalmer, 2003.

Robinson, D. H. Textbook Selection: Watch Out for "Inconsiderate" Texts. In K. W. Prichard and R. M. Sawyer (Eds.), *Handbook of College Teaching: Theory and Applications.* Westport, CT: Greenwood Press, 1994.

Shepperd, J. A., Grace, J. L., and Koch, E. J. "Evaluating the Electronic Textbook: Is It Time to Dispense with the Paper Text?" *Teaching of Psychology,* 2008, *35*(1), 2–5.

Stark, J. S. "Planning Introductory College Courses: Content, Context and Form." *Instructional Science*, Sept. 2000, *28*, 413–438.

Stinebrickner, T., and Stinebrickner, R. "The Causal Effect of Studying on Academic Performance." Working Paper W13341. Cambridge, MA: National Bureau of Economic Research, Aug. 2007.

Suskie, L. A. *Assessing Student Learning: A Common Sense Guide.* Bolton, MA: Anker, 2004.

Toohey, S. *Designing Courses for Higher Education.* Philadelphia: Society for Research into Higher Education and Open University Press, 1999.

Wankat, P., and Oreovicz, F. "Content Tyranny." *ASEE PRISM*, 1998, *8*(2), 15.

Whetten, D. A. "Principles of Effective Course Design: What I Wish I Had Known About Learning-Centered Teaching 30 Years Ago." *Journal of Management Education*, 2007, *31*(3), 339–357.

Wiggins, G., and McTighe, J. *Understanding by Design.* (expanded 2nd ed.) Alexandria, VA: Association for Supervision and Curriculum Development, 2005.

Wulff, D. H. (Ed.). *Aligning for Learning: Strategies for Teaching Effectiveness.* San Francisco: Jossey-Bass/Anker, 2005.

2

The Comprehensive Course Syllabus

A course syllabus, placed on the Web or handed out on the first day of class, gives students an immediate sense of what the course will be about, what they will learn, and how their academic progress will be evaluated.

All courses can benefit from a syllabus. The act of preparing a syllabus helps you organize your course and set the schedule. You can also describe to students what they will need to know and do to succeed in your class.

General Strategies

Understand the multiple roles a comprehensive syllabus plays. Experts have identified various purposes a syllabus can serve: an implicit teaching-learning contract, outlining the reciprocal roles and responsibilities of students and the instructor; a diagnostic tool, helping students assess their readiness for a course by identifying prerequisites and required levels of academic preparation and describing workload and course challenges; an unambiguous source of policies and procedures for course operations; a learning tool, piquing students' interest and providing them with the information, resources, and links they will need to succeed in the course; and a set of promises—what the instructor promises students will learn and the activities students will undertake to fulfill those promises. (Sources: Bain, 2004; Collins, 1997; Eberly et al., 2001; Grunert O'Brien et al., 2008; Lang, 2008; Parkes and Harris, 2002)

Look over the syllabi of other faculty members. If your department does not have a standard format, ask to see your colleagues' syllabi. Other sources of samples include George Mason University's Syllabus Finder, and the University of Texas's World Lecture Hall. Brown University and the University of Minnesota offer online syllabus construction workshops and Honolulu Community College has made syllabus templates available online. In addition, professional associations in your field may have compiled syllabi for introductory and advanced courses.

Anticipate the general questions that will be in the minds of students. What will your students want to know about your course? The three most common concerns of students on the first day of class are likely to be, Will I be able to do the work? Will I like the professor? Will I get along with my classmates? Students may also be asking themselves, Why should I take *this* course? How does this course fit into the larger curriculum or the general education program? Where does it lead intellectually and practically? (Source: Rubin, 1985)

Keep the syllabus flexible. Some classes move more slowly than others. You might anticipate such variations by indicating the topics week by week rather than session by session. Or you might plan to issue a revised schedule midway through the term to account for students' heightened interest in certain topics. Let students know that the course schedule may change, but that the dates for exams and deadlines for assignments are fixed.

Post the syllabus online as early as possible. Students with disabilities may require extra time to convert the readings into alternative media formats.

Creating a Syllabus

Include more rather than less material. Your syllabus need not include all the components mentioned here, but experienced faculty agree that a comprehensive syllabus can be a valuable learning tool for students and can lessen their initial anxieties about the course. Be careful, however, not to include so many details about rules, contingencies, and dos and don'ts that the syllabus loses its intellectual focus. (Sources: Collins, 1997; Garavalia et al., 1999; Grunert O'Brien et al., 2008)

Use a simple layout for the hard-copy syllabus handout. Use headings, text boxes, bulleted lists, and graphics to highlight important information. Some faculty have found that distributing a one-page graphic syllabus to accompany a comprehensive syllabus helps students understand the flow of the course and the logical and chronological relationships among the topics. Other faculty have replaced their text syllabus with an entirely graphic representation of the course. (Source: Nilson, 2007)

Provide basic information. Include the name of the university, current year and term, the course title and number, the number of units, and the meeting time and location. Indicate any course meetings that are not scheduled for the assigned room. List your name (and what you prefer to be called), office address (include a map if your office is hard to locate), office phone number, department phone number, mobile phone (if you wish, and indicate whether you take voice or text messages), e-mail address, fax number, and office hours. For your office hours, indicate whether students need to make appointments in advance or may just stop in. Let students know your preferred mode of communication: e-mail, telephone, text message, or through the learning management system or a social networking site. Indicate the link for your Web page and the course Web page. List the days, hours, and access addresses for online chat, if your course has this component, and the mail-list for the class if you have established one. Include the names, offices, e-mails, phone numbers, and Web addresses of any teaching or laboratory assistants.

Describe the prerequisites to the course. Help students realistically assess their readiness for your course by listing the knowledge, skills, or experience you expect them to have already or the courses they should have completed. Give students suggestions on how they might refresh their skills if they feel uncertain about their readiness. Show how skills and knowledge from past courses will be used in your course. It is also helpful to clarify the target audience for the course: is the course required for the major in your field? required for the major in other departments? a general elective?

Indicate any instructional technology requisites. Do students need to bring a laptop to class? Do students need to know particular software? If so, let students know where they might go for training.

Give an overview of the course's purpose. Provide an introduction to the subject matter and show how the course fits in the college or department curriculum. Explain what the course is about and why students would want to learn the material. How does the course relate to other courses students have taken? One faculty member writes an essay about the purpose of the course and includes it in the syllabus. He makes an effort to refer to the essay periodically during the term. Another faculty member begins with a story that leads into what students will learn and the challenges and benefits they will encounter. (Sources: Bain, 2004; Shea, 1990)

State the general learning goals, objectives, or outcomes. This clarifies for students what they will learn and be evaluated against. List three to five major objectives that you expect all students to strive for: What will students know or be able to do better after completing this course? What skills or competencies do you want to develop in your students? In formulating objectives, use active verbs ("interpret" "explain") and consider skills, knowledge, values, and attitudes. An example of a student learning objective is "Upon completion of this course, you will be able to explain methods of sampling and determination of sample size." Some faculty members ask students to develop their own learning goals: what they want to know or be able to do after completing the course. (Sources: Collins, 1997; Lang, 2008; Matejka and Kurke, 1994; Smith, 1993; Smith and Razzouk, 1993; Woolcock, 1997)

Clarify the conceptual structure used to organize the course. Students need to understand why you have arranged topics in a given order and the logic of the themes or concepts you have selected.

Describe the format or activities of the course. Let students know the components of the course (for example, discussion sections, fieldwork activities, labs) and how they will be spending class time (listening to lectures? participating in small group work? giving oral presentations? collaborating online?). Select instructional activities inside and outside of class that reinforce the learning you want to encourage.

Specify the textbook, readings, and coursepack information. A coursepack (also called a *reader* or *course reader*) contains instructor-compiled published articles, book chapters, and unpublished documents. Using a coursepack requires obtaining copyright permission for published material. For textbooks, give author, title, edition, ISBN, and availability of electronic or alternative formats for students with disabilities, if known. If appropriate, show the relationship between the readings and the course objectives, especially if you assign chapters in a textbook out of sequence (Rubin, 1985). Let students know whether they are required to do the reading before each class meeting.

Identify additional materials or equipment needed for the course. For example, do students need lab or safety equipment, art supplies, particular software, drafting materials? Be specific about safety issues: why they are in place and needed. (Source: Collins, 1997)

List assignments, term papers, and exams. State the nature and format of the assignments, the expected length of essays, and their deadlines. Indicate how the assignments are related to the goals of the course. Give the examination dates and briefly indicate the nature of the tests (multiple-choice, essay, short-answer, take-home tests). In setting up the syllabus, try to keep the work load evenly balanced throughout the term.

State how students will be evaluated and how grades will be assigned.
Students' behaviors are strongly influenced by the ways in which their learning
will be evaluated. Describe the grading procedures, including the components
of the final grade and the weights assigned to each component (for example,
homework, term papers, midterms, and final exams) and how final grades in the
course will be calculated. Students appreciate knowing the weighting because it
helps them budget their time. Will you grade on a curve or use an absolute scale?
Will you accept extra-credit work to improve grades? See Chapter 43, "Grading
Practices." Bain (2004) encourages faculty to share with students how they jointly
can better understand students' intellectual progress during the term.

List other course requirements. For example, are students required to attend an
office hour, post comments to the discussion board, or form a study group in a
social networking site?

Discuss course policies. State your policies regarding class attendance; tardiness;
class participation; turning in late work; missing homework, tests or exams; make-
ups; extra credit; requesting extensions; reporting illnesses; and standards of academic honesty. Try to phrase policies positively in a friendly tone so that you don't
come across as a tyrant or as someone who expects the worst in students. At least
one instructor (Warma, 1998), though, devotes several paragraphs in the syllabus
to such personally annoying student behaviors as coming late to class, leaving early,
and carrying on private conversations while the instructor is lecturing. If you list
acceptable and unacceptable classroom behavior, give reasons ("Please refrain from
eating during class because it is disturbing to me and other students. If you need
to bring food into class for health or medical reasons, please see me privately.").
Giving reasons for policies may be more likely to gain students' cooperation. Some
instructors (DiClementi and Handelsman, 2005) have had success in letting the
class as a whole generate rules and strategies for managing rules violations around
such issues as eating in class, sleeping in class, using cell phones, and the like.

Invite students with special needs to contact you. Let students know that if
they need an accommodation for any type of physical or learning disability, medical needs, or other reasons, they should set up a time right away to meet with the
student disability services office and then meet with you privately to discuss what
modifications are necessary to ensure their full participation in the course.

**Ask students who have conflicts with the dates of the exams to contact you
early in the term.** Some students may miss exams because of foreseeable conflicts,
such as medical/graduate school interviews, athletic competition, and religious

observance. Ask students to set up a time to meet with you during the first weeks of the course to discuss options.

Provide a course calendar or schedule. The schedule states the sequence of course topics, preparations or readings, and the assignments due. If appropriate, pique students' interest by posing provocative questions or using compelling titles for class sessions. For the readings, give page numbers in addition to chapter numbers—this will help students budget their time. Consider giving students pointers on the reading, as necessary ("This is a particularly challenging article. You may find it useful to review Chapter Five in the text beforehand.").

Take holidays and campus events into account. Try to schedule exams and due dates for assignments so that they do not conflict with major religious holidays and significant campus events. Lists of religious holidays are available at www.interfaithcalendar.org. Ask students to inform you immediately of any scheduling conflicts you may have overlooked. Also be mindful of the topics you schedule immediately after midterms or deadlines for projects, when students' energy levels may not be as high.

Schedule time for gathering feedback from your students. Set a time midway through the term when you can solicit from students their reactions to the course so far. See Chapter 52, "Early Feedback to Improve Teaching and Learning," for ways to get feedback from students. You might also include an example or two of how student feedback has improved the course. (Source: Chen and Hoshower, 2003)

List important drop dates. Include on the course calendar the last day students can withdraw from the course without penalty.

Estimate student work load. Give students a sense of how much preparation and work the course will involve. How much time should they anticipate spending on reading assignments, problem sets, lab reports, or research? See Chapter 1, "Designing or Revising a Course."

Include supplementary material as appropriate. For example, consider providing one or more of the following:

- tips on how to study, take notes, and prepare for exams
- glossary of technical terms
- lecture notes or study guides
- bibliography of supplemental readings at a higher or lower level of difficulty in case students find the required text too simple or too challenging

- copies of past exams, model papers, or projects
- areas of difficulty experienced by students in past classes
- characteristics and behaviors of students who have done well in the past classes
- information on the availability of webcasts or podcasts of lectures
- a list of campus resources for tutoring, academic support, and time management (including contact information, physical location, hours of operation)
- calendar of campus lectures, plays, events, exhibits, or other activities of relevance to your course

Include a statement of copyright. Check with legal counsel on your campus about adding language that gives you copyright and ownership of the content and component elements of the course, including the syllabus.

Include a statement on civility and academic freedom. Let students know that you expect them to listen to and respect points of view other than their own. Course content that may be controversial could benefit from a brief note that students' perspectives may be challenged and that they may encounter attitudes, opinions, and information counter to what they believe or think. (Source: Parkes and Harris, 2002)

Describe procedures for emergencies. Indicate what to do if there is an earthquake, fire, bomb threat, or other emergency during class. Identify the location and phone number of campus security. Clarify notification procedures for inclement weather conditions which may force the cancellation of classes.

For the hard-copy syllabus, provide space for names and contact information of two or three classmates. Encourage students to identify people in class they can call if they miss a session or want to study together.

Provide a disclaimer. Let students know what aspects of the schedule may be subject to change (for example, guest speakers, some topics). Dates of exams and deadlines for assignments should not change. If the schedule does change, inform students as early as possible both in writing and orally in class.

End the syllabus in a positive, upbeat fashion. For example, describe that the class will be a joint intellectual discovery. Or end with a meaningful quote, relevant graphic or cartoon, a final thought, or words of encouragement. (Source: Matejka and Kurke, 1994)

Review your syllabus against the checklist in Exhibit 2.1 to decide what you want to include. The checklist summarizes the key components of a comprehensive syllabus.

Exhibit 2.1. Checklist: Components of a Comprehensive Course Syllabus

Basic Information

- **Name of university, semester, year**
- **Course title, number, unit value**
- **Course meeting times and location**
- **Instructor, GSI names**
- **How to contact instructor/GSIs:**
  – in-person office hours: times and location (with map if needed); drop-in or by appointment?
  – online office hours: times and how to access (URL)
  – e-mail addresses
  – phone numbers: private office and department lines; mobile, if you wish, for text messages
  – preferred mode of communication (e-mail, phone, text messages, in person, instant messages, through learning management system, through social networking site, etc.)
  – fax number
  – optional: times other than office hours when instructor can be reached
- **Instructor Web page URL**
- **Course Web page URL**
- **Online chat days, hours, and access address, if available**
- **Group mail-list address, if available**

Course Description

- **Prerequisites:**
  – prior courses
  – knowledge/skills needed to succeed in this course
  – permission of instructor needed?
- **Technology requirements:**
  – laptops for class work
  – software
  – clickers
  – learning management system
- **Overview of course:**
  – what is the course about: its purpose, rationale?
  – what are the general topics or focus?
  – how does it fit with other courses in the department or on campus?
  – who is the course aimed at?
  – why would students want to take this course and learn this material?
- **Student learning objectives:**
  – what will students be expected to know or do after this course?
  – what competencies/skills/knowledge will students be expected to demonstrate at the end of the course?
- **Methods of instruction:**
  – lectures
  – discussion
  – group work
  – field work
  – other methods
- **Workload:**
  – estimated amount of time to spend on course readings
  – estimate amount of time to spend on course assignments and projects

Materials

- **Primary or required books/readings for the course:**
  – author, title, edition ISBN
  – costs, where available
  – availability of electronic or alternative formats, for students with disabilities
- **Supplemental or optional books/readings**
- **Web sites and links**
- **Other materials:**
  – lab equipment
  – art supplies
  – software
  – other types of material

Requirements

- **Exams and quizzes:**
  - how many
  - what kind (e.g., open/closed book; essay/multiple choice)
  - type of knowledge and abilities tested
  - place, date, and time of final exam
- **Assignments/problem sets/projects/reports/research papers:**
  - general information on type, length, and when due (detailed information can be distributed during the term)
  - relationship between the learning objectives and assignments
  - criteria for assessing student work
  - format for submitting work (online or in hard copy)
  - for research papers and projects:
    - steps in conducting research
- shorter assignments that build to the research paper (e.g., annotated bibliography of primary sources, thesis statement, fact sheet, etc.)
- skills and knowledge students needed to complete the research assignments
- connection between research assignments and course goals and student learning objectives
- **Other requirements:**
  - attend an office hour?
  - post comments to the discussion board?

Policies

- **Grading procedures:**
  - describe how students will be graded: on a curve or absolute scale?
  - clarify weighting of course components
  - explain policies regarding incompletes, pass/not pass
  - describe grade appeals
- **Attendance and tardiness**
- **Class participation**
- **Classroom decorum**
- **Interrupted exams (e.g., fire alarms)**
- **Missed exams/makeup exams**
- **Missed assignments**
- **Late assignments/extensions**
- **Reporting illness and family emergencies**
- **Extra credit opportunities**
- **Permissible and impermissible collaboration**
- **Standards for academic honesty and penalties for infractions**

Schedule

- **Tentative calendar of topics and readings:**
  - by week rather than by session
  - or leave some sessions empty for flexibility
- **Firm dates for exams and written assignments**
- **Dates of special events:**
  - field trips
  - performances
  - exhibits
  - other special events
- **Last day to switch to pass/not pass**
- **Last day to withdraw from the course**

Resources

- **Tips for success**
  - how students might approach the material
  - how students can manage their time
  - tips for studying, taking notes, preparing for exams
  - common student mistakes or misconceptions
- **Copies of past exams or model student papers**
- **Glossaries of technical terms**
- **Links to appropriate support material on the Web** (e.g., style manuals, past student projects, Web-based resources, etc.)
- **Academic support services on campus**
- **Information on the availability of podcasts or webcasts**
- **Space for students to identify two or three classmates' names and their contact information**
  - in case they miss class
  - to form a study group

Statement on Accommodation

- **A request that students see the instructor to discuss accommodations for:**
  - physical disabilities
  - medical disabilities
  - learning disabilities
- **A statement on reasonable accommodation for students'** religious beliefs, observations, and practices; for students' foreseeable conflicts because of athletic competition, medical/graduate school interviews

Evaluation of the Course and Assessment of Student Learning

- **Student feedback strategies during the semester** (other than quizzes and tests)
- **End-of-course evaluation procedures**

Rights and Responsibilities	Safety and Emergency Preparedness	Disclaimer
• Students' and instructor's rights to academic freedom (e.g., respect the rights of others to express their points of view) • Students' and instructor's adherence to campus principles of community (e.g., civility in personal interactions) • Statement on copyright protection for the contents of the course, as appropriate	• What to do in case of an earthquake, fire, hazardous spill, accident or injury, bomb threat, or other emergency • Notification procedures for inclement weather • Evacuation procedures • Lab safety precautions	• Syllabus/schedule subject to change

Creating Your Syllabus Online

Check with your department for guidelines for online syllabi. Some campuses have preferred learning management systems or collaborative and learning environments for uploading syllabi. Other campuses let faculty design their own course Web sites however they wish. Some departments no longer cover the costs of reproducing hard copy syllabi. Check with your department to see what policies are in place and what resources are provided.

Add links to campus resources. Supply links to campus policies (for example, academic honesty, academic freedom), the bookstore, academic support services, library resources, disabled students services, and relevant campus events. Some campuses have standard templates that include links to academic departments, libraries, and course catalogs. (Sources: Palmiter and Renjilian, 2003; Rankin, 2000)

Add links to off-campus resources. Link to sites that are relevant to your course such as disciplinary databases, topical bibliographies (available through libraries), or style manuals from your professional association.

Provide an e-mail link for students to contact you. Include your e-mail address and a link that students can click on to send you an e-mail. Remind students that it may take you 24–48 hours to respond. (Sources: Palmiter and Renjilian, 2003; Rankin, 2000)

Supply a class roster. If the class agrees, is small enough, and this does not violate campus policy, include a list of all the students in the course and their contact information. If the class agrees, include photos of students.

Create an announcement section. Whenever you announce in class any change in the schedule or a new event, post that information online as well.

Clarify online requirements. Describe your expectations: Will students be submitting work online? Are students required to participate in a discussion forum? Will they have assignments using wiki?

Post an FAQ (frequently asked questions). Provide answers to commonly asked questions about course procedures and policies or the course material.

Add a link to "netiquette" rules. If your course Web site or learning management system has active discussion boards, posts on walls in social networking sites, or class mail-lists, remind students of basic online etiquette. Stewart (2000) offers the following advice for e-mail:

- Use meaningful subject lines.
- Don't use ALL CAPS.
- Quote selected parts of a previous e-mail.
- Don't forward e-hoaxes or chain letters.
- Avoid attachments.
- Forward messages only with the sender's permission.
- Recognize that your message might be forwarded without your permission.

Stewart (2000) also offers tips for chat rooms and discussion boards:

- Avoid personal attacks and name calling.
- Don't repeat the same message over and over.
- Don't flirt in a chat room.
- Be welcoming and courteous to newcomers.

Regularly update the syllabus and list the date it was last revised. One advantage of posting material online is the ease with which you can revise it to reflect changes in scheduling or emphasis. Date the pages so that students will know the information is current. (Sources: Rankin, 2000; Richards, 2003)

Password-protect the site. If the site includes student information or other information that should not be widely distributed, limit access to those who are enrolled in the course.

Keep permanent file copies. If you create an online syllabus, be sure to keep backup files and a complete hard-copy printout. The hard copy will be useful the next time you offer the course, and you may need it for accreditation reviews, curricular analysis, or your merit and promotion decisions.

If you are designing your own online syllabus, give special attention to the layout. Professional Web designers recommend keeping it simple, using color, breaking up text with a limited number of graphics, and paying attention to navigational aids. They recommend using frames (no more than three), with only one window scrollable. They also suggest avoiding underlining for emphasis or in citations because underlining on the Web indicates a link. Instead, designers recommend using color, bold, italics, or different fonts for emphasis. Keep in mind that students may be printing from the

Web site, so the hard copy should be as easy to read as the Web site. (Source: Richards, 2003)

Motivating Students to Read and Use the Syllabus

Highlight information of most interest to students. Not surprisingly, students do not attend equally to all information in a syllabus. When queried, students indicate that they pay most attention to information about exams and assignments (the dates, formats, and length), the reading list, and the course schedule and activities. Further, differences exist among new and continuing students, with new first-semester students more interested in prerequisites and available support services. (Sources: Becker and Calhoon, 1999; Garavalia et al., 1999; Smith and Razzouk, 1993)

Place the syllabus in the coursepack or reader. Besides distributing an online or print version, consider placing a hard copy of the syllabus in the coursepack so that students won't lose it and can refer to it easily during the term.

Ask students to tape the calendar portion of the syllabus to their textbook. One faculty member takes the schedule of readings and dates for exams and assignments to class with a roll of tape. He passes out both and asks students to tape the abbreviated syllabus to the inside of the textbook. (Source: Smith, 1993)

Consider giving students a short quiz or assignment on the syllabus. Some faculty test students on the information in the syllabus, giving extra credit to students who score above a certain threshold or weighting the quiz the same as problem sets. One faculty member asks students to write a paragraph about their expectations for the course, given what they know about themselves as learners. He also asks students to identify those aspects of the course they are looking forward to and those aspects they have concerns about. This assignment is the basis of small-group discussion in the next class session. (Sources: Hammons and Shock, 1994; Raymark and Connor-Greene, 2002)

Go over important information orally in class. Highlight for students the most critical information in the syllabus. Let them know how to use the syllabus effectively. Revisit the syllabus throughout the term, in print or online, as information becomes more relevant. For example, before assignments are due, restate the penalties for late work. (Source: Grunert O'Brien et al., 2008)

Experiment with a student-written syllabus. One faculty member used the first sessions of class to work with students in an English composition class to design their own syllabus. The syllabus included mutually agreed-on outcomes students wanted to achieve, policies on grading and attendance, and in-class and out-of-class activities. Another faculty member tossed his syllabus, began class with only a tentative set of readings for the first few weeks, and evolved the syllabus in partnership with students over the course of the term. Check with your department to see if any university policies prevent this. (Source: Dahlin, 1994; Singham, 2005)

References

Bain, K. *What the Best College Teachers Do.* Cambridge, MA: Harvard University Press, 2004.

Becker, A. H., and Calhoon, S. K. "What Introductory Psychology Students Attend to on a Course Syllabus." *Teaching of Psychology*, 1999, *26*(1), 6–11.

Chen, Y., and Hoshower, L. B. "Student Evaluation of Teaching Effectiveness: An Assessment of Student Perception and Motivation." *Assessment and Evaluation in Higher Education*, 2003, *28*(1), 71–88.

Collins, T. For Openers . . . An Inclusive Course Syllabus. In W. E. Campbell and K. A. Smith (Eds.), *New Paradigms for College Teaching.* Edina, MN: Interaction Book Company, 1997.

Dahlin, A. "A Student-Written Syllabus for Second-Semester English Composition." *Teaching English in the Two-Year College*, 1994, *21*(1), 27–32.

DiClementi, J. D., and Handelsman, M. M. "Empowering Students: Class-Generated Course Rules." *Teaching of Psychology*, 2005, *32*(1), 18–21.

Eberly, M. B., Newton, S. E., and Wiggins, R. A. "The Syllabus as a Tool for Student-Centered Learning." *Journal of General Education*, 2001, *50*(1), 56–74.

Garavalia, L. S., Hummel, J. H., Wiley, L. P., and Huitt, W. G. "Constructing the Course Syllabus: Faculty and Student Perceptions of Important Syllabus Components." *Journal on Excellence in College Teaching*, 1999, *10*(1), 5–21.

Grunert O'Brien, J., Millis, B. J., and Cohen, M. W. *The Course Syllabus.* (2nd ed.) San Francisco: Jossey-Bass, 2008.

Hammons, J. O., and Shock, J. R. "The Course Syllabus Re-Examined." *Journal of Staff, Program and Organizational Development*, 1994, *12*(1), 5–17.

Lang, J. M. *On Course: A Week-By-Week Guide to Your First Semester of College Teaching.* Cambridge, MA: Harvard University Press, 2008.

Matejka, K., and Kurke, L. B. "Designing a Great Syllabus." *College Teaching*, 1994, *42*(3), 115–117.

Nilson, L. B. *The Graphic Syllabus and the Outcomes Map: Communicating Your Course.* San Francisco: Jossey-Bass, 2007.

Palmiter, D., and Renjilian, D. "Improving Your Psychology Faculty Home Page: Results of a Student-Faculty Online Survey." *Teaching of Psychology*, 2003, *30*(2), 163–166.

Parkes, J., and Harris, M. B. "Purpose of a Syllabus." *College Teaching*, 2002, *50*(2), 55–61.

Rankin, W. "A Survey of Course Web Sites and Online Syllabi." *Educational Technology*, March–April 2000, 38–42.

Raymark, P. H., and Connor-Greene, P. A. "The Syllabus Quiz," *Teaching of Psychology*, 2002, *29*(4), 286–288.

Richards, S. L. F. "The Interactive Syllabus: A Resource-Based, Constructivist Approach to Learning." *The Technology Source*, July/August 2003. http://www.technologysource.org/article/interactive_syllabus

Rubin, S. "Professors, Students and the Syllabus." *Chronicle of Higher Education*, Aug. 7, 1985, 56.

Shea, M. A. *Compendium of Good Ideas on Teaching and Learning*. Boulder: Faculty Teaching Excellence Program, University of Colorado, 1990.

Singham, M. "Moving Away from the Authoritarian Classroom." *Change*, May/June 2005, 50–57.

Smith, M. F., and Razzouk, N. Y. "Improving Classroom Communication: The Case of the Course Syllabus." *Journal of Education for Business*, 1993, *68*(4), 215–221.

Smith, R. A. "Preventing Lost Syllabi." *Teaching of Psychology*, 1993, *20*(2), 113.

Stewart, B. "Commonsense Netiquette Rules." 2000. http://www.westpagepublishing.com/netiquetterules.htm

Warma, S. J. "Classroom Demeanor: An Excerpt from One Syllabus." *Chronicle of Higher Education*, March 27, 1998, 12.

Woolcock, M. J. *Constructing a Syllabus: A Handbook for Faculty, Teaching Assistants and Teaching Fellows*. Providence, RI: Sheridan Center for Teaching and Learning, Brown University, 1997. http://www.brown.edu/Administration/Sheridan_Center/publications/syllabus.html

3

The First Days of Class

The first day of class sets the tone for the rest of the term. It is natural for both students and instructors to feel anticipation, excitement, anxiety, and uncertainty. To pique students' interest, convey your enthusiasm for the topics that will be covered during the term. To put students at ease, try to create a relaxed, open classroom environment conducive to inquiry and participation, and let students know what you will expect from them and what they can expect from you and the course. The following suggestions, intended to help you get your class off to a good start, address three important tasks of the first day: handling administrative matters including course policies and procedures, creating a positive classroom environment, and setting course expectations and standards.

General Strategies

Visit the classroom before the first meeting. Test the room's lights, blinds, electrical outlets, thermostat, and ventilation. Check any equipment (microphone, projector screen, laptop, chalkboard) that you will be using, and find out how to obtain help if the equipment malfunctions. If the classroom is large, practice speaking to the far corners of the room and make sure your board work will be legible from the back row.

Build a sense of community in the classroom. Students learn more and work harder in classes that spark their intellectual curiosity and allow for active involvement and participation. For the first day, plan an activity that provides opportunities for students to speak to one another or to solve problems. Students also tend to work harder when they feel that their instructor views them as individuals rather than as anonymous faces in the crowd. From the start, make an effort to get to know your students and express your interest in working with them during the term. (Source: Astin, 1993)

Address students' concerns. Students enter a new class with several questions: Is this the right course for me? Does the teacher seem competent and fair? How much work will be required? How will I be evaluated? Use the first days to answer these questions and demonstrate your commitment to helping your students learn. (Source: Forsyth, 2003)

Set the tone for the rest of the term. Greet students when they enter the class-room. Start and finish class on time. Encourage questions, and give students the opportunity to talk. Stay after class to answer questions, or invite students to walk with you back to your office. Students with positive first-day experiences report higher levels of motivation and achieve higher grades than students with negative first-day experiences. (Source: Wilson and Wilson, 2007)

Make the time worthwhile. As time permits, plunge into substantive material. Choose a topic or an activity that will engage students: stage a provocative dem-onstration, pose a controversial issue, make a counterintuitive argument, or work through a compelling case study.

Expect some awkwardness. All teachers, especially beginning instructors, feel a twinge of apprehension before the first class. Do your best to assume a confident attitude. Keep in mind that your students are likely to perceive your nervousness as energy and enthusiasm. Arriving early on the first day of class and talking informally to students may help you relax.

Taking Care of Administrative Tasks

Identify the course name and number and your name on the screen or chalkboard. This message will alert any students who are in the wrong class-room to leave before you begin. If your name is difficult to pronounce, include the phonetic spelling.

Take attendance, if class size permits. Call the roll or ask students to sign in. Make allowances for students who arrive late and have a contingency plan if more students arrive than you can accommodate. If your department does not have a policy for handling excess enrollment demand, you may want to give preference to graduating seniors or to majors, or you may prefer to hold a lottery. If your course is an elective, consider admitting a few extra students to compensate for those who are likely to drop the course.

Mention campus enrollment policies. Explain procedures for wait lists, deadlines for adding and dropping courses, and so on. Know where to refer students who have problems in these areas.

Clarify your policies on attendance. Researchers have examined the effects of classroom attendance. Students who regularly attend class tend to earn higher grades than students who attend sporadically. More significantly, classroom attendance has a more positive effect on overall student performance than time spent studying outside of class. Absenteeism—which in large universities may approach 40 percent on a typical day according to Romer (1993)—declines when students perceive the course content to be relevant to their interests or needs, when the quality of teaching is high, and when expectations for attendance are explicit. (Sources: Gump, 2005; Marburger, 2001; Rocca, 2003; Schmidt, 1983; Wyatt, 1992)

Explain the procedures for sections. If your course has sections, make sure that all students know which section they are enrolled in, who their graduate student instructor is, and when and where the section meets. Describe the relationship between the course and the sections and how sections will be run. Have the graduate student instructors introduce themselves.

Review any prerequisites for the course. Let students know what skills or knowledge they are expected to have and whether alternate experience or course work will be accepted. Is help available for those who do not have all the prerequisite skills? Some faculty list tasks that students should be able to perform if they have the prerequisite skills and knowledge, and they announce that the first graded test will include those tasks. (Source: Brent and Felder, 1999)

Go over course requirements and give estimates of workload. Discuss the written assignments and exams, other requirements (for example, class participation, group activities, field trips), and your estimate of how much time students will need to devote to the course outside of class.

Discuss the course syllabus. See Chapter 2, "The Comprehensive Course Syllabus."

Explain your grading policies. Let students know what they will need to do to succeed in your class. Students who believe that they can excel in a course are more likely to work harder, take an active role in their learning, and learn more. As appropriate, provide grade distributions from prior offerings of the course and let the class know what past students have done to earn As. (Source: Forsyth, 2003)

Tell students about campus policies on academic honesty. State your expectations, and let students know what activities constitute cheating and impermissible collaboration. See Chapter 38, "Promoting Academic Honesty."

Invite students to attend your office hours. Tell students where your office is and encourage them to stop by with questions and course-related problems. Ask students who need academic accommodations for a physical or learning disability to see you during the first or second week of the term. Invite students who may have foreseeable conflicts, such as student athletes or students with medical school interviews, to meet with you to arrange for makeup exams or assignments.

Review safety precautions and emergency procedures. If your course requires lab work or fieldwork, review safe practices for using equipment and supplies and discuss emergency procedures. Show students how to use equipment safely and appropriately. Let students know what to do in case of fire, tornado, hurricane, earthquake, evacuation, or other emergency.

Record the session, if appropriate. For students who miss the first day of class, make available a webcast or podcast that they can review on their own. If recording is impractical, ask latecomers to obtain notes from a classmate.

Give a catch-up assignment to students who want to add the class after the first or second session. To ensure that students catch up on the reading assignments, one faculty member asks students to submit five multiple-choice exam questions for each class session they missed.

Creating a Positive Classroom Environment

Introduce yourself to your class. Let students know how you prefer to be addressed (first name, or last name prefaced by Dr., Professor, Mr., or Ms.). You might also briefly share some information about where you are from, the schools you attended, how you first became interested in the subject, your publications and research, how long you have been at the university, and why you are teaching the course. Convey your enthusiasm for the field and the subject. For many students, the instructor's enthusiasm about the course material is a key motivator for learning. (Source: Wolcowitz, 1984)

Gather information about the students in your class. If class size is appropriate, ask students to complete a questionnaire in class or online: name (and what they like to be called), hometown, campus address, e-mail address, phone numbers and preferred method of contact, year in school, and major field. Some faculty ask students to list related courses or prerequisites they have completed or other courses they are taking during the current term; reasons for enrolling in the course or what they hope to learn in the course; tentative career plans; outside interests, hobbies, and current employment. Some faculty have asked other questions: What should this class *not* be like? How do you learn the best? What question is uppermost in your mind about this course? How well prepared are you for this course? Approximately how many hours outside of class do you plan on studying for this course?

Ask students to write a letter of introduction. Some faculty ask students to write a paragraph or two about themselves and attach a photo. The letters are not graded or returned. (Source: Armstrong, 2008)

Begin to learn students' names. Learning students' names signals your interest in their performance and encourages student motivation and class participation. If you call roll, ask for the correct pronunciation and how the student prefers to be addressed. California State Polytechnic University, Pomona, has developed a pronunciation guide for Cambodian, Cantonese, Filipino, Mandarin, Indonesian, Japanese, Korean, Thai, and Vietnamese names. If your course enrolls fewer than twenty or thirty students, call the roll for several class meetings to help you learn names. During the term, ask students to give their name when they pose a question in class, call students by name when you return homework or quizzes, and use names frequently in class. Even if you can't learn everyone's name, students appreciate your making the effort. Here are a some other strategies for learning students' names:

- *Photographs.* Ask students to pose in groups of four or five. Post online copies of the photographs with students' names. If your campus supplies faculty with photos of enrolled students, append these photos to your online files. Or, with students' permission, post individual photos on the course Web site.
- *Name cards.* For a seminar class, place name cards in front of each student. In a studio or lab course, post students' names above their workstations.
- *Seating chart.* Ask students to sit in the same seats for the first few weeks, and prepare a seating chart. Try to memorize four or five names at each class session.
- *Alphabetical order.* In a small class, have students arrange themselves along one wall of the classroom in alphabetical order by first name.
- *Introductions.* In a large class, at the beginning of each class period, ask six or eight students to introduce themselves.
  (Sources: McGlynn, 2001; Ricci, 2004; Smith and Malec, 1995)

Give students an opportunity to know who is in the class. Ask students to raise their hands if their answer is yes to questions you pose (and if they feel comfortable sharing with information with the entire class). Examples of questions include year in school, major, favorite sports teams, place of birth, languages spoken.

Ask students to interview each other outside of class. If your course is small and has a writing component, assign students to write a brief description of a classmate. The class could agree on the interview questions beforehand, or students can improvise. (Source: Scholl-Buckwald, 1985)

Ask small groups to explore characteristics of effective learning. In the first round, each group generates a list of the three or four best practices of successful students. Groups are then paired to share their lists and agree on a single list of four practices. This sharing of lists can be repeated several times, as needed, and the final lists can be posted for the entire class.

Ask small groups to explore characteristics of effective teaching. In the first round, each group generates a list of the three or four best practices of successful teachers. Groups are then paired to share their lists and agree on a single list of four practices. This sharing of lists can be repeated several times, as needed, and the final lists can be posted for the entire class and for you to comment on.

Consider using an icebreaker. Icebreakers can help people get to know one another and engage students immediately in the class. However, research indicates that students may not like icebreakers (Perlman and McCann, 1999) because they engage in icebreakers in many other parts of their campus lives, and may suffer from icebreaker fatigue (Lang, 2008) . If you decide to use an icebreaker, make sure that it doesn't make students uncomfortable or reveal information they would not rather share. Linking your icebreaker to the content of the course may make it more palatable to students. Here are some examples of icebreakers culled from the Web:

- *Birthday buddies.* Ask students to find someone whose birthday is closest to theirs (day and month only). Ask the pairs to identify two academic or course-related things they have in common.
- *Find someone.* Students write three statements related to the course content on a single index card, such as "Marine biology has been an interest of mine since I visited the Monterey Aquarium when I was 12"; "I am a certified scuba diver;" "In Hawaii, I swam with the dolphins." Cards are distributed so that no one has their own card and students circulate to find and meet the person who has their card.

- *True or false.* Students write three statements about themselves: one is true and two are false. In small groups, students have to identify the true statement.

Distribute rosters. With students' permission, post online the roster and contact information. Encourage students to contact classmates about missed classes, homework assignments, and study groups. Or ask students to exchange contact information with two or three classmates.

Setting Course Expectations and Standards

Discuss the objectives of the course. Tell your students what you plan to accomplish and why, and ask what they want to learn from you. Be sure to carefully acknowledge students' contributions. How you respond to students' ideas on the first day will set the tone for student participation throughout the term. (Source: McKeachie and Svinicki, 2006)

Ask students to list the goals they hope to achieve by taking the course. Have students, in small groups or individually, list two or three goals in the form of statements about knowledge, skills, interests, or attitudes. Students can also rank their goals in terms of how difficult they may be to achieve. Use these lists to identify your class's interests and likely problem areas. (Source: Angelo and Cross, 1993)

Describe how you propose to spend class time. How will sessions be structured? How will discussions be organized? Will a specific time be set aside for questions, or may students ask questions as they arise? Should questions requiring a lengthy response be saved for office hours?

Give your students advice about how to succeed in your class. Discuss strategies for approaching the material and for studying, and give examples of questions students might want to think about. Tell students how much time they will need to devote to studying for the course, and let them know about campus academic support services. Some faculty distribute advice solicited from students in previous offerings of the course. If you teach a large-enrollment course, you may want to mention research findings about seat location and course performance: students who sit near the front of the room are more likely to receive As than students who sit in the back of the room, and students who prefer to sit in the back but nonetheless move forward tend to receive higher grades than those who remain in the back. (Sources: Benedict and Hoag, 2004; Brent and Felder, 1999; Brinthaupt, 2004; Perkins and Wieman, 2005)

Give a brief diagnostic pretest or survey. Administer a short, scored, but ungraded exercise that will show you and your students what topics or skills they have already mastered. Some science disciplines have widely used diagnostic tests (for example, the Force Concept Inventory in Physics and the California Chemistry Diagnostic Test). The Knowledge Surveys from the Science Education Resource Center (SERC) at Carleton College ask students to rate their level of confidence on various course topics. If your field does not have an established test, you can develop your own. For example, you could create a list of key concepts, facts and figures, or major ideas and ask students to indicate their familiarity with each. Or you could have students solve problems, define terms, and complete short-answer items. In a writing course you might assign a short essay that will allow you to identify students' strengths and weaknesses.

A diagnostic pretest or knowledge survey can be used in a variety of ways. Some faculty administer the same exercise at the end of the term and then return the pretest to students for comparison. Other faculty ask students to take the test anonymously, and some give the answers in the subsequent class so that students can assess their readiness to take the course. Some faculty include questions to assess students' motivation and study habits, since students who do poorly on a diagnostic test might do well in the class with adequate academic support and disciplined study. (Sources: Eckert et al., 1997; Lang, 2008; Nuhfer and Knipp, 2003; Ochs, 1998)

Ask students to work through a problem. Begin to teach students how to participate in your class. Engaging students in coursework during the first session gives them an idea of what class will be like. Here are some suggestions from faculty in a variety of fields (Brent and Felder, 1999; Erickson et al., 2006; Henderson and Mirafzal, 1999; Higgins, 1999; Keeports, 2000; Scholl-Buckwald, 1985):

- Some professors select keywords from the course title, ask students to propose related ideas, and use those responses to give a thematic overview of the course.
- A sociology professor asks small groups of students to come up with a list of the ten most important events (or people) in history. After ten or fifteen minutes, the groups' responses are placed on the board for discussion and interpretation.
- An English professor divides the class into small groups and gives each member a line from a poem, which the group is asked to reassemble.

- A physics instructor discusses with the class how normal observations lead to false conclusions about gravity, velocity, inertia, and other laws of nature, using everyday examples: swinging a golf club, looking in the mirror, dropping a feather.
- A sociology faculty member uses a demonstration to show how context can define meaning by having a student provide a small amount of saliva in a sterilized spoon. The instructor then asks whether any students want to swallow the saliva on the spoon. When all students decline, the faculty member launches into a discussion of how sharing a soft drink or kissing is an acceptable exchange of saliva but swallowing a spoonful is not.
- A chemistry professor describes a case study about finding white powdery substances near the household cleaning products and an odorless crystalline powder in the pantry. Students are then asked to describe experiments that would help them identify the sample materials.

Give an assignment for the next session. By moving immediately into the first topic, you are indicating to students that the course is well organized and well paced. Avoid giving a graded assignment, however, because students may be adding or dropping your course during the first week or two. (Source: Povlacs, 1986)

Ask students to write their reactions to the first day. Take two minutes at the end of class to have students jot down unsigned comments about what went well and what questions or concerns they have about the course. Review their comments and report back to students at the next session, correcting any misconceptions or inaccuracies. (Source: McKeachie and Svinicki, 2006)

References

Angelo, T. A., and Cross, K. P. *Classroom Assessment Techniques: A Handbook for College Teachers.* (2nd ed.) San Francisco: Jossey-Bass, 1993.

Armstrong, J. "Write Me a Letter: Challenging Anonymity in Large-Enrollment Classes." *College Teaching*, 2008, *56*(1), 63.

Astin, A. W. *What Matters in College? Four Critical Years Revisited.* San Francisco: Jossey-Bass, 1993.

Benedict, M. E., and Hoag, J. "Seating Location in Large Lectures: Are Seating Preferences or Location Related to Course Performance?" *Journal of Economic Education*, 2004, *35*(3), 215–231.

Brent, R., and Felder, R. M. "It's a Start." *College Teaching.* 1999, *47*(1), 14–18.

Brinthaupt, T. M. "Providing a Realistic Course Preview to Students." *Teaching of Psychology*, 2004, *31*(2), 104–106.

Eckert, C. M., Bower, D. J., Hinkle, A. J., Stiff, K. S., and Davis, A. R. "Students' Knowledge and Faculty Members' Expectations: The Case for Classroom Assessment." *Teaching Sociology*, 1997, *25*(2), 150–159.

Erickson, B. L., Peters, C. B., and Strommer, D. W. *Teaching First-Year College Students*. San Francisco: Jossey-Bass, 2006.

Forsyth, D. R. *The Professor's Guide to Teaching: Psychological Principles and Practices*. Washington, DC: American Psychological Association, 2003.

Gump, S. E. "The Cost of Cutting Class: Attendance as a Predictor of Student Success." *College Teaching*, 2005, *53*(1), 21–26.

Henderson, L. L., and Mirafzal, G. A. "A First-Class Meeting Exercise for General Chemistry: Introduction to Chemistry through an Experimental Tour." *Journal of Chemical Education*, 1999, *76*(9), 1221–1223.

Higgins, P. "Unconventional First Days: Encouraging Students to Wonder about Social Life and Learning." *Teaching Sociology*, 1999, *27*(3), 258–263.

Keeports, D. "Addressing Physical Intuition—A First Day Event." *The Physics Teacher*, 2000, *38*(5), 318–319.

Lang, J. M. *On Course: A Week-By-Week Guide to Your First Semester of College Teaching*. Cambridge, MA: Harvard University Press, 2008.

Marburger, D. R. "Absenteeism and Undergraduate Exam Performance." *Journal of Economic Education*, 2001, *32*(2), 99–109.

McGlynn, A. P. *Successful Beginnings for College Teaching: Engaging Your Students from the First Day*. Madison, WI: Atwood, 2001.

McKeachie, W. J., and Svinicki, M. *McKeachie's Teaching Tips*. (12th ed.) Boston: Houghton Mifflin, 2006.

Nuhfer, E., and Knipp, D. The Knowledge Survey: A Tool for All Reasons. In C. M. Wehlburg and S. Chadwick-Blossey (Eds.), *To Improve the Academy*. Vol. 21. San Francisco: Jossey-Bass/Anker, 2003.

Ochs, R. S. "The First-Day Quiz as a Teaching Technique." *Journal of Chemical Education*, 1998, *75*(4), 401–403.

Perkins, K. K., and Wieman, C. E. "The Surprising Impact of Seat Location on Student Performance." *The Physics Teacher*, 2005, *43*(1), 30–33.

Perlman, B., and McCann, L. I. "Student Perspectives on the First Day of Class." *Teaching of Psychology*, 1999, *26*(4), 277–279.

Povlacs, J. T. "101 Things You Can Do the First Three Weeks of Class." *Teaching at the University of Nebraska, Lincoln*, 1986, *8*(1), 1–4. (Newsletter available from the Teaching and Learning Center, University of Nebraska, Lincoln.)

Ricci, C. W. "The Impacts of Professors' Knowledge of Students' Names." *Journal on Excellence in College Teaching*, 2004, *15*(3), 85–104.

Rocca, K. A. "Student Attendance: A Comprehensive Literature Review." *Journal on Excellence in College Teaching*, 2003, *14*(1), 85–107.

Romer, D. "Do Students Go to Class? Should They?" *Journal of Economic Perspectives*, Summer 1993, *7*(3), 167–174.

Schmidt, R. M. "Who Maximizes What? A Study in Student Time Allocation." *American Economic Review*, May 1983, *73*(2), 23–28.

Scholl-Buckwald, S. "The First Meeting of the Class." In J. Katz (Ed.), *Teaching As Though Students Mattered*. New Directions for Teaching and Learning, no. 21. San Francisco: Jossey-Bass, 1985, pp. 13–21.

Smith, D. H., and Malec, M. M. "Learning Students' Names in Sociology Classes: Interactive Tactics, Who Uses Them, and When." *Teaching Sociology*, 1995, *23*(3), 280–286.

Wilson, J. H., and Wilson, S. B. "The First Day of Class Affects Student Motivation: An Experimental Study." *Teaching of Psychology*, 2007, *34*(4), 226–230.

Wolcowitz, J. The First Day of Class. In M. M. Gullette (Ed.), *The Art and Craft of Teaching*. Cambridge, MA: Harvard University Press, 1984.

Wyatt, G. "Skipping Class: An Analysis of Absenteeism among First-Year College Students." *Teaching Sociology*, 1992, *20*(3), 201–207.

4

Classroom Conduct and Decorum

Feldmann (2001, p. 137) defines classroom incivility as "any action that interferes with a harmonious and cooperative learning atmosphere in the classroom." Examples of disruptive student behavior include disturbing others when arriving late or leaving early; packing up books before class is over; dozing in class; reading the newspaper; noisy eating or drinking; checking social networking sites, shopping, or playing games on laptops; text messaging on cell phones; conducting side conversations; and hostile public challenges to course policies and procedures.

The following suggestions are intended to help you maintain a sense of decorum in your classroom. When improprieties occur, you will want to promptly address them: the longer inappropriate behavior persists, the more difficult it is to stop (Sorcinelli, 1994).

General Strategies

Define and distribute policies at the start of the term. Some faculty spend a portion of class time generating guidelines as a class on what is acceptable and unacceptable classroom behavior. For example, consider asking students in small groups to give specific behavioral examples of "best effort" and "mutual respect." Research shows that students are more civil when given the opportunity to develop their own rules and sanctions. Other faculty set their own standards and detail them in the syllabus and course Web site. Set only those rules and penalties that you are willing and able to enforce. It is usually better to be firm at the beginning and later relax your policies rather than try to impose a stricter regime as the term progresses. (Sources: Bayer, 2004: DiClementi and Handelsman, 2005)

Emphasize the value of civility. Help students see the effect of their actions on others. Share with students the responsibility for maintaining norms: let students know that they should feel free to tell talkative students to be quiet. (Source: Forsyth, 2003)

Set a good example. Researchers have identified faculty behaviors that set a negative tone for students and affect their academic and intellectual development (Braxton et al., 2004; Buttner, 2004):

- *Inadequate preparation:* failure to order required texts or readers in a timely fashion; inadequate communication about due dates for assignments or about policies on missed or makeup exams; incomplete syllabus.
- *Poor in-class interactions with students:* treating students in a condescending, insensitive, or demeaning manner; putting students down in front of classmates; ignoring students' perspectives; lack of respect for students as individuals.
- *Lack of integrity:* grading students' work on criteria other than merit; treating students unfairly.
- *Failure to provide help:* ignoring students' questions or reacting angrily or defensively when challenged; refusing to provide assistance with assignments.
- *Repeatedly arriving late, running overtime, or ending class early.*

Handling Incivilities

Deal with incivilities promptly and consistently. Responding immediately and consistently to misbehavior will discourage future misconduct. Try to size up the student's frame of mind (for example, disengaged, uninterested, disrespectful, disruptive, defiant, disturbed) and intentions. Address the student politely and calmly, name the behavior that is disrupting the class, and give clear instructions or options about what you want the student to do. If the problem is more complicated, ask the student to see you during office hours. (Sources: Boice, 1996; Feldmann, 2001; González and López, 2001)

Anticipate problems at the back of the room. The back of the classroom is the traditional gathering spot for bored and disruptive students. If your classroom has many unoccupied seats, instruct the class to use only so many rows, starting from the front. Mention that research shows that students who sit in the front of the classroom earn higher grades. Or consider asking students to change their seats periodically, asking those in the back to sit in the front at the next session. (Sources: Benedict and Hoag, 2004; McKeachie and Svinicki, 2006; Perkins and Wieman, 2005)

Make disrupters aware of the problem. Disruptive students may not be aware of the problems they are causing. To interrupt a side conversation, you could move towards the talkers, making eye contact; or ask the students if they would like to share their ideas with the class; or you could pause until everyone quiets down and say, "When people have side conversations, it's hard for the rest of us to concentrate. Please save it for after class." To keep laptop users from playing online games, perusing Facebook or YouTube, and the like, let students know that it is distracting to those behind and to the sides of them. (For more suggestions on laptop etiquette, see Chapter 33, "Mobile Learning.") Ask students to silence their cell phones.

Monitor comings and goings. Some faculty advise students to sit near the door if they arrive late or need to leave early. One instructor discourages late arrivals by addressing the individual by name before he or she sits down and asking, good-naturedly, a course-relevant question related to that person's own experience, then following up with more questions to the same person. (Source: Carbone, 1999)

Acknowledge negative emotions, but do not explore them in class. When a student's incivility is prompted by negative feelings, show empathy by acknowledging the feeling ("I'm guessing that you're angry because you think this is unfair"), and invite the student to discuss the matter with you after class. Refrain from showing anger, impatience, or hostility. (Source: Meyers, 2003)

Speak with the student in private. In class, enforce your policies. As needed, arrange to speak with a disruptive student outside class, either in a neutral space or in your office. Explain the problem as you see it and ask for the student's perspective. If a student becomes argumentative, agitated, or highly defensive, stop the conversation and arrange for another meeting. Look for common ground in terms of the student's interests and the reasons the student is taking the course. (Source: Downs, 1992)

Deal with grumpy consumers. Some students feel that since they pay tuition, you are a service provider and their preferences take precedence over your classroom rules. Don't extend such arguments in class, but invite the student to meet with you privately. At that time talk about your role and responsibilities to all the students in your class and how you view your role in relation to students (for example, expert and apprentices, not service provider and customers).

Expect some cyber-complaining, but establish limits. Blogs and Web sites such as YouTube and Facebook give students new ways to scrutinize and vent about instructors and courses. Try to take any negative comments with good humor. Let students know if your college or university has policies against filming instructors in class without their permission or if your state makes it illegal to secretly film someone. When complaints cross over into threats, bullying, or misconduct, or when students impersonate and misrepresent you online, take up the matter with your department chair. (Source: Summerville and Fischetti, 2005)

Explain the student grievance process. All campuses should have in place procedures to investigate students' complaints and concerns, if they cannot be resolved adequately by the parties in conflict. Find out about the process on your campus and refer students, as needed, to the appropriate resources. Similarly, find out what recourse your campus has for instructors who face hostile, unruly, or belligerent students.

Teaching in Times of Crisis and Tragedy

Think about how you can help your students cope with tragic events. International crises, shooting rampages on college campuses, natural disasters, the unexpected death of a fellow student or teacher, and other events may make it difficult to conduct class as usual. Studies conducted after September 11, 2001, found that on some American campuses, fewer than two-thirds of instructors mentioned the terrorist attacks in class, and this lack of response surprised, frustrated, and disappointed most students. Students said they were grateful and found it helpful when faculty acknowledged the tragedy and how it affected them. (Source: Huston and DiPietro, 2007)

If warranted, cancel class. If you are unsure about canceling class, check with your department chair. If you cannot notify all your students in advance, show up at the appointed time and explain why you are canceling class—don't just post a note on the door. Let students know what campus resources are available to them, and stay to answer any questions they may have.

When you meet your class, acknowledge the tragedy. Some instructors mention an event but choose not to discuss it in class; others devote a few moments of class time to such discussion. Still other instructors ask students at the start of class whether they want to discuss the event for a portion of the meeting. And some instructors invite concerned students to come to a special office hour.

Here are some other ways that faculty have responded to tragic events:

- Observe a moment of silence to remember the victims.
- Read an inspirational or comforting poem or passage from a book.
- Sign and send a card to students on the affected campus.

- Post contact information for the campus counseling center so students know resources are available.
- Postpone a test; extend the deadlines for assignments and homework.
- Change the syllabus for the following week to accommodate a reduced workload.
- Ask students to write about their feelings and responses.
- Tell students about candlelight vigils on campus and other memorial events.
- Let students know about ways to help (giving blood, collecting donations, volunteering).
- Review with students campus emergency and security procedures.

Recognize that some students may need extra support. Some students may be personally affected by local, national, or international events, and they may need referrals, psychological services, or assignment extensions to accommodate sudden travel plans.

If you discuss the events in class, encourage students to be empathetic listeners. Open the discussion by acknowledging that people have different ways of coping with crises and that all are valid. Some of your students will want to talk and try to understand what has happened, while others will feel that talking and listening will upset them. Some students will share their feelings, but others would be uncomfortable doing so, and some students will welcome the resumption of ordinary routines that convey a sense of security and safety.

Try to introduce and close the session on a supportive note; for example, you might begin by mentioning your reasons for holding the discussion and end by telling students how they can continue the discussion in other venues on campus. Help your class establish ground rules for the discussion: respect one another's points of view, including the preferences of students who wish to remain silent; avoid speculation and rumor; politely remind each other not to monopolize the conversation.

Experts also recommend other guidelines:

- Pose a question or two to get the discussion started: What makes this hard to talk about? In what ways are you affected by these events? How might these events affect your future action and behavior? What questions and fears do you have? How can you become better informed? What positive actions can individuals take in response to this event?
- Balance the emotional and intellectual aspects of the discussion and help students distinguish between the two.

- Invite students who do not wish to participate in the discussion to leave.
- Give students a chance to write before speaking.
- Stop the discussion if it veers off in unproductive directions.

    (Sources: Web sites of the University of Michigan, University of Washington, Vanderbilt University, and the University of California, Berkeley)

As appropriate, develop class assignments related to the tragedy. Some professors have asked their students to gather newspapers from around the world and examine the attitudes expressed in the reporting; to follow online coverage in one or two newspapers over the course of several days; to write a "memoir" of their reactions to the events, with the thought that they might reread their account in twenty-five or thirty years.

Strive to restore some sense of normalcy. Try to avoid overreacting to the tragedy. Let students know that the school year will proceed. Reassure them if they are having problems concentrating, and ask them to talk with you about options for completing the semester.

References

Bayer, A. E. "Promulgating Statements of Student Rights and Responsibilities."*New Directions for Teaching and Learning*, no. 99. San Francisco: Jossey-Bass, 2004, pp. 77–87.

Benedict, M. E., and Hoag, J. "Seating Location in Large Lectures: Are Seating Preferences or Location Related to Course Performance?" *Journal of Economic Education*, 2004, *35*(3), 215–231.

Boice, B. "Classroom Incivilities." *Research in Higher Education*, 1996, *37*(4).

Braxton, J. M., Bayer, A. E., and Noseworthy, J. A. "The Influence of Teaching Norm Violations on the Welfare of Students as Clients of College Teaching." *New Directions for Teaching and Learning*, no. 99. San Francisco: Jossey-Bass, 2004, 41–46.

Buttner, E. H. "How Do We 'Dis' Students? A Model of (Dis)respectful Business Instructor Behavior." *Journal of Management Education*, 2004, *28*(3), 319–334.

Carbone, E. "Students Behaving Badly in Large Classes." In S. M. Richardson (Ed.), *Promoting Civility: A Teaching Challenge*. New Directions for Teaching and Learning, no. 77. San Francisco: Jossey-Bass, 1999.

DiClementi, J. D., and Handelsman, M. M. "Empowering Students: Class-Generated Course Rules." *Teaching of Psychology*, 2005, *32*(1), 18–21.

Downs, J. R. "Dealing with Hostile and Oppositional Students." *College Teaching*, 1992, *40*(3), 106–108.

Feldmann, L. J. "Classroom Civility Is Another of Our Instructor Responsibilities." *College Teaching*, 2001, *49*(4), 137–140.

Forsyth, D. R. *The Professor's Guide to Teaching: Psychological Principles and Practices*. Washington, DC: American Psychological Association, 2003.

González, V., and López, E. "The Age of Incivility: Countering Disruptive Behavior in the Classroom." *AAHE Bulletin*, April 2001.

Huston, T. A., and DiPietro, M. In the Eye of the Storm: Students' Perceptions of Helpful Faculty Actions Following a Collective Tragedy. In D. R. Robertson and L. B. Nilson (Eds.), *To Improve the Academy*. Vol. 25. San Francisco: Jossey-Bass/Anker, 2007.

McKeachie, W. J., and Svinicki, M. *McKeachie's Teaching Tips*. (12th ed.). Boston: Houghton Mifflin, 2006.

Meyers, S. A. "Strategies to Prevent and Reduce Conflict in College Classrooms." *College Teaching*, 2003, *51*(3), 94–98.

Perkins, K. K., and Wieman, C.E. "The Surprising Impact of Seat Location on Student Performance." *The Physics Teacher*, 2005, *43*(1), 30–33.

Sorcinelli, M. D. Dealing with Troublesome Behaviors in the Classroom. In K. W. Prichard and R. M. Sawyer (Eds.), *Handbook of College Teaching: Theory and Applications*. Westport, CT: Greenwood Press, 1994.

Summerville, J., and Fischetti, J. C. "How to Foil Cyberbullies." *Chronicle of Higher Education*, June 24, 2005, *51*(42).

PART II

Responding to a Changing Student Body

5

Diversity and Inclusion in the Classroom

As campuses continue to become more diverse, faculty members need to be attentive to prejudice, bias, and discriminatory behavior—their own and that of their students. Some historically underrepresented students describe feeling like unwelcome outsiders and encountering subtle forms of bias and unwitting insensitive comments from peers and instructors that have led to a sense of alienation and detachment (Carroll, 1998; Davis et al., 2004; Engberg, 2004; Harris and Nettles, 1996; Nora and Cabrera, 1996; Steele, 1997; Suarez-Balcazar et al., 2003; Sue et al., 2007). You can begin to explore attitudes and conduct by asking yourself (or your students) the following kinds of questions (adapted from Adams et al., 1997; Chin et al., 2002; and Gay, 2000):

- Do you interact with men and women in ways that manifest double standards?
- Do you inadvertently undervalue comments made by speakers whose English is accented differently from your own?
- Do you assume that students of some racial or ethnic groups will need additional help? Or that students of some racial or ethnic groups will do better than others?
- Are you comfortable around people whose racial, ethnic, or sexual identity differs from your own?
- Are you comfortable disclosing your knowledge of and experiences with diversity?
- How do you handle your own doubts or ambivalence about multicultural issues?

You may also discover that for some students, issues related to group identity assume great importance because college presents their first opportunity to affirm their identity and join single-identity organizations or groups.

The following ideas, based on the teaching practices of faculty and on current research, are intended to help you work effectively with the broad range of students enrolled in your classes.

General Strategies

Become aware of any biases or stereotypes you may have absorbed. We are all shaped and influenced by our backgrounds and experiences that have led to biases and assumptions about ourselves and others. Your attitudes and values not only influence the attitudes and values of your students, but they can affect the way you teach, particularly your assumptions about students based on race or ethnicity, which can lead to unequal learning outcomes for those in your classes. (Sources: American Psychological Association, 2003; Bensimon, 2005; Fouad and Arredondo, 2006; Hurtado et al., 1999; Sue, 2001)

Treat each student as an individual. Each of us shares some characteristics with others of our gender, race, place of origin, and sociocultural group, but these are outweighed by the many differences among members of any group. We tend to recognize this point about groups we belong to ("I'm not like all those other Texans you may know"), but we sometimes fail to recognize it about others. Try not to project your experiences with, feelings about, or expectations of an entire group onto any one student.

Monitor the climate in your classroom. Ask students to let you know if you inadvertently offend them, and tell them you'll let them know if they unintentionally offend you. Invite students to send you a note (signed or unsigned), or add one or more of the following questions to your midsemester course evaluation (adapted from Hyde and Ruth, 2002):

- Does the instructor treat students equally and evenhandedly?
- How comfortable do you feel participating in this class? What makes it easy or difficult for you?
- Do you feel that your ethnicity, race, sexuality, or gender affects your interactions with the teacher in this class? With other students?
- Do you have suggestions for encouraging open and candid discussion in class?

Introduce discussions of diversity at department meetings. Propose that the agenda of your department meetings include topics such as classroom climate, course content and course requirements, graduation and placement rates, extracurricular activities, orientation for new students, academic support services, and opportunities for undergraduate research or service-learning experiences.

Recognize the complexity of diversity. Diversity can include race, ethnicity, culture, gender, sexuality, disability, age, religion and spirituality, language, family responsibilities, immigrant status, socioeconomic status, worldview, political persuasion, academic preparation, and regional and national identity. In addition, even a category like "ethnic group" can have numerous intragroup differences. For example, the U.S. Census in 2000 listed sixty categories for Asian/Pacific Islanders. Latinas/os may come from one of twenty-five culturally different Spanish-speaking countries or territories. As of 2007, the U.S. government recognized 561 Native American tribes, each with its own language, traditions, and customs.

Students enter college with multiple, evolving, and shifting identities. Some group characteristics are fixed (for example, age) and others are fluid (for example, income level); some identities are more salient than others (for example, race over religion) and may shift from one to the other depending on the context (disability among people without disabilities but sexual orientation among people with disabilities) or at different times in students' lives. Avoid making assumptions about students based on only one of their group characteristics and neglecting the complexities in their lives and experiences. Keep in mind that differences within groups can be as great or greater than differences across groups. (Sources: Sue, 2001; Tatum, 2003; Torres et al., 2003)

Communicating and Fostering Respect

Be attentive to terminology. Terminology changes over time, as ethnic and cultural groups continue to define their identity, their history, and their relationships to other groups. Racial categories are regularly "created, inhabited, transformed and destroyed" (Omi and Winant, 1994, p. 55), and individuals within groups can disagree about preferred designations. Ask your students or your faculty diversity officer about terms that are used on your campus. For example, *minority student* has become outdated, especially on campuses where the former minority now constitutes the numerical majority. Some people favor the omnibus term *students of color,* while others dislike it because it implies that white is the norm. Some campuses use *historically underrepresented students* in discussing recruitment and retention.

Ask whether students have a preference for *African American* or *black.* Some in the community want to distinguish those who are descended from slaves from those who have recently immigrated from the Caribbean, South America, or Africa. Do students of mixed racial heritage use terms such as *multiracial, biracial,* or *mixed*?

In some parts of the country, Americans of Mexican ancestry prefer *Chicana/o, Mexicano/a,* or *Mexican American* to *Hispanic,* which carries the echo of Spanish colonialism. But in the Southwest, some descendants of the Spanish colonists prefer *Hispanic* as do some people in Florida, which has large populations of

Cuban Americans, Puerto Ricans, and South Americans. Others use *Latina/o* to refer to people whose forebears came from Spanish- or Portuguese-speaking regions of the Western Hemisphere. *Mestizo* reflects a mix of Native American and European backgrounds.

Oriental has long been considered a derogatory by-product of British imperialism. Because Asia is so large and diverse, many individuals prefer to be identified not by the continent but by the nationality of their ancestors (for example, Thai American, Korean American). In California, *Pacific Islander* is currently preferred by students whose forebears are from that region, rather than being grouped with *Asian American*.

Among descendants of the indigenous peoples of North America, some prefer the term *Native Americans*, others prefer *American Indians, Indians, Indigenous Peoples*, or a tribal name. In Canada, the preferred term is *First Nations*. Because Alaskan Natives include groups other than Eskimos, the preferred term is *Inuit* (*Inuk* for singular).

On some campuses, *gay* and *lesbian* have given way to *LGBTQ* (Lesbian, Gay, Bisexual, Transgender, Questioning) or *LGBTQ2IA* (Lesbian, Gay, Bisexual, Transgender, Queer, Questioning, Intersex, Allies). Some within the community use *queer* as an inclusive term, but others view *queer* as pejorative. *Sexual orientation, sexual identity,* and *sexuality* are all in use; *sexual preference* is dismissed as inaccurate because most people do not believe that their sexuality is a matter of choice.

Immigrant communities are described by researchers as First Generation (adults who are born and educated outside the United States), Generation 1.5 (individuals who are born outside the United States and partially educated where they were born and partially U.S.-educated), and Second Generation (children of immigrants who are U.S.-born and -educated).

Because terminology changes and can be confusing, it is tempting to just give up. But how we refer to groups can make a difference to students. When in doubt, err on the side of being more specific, not less—use *Cambodian American* instead of *minority* or *Asian American*.

Learn about groups other than your own. Cultures, for example, differ in the value they place on personal independence, competition and ambition, social harmony, and attitudes toward authority—all of which may affect a student's learning and conduct. Culture in the United States has a preference for individuals who are independent, competitive, and focused on achieving success. Individuals with origins in cultures of East Asia may prefer conformity and harmony over individualism and personal achievement. Some cultures expect professors to be experts and final authorities, whereas others recognize that professors may not know all the answers. Students from cultures that teach respect for the wisdom of their elders may be reluctant to share their opinions, to disagree with the readings, or to challenge their professors. Some cultures value memorization as a critical component of learning, and students from those cultures can become confused when instructors dismiss memorization in favor of analysis, synthesis, and critical evaluation.

Sources of information about cultural differences include student organizations, professional development workshops and conferences, ethnic film festivals and museums, and both fiction and nonfiction literature. Perhaps the best source is students themselves, if you openly share your ignorance and express a genuine curiosity to learn about groups different from your own. (Sources: American Psychological Association, 2003; Johnson, 1997; Pratt et al., 1999; Shield, 2004–05; Yeh, 2004–05)

Convey the same level of confidence in the abilities of all your students. Students who sense that more is expected of them tend to outperform students who believe that less is expected of them, regardless of their actual abilities. Conversely, the perception that one belongs to a stigmatized group can result in underperformance, called "stereotype threat," which occurs when a student's anxieties about confirming a negative stereotype cause the student to perform poorly. To address self-fulfilling prophecies and stereotype threat, convey your clear conviction in each student's intellectual potential and let students know you expect them to work hard in class, that you want them to be challenged by the material, and that you hold high standards for their academic achievement. And then practice what you have said: expect your students to work hard, be challenged, and achieve high standards. (Sources: Gay, 2000; Steele, 1997; Steele and Aronson, 1995)

Don't try to "protect" any group of students. If you refrain from challenging or criticizing the performance of students because of their membership in a demographic group, or if you in some way favor those students, you are likely to undermine their self-esteem and their view of their abilities and competence. (Source: Cohen et al., 1999)

Be evenhanded in acknowledging students' accomplishments. Praise students for good work, but avoid lavish displays that may make students uncomfortable ("Why is he so surprised that I'm doing well?") or anxious ("Will I be able to maintain this high level of achievement?"). Note also that in some cultures being singled out for personal accomplishments is neither valued nor appreciated. (Sources: Cohen et al., 1999; Guiffrida, 2005; Lynch, 1997)

Be aware of possible misinterpretations of students' nonverbal behaviors. Eye contact, nodding, verbal utterances, physical contact, smiling, pauses after speaking, physical distance between individuals—all these behaviors differ across cultural groups. For example, in some cultures the pause time between speakers is four or five seconds, compared to one second in American English; looking away from the speaker is a sign of attention, not inattention; and a pat on the shoulders is a source of shame and embarrassment—not a signal of "job well done." (Sources: Al-Issa, 2004; Lynch, 1997; Suinn, 2006)

Pedagogical Approaches

Use inclusive language and examples. Try to use language that acknowledges the diversity in the class:

- Use nongendered terms such as *parenting* rather than *mothering*; *chair* or *chairperson* rather than *chairman* or *chairwoman*.
- Use the more-inclusive *house of worship* rather than *church*.
- Refrain from comments that imply assumptions about students' lives ("Now, when your parents were in college . . .").
- Use inclusive terms such as *significant other* or *partner* rather than *boyfriend* or *girlfriend*.
- Avoid comments that diminish students' perspectives ("Don't be so sensitive").
- Draw examples and anecdotes from a variety of cultural and social contexts.
  (Sources: Allan and Madden, 2006; Hall and Sandler, 1982; Sue et al., 2007)

Learn to correctly pronounce students' names. Ask students directly and jot down their names phonetically. There's nothing wrong with saying, "I'm really trying to learn how to say your name correctly. Can you tell me again how to pronounce it?" California State Polytechnic University, Pomona, has developed an online pronunciation guide for Cantonese, Chinese/Mandarin, Filipino, Indonesian, Japanese, Korean, Thai, and Vietnamese names.

Look for opportunities to give personal attention and validation to students. Research shows the critical role of faculty-student interaction in students' academic success and satisfaction. Students benefit when a faculty member gets to know them outside of class, provides opportunities for them to experience themselves as capable learners, and encourages them to succeed. (Sources: Allen, 1992;

Anaya and Cole, 2003; Cole, 2007; Fischer, 2007; Flowers, 2004–05; Hernández and López, 2004–05; Hurtado et al., 1999; Rendón, 1994)

Cultivate an inclusive classroom. As needed, diversify the perspectives included in class materials, intervene if any students act disrespectfully to others, and make students feel comfortable in asking for help. For discipline-specific advice, see Chin, Berheide, and Rome (2002) on incorporating diversity into courses in sociology; Fowler and Villanueva (2002) on English courses; and Trent (2002) on communication courses. (Sources: Evans, 2000; Hurtado et al., 1998)

Recognize your own culture-bound assumptions. If you have earned your academic credentials in an American college or university, you know that American higher education tends to reward students who question assumptions, challenge points of view, speak out, and participate actively. Some of your students, however, may have been raised to believe that challenging their instructors is disrespectful or rude. Others may be reluctant to ask questions or speak out because they are afraid of reinforcing stereotypes about their ignorance. (Sources: Collett, 1990; Institute for the Study of Social Change, 1991)

Assign group work and collaborative learning activities. In addition to enhancing academic achievement, group work can reduce prejudice and bias by giving students opportunities to interact with others from different backgrounds. Students report acquiring a strong understanding of diversity as a side effect of group projects and community service. Moreover, diverse groups and viewpoints lead to better problem solving and decision making. Small-group work during class can be as simple as counting off three to five students to solve a problem or to answer a question. (Sources: Aronson, 2002; Gurin and Nagda, 2006; Hurtado et al., 1999; Institute for the Study of Social Change, 1991; Page, 2007; Slavin, 1995)

Course Content and Material

Try to select texts and readings whose language is gender neutral and free of stereotypes. If you assign readings that use only masculine pronouns or that incorporate stereotypes, point out these shortcomings in class and give students an opportunity to discuss them.

Aim for an inclusive curriculum. Try to structure your course so that students view concepts, events, and themes from diverse perspectives, rather than treating one group's experience as the standard against which everyone else is defined. Use the following strategies as appropriate:

- Assign texts and readings that reflect scholarship and research about previously underrepresented groups.
- Discuss the contributions made to your field by historically underrepresented groups.
- Describe how recent scholarship about gender, race, sexual identity, and class is changing your field of study.

(Source: Banks, 2006)

Do not assume that all students will recognize cultural, literary, or historical references familiar to you. Your students may not share the cultural experiences, literary allusions, and historical references that you consider canonical. If a certain type of cultural literacy is prerequisite to your course, discuss that prerequisite on the first day of class. (Of course, you may want to refer to individuals or events unfamiliar to your students in order to encourage them to do some individual research or a group wiki project where they submit questions and post definitions.)

Bring in guest lecturers. Broaden and enrich your course by asking faculty or off-campus professionals of different ethnic and cultural groups to make presentations to your class.

Class Discussion

Emphasize the importance of considering different approaches. Help students appreciate different points of view. Encourage them to evaluate their own beliefs and explore how an individual's premises, observations, and interpretations are influenced by social identity and background.

Make it clear that you value all comments. Students need to feel free to voice an opinion and feel empowered to defend it. If some students seem to be ignoring the viewpoints of others, reintroduce the overlooked comments into the discussion. If you see a student frowning or making disapproving gestures while another student is talking, ask the frowner to explain his or her point of view. As appropriate, address the concern that students may be censoring themselves out of fear of being viewed as insensitive or overly sensitive to identity issues.

Balance openness and safety. Students need a balance of openness—the freedom to explore ideas that may be unpleasant or harsh—and safety, which calls for setting limits to prevent personal or disrespectful comments. Openness demands that all points of view be aired, but safety requires interrupting offensive speech—an action that some students will interpret as censorship. The ideal classroom environment is one in which all students feel as if they belong and as if their points of view matter. Early in the term, ask students to break into small groups and discuss behaviors that discourage them from participating in class discussions. Or ask the groups to define what a "safe" classroom means to them. (Sources: Adams et al., 1997; Canetto et al., 2003)

Encourage all students to participate in class discussion. From the start of the term, try to prevent any one group of students from monopolizing the discussion. Solicit alternate viewpoints, and encourage students to listen to and value comments made from perspectives other than their own. Keep in mind that some students may be reluctant to speak up in class for fear of being wrong. Having students work in small groups early in the term may make it easier for them to speak up in a larger setting. (Sources: Carroll, 1998; Steele, 1997)

Monitor your behavior in responding to students. Research studies show that teachers tend to interact differently with men and women students and with students who are—or whom the instructor perceives to be—high or low achievers. More often than not, these patterns of behavior are unconscious, but they can demoralize students. As you teach, try to be evenhanded in the following matters:

- recognizing students who raise their hands in class
- listening and responding to students' comments and questions
- addressing students by name
- prompting students to provide a fuller answer or an explanation
- giving students time to answer a question before moving on
- not interrupting students or allowing them to be interrupted by their peers
- crediting student comments during your summary ("As Akim said, . . .")
- giving feedback and balancing criticism and praise
- making eye contact

    (Sources: Gay, 2000; Green, 1989; Hall and Sandler, 1982; Sadker and Sadker, 1990)

Speak up if a student makes a distasteful remark—even jokingly. Don't let a disparaging comment pass unnoticed. Students may take your silence as condoning the behavior. Consider slowly repeating back the exact words as accurately as possible to the person who made the comment and give that student an opportunity to rephrase. Or explain why the comment is offensive or insensitive—for example, "What you said made me feel uncomfortable. Although you didn't mean it, it could be interpreted as saying . . . ." Or depersonalize the situation: "Some people think that way. What assumptions are they making?" Or ask students to comment. Keep the discussion focused on issues, not individuals, so that students can gracefully retreat from untenable positions. Try not to get rattled by inappropriate remarks and, as appropriate, protect the lone voice (the attacked or the attacker) regardless of his or her position. (Sources: Fouad and Arredondo, 2006; Frederick, 1995; Vacarr, 2001)

Defuse heated remarks. If hurtful comments are made, stop the discussion, have students take a minute to write about the incident, and ask pairs to exchange their points of view before you restart the discussion. Or step back to focus on group dynamics and how the group wants to work. Try not to intervene too quickly: give students a chance to learn that they can handle difficult discussions on their own. (Source: Frederick, 1995)

Do not treat students as spokespersons for their demographic group. Asking a student to speak for his or her entire race, nationality, or other group both ignores the heterogeneity of viewpoints among members of any group and also reinforces the mistaken notion that every member of a particular group is an authority on his or her group. An example to avoid: after lecturing on research about the relationship between race and heart disease, an instructor called on an African American student and asked him to describe how black health professionals were reacting to the research.

Assignments and Exams

Be sensitive to students whose first language is not English. Most colleges in the United States require students who are nonnative speakers of English to achieve oral and written competency by taking English courses. Ask specialists on your campus for advice about how to grade papers and for information about typical patterns of errors related to a student's native language. For example, some languages do not have two-word verbs, and speakers of those languages may need extra help—and patience—as they try to master English idioms. Such students should not be penalized for misusing, say, *take after, take in, take off, take on, take out,* and *take over.*

Help students form study teams. Peer support is an important factor in student persistence in school. By arranging for times and rooms where groups can meet, you can encourage students to make friends beyond their own personal networks. See Chapter 21, "Learning in Groups," for suggestions on how to form study teams. (Source: Pascarella and Terenzini, 2005)

Give assignments and exams that recognize students' diverse backgrounds and special interests. As appropriate to your field, you can develop paper topics or term projects that encourage students to explore the roles, status, contributions, and experiences of groups traditionally underrepresented in scholarly research studies or in academia.

Use a variety of names in classroom examples and test questions. Draw from different cultural groups: Fatima, Keisha, Tran, Francisco, Juanita, Adam, Carol, Yu-Tin, and so on.

Advising, Mentoring, and Out-of-Class Activities

Meet with students informally. Frequent and rewarding informal contact with faculty members is a strong predictor of student success and persistence to complete a degree. Ongoing contact outside the classroom also provides strong motivation for students to perform well in your class and to participate in the broad social and intellectual life of the institution. Encourage students to come to office hours, invite groups of students for coffee or lunch, and consider participating in campus orientation and academic advising programs. See Chapter 57, "Academic Advising and Mentoring Undergraduates." (Sources: Astin, 1993; Tinto, 1993)

Involve students in your research and scholarly activities. When you invite students to examine or contribute to your work, you are teaching them about your field, giving them a view of faculty life, and helping them feel more a part of the college community. Consider sponsoring students in independent study courses, arranging internships, and providing opportunities for undergraduates to participate in research. See Chapter 27, "Undergraduate Research."

Help students establish departmental organizations. If your department does not have an undergraduate association, encourage students to create one. Student organizations can provide peer tutoring and advising as well as social and academic programs. In fields in which certain demographic groups have traditionally been underrepresented, some students may prefer to form caucuses based on their gender or cultural affinities.

Encourage students to join school organizations. Extracurricular activities give students the opportunity to make new friends, find their niche, and become part of a caring and supportive community. Students who are involved in formal social and extracurricular activities attain higher grades and are significantly less likely to leave college. (Sources: Fischer, 2007; Hernández and López, 2004–05)

Direct students to relevant campus resources. Let your students know about campus mentoring programs, workshops, support services, and resource centers.

References

Adams, M., Bell, L., and Griffin, P. (Eds.) *Teaching for Diversity and Social Justice: A Sourcebook.* New York: Routledge, 1997.

Al-Issa, A. "Global Nomads and the Search for Cultural Identity: Tips from the Classroom." *College Teaching*, 2004, *52*(1), 31–32.

Allan, E. J., and Madden, M. "Chilly Classrooms for Female Undergraduate Students at a Research University: A Question of Method?" *Journal of Higher Education*, 2006, *77*(4), 684–711.

Allen, W. R. "The Color of Success: African American College Student Outcomes at Predominantly White and Historically Black Public Colleges and Universities." *Harvard Educational Review*, 1992, *62*(1), 26–44.

American Psychological Association. "Guidelines on Multicultural Education, Training, Research, Practice and Organizational Change for Psychologists." *American Psychologist*, 2003, *58*(5), 377–402.

Anaya, G., and Cole, D. Active Involvement in Latina/o Student Achievement. In J. Castellanos and L. Jones (Eds.), *The Majority in the Minority: Expanding the Representation of Latina/o Faculty, Administrators and Students in Higher Education.* Sterling, VA: Stylus, 2003.

Aronson, J. M. (Ed.). *Improving Academic Achievement: Impact of Psychological Factors on Education.* San Diego, CA: Academic Press, 2002.

Astin, A. W. *What Matters in College? Four Critical Years Revisited.* San Francisco: Jossey-Bass, 1993.

Banks, J. A. Approaches to Multicultural Curriculum Reform. In J. A. Banks and C. A. M. Banks (Eds.), *Multicultural Education: Issues and Perspectives.* (6th ed.) Boston: Allyn and Bacon, 2006.

Bensimon, E. M. "Closing the Achievement Gap in Higher Education: An Organizational Learning Perspective." *New Directions for Higher Education*, no. 131. San Francisco: Jossey-Bass, 2005, pp. 99–111.

Canetto, S. S., Timpson, W. M., Borrayo, E. A., and Yang, R. Teaching about Human Diversity: Lessons Learned and Recommendations. In W. M. Timpson, S. S. Canetto, E. A. Borrayo, and R. Yang (Eds.), *Teaching Diversity: Challenges and Complexities, Identities and Integrity.* Madison, WI: Atwood, 2003.

Carroll, G. *Environmental Stress and African Americans: The Other Side of the Moon.* Westport, CT: Praeger, 1998.

Chin, J., Berheide, C. W., and Rome, D. (Eds.). *Included in Sociology: Learning Climates That Cultivate Racial and Ethnic Diversity.* Washington, DC: American Association for Higher Education in cooperation with American Sociological Association, 2002.

Cohen, G. L., Steele, C. M., and Ross, L. D. "The Mentor's Dilemma: Providing Critical Feedback across the Racial Divide." *Personality and Social Psychology Bulletin*, 1999, *25*(10), 1302–1318.

Cole, D. "Do Interracial Interactions Matter? An Examination of Student-Faculty Contact and Intellectual Self-Concept." *Journal of Higher Education*, 2007, *78*(3), 249–281.

Collett, J. "Reaching African-American Students in the Classroom." In L. Hilsen (Ed.), *To Improve the Academy.* Vol. 9. Stillwater, OK: New Forums Press, 1990.

Davis, M., Dias-Bowie, Y., Greenberg, K., Klukken, G., Pollio, H.R., Thomas, S. P., and Thompson, C. L. "'A Fly in the Buttermilk': Descriptions of University Life by Successful Black Undergraduate Students at a Predominantly White Southeastern University." *Journal of Higher Education*, 2004, *75*(4), 420–445.

Engberg, M. E. "Improving Intergroup Relations in Higher Education: A Critical Examination of the Influence of Educational Interventions on Racial Bias." *Review of Educational Research*, Winter 2004, *74*(4), 473–524.

Evans, N. J. "Creating a Positive Learning Environment for Gay, Lesbian, and Bisexual Students." *New Directions for Teaching and Learning*, no. 82. San Francisco: Jossey-Bass, Summer 2000, pp. 81–87.

Fischer, M. J. "Settling into Campus Life: Differences by Race/Ethnicity in College Involvement and Outcomes." *Journal of Higher Education*, 2007, *78*(2), 125–161.

Flowers, L. A. "Retaining African-American Students in Higher Education: An Integrative Review." *Journal of College Student Retention*, 2004–05, *6*(1), 23–35.

Fouad, N. A., and Arredondo, P. *Becoming Culturally Oriented: Practical Advice for Psychologists and Educators.* Washington, DC: American Psychological Association, 2006.

Fowler, S. B., and Villanueva, V. (Eds.). *Included in English Studies: Learning Climates That Cultivate Racial and Ethnic Diversity.* Washington, DC: American Association for Higher Education in cooperation with National Council of Teachers of English, 2002.

Frederick, P. "Walking on Eggs: Mastering the Dreaded Diversity Discussion." *College Teaching*, 1995, *43*(3), 83–92.

Gay, G. *Culturally Responsive Teaching: Theory, Research, and Practice.* New York: Teachers College Press, 2000.

Green, M. F. (Ed.). *Minorities on Campus: A Handbook for Enriching Diversity.* Washington, DC: American Council on Education, 1989.

Guiffrida, D. "Othermothering as a Framework for Understanding African American Students' Definitions of Student-Centered Faculty." *Journal of Higher Education*, 2005, *76*(6), 701–723.

Gurin, P., and Nagda, B. A. "Getting to the 'What,' 'How,' and 'Why' of Diversity on Campus." *Educational Researcher*, 2006, *35*(1), 20–24.

Hall, R. M., and Sandler, B. R. *The Classroom Climate: A Chilly One for Women?* Washington, DC: Association of American Colleges, 1982.

Harris, S. M., and Nettles, M. T. "Ensuring Campus Climates That Embrace Diversity." In L. I. Rendón and R. O. Hope (Eds.), *Educating a New Majority: Transforming America's Educational System for Diversity.* San Francisco: Jossey-Bass, 1996.

Hernández, J. C., and López, M. A. "Leaking Pipeline: Issues Impacting Latina/o College Student Retention." *Journal of College Student Retention*, 2004–05, *6*(1), 37–60.

Hurtado, S., Milem, J. F., Clayton-Pedersen, A. R., and Allen, W. R. "Enhancing Campus Climates for Racial/Ethnic Diversity: Educational Policy and Practice." *Review of Higher Education*, 1998, *21*(3), 279–302.

Hurtado, S., Milem, J. F., Clayton-Pedersen, A. R., and Allen, W. R. *Enacting Diverse Learning Environments: Improving the Climate for Racial/Ethnic Diversity in Higher Education.* ASHE-ERIC Higher Education Report, *26*(8). Washington, DC: The George Washington University, Graduate School of Education and Human Development, 1999.

Hyde, C. A., and Ruth, B. J. "Multicultural Content and Class Participation: Do Students Self-Censor?" *Journal of Social Work Education*, 2002, *38*(2), 241–256.

Institute for the Study of Social Change. *The Diversity Project: Final Report.* Berkeley: University of California, 1991.

Johnson, E. "Cultural Norms Affect Oral Communication in the Classroom." *New Directions for Teaching and Learning*, no. 70. San Francisco: Jossey-Bass, 1997, pp. 47–52.

Lynch, E. W. Instructional Strategies. In A. I. Morey and M. K. Kitano (Eds.), *Multicultural Course Transformation in Higher Education: A Broader Truth.* Boston: Allyn and Bacon, 1997.

Nora, A., and Cabrera, A. F. "The Role of Perceptions of Prejudice and Discrimination on the Adjustment of Minority Students to College." *Journal of Higher Education*, 1996, *67*(2), 119–148.

Omi, M., and Winant, H. *Racial Formation in the United States from the 1960s to the 1980s.* (2nd ed.) New York: Routledge, 1994.

Page, S. E. *The Difference: How the Power of Diversity Creates Better Groups, Firms, Schools and Societies.* Princeton, NJ: Princeton University Press, 2007.

Pascarella, E. T., and Terenzini, P. T. *How College Affects Students: A Third Decade of Research.* Vol. 2. San Francisco: Jossey-Bass, 2005.

Pratt, D. D., Kelly, M., and Wong, W. S. S. "Chinese Conceptions of 'Effective Teaching' in Hong Kong: Towards Culturally Sensitive Evaluation of Teaching." *International Journal of Lifelong Education*, 1999, *18*(4), 241–258.

Rendón, L .I. "Validating Culturally Diverse Students: Toward a New Model of Learning and Student Development." *Innovative Higher Education*, 1994, *19*(1), 33–51.

Sadker, M., and Sadker, D. Confronting Sexism in the College Classroom. In S. L. Gabriel and I. Smithson (Eds.), *Gender in the Classroom: Power and Pedagogy.* Urbana: University of Illinois Press, 1990.

Shield, R. W. "The Retention of Indigenous Students in Higher Education: Historical Issues, Federal Policy, and Indigenous Resilience." *Journal of College Student Retention*, 2004–05, *6*(1), 111–127.

Slavin, R. E. Cooperative Learning and Intergroup Relations. In J. A. Banks, and C. A. M. Banks (Eds.), *Handbook of Research on Multicultural Education.* New York: MacMillan, 1995.

Steele, C. M. "A Threat in the Air: How Stereotypes Shape Intellectual Identity and Performance." *American Psychologist*, 1997, *52*(6), 613–629.

Steele, C. M., and Aronson, J. "Stereotype Threat and the Intellectual Test Performance of African Americans." *Journal of Personality and Social Psychology*, 1995, *69*(5), 797–811.

Suarez-Balcazar, Y., Orellana-Damacela, L., Portillo, N., Rowan, J. M., and Andrews-Guillen, C. "Experiences of Differential Treatment among College Students of Color." *Journal of Higher Education*, 2003, *74*(4), 428–444.

Sue, D. W. "Multidimensional Facets of Cultural Competence." *Counseling Psychologist*, 2001, *29*(6), 790–821.

Sue, D. W., and others. "Racial Microaggressions in Everyday Life: Implications for Clinical Practice." *American Psychologist*, 2007, *62*(4), 271–286.

Suinn, R. M. Teaching Culturally Diverse Students. In W. J. McKeachie and M. Svinicki, *McKeachie's Teaching Tips*. (12th ed.) Boston: Houghton Mifflin, 2006.

Tatum, B. D. *Why Are All the Black Kids Sitting Together in the Cafeteria?* New York: Basic Books, 2003.

Tinto, V. *Leaving College: Rethinking the Causes and Cures of Student Attrition*. (2nd ed.) Chicago: University of Chicago Press, 1993.

Torres, V., Howard-Hamilton, M. F., and Cooper, D. L. *Identity Development of Diverse Populations: Implications for Teaching and Administration in Higher Education*. ASHE-ERIC Higher Education Report, *29*(6). San Francisco: Jossey-Bass, 2003.

Trent, J. S. (Ed.). *Included in Communication: Learning Climates That Cultivate Racial and Ethnic Diversity*. Washington, DC: American Association for Higher Education in cooperation with the National Communication Association, 2002.

Vacarr, B. "Moving Beyond Polite Correctness: Practicing Mindfulness in the Diverse Classroom." *Harvard Educational Review*, 2001, *71*(2), 285–295.

Yeh, T. L. "Issues of College Persistence between Asian and Asian Pacific American Students." *Journal of College Student Retention*, 2004–05, *6*(1), 81–96.

6

Students with Disabilities

Campuses and faculty are required, under federal law (the Americans with Disabilities Act of 1990) and most state laws, to make reasonable academic accommodations for students who have a documented disability. These accommodations are intended to ensure that all students have an equal opportunity to learn, to demonstrate what they have learned, and to meet the institution's standards of intellectual rigor. When students with disabilities are provided with appropriate accommodations, other students and faculty benefit: a class functions best when all students can contribute to their fullest to the intellectual enterprise.

On most campuses a disability services office verifies a student's disability and helps faculty implement appropriate accommodations. Many accommodations are easy to provide and often benefit many other students in your class. If you have concerns about the effects of a proposed accommodation, discuss these with staff at the disability services office. As they will explain, an accommodation is not considered "reasonable" if it fundamentally alters the nature of a program or activity—for example, if it substantially alters course objectives, essential course requirements, or academic standards, or if it presents undue financial or administrative hardships (Scott, 1997; Simon, 2000).

Approximately 6–9 percent of college students report having a physical, psychological, or learning disability that requires accommodation (Henderson, 2001; National Center for Education Statistics, 2002). Some disabilities are readily apparent, but others are not, including learning disabilities (for example, dyslexia), mild to moderate sensory deficits (low-level vision, slight hearing impairment), psychological conditions (depression, bipolar disorder, Asperger's syndrome), and chronic medical conditions (diabetes, seizure disorders, lupus, cancer, HIV).

General Strategies

Place a statement in your syllabus inviting students with disabilities to meet with you privately. Ask students to make their needs known at the beginning of the semester so that the logistics and academic adjustments can be made in a timely manner. Here's a sample syllabus statement:

> I am available to discuss privately appropriate academic accommodations for students with disabilities. Please see me as soon as possible so that we can work out the necessary arrangements. Students with disabilities are also encouraged to meet with specialists in Student Disability Services for advice and to verify eligibility for appropriate accommodations.

Make an announcement in class. In addition to putting a statement in your syllabus, make a general announcement at the beginning of the term:

> If you may need accommodations for any physical, psychological, or learning disability and have not yet contacted the student disability services office, please do so as soon as possible. Feel free to speak to me privately, either after class or during my office hours, about your accommodations needs.

Remember that all information about a student's disability is confidential. (Sources: Hartman-Hall and Haaga, 2002; Hodge and Preston-Sabin, 1997)

Avoid counterproductive approaches. Experts caution against the following attitudes (adapted from Aune, 2000; Bourke et al., 2000; Burgstahler, 2003; Kleege, 2002):

- being overly lenient with students with disabilities or holding different expectations for them
- viewing students with disabilities as tragic or helpless or as heroic and inspirational
- suspecting that students with disabilities wish they had the abilities they lack
- treating learning disabilities as "less real" than physical disabilities
- assuming that fairness means sameness
- viewing accommodations as preferential treatment

The University of Washington, through its DO-IT project, offers self-paced online instruction, downloadable multimedia presentations, and extensive resources to help faculty learn more about students with disabilities.

Be alert to the power of language. Listen to how students refer to their disability and follow their lead or ask them about terminology. Some will prefer phrases that mention the person first and the disability second: *students with mobility* *disabilities, people who have schizophrenia* (but not people "*suffering* from X" or "*afflicted* with Y"). Others will use terms in which the disability comes first (*deaf people, blind people, disabled people*). Language that tends to offend includes euphemisms (*physically challenged, special needs*) and terms that emphasize a deficit (*hearing impaired, invalid*) or weakness (*wheelchair bound, handicapped*). But don't worry about everyday metaphors: students who are blind "see" ideas or concepts, just as students who are deaf "hear" what someone means, and wheelchair users "walk" to class. (Sources: American Psychological Association, 1999; Gill et al., 2003; Lewiecki-Wilson and Brueggemann, 2008; Longmore, 2003; Michalko, 2002; Olkin, 2002; Pledger, 2003)

Help students get the supplemental academic support they need. A student may have a legally mandated accommodation of an in-class aide (a note taker, sign-language interpreter, amanuensis), but these aides are not academic tutors. Students with disabilities may benefit from nonmandated services such as ongoing tutorial assistance. They may also benefit from specialized courses for students with disabilities to help them increase their knowledge and understanding of their disability, become more effective self-advocates, use appropriate assistive technology, and apply cognitive principles to become more effective self-sufficient learners. Chiba and Low (2007) describe a successful course for students with learning disorders.

Treat disability accommodations matter-of-factly as part of a broader range of ways in which you ensure effective learning and recognize all students as individuals. Consider, for instance, asking students on the first day to fill out an index card (or complete an online questionnaire) with standard contact information and additional details (like year in school and major), but also with anything they want to tell you about their personal situations that may bear on their work in the course: are they working many hours, commuting, parenting, and so on? Mentioning disability accommodations within a broader list conveys a quietly inclusive message.

Physical Access

Be attentive to classroom access. Most campus buildings have entrances that are accessible to students who use mobility aids (wheelchairs, canes, crutches, and walkers), but individual classrooms and laboratories may be less accessible—check with the room scheduling office and be prepared to request a change of rooms if a student with a mobility disability enrolls in your course If a student with limited mobility uses an elevator to get to your classroom, keep an eye on whether the elevator is working and arrange for a room change if repeated breakdowns occur. The scheduling office will also have a list of classrooms equipped with infrared listening systems, which work independently or in conjunction with students' hearing aids.

Observe seating needs. Students who use canes, crutches, or walkers appreciate having a seat that is close to the door and that can be reached without struggling with steps or uneven surfaces. Students who use service dogs may appreciate a corner seat. Wheelchair users need flat or ramped access and desks with enough clearance for their legs. Some students may want to sit near the front of the class to see and hear better, and some may prefer to be away from windows. Aides (lab assistants, readers) may need adjacent seating. Offer physical assistance only if a student requests help or if the need is obvious, but never touch students unless they have explicitly indicated assistance is appreciated.

Ensure access to out-of-class activities. Include students in out-of-class activities rather than suggesting alternatives. Be sensitive to questions of access when planning field trips and recommending visits to museums, attendance at off-campus lectures and dramatic presentations, and the like. Some students may need transportation assistance, special seating, frequent rest breaks, or interpretive aides or devices. The disability services office is usually the best place to start when seeking creative solutions to curriculum access issues. When scheduling office hours, if possible, avoid early morning which are sometimes hard for students to attend who rely on personal care assistants to help start their days.

Barrier-Free Learning

Follow good teaching practices. Many techniques that help students who have sensory or learning disabilities will also benefit the other students in your class. Here are some examples:

- Face the class when you are speaking. When you write on the board or narrate a slide presentation, try to avoid talking while facing the board or the screen.
- Speak clearly and at an appropriate volume and pace. Pause after important points. After you pose a question to students, pause before calling on someone for a response.

- Open each session with a brief review of the previous session and an outline of that day's topic. Conclude each session with a summary of key points.
- Present new or technical vocabulary orally and in writing.
- Describe the content of all visual aids (computer displays, board work, demonstrations). As you work at the board, narrate the procedure: "Adding all the scores and dividing by the number of scores gives us the mean" (rather than "Adding all these and dividing by that gives us this").
- Provide different ways of learning: group work, hands-on activities, individual work. Vary instructional formats so that students aren't passively listening the entire class session. At the same time be alert to problems created for some students with disabilities by varied formats. In-class writing poses difficulties for students who need amanuenses or assistive technology to complete writing assignments; students with communication impairments may not be able to participate verbally in small-group work. Consider notifying these students in advance so they can come to class with in-class work already completed.
- When making assignments, give instructions both orally and in writing.
- Give students opportunities for questions, clarification, and review.
- Provide students with frequent and ongoing feedback on their academic performance through multiple exams and reviews of early drafts of term papers.

Incorporate "universal design" principles into your course. The premise of universal design is that the everyday built environment should be equally accessible to everyone, disabled and nondisabled alike, without need for special modifications. The "curb cut" is the classic example of universal design: it is not only wheelchair-friendly but also friendly to skateboarders, rollerbladers, people pushing strollers, travelers with rolling luggage, and pedestrians using crutches, walkers, or canes. Similarly, universal instructional design aims to make the learning environment accessible to all types of learners without the need for special adaptations. For example, Keller's Personalized System of Instruction (Keller, 1968) allows students to work at their own pace, to retake tests as many times as needed to demonstrate mastery, and to learn course content through print or digital materials. Universal test design calls for tests to be constructed and administered so that accommodations are unnecessary, for example, administering exams without time limits.

Universal design in higher education views learning differences as a continuum, with students with disabilities at one end rather than as a separate or distinct group. Universal design relies on using an array of instructional materials, a variety of teaching strategies, and a flexible approach to measuring students' level of learning or knowledge. The Association for Higher Education and Disability (AHEAD) Web site contains a comprehensive listing of resources which can help you implement universal design (ahead.org/resources/ud). (Sources: Belch,

2004–05; Brothen et al., 2002; Burgstahler and Cory, 2008; Scott et al., 2003; Silver et al., 1998; Sireci, 2005)

Design course Web sites that are universally accessible. Ask your campus instructional technology professionals for advice on accessible Web site design. Typical strategies include the following:

- providing auditory descriptions for all visual content and text alternatives for all audio content
- captioning all videos
- uniquely labeling all links and controls
- relying on keyboard commands in addition to clicking on images
- avoiding flashing or blinking elements (which may cause seizures in those with photosensitive epilepsy)
- offering customized options for text size, color, and contrast

Guidelines are available from the Web Accessibility Initiative (www.w3.org/ WAI) which also reviews commercially available and open source software to test Web accessibility. WebAIM (www.webaim.org), created by Utah State and the Center for Persons with Disabilities, also offers resources for making Web sites accessible.

Ensure equal access to information. If you have a deaf/hard-of-hearing student in your class, when you show films, videos, or DVDs make sure they are open- or closed-captioned whenever possible. Provide electronic versions of print handouts so that students can use screen readers and assistive technology to create a more accessible version. To the extent possible, select textbooks, reading materials, journal articles, and newspaper articles that are available in digital format as well as print. For information on making course materials and collaboration tools (discussion boards, chat rooms, videoconferencing) accessible, see Barstow et al., 2002. Most campuses have resources to help pay the cost of transferring information from hard copy to an alternative medium.

Provide captioners or sign language interpreters with terms and names in advance. Whenever possible, provide a written list of technical terms and proper names you will use in class to ensure that they are spelled correctly. As appropriate, provide a copy of your notes before class begins. Become familiar with accessible technologies.

Ask your campus disability services office about personal and classroom accessible technologies. Personal devices include voice-recognition software, modified keyboards, mouthsticks and headwands, screen magnifiers, speech synthesizers,

Braille or large-print output devices, screen-reading programs, and personal information managers. Classroom accessible technology may include real-time captioning, whereby captioners transcribe lectures and discussions to a computer screen that students read at their desks in real time. (The captioners need not be present in the classroom as long as they can hear what is going on.) Trained keyboarders using technologies such as C-Print (www.ntid.rit.edu/cprint) transcribe lectures in real time and project the results on a laptop screen for the individual student or onto a classroom screen for the entire class to view; these transcriptions benefit students who have difficulty hearing and also students whose first language is not English. The notes can be posted on a course Web site after class.

Wear a cordless microtransmitter, if asked. Students who cannot take notes and need to record class sessions and students who use assistive listening devices may ask you to wear a cordless microphone. When you do so, remember to describe the visual elements of your presentation (computer displays, board work, demonstrations). If you are concerned about a student's reuse of the course material, ask the student to sign an agreement not to make copies of the recordings, not to share the recordings with others, and to erase the recordings at the end of the term.

Provide pointers on how to master the material. Advice can be helpful to all students, not just those with disabilities. Consider the following teaching strategies (adapted from Stage and Milne, 1996; Swanson and Hoskyn, 1998; Tincani, 2004):

- List key objectives for the week's readings.
- When lecturing, use advance organizers that build on what students already know and provide the context for new information.
- When lecturing, make easily recognizable the step-by-step progression from subtopic to subtopic.
- Use concrete examples and visual demonstrations to reinforce learning.
- Review effective study strategies such as underlining important concepts, constantly reviewing the material, blocking out time for studying, spending time in the library in a study atmosphere, and setting goals on a short-term daily checklist.
- Distribute practice test questions for midterms and finals.
- Encourage students to form study groups that meet outside of class.

Make reading lists available in advance. Students who rely on readers or need Braille, large-print, computer disks, or tape-recorded versions of books and articles will appreciate as much notice as possible. By midsemester these students hope to obtain the reading lists for the courses they anticipate taking the following term.

Class Participation

Arrange for classroom participation or an alternative activity. Students whose disability prevents them from raising their hand to answer or ask questions may feel isolated or ignored in class. During your first private meeting with such a student, ask how he or she wishes to be recognized in the classroom. Some students will want to be called on; others may wish to make other arrangements for getting their questions answered. Students whose disability prevents them from reading aloud or answering questions in class may wish to develop alternatives.

Address the student, not the aide. When talking to a student who has an assistant, briefly greet and acknowledge the assistant's presence but look at and address the student. If you are engaging in more than a quick exchange with a student who uses a wheelchair, pull up a chair, sit down, and talk at eye level (but do not lean on, touch, or push the wheelchair unless you are asked to).

Actively moderate all class discussions. As needed, repeat students' comments or questions and identify the speaker. Try to ensure that only one student speaks at a time. Listen attentively when a student with a speech disability is speaking; do not finish a student's sentences or interrupt. If you are having difficulty understanding a student, repeat what you have understood and ask the student to confirm, repeat, or rephrase.

Give alternatives for oral presentations, as needed. Oral presentations may pose difficulties for students who have a speech disability. Some students will want to give their presentations without assistance, but others may want the help of an interpreter. Still others may want to write out their presentation and ask an interpreter or another student to read it to the class.

Exams

Be attentive to the format of exams. Exams are supposed to measure students' knowledge or mastery of course content, but the format of an exam inevitably tests other skills as well. For example, success on a print test depends on visual-processing capabilities, success on an essay test depends on fine-motor skills, and success on an oral exam depends on auditory-processing skills. When a student's disability interferes with his or her opportunity to demonstrate mastery, an accommodation may be needed. (Sources: Barstow et al., 2002; Brinckerhoff et al., 2002)

Design print exams for universal access. The Disabled Students' Program at the University of California at Berkeley recommends the following:

- Use a large, dark font, and double-space or triple-space between test items.
- Avoid cramming too many questions or math problems on a single page.
- Group similar types of items together (for example, true-false, short answer) with extra space between types.
- If possible, eliminate matching items that are difficult to read aloud or on tape.
- As appropriate, allow students to circle answers on the test rather than fill in ovals on a Scantron sheet.

Provide appropriate test-taking conditions. The disability services office may authorize one or more of the following accommodations:

- an aide to read the test aloud or to write down the student's dictated answers
- a large-print version of the test
- a room that has better lighting, fewer distractions, or special technology
- an extended exam period, with or without scheduled breaks
- the option of substituting an oral exam for a written exam, or a written exam for an oral exam, or a multiple-choice exam for an essay exam

Grade exams as you usually do. When students receive accommodations for taking an exam, there is no need to extend leniency to grading. Of course, grading students more harshly because they had, say, the "advantage" of extra time would nullify the effect of the accommodation.

Laboratory Courses

Review safety and evacuation procedures. Ask your campus facilities office about adding auditory or visual emergency warning systems as needed.

As needed, adjust the furniture, equipment, and experiments. Give students a tour of the lab and ask what accommodations might be necessary. Consult with your campus facilities office for guidelines and temporary adjustments—for example, how to make counters, sinks, equipment, and fume hoods accessible to students who use wheelchairs. Adaptive lab equipment such as talking thermometers, tactile timers, tactile syringes, and light probes may make it possible for students with visual disabilities to conduct lab experiments. Providing C-clamps for holding objects and single-action-lever controls in place of knobs can be helpful to students who have mobility disabilities. Labeling equipment, tools, and materials can be helpful to students with learning disabilities. For detailed advice, see the University of Washington DO-IT Web site on "Science Labs."

Provide a personal lab assistant. A faculty-selected personal lab assistant familiar with lab procedures can help students carry out tasks they would otherwise be unable to accomplish. (Source: Pence et al., 2003)

Consider alternative arrangements. You may be able to adapt lab exercises and experiments to accommodate a student's disability by substituting easier-to-use equipment, by structuring some lab assignments as group work, or by providing a lab assistant. (Source: Womble and Walker, 2001)

Explore virtual lab experiments. Some students may benefit from performing experiments online, where the levels of dexterity and strength are less demanding than in a lab. (Source: Martínez-Jiménez et al., 2003)

Behavioral Risk Assessment

Be alert for worrisome behavior. The transition to college life may be particularly stressful for students with disabilities. These difficulties are compounded when students choose not to take their medication. If you are concerned about a student's behavior—acting out, severe withdrawal, or excessively violent or bizarre writing—consult with campus counseling experts for best next steps. Mental health experts offer these recommendations (adapted from Cohen, 2007):

- Be specific as possible with the student in stating your observations and reasons for concern.
- Let the student discuss his or her feelings and thoughts.
- Avoid criticizing or making judgments.

- Listen carefully and, as necessary, confirm your understanding by repeating what the student has said.
- Do not try to counsel the student. Make a referral to your campus counseling center, or schedule an appointment by phone while the student is in your office.
- If a student resists referral, contact your counseling service and express your concerns.

Try to distinguish between psychological distress and rebellious behavior or an active imagination. In their attire and conduct, college students are experimenting with new roles and attitudes. Not every student who wears sunglasses indoors and sits alone in the back row is in need of counseling. Similarly, not every short story that features mayhem and violence is a symptom of psychosis. Sometimes, though, dramatic behavior is a cry for help or a cry for attention, and these should not be ignored. In particular, threats directed at any member of the campus community should be immediately addressed by bringing the issue to your department chair. The Virginia Tech English department has developed a helpful guide for instructors called "Responding to Disturbing Creative Writing" (available on the Virginia Tech Web site) which describes steps to take when a student's creative work raises concerns.

Deal directly with students' extreme emotional states. Experts at University of California at Berkeley's Counseling and Psychological Services make these recommendations:

- Maintain a poised, not fearful, posture, and place yourself behind a table or chair or near an exit, if possible.
- Speak in a calm, matter-of-fact tone.
- Limit interaction: don't press for explanations; don't argue; don't become hostile or punitive.
- State instructions and consequences clearly; repeat as necessary.

Discuss your concerns with others on campus. If you fear that a student poses a danger to self or others, alert your department chair or dean. If your campus has a behavioral risk assessment team, contact them as well.

References

American Psychological Association. *Enhancing Your Interactions with People with Disabilities.* Washington, DC: American Psychological Association, Public Interest Directorate, 1999.

Aune, B. "Career and Academic Advising." In H. A. Belch (Ed.), *Serving Students with Disabilities*. New Directions for Student Services, no. 91. San Francisco: Jossey-Bass, 2000, pp. 55–67.

Barstow, C., McKell, M., Rothberg, M., and Schmidt, C. "IMS Guidelines for Developing Accessible Learning Applications." 2002. http://www.imsglobal.org/accessibility/accessiblevers/index.html

Belch, H. A. "Retention and Students with Disabilities." *Journal of College Student Retention*. 2004–05, *6*(1), 3–22.

Bourke, A. B., Strethorn, K. C., and Silver, P. "Faculty Members' Provision of Instructional Accommodations to Students with LD." *Journal of Learning Disabilities*, 2000, *33*(1), 26–32.

Brinckerhoff, L. C., McGuire, J. M., and Shaw, S. F. *Postsecondary Education and Transition for Students with Learning Disabilities*. (2nd ed.) Austin, TX: PRO-ED, 2002.

Brothen, T., Wambach, C., and Hansen, G. "Accommodating Students with Disabilities: PSI as an Example of Universal Instructional Design." *Teaching of Psychology*, 2002, *29*(3), 239–240.

Burgstahler, S. E. "Accommodating Students with Disabilities: Professional Development Needs of Faculty." In C. M. Wehlburg and S. Chadwick-Blossey (Eds.), *To Improve the Academy*. Vol. 21. San Francisco: Jossey-Bass/Anker, 2003.

Burgstahler, S. E., and Cory, R. C. (Eds.). *Universal Design in Higher Education: From Principles to Practice*. Cambridge, MA: Harvard Education Press, 2008.

Chiba, C., and Low, R. "A Course-Based Model to Promote Successful Transition to College for Students with Learning Disorders." *Journal of Postsecondary Education and Disability*, 2007, *20*(1), 40–53.

Cohen, A. S. *From Documentation to Accommodation: The Disability Service Provider's Guide to Supporting Students with Psychiatric Disabilities*. Horsham, PA: LRP Publications, 2007.

Gill, C. J., Kewman, D. G., and Brannon, R. W. "Transforming Psychological Practice and Society: Policies That Reflect the New Paradigm." *American Psychologist*, 2003, *58*(4), 305–312.

Hartman-Hall, H. M., and Haaga, D. A. "College Students' Willingness to Seek Help for Their Learning Disabilities." *Learning Disability Quarterly*, 2002, *25*(4), 263–74.

Henderson, C. *College Freshmen with Disabilities, 2001: A Biennial Statistical Profile*. Washington, DC: American Council on Education/HEATH Resource Center, 2001.

Hodge, B. M., and Preston-Sabin, J. *Accommodations—Or Just Good Teaching? Strategies for Teaching College Students with Disabilities*. Westport, CT: Praeger, 1997.

Keller, F. S. "Good-Bye, Teacher . . . ." *Journal of Applied Behavior Analysis*, 1968, *1*(1), 79–89.

Kleege, G. Disabled Students Come Out: Questions without Answers. In S. L. Snyder, B. J. Brueggemann, and R. Garland-Thomson (Eds.) *Disability Studies: Enabling the Humanities*. New York: Modern Language Association of America, 2002.

Lewiecki-Wilson, C., and Brueggemann, B. J. (Eds.). *Disability and the Teaching of Writing: A Critical Sourcebook*. Boston: Bedford/St. Martin's, 2008.

Longmore, P. K. *Why I Burned My Book and Other Essays on Disability*. Philadelphia: Temple University Press, 2003.

Martínez-Jiménez, P., Pontes-Pedrajas, A., Polo, J., and Climent-Bellido, M. "Learning in Chemistry with Virtual Laboratories." *Journal of Chemical Education*, 2003, *80*(3), 346–52.

Michalko, R. *The Difference That Disability Makes*. Philadelphia, PA: Temple University Press, 2002.

National Center for Education Statistics. *Profile of Undergraduates in U.S. Postsecondary Institutions: 1999–2000.* National Postsecondary Student Aid Study. Washington, DC: National Center for Education Statistics, U.S. Department of Education, 2002.

Olkin, R. "Could You Hold the Door for Me? Including Disability in Diversity." *Cultural Diversity and Ethnic Minority Psychology,* 2002, *8*(2), 130–137.

Pence, L. E., Workman, H. J., and Riecke, P. "Effective Laboratory Experiences for Students with Disabilities: The Role of a Student Laboratory Assistant." *Journal of Chemical Education,* March 2003, *80*(3), 295–298.

Pledger, C. "Discourse on Disability and Rehabilitation Issues: Opportunities for Psychology." *American Psychologist,* 2003, *58*(4), 279–284.

Scott, S. S. "Accommodating College Students with Learning Disabilities: How Much Is Enough?" *Innovative Higher Education,* 1997, *22*(2), 85–99.

Scott, S. S., McGuire, J. M., and Shaw, S. F. Universal Design for Instruction: A New Paradigm for Adult Instruction in Postsecondary Education. *Remedial and Special Education,* 2003, *24*(6), 369–379.

Silver, P., Bourke, A., and Strehorn, K. C. Universal Instructional Design in Higher Education: An Approach for Inclusion. *Equity and Excellence in Education,* 1998, *31*(2), 47–51.

Simon, J. "Legal Issues in Serving Students with Disabilities in Postsecondary Education." In H. A. Belch (Ed.), *Serving Students with Disabilities.* New Directions for Student Services, no. 91. San Francisco: Jossey-Bass, 2000, pp. 69–81.

Sireci, S. G. "Unlabeling the Disabled: A Perspective on Flagging Scores from Accommodated Test Administrations." *Educational Researcher,* 2005, *34*(1), 3–12.

Stage, F. K., and Milne, N. V. "Invisible Scholars: Students with Learning Disabilities." *Journal of Higher Education,* 1996, *67*(4), 426–445.

Swanson, H. L., and Hoskyn, M. "Experimental Intervention Research on Students with Learning Disabilities: A Meta-Analysis of Treatment Outcomes." *Review of Educational Research,* 1998, *68*(3), 277–321.

Tincani, M. "Improving Outcomes for College Students with Disabilities: Ten Strategies for Instructors." *College Teaching,* 2004, *52*(4), 128–132.

Womble, M. D., and Walker, G. R. "Teaching Biology to the Visually Impaired: Accommodating Students' Special Needs." *Journal of College Science Teaching,* 2001, *30*(6), 394–396.

7

Reentry and Transfer Students

Reentry students (often defined as students twenty-five years and older who have not attended school for at least two years) and transfer students constitute more than half the undergraduate student body nationwide (Bash, 2003). Despite their numbers, reentry and transfer students may feel out of step with students who started on campus as freshmen.

Compared to younger students, reentry students tend to be more motivated and to bring a more practical, problem-solving orientation to learning; they often treat their professors as peers; and they are usually clearer about their educational goals (Bean and Metzner, 1985; Bishop-Clark and Lynch, 1992). Most reentry students arrive with work-related goals (Aslanian, 2001; Hagedorn, 2005), and they tend to outperform younger students in the classroom (Hagedorn, 2005; Richardson and King, 1998). Faculty have described reentry students as highly motivated and excited about learning (Giczkowski, 1992), and their presence and participation can considerably enrich the educational experiences of all students.

Some transfer students are also older (Cohen and Brawer, 2002), but the average age of transfer students has been declining (Adelman, 2005). At the same time, the number of transfer students attending four-year schools has been rising. Contrary to stereotypes, students transferring from two-year schools can be the academic equals of their third-year classmates at the destination school.

One common challenge for transfer students, regardless of age, is the culture shock they feel on a new campus with a different (often less teaching-focused) system of instruction and where they have few friends or extracurricular ties (Bingham-Newman and Hopkins, 2004). They may feel less connected to the campus and to their classmates.

The suggestions on the following pages can help you meet the challenges and opportunities of working with reentry and transfer students.

General Strategies

Avoid stereotyping your students. For example, do not make assumptions about your students' academic abilities based on their status as reentry or transfer students and avoid considering them a homogeneous group with the same challenges, values, attitudes, or goals. (Source: Donaldson and Townsend, 2007)

Be aware of the dynamics between younger and older students. In general, both younger and older students view the mixed-age classroom as a positive experience. Help students appreciate each other's viewpoints and help them recognize how different perspectives enliven and enrich discussions. (Sources: Howard et al., 1996; Lynch and Bishop-Clark, 1993)

Help students make the transition to a four-year college. Older students who have never attended college or who did poorly in college the first time around may feel nervous about their academic abilities. Help these students feel comfortable in your classroom by offering reassurance and expressing confidence in their skills. (Source: Ross-Gordon, 2003)

Be sensitive to students' logistical constraints. Many reentry students are juggling family responsibilities, job commitments, social and community obligations, and commuting. Attending field trips and weekend or evening activities may pose special problems for these students, and commuting students may have limited access to campus resources, labs, and tutorial services. As appropriate, try to develop online resources that can surmount logistical problems.

Creating Connections

Encourage students to participate in campus life. All students thrive when they feel comfortable and connected to the intellectual life of the campus. Make efforts to help your students feel a part of campus life, and encourage reentry and transfer students to network and problem-solve with one another. As appropriate, help students make contact with other faculty and staff. Small groups, discussions, and other interactive strategies can foster peer connections. (Source: Donaldson et al., 2000; Ross-Gordon, 2003)

Help reentry and transfer students find on-campus jobs. Approximately 50 percent of four-year college students and 80 percent of two-year college students work part-time. Research shows that those who work on campus, rather than off campus, tend to be more satisfied with their undergraduate experience and tend to feel more connected to the campus—two factors that lead to higher graduation rates. (Source: Astin, 1993; Kodama, 2002; National Center for Education Statistics, 2005)

Help transfer students with recommendations. Transfer students are at a disadvantage because they have a shorter time to build relationships with their instructors, which lay the basis for a recommendation to graduate school or career opportunity. Be open to writing recommendations for these students.

Teaching Practices

Emphasize teaching practices known to be especially effective with adult learners. These good teaching practices will help all students: presenting material clearly, being well organized, creating a comfortable learning environment, adapting to students' diverse needs, incorporating active learning strategies into the course, and demonstrating concern for students' learning. (Source: Donaldson et al., 1993)

Adopt participatory pedagogical styles. All students benefit from active learning strategies, but older students are less likely to tolerate being lectured to; they will want to interact, discuss, ask questions, and experiment. (Source: Wircenski et al., 1999)

Incorporate group work into instruction. The life experiences of reentry students can enrich classroom discussion by providing examples that illustrate theories and general principles. Capitalize on these resources by assigning collaborative learning activities that permit students to work together in small groups.

Take advantage of reentry students' capacity for self-direction. Most reentry students are used to working independently and autonomously. Opportunities for independent study and choices in assignments acknowledge and reinforce these students' learning abilities and styles. See Chapter 27, "Undergraduate Research." (Source: Ross-Gordon, 2003)

Vary the way you present course content. When working with traditional-age students, one business professor finds it most effective to introduce a new concept or idea by first discussing the theory and then presenting some applications. With older students, in contrast, he finds that they become more engaged when he begins with the applications and then moves to the theory. (Source: Watkins, 1990)

Returning Veterans

Avoid stereotyping veterans. Some veterans have seen combat, others have not. Some veterans have political views that differ from the majority of students on campus, others do not. Some have symptoms of post-traumatic stress disorder, others do not. In other words, do not make assumptions about a student's experiences, values, or mental health based solely on his or her military service.

Help veterans cope with culture shock and make the transition to college life. Returning to campus life after active duty may leave students feeling out of place, disconnected, or anxious about their academic performance or the possibility of being redeployed. Be patient with students as they adjust to new circumstances and, as needed, encourage them to take advantage of campus support services such as tutoring and counseling. Some veterans may be worried about competing academically. Help them see their strengths and resiliency, and let them know you have confidence in their ability to succeed. Experts who work with veterans at the University of Texas, University of California at Berkeley, and University of Minnesota also make the following recommendations for veterans entering college:

- Limit the number of units each term to a reasonable course load or seek a reduced load.
- Get involved in school activities or organizations to connect to the larger campus community and build a support network.
- Limit exposure to traumatic information from news outlets.
- Volunteer on or off campus in activities of interest.
- Follow a daily schedule to stay organized.

Become familiar with campus support services. Your campus may have a veterans office that can help returning military personnel find tutors, arrange for work-study employment, make connections with local veterans groups, and advise about campus and military paperwork. Veterans who have a disability are entitled to services from your campus's disability programs. For advice on students with disabilities, see Chapter 6, "Students with Disabilities."

Respect students' privacy. Some students may prefer that others do not know about their military service. Some may mention their service to an instructor but not to other students because they do not want to risk being stereotyped or they do not want to be asked about their experiences.

References

Adelman, C. *Moving into Town—and Moving On: The Community College in the Lives of Traditional-Age Students*. Washington, DC: U.S. Department of Education, 2005.

Aslanian. C. B. *Adult Students Today*. New York: College Board, 2001.

Astin, A. W. *What Matters in College? Four Critical Years Revisited*. San Francisco: Jossey-Bass, 1993.

Bash, L. *Adult Learners in the Academy*. San Francisco: Jossey-Bass/Anker, 2003.

Bean, J. P., and Metzner, B. S. "A Conceptual Model of Nontraditional Undergraduate Student Attrition." *Review of Educational Research*, 1985, *55*(4), 485–540.

Bingham-Newman, A. M., and Hopkins, R. L. Transfer Students: An Overview. In T. J. Kerr, M. C. King, and T. Grites (Eds.), *Advising Transfer Students: Issues and Strategies*. National Academic Advising Association, Monograph Series, no. 12, 2004.

Bishop-Clark, C., and Lynch, J. M. "The Mixed-Age College Classroom." *College Teaching*, 1992, *40*(3), 114–117.

Cohen, A. M., and Brawer, F. B. *The American Community College*. (4th ed.) San Francisco: Jossey-Bass, 2002.

Donaldson, J. F., Flannery, D., and Ross-Gordon, J. "A Triangulated Study Comparing Adult College Students' Perceptions of Effective Teaching with Those of Traditional Students." *Continuing Higher Education Review*, 1993, *57*(3), 147–165.

Donaldson, J. F., Graham, S. W., Martindill, W., and Bradley, S. "Adult Undergraduate Students: How Do They Define Their Experiences and Their Success?" *Journal of Continuing Higher Education*, 2000, *48*(2), 2–11.

Donaldson, J. F., and Townsend, B. K. "Higher Education Journals' Discourse about Adult Undergraduate Students." *Journal of Higher Education*, Jan/Feb 2007, *78*(1), 27–50.

Giczkowski, W. "The Influx of Older Students Can Revitalize College Teaching." *Chronicle of Higher Education*, March 25, 1992, B3.

Hagedorn, L. S. "Square Pegs: Adult Students and Their 'Fit' in Postsecondary Institutions." *Change*, Jan.–Feb., 2005, 22–29.

Howard, J. R., Short, L. B., and Clark, S. M. "Students' Participation in the Mixed-Age College Classroom." *Teaching Sociology*, 1996, *24*(1), 8–24.

Kodama, C. M. "Marginality of Transfer Commuter Students." *NASPA Journal*, 2002, *39*(3), 233–250.

Lynch, J. M., and Bishop-Clark, C. "Traditional and Nontraditional Student Attitudes Toward the Mixed-Age College Classroom." *Innovative Higher Education*, 1993, *18*(2), 109–121.

National Center for Education Statistics. *Indicator 30: Employment of College Students*. Washington DC: U.S. Department of Education, 2005.

Richardson, J.T.E., and King, E. "Adult Students in Higher Education: Burden or Boon?" *Journal of Higher Education*, 1998, *69*(1), 65–88.

Ross-Gordon, J. M. "Adult Learners in the Classroom." *New Directions for Student Services*, no. 102. San Francisco: Jossey-Bass, Summer, 2003, 43–52.

Watkins, B. T. "Growing Number of Older Students Stirs Professors to Alter Teaching Styles." *Chronicle of Higher Education*, Aug. 1, 1990, A1, A12.

Wircenski, M., Walker, M., Allen, J., and West, L. "Age as a Diversity Issue in Grades K–12 and in Higher Education." *Educational Gerontology*, 1999, *25*(6), 491–500.

8

Teaching Academically Diverse Students

Many undergraduate classes—especially large introductory and survey courses—include students who have a range of academic abilities, interests, skills, and goals. For instructors, the goal is to prevent the stronger students from becoming bored or frustrated and yet to avoid overwhelming the weaker students. The suggestions below are intended to help you meet the needs of both groups.

General Strategies

Determine what preparation students need before enrolling in your course. Analyze how your course relates to lower-level and higher-level courses in your department. In your course description and syllabus and during the first class meeting, be clear about what knowledge or skills students must already possess in order to succeed in your course.

Give students a pretest to help them determine whether they are prepared for your course. At the first class meeting, give an in-class or online pretest, ask for a writing sample, or make an introductory assignment that covers the material you expect students to know. Direct inadequately prepared students to other courses or resources, or assign them supplementary work early in the term. If underprepared students want to enroll, remind them that they are responsible for catching up.

Teach to the level you expect students to reach. For most undergraduate classes, you will want to teach at the level of the B student. When in doubt, it is better to overestimate rather than underestimate the level of the class. Students tend to learn more when a course is conducted just above their comfort level. (Source: Lucas, 1990)

Course Structure

Prepare a reading list that reflects the academic diversity of the class. Your reading list could include three sections: background reading for students who need to review or acquire skills or knowledge to succeed in class; basic reading essential to the course; and in-depth reading, grouped by topic, for students who wish to delve deeper.

Offer a "cafeteria menu" of assignments. Allow students to choose various combinations of assignments—each worth a specified number of points, reflecting the difficulty or time required—to meet the course requirements. Weaker students may prefer to submit a larger number of shorter or easier assignments, while stronger students may choose to do one or two longer, more complex assignments.

Encourage students to learn from each other. Help students organize study groups of five or six members; see Chapter 21, "Learning in Groups." Or assign partners to work on projects: the stronger student will develop skills in explaining and analyzing material, and the struggling student will benefit from the peer tutoring. You might also encourage students to exchange drafts with classmates for peer editing; see Chapter 34, "Helping Students Write Better in All Courses."

Do not grade on a curve. Grading on a curve disadvantages the less well-prepared students. Instead, grade students on clearly defined criteria. See Chapter 44, "Calculating and Assigning Grades."

Monitoring Students' Learning

Arrive early for class. Use the time before class to chat with students about how well they are understanding the material and to answer questions they may have from the last session or from the homework.

Ask questions during class. Asking questions about key concepts and ideas will help you judge whether students are keeping up or falling behind. Have students give definitions, associations, and applications of the ideas, or ask students to name two or three key concepts or main ideas from the day's session. See Chapter 32, "Informally Assessing Students' Learning."

Be aware of who is talking in class. Do the stronger students tend to dominate the discussion? If so, be sure to direct your comments and questions to the entire class, and ask follow-up questions of all students; see Chapter 9, "Leading a Discussion."

Watch for nonverbal cues. If you see students having trouble taking notes or sitting with blank or quizzical looks on their faces, stop and say, "I seem to be losing some of you; let me explain this point another way."

Helping Students Who Are Having Difficulty

Early in the course, identify students who are struggling. If you give a quiz or test during the first two or three weeks, you and your students will know how well they are doing. Watch class attendance as well. When students feel lost or overwhelmed by a course, they may stay away.

Ask to see students whose papers or tests are weak. At the top of the assignment, issue an encouraging invitation: "I have some advice that will help you do better work. See me during my office hours." (Source: Eaton and Sleigh, 2003)

Try to determine the source of difficulty. When 250 students on academic probation were asked to name the source of their problems, inadequate academic preparation was not among these top ten answers: procrastination, missed class, stress, lack of time management, lack of motivation, lack of study skills, test-taking problems, poor study environment, inadequate study time, and inability to concentrate. Some of these problems are, of course, beyond your control, but you might be able to help procrastinators and students with poor time management skills by adding more structure or intermediate deadlines to assignments. Other struggling students may benefit from a referral to the campus tutoring center. (Source: Kamphoff, n.d.)

Prepare supplementary materials. If some students find the assigned readings too challenging, recommend other texts that explain the concepts in a different way. Prepare or call attention to glossaries that include short definitions and examples.

Hold review sessions during office hours. Instead of slowing the pace of the class, invite students who are having trouble with a particular topic to meet for a group review during your office hours; schedule a classroom if your office is too small.

Show students how to do the tasks you set for the class. Struggling students are unlikely to benefit from broad admonitions to work harder. Often they need advice on specific skills (how to read a journal article critically, how to move from topic to thesis when writing a paper). Give students suggestions on four topics: reading text material for comprehension and retention, taking and reviewing notes, studying and the amount of time to spend studying, and preparing for exams. (Source: Forsyth, 2003)

Distribute copies of good papers or lab reports. Circulating copies of good (B or B+) but not outstanding work helps students understand your standards and expectations. Students can also compare their work against the models. Always obtain permission from students before distributing their work.

Encourage graduate students or advanced undergraduates to mentor younger students. Older, more advanced students, especially those who have overcome academic difficulties of their own, can help first-year students work through problems related to time management and study habits. (Source: Bartlett, 2004)

Encouraging Your Best Students

Prepare supplementary materials. Give your best students opportunities for special assignments such as recommended readings, additional papers, or fieldwork. Even those who do not follow through will appreciate the extra attention.

Use office hours for advanced exploration of a topic. During an office hour, provide a group of students with an in-depth analysis of a topic that was covered only briefly in class. Suggest follow-up independent study. For students who wish to pursue specific topics in more detail, recommend enrollment in an independent research course the following term.

Engage your best students in research. See Chapter 27: "Undergraduate Research."

References

Bartlett, T. "Back from the Brink: More Colleges Try to Help Students Who Struggle with Their Courses." *Chronicle of Higher Education*, May 14, 2004.

Eaton, R. F., and Sleigh, M. J. "Going the Extra Mile: Identifying and Assisting Struggling Students." *APS Observer*, 2003, *16*(2), 21–22, 30–31.

Forsyth, D. R. *The Professor's Guide to Teaching: Psychological Principles and Practices.* Washington, DC: American Psychological Association, 2003.

Kamphoff, C. S. "Helping Students on Probation." *On Course Newsletter.* n.d. http://www.oncourseworkshop.com/Miscellaneous013.htm

Lucas, A. F. "Using Psychological Models to Understand Student Motivation." In M. D. Svinicki (Ed.), *The Changing Face of College Teaching.* New Directions for Teaching and Learning, no. 42. San Francisco: Jossey-Bass, 1990, pp. 103–114.

PART III

Discussion Strategies

9

Leading a Discussion

Class discussion provides students with opportunities to develop their communication skills and to acquire knowledge and insight through the face-to-face exchange of information, ideas, and opinions. A lively, productive give-and-take discussion allows students to articulate their ideas, respond to their classmates' points, and develop skills in thinking through problems and organizing evidence using the language and methodologies of an academic discipline (McGonigal, 2005).

In large-enrollment courses, instructors can divide the class into smaller groups for discussion; see Chapter 18, "Encouraging Student Participation in the Large-Enrollment Course."

General Strategies

Clarify your expectations at the beginning of the term. During the first week of class and in the syllabus, define the role discussion will play in the course and describe students' responsibilities. Let students know that you expect everyone to participate, that discussion is a time to test ideas and new perspectives, and that the discussion will be more worthwhile if they come prepared.

Plan how you will conduct each discussion session. You will want to devise assignments that prepare students for the discussion, compose a list of questions to guide and focus the discussion, and identify appropriate in-class activities such as pair work and brainstorming. Have in mind two or three ways that you might begin the discussion, and leave time for an end-of-session wrap-up and synthesis. Because discussion patterns tend to gel early in the term, devote extra effort to the early sessions. (Source: Faust and Courtenay, 2002)

Sharpen students' discussion skills. Help students develop the attitudes and skills they need to participate. For example, identify the roles that make for lively, purposeful discussion, including "detective" (listening for unchallenged biases) and "umpire" (listening for judgmental comments). Explain that conflicts are a natural part of the discussion process, and describe ways to handle conflicts. Talk about the value of staying on point and not succumbing to digressions. (Sources: Brookfield and Preskill, 2005; Kramer and Korn, 1999)

Sharpen your discussion skills. An effective discussion leader must be involved in the discussion but also mindful of the group process. You will need to serve as a gatekeeper ("Makayla, you've been quiet. Do you have something to add?"), a mirror ("The group seems to be focusing on . . ."), an observer ("Why do we drift into tangents whenever . . . comes up?"), a validator ("Great point!"), a negotiator ("Can we come to consensus on this?"), and a reality tester ("Do you realize how our comments can be interpreted?"). (Source: Forsyth, 2003)

Take cultural norms into account. Some of your students may have been taught to be silent and respectful in class; others may have been taught that interrupting and speaking loudly are natural when one feels passionately about a topic. Help your students by identifying ground rules for discussion and asking students who want additional guidance to see you after class. (Source: Eberly Center for Teaching Excellence and Intercultural Communication Center, n.d.)

Setting the Context for Discussion

Explain the ground rules for participation. For example, do students have to raise their hand to speak? If you will call on students at random, do they have a right to "pass" without penalty? If the class is small, you might involve the students in setting the ground rules. (Source: Brookfield and Preskill, 2000)

Ask students what makes for an excellent class discussion. Either in writing or small groups have students develop guidelines that they can refer to during the term. Faculty who have posed this question report that students paint a vivid picture of an engaged, energetic class: well-prepared students; wide participation; respect for different opinions; thought-provoking questions; and thoughtful listeners. (Source: teachers listserv of the University of California, Berkeley)

Give pointers about how to participate in a discussion. Explain that the purpose of discussion is exploration—the search for more information and new viewpoints to compare and test—not advocacy or battle. Stress the value of listening carefully, tolerating opposing viewpoints, suspending judgment until all sides have spoken, realizing that there may not be one right answer or conclusion, and recognizing when one has not understood a concept or idea. Tiberius (1999, adapted from p. 64) recommends distributing a list of suggestions for discussion participants:

- Seek the best answers rather than try to convince other people.
- Try to keep an open mind and not let your previous opinions or ideas get in the way of your willingness to listen to others' ideas.
- Practice listening by putting into your own words the point that the previous speaker made before adding your own contribution.
- Avoid disrupting the discussion by introducing new issues; instead, wait until the current topic reaches its natural end; if you wish to introduce something new, let the group know that what you are about to say will raise a new topic and that you are willing to hold your comment until people are finished discussing the current topic.
- Stick to the subject and talk briefly.
- Avoid long stories, anecdotes, or examples.
- Give encouragement and approval to others.
- Seek out differences of opinion; they enrich the discussion.
- Be sympathetic and understanding of other people's views.

Assign preparation activities. Accompany a reading assignment with questions likely to arise during the discussion. Or ask students to conduct a "fact-finding mission" to search the texts for factual evidence that clarifies a particular concept or problem. Or ask students to come to class with a one- or two-paragraph position piece or several questions they would like to be discussed. (Sources: Clarke, 1988; Cross, 2002)

Starting a Discussion

Refer to the study questions. Begin the discussion by raising one of the study questions or by asking the class which of the study questions they found most provocative or most difficult to answer.

Phrase questions so that students feel comfortable responding. Open with a question that does not have a single correct answer. For example, instead of asking for a definition ("What is entropy?"), ask the students to mention something new that they learned ("What about entropy stands out in your mind?") or to give an example of the concept. Or give students a few minutes to write a response to the question "What is the most important word in the first (or last) paragraph of the reading? Why?" and begin the discussion with that question. (Sources: Kloss, 1996; Lowman, 1995; McKeachie and Svinicki, 2006)

Ask for students' questions. Tell students to come to class with one or two questions about the reading: "Bring a provocative, intriguing question and a sentence or two about why you would like the question to be discussed." From these questions, pick one at random to start the discussion. Or have students divide into small groups to discuss their questions. (Source: Frederick, 1981)

Pose an opening question and have students divide into pairs to discuss. Give pairs, trios, or small groups of students an explicit task: "Identify the two most obvious differences between today's and last week's readings" or "Identify three themes common to the reading assignments." Give the groups a time limit and ask them to select a spokesperson who will report back to the entire class. (Source: Frederick, 1981)

Pose an opening question and have students spend five minutes writing a response. Beginning a discussion with a short writing task gives students time to think and enriches subsequent discussion. (Source: Lang, 2008)

Ask students to recall specific images from the reading assignment. Ask students to volunteer one memorable image, scene, event, or moment from the reading: "What images remain with you after reading the account of Wounded Knee?" List these on the board and explore the themes that emerge. (Source: Frederick, 1981)

Pose a controversial question and have students take a position. Ask students for pro and con arguments or strong examples that support each position. You can also ask students to argue the counterposition to a point they agree with. This approach can lead students to understand the complexities of a controversy, rather than simply reinforce their initial views. (Source: Budesheim and Lundquist, 1999)

Brainstorm. In a brainstorming exercise, anyone can contribute an idea (no matter how bizarre or far-fetched), and each idea is written on the board or screen. Free association, creativity, and ingenuity are the goal; no idea is questioned, praised, or criticized during the exercise. Use brainstorming to encourage students to produce a range of possible causes, consequences, solutions, reasons, or contributing factors. After a set time (five minutes, for example) or when students have run out of ideas, the group begins to evaluate all the ideas.

Ask students to respond to a brief questionnaire. Post or distribute a brief set of questions and use the signed responses to open the discussion. "Amir, I see you answered the first question in the negative. Ebba, I note that you disagree with Amir" or "Minh, your answer to question four is intriguing. Can you tell us more?" (Source: Davis, 1976)

Have students write a few facts on index cards. Hand out blank index cards and ask your students to write down two or three facts about a given topic; these cards are not signed. Collect the cards, shuffle the deck, and draw a card at random. Read one fact from the card and ask students to comment or add related information. (Source: Devet, 1995)

Use sentence completion exercises. Brookfield and Preskill (2005) suggest the following prompts: "The question I'd most like to ask the author is ____"; "The idea I most take issue with is ____"; "The part of the readings that is most confusing is ____."

Guiding the Discussion

Take rough notes. Use these for summarizing the session. You might also note areas that need clarification as well as students' comments that can be used to segue to other points.

Keep the discussion focused. List the day's questions or issues on the screen or board so that the class can see where the discussion is heading. Brief interim summaries of the discussion are helpful, as long as the summaries do not cut off the discussion prematurely.

Use nonverbal cues to encourage participation and maintain the flow. Eye contact, nods of approval, and other signals will help keep students engaged. To shift the mood and pace, you can move around, sit down, stand up, or write on the board. (Sources: Faust and Courtenay, 2002; Rosmarin, 1987)

Return the discussion to the key issues. Redirect a discussion that gets off track: "We seem to have lost sight of the original point. Let's pick up the notion that . . ." or "This is all very provocative, but we also need to talk about the government's response before we end today."

Listen carefully to what students say. Be attentive to (adapted from Christensen, 1991):

- *Content, logic, and substance.* Does the student see the strengths and weaknesses of his or her point? Has something important been left unsaid?
- *Nuance and tone.* Does the student sound confident or doubtful, engaged or indifferent?

- *Context.* Does the student's comment build on previous points and strengthen the flow of the discussion?
- *Consensus.* Do students agree or disagree with the student's comment?

Clarify students' misunderstandings. Don't let the discussion become bogged down in confused statements: "Let's clear up this misunderstanding before we continue"; "We've covered some important points so far. Are you persuaded or troubled by this line of thinking?" (Source: Lowman, 1995)

Vary the pace and tone. To spark participation, ask specific rather than general questions, or call on students who tend to express strong opinions. To calm a discussion, pose abstract or theoretical questions, slow the tempo of your voice, and avoid calling on opinionated students. (Sources: Christensen, 1991; Rosmarin, 1987)

Be alert for signs that a discussion is faltering. Expect one or two lulls in the discussion, but be prepared to move on when students' attention is wandering. Signs that a discussion is foundering include excessive hair-splitting or nitpicking, repetition of points, private conversations, refusals to compromise, disruptive attacks, and apathetic participation. Introducing a new question or activity can jump-start the discussion. (Source: Tiberius, 1999)

Avert heated arguments. Remind students that intellectual conflict is essential to academic discovery, but also point out the importance of cooperating, avoiding personal attacks, and being tolerant of divergent points of view. If a discussion risks becoming too heated, offer a calm remark ("Let's slow down a moment" or "Wait. It's not helpful when five people speak at once") and move on. (Source: Johnson and Johnson, 1997)

Bring closure to the discussion. Announce that the discussion is ending: "Are there any final comments before we pull these ideas together?" Use your closing summary to emphasize two or three key points and to provide a framework for the next session. (Source: Clarke, 1988)

Assign students to conduct the summary. At the beginning of the discussion, select one or two students to be the summarizers of the major issues, concerns, and conclusions generated during discussion. Or tell the class that you will call on someone at the end of class to summarize. This strategy encourages students to listen more carefully because they may be called upon to give the summary.

Ask students to write down and submit the question uppermost in their minds. During the closing minutes of class, ask students to list one or two questions and to turn these in anonymously. Use these questions to start the next class meeting.

Evaluating the Discussion

Ask yourself a few evaluative questions. After class, spend a few minutes thinking about these questions:

- What portion of the class contributed to the discussion?
- How much did you dominate the session?
- What was quality of students' comments?
- What questions worked especially well?
- How satisfied did the group seem?
- Did students learn something new about the topic?

Occasionally save a few minutes for the students to assess the discussion. Ask students to discuss or write their responses to the following questions: What is going well with class discussion? What could be improved? Are you satisfied with your participation in class discussion? (Source: Hollander, 2002)

Video-record the discussion. If you want to make a detailed analysis of how you conduct discussions, video-record a session. One way to analyze the recording is to note who undertakes which of the following activities (adapted from Davis, 1976, pp. 85–86):

- *Initiating:* proposing tasks or procedures, defining problems, identifying action steps
- *Eliciting:* requesting information, inviting reactions, soliciting ideas
- *Informing:* offering information, expressing reactions, stating facts
- *Blocking:* introducing irrelevancies, changing the subject, questioning others' competence
- *Entrenching:* expressing cynicism, posing distractions, digging in
- *Clarifying:* clearing up confusions, restating others' contributions, suggesting alternative ways of seeing problems or issues
- *Clouding:* creating confusion, claiming that words can't "really" be defined, remaining willfully puzzled, quibbling over semantic distinctions, obscuring issues

- *Summarizing*: pulling together related ideas, offering conclusions, stating implications of others' contributions
- *Interpreting*: calling attention to individual actions and what they mean
- *Consensus proposing*: asking whether the group is nearing a decision, suggesting a conclusion for group agreement
- *Consensus resisting*: persisting in a topic or argument after others have decided or lost interest, going back over old ground, finding endless details that need attention
- *Harmonizing*: trying to reconcile disagreements, joking at the right time to reduce tensions, encouraging inactive members
- *Disrupting*: interfering with the work of the group, trying to increase tensions, making jokes as veiled insults or threats
- *Evaluating*: asking whether the group is satisfied with the proceedings or topic, pointing out implicit or explicit standards the group is using, suggesting alternative tasks and practices

As you observe your students' behavior and your own, think about ways to increase productive activities and decrease counterproductive ones. Ask a trusted colleague or a faculty development expert on your campus to analyze and review your recording with you.

References

Brookfield. S. D., and Preskill, S. Getting Lecturers to Take Discussion Seriously. In M. Kaplan and D. Lieberman (Eds.), *To Improve the Academy: Resources for Faculty, Instructional, and Organizational Development*. Vol. 18. Bolton, MA: Anker, 2000.

Brookfield, S. D., and Preskill, S. *Discussion as a Way of Teaching: Tools and Techniques for Democratic Classrooms*. (2nd ed.) San Francisco: Jossey-Bass, 2005.

Budesheim, T. L., and Lundquist, A. R. "Consider the Opposite: Opening Minds through In-Class Debates on Course-Related Controversies." *Teaching of Psychology*, 1999, *26*(2).

Christensen, C. R. The Discussion Teacher in Action: Questioning, Listening, and Response. In C. R. Christensen, D. A. Garvin, and A. Sweet (Eds.), *Education for Judgment: The Artistry of Discussion Leadership*. Boston: Harvard Business School, 1991.

Clarke, J. H. "Designing Discussions as Group Inquiry." *College Teaching*, 1988, *36*(4), 140–143.

Cross, K. P. "The Role of Class Discussions in the Learning-Centered Classroom." *The Cross Papers*. League for Innovation in the Community College, Educational Testing Service, March 2002, no 6.

Davis, J. R. *Teaching Strategies for the College Classroom*. Boulder, CO: Westview Press, 1976.

Devet, B. "Using Index Cards to Introduce a Subject." *College Teaching*, 1995, *43*(1), 40.

Eberly Center for Teaching Excellence and Intercultural Communication Center. "Recognizing and Addressing Cultural Variations in the Classroom." Carnegie Mellon University, n.d.

http://www.cmu.edu/teaching/resources/PublicationsArchives/InternalReports/
culturalvariations.pdf

Faust, D. F., and Courtenay, B. C. "Interaction in the Intergenerational Freshman Class:
What Matters." *Educational Gerontology*, 2002, *28*(5), 401–422.

Forsyth, D. R. *The Professor's Guide to Teaching: Psychological Principles and Practices*. Washington,
DC: American Psychological Association, 2003.

Frederick, P. "The Dreaded Discussion: Ten Ways to Start." *Improving College and University
Teaching*, 1981, *29*(3), 109–114.

Hollander, J. A. "Learning to Discuss: Strategies for Improving the Quality of Class
Discussion." *Teaching Sociology*, 2002, *30*(3), 317–327.

Johnson, D. W., and Johnson, R. T. Academic Controversy: Increase Intellectual Conflict and
Increase the Quality of Learning. In W. E. Campbell and K. A. Smith (Eds.), *New Paradigms for College Teaching*. Edina, MN: Interaction Book Company, 1997.

Kloss, R. J. "Writing Things Down vs. Writing Things Up: Are Research Papers Valid?"
College Teaching, 1996, *44*(1), 3–7.

Kramer, T. J., and Korn, J. H. Class Discussions: Promoting Participation and Preventing
Problems. In B. Perlman, L. I. McCann, and S. H. McFadden (Eds.), *Lessons Learned: Practical
Advice for the Teaching of Psychology*. Washington, DC: American Psychological Society, 1999.

Lang, J. M. *On Course: A Week-By-Week Guide to Your First Semester of College Teaching*. Cambridge,
MA: Harvard University Press, 2008.

Lowman, J. *Mastering the Techniques of Teaching*. (2nd ed.) San Francisco: Jossey-Bass, 1995.

McGonigal, K. "Using Class Discussion to Meet Your Teaching Goals." *Speaking of Teaching*,
2005, *15*(1). (Newsletter of the Center for Teaching and Learning, Stanford University)
http://ctl.stanford.edu/Newsletter/discussion_leading.pdf

McKeachie, W. J., and Svinicki, M. *McKeachie's Teaching Tips*. (12th ed.) Boston: Houghton
Mifflin, 2006.

Rosmarin, A. The Art of Leading a Discussion. In C. R. Christensen and A. J. Hansen
(Eds.), *Teaching and the Case Method*. Boston: Harvard Business School, 1987.

Tiberius, R. G. *Small Group Teaching: A Trouble-Shooting Guide*. London: Kogan Page, 1999.

10

Encouraging Student Participation in Discussion

Students' enthusiasm and willingness to participate affect the quality of class discussion. Your challenge is to engage your students, keep them talking to each other, and help them develop insights into the material. Roby (1988) warns against falling into quasi-discussions—encounters in which students talk but do not develop or criticize their own positions. Two common forms of quasi-discussion are "quiz shows" (where the teacher has the right answers) and "bull sessions" (which are characterized by clichés, stereotypes, empty generalizations, and aimless talking).

Class participation tends to increase when students feel confident, are interested in the topic, and have good rapport with one another (Fassinger, 1997). The following suggestions are intended to help you create a classroom in which students feel comfortable testing and sharing ideas.

General Strategies

Get to know your students. In classes of thirty or fewer, learn all your students' names; see Chapter 3, "The First Days of Class" for suggestions. If you require students to come to your office once during the first few weeks of class, you can also learn about their interests. Class participation may improve after students have had an opportunity to talk informally with their instructor.

Arrange seating to promote discussion. At a long seminar table, seat yourself along the side rather than at the head. If it's feasible, ask students to sit in a semicircle so that they can see one another. If the discussion tends to be dominated by students sitting closest to you, suggest that students change seats. (Sources: Brookfield and Preskill, 2005; Faust and Courtenay, 2002; Jensen et al., 2005)

Encourage students to meet one another. Students are more likely to participate in class if they feel they are among friends. During the first week or two of class, plan some activities that will help students get to know one another. For example, ask students to introduce themselves and describe their background in the subject. These introductions may also give you some clues about framing discussion questions that address students' interests. See Chapter 3, "The First Days of Class" for suggestions. (Source: Faust and Courtenay, 2002)

Help students dispel faulty assumptions about class participation. Trosset (2000) has identified the following false assumptions that hinder students from participating:

- Participation requires advocating a particular position.
- Matters should not be discussed if the result is unlikely to be agreement.
- Personal experience is the only source of legitimate knowledge.
- All knowledge is merely opinion.
- People have the right not to be challenged.
- No one in the group should experience discomfort.

Increasing Student Participation

Create opportunities for all students to talk in class during the first two weeks. The longer a student goes without speaking in class, the more difficult it will be to speak up. Use small-group or pair work early in the term so that all students can participate in nonthreatening circumstances.

Allow the class time to warm up. Arrive a few minutes early and talk informally with students. Or open the class with a few minutes of conversation about relevant current events, campus activities, or administrative matters.

Limit your own comments. Avoid the temptation to respond to every student's contribution. Instead, allow students to develop their ideas and respond to one another.

Periodically divide students into small groups. Students may find it easier to speak to groups of three or four. Divide students into small groups, have them discuss a question for five or ten minutes, and then reconvene the class. Choose topics that are focused and straightforward: "What are the two most important characteristics of goal-free evaluation?" or "Why did the experiment fail?" Once students have spoken in small groups, they may be less hesitant to speak to the class as a whole.

Assign leadership roles to students. Ask two or three students to lead a discussion session during the term. Meet with the discussion leaders beforehand to go over their questions and proposed format. Have the leaders distribute three to six discussion questions to the class a week before the discussion.

Use tokens to encourage discussion. Try a "token economy" in which you award tokens for participation that students can accumulate for extra credit or parlay into an option such as not having to take a quiz. Or use poker chips when over- or under-participation is a problem. One faculty member distributes three poker chips to each student in her class. Each time a student speaks, a chip is turned over to the instructor. Students must spend most of their chips by the end of the period. Another faculty member uses sticky notes which students place on their desk each time they speak. This gives an immediate visual sense of the contributions of each student. (Sources: Boniecki and Moore, 2003; Cross, 2002; Lang, 2008)

Keeping the Discussion Going

Build rapport with students. Comment positively about a student's contribution and reinforce good points by paraphrasing or summarizing them. If a student makes a good observation that is ignored by the class, point this out: "Thank you, Steve. Karen also raised that issue earlier, but we didn't pick up on it. Perhaps now is the time to address it. Thank you for your patience, Karen." (Source: Tiberius, 1999)

Bring students' outside comments into class. When students make a good comment after class, through e-mail, or during office hours, ask if they are willing to raise the idea in class. If they agree, introduce the comment in class by saying something like "Jin, you were saying something about that in the hall yesterday. Would you repeat it for the rest of the class?" If the student is reluctant, bring up the issue yourself and give credit to the student.

Use nonverbal cues to encourage participation. Smile expectantly and nod as students talk. Maintain eye contact with students. Look relaxed and interested.

Draw all students into the discussion. You can involve more students by asking whether they agree with what has just been said or whether someone can provide another example to support or contradict a point: "How do the rest of you feel about that?" or "Does anyone who hasn't spoken care to comment on the plans for greening the campus?"

Give quiet students special encouragement. Some quiet students are just waiting for a nonthreatening opportunity to speak. To help these students, you can try these strategies:

- Arrange small-group (two to four students) discussions.
- Pose casual questions that don't have a single correct answer: "What do you remember most from the reading?" or "Which of the articles did you find to be the easiest to understand?" (McKeachie and Svinicki, 2006).
- Assign a small specific task to a quiet student: "Carrie, would you find out for next class session what Chile's GNP was last year?"
- Bolster students' self-confidence by writing their comments on the board.
- Stand or sit next to someone who has not contributed; your proximity may draw a hesitant student into the discussion.

Discourage students who monopolize the discussion. Here are some ways to handle dominating students:

- Ask everyone to jot down a response to your question; then choose someone to speak.
- Enforce a minute or so of silent wait time after posing a question, allowing students to structure a response (Bean and Peterson, 1998).
- Restate your desire for greater student participation: "I'd like to hear from others in the class."
- Avoid making eye contact with the talkative.
- Explain that the discussion has become too one-sided and ask the monopolizer to help by remaining silent: "Larry, since we must move on, would you summarize your remarks, and then we'll hear the reactions of other group members."
- Acknowledge the time constraints: "Our time is running out. Let's set a thirty-second limit on everybody's comments from now on."
- Speak to the monopolizer after class or during office hours. Tell the student that you value his or her participation and wish more students contributed. If this student's comments are good, say so; but point out that learning results from give-and-take and that everyone benefits from hearing a range of opinions and views.

Tactfully correct wrong answers. Any type of put-down or disapproval will inhibit students from speaking up. Say something positive about those aspects of the response that are insightful or creative and point out those aspects that are off base. Provide hints, suggestions, or follow-up questions that will enable students to understand and correct their own errors.

Grading Class Participation

Decide whether you want to grade student participation. Some faculty grade students on their classroom participation, and on some campuses the practice is common. This may benefit students who test poorly but who demonstrate a depth of understanding by their comments during class. However, grading class participation may discourage free and open discussion, making students hesitant to talk for fear of revealing their ignorance or being perceived as trying to gain grade points. Faculty also argue that thoughtful silence is not unproductive, and that shy students should not be placed at a disadvantage simply because they are shy. Some faculty regard the grading of participation as too subjective to be defended if challenged. (Sources: Bean and Peterson, 1998; Hollander, 2002)

If you grade participation, select appropriate standards. Brookfield's many examples of kinds of participation (2006) include bringing in an article or a Web URL that adds new information or perspectives; asking the group for a moment of silence that gives others time to think; and paraphrasing or summarizing previous comments. Bean and Peterson (1998) recommend using holistic rubrics for scoring participation; for example, from "1" (is disruptive and rude) to "6" (is well prepared, advances the conversation, shows interest and respect for others). If you use rubrics, share them with students at the beginning of the term so they know how they will be graded.

Dancer and Kamvounias (2005) ameliorate the problem of the instructor's subjectivity by incorporating peer-to-peer evaluations. You can ask students to rate each other: "How much did student X contribute to your learning in this course?" You can involve the class in defining the criteria for assessment. For example, classes have generated criteria such as "willing to take risks," "limiting participation to a reasonable amount," and "providing new ways of thinking about the material."

Zaremba and Dunn (2004) and Lang (2008) describe examples of self-evaluation measures in which students rate their preparation and verbal and nonverbal participation after each class session. When the student's self-evaluation is consistent with the instructor's assessment, the student's rating is recorded. When they differ, the instructor's takes precedence, and students receive an explanation for the instructor's rating.

Melvin (1988) describes a grading scheme based on peer and professor evaluation: students are asked to rate the class participation of each of their classmates as high, medium, or low. If the median peer rating is higher than the instructor's rating of that student, the two ratings are averaged. If the peer rating is lower, the student receives the instructor's rating.

Faculty who grade participation tend to make it 10–20 percent of the final grade in the course.

References

Bean, J. C., and Peterson, D. "Grading Classroom Participation." *New Directions for Teaching and Learning*, no. 74. San Francisco: Jossey-Bass, 1998, pp. 33–40.

Boniecki, K. A., and Moore, S. Breaking the Silence: Using a Token Economy to Reinforce Classroom Participation. *Teaching of Psychology*, 2003, *30*(3), 224–227.

Brookfield, S. D. *The Skillful Teacher: On Technique, Trust, and Responsiveness in the Classroom.* (2nd ed.) San Francisco: Jossey-Bass, 2006.

Brookfield, S. D., and Preskill, S. *Discussion as a Way of Teaching: Tools and Techniques for Democratic Classrooms.* (2nd ed.) San Francisco: Jossey-Bass, 2005.

Cross, K. P. The Role of Class Discussions in the Learning-Centered Classroom. *The Cross Papers.* League for Innovation in the Community College, Educational Testing Service, March 2002, no. 6.

Dancer, D., and Kamvounias, P. "Student Involvement in Assessment: A Project Designed to Assess Class Participation Fairly and Reliably." *Assessment and Evaluation in Higher Education*, 2005, *30*(4), 445–454.

Fassinger, P. A. "Classes Are Groups: Thinking Sociologically about Teaching." *College Teaching*, 1997, *45*(1), 22–25.

Faust, D. F., and Courtenay, B. C. "Interaction in the Intergenerational Freshman Class: What Matters." *Educational Gerontology*, 2002, *28*(5), 401–422.

Hollander, J. A. "Learning to Discuss: Strategies for Improving the Quality of Class Discussion." *Teaching Sociology*, 2002, *30*(3), 317–327.

Jensen, M., Farrand, K., Redman, L., Varcoe, T., and Coleman, L. "Helping Graduate Teaching Assistants Lead Discussions with Undergraduate Students: A Few Simple Teaching Strategies." *Journal of College Science Teaching*, 2005, *34*(7), 20–24.

Lang, J. M. *On Course: A Week-By-Week Guide to Your First Semester of College Teaching.* Cambridge, MA: Harvard University Press, 2008.

McKeachie, W. J., and Svinicki, M. *McKeachie's Teaching Tips.* (12th ed.) Boston: Houghton Mifflin, 2006.

Melvin, K. B. "Rating Class Participation: The Prof/Peer Method." *Teaching of Psychology*, 1988, *15*(3), 137–139.

Roby, T. W. Models of Discussion. In J. T. Dillon (Ed.), *Questioning and Discussion: A Multidisciplinary Study.* Norwood, NJ: Ablex, 1988.

Tiberius, R. G. *Small Group Teaching: A Trouble-Shooting Guide.* London: Kogan Page, 1999.

Trosset, C. Obstacles to Open Discussion and Critical Thinking: The Grinnell College Study. In D. DeZure (Ed.), *Learning from Change: Landmarks in Teaching and Learning in Higher Education from* Change Magazine, *1969–1999.* Sterling, VA: Stylus Publishing, 2000.

Zaremba, S. B., and Dunn, D. S. "Assessing Class Participation through Self-Evaluation: Method and Measure." *Teaching of Psychology*, 2004, *31*(3), 191–193.

11

Online Discussions

Successful online discussion requires careful planning of purpose and structure, as well as active instructor supervision. In the absence of these factors, online discussions are often of little value, and students show little enthusiasm for them (Pena-Shaff et al., 2005; Williams and Pury, 2002). Be clear on what you want your online discussion to accomplish. Online discussion should be an integral part of the course, not an add-on and not busywork. If online discussion appeals to you as a way to have more class time to lecture, consider moving some lecture material online in order to free some class time for discussion (Keefe, 2003; Silverstein, 2006). If regular participation in an online discussion group is a course requirement, reduce the other homework accordingly.

General Strategies

Use your campus learning management system. Your learning management system or collaborative and learning environment may include software for conducting online discussions. Current technology offers three ways to structure online discussion:

- *Mail-lists* and *listservs* allow instructors and individual students to exchange e-mail messages with everyone in the class.
- *Discussion boards* (bulletin boards, forums) are Web sites where students can post messages and read all their classmates' messages. The messages are usually threaded (grouped by subject line and displayed in chronological sequence).
- *Chat sessions* allow for real-time typed conversations at a Web site.

Real-time online chat is useful for distance learning, but it seems to be less effective than discussion boards for classes that have face-to-face meetings. Online chat also poses difficulties in maintaining focus; sometimes, too, it is hard to tell whether a participant has completed a response or is pausing to compose a thoughtful comment. For these reasons and others, most instructors prefer discussion boards to online chat. (Sources: Bauer 2002; Kirkpatrick, 2005)

Create a course blog. Some instructors use blogging software to organize online course materials and to facilitate online exchanges among students. Other instructors have found that blogging is not particularly effective for promoting student interaction. (Source: Krause, 2005)

Planning a Discussion Board

Coordinate online, offline, and in-class work. For example, will students identify questions in class that they will then explore in online discussion? Will students be assigned projects to complete in online groups? How will ideas or consensus opinions generated online be introduced into classroom discussion, papers, or tests? Instructors who use online discussion agree that it does not supplant the need for face-to-face discussion in the classroom. (Source: de Bruyn, 2004)

Control the size of online discussion groups. Experienced faculty recommend that groups contain four to twelve students, and no more than twenty students. In large courses, you can list a set of discussion topics and let students choose which discussion to join. Or you can divide your class into three groups—one to pose questions, one to respond to questions, and one to summarize and comment—and have students rotate groups throughout the term. One instructor suggests dividing a class of twenty-five students into two groups, which post online during alternate weeks. (Source: Bryant, 2005)

Set expectations for participation. Tell students how many times (or how often) you expect them to log on and to post; experienced faculty recommend twice a week. State how their online participation (both attendance and quality of participation) will affect their course grades. Some faculty assign bonus points for high-quality contributions; others weigh online participation as 10 percent or less the course grade. Bauer (2002) provides examples of rubrics for grading student participation in online discussions, including type of comments. (Sources: Bauer, 2002; Bender, 2003)

Devise focused questions or specific tasks. It is usually better to dedicate online discussion to problem-solving rather than to broad questions, although it can be effective to ask students to explore and reach consensus on an open-ended question within a set time period. Other tasks for discussion boards include creating exam questions for the midterm or final; making a substantive reply to four classmates, with each student then posting how the feedback has affected his or her thinking; engaging a guest discussant who is an author of one of the readings; and conducting a debate in which students argue for or against a particular position. (Source: Greenlaw and DeLoach, 2003)

Explain the ground rules. The following guidelines are adapted from Gajadhar and Green (2005); Palloff and Pratt (2007); Pena-Shaff, Altman, and Stephenson (2005); Sevilla and Wells (2002); and Wakley (2002):

- Write informative subject lines.
- When responding to a previous comment, mention the specific point to which you are responding.
- Keep comments short but include supporting logic and details. Avoid postings like "Me too," "Good point," or "Don't think so."
- When you present an opinion, support it with evidence or data.
- Ask for clarification if you don't understand a point someone has made.
- Communicate agreement as well as disagreement, and state your reasons.
- Carefully proofread your post.
- Assume that all participants have good intentions.
- Wait 24 hours before responding to a post that you perceive as negative to let your emotions settle down.
- Expect conflict as part of the group process.
- Be willing to change your mind.
- Adhere to general rules of civility, courtesy, and mutual respect.

Establish the style of response. How formal or informal do you expect students' posts to be? Describe and give examples of the style you expect them to follow. You may also wish to set standards for permissible language and to require all participants to identify themselves by name. Students who are new to discussion boards may appreciate seeing examples of thoughtful and courteous posts. (Sources: Bender, 2003; Lawrence et al., 2005)

Help students manage the message volume. Students may need tips on sorting and keeping track of the threads or e-mail messages that most interest them. Suggest that students scan the posts every day or two, rather than face an overwhelming stack of messages twice a week. (Source: Aitken and Shedletsky, 2002)

Conducting Online Discussions

Launch the discussion. Establish a welcoming, encouraging tone, and let students see that you are paying attention. Compliment participants online and in or after class, and incorporate, as appropriate, students' comments into your postings. Make an occasional short substantive comment, but focus on prompting students to expand their comments: "Miguel, is what you're saying consistent with what Sumi said?" or "Sumi, what alternative explanations could you add to the one you've stated?" When discussion is flowing well, praise the quality of discussion. (Sources: Bender, 2003; Muilenburg and Berge, 2000)

Pose questions at different levels. Effective questions are the key to starting and maintaining discussion (see Chapter 12, "Asking Questions"). Students tend to ignore vague or overly broad questions. You can also prompt discussion with sentence-completion exercises, a problem or scenario, or by playing devil's advocate. (Sources: Bender, 2003; Muilenburg and Berge, 2000)

Facilitate the discussion. Encourage active student-to-student participation. Ask for clarification, point out contradictory statements, or energize the discussion if needed, but try to stay in the background. Research shows that frequent postings by instructors do not result in greater student participation. (Sources: Mazzolini and Maddison, 2003; Oren et al., 2002)

Launch and manage discussion threads. Start a thread for procedural questions, so that these exchanges will be separate from the substantive discussion. Announce general topics for discussion, and seed the discussion by posing an opening question. Archive any threads that have served their purpose and are cluttering the site. Especially at the beginning of the course, monitor how well students are respecting the boundaries of existing threads and starting new ones when appropriate. In a threaded discussion, require students to comment on previously posted questions before adding comments of their own. Remind students to respond to pertinent comments on their own earlier questions or comments. (Source: de Bruyn, 2004)

Watch out for orphaned comments and silent students. Sometimes students' comments or questions get little or no response from other students. The authors of these orphaned comments may become discouraged and drop out of the discussion. If you see this dynamic, gently remind students to respond to the orphaned comment. When quieter students participate, give them a supportive response. (Source: Pena-Shaff et al., 2005)

Monitor and instruct students in the use of subject lines. Remind students that each message should have an accurate subject line that indicates both the point the message is addressing ("Re: Kim's pro-incentive argument") and what the message will add ("—but what about New Zealand?"). Do not let students develop the lazy habit of simply adding "Re" before the subject line of an earlier comment. (Source: Sevilla and Wells, 2002)

Provide for summary and synthesis. To avoid letting a threaded discussion lose its way or simply fade out, periodically pose questions that require synthesis and summary of the thread. You could also assign this task and other moderating roles to individual students. (Source: de Bruyn, 2004)

Assess online participation. Whether or not online participation counts toward course grades, give students some comments about the quality of their participation. Most online discussion software allows you to preserve and archive contributions and then review these when evaluating the quantity and quality of participation. (Sources: Knowlton, 2003; Murphy and Loveless, 2005; Wang and Tucker, 2001)

References

Aitken, J. E., and Shedletsky, L. J. "Using Electronic Discussion to Teach Communication Courses." *Communication Education*, 2002, *51*(3), 325–331.

Bauer, J. F. "Assessing Student Work from Chatrooms and Bulletin Boards." *New Directions for Teaching and Learning*, no. 91. San Francisco: Jossey-Bass, 2002, pp. 31–36.

Bender, T. *Discussion-Based Online Teaching to Enhance Student Learning: Theory, Practice, and Assessment*. Sterling, VA: Stylus, 2003.

Bryant, B. K. "Electronic Discussion Sections: A Useful Tool in Teaching Large University Classes." *Teaching of Psychology*, 2005, *32*(4), 271–275.

de Bruyn, L. L. "Monitoring Online Communication: Can the Development of Convergence and Social Presence Indicate an Interactive Learning Environment?" *Distance Education*, 2004, *25*(1), 67–81.

Gajadhar, J., and Green, J. "The Importance of Nonverbal Elements in Online Chat." *Educause Quarterly*, 2005, *28*(4), 63–64.

Greenlaw, S. A., and DeLoach, S. B. "Teaching Critical Thinking with Electronic Discussion." *Journal of Economic Education*, 2003, *34*(1), 36–52.

Keefe, T. J. "Using Technology to Enhance a Course: The Importance of Interaction." *Educause Quarterly*, 2003, *26*(1), 24–34.

Kirkpatrick, G. "Online 'Chat' Facilities As Pedagogic Tools." *Active Learning in Higher Education*, 2005, *6*(2), 145–159.

Knowlton, D. S. "Evaluating College Students' Efforts in Asynchronous Discussion: A Systematic Process." *Quarterly Review of Distance Education*, 2003, *41*(1), 31–41.

Krause, S. D. "Blogs as a Tool for Teaching." *Chronicle of Higher Education*, June 24, 2005.

Lawrence, M., O'Dell, B., and Stephan, L. Aligning Online. In D. H. Wulff (Ed.), *Aligning for Learning: Strategies for Teaching Effectiveness*. Bolton, MA: Anker, 2005.

Mazzolini, M., and Maddison, S. "Sage, Guide or Ghost? The Effect of Instructor Intervention on Student Participation in Online Discussion Forums." *Computers and Education*, 2003, *40*(3), 237–253.

Muilenburg, L., and Berge, Z. L. "A Framework for Designing Questions for Online Learning." *DEOSNEWS*, 2000, 10(2). http://www.ed.psu. edu/acsde/deos/deosnews/deosnews10_2.asp

Murphy, E., and Loveless, J. "Students' Self Analysis of Contributions to Online Asynchronous Discussions." *Australasian Journal of Educational Technology*, 2005, *21*(2), 155–172.

Oren, A., Mioduser, D., and Nachmias, R. "The Development of Social Climate in Virtual Learning Discussion Groups." *International Review of Research in Open and Distance Learning*, 2002, *3*(1), 1–19.

Palloff, R. M., and Pratt, K. *Building Online Learning Communities*. (2nd ed.) San Francisco: Jossey-Bass, 2007.

Pena-Shaff, J., Altman, W., and Stephenson, H. "Asynchronous Online Discussions as a Tool for Learning: Students' Attitudes, Expectations, and Perceptions." *Journal of Interactive Learning Research*, 2005, *16*(4), 409–430.

Sevilla, C., and Wells, T. "Guiding and Evaluating Online Discussion: Practical Tips to Make Your Courses Successful." *E-Learning*, February 2002.

Silverstein, S. "The iPod Took My Seat." *Los Angeles Times*, January 17, 2006.

Wakley, D. "The New Rules of Engagement: Keeping Online Students Involved and On Track in Asynchronous Discussion Forums." *Journal of Instruction Delivery Systems*, 2002, *16*(2), 6–12.

Wang, A. Y., Newlin, M. H., and Tucker, T. L. "A Discourse Analysis of Online Classroom Chats: Predictors of Cyber-Student Performance." *Teaching of Psychology*, 2001, *28*(3), 222–226.

Williams, S., and Pury, C. "Student Attitudes toward and Participation in Electronic Discussion." *International Journal of Educational Technology*, 2002, *3*(1).

12

Asking Questions

The give-and-take of asking and answering questions is central to learning and to effective teaching. The types of questions instructors pose and the sequencing of questions should capture students' attention, arouse their curiosity, reinforce important points, encourage reflection, and promote active learning.

General Strategies

Formulate questions in advance. As you prepare for class, identify questions and anticipate the range of student responses. Select and discard questions from your list as the discussion proceeds, depending on what topics your students want to pursue. To improve students' inquiry skills, use your opening questions to stimulate students to form their own questions. Ask a few questions that you are not quite sure how to answer. You may be impressed by your students' ideas. (Source: Haroutunian-Gordon, 1998; Windschitl and Buttemer, 2000)

Place your questions in order. You might want to move from the general to the specific, from the simple to the complex, or from the convergent (one answer possible) to the divergent (many answers possible). Select an order that will allow students to answer successfully the first time, especially to your opening questions. (Source: Pennell, 2000)

Prepare strategies for asking questions. Think about different ways to pose your questions: to the class as a whole, to pairs of students, to small groups. Create questions designed to prompt brainstorming, consensus building, or debate. (Source: Kasulis, 1984)

Decide how you will call on students. Some faculty call only on students who raise their hands; other faculty prefer to draw all students into the discussion by pointing to someone and requesting a response. If you go around the room calling on students in order, some students' attention may wander until it is their turn. If you choose to "cold-call" randomly on students with questions, warm up the situation first. For example, consider asking students to turn to a neighbor to answer the question; pausing before calling on someone to give students time to think; writing the question on the board to help students gather their thoughts; or allowing students a moment to write a response, jotting down a few key points. (Source: Dallimore et al., 2004)

Convey a sense of spirited inquiry. Let your tone of voice, facial expression, and gestures suggest that you are seeking knowledge, not interrogating the troops. Be demographically inclusive in directing your questions and calling on students. (Source: Payne and Gainey, 2003)

Keep notes on class participation. Take a few minutes after each class session to note which questions generated the most lively exchanges. (Source: Kasulis, 1984)

Evaluate your questioning skills. The University of Illinois at Urbana-Champaign has developed guidelines for evaluating instructors' questioning skills ("Methods for Assessing Questioning Skills," n.d.) including sample surveys to administer to students to get their feedback. Acheson and Gall (2003) suggest dimensions on which students or instructors can evaluate an instructor's questioning behavior, including use of a variety of questioning strategies and behaviors that elicit student participation. See also Chapter 53, "Video Recordings and Classroom Observations" for advice.

Levels and Types of Questions

Vary the kinds of questions you ask. Move from simple questions to those that require more thought (adapted from Christensen, 1991; Elder and Paul, 2005; McKeachie and Svinicki, 2006; Rosmarin, 1987; Yip, 2001):

- *Exploratory questions* probe facts and basic knowledge: "What research evidence supports the theory of a cancer-prone personality?"
- *Challenge questions* examine assumptions, conclusions, and interpretations: "How else might we account for the findings of this experiment?" "What assumptions underlie this point of view?"
- *Relational questions* ask for comparisons of themes, ideas, or issues: "What premises of *Plessy v. Ferguson* did the Supreme Court throw out in deciding *Brown v. Board of Education*?"
- *Diagnostic questions* probe motives or causes: "Why did Simone assume a new identity?"

- *Action questions* call for a conclusion or action: "In response to a sit-in at California Hall, what should the chancellor do?"
- *Connective and cause-and-effect questions* ask for causal relationships between ideas, actions, or events: "If the government stopped farm subsidies for wheat, what would happen to the price of bread?"
- *Extension questions* expand the discussion: "How does this comment relate to what we have previously said?"
- *Hypothetical questions* pose a change in the facts or issues: "Suppose Sergei had been rich instead of poor. Would the outcome have been the same?"
- *Priority questions* seek to identify the most important issue: "From all that we have talked about, what is the most important cause of the decline of American competitiveness?"
- *Summary questions* elicit syntheses: "What themes or lessons have emerged from today's class?"

Tap different cognitive skills. Another way of categorizing questions follows from Bloom's classic hierarchy of cognitive skills (1956):

- *Knowledge* (remembering previously learned material such as definitions, principles, formulas): "Define *shared governance*." "What are Piaget's stages of development?"
- *Comprehension* (understanding the meaning of remembered material, usually demonstrated by restating or citing examples): "Explain the process of mitosis." "Give some examples of alliteration."
- *Application* (using information in a new context to solve a problem, answer a question, perform a task): "How does the concept of price elasticity explain the cost of oat bran?" "How would you graph the data in a sample like this one?"
- *Analysis* (breaking a concept into its parts and explaining their interrelationships; distinguishing relevant from extraneous material): "What factors affect the price of gasoline?" "Point out the arguments the author uses to support his thesis about polar ice melts."
- *Synthesis* (putting parts together to form a new whole; solving a problem requiring creativity or originality): "How would you design an experiment to show the effect of education on income, holding other factors constant?" "How would you reorganize Bloom's taxonomy in light of new research in cognitive science?"
- *Evaluation* (using criteria to arrive at a reasoned judgment of the value of something): "To what extent does the proposed package of tax increases resolve the budget deficit?" "If cocaine were legalized, what would be the implications for public health services?"

Higher-level questions may also be sorted into three main types (adapted from Edwards and Bowman, 1996):

- *Convergent* questions invite the analysis and integration of existing data with the aim of arriving at a single conclusion.
- *Divergent* questions invite the respondent to elaborate on a conclusion to reach further implications or synthesis with other ideas.
- *Evaluative* questions involve making considered judgments based on data or evidence.

"What's the next important question we should ask?" is an excellent high-level question that shares with students the responsibility for directing the discussion (O'Hare, 1993). At times, you will also want to ask questions that encourage hunches, intuitive leaps, and educated guesses.

Effective Questioning

Ask one question at a time. In an effort to elicit a response, instructors sometimes attempt to clarify a question by rephrasing it. But often the new wording poses an entirely new question, which sends students off in another direction. The better strategy is to ask a brief question and wait for a response. Instead of "How are Lacan and Freud alike, for example, in their view of the unconscious, or how about their approach to psychoanalysis?" ask, "How is Lacan's theory of the unconscious similar to Freud's?" (Source: Hyman, 1989)

Avoid asking, "Any questions?" The question "Any questions?" often does not elicit any questions. A better approach is to imply that you are expecting questions and encourage students to ask them. For example, you might say, "At this point, I'm sure you have some questions" or "That was complicated. What did I leave out?" or "What questions are uppermost in your mind?" (Sources: Felder, 1994; Pennell, 2000)

Avoid asking yes-or-no questions. The discussion will stall if you ask questions that invite a one-word or short-phrase response. Instead, ask *why* or *how* questions that lead students to try to explain things. Instead of "Is radon considered a pollutant?" ask, "Why might radon be considered a pollutant?" Leading questions ("Don't you agree that climate change is the most serious environmental hazard we face?") also close off avenues for discussion. And the discussion will come to a halt if you answer your own question: "Why can't we use the chi-square test here? Is it because the cells are too small?"

Pose questions that invite multiple answers. A chemical engineering instructor avoids asking for the correct number by saying, "Before you calculate the answer, how do you predict the system will behave in general?" A history professor asks questions for which a number of hypotheses are equally plausible—"Why did the birth rate rise in mid-eighteenth-century England?" or "Why did Napoleon III agree to Cavour's plans?"—and emphasizes to students that these questions are matters of controversy or puzzlement to scholars. She also shows how different answers lead in very different directions. (Source: Felder, 1994)

Ask focused questions. An overly broad question such as "What about the fall of the Berlin Wall?" may lead students far off the topic. Instead ask, "How did the fall of the Berlin Wall—the reunification of Germany—affect European economic conditions?"

After you ask a question, wait silently for an answer. Do not be afraid of silence. Be patient. Students may need 10–30 seconds to form an answer to a question. Don't misinterpret silence as a signal of apathy, resistance, or laziness. Give students time to think and to word a response. Count to yourself while students are thinking; the silence rarely lasts more than 10–15 seconds. Waiting indicates that you want thoughtful participation, and if you communicate an air of expectation, someone will break the silence, if only to say, "I don't understand the question."

If the silence exceeds 30 seconds, ask your students what the silence means: "The room has grown quiet. Why?" Or encourage them by saying, "Could someone get us started?" Even then, you might delay calling on someone until several hands are raised; pausing lets students know that replies do not have to be formulated quickly. Wait again after a student has responded, in order to indicate that the response is worth thinking about. Waiting helps students focus on what their peers say instead of planning their next remark. (Sources: Biggs, 2003; Pennell, 2000)

Search for common ground. If one student immediately gives a response, follow up by asking others what they think. "Hadley, how strongly do you agree or disagree with that?" is a good way to involve more students in the discussion.

Ask questions that require students to demonstrate their understanding. Instead of "Do you understand?" or "Do you have any questions about this?" ask, "What are the considerations to keep in mind when you want your evaluation results to be used?" Instead of "Do you understand this program command?" ask, "How would we change the program if we wanted to sort the numbers in ascending order rather than descending order?" Instead of "Does everybody see how I got this answer?" ask, "Why did I substitute the value of delta in this equation?" (Source: Pennell, 2000)

Structure your questions to encourage student-to-student interaction. Students become more attentive when you ask questions that require them to respond to each other. For example, ask Molly, "Could you relate that to what Sam said earlier?" and, if needed, help Molly recall what Sam said. (Source: Kasulis, 1984)

Draw out reserved or reluctant students. A disguised question may encourage students who are hesitant to speak. For example, instead of "What is the essence of John Dewey's work?" saying, "I wonder if it's accurate to describe John Dewey's work as learning by doing" gives a student a chance to comment without feeling put on the spot. Similarly, these kinds of questions are more likely to engage quiet students: "What aspects of the readings do you think we should discuss?" "What part of the reading surprised you the most?" "Can you give me one or two points from the chapter that seem especially important?"

Use questions to change the tempo or the direction of the discussion. Use questions to pace or redirect the conversation (adapted from Kasulis, 1984):

- *To lay out perspectives:* "If you had to pick just one factor . . ." or "In a few words, name the most important reason . . . ." This form of questioning can also be used to cap talkative students.
- *To move from abstract to concrete, or general to specific:* "If you were to generalize . . ." or "Can you give some specific examples?"
- *To acknowledge good points made previously:* "Zhong, would you tend to agree with Carmen on this point?"
- *To summarize or conclude:* "Sabah, if you had to pick two or three themes that were most frequently expressed today, what would they be?"

Use probing strategies. Probes are follow-up questions that focus students' attention on ideas or assumptions implicit in their first answer. Probes can ask for specifics, clarifications, consequences, elaborations, parallel examples, relationships, or explanations. Probes are important because they help students explore and express what they know, even when they aren't sure they know it (Hyman, 1980). Here are some examples of probing (based on Goodwin et al., 1985):

INSTRUCTOR: What are some ways we might solve the energy crisis?
STUDENT: Peak-load pricing by utility companies.

INSTRUCTOR: What assumptions are you making about consumer behavior when you suggest that solution?

INSTRUCTOR: What is neurosis?
STUDENT: It's a condition in which . . . a state in which . . . (*pause and shrug*)
INSTRUCTOR: What are the characteristics of a neurotic person?

INSTRUCTOR: How far has the ball fallen after three seconds?
STUDENT: I have no idea.
INSTRUCTOR: Well, what is happening to the speed of the ball?

Occasionally poll the class. Ask for a show of hands: "Who believes that military dictatorship was, more or less, a foreseeable outcome of the French Revolution?" Follow up by asking individual students to offer reasons for raising or not raising their hand.

Responding to Students' Responses

Listen to the student. Do not interrupt a student's answer, even if you think the student is heading toward an incorrect conclusion. Interrupting signals your impatience and hinders participation. Instead, wait a second or two after a student responds to be sure that the student is finished speaking.

Use nonverbal cues to indicate your attention. Maintain eye contact with the student who is speaking. Nod your head, use facial expressions or hand gestures to prompt the student to continue, or adopt a stance that signals you are ready to move on.

Vary your reactions to students' answers. Depending on the student's comments, you might respond in one of the following ways (adapted from Hyman, 1989; Kovacs-Boerger, 1994; Yelon and Cooper, 1984):

- Reinforce the point by restating what the student has said.
- Paraphrase the student's response without judging its correctness to give the student time to rethink the answer, especially if the paraphrase highlights underlying assumptions.
- Ask for clarification: "Could you be more specific about . . .?"
- Invite the student to elaborate: "We'd like to hear more about . . . ."
- Expand the student's contribution: "That's right, and following up on what you said . . . ."

- Acknowledge the student's contribution and ask for another view: "You're right about children's linguistic capabilities, but what about their social development?"
- Acknowledge the originality of a student's ideas: "Self-selection factors could be responsible for the outcome. I didn't think of that."
- Nod or look interested but remain silent. You don't need to comment on every response. A silent nod keeps the focus on the students' responses. After a few students have commented, you can condense or combine their comments, and relate them to each other.

Judiciously praise correct answers. Students look to their instructors for guidance and support. Be enthusiastic in your praise rather than offering a bland "OK," "Yes," or "All right." If you want to elicit more responses, however, follow the praise with another question: "Combustion? That's very good. What other outcomes are possible?" The downside of praising every answer is that it becomes awkward when a student gives a vague or irrelevant answer. (Sources: Hyman, 1989; Tiberius, 1999)

Tactfully correct wrong answers. Wait a few seconds before responding to an incorrect answer, in case another student volunteers a better response. Or look to another student to provide help rather than providing help yourself. When an answer is partly correct, avoid responding "Yes, but . . . ." Instead, encourage students to rephrase or revise incorrect answers. Try to correct the answer, not the student: "I don't believe that answer is correct" instead of "Gary, you are wrong." Look beyond the answer to the thought process: "This is a hard concept to grasp. Let's take this a step at a time" or "You're right about one part, but let's figure out the rest together." Sometimes wrong answers or incorrect but logical directions can be used to help the class figure out the correct answer, for example, in designing multistep experiments to answer scientific questions.

References

Acheson, K. A., and Gall, M. D. *Clinical Supervision and Teacher Development: Preservice and Inservice Applications.* (5th ed.) New York: Wiley, 2003.

Biggs, J. *Teaching for Quality Learning at University.* (2nd ed.) New York: Open University Press/McGraw-Hill, 2003.

Bloom, B. S., Engelhart, M. D., Furst, E. J., Hill, W. H., and Krathwohl, D. R. (Eds.). *Taxonomy of Educational Objectives: The Classification of Educational Goals.* Handbook I: Cognitive Domain. New York: David McKay, 1956.

Christensen, C. R. The Discussion Teacher in Action: Questioning, Listening, and Response. In C. R. Christensen, D. A. Garvin, and A. Sweet (Eds.), *Education for Judgment: The Artistry of Discussion Leadership.* Boston: Harvard Business School, 1991.

Dallimore, E. J., Hertenstein, J. H., and Platt, M. B. "Faculty-Generated Strategies for 'Cold Calling' Use: A Comparative Analysis with Student Recommendations." *Journal on Excellence in College Teaching*, 2004, *16*(1).

Edwards, S., and Bowman, M. A. "Promoting Student Learning through Questioning: A Study of Classroom Questions." *Journal on Excellence in College Teaching*, 1996, *7*(2), 3–24.

Elder, L., and Paul, R. *The Miniature Guide to the Art of Asking Essential Questions*. (3rd ed.) Dillon Beach, CA: Foundation for Critical Thinking, 2005.

Felder, R. M. "Any Questions?" *Chemical Engineering Education*, 1994, *28*(3), 174–175.

Goodwin, S. S., Sharp, G. W., Cloutier, E. F., and Diamond, N. A. *Effective Classroom Questioning*. Urbana: Office of Instructional Resources, University of Illinois, 1985. http://www.oir.uiuc.edu/Did/docs/questioning.htm

Haroutunian-Gordon, S. "A Study of Reflective Thinking: Patterns in Interpretive Discussion." *Educational Theory*, 1998, *48*(1), 33–58.

Hyman, R. T. *Improving Discussion Leadership*. New York: Teachers College Press, 1980.

Hyman, R. T. Questioning in the College Classroom. In R. A. Neff and M. Weimer (Eds.), *Classroom Communication: Collected Readings for Effective Discussion and Questioning*. Madison, WI: Atwood, 1989.

Kasulis, T. P. Questioning. In M. M. Gullette (Ed.), *The Art and Craft of Teaching*. Cambridge, MA: Harvard University Press, 1984.

Kovacs-Boerger, A. E. "Responding to Students in Ways That Encourage Thinking." *Journal of Chemical Education*, 1994, *71*(4), 302–303.

McKeachie, W. J., and Svinicki, M. *McKeachie's Teaching Tips*. (12th ed.) Boston: Houghton Mifflin, 2006.

"Methods for Assessing Questioning Skills." Center for Teaching Excellence, University of Illinois at Urbana-Champaign, n.d. http://www.cte.uiuc.edu/Did/docs/QUESTION/quest4.htm

O'Hare, M. "Talk and Chalk: The Blackboard as an Intellectual Tool." *Journal of Policy Analysis and Management*, 1993, *12*(1), 238–246.

Payne, B. K., and Gainey, R. R. "Understanding and Developing Controversial Issues in College Courses." *College Teaching*, 2003, *51*(2), 52–58.

Pennell, M. L. "Improving Student Participation in History Lectures: Suggestions for Successful Questioning." *Teaching History: A Journal of Methods*, 2000, *25*(1), 25–35.

Rosmarin, A. The Art of Leading a Discussion. In C. R. Christensen and A. J. Hansen (Eds.), *Teaching and the Case Method*. Boston: Harvard Business School, 1987.

Tiberius, R. G. *Small Group Teaching: A Trouble-Shooting Guide*. London: Kogan Page, 1999.

Windschitl, M., and Buttemer, H. "What Should the Inquiry Experience Be for the Learner?" *American Biology Teacher*, 2000, *62*(5), 346–350.

Yelon, S. L., and Cooper, C. R. "Discussion: A Naturalistic Study of a Teaching Method." *Instructional Science*, 1984, *13*(3), 213–224.

Yip, D. Y. "Assessing and Developing the Concept of Assumptions in Science Teachers." *Journal of Science Education and Technology*, 2001, *10*(2), 173–179.

13

Fielding Students' Questions

When answering a student's question, instructors must think about the content, the tone, and the timing of their response. The following tips describe techniques for handling both routine and difficult questions and questioners.

General Strategies

Answer most questions directly. Offering a direct response signals that the question is worthwhile: "Yes, I do think that historians have portrayed the Trail of Tears inaccurately." But sometimes it is worthwhile to give students a chance to answer. If you redirect a question to the class at large, let the questioner know that you are not avoiding or dismissing the question: "After we hear what everyone else wants to say, I'll see if there's anything left to add." (Sources: Cashin, 1995; Duell, 1994; Hyman, 1989)

Point students toward an answer. Sometimes you can rephrase a student's question in a way that points toward an answer ("Sarah, have you thought about . . . ?") A faculty member in architecture turns students' questions about design issues back to them. When a student asks, "Should I put the kitchen on the north or south end?" the instructor asks the student, "Why might you want the kitchen on the north end?" Or you can turn some students' questions back to the class: "What do others of you think are the reasons the Treaty of Guadalupe Hidalgo was ignored?" Doing so not only encourages more class participation but also reminds students that their peers are a resource.

Avoid comments or gestures that discourage students' questions. Students may refrain from asking questions if they sense that their instructor doesn't want to hear them. A dismissive response to a student's question ("We discussed that last time" or "That question is not really on point") discourages future questions. Other disincentives include interrupting the questioner, avoiding eye contact, answering questions hurriedly or incompletely, and treating questions as distractions rather than as contributions to the learning process. (Source: Hyman, 1989)

Admit when you don't know the answer. If you are uncertain about the correct answer, it is usually better to say so ("I'm not sure; let me think about it. It's a good question") than to give a wrong answer and have to correct yourself later. Other ways to respond include the following (adapted from Cashin, 1995):

- Ask whether a student has an answer (and check the answer before the next class).
- Suggest resources that would enable the questioner to answer the question (but note that assigning students to look up answers to their questions may lead students to ask fewer questions).
- Show students how to think out loud about the answer.
- Volunteer to find the answer yourself and report back at the next session.

In scientific fields, sometimes a question may not yet have an answer. The best you can do is mention the cutting-edge nature of the question and speculate on possible responses.

Answering Routine Questions

Call on questioners in the order in which they sought recognition. If several students want to ask a question, announce an order ("Lizzie first, then Joe, then Alex"). Remember that students may stop listening once their hands go up and they know what they want to say.

Thank the student for having asked a question. "Excellent question" and "Thanks for asking that" are comments that reinforce the behavior of asking questions. Better still, mention what makes the question a good one: "That question takes us directly to the relationship between inflation and wages."

Repeat and paraphrase some questions. Use repetition and paraphrase to make sure that everyone has heard the question and to test your understanding of it. Sometimes a paraphrase may help the student answer his or her own question. But do not repeat or paraphrase every question. Such repetition dissuades students from listening to one another and runs the risk of boring the class. Asking students to rephrase or restate a question (your own or one posed by another student) and asking them to compare different ways of posing a question may help them answer it. (Sources: Cashin, 1995; Dillon, 1998)

Prompt students to clarify their questions. If you don't understand a student's question, ask for clarification: "Give me an example" or "Do you mean . . .?" Instead of "Your question isn't clear," say, "I'm sorry, I don't understand your question."

Don't answer a question that is based on a false presupposition. If you recognize that a student's question is based on an incorrect assumption, address that assumption, perhaps by asking the other students to comment on it. (Source: van der Meij, 1998)

Delay answers to questions that will be covered later. If the question will be addressed later in the session, mention this and return to the question at the appropriate time. When you reach the topic, let the student know you have remembered the question: "Here is the answer to the question you asked before, Harun." (Source: Cashin, 1995)

When responding, talk to the whole class. Don't focus solely on the questioner, but look around the room to include all the students in your comments.

Check back with the questioner. Before moving on, confirm with the student that his or her question has been answered satisfactorily: "Was that what you were asking?" or "Did that help you?" (Source: van der Meij, 1998)

Handling Difficult Questions and Questioners

Avoid dismissing a naïve question. Sometimes a simple-sounding question can provoke an animated discussion, and even the oddest question deserves a tactful response. Because your students empathize with the questioner, your efforts to put a nervous or confused questioner at ease will win you the class's goodwill (Sprague and Stuart, 2005). Consider the following two sets of responses (Sprague and Stuart, p. 403):

Not: "Well, as I already said . . . ."
But: "Let me go over those data again."
Not: "You've totally confused fission and fusion."
But: "Many of those problems relate to nuclear fission. The fusion reaction is quite different. It works like this . . . ."

Try to answer twice, then let a student try. If your first and second answers don't satisfy the questioner, ask your class for help: "Sorry, I've gotten myself stuck here. Could someone help me by explaining it in their own words?" When answering the question would take the class too far afield, or when students continue to disagree, suggest meeting outside of class for further discussion. (Sources: McAllister, 1994; McNinch, 1999)

When students raise complex or tangential questions, ask them to stop by after class. Some questions go beyond the topic of discussion: they anticipate an upcoming topic, seek more detail, or raise a new issue. When such questions require a lengthy response or a detour from the topic, offer to answer them after class or during office hours.

Be patient with students who ask questions you have already answered. Although you may have already discussed a topic or even answered an identical question, students may not have understood the point at the time. Only later, when the material makes sense to them, does the particular point become meaningful. When answering repetitive questions, try to use different language and examples so that you don't bore students who grasped the idea earlier. Or consider asking another student in class to answer the question.

Preempt long-winded questioners. Occasionally, a student may incorporate extraneous opinions and comments into a question. One way to respond is to answer what appears to be the student's main point, and then recognize another student. For example: "You want to know why the university refuses to divest. The Regents' position is that the Global Sullivan Principles of Social Responsibility are sufficient. Let's hear from Jean; she's had her hand up for a long time." (Source: Sprague and Stuart, 2005)

Preempt the serial answerer/questioner. Some students will eagerly answer every question you pose or dominate the class with their own questions. Here are some tips on responding to these students (adapted from PsychTeacher and POD listserv):

• Meet privately with the student. Tell the student how pleased you are that he is so engaged in the class and has so many interesting things to say. Explain that your goal is to give everyone a chance to participate, and ask this student to wait at least 30 seconds before raising his hand to answer a question. You could also set a limit on the number of times you will call on this student in class and have the student come to office hours to discuss any remaining questions.

- Announce the order of students you will call on. "Bryan, in a minute I'm going to ask people to describe a real-life example of a workplace conflict. Will you please be first? Then, Michele and Debbie, will you be second and third?"
- Before calling on the serial answerer say, "I'd like to hear from someone who hasn't said much today." To reassure serial students, call on them at least once during class.
- Ask students to put their answers in writing and share their responses with their neighbors.
- Move around the room and stand with your back to the serial answerer when you ask a question.

Cut off students who want an extended dialogue. If a student is reluctant to relinquish the floor, end the exchange and offer a compliment or an invitation: "You've raised quite a number of excellent points. Maybe you can come to my office later and talk with me further." Or "You've made a number of good comments; why don't we hear from someone else as well?" (Source: Sprague and Stuart, 2005)

References

Cashin, W. E. *"Answering and Asking Questions."* IDEA Paper No. 31. Manhattan, KS: Center for Faculty Evaluation and Development, Kansas State University, January, 1995.

Dillon, J. T. Theory and Practice of Student Questioning. In S. A. Karabenick (Ed.), *Strategic Help Seeking: Implications for Learning and Teaching*, Chapter 8. Mahwah, NJ: Erlbaum, 1998.

Duell, O. K. "Extended Wait Time and University Student Achievement." *American Educational Research Journal*, 1994, *31*(2), 397–414.

Hyman, R. T. Questioning in the College Classroom. In R. A. Neff and M. Weimer (Eds.), *Classroom Communication: Collected Readings for Effective Discussion and Questioning.* Madison, WI: Atwood, 1989.

McAllister, B. "Dumb Questions: Can't Live With 'Em, Can't Live Without 'Em." 1994. http://trc.virginia.edu/Publications/Teaching_Concerns/Fall_1994/TC_Fall_1994_McAllister.htm

McNinch, J. "Dealing with Difficulties in the Classroom." *Teaching and Learning in Higher Education* (Newsletter), April 1999.

POD Listserv: An unmoderated online community for instructors and administrators with interests in teaching and learning in higher education; see http://podnetwork.org.

PsychTeacher Listserv: A moderated online community for instructors involved in teaching psychology; teachpsych.org/news/psychteacher.php.

Sprague, J., and Stuart, D. *The Speaker's Handbook.* (7th ed.) Belmont, CA: Wadsworth/ Thomson Learning, 2005.

van der Meij, H. The Great Divide between Teacher and Student Questioning. In S. A. Karabenick (Ed.), *Strategic Help Seeking: Implications for Learning and Teaching*, Chapter 9. Mahwah, NJ: Erlbaum, 1998.

PART IV

The Large-Enrollment Course

14

Preparing to Teach the Large-Enrollment Course

A sizable portion of the work involved in teaching a large-enrollment course takes place well before the first day of class. In a seminar you can make a spur-of-the-moment assignment, but in large classes you need to distribute and post guidelines. Indeed, every aspect of the large course requires planning and organization. Many of the following suggestions for teaching large classes are also applicable to small classes: good teaching practices are effective in classes of any size.

General Strategies

Become comfortable with the material. In an introductory survey course you may be covering topics outside your specialty. As you read up on those topics, try to anticipate questions that beginning students might ask. Review the course materials, assignments, and reading lists of colleagues who have taught the course before. Consider viewing a webcast or sitting in on courses taught by colleagues who are effective teachers of large classes to see what ideas and techniques work well, or ask them about their experiences teaching large courses.

Capitalize on the strengths of lecturing. A well-crafted, well-delivered lecture can impart information as well as motivate and inspire students by conveying how an expert thinks about complex content, organizes knowledge, and applies the methods of the discipline. Help your students gain the most from your lectures by explicitly sharing with them the kinds of analysis and arguments that shape your field. (Sources: Brown and Race, 2002; Burgan, 2006; Chanock, 1999; Cooper et al., 2000; deWinstanley and Bjork, 2002; Saroyan and Snell, 1997; Twigg, 2003)

Recognize the limitations of lecturing. Research shows that lecturing is as effective as other instructional methods, such as discussion, in imparting information but less effective in encouraging independent thought, developing critical thinking skills, and meeting individual students' pedagogical needs. (Sources: Bligh, 2000; Laurillard, 2002; Wood and Gentile, 2003)

Don't plan to lecture for a full period for every class meeting. Studies show that incorporating opportunities for discussion or problem-solving exercises into a lecture—activities that encourage students to make the material their own—will enhance learning and increase long-term retention. Ask students to solve a problem at their seats or in small groups sitting near one another, pose a question to the entire class and have students yell out answers or respond using clickers, or give a demonstration. (Sources: Bridges and Desmond, 2000; Hake, 1998; Huxham, 2005; Leamnson, 1999; Weimer, 2002; Wood and Gentile, 2003)

Manage your own time. Teaching a large-enrollment course takes a great deal of time and energy. Set up weekly work schedules for yourself, and plan how best to handle the onslaught of midterms and finals. Try to scale back other obligations if you can. (Source: Stanley and Porter, 2002)

Decide whether to permit the capture of your lectures for later use. Some faculty worry about declining attendance if their course is webcast or podcast; others dismiss recorded lectures as a crutch for students who lack the motivation or organizational skills to attend class; and others worry about students becoming too dependent on technology as a replacement for meaningful in-class engagement. Defenders of capturing lectures believe it is helpful for students to be able to review and study complex material after the lecture and before exams, and that captured lectures are especially valuable for students who learned English as a second language. In addition, faculty point out that webcasting allows them to view and critique their own lectures.

Research shows that students are most likely to view a webcast right after a lecture or right before an exam. They do not watch the entire lecture but use search tools to locate particular topics. Lecture capture has not depressed attendance and has not shown a measurable effect on students' grades. Lecture capture does seem to encourage extra review activities, and students value and appreciate this resource. If you are concerned about drops in attendance, consider delaying availability of the recorded lecture until a week after each class session, giving in-class quizzes, or turning off the camera when discussing upcoming exams. (Source: Brotherton and Abowd, 2004; Deal, 2007; Rowe et al., 2001; Young, 2008)

Organizing the Course

Decide what content to include. After reviewing your department's guidelines or sample curricula, set your broad goals for the course. The goals of an introductory survey course might include stimulating students' interest in the field and providing them with the foundation to pursue that interest. Identify specific student learning objectives: What do you want students to know or be able to do?

Next, make a list of topics you feel are important to include. Estimate the amount of time required to address these topics, and then increase your estimate by 50 percent to allow time for taking questions from students and for the inevitable slippage in large groups. For suggestions on how to reduce the number of topics to fit the length of the course, see Chapter 1, "Designing or Revising a Course." (Sources: Christensen, 1988; Wankat, 2002)

Organize the topics in a meaningful sequence. Arrange the topics chronologically, spatially, by problem and solution, or according to some other scheme:

- *Topical.* A psychology course examines how four groups of theorists approach human behavior: social learning theorists, developmental theorists, psychoanalytic theorists, and cognitive theorists.
- *Causal.* An economics course explores factors that affect the distribution of wealth: the labor market, tax policy, investment policy, and social mobility.
- *Sequential.* A course on education in the United States discusses the school system in five stages: preschool, elementary school, secondary school, college, and graduate school.
- *Symbolic or graphic.* An integrative biologist begins each lecture by projecting the same detailed diagram of the human brain. She then highlights the structural details relevant to that day's lecture.
- *Structural.* A physiologist uses the same format to discuss each anatomical system: its organs, the functions of the organs, how the organs are regulated, and the relationship of the system to other systems.
- *Problem-solution.* An engineering course looks at a series of structural failures in various types of buildings.

Mention the organizational principle in the syllabus, at the beginning of the course, and throughout the term. Periodically devote a part of your lecture to the broader view.

Vary the types of lectures you deliver. Choose formats that suit the content:

- The *expository lecture* treats a single question or problem, typically with a hierarchical organization of major and minor points. This approach is useful for efficiently presenting broad concepts and foundational information.
- In the *participatory lecture,* the speaker intersperses one or more activities. This type of lecture is variously called *interactive, spaced, punctuated, feedback, change-up,*

modified, mediated, responsive, engaged, or *enhanced,* with nuanced distinctions among them. In a participatory lecture, the speaker may begin with a question to the class ("Call out what you know about DNA") and then sort the responses into categories, with the flow of examples and counterexamples, generalizations and specifics, or rules and exceptions encouraging students to grapple with the topic. Or a lecturer may initiate a period of small-group work, a quick writing task, or individual or paired problem solving—any activity that lets students shift from listeners to actors. Some faculty use these breaks at the same time each session, others incorporate them as appropriate, and still others alternate class periods of lecture with class periods of small-group work.

- In *interteaching,* the instructor presents a series of questions that students use to prepare for the next class period. At that session, students form pairs or trios and discuss the questions. The instructor moves down the aisles, answering questions and monitoring students' understanding. At the end of the session, students fill out an interteaching record that states which questions were difficult to answer, which questions they would like reviewed in lecture, and other comments that might be useful to the instructor in preparing a clarifying lecture for the next class period. Some instructors schedule interteaching sessions on a regular basis, and others use it for almost every class, with students forming new groups each session.

- *Problem solving, demonstrations, proofs, and mysteries* begin with the instructor posing a question, paradox, mystery, or enigma—some provocative problem that whets students' interest. The answer unfolds during the class period, with students actively or passively anticipating or pointing toward solutions.

- In the *case study method,* the lecture follows a realistic situation step-by-step to illustrate a general principle or problem-solving strategy. Depending on the level of the students, either the instructor takes the lead or the students direct the solution. See Chapter 24, "Case Studies."

- The *structured lecture* begins with a short presentation that sets the stage and then poses a problem, task, or question ("What causes lake acidification?"). Students work in trios or small groups to come up with an answer; the instructions they are given include guidance on how to proceed and a time limit. The class closes with another short lecture that pulls together the major themes or issues.

(Sources: Bligh, 2000; Bonwell, 1996; Boyce and Hineline, 2002; Chaney, 2005; Frederick, 1986; Jenkins, 1992; Lowman, 1995; Middendorf and Kalish, 1996; Saville and Zinn, 2006)

In each lecture, incorporate at least one example or demonstration that excites you. Students respond to an instructor's enthusiasm, and they can often tell when a lecturer is bored. Try to insert into each lecture at least one moment that you genuinely look forward to: a riveting example, a clever experiment, or a humorous anecdote. One faculty member begins a difficult lecture on policy and regulation with this mystery: "After a three-year slide of 10 percent in tobacco consumption in the United States during the late 1960s, Big Tobacco did something that had the extraordinary effect of ending the decline, boosting consumption, and slashing advertising expenditures by a third. What was it?" (They voluntarily agreed to stop advertising on television.) Another faculty member begins a dense lecture on mollusks by projecting an image of a brownish blob and asking, "What is this thing? Is it alive? Is it a plant, animal, alien, or forgotten leftovers from the fridge?" (The object is a clam.) (Sources: Cialdini, 2005; Jones, 2003; Schwartz and Bransford, 1998)

Consider the abilities and interests of your students. In preparing your course, ask yourself, How much will students know about the subject matter? How interested will they be in the material? What experiences or attitudes might students have that I can use to draw them into the subject?

Prepare a detailed syllabus for students. The more information you give your students, the fewer problems you are likely to have later on; see Chapter 2, "The Comprehensive Course Syllabus." During the term, try to stick to the schedule contained in the syllabus. If you must deviate, make it clear when and why you are departing from the schedule.

Meet with your graduate student instructors before the term begins. Discuss course procedures, their responsibilities, grading, and the most effective ways for them to conduct sections. See Chapter 58, "Guiding, Training, Supervising, and Mentoring Graduate Student Instructors."

Visit the classroom before the first meeting. Notice the instructor's area, the location of light switches and technology controls, and other features. Make arrangements for any instructional equipment you will need. When you visit the classroom, stand where you will lecture, practice using the equipment, and write on the board. Check whether your board work can be seen from the back of the room.

Preparing Lecture Notes

Carefully prepare your lectures. Thorough preparation can prevent last-minute headaches. Take time to arrange your points, develop your examples, write out definitions, and solve equations. No matter how well you know the topic, you will want to have a set of notes to remind you of the sequence of points, the best examples, or alternative solutions. Some faculty prepare their lectures well in advance and revise them during the term to take into account students' responses to previous lectures. Other faculty emphasize the value of the preparation done immediately after class, when the experience of what worked and what didn't is still fresh. New faculty typically complete the bulk of preparatory reading before the course starts and then keep about one or two weeks ahead of their students. Faculty report spending anywhere from two to ten hours to prepare a lecture. Some faculty recommend working under a strict self-imposed time limit. (Sources: Eble, 1988; Heppner, 2007; Wankat, 2002)

Avoid reading a prepared text. If you stand at a lectern and read from a script or set of slides, you will be unable to maintain eye contact with your students, your voice will be cast down toward your notes instead of out toward the lecture hall, and you run the risk of your students becoming disengaged. Writing out lectures is also extremely time-consuming: a script for a fifty-minute lecture might run twenty-five or thirty double-spaced pages. If you do feel the need to write out a draft of a lecture, reduce that draft to an outline of key words and phrases, and lecture from this outline; see Chapter 15, "Delivering a Lecture" and Chapter 51, "PowerPoint Presentations."

Experiment with different formats for your lecture notes. Some topics lend themselves to the traditional outline, with headings and subheadings. If you are very familiar with the material, a list of major points or key terms may suffice. Some instructors prepare tree diagrams or flowcharts that include major points, optional stopovers, and illustrations or examples. Other instructors sketch the drawings that will be placed on the board.

Prepare your notes to aid your delivery. Experiment with using your laptop, sheets of paper, five-by-eight index cards, or smaller cards. Highlight difficult points, distinctions between major examples, and important information. Include notations that indicate times to pause or to ask for questions, and include reminders ("Ask students to jot down a response" or "If less than ten minutes left, skip to the conclusion").

Write down facts and formulas for easy reference. Within the body of your lecture notes or on a separate file or sheet of paper, write out all the key facts, quotations, computations, and complex analyses.

Write down vivid examples. Experienced faculty recommend that you give special attention to preparing memorable examples, counterexamples, illustrations, and demonstrations. Research shows that an important characteristic of an effective teacher is the ability to present difficult concepts in ways that students can understand, through the use of metaphors, analogies, and examples; see Chapter 16, "Explaining Clearly." (Sources: Erickson et al., 2006; Schwartz and Bransford, 1998; Stones, 1992)

Prepare your lecture for the ear, not the eye. When students are listening to a lecture, they cannot go back and reread a sentence or look up a word in the dictionary. Here are some tips to facilitate comprehension:

- Use short, simple words and informal diction, including personal pronouns; be conversational.
- Speak succinctly, in short, straightforward sentences.
- Offer signposts for transitions and structure: "the third objection," "let's look at this argument from another angle," "in contrast," "as we have seen," "now we can turn to."
- Restate and periodically summarize key points.

Compensate for dips in students' attention. Studies show that students' recall of material presented during a fifty-minute lecture improves when they have an opportunity to apply the material shortly after it is presented. Students are also more likely to remember information presented at the beginning and at the end of a lecture. As you plan your lecture, try to incorporate a student activity or another novel element for the midpoint. (Sources: Bligh, 2000; Fry et al., 2003)

Rehearse your lecture. Run through a newly prepared lecture to increase your confidence and to gauge the length of your presentation. If your time for practice is short, you might practice only the most difficult sections or the opening and ending.

Structuring a Lecture

Begin by writing out the main theme and why students should learn about it. Identify what you most want your students to remember about the topic. It is better to teach two or three major points well than to inundate students with information they are unlikely to remember. Brown and Atkins (1988, pp. 35–38) recommend the following process for writing a lecture:

- Specify the main topic or topics.
- Free-associate words, facts, ideas, and questions as they come to you.
- State a working title or a general question based on the groupings from your free association.
- Prepare a one-page sketch of the lecture.
- Read selectively, as needed, and take notes on important ideas and structure.
- Draft an outline and flesh it out with examples and illustrations; identify your key points.
- Check the opening and ending.

Organize your material. Typical approaches include moving in chronological order, working from general principle to specific instances, building up from the parts to the whole, tracking one idea across different places, posing a problem and its solution, and announcing a thesis and providing evidence for it.

Structure your lectures to emphasize the most important points. Consider the difficulty of the material and your students' abilities. Help students identify and focus on the key points by including the following elements:

- attention-getting introduction
- brief overview of the main points
- quick statement of background or context
- detailed explanation of no more than three major points, with the most important first
- concluding summary to reinforce key themes

Create lectures that help students process the information. Students are more apt to understand the material when you (adapted from deWinstanley and Bjork, 2002):

- Avoid dividing their attention. Learning suffers when students are trying to listen and read at the same time. If you are projecting slides, give students a moment to read the slide and then resume talking; see Chapter 51, "PowerPoint Presentations."
- Relate new information to information your students already have.
- Repeat important points during two or more class sessions.

- Present concepts from more than one angle.
- Demonstrate the relevance of key ideas in several contexts.
- Provide opportunities for students to use the information—to do something in addition to listening and taking notes.
- Avoid cognitive overload (presenting too much information); see Chapter 29, "Helping Students Learn."

Structure your lecture to make your points unforgettable. Set aside your knowledge and expertise for a moment, and try to identify with students who know nothing about the topic. According to Heath and Heath (2007), research studies show that novice learners respond to lectures with the following characteristics:

- *Simplicity:* focus on the core of the idea, stripped of any elaboration.
- *Concreteness:* use specific, clear language.
- *Emotion:* when you care about what you are saying, students will care.
- *Surprise:* surprise, suspense, and the unexpected will attract students' curiosity and hold their attention.
- *Storytelling:* narratives are memorable, and they help students organize new material.

Include verbal signposts. Provide cues that signal transitions ("The second reason is . . .") and that emphasize the links between new information and old information. (Source: Saroyan and Snell, 1997)

Design your lectures in ten- or fifteen-minute blocks. Each block should cover a single point, provide examples, and end with a brief summary and transition to the next section. If you find yourself running out of time, cut an entire block or shorten the middle section of a block rather than rush the summary.

Budget time for questions. Whether or not you open the floor for questions, leave time for students to ask you to repeat material or to supply additional explanations. Some faculty ask for students' questions at the beginning of class, list them on the board or screen, and pledge to answer them sometime during the hour.

Begin and end with a summary statement. Continuity and closure are important: students need to see how each new topic relates to what they have already learned as well as to what they will be learning in the coming weeks. To bring your points home, use different words and examples in your opening and closing summaries.

Managing a Large-Enrollment Course

Establish reasonable rules for student behavior. Decide on your policies regarding latecomers, eating during class, and the like. Explain your rules during the first week, state them in the syllabus, and stress the value of cooperation and consideration. For example, some faculty set limits on when students can pack up and leave: "You're mine until 2 PM" or "When the cartoon appears on the screen you can go" or "I will end each session one minute early so that I won't have to talk over the commotion of packing up." See Chapter 4, "Classroom Conduct and Decorum." (Source: Carbone, 1998)

Plan how to handle wait lists. The wait list for an oversubscribed large-enrollment course can steal a considerable amount of your time. Be prepared for enrolled students who dither for a week or more about whether to drop your course, enrolled students who do not appear until two weeks into the term, and wait-listed students who refrain from doing the assignments (because they don't know if they will be admitted) or who energetically pester you about adding the class. If there are no departmental or collegewide policies about wait lists, consider setting policies that limit wait lists to a reasonable percentage of the enrollment, that clear wait lists on the first or second day of class, and that drop students who do not attend the first and second class meetings.

Plan how to handle student announcements. Some instructors prohibit any student announcements in class. Others adopt one or more of the following strategies (adapted from UC Berkeley listserv on teaching):

- *Announcements in class:* Some faculty restrict in-class announcements to one minute and allow a maximum of two announcements per class session. Some faculty require students to e-mail proposed announcements for clearance beforehand. Some faculty also limit announcements to those directly related to the content of the course.
- *Announcements by course e-mail:* Faculty typically inform students that they will edit all proposed announcements for length, clarity, and relevancy and that these announcements will be limited to two or three a week.
- *Announcements written on a designated panel of the chalkboard.*
- *Leafleting:* Students may distribute flyers outside the door of the classroom to entering students, but they may not leaflet inside or leave flyers on students' seats.

Plan how to grade homework. If you do not have a graduate student instructor (GSI) or reader, grade samples of homework assignments to save time. For the assignments you do not grade, post the answers so that students can assess their own performance. See Chapter 19, "Maintaining Instructional Quality with Limited Resources."

Plan how to collect and return homework. The following procedures can expedite the return of homework and avoid the misdirection of items:

- Use your learning management system or collaborative and learning environment to accept and return homework.
- Set up boxes with a homework folder for each student. For the sake of privacy, fold and staple the paper before placing it in the folder or ask students to submit their work with a cover page that has only their name on it.
- Place students' work in alphabetical stacks (A–G, H–N, etc.). Give each of your readers or GSIs a stack and have students go to different parts of the room to receive their work. Or have students line up in alphabetical order and march past you as you return their work.
- Return homework during office hours.
- Collect and hand back work in sections (if your course has sections).
- Post the correct answers online, but don't return any homework.

Stagger due dates for essay or research papers. One faculty member requires all three hundred of his students to write one paper during the semester, but students write on different topics and the papers are due on different dates. At the beginning of the term, he randomly divides the class into ten groups of thirty students each. He announces the dates when the various groups are to turn in their papers. All students receive their paper topics two weeks before their due date. Using this approach, the instructor is able to read and respond to all three hundred papers but never reads more than thirty in a given week. (Source: Erickson et al., 2006)

Use multiple-choice tests as an alternative. Use your learning management system to design tests that can be scored online. Multiple-choice exams can measure both fundamental knowledge and complex concepts. To give students practice in writing and grappling with open-ended questions, include two or three items that call for a few paragraphs of explanation or analysis. If you do not use a learning management system for testing, optical scanning and scratch-off technology allow for the quick and reliable scoring of in-class exams.

References

Bligh, D. A. *What's the Use of Lectures?* San Francisco: Jossey-Bass, 2000.

Bonwell, C. C. "Enhancing the Lecture: Revitalizing the Traditional Format." *New Directions for Teaching and Learning*, 1996, no. 67, pp. 31–44.

Boyce, T. E., and Hineline, P. N. "Interteaching: A Strategy for Enhancing the User-Friendliness of Behavioral Arrangements in the College Classroom." *Behavior Analyst*, 2002, *25*(2), 215–226.

Bridges, G. S., and Desmond, S. (Eds.). *Teaching and Learning in Large Classes*. Washington, DC: American Sociological Association, 2000.

Brotherton, J. A., and Abowd, G. D. "Lessons Learned from eClass: Assessing Automated Capture and Access in the Classroom." *ACM (Association for Computing Machinery) Transactions on Computer-Human Interaction*, 2004, *11*(2), 121–155.

Brown, G., and Atkins, M. *Effective Teaching in Higher Education*. London: Methuen, 1988.

Brown, S., and Race, P. *Lecturing: A Practical Guide*. London: Kogan Page, 2002.

Burgan, M. "In Defense of Lecturing." *Change*, Nov./Dec. 2006, *38*(6), 30–34.

Carbone, E. L. *Teaching Large Classes: Tools and Strategies*. Thousand Oaks, CA: Sage, 1998.

Chaney, W. R. "Top-of-the Hour Break Renews Attention Span." *Teaching Professor*, June/July 2005, *19*(6), 1, 5.

Chanock, K. "One Good Thing about Lectures: They Model the Approach of the Discipline." *Journal of General Education*, 1999, *48*(1), 38–52.

Christensen, N. Nuts and Bolts of Running a Lecture Course. In A. L. Deneff, C. D. Goodwin, and E. S. McCrate (Eds.), *The Academic Handbook*. Durham, NC: Duke University Press, 1988.

Cialdini, R. B. "What's the Best Secret Device for Engaging Student Interest? The Answer Is in the Title." *Journal of Social and Clinical Psychology*, 2005, *24*(1), 22–29.

Cooper, J. L., MacGregor, J., Smith, K. A., and Robinson, P. (Eds.). "Implementing Small-Group Instruction: Insights from Successful Practitioners." *New Directions for Teaching and Learning*, no. 81. San Francisco: Jossey-Bass, 2000, pp. 63–76.

Deal, A. "Podcasting." A Teaching with Technology White Paper. Carnegie Mellon University, 2007. http://www.cmu.edu/teaching/resources/PublicationsArchives/StudiesWhitepapers/Podcasting_Jun07.pdf

deWinstanley, P. A., and Bjork, R. A. "Successful Lecturing: Presenting Information in Ways That Engage Effective Processing." *New Directions for Teaching and Learning*, no. 89. San Francisco: Jossey-Bass, 2002, pp. 19–31.

Eble, K. E. *The Craft of Teaching*. (2nd ed.) San Francisco: Jossey-Bass, 1988.

Erickson, B. L., Peters, C. B., and Strommer, D. W. *Teaching First-Year College Students*. San Francisco: Jossey-Bass, 2006.

Frederick, P. J. "The Lively Lecture—Eight Variations." *College Teaching*, 1986, *34*(2), 43–50.

Fry, H., Ketteridge, S., and Marshall, S. *A Handbook for Teaching and Learning in Higher Education: Enhancing Academic Practice*. (2nd ed.) New York: RoutledgeFalmer, 2003.

Hake, R. R. "Interactive-Engagement vs. Traditional Methods: A Six-Thousand-Student Survey of Mechanics Test Data for Introductory Physics Courses." *American Journal of Physics*, 1998, *66*(1), 64–74.

Heath, C., and Heath, D. *Made to Stick: Why Some Ideas Survive and Others Don't*. New York: Random House, 2007.

Heppner, F. *Teaching the Large College Class: A Guidebook for Instructors with Multitudes*. San Francisco: Jossey-Bass, 2007.

Huxham, M. "Learning in Lectures: Do 'Interactive Windows' Help?" *Active Learning in Higher Education*, 2005, *6*(1), 17–31.

Jenkins, A. Active Learning in Structure Lectures. In G. Gibbs and A. Jenkins (Eds.), *Teaching Large Classes in Higher Education: How to Maintain Quality with Reduced Resources*. London: Kogan Page, 1992.

Jones, L.L.C. "Are Lectures a Thing of the Past? Tips and Techniques for Success." *Journal of College Science Teaching*, 2003, *32*(7), 453–457.

Laurillard, D. *Rethinking University Teaching: A Framework for the Effective Use of Learning Technologies*. (2nd ed.) London: RoutledgeFalmer, 2002.

Leamnson, R. *Thinking about Teaching and Learning: Developing Habits of Learning with First Year College and University Students*. Sterling, VA: Stylus, 1999.

Lowman, J. *Mastering the Techniques of Teaching*. (2nd ed.) San Francisco: Jossey-Bass, 1995.

Middendorf, J., and Kalish, A. "The Change-Up in Lectures." *National Teaching and Learning Forum*, 1996, *5*(2), 1–5.

Rowe, L. A., Harley, D., Pletcher, P., and Lawrence, S. *BIBS: A Lecture Webcasting System*. Berkeley: Center for Studies in Higher Education, University of California, 2001.

Saroyan, A., and Snell, L. S. "Variations in Lecturing Styles." *Higher Education*, 1997, *33*(1), 85–104.

Saville, B. K., Zinn, T. E., Neef, N. A., Van Norman, R., and Ferreri, S. J. "A Comparison of Interteaching and Lecture in the College Classroom." *Journal of Applied Behavior Analysis*, 2006, *39*(1), 49–61.

Schwartz, D. L., and Bransford, J. D. "A Time for Telling." *Cognition and Instruction*, 1998, *16*(4), 475–522.

Stanley, C. A., and Porter, M. E. (Eds.). *Engaging Large Classes: Strategies and Techniques for College Faculty*. Bolton, MA: Anker, 2002.

Stones, E. *Quality Teaching: A Sample of Cases*. New York: Routledge, 1992.

Twigg, C. A. "Improving Quality and Reducing Cost: Designs for Effective Learning." *Change*, July/Aug. 2003, *35*(4), 22–29.

Wankat, P. C. *The Effective, Efficient Professor: Teaching, Scholarship and Service*. Boston: Allyn and Bacon, 2002.

Weimer, M. *Learner-Centered Teaching: Five Key Changes to Practice*. San Francisco: Jossey-Bass, 2002.

Wood, W. B., and Gentile, J. M. "Teaching in a Research Context." *Science*, 2003, *302*(5650), 1510.

Young, J. R. "The Lectures Are Recorded, So Why Go to Class?" *Chronicle of Higher Education*, May 16, 2008, *54*(36), A1.

15

Delivering a Lecture

Lecturing is not simply a matter of standing in front of a class and reciting what you know. The classroom lecture is a special form of communication in which voice, gesture, movement, facial expression, and eye contact can either complement or detract from the content. No matter what your topic, your delivery and manner of speaking immeasurably influence your students' attentiveness and learning. The following suggestions, based on the teaching practices of faculty and on research studies in speech and communication, are intended to help you capture and hold students' interest and increase their retention.

General Strategies

Observe excellent teachers. If your college gives out teaching awards, ask to visit the classes of those who have been designated excellent lecturers or watch them on a webcast. Take note of teaching strategies that work that are different from yours. UC Berkeley has short clips, with explanatory text, of faculty who have received the Distinguished Teaching Award (teaching.berkeley.edu/video.html).

Watch yourself on video. Often we need to see our good behaviors in order to exploit them and see our undesirable behaviors in order to correct them. If you want to improve your public speaking skills, viewing a video recording of yourself can be invaluable; see Chapter 53, "Video Recordings and Classroom Observations."

Learn how not to read your lectures. At its best, lecturing resembles a natural, thoughtful conversation between instructor and student, with each student feeling as though the instructor is speaking to an audience of one. If you read your lectures—even if you are a dynamic reader—your presentation will seem formal and distant, and you forfeit the expressiveness, animation, and spontaneity of plain talking. Reading from notes also reduces your opportunities to engage your class in conversation and prevents you from maintaining eye contact. On this point all skilled speakers agree: use notes, but don't read your presentation.

Prepare yourself emotionally for class. Some faculty play rousing music before lecturing. Others set aside fifteen or thirty minutes of solitude to review their notes. Still others walk through an empty classroom gathering their thoughts. Try to identify for yourself an activity that gives you the energy and focus you need to speak enthusiastically and confidently. (Source: Lowman, 1995)

Opening a Lecture

Take a moment to warm up. Go to class a little early and talk informally with students. Or walk in the door with students and engage them in conversation. Using your voice informally before you begin to lecture will help you maintain a conversational tone.

Minimize nervousness. Some nervousness is normal. Take a few deep breaths before you begin, or tighten and then release the muscles of your body from your toes to your jaw. Once you are under way, your nervousness will lessen. If you freeze up during the lecture, experienced instructors recommend that you take a sip of water, which gives you time to collect your thoughts, then smile and continue.

Signal that the lecture is beginning. Give students a cue to quiet down: dim or flicker the lights, change the slide that is projected on the screen, or bang a gavel. Select any visual or auditory device that doesn't require you to yell over the din.

Grab students' attention with your opening. Open with a provocative question, startling statement, unusual analogy, striking example, personal anecdote, dramatic contrast, powerful quote, short questionnaire, demonstration, or mention of a recent news event. Here are some sample openings:

- From a sociology lecture: "How many people would you guess are sent to prison each week in the state of California? Raise your hand if you think 50 people or fewer. How about 51 to 100? 101 to 150? Over 150? (*Pause.*) In fact, over 250 people are placed in custody every week."
- From a business lecture: "Teddy has been with the company for nearly four years and is considered a good worker. Recently, though, he's been having problems. He's late for work, acts brusque, and seems sullen. One morning he walks into the office, knocks over a pile of papers, and leaves them lying on the floor. His supervisor says, 'Teddy, could you please pick up the papers so

that no one trips over them?' Teddy says loudly, 'Pick them up yourself.' If you were the supervisor, what would you do next?"

- From a rhetoric lecture: "The number-one fear of Americans—more terrifying than the fear of death—is public speaking."
- From an economics lecture: An economist shows a slide of farmers dumping milk from trucks or burning cornfields and asks, "Why would people do this?"
- From a physics lecture: "Watch what happens to this balloon when the air is released."
- From an architecture lecture: "How many of you believe that 'high-rise' housing means 'high-density' housing?"
- From a social welfare lecture: "Nearly three-quarters of all assaults, two-thirds of all suicide attempts, half of all suicides, and half of all rapes are committed by people under the influence of what drug? How many think crack? Heroin? Marijuana? None of the above? The correct answer is alcohol."
- From a psychology lecture: "Look at this incomplete image of a penny, something you see every day. What is missing?"

Announce the objectives for the class. Tell your students what you expect to accomplish during the class, or list your objectives on the screen or board. Place the day's lecture in context by linking it to material from earlier sessions.

Establish rapport with your students. Warmth and rapport have a positive effect on any audience. Students will feel more engaged in the class if the opening minutes are personal, direct, and conversational. (Source: Heppner, 2007)

Capturing Students' Interest

Watch your audience. Focus on your students as if you were talking to a small group. One-on-one eye contact will increase students' attentiveness and enable you to catch facial expressions and body language that indicate whether you are speaking too slowly or too quickly, or whether students need another example or explanation. A common mistake lecturers make is to become so absorbed in the material that they fail to notice whether students are paying attention and following along.

Vary your delivery to keep students' attention. Students' attention is likely to wander over the course of a class period. To extend students' attention spans and recapture wandering minds, try the following techniques:

- Ask questions at strategic points or ask for comments or opinions about the subject.
- Play devil's advocate or invite students to challenge your point of view.
- Have students solve a problem individually, or have them break into pairs, trios, or quartets to brainstorm or answer a question or discuss a topic.
- Pause to allow students to catch up on their notetaking.
- Intersperse slides, charts, graphs, videos, or film clips.

(Sources: Bligh, 2000; Heppner, 2007; Wilson and Korn, 2007)

Make the organization of your lecture explicit. Put an outline on the screen or board before you begin, outline the development of ideas as they occur, or post a list of major points online before class. Outlines help students take better notes and focus on the progression of the material. If their attention does wander, students can more readily catch up with the lecture if they have an outline in front of them.

Convey enthusiasm for the material. Think back to what inspired you as an undergraduate and to the reasons you chose your academic field. Even if you have little interest in a particular topic, try to come up with a new way of looking at it and do what you can to stimulate students' enthusiasm. Everyone agrees that if you appear bored with the topic, students will quickly lose interest. Researchers recommend vocal and physical animation. To be vocally animated, draw attention to important words by lowering your pitch, use rising inflections to signal a climax, and occasionally speak softly, which forces students to listen more carefully. Recommended physical gestures include making eye contact with students, using varied facial expressions, changing gestures and posture for emphasis and to command attention, and moving vigorously about the stage. (Sources: Brown and Race, 2002; Tauber and Mester, 2007; Zimbardo, 1997)

Be conversational. Use conversational inflections and tones, varying your pitch just as you do in ordinary conversation. If you focus on the meaning of what you are saying, you will instinctively become more expressive. Choose informal language, and try to be natural and direct.

Use concrete, simple, colorful language. Use first-person and second-person pronouns (*I, we, you*). Choose dramatic adjectives; for example, "vital point" rather than "main point" or "next point." Eliminate jargon, empty words, and unnecessary qualifiers ("little bit," "sort of," "kind of"). If your class includes students who do not speak English well, avoid slang and allusions that may be unfamiliar to them.

Incorporate anecdotes and stories into your lecture. When you are in a storytelling mode, your voice becomes conversational and your face more expressive, and students tend to listen more closely. Use anecdotes to illustrate your key points, but resist the impulse to incorporate tangential details that do not support your learning objectives. For example, when explaining the meteorological processes involved in the formation of lightning, don't distract students with statistics about the number of people struck by lightning. (Source: Harp and Maslich, 2005)

Don't talk into your notes. If you are not using a lectern and you need to refer to your note cards, raise the cards (rather than lower your head) and take a quick glance at them. You will have an easier time if your notes are brief and in large letters.

Maintain eye contact with the class. Look directly at your students one at a time, for about three to five seconds—a longer glance will make most students uncomfortable. Beware of aimless scanning or swinging your head back and forth. Mentally divide the lecture hall into three to five sections, and address comments, questions, and eye contact to each section during the course of your lecture, beginning in the center rear of the room. Pick out friendly faces, but try to include others. Don't waste time hoping to win over the visibly uninterested; concentrate on the attentive. If direct eye contact upsets your concentration, look between two students or look at foreheads.

Use movement to hold students' attention. A moving object is more compelling than a static one. Occasionally, move about the room. Use deliberate, purposeful, sustained gestures: hold up an object, take off your glasses, push up your sleeves. To invite students' questions, adopt an open, casual stance. Beware of nervous foot shifting.

Use movement to emphasize an important point or to lead into a new topic. Some faculty move to one side of the table or the lectern when presenting one side of an argument and to the other side when presenting the opposing view. This movement not only captures students' attention but reinforces the opposition between the two points of view. (Sources: Heppner, 2007; Tauber and Mester, 2007; Weimer, 1988)

Use facial expressions to convey emotions. If you appear enthusiastic and eager to talk, students will be more enthusiastic about listening to you. Use your eyes, eyebrows, forehead, mouth, and jaw to convey enthusiasm, conviction, curiosity, and thoughtfulness. (Source: Lowman, 1995; Tauber and Mester, 2007)

Laugh at yourself when you make a mistake. If you mispronounce a word or drop your notes, your ability to see the humor of the situation will put everyone at ease. Don't let your confidence be shaken by minor mistakes.

Avoid a boring lecturing style. Researchers have identified several characteristics of boring lecturers: they ramble, go into too much detail, have a low rate of activity, talk in a monotone at a sluggish pace, make little eye contact and have few facial expressions, show little emotion and with flat affect, react minimally to students' questions, and conduct class and lecture in a predictable routine. (Source: Forsyth, 2003)

Keep track of time. Be aware of how long you are taking to make your points. Decide in advance what material you should have covered halfway through the class period and what material you will leave out if you are behind schedule. Do not try to speed up to cover everything in your notes. Have a plan for what to omit: If I don't have fifteen minutes left when I reach this heading, I'll give only one example and post the other examples online.

Mastering Delivery Techniques

Vary the pace at which you speak. Students need time to assimilate new information and to take notes, but if you speak too slowly, they may become bored. Try to vary the pace to suit your own style, your message, and your audience. For example, present important points more deliberately than anecdotal examples. If you tend to speak quickly, try to restate your major points so that students can absorb them. Research shows that a speaking rate of about 100 words a minute is optimal for students' comprehension; understanding suffers when the rate approaches 150–200 words a minute. (Source: Robinson et al., 1997)

Project your voice or use a microphone. Ask students whether they can hear you, or have a graduate student instructor sit in the back corner to monitor the clarity and volume of your lecture. When using a microphone, speak in a normal voice and do not lean into the microphone.

Vary your pitch, volume, and intonation. Communication experts recommend placing the emphasis on key nouns and verbs and building sentences to an emphatic conclusion, rather than letting them trail away. Try not to let the volume of your voice drop at the end of sentences. Practice these techniques and apply them to the first few sentences or minutes of your lecture. Over time you will naturally expand these techniques to the entire lecture. Lowman (1995) describes a series of voice exercises to improve projection, articulation, and tonal quality. (Sources: Lang, 2008; Tauber and Mester, 2007)

Pause. The pause is one of the most powerful tools in public speaking. It is an important device for gaining attention. Pauses can be used as punctuation—to mark a thought, sentence, or paragraph—and also for emphasis, before or after a key concept or idea. If you suddenly stop in midsentence, students will look up from their notes to see what happened. Planned pauses also give you and your audience a short rest. Some faculty take a sip of coffee or water after they say something they want students to stop and think about. Other faculty deliberately pause, announce, "This is the really important consideration," and pause again before proceeding.

Watch out for vocalized pauses. Try to avoid saying "um," "well," "you know," "OK," or "so." Silent pauses are more effective.

Adopt a natural speaking stance. Balance yourself on both feet with your toes and heels on the ground. Beware of swaying or rocking back and forth. Keep your knees slightly relaxed. Shoulders should be down and loose, with elbows cocked, and your hands at waist level. If you use a lectern, don't grip the sides, elbows rigid; instead, keep your elbows bent and lightly rest your hands on the lectern, ready for purposeful gestures.

Breathe normally. Normal breathing prevents vocal strain that impairs the pitch and quality of your speech. Keep your shoulders relaxed, your neck loose, your eyes fully open, and your jaw relaxed.

Closing a Lecture

Draw a conclusion. Help students see that a purpose has been served, that something has been gained during the class session. A well-planned conclusion rounds out the presentation, ties up loose ends, suggests ways for students to follow up on the lecture, and provides a sense of closure.

Finish forcefully. Don't allow your lecture to trail off or end in midsentence because the period is over, and avoid the last-minute "Oh, I almost forgot . . . ."

An impressive ending will echo in students' minds and prompt them to prepare for the next meeting. End with a thought-provoking question or problem, a quotation that sets an essential theme, a summation of the major issue, or a preview of coming attractions. For example, a physics professor ended a lecture by asking a volunteer to come up to the front, stand with his back to the wall, and try to touch his toes. She challenged the class to think about why the volunteer was not successful in this task. In this way, she dramatically introduced the topic of the next lecture, center of gravity. Don't worry if you finish a few minutes early; explain that you have reached a natural stopping point. (But don't make a habit of quitting early.)

End your lecture with the volume up. Make your voice strong, lift your chin up, keep your eyes on your audience. To signal class is over, say "See you on Wednesday" or "Have a good weekend." If the room is available, stay after class for a few minutes to answer students' questions, or walk out with students.

Improving Your Lecture Style

Make notes to yourself immediately after each lecture. Consider the timing, the effectiveness of your examples, the clarity of your explanations, and the like. Jot down questions students asked or comments they made. These notes will help you be more effective the next time you give that lecture.

Record a video of your lecture. When reviewing a video recording of yourself lecturing, you can watch the entire video, watch the video with the sound turned off, or listen to the video without watching it. For advice on analyzing your video, see Chapter 53, "Video Recordings and Classroom Observations."

If you are listening to only the sound track, the following procedure is effective (adapted from Lowman, 1995):

- Listen first straight through, without stopping or taking notes. What is your overall impression of the voice you are hearing?
- Replay the recording, and jot down words that best describe your voice.
- Replay the recording again, this time focusing on the use of extraneous words, the level of relaxation and fluency in the voice, patterns of breathing, volume, pitch and pace, emphasis, and articulation.

You may be pleasantly surprised to discover that the nervousness you felt was not visible to your class.

Work with a communication consultant. Communication consultants can help you develop effective delivery skills. Ask your campus faculty development office for names of consultants or for a schedule of workshops on lecturing and public speaking.

References

Bligh, D. A. *What's the Use of Lectures?* San Francisco: Jossey-Bass, 2000.

Brown, S., and Race, P. *Lecturing: A Practical Guide.* London: Kogan Page, 2002.

Forsyth, D. R. *The Professor's Guide to Teaching: Psychological Principles and Practices.* Washington, DC: American Psychological Association, 2003.

Harp, S. F., and Maslich, A. A. "The Consequences of Including Seductive Details during Lecture." *Teaching of Psychology,* 2005, *32*(2), 100–103.

Heppner, F. *Teaching the Large College Class: A Guidebook for Instructors with Multitudes.* San Francisco: Jossey-Bass, 2007.

Lang, J. M. *On Course: A Week-By-Week Guide to Your First Semester of College Teaching.* Cambridge, MA: Harvard University Press, 2008.

Lowman, J. *Mastering the Techniques of Teaching.* (2nd ed.) San Francisco: Jossey-Bass, 1995.

Robinson, S. L., Sterling, H. E., Skinner, C. H., and Robinson, D. H. "Effects of Lecture Rate on Students' Comprehension and Ratings of Topic Importance." *Contemporary Educational Psychology,* 1997, *22*(2), 260–267.

Tauber, R. T., and Mester, C. S *Acting Lessons for Teachers: Using Performance Skills in the Classroom.* (2nd ed.) Westport, CT: Praeger, 2007.

Weimer, M. G. "Ways and Means of Communicating Structure." *Teaching Professor,* 1988, *2*(7), 3.

Wilson, K., and Korn, J. H. "Attention during Lectures: Beyond Ten Minutes." *Teaching of Psychology,* 2007, *34*(2), 85–89.

Zimbardo, P. G. A Passion for Psychology: Teaching It Charismatically, Integrating Teaching and Research Synergistically, and Writing about It Engagingly. In R. J. Sternberg (Ed.), *Teaching Introductory Psychology: Survival Tips from the Experts.* Washington, DC: American Psychological Association, 1997.

16

Explaining Clearly

Research has shown that student achievement correlates most highly with two characteristics of effective teachers (Feldman, 1989). One is preparation and organization. The other is clarity and "understandableness." The suggestions below will help you communicate clearly and intelligibly to stimulate students' thinking and maximize their learning.

General Strategies

Give students a road map. At the beginning of class, provide a brief outline (on the board or screen) of that day's class. During the session, refer to the outline to alert students to transitions and to the relationships between points. In addition, if not available in the textbook, place on the course Web site definitions of new terms; complex equations and formulas; and graphs, charts, and drawings.

Place key concepts in a larger context. To give students a sense of continuity and meaning, introduce a new topic by explaining how it relates to earlier material and to the course's main themes. To capture students' attention, emphasize the importance of the topic in addressing a specific problem or explaining a particular phenomenon. Students care about the relevance and application of ideas and concepts, and they appreciate real-world examples. (Source: Bain, 2004)

Be selective. Students become confused, overwhelmed, or bored when they feel inundated with information. Deliver the most essential information in manageable chunks. Focus on the fundamentals, use generalizations, and do not give too many exceptions to the rule.

Set an appropriate pace. Talk more slowly when students are taking notes and when you are explaining new material, complex topics, or abstract issues. You can pick up the pace when relating stories, summarizing previous points, or presenting examples.

Assess your own clarity. Pay attention to puzzled expressions, dramatic fall-offs in attendance, and low ratings for clarity on evaluations of your teaching. As you complete a topic, ask students to identify the main points, to state any questions that remain unanswered, and to identify the point that remains most unclear. Address misunderstandings promptly. (Source: Hativa, 1998)

Address possible barriers of an accent. American students may have trouble understanding instructors from other countries who speak something other than the usual range of American English. To address issues of accent, experts recommend that you give assignments in writing; use verbal signals when you speak ("Well, let's get started"); and say the same thing in a few different ways. (Source: Sarkisian, 2006)

Aiding Students' Comprehension

Build on students' prior knowledge and current understanding. If an explanation is beyond students' level of understanding or fails to take into account their misunderstandings or faulty knowledge about a topic, then comprehension breaks down. (Source: Wittwer and Renkl, 2008)

Identify points that may be hard for students to understand. Think about your students' general level of preparation and try to anticipate what they may or may not know. Researchers recommend that you look at your notes before class and identify terms or concepts that may be unfamiliar. Add definitions for unusual words or expressions as well as for technical terms. Introduce new terms one at a time, and project each on the screen or write it on the board. Be ready to illustrate concepts with examples. (Source: Sorcinelli, 2005)

Alert students to the start of a complex point. Cue students to the most difficult ideas ("Almost everyone has difficulty with this one, so listen closely"). Because students' attention wanders throughout the hour, try to recapture their interest before you explain a difficult point.

Create a sense of order. Convey the structure of the session with the following techniques:

- *Forecasting the topic:* "Today I want to discuss three reasons why the government wants to mandate assessment of student learning in higher education."
- *Announcing transitions:* "The first pressure, then, came from concerns about affordability and the increasing costs of higher education. Now let's look at

a second factor: how political candidates emphasized 'accountability' as a campaign promise."

- *Restating the main ideas:* "We've looked at three pressures on colleges to institute assessment procedures: the government's desire for cost-effectiveness, the appeal of campaign slogans in the past election, and public disenchantment with higher education."

Move from the simple to the complex, from the familiar to the unfamiliar. Lay out the most basic ideas first and then introduce complexities. Start with what students know and then move to new territory. (Source: Bain, 2004)

Begin with general statements and then provide specific examples. Research shows that students generally remember facts or principles if they are first presented with the general rule; then given specific examples, illustrations, or applications; and then offered a restatement of the rule, generalization, or principle. For complicated ideas, however, you might first offer an easy example that illustrates the principle, then provide the general statement and explanation of the principle, and then offer a more complex example or illustration. (Sources: Brown, 1978; King, 1994; Wittwer and Renkl, 2008)

Give students opportunities to apply the explanations they hear or read. By performing a task, solving a problem, or generating a self-explanation, students can extend and deepen their understanding. (Source: Wittwer and Renkl, 2008)

Presenting Key Points and Examples

Limit the number of points you make in a lecture. Research shows that students can absorb three to five points in a fifty-minute period and four to five points in a seventy-five-minute class. Be ruthless in paring down the number of major points you make, and be more generous with examples and illustrations that clarify your arguments. Cut entire topics rather than condense each one. Refer interested students to resources that provide a more detailed treatment. (Source: Lowman, 1995)

Call attention to important points. Your students may not grasp the importance of a point unless you announce it: "This is really important, so listen up" or "The most important thing to remember is . . ." or "This is so important that you should have it engraved on a plaque" or "You don't have to remember everything in this course, but you should remember . . . ." Follow through by explaining *why* the particular point is important.

Demonstrate a process rather than describe it. Instead of telling students how to present a logical argument, present a logical argument and help them analyze it. Instead of describing how to solve a problem, solve it in front of them, labeling the steps as you go along.

Use multiple examples to show how the same idea applies in different contexts. As examples of aerodynamic oscillation, one instructor describes holding a scarf out the window of a moving car, holding a thin piece of paper near an air conditioner, and traveling across a suspension bridge battered by gale winds.

Use analogies, anecdotes, and vivid images. People tend to remember images and strong anecdotes. Help students understand and recall important concepts by pairing abstract content with a vivid image, a revealing anecdote, or a concrete association. A physics professor describes velocity by presenting the image of a speeding bullet. An integrative biology instructor compares the size, texture, and other qualities of body organs to familiar objects such as a walnut or a grapefruit. An economics professor defines a trillion by saying how long it would take to count off a trillion seconds (31,700 years). (Sources: Ford, 2002; Kaufman and Bristol, 2001; Lowman, 1995)

Using Repetition and Reinforcement

Use repetition to emphasize important material. Although it is commonly believed that students can only pay attention for about fifteen minutes before their minds begin to drift (Davis, 1993; McKeachie and Svinicki, 2006; Middendorf and Kalish, 1996), researchers have found little empirical support for a fifteen-minute attention span (Wilson and Korn, 2007). Students' attention does wander, but not at precise intervals. To underscore the importance of a point, plan to say it more than once.

Find different ways to make the same point. No single explanation will be clear to all students, so rephrase major points, and let students know you are doing so. You might make a point twice, once in formal language and once colloquially. Or you might present the same point in two or three different modes—verbally, graphically, and numerically—or with different examples.

Use redundancy to let students catch up with the material. Students will have trouble moving on to a second topic if they are still grappling with the first. Give students a chance to catch up by building in redundancy, repetition, and pauses.

References

Bain, K. *What the Best College Teachers Do.* Cambridge, MA: Harvard University Press, 2004.

Brown, G. *Lecturing and Explaining.* New York: Methuen, 1978.

Davis, B. G. *Tools for Teaching.* San Francisco: Jossey-Bass, 1993.

Feldman, K. A. "The Association between Student Ratings of Specific Instructional Dimensions and Student Achievement." *Research in Higher Education,* 1989, *30*(6), 583–645.

Ford, D. G. "Teaching Anecdotally." *College Teaching,* 2002, *50*(3), 114–115.

Hativa, N. "Lack of Clarity in University Teaching: A Case Study." *Higher Education,* 1998, *36*(3), 353–381.

Kaufman, J. C., and Bristol A. S. "When Allport Met Freud: Using Anecdotes in the Teaching of Psychology." *Teaching of Psychology,* 2001, *28*(1), 44–46.

King, A. Inquiry as a Tool in Critical Thinking. In D. F. Halpern and associates (Eds.), *Changing College Classrooms: New Teaching and Learning Strategies for an Increasingly Complex World.* San Francisco: Jossey-Bass, 1994.

Lowman, J. *Mastering the Techniques of Teaching.* (2nd ed.) San Francisco: Jossey-Bass, 1995.

McKeachie, W. J., and Svinicki, M. *McKeachie's Teaching Tips.* (12th ed.) Boston: Houghton Mifflin, 2006.

Middendorf, J., and Kalish, A. "The Change-Up in Lectures." *National Teaching and Learning Forum,* 1996, *5*(2), 1–5.

Sarkisian, E. *Teaching American Students: A Guide for International Faculty and Teaching Assistants in Colleges and Universities.* (3rd ed.) Cambridge, MA: Harvard University Press, 2006.

Sorcinelli, M. D. "IDEA Item #10: Explained Course Material Clearly and Concisely." *POD-IDEA Center Notes,* July 2005. http://www.idea.ksu.edu/podidea/Item10Formatted.pdf

Wilson, K., and Korn, J. H. "Attention during Lectures: Beyond Ten Minutes." *Teaching of Psychology,* 2007, *34*(2), 85–89.

Wittwer, J., and Renkl, A. "Why Instructional Explanations Often Do Not Work: A Framework for Understanding the Effectiveness of Instructional Explanations." *Educational Psychologist,* 2008, *43*(1), 49–64.

17

Personalizing the Large-Enrollment Course

Classes of more than a hundred students pose special challenges for instructors. It is easy for students to feel anonymous or isolated in large courses and difficult for them to get to know one another for support and group study. By nature, large courses include students of varying abilities, interests, and aspirations, but they offer few opportunities for individual attention. The following suggestions are designed to help you give your students a sense that their presence and participation matter.

General Strategies

Be as flexible as your class plan will allow. Provide a "warm" classroom environment that includes time for you to entertain students' comments and give immediate responses to their questions.

Share your enthusiasm and interests. The best lecturers give the impression that they are talking to a few friends about topics of great personal and professional concern. Let your students see that your interests and values extend beyond the classroom. Before class begins, one science faculty member plays the music of the composer or musician whose birthday is closest to that day, or a piece of music that sets the tone for the class: soothing jazz for an exam, hard rock on a Friday.

Be attentive to the physical environment of the classroom. Make sure that the lights are adequate for note taking, that glare does not interfere with the students' view of the screen or chalkboard, and that the room temperature is comfortable. Encourage students to increase their comfort by closing the blinds or opening the windows.

Make the space seem small. A large lecture room will seem smaller if you stand in front of the lectern, not behind it. Move about the room as you lecture, using the aisles if appropriate. If you have graduate student instructors, join with them in distributing class materials. (Source: Gleason, 1986)

Creating a Sense of Community

Encourage students to get to know one another. Students who feel anonymous in class are less motivated to learn and less likely to work hard, while students who feel a sense of community pay more attention and participate more. On the first day of class, ask students to introduce themselves to one or two others sitting nearby. If your class does not have sections, explain how study groups operate, and set aside class time to organize the groups (see Chapter 21, "Learning in Groups"). Give short group assignments, or have the class form teams of two or three students to submit test questions, work on in-class projects, and so on. Ask students to exchange contact information with two other people in the class or to look each other up on an online social networking site. For more ideas, see Chapter 3, "The First Days of Class."

Make an attempt to meet informally with students. In a large class, you will not be able to meet each of your students, but it is worthwhile to get to know some of them. Some faculty extend an invitation for students to drop by a café for conversation. Others select two or three students a week from the class roster and invite them to lunch. Still others hold afternoon teas in their offices throughout the semester. One faculty member invites groups of students to a local ball game. (Source: Padian, 1992)

Try to learn the names of some students and refer to students by name. Students in a large class seem to appreciate an instructor's attempts to learn some names. If a student brings up a point, ask for the student's name, and refer to that point or question as his or hers. The effect of this personal address carries over to all the students. (Source: Benjamin, 1991)

Ask students to submit autobiographical information. If class size permits, during the first week of class ask students to complete a brief questionnaire with their name, contact information, year in college, hometown, reasons for taking the course, expectations, hobbies or interests, work experience, and so on. Summarize this information so that students know about their classmates. You can also use this information to select course activities or match your examples to students' interests.

Hold an in-class orientation for freshmen and transfer students. One science faculty member dismisses his large introductory lecture class twenty minutes early during the second week of the semester and invites first-year students to stay. At this meeting, he reintroduces himself and the graduate student instructors, learns a bit about the backgrounds of the students, and gives them advice on how to study, the importance of attending class, the value of forming study groups, campus resources for counseling and tutoring, and how to get to know professors at a large university. (Source: Padian, 1992)

Provide extra-credit competitions. One faculty member offers students in a large computer science course the chance to enter up to three contests per term to earn extra credit. He reports that about 10 percent of his class of four hundred students take up the offer. Contests have included programmed adventure games, robotics, and computer animations. He gives all the winners a certificate, extra-credit points, and an invitation to dinner at his house the following term. Such contests can challenge, encourage, and motivate the best students. (Source: Levy, 2004)

Minimizing the Distance Between Teacher and Student

Let students know that they are not faces in an anonymous audience. In large courses students often think that their classroom behavior (eating, talking, nodding off, arriving late, leaving early) goes unnoticed. By your word and deed, let students know that you are aware of what is happening in class.

Ask students to refrain from sitting in certain rows. One math professor asks students not to sit in rows 3, 6, 9, and 12, so that she can walk between the seats and observe students when they are working on problems during class.

Invite specific students to sit in the front row. Before each class begins, one faculty member writes a list of students' names on the board; those students are requested to sit in the front row. Over the course of the semester, every student sits up front at least once. During the first few minutes of class, before he begins lecturing, the instructor talks informally to the front row about the homework, their other courses, and the like. He reports that his students appreciate this interaction, and most rate it as a positive experience. (Source: Wheeler, 2000)

Recognize students' outside accomplishments. Read your campus newspaper, scan the dean's list, pay attention to undergraduate awards and honors, and let students know you are aware of their achievements.

Occasionally attend lab or discussion sections. Attending sections gives you an opportunity to meet students and answer questions in a more personal setting.

Capitalize on outside events or situations, as appropriate. Relate major world events or events on campus both to topics in your class and to the fabric of your students' lives outside the classroom. Consider posting a calendar or setting aside class time to mention local events (plays, lectures, performances) that will enhance their understanding of the subject matter.

Arrive early and chat with students. Ask how the course is going, whether they are enjoying the readings, whether there is anything they want you to include in lectures. Or ask students to walk back with you to your office after class.

Read a sample of assignments and exams. If you have graduate student instructors who do most of the grading, let students know you will be reading and grading some of their assignments and exams.

Seek out students who are doing poorly in the course. Write "I know you can do better; see me during my office hours" on all exams graded C– or below. Offer early assistance to students having difficulty.

Acknowledge students who are doing well in the course. Write "Good job! See me after class" on all exams graded A– or above. Take a moment after class to compliment students who are excelling. Some teachers send "A" students a letter of congratulation at the end of the term.

Schedule topics for office hours. To encourage more students to come to your office hours, periodically schedule a help session on a particular topic; see Chapter 55, "Holding Office Hours."

Talk about questions students have asked in previous terms. Mention specific questions that former students have asked and explain why they are excellent questions. This acknowledgement lets students know that you take their questions seriously and that their questions will contribute to future offerings of the course. (Source: Gleason, 1986)

Listen attentively to all questions and answer them directly. If the answer to a question will appear in an upcoming segment of your lecture, acknowledge the aptness of the question, ask the student to hold onto the question for a bit, and answer the question directly when you arrive at that subject; see Chapter 13, "Fielding Students' Questions."

Try to empathize with beginners. Remember that not all of your students are as highly motivated and interested in the discipline as you were when you were a student. Slow down when explaining complex ideas, and acknowledge the difficulty and importance of certain concepts or operations. Try to recall your first encounter with a concept—what examples, strategies, or techniques helped clarify it for you? By describing that encounter and its resolution to your students, you not only explain the concept but also convey the struggle and rewards of learning. (Source: Gleason, 1986)

Monitoring Students' Progress

Ask questions. By asking questions, you turn students into active participants and you can also get a sense of their interests and comprehension. For example, you might leave the last ten or fifteen minutes for students' questions, and if several questions concern one topic, incorporate a presentation on that topic into your next lecture. If your class is too large for an open discussion, identify participation areas of the room (the northeast quadrant one period, the southwest the next) and engage that day's group in discussion. Consider using clickers or other strategies to check on students' understanding. See Chapter 32, "Informally Assessing Students' Learning."

Take an extra pause to look out at the class after you have made a key point. Be alert to nonverbal reactions that indicate that you have lost your students. For example, are students asking their neighbors about a point they missed? If so, try to identify the sticking point, or ask students to supply elaborations or illustrations.

If you have graduate student instructors, ask for periodic reports on problems students are having. At the end of each week ask your graduate student instructors to list two or three points that caused students the most difficulty in discussion sections. You might also ask for their observations about students' responses to your lectures.

Give frequent quizzes and two or more midterms. Frequent quizzes (graded or ungraded) give students more opportunities to do well in your course, and they give you a better sense of students' progress. See Chapter 39, "Quizzes, Tests, and Exams."

Gather feedback during the semester. See Chapter 52, "Early Feedback to Improve Teaching and Learning," and Chapter 32, "Informally Assessing

Students' Learning," for a variety of informal ways to check students' progress and gauge how and what they are learning.

References

Benjamin, L. T. "Personalization and Active Learning in the Large Introductory Psychology Class." *Teaching of Psychology*, 1991, *18*(2), 68–74.

Gleason, M. "Better Communication in Large Courses." *College Teaching*, 1986, *34*(1), 20–24.

Levy, D. "Contests Motivate Top Students in Large Classes." *Stanford Report*, December 3, 2004.

Padian, K. "Three Suggestions for Improving Contact with Students." *Journal of College Science Teaching*, 1992, *21*(4), 205–206.

Wheeler, D. E. "To the Front of the Class." *Journal of Chemical Education*, 2000, *77*(11), 1440.

18

Encouraging Student Participation in the Large-Enrollment Course

Traditional lecturing suffers from a major defect: it is one-way communication in which students sit, listen, and take notes. But students learn best when they take an active role, when they discuss what they are reading, practice what they are learning, and apply concepts and ideas. The following techniques have been used successfully by faculty in various fields to engage large undergraduate classes in student-student and student-faculty interaction, both to enhance learning and to break up the potential tedium of straight lecturing. Though oriented toward large-enrollment courses, these ideas can be implemented in classes of any size. See also Chapter 22, "Informal Group Learning Activities."

General Strategies

Challenge students' notions about the large class. Many students assume that they can sit silently in a large class, taking notes and watching the instructor do all the work. To prepare students to take part in learning activities during class, explain your teaching strategies and expectations at the beginning of the term. Discuss the relationship between participation and learning, and let students know that the in-class activities will give them a head start on homework and on studying for exams. Begin engaging students at the first class session, when norms for the class are being established. (Sources: Felder and Brent, 2003; Freisem and Coutu, 2005; Messineo et al., 2007)

Plan how to engage students. As you prepare your lectures, decide at what points you will stop lecturing and give students a task or exercise (as individuals, pairs, or small groups) of a specific duration (fifteen seconds to fifteen minutes). Consider also how you will handle reporting back: call on individuals for responses, ask for volunteers, or provide your own response. Aim for variety in the type of activity, size of groups, and the interval between lecture and activity.

In the largest classes, of course, students will need more time to break into small groups and to wrap up their work. (Source: Felder and Brent, 2003)

Breaking the Class into Small Groups

Group students in pairs or trios. At the beginning of a class session, ask students to pair off with someone sitting beside or behind them for the purpose of discussing an issue or solving a problem later in the hour. At a stopping point in your lecture, ask the pairs to define a term ("Describe the Doppler effect to your partner"), to pose a "why" or "how" question from the reading, to solve a problem, to answer a question, or to identify the major points in the lecture. To dispel any misinformation, offer a brief answer to the entire class when the pairs are done. Studies show the effectiveness of this strategy on students' short-term and long-term retention. (Source: Prince, 2004)

Use learning dyads. Give an assignment that students are to complete before the next class meeting. The assignment may entail reading, problem solving, undertaking a field trip, conducting a laboratory experiment, or some other activity. In addition to doing the assignment, each student is to prepare two or three questions about the assignment; for example, "Why did Congress pass the Repatriation Act of 1935?" In class, have the students pair off and ask their partners a question from their list; students should alternate in the roles of questioner and responder. At successive meetings, have students form new partnerships.

Form small working groups. Ask your class to form groups of three or four students, and pose a task that the groups can resolve in two or three minutes. For instance, ask the groups to rank several items, to identify the causes of a given occurrence, to generate examples that illustrate a particular point, or to suggest ways to remedy or change something. In a cognitive psychology class, a faculty member asks groups to "identify which aspect of artificial intelligence has the greatest impact on our lives: robotics, expert systems, pattern recognition, or natural language." In a math class, a faculty member hands out a short problem for the groups to solve at their seats, but he distributes only one copy per group, which compels the students to collaborate rather than work on their own.

If class size permits, let students know that you will be soliciting responses from each group—this provides additional incentive for students to do the work. If the class is too large, ask one or two groups to state their conclusions, and ask how many of the groups agree.

Use the snowball discussion technique. Ask the class to pair off. Pose a general question that will generate several ideas from even the least sophisticated student: "Who are the key professionals, besides the architect, involved in designing, financing, and constructing a building?" Ask each pair to generate as many responses as possible during a designated period (three or four minutes), with one member recording the responses. When time is up, ask each pair to join with a nearby pair to form a four-person group. The quartet can combine their ideas into one list and add new ideas to it. If desired, the quartets can combine again to form octets. During the last round, ask the students to select one member of the group to report back to the class.

This technique is helpful early in the term because it gets students thinking about the subject matter, lets you see how much they already know about the field, helps students overcome the isolation and impersonality of a large class, and sets a pattern of student participation for the term. You can repeat the process later in the term with a more sophisticated topic.

Convene simultaneous discussion groups. Announce a topic or question and have students divide into discussion sections (twenty to twenty-five people) that meet in corners of the lecture hall or move into empty neighboring classrooms. Briefly sit in with each group to answer questions, comment on the topic, and help the groups stay on track. It is helpful to give students guidelines on how to participate in a discussion (see Chapter 9, "Leading a Discussion"). As time permits, reconvene the class to summarize the groups' activities.

Use the thirty-five/five rule. When 35 percent of the groups have completed an in-class task, the remaining groups have about five more minutes to finish. (Source: Michaelsen, 2004)

Engaging the Entire Class

Ask students to brainstorm. Some faculty, even in classes of up to four hundred students, pose a general open-ended question to the entire class and ask students to brainstorm, that is, to offer as many suggestions as possible without judging their validity. For example, "What factors contributed to the formation of OPEC?" Give your students these guides for brainstorming:

- Quantity is the goal: the more suggestions, the greater the likelihood of obtaining good ones.
- No one should criticize any suggestion.
- Freewheeling ideas are welcome.

　　Write your students' suggestions on the screen or board in rough categories (for example, social, economic, and political factors) but do not label the categories; instead, ask your students to name the categories or themes. Or you can sift through the list, combine related ideas, and provide the major conclusions yourself. Some faculty stop in the middle of a lecture and ask students to write their thoughts on the subject being discussed. (Sources: Bligh, 2000; Frederick, 1986)

Post questions or problems. Begin the period by asking students to raise questions or problems. Write these on the screen or board, but do not answer the questions—just help your students state their problems. Once the list is finished, you can sort the items into categories. If the list is long and time is limited, ask the class to vote on which problems should be given priority. You can then either respond to the questions yourself or assign questions to groups of students. Some of the benefits of posting questions include increased participation, an attitude toward problems as challenges rather than as evidence of inadequacy, and increased self-confidence as students help others and are helped by them. (Source: McKeachie and Svinicki, 2006)

Devise an online questionnaire. Create a short questionnaire covering one or more controversial topics (theories, research findings, positions on issues) that will be addressed during the course. After each controversial statement, list five response categories: strongly agree, agree, neither agree nor disagree, disagree, strongly disagree. Have students complete the questionnaires online.

　　Throughout the semester, reveal selected results from the survey as they relate to new concepts or issues covered in lectures or readings. Offer the class a snapshot or profile of itself so that each student can see how his or her views match those of classmates. If time permits, ask one or more members of the class who took a "strongly agree" or "strongly disagree" position to state their reasons and evidence. Such discussions bring controversies to life, and students tend to be interested in hearing the opinions and reasoning of fellow students.

Pause during your lecture to pose a quick problem or ask a question. Give students a few minutes to solve a problem at their seats; after you explain the answer, proceed with your lecture. For example, ask students to reorder a set of randomly sequenced steps, to correct the error in a weak argument, or to select a response to a multiple-choice question. (Or use clickers to call for votes on an issue or answer; see Chapter 32, "Informally Assessing Students' Learning.") Or you might ask questions that have a one- or two-word answer—" What's the next number in the Fibonacci sequence 0, 1, 1, 2, 3, 5, 8, _____?" "Who painted *Expulsion from Paradise*?" Keep the pace brisk, move about the class, and call on people with direct eye contact. (Sources: Cooper and Robinson, 2000; Gleason, 1986)

Pause during your lecture for a short ungraded writing activity. See Chapter 34, "Helping Students Write Better in All Courses" for a variety of informal in-class writing activities.

Ask students to become experts on a key term. At the beginning of the semester, post a list of concepts, ideas, people, organizations, or events. Ask each student to select one term (in large classes, groups of students may choose the same term). For their first assignment, students submit a one-page "definition" of their term. Throughout the semester, students are encouraged to read in depth on their term and to serve as in-house experts when that term comes up in lecture. (Source: Christensen, 1988)

Encourage students to ask questions. If the class is too large for you to call on students, ask students to write their questions on index cards and pass them to the aisles. If there are only a few questions, you can quickly sort them and give answers on the spot. If you receive many questions, tell students you will address them during the next session. A variation is to shuffle and redistribute the cards and have individual students read a question aloud and give a response. (Source: Staley, 2003)

Conduct a large-group discussion. To hold a discussion with several hundred students, let disagreement play a major part. After a student expresses a point of view, ask the rest of the class to indicate whether or not they agree. Once agreement is registered by a show of hands, ask for points of disagreement or alternative views and put these to a show of hands. Keep the discussion moving by searching for different ideas and inviting comments that support different views. (Source: Maier, 1963)

Periodically cut short your lecture. Occasionally end your lecture half an hour early and use that time for informal discussion. One faculty member allows students to leave the room at that point; for those who stay, he reports holding lively discussions about the lectures, reading assignments, and the discipline. (Source: Padian, 1992)

Avoid starting a serious discussion near the end of the period. As class draws to a close, students' questions or comments may be stifled by peer pressure for the dismissal of class.

Allow time for students to write a summary of what has been presented. Periodically, at the end of the class session, ask students to jot down the two or three key points of the day's lecture or the question that is uppermost in their minds. Collect their responses and review a sample as a check on what they have learned.

References

Bligh, D. A. *What's the Use of Lectures?* San Francisco: Jossey-Bass, 2000.

Christensen, T. "Key Words Unlock Students' Minds." *College Teaching*, 1988, *36*(2), 61.

Cooper, J. L., and Robinson, P. "Getting Started: Informal Small-Group Strategies in Large Classes." *New Directions for Teaching and Learning*, no. 81. San Francisco: Jossey-Bass, 2000, pp. 17–24.

Felder, R. M., and Brent, R. "Learning by Doing." *Chemical Engineering Education*, 2003, *37*(4), 282–283.

Frederick, P. J. "The Lively Lecture—8 Variations." *College Teaching*, 1986, *34*(2), 43–50.

Freisem, K., and Coutu, L. M. Aligning in Large Class Instruction. In D. H. Wulff (Ed.), *Aligning for Learning: Strategies for Teaching Effectiveness*. Bolton, MA: Anker, 2005.

Gleason, M. "Better Communication in Large Courses." *College Teaching*, 1986, *34*(1), 20–24.

Maier, N.R.F. *Problem-Solving Discussions and Conferences*. New York: McGraw-Hill, 1963.

McKeachie, W. J., and Svinicki, M. *McKeachie's Teaching Tips*. (12th ed.) Boston: Houghton Mifflin, 2006.

Messineo, M., Gaither, G., Bott, J., and Ritchey, K. "Inexperienced versus Experienced Students' Expectations for Active Learning in Large Classes." *College Teaching*, 2007, *55*(3), 125–133.

Michaelsen, L. K. Team-Based Learning in Large Classes. In L. K. Michaelsen, A. B. Knight, and L. D. Fink (Eds.), *Team-Based Learning: A Transformative Use of Small Groups in College Teaching*. Sterling, VA: Stylus, 2004.

Padian, K. "Three Suggestions for Improving Contact with Students." *Journal of College Science Teaching*, 1992, *21*(4), 205–206.

Prince, M. J. "Does Active Learning Work? A Review of the Research." *Journal of Engineering Education*, 2004, *93*(3), 223–231.

Staley, C. *Fifty Ways to Leave Your Lectern*. Belmont, CA: Wadsworth/Thomson, 2003.

19

Maintaining Instructional Quality with Limited Resources

In large classes, compared to small classes, the curriculum is more tightly prescribed, student-instructor interaction is more limited, and procedures are more formalized (Hattie, 2005). Although students and faculty may prefer small classes, the financial constraints of many colleges and universities, especially those in the public sector, necessitate large-enrollment courses. More challenging still, these courses are often taught without graduate student instructors (GSIs) or readers, and with little or no funding for guest lecturers, classroom technology, laboratory sessions, or field trips.

Professors who teach these large courses must decide how to handle the responsibilities and tasks that were once entrusted to GSIs and readers: How will tests and writing assignments be graded? What will replace weekly sections? This chapter discusses how to provide quality education on a tight budget by restructuring courses and adopting cost-efficient teaching and testing techniques.

General Strategies

Use technology as part of course redesign. Instructors can use learning management software to create online tutorials, exercises, and other resources that address core skills and foundational principles that were traditionally handled in GSI-led sections. Research shows that after an initial outlay for development, cost savings can be achieved through technology without risks to students' grades, retention, or conceptual understanding. (Sources: Guskin and Marcy, 2003; Harley et al., 2003; Twigg, 2003)

Develop students' independence. Help students develop the skills they need to become independent, self-regulated learners. It can be both cost-effective and educationally desirable to invest in efforts to promote students' autonomy early in their college years. See Chapter 29, "Helping Students Learn." (Source: Gibbs and Jenkins, 1992)

Prepare students for new ways of learning. If you implement group testing, peer teaching, or other nontraditional strategies, discuss these approaches with your students and give them the skills they need to succeed at these tasks. Be explicit about learning objectives, assessment requirements and criteria, and levels of academic support. (Source: Gibbs and Jenkins, 1992)

Administering and Grading Tests without Readers and GSIs

Ask students to submit proposed test questions. Faculty have had success in adapting students' items for midterm exams. See Chapter 39, "Quizzes, Tests, and Exams."

Consider group testing. In group testing, pairs or small groups of students complete a single test. The challenge of group testing is assessing performance in ways that are fair to individuals when the evidence is a single exam. One option is to give all members of the group the same grade. Another option lets students distribute grades among themselves. For example, if a test receives a score of 80, the four students who worked together on the test would have 320 (80 × 4) points to distribute among themselves. If you want to use this kind of strategy, describe the process and have students determine the criteria for allocating points before they submit the exam. See Chapter 39, "Quizzes, Tests, and Exams." (Source: Cannon and Newble, 2000)

Consider peer grading. For midterms or quizzes (but not the final exam), arrange to have each test individually graded by two different students during class time (with you as the third reader if the two student graders disagree). Students need training, scoring guidelines, and practice for this strategy to be effective. But it does provide students an additional opportunity to learn. See Chapter 39, "Quizzes, Tests, and Exams." (Source: Race et al., 2005)

Develop rubrics and grading criteria. For short answer and essay questions, rubrics can significantly cut down grading time. In addition, if the guidelines are distributed to students in advance of the exam, students may write higher quality answers which can lead to easier grading. See Chapter 36, "Evaluating Students' Written Work." (Source: Race et al., 2005)

Assigning and Grading Writing Assignments without Readers and GSIs

Don't read and grade every piece of writing. Even if you cannot respond to each writing assignment, students will learn more about the topic if they write about it. Ask students to analyze or critique each other's work in small groups during or outside of class. Or have students write for their own purposes, without any feedback. Students will learn that they are writing in order to think more clearly, not to obtain a grade. As time permits, collect a sample of papers and skim them.

Assign brief in-class writing. Before discussing a topic, ask students to write a paragraph or two summarizing what they know about the topic or what opinions they hold. Do not collect these; the purpose is to focus students' attention. Or you can ask students to write in response to short-answer questions you pose during class. For example, you could ask three or four questions that test students' recall of the assigned readings. (Source: Tollefson, 2002)

Use peer response groups. Divide the class into groups of three or four students and schedule a critique session during which students read and comment on each other's rough drafts. Provide the groups with guidelines for responding to the drafts (see Chapter 34, "Helping Students Write Better in All Courses"). Faculty who have had students grade other students' work report that the grades students assign closely match the faculty member's own assessment. (Source: Erickson et al., 2006)

Develop a standard feedback sheet. Include common student errors with space for check marks and assessment criteria with space for brief comments. (Source: Race et al., 2005)

Assigning and Grading Problem Sets without Readers and GSIs

Give frequent homework but do not grade every assignment. Some instructors collect all the homework assignments and grade only one or two problems on each; other instructors collect two or three problems a week for grading. Some faculty ask their students to place all their homework in a notebook and to submit the notebook for checking every few weeks. You can also give and grade short in-class quizzes based on the problem sets. For ungraded assignments, post an answer sheet online or distribute one in class on the day the homework is due and have students check their own work. (Source: Zietz and Cochran, 1997)

Encourage students to collaborate on homework or projects. Students can learn from each other by working together. Ask students to work in small groups and submit a single homework assignment. For suggestions on grading group work, see Chapter 21, "Learning in Groups."

Evaluate some class requirements on a pass/fail basis. Instead of assigning a numerical grade or a letter grade to every piece of homework, use two-point system (pass/not pass) or a three-point system (check, check plus, or zero).

Holding Discussion Sections without Readers and GSIs

Build discussion online. Use learning management or other software to create online student discussion groups or chat rooms. Keep in touch with students electronically through a message board; see Chapter 11, "Online Discussions."

Use undergraduate teaching assistants (UTAs). Some departments allow advanced undergraduates to earn credit by tutoring and teaching sections of first-year students. These UTAs can respond to papers, grade tests, and conduct review sessions. Students report that UTAs are often effective tutors because they are better able to remember their own difficulties in learning the material. If you do use UTAs, plan to provide pedagogical guidance and mentoring, including a pre-semester orientation, weekly meetings to discuss logistics and pedagogy, classroom observation, and the like. Also, if your campus has a teaching assistants' union, work with the union in devising a plan for using UTAs. (Source: Civikly-Powell and Wulff, 2002; McKeegan, 1998; Miller et al., 2001; Twigg, 2003)

Offer a substitute for discussion sections. In lieu of small, weekly, GSI-led section meetings, offer fewer, larger, open-ended sections that any student in the class can attend. Encourage students to teach one another during these sections. Students, of course, will be less knowledgeable and adept than GSIs, but they will benefit from the experience of learning how to explain concepts to peers. (Source: Gibbs and Jenkins, 1992)

References

Cannon, R., and Newble, D. *A Handbook for Teachers in Universities and Colleges: A Guide to Improving Teaching Methods*. (4th ed.) London: Kogan Page, 2000.

Civikly-Powell, J., and Wulff, D. H. Working with Teaching Assistants and Undergraduate Peer Facilitators to Address the Challenges of Teaching Large Classes. In C. A. Stanley and M. E. Porter,. *Engaging Large Classes: Strategies and Techniques for College Faculty.* San Francisco: Jossey-Bass, 2002.

Erickson, B. L., Peters, C. B., and Strommer, D. W. *Teaching First-Year College Students.* San Francisco: Jossey-Bass, 2006.

Gibbs, G., and Jenkins, A. (Eds.). *Teaching Large Classes in Higher Education: How to Maintain Quality with Reduced Resources.* London: Kogan Page, 1992.

Guskin, A. E., and Marcy, M. B. "Dealing with the Future Now: Principles for Creating a Vital Campus in a Climate of Restricted Resources." *Change,* July/Aug. 2003, *35*(4), 10–21.

Harley, D., Maher, M., Henke, J., and Lawrence, S. "An Analysis of Technology Enhancements in a Large Lecture Course." *Educause Quarterly,* 2003, *26*(3), 26–33.

Hattie, J. "The Paradox of Reducing Class Size and Improving Learning Outcomes." *International Journal of Educational Research,* 2005, *43*(6), 387–425.

McKeegan, P. "Using Undergraduate Teaching Assistants in a Research Methodology Course." *Teaching of Psychology,* 1998, *25*(1), 11–14.

Miller, J. E., Groccia, J. E., and Miller, M. S. (Eds.). *Student-Assisted Teaching: A Guide to Faculty-Student Teamwork.* Bolton, MA: Anker, 2001.

Race, P., Brown, S., and Smith, B. *500 Tips on Assessment.* (2nd ed.) London: RoutledgeFalmer, 2005.

Tollefson, S. K. *Encouraging Student Writing.* (rev. ed.) Berkeley: Office of Educational Development, University of California, 2002.

Twigg, C. A. "Improving Quality and Reducing Cost: Designs for Effective Learning." *Change,* July/Aug. 2003, *35*(4), 22–29.

Zietz, J., and Cochran, H. H. "Containing Cost without Sacrificing Achievement: Some Evidence from College-Level Economics Classes." *Journal of Education Finance,* 1997, *23,* 177–192.

PART V

Alternatives and Supplements to Lectures and Discussion

20

Web 2.0

The term *Web 2.0* was coined in 2004 to refer to Web sites and applications that foster collaboration, user participation, interactivity, and content sharing. Web 2.0 includes blogs, microblogs, wikis, social networks, tagging and bookmarking, online discussion boards, multimedia and file sharing, syndication, podcasts, and multi-user virtual environments. The following list summarizes the principal concepts underlying Web 2.0 (adapted from Anderson, 2007; Brown and Adler, 2008; David, 2007; Solomon and Schrum, 2007; Sreebny, 2007):

- facilitating the individual creation and manipulation of digital information and artifacts
- offering strong support for and low barriers to sharing individual creations
- harnessing the "power of the crowd," the collective intelligence of large groups of people, in problem solving, forecasting, and other activities in which the independent judgments of participants are aggregated
- maximizing the architecture of participation, whereby the precision or value of an application or service improves over time as usage increases
- affirming openness in source software and content distribution that allows users to access, reuse, and recombine (mashup) digital materials

This chapter gives some examples of how instructors have integrated Web 2.0 into their courses. Online discussion boards are treated in Chapter 11, "Online Discussions"; multi-user virtual environments are introduced in Chapter 25, "Simulations"; and podcasting is discussed in Chapter 33, "Mobile Learning."

General Strategies

Be open to new developments. Try to stay informed about new applications and media, but don't worry if you can't keep up. As appropriate, rely on colleagues and your campus's information technology staff. If you have interests in this area, a helpful resource is the *Horizon Report*, an annual publication of the New Media Consortium and Educause Learning Initiative that identifies and describes emerging technologies likely to impact teaching, learning, and creative expression in higher education. However, most faculty will want to think twice before joining the early adopters, who run the risk that start-up companies may discontinue operations or tech support. Some college libraries have set up online self-study programs (called Learning 2.0) where instructors can explore and expand their knowledge of Web 2.0. (Sources: Anderson, 2007; David, 2007)

Select technologies based on pedagogical principles. In the broadest terms, the general tasks of instructors include identifying course content, organizing students' learning experiences, assessing student performance, and providing feedback to learners. The general tasks of students include reading, searching, collecting, and analyzing content; practicing what is being learned; presenting a point of view; and demonstrating mastery. Consider which Web 2.0 technologies to incorporate into your course in light of these teaching and learning activities. For example, with forums or discussion boards students can present their points of view; with multimedia sharing, they can demonstrate what they have learned. (Source: McGee and Diaz, 2007)

Recognize the educational opportunities and challenges posed by Web 2.0. It is too soon for researchers to have examined whether Web 2.0 applications improve student learning, although common sense suggests that online collaborative activities will enhance motivation and learning for many students. Some commentators, however, warn that Web 2.0 heralds an amateur do-it-yourself culture that prizes opinion over expertise and that ignores traditional methods for authenticating knowledge and designating authority. Other challenges posed by Web 2.0 include the following (from Anderson, 2007; David, 2007; McGee and Diaz, 2007):

- the speed with which new technologies emerge versus the length of time instructors need to adopt and integrate technology into their courses
- clashes over privacy, shared authorship, intellectual property rights, and ownership of content
- difficulties in determining whether material comes from a trusted source and is accurate and up-to-date
- students' struggles to adapt to using the new media and applications for educational purposes rather than for entertainment

Weigh the pros and cons of using Web-based versions of desktop applications. For word processing, spreadsheets, e-mail, and other tasks, Web-based applications are alternatives to applications that reside on users' computers. Perhaps the best-known are the many tools and applications developed by Google. Issues to consider in deciding whether to adopt these free tools for classroom use include ease of use, security and privacy, data backup, advertising and marketing, and support and training.

A Sample of Applications

Blogs. A typical blog consists of a series of time-stamped entries posted by the blog's creator, each of which is followed by comments contributed by readers; a vlog (video blog) uses video as the primary media source. Many campuses have learning management systems or collaborative learning environments that make it easy for instructors and students to create and maintain blogs. Faculty and students can also use free open-source technology (see, for example, the tools available at www.blogger.com). Blogs are updated from several times a day to several times a week; they tend to use an informal, conversational tone; and they offer easy ways to alert readers when new posts or comments are added.

Instructors can use blogs for the following purposes (adapted from Britt, 2007; Educause Learning Initiative, August 2005a; Educause Learning Initiative, August 2005b; Warlick, 2007):

- to provide answers to questions about course content or course procedures as they arise
- to give students their unvarnished point of view and invite conversation, reaction, and comments
- to create a class Web site, using plug-ins that allow for e-mail, voice mail, and quick polling
- to provide a forum for peer review, with students posting their drafts or final versions of papers so that other students can read and comment on them

Microblogs. With microblog services, users can send text-based updates or post short messages via Web sites, instant messaging, and mobile devices to people who have subscribed to receive them. Currently, messages are limited to 140 characters (for example, in Twitter). Here are some suggested instructional uses of microblogging (adapted from the PsychTeacher listserv):

- to make students aware of a news item or timely event related to the course content ("See today's New York Times article on depression")
- to request answers to simple questions ("homework helpful for today's class topic?")
- to give the class real-time feedback while grading their papers ("thesis statements need work")

- to let students know in real time when you are in your office available to see students ("in office; no students waiting")
- to encourage students to comment about a shared experience as it is happening; for example, while watching a laboratory demonstration

Wikis. A wiki allows multiple users to write and edit a Web document. The online encyclopedia *Wikipedia* exemplifies the advantages and disadvantages of collective composition: the collaboration of many contributors lends breadth and depth to the entries even as it endangers accuracy and objectivity. Newer wiki reference works seek to overcome these difficulties by requiring contributors to use their real names or by relying on established scholars and anonymous peer-review.

     To create a wiki for a course or a department, faculty use either a campuswide learning management system or an open source program such as www.wikispaces .com. Here are some typical wiki projects (adapted from Educause Learning Initiative, July 2005; Parry, 2008; Warlick, 2007):

- Ask students to fact-check and then update an article in *Wikipedia* that is relevant to the content of the course. Or ask students to pick a controversial article in *Wikipedia* (for example, global warming), review the history of the article and the contributors' ongoing discussion and debate (accessed by tabs at the top of the article), and then analyze themes and discourse that led to the current entry. Or ask students to use primary source documents to prepare an entry for *Wikipedia* on a topic from the course.
- Assign group projects and have students use wikis for collaboration and group authoring. For example, teams of students might be asked to interpret a group of poems, post their comments on a wiki page, and respond to one another's remarks. Or different teams of students might summarize different subsets of the readings that they then put together into a comprehensive summary of course readings.
- Have students draft, revise, and submit an individual assignment on a wiki site. The wiki's automatic revision history will save each draft of the assignment, allowing the instructor to see the evolution of the paper.
- Create wikis for students to produce a collaborative set of class notes, a course bibliography or reference list, or a summary of key points at the end of a course unit.
- Establish a wiki to facilitate cross-disciplinary or cross-institutional collaboration.

Social bookmarking and tagging. Using social bookmarking (to create a list of Web links) and tagging (to provide keywords for each link), students can collect a set of Web resources, share their list with others, and provide a classification scheme for those resources. In an academic context, tagging serves as an analytic exercise that requires students to identify overarching themes, major points, and the value of their resource list for classmates and other audiences. (Source: Educause Learning Initiative, May 2005)

RSS and syndication. Through Web syndication, content producers can make their text, video, or audio files available to individual subscribers and to other Web sites. Content producers use RSS (Really Simple Syndication) or other feeds to inform subscribers about updates to a Web site, blog, or podcast. Clicking on a small icon on Web pages and blogs allows users to register and to receive regular feeds from that site on their computer or mobile device. The RSS feed may consist of headlines, short bits of text, photos, or entire podcasts.

Peterson's maintains a College and University Feed Directory (directory.edufeeds.com) that catalogs hundreds of higher education RSS feeds organized by topic. Faculty can also use RSS to keep in touch with students concerning course work, other academic activities, and developments in their fields of study, without having to go from Web site to Web site. (Sources: Anderson, 2007; David, 2007; Educause Learning Initiative, April 2007; Solomon and Schrum, 2007)

Social networking. Originally, social networking sites emphasized setting up groups of friends and relationships. Each participant in a social networking site creates a personal profile of interests and activities using text, photos, videos, music, and links to other profiles or Web sites. Participants also create networks of people to whom they grant various types of access and updates. On campus, locally hosted social networking sites (for example, through Ning) may be limited to students in a course, department, or interdisciplinary program and created around academic topics. Social networking sites have now expanded to include blogs, asynchronous dialogs, and more content, evolving into general media platforms.

Current social networking sites can enhance learning and motivation by facilitating collaboration and information sharing. Most of the scant research on social networking in higher education, however, has focused on self-presentation (how individuals shape identity online), friendship performance, network structure, online/offline connections, and privacy issues (boyd and Ellison, 2007). Some research has begun to explore issues of race, ethnicity, and class in social network sites. Hargittai (2007), for example, found that white students gravitate toward Facebook, while Chicano/a–Latino/a–Hispanic students are more likely to have MySpace pages. Asian American students prefer Facebook to MySpace but use other social network sites, like Xanga.

Some faculty participate in commercial social network sites as a way of staying in contact with current and former students and advisees. Some students appreciate this participation (Mazer et al., 2007), but others see faculty as interlopers (Lipka, 2007). One general caution about commercial sites—which you may wish to share with your students—is that participants have no control over what may happen to materials on the site after a change in policy or ownership.

Here are some tips on using current campus and commercial social network sites for instructional purposes (from boyd and Ellison, 2007; Cho et al., 2007; Lemuel, 2006; Lipka, 2007; Mazer et al., 2007; Miller and Jensen, 2007):

- Your profile will likely be intensely scrutinized by students. Keep your entries professional and related to educational topics. Present yourself as a trustworthy individual who has students' best interests in mind.
- Respect students' privacy. Don't use a social network site to gossip or spy on students. Don't lecture or criticize students regarding items in their profiles.
- Look up students who are your advisees before you meet with them so that you will have a better understanding of their current circumstances.
- Post pictures from class field trips or research activities.
- Check in with a student who has missed several classes to see if all is well.
- Post requests to recruit students for undergraduate research projects.
- Be cautious about "friending"; accept requests from students but don't initiate any.
- Let students know whether they can form study groups through social networking sites to exchange advice, tips, and ideas about homework assignments or whether study groups should be formed only through the learning management system or collaborative learning environment.

Peer-to-Peer file sharing As defined by *Wikipedia, file sharing* "refers to the providing and receiving of digital files over a network, usually following the peer-to-peer (P2P) model, where the files are stored on and served by personal computers of the users." Typically, students both provide (upload) and receive (download) files, often through flash drives. File sharing is wildly popular for swapping music and movies, frequently from unauthorized sources, despite efforts by the entertainment industry to litigate over copyright infringement. Currently, educational applications of P2P file sharing are limited though some universities are working on projects for exchanging files among educational institutions globally.

Multimedia sharing. Various Web sites allow users to upload, view, annotate, and share photographs, audio clips, and video clips on a variety of devices (desktop computers, laptops, MP3 players, mobile phones). Users can also create play lists of their favorites and subscribe to others' videos. Instructors can select educational videos from online repositories, post their own videos (for example, end-of-unit summaries or lab experiments), and incorporate multimedia into students' projects and assignments. One faculty member asked students to identify videos on YouTube that related to particular topics in the course readings. Another instructor assigned students to search for photographs that illustrated important course concepts. Some universities have posted entire courses on YouTube, along with panel discussions, poetry readings, and campus events. (Sources: Lang, 2008; Solomon and Schrum, 2007; Trier, 2007)

Data mashups. As defined by *Wikipedia*, a *mashup* is a Web application that "combines data from more than one source into a single integrated tool." An example of a data mashup is a map of air quality in the United States, created by the U.S. Environmental Protection Agency (EPA), that combines Google Earth with data on the amount and kind of pollutants emitted by businesses. Faculty are using mashups to help students better understand crime patterns, for example, or government and nonprofit responses to natural disasters. (Source: New Media Consortium and Educause Learning Initiative, 2008)

Personal learning environments. Some educators use the term "personal learning environment" (PLE) to refer to online tools that allow students to manage their academic work by selecting the Web applications and materials they need to acquire, document, and communicate the skills and information they are learning. In contrast, instructor- and institution-controlled learning management systems restrict the content, services, and applications to a centralized repository.

PLEs may include applications and tools for the production of blogs, wikis, podcasts, social bookmarking, instant messaging, social networking and aggregation, and digital recombination and mashups. Indeed, so many applications are available that the first challenge for students and faculty is selecting and learning to use the different tools. (Sources: PLE, 2008)

Online academic exchange. A large-scale example of online academic exchange is Harvard University's H2O project, an open source site that has two components: the Idea Exchange and the Rotisserie. The Idea Exchange includes all features needed to host a course entirely on H2O, including applications for uploading resources (readings, notes, videos, and so on) and for running discussion boards. The system also facilitates the collaborative development of course materials by allowing project leaders to browse, search, and import the materials of other project leaders. Because materials created on the Idea Exchange are covered by a Creative Commons license, all project leaders share in the free exchange of educational content. The Rotisserie hosts discussion boards that encourage thoughtful discourse. Faculty have organized H2O projects on such topics as power, politics, and the state; world religions; and bringing chemistry to life. (Sources: Anderson, 2007; David, 2007; Harvard H2O Web site; Solomon and Schrum, 2007)

References

Anderson, P. *What Is Web 2.0? Ideas, Technologies and Implications for Education.* UK: Joint Information Systems Committee, 2007. http://www.jisc.ac.uk/media/documents/techwatch/tsw0701b.pdf

boyd, d. m., and Ellison, N. B. "Social Network Sites: Definition, History and Scholarship." *Journal of Computer-Mediated Communication,* 2007, *13*(1) 210–230.

Britt, M. A. "Setting Up a Blog or Podcast for the Teaching of Psychology: A 'How To' and 'Why To.'" *Excellence in Teaching,* Society for the Teaching of Psychology, October 2007.

Brown, J. S., and Adler, R. P. "Minds on Fire: Open Education, the Long Tail and Learning 2.0." *Educause Review,* January–February 2008, *43*(1), 16–33.

Cho, H., Gay, G., Davidson, B., and Ingraffea, A. "Social Networks, Communication Styles, and Learning Performance in a CSCL Community." *Computers and Education,* 2007, *49*(2), 309–329.

David, C. "Working the Web." *University Business,* April 2007, *10*(4), 64–68.

Educause Learning Initiative. "7 Things You Should Know about Social Bookmarking." May 2005. http://connect.educause.edu/library/abstract/7ThingsYouShouldKnow/39378

Educause Learning Initiative. "7 Things You Should Know about Wikis." July 2005. http://connect.educause.edu/library/abstract/7ThingsYouShouldKnow/39381

Educause Learning Initiative. "7 Things You Should Know about Blogs." August 2005a. http://connect.educause.edu/Library/ELI/7ThingsYouShouldKnowAbout/39383

Educause Learning Initiative. "7 Things You Should Know about Videoblogging." August 2005b. http://connect.educause.edu/Library/ELI/7ThingsYouShouldKnowAbout/39382

Educause Learning Initiative. "7 Things You Should Know about RSS." April 2007. http://connect.educause.edu/library/abstract/7ThingsYouShouldKnow/39401

Hargittai, E. "Whose Space? Differences among Users and Non-Users of Social Network Sites." *Journal of Computer-Mediated Communication,* 2007, *13*(1), 276–297.

Harvard H2O. Home page, n.d. http://h2o.law.harvard.edu/index.jsp

Lang, J. M. *On Course: A Week-By-Week Guide to Your First Semester of College Teaching.* Cambridge, MA: Harvard University Press, 2008.

Lemuel, J. "Why I Registered on Facebook." *Chronicle of Higher Education,* September 1, 2006.

Lipka, S. "For Professors, 'Friending' Can Be Fraught." *Chronicle of Higher Education,* December 7, 2007, *54*(15), A1.

Mazer, J. P., Murphy, R. E., and Simonds, C. J. "I'll See You on Facebook: The Effects of Computer-Mediated Teacher Self-Disclosure on Student Motivation, Affective Learning, and Classroom Climate." *Communication Education,* 2007, *56*(1), 1–17.

McGee, P., and Diaz, V. "Wikis and Podcasts and Blogs! Oh My! What Is a Faculty Member Supposed to Do?" *Educause Review*, Sept./Oct. 2007, *42*(5), 28–40.

Miller, S. E., and Jensen, L. A. "Connecting and Communicating with Students in Facebook." *Computers in Libraries*, 2007, *27*(8), 18–22.

New Media Consortium and Educause Learning Initiative. *Horizon Report*, 2008. http://www.nmc.org/publications/2008-horizon-report

Parry, D. "Wikipedia and the New Curriculum." *Science Progress*, 2008. http://www.scienceprogress.org/2008/02/wikipedia-and-the-new-curriculum/

"PLE (Personal Learning Environment)." Learning Technologies Center Wiki, University of Manitoba, May 2008. http://ltc.umanitoba.ca/wiki/Ple

Solomon, G., and Schrum, L. *Web 2.0: New Tools, New Schools*. Washington, DC: International Society for Technology in Education, 2007.

Sreebny, O. "Digital Rendezvous: Social Software in Higher Education." *Educause Center for Applied Research*, 2007, no. 2.

Trier, J. "Cool Engagements with YouTube: Part 1." *Journal of Adolescent and Adult Literacy*, 2007, *50*(5), 408–412.

Warlick, D. F. *Classroom Blogging*. (2nd ed.) Raleigh, NC: Landmark Project, 2007.

21

Learning in Groups

Researchers report that, regardless of the subject matter, students working in small groups tend to learn more and demonstrate better retention than students taught in other instructional formats. Students who work in groups also appear more satisfied with their classes, and group work provides a sense of shared purpose that can increase morale and motivation. In addition, group work introduces students to the insights, values, and worldviews of their peers, and it prepares students for life after school, when many will be working on teams (Astin, 1993; Barkley et al., 2004; Johnson et al., 1991; Millis and Cottell, 1998; Pascarella and Terenzini, 2005; Prince, 2004; Slavin, 1996; Springer et al., 1999).

Group work can be incorporated into almost any course, regardless of enrollment or content. The methods and techniques go by many names, so the jargon can be confusing. Moreover, the distinctions among them are not always clear. One way to sidestep the internecine debates about terminology is to sort the various approaches by principal focus:

- terms that reinforce the notion that the learner or student is the primary focus of instruction: *learner-centered instruction, student-centered instruction, student-driven methods, student active teaching*
- terms that emphasize the importance of interaction and "doing": *hands-on learning, participative learning, authentic learning, constructivist learning, interactive engagement, pedagogies of engagement, interactive teaching and learning, inductive teaching and learning*
- terms that stress the importance of working in groups: *cooperative learning, collaborative learning, collective learning, learning communities, peer teaching, peer learning, reciprocal peer learning, team learning, syndicate learning, study groups, base groups, work groups*
- terms that describe structured approaches to developing solutions to real-world problems: *problem-based learning, project-based learning, guided design, inquiry learning, discovery learning*

Some people use the umbrella term *active learning* to encompass all these types of pedagogies, but others point out the term is misleading and that "passive learning" is a state that does not really exist (Lyons et al., 2003).

All these strategies share several assumptions (adapted from Bonwell and Eison, 1991; Meyers and Jones, 1993):

- Listening to lectures and taking notes will carry students only so far in their academic and intellectual development. Students need opportunities to do more than listen and watch others.
- In addition to promoting the transmission of information, higher education should help students develop their skills and capacities for higher-order thinking.
- College students are mature enough to assume some responsibility for teaching themselves and for teaching others.
- Students benefit from reflecting on what they are doing and what they have learned.

To implement these concepts, college instructors most often look to three types of group work: informal learning groups, formal learning groups, and study groups (adapted from Johnson et al., 1991).

Informal learning groups are ad hoc clusterings of students during a single class session. Informal learning groups can be initiated, for example, by asking students to turn to several neighbors and spend two minutes discussing a question you have posed. Instructors can organize informal groups at any time in a class of any size to check on students' understanding of the material, to give students an opportunity to apply what they are learning, or to provide a change of pace.

Formal learning groups are established to complete a specific task (conduct a lab experiment, write a position paper, carry out a project). These tasks may extend over several weeks or the entire term. Students work together until the task is finished and their project is evaluated or graded.

Study groups are long-term groups (usually over the course of a semester) with stable membership whose primary responsibility is to provide support, encouragement, and assistance in completing course requirements and assignments. Study groups also help members catch up when they have missed a class. The larger the enrollment and the more complex the subject matter, the more valuable study groups can be.

The suggestions below are designed to help you set up formal learning groups and study groups. Three other chapters—22, "Informal Group Learning Activities"; 9, "Leading a Discussion"; and 18, "Encouraging Student

Participation in the Large-Enrollment Course"—describe a variety of ways to incorporate informal learning groups into your courses. Chapter 34, "Helping Students Write Better in All Courses," discusses informal collaborative writing activities. Chapter 20, "Web 2.0," describes ways technology can be used to promote learning in groups. Chapter 23, "Formal Group Learning Activities," offers brief descriptions of pedagogies that faculty have used to incorporate real-world problems into their courses.

General Strategies

Plan for each stage of group work. When you are writing your course syllabus, decide which topics, themes, or projects might lend themselves to formal group work. Think about how you will organize students into groups, help group members negotiate among themselves, provide feedback to the groups, and evaluate the products of group work. (Source: Race, 2000)

Carefully explain to your class how the groups will operate and how students will be graded. Take a bit of extra time to explain the objectives of the group task and define relevant concepts. Students will need advice about what group membership means, how to get started, and how to know when their task is done. Students will also want to know how they will be graded. Keep in mind that group work is more successful when students are graded against a set standard rather than against each other (on a curve). (Source: Bacon et al., 1999)

Help students develop the skills they need to succeed in groups. Many students will need tips about active and tolerant listening, helping one another master content, giving and receiving constructive criticism, and managing disagreements and conflicts. Discuss these skills with your students, provide resources as needed, and model and reinforce these skills during class. Studies show that interpersonal skills training is a key to successful learning for students working in groups. (Sources: Prichard et al., 2004, 2006; Stein and Hurd, 2000)

Consider using written contracts. Some faculty have students sign contracts, generated by the students or by the instructor, that list members' obligations to their group and penalties for slacking off. Responsibilities include being prepared and ready to share, listening actively, and being supportive of others. Sample penalties include taking on extra work and making up missed assignments. (Source: Barkley et al., 2004)

Designing Group Work

Create group tasks that require interdependence. Mutual reliance is a powerful motivator for learning, and group work is most effective when students know that they "sink or swim" together, when each member feels responsible to and dependent on the others, and when no one student can succeed unless all in the group succeed. Strategies for promoting interdependence include specifying common rewards for the group, encouraging students to divide up the labor, and formulating tasks that compel students to reach a consensus. (Sources: Engle and Conant, 2002; Johnson et al., 1991)

Assign tasks that are integral to the course objectives. Some faculty recommend assigning tasks that require the analysis of complex issues and that rely on judgment and decision making. As reported by Johnson, Johnson, and Smith (1991), for example, in an engineering class, a faculty member gives groups a problem to solve: Determine whether the city should purchase twenty-five buses or fifty. Each group prepares a report, and a representative from each group is randomly selected to present the group's solution. The approaches used by the various groups are compared and discussed by the entire class.

Create assignments that fit the students' skills, interests, and abilities. Early in the term, assign relatively easy tasks; as the term progresses, increase the difficulty. For example, a faculty member teaching research methods begins by having students identify various research designs and sampling procedures. Later, group members generate their own research designs. At the end of the term, each group prepares a proposal for a research project and submits it to another group for review and evaluation.

Assign tasks that allow for a fair division of labor. Try to structure the tasks so that each group member can make an equal contribution. For example, one instructor asks groups to write a report on alternative energy sources. Each member of the group is responsible for research on one source, and all the members work together to incorporate the individual contributions into the final report. Another faculty member asks groups to prepare a medieval newspaper. Students research aspects of life in the Middle Ages, and each student contributes one major article for the newspaper, which includes news stories, features, and editorials. Students conduct their research independently and use group meetings to share information, critique and edit articles, proofread, and design the layout. (Source: Tiberius, 1999)

Consider administering group tests. Faculty who have used group exams report that groups consistently achieve higher scores than individuals and that students enjoy collaborative test taking. Faculty who use this technique recommend the following steps for in-class exams:

- Assign group work at the beginning of the term so that students develop skills for working in groups.
- Use multiple-choice tests that include higher-level questions. Allow about three minutes of discussion per item (for example, fifteen multiple-choice questions for a forty-five-minute exam).
- Divide students into groups of no more than five.
- Have students take the test individually and turn in their responses. Then have the group convene to arrive at a consensus answer for each question. For each correct response a group attains, add bonus points to the test score of every student in the group.

See Chapter 39, "Quizzes, Tests, and Exams." (Sources: Cottell, 2000; Michaelsen et al., 2004; Toppins, 1989)

Organizing Learning Groups

Decide how the groups will be formed. Ideally, all students will have equal opportunities to participate and feel included in their group. You may need to make an extra effort to reduce the chances that a student who appears different from others in the class will feel isolated; for example, a male in a predominantly female class or a student with a visible disability. Openly discuss with students how differences (in culture, ethnicity, nationality, disability, sexuality, age, language, background, ways of thinking) do not hinder the task at hand but actually strengthen a group by providing greater diversity of perspectives, knowledge, and insights. Research shows that diverse groups of problem solvers consistently outperform groups composed entirely of individuals who are highly skilled at solving problems (Page, 2007).

Here are some common approaches to forming groups:

- *Assign students to groups based on specific criteria.* Some faculty try to maximize group heterogeneity, creating a mix of males and females, verbal and quiet students, the cynical and the optimistic, the stellar and the struggling. Sometimes, though, students will distrust the process or feel that favoritism is at work.
- *Assign students to groups randomly.* Some faculty assign students to groups using the first letter of the students' last names, a table of random numbers, or a count-off procedure. One faculty member uses an activity to randomly form

groups in small classes: the class forms two parallel lines, one for men and one for women ordered by height. The lines then merge alternately if the number of men and women are about equal, or one to two or more if numbers are disproportionate. The resulting single line counts off "1, 2, 3, . . . n" to form n groups. Random assignment, however, can produce unbalanced teams in terms of skill sets and diversity.

- *Have students choose their teammates.* Self-selected groups seem to work best when students already know one another; for example, in small classes and in small residential colleges. Some research shows that self-selected groups are initially more cohesive, which improves performance, and better able to manage interpersonal conflicts. Self-selected groups, however, tend to be based on affinities (friends, teammates, members of the same ethnic group). This may be uncomfortable for students who are shy or who don't belong to one of the major groups in a course and may feel left out ("last one chosen"). If you ask students to create their own groups, remind them that diversity strengthens a group by including a variety of points of view, skills, and values. Another pitfall of self-selection is "groupthink"—the failure to conduct adequate research and examine alternatives in order to maintain group solidarity.

- *Use a combination strategy.* Some faculty select the groups after asking students to express their preferences ("Name the three students you would most like to work with") and assign students into groups with at least one classmate for whom they expressed a preference. Other faculty specify the criteria for the groups—for example, a mix of genders, majors, and nonmajors—and allow students to select their teammates. For large classes, some faculty use open source software to make the assignments: students complete a short question-naire that includes preferences for teammates, and the software makes assign-ments that satisfy both the instructor's criteria and the students' preferences.

- *Use student self-assessment to form groups.* Identify the three or four most important skills for success in the group project (such as communication skills, analyti-cal skills, technology skills, and background in a particular content area) and add the generic "jack of all trades." Have students rank their strengths in these categories from highest to lowest skill level. Then, using a portion of class time, ask students to raise their hands if they rated themselves highly as each skill is announced and randomly assign students to n groups. Students raise their hands only once unless not placed in a group.

Since the methodologies for assigning students to groups have strengths and drawbacks, some faculty vary the methods they use over the term. (Sources: Bacon et al., 1999; Barkley et al., 2004; Blowers, 2003; Jaques and Salmon, 2007; Johnson et al., 1991; Walvoord, 1986)

Be conscious of group size. In general, groups of four or five members work best; in larger groups, students have fewer opportunities to participate. Groups of four allow for some pair work, but groups of five preclude tie votes. Students who are less skillful tend to work best in smaller groups, and shorter tasks are also conducive to smaller groups. (Sources: Bean, 1996; Brufee, 1999; Cooper et al., 2003; Johnson et al., 1991)

Encourage students to begin with a team-building exercise. For example, ask students to take two items from their backpack, handbag, or pocket and then introduce themselves to the group using the items to describe themselves. Or ask each group to come up with a name, logo, or slogan that represents it. (Source: Deeter-Schmelz et al., 2002; Stein and Hurd, 2000)

Help students get off to a good start. As a first assignment ask each group to prepare a collective response to questions such as the following (adapted from POD listserv):

- What specific factors or conditions lead to a well-functioning and effective group?
- How will you help your group meet each of those conditions for success?
- How will your group handle a group member who misses a group meetings, fails to complete assignments in a timely fashion, or interacts poorly with others?
- What specifically can each individual do to help the group work harmoniously and productively?

Keep groups together. When a group is not working well, avoid breaking it up, even if the group requests it. The addition of the floundering group's members to ongoing groups may throw off their group process, and the bailed-out troubled group does not learn to cope with its unproductive interactions. (Source: Barkley et al., 2004)

But consider rotating group membership throughout the semester. Let students know that they will have the opportunity to work in groups with a different set of students later in the term.

Guiding Learning Groups

Help groups plan how to proceed. Ask each group to devise a plan of action: who will be doing what and when. Review the written plans or meet with each group to discuss its plan.

Give advice on how to make group decisions. Discuss various methods for decision making (adapted from Barkley et al., 2004):

After a period of discussion, the group can vote and the *majority* wins; the drawback to this process is that a narrow majority can overwhelm the minority and encourage factionalism.

In a variation called *negative minority* the group discusses a list of suggestions and votes to eliminate the most unpopular one; discussion and elimination continue until only one suggestion remains. This method has the advantage of creating consensus when there are many ideas and few voters, although it is time consuming and some members will be unhappy when their ideas are voted down.

In *consensus* the group discusses and negotiates a decision until everyone is satisfied. This technique has the advantage of allowing all members the opportunity to be heard and to influence the decision, although the process may be stressful and time consuming.

Using *criteria* to make decisions has the advantage of giving an objective measure of the quality of a solution, but students may struggle to agree on appropriate criteria.

Compromise avoids either-or decisions but can take a long time because students must engage in give-and-take on each idea under consideration.

Regularly check in with the groups. When the task spans several weeks, you will want to establish checkpoints with the groups. Ask groups to turn in outlines or drafts or to meet with you.

Minimize student resistance to group work. If some students undermine the group, complain about group work, or seem hostile, try to determine the reasons for the resistance. Help students see how group work fits into your overall goals for the course. Discuss a sample group task and explain how groups often come up with more and better solutions than an individual. (Sources: Barkley et al., 2004; Cooper et al., 2003)

Provide mechanisms for groups to deal with uncooperative members. Some faculty structure group tasks to include anonymous follow-up assessments in which each student comments on the participation of other group members, identifying who did extra work and who shirked. If several people indicate that a student was a shirker, he or she receives a lower grade than the rest of the group. This system works best when groups have a mid-project discussion of whether any members are not doing their share. Members who are perceived as shirkers then have an opportunity to make amends.

Here are some other options for dealing with shirkers (from Oakley, 2002; Race, 2000; Walvoord, 1986):

- Limit groups to three students: it is hard to be a shirker in a small group.
- Give the groups some advice on handling unproductive group behavior:
  - As a group, agree on expectations of members and the consequences for violations.
  - Address problem behaviors as soon as they occur rather than hoping they will get better over time.
  - If a group member doesn't respond to e-mails or phone messages, don't waste more time trying to follow up.
  - If a student misses meetings and fails to turn in satisfactory work, his or her name will not go on the finished product.
- Allow the groups, by majority vote, to dismiss a member who is not carrying a fair share. Students who are dropped have four options: persuade the group to reconsider, find acceptance in another group, complete the project on their own, or take a failing grade for the project.

Perhaps the best way to assure comparable effort by all group members is to design activities in which there is a clear division of labor and each student must contribute if the group is to reach its goal.

Encourage students to use technology to facilitate coordination. Remind students that they can replace meetings with audio and video conferences, online bulletin boards and chat rooms, and e-mail. Use a learning management system, such as Blackboard, or a collaborative and learning environment such as Sakai, or a social networking site, such as Facebook, that has private space (for groups to post and review materials, have online conversations, and so on) and public space (for classmates and faculty to view ongoing work). (Sources: Clyde and Delohery, 2005; Duarte and Snyder, 1999)

Evaluating Group Work

Ensure that the groups know how each member is doing. Groups need to know who needs more assistance in completing the assignment, and members need to know they cannot sit back and let others do all the work. You can see how individual students are progressing by giving spot quizzes and calling on students to give a status report on their group. (Source: Johnson et al., 1991)

Give students an opportunity to evaluate the effectiveness of their group. Once or twice during the group task, ask group members to discuss two questions: What action has each member taken that was helpful for the group? What action could each member take to make the group more effective?

At the end of the project, consider asking students to complete a brief confidential evaluation of the effectiveness of the group and its members. Develop the form in collaboration with your students; Web-based templates can make data collection and analysis easier. Here are some typical questions:

- Overall, how effectively did [name of team member] work on this task?
- To what extent did [name of team member]
  - prepare
  - listen carefully
  - participate
  - deliver on promises
  - ask for reactions to own contributions
  - encourage others to participate
  - respect others' ideas
  - deal constructively with conflicts
- Give an example of something you learned from [name of team member]

Some studies have found that end-of-course peer evaluations can undercut team cohesion and effectiveness (Bacon et al., 1999), perhaps because students will tolerate bad situations, rather than confronting team members, with the plan of "getting even" on the peer evaluation form. You can minimize this outcome by emphasizing that groups should have frequent, open conversations about their internal dynamics. (Sources: Barkley et al., 2004; Freeman and McKenzie, 2002; Gueldenzoph and May, 2002; Johnson et al., 1991; Walvoord, 1986)

Give students an opportunity to evaluate themselves. Help students reflect on what they have learned and how they have learned it. Consider asking students to complete a short questionnaire with items such as these (adapted from Barkley et al., 2004):

- In what ways did you help or hinder the progress of the group?
- From this experience, what did you learn about the course content?
- From this experience, what did you learn about how you interact with others?
- How will you apply what you have learned to new situations, your future goals, your study habits?
- What was the best/worst/most challenging thing that happened?

Decide how to grade members of the group. Explain your grading system to students before they begin their work. The system should encourage teamwork, positive interdependence, and individual accountability. Some faculty assign all students in the group the same grade on the group task. Grading students individually, they argue, inevitably leads to competition within the group and thus subverts the benefits of group work. However, students may view group grades as unfair to those who may not have carried their load. Other faculty grade the contribution of each student on the basis of individual test scores and the group's evaluation of each member's work.

If you are going to take into account the group's evaluation of each member's work, research shows that it is best to have students evaluate each other independently and confidentially, using holistic criteria (Sharp, 2006). Three methods for incorporating student evaluations are most commonly used:

- *Ask students to allocate points to themselves and others in the group based on their level of effort.* For example, if a group has four members, members are to allocate four points. If Kevis did more work than the others, Kevis might receive 1.3 points. If Jared and Julie did an equal amount of work, they would each receive 1 point. Oliver, who contributed less, would receive 0.7 point. Then if the group project receives a score of 80 percent from the instructor, Kevis would earn an individual score of 104 percent (1.3 × .80), Jared and Julie would each score 80 percent (1 × .80), and Oliver would score 56 percent (0.7 × .80).
- *A variant method asks students to assign percentages to members of the group.* Amanya and Anil, who did everything expected, would each be awarded 100 percent. Gina, who missed meetings and did work of inferior quality, might be awarded 80 percent, and Nadir, who picked up the slack, would be awarded 120 percent. Each student's percentage is used as a multiplier to determine the student's individual score on the project. If this group's project earns 40 points (out of 50), Amanya and Anil would each receive 40 points (100 percent × 40), Gina would receive 32 points (80 percent × 40 points), and Nadir would receive 48 points (120 percent × 40).
- *Ask students to give themselves and other group members a letter grade based on criteria established at the start of the project.* Each student then receives a grade that represents the average of the instructor's grade for the group's project, the student's grade of his or her own effort, and the grades the student received from the other students in the group.
- *Use statistical formulas to calculate student grades.* For example, one formula is Final Student Grade = IWF (Individual Weighting Factor) × Final Group Project Grade, where IWF = Individual Effort Rating divided by Average Effort

Rating for the Group. Statistical methods for calculating individual students' grades on the basis of their contributions are described in Sharp (2006).

If you choose to assign the same grade to all members in a group, the grade should not account for more than a small part of a student's grade in the class, since the group grade may reflect the average abilities of the students in the group rather than the individual's efforts and ability. Some faculty use class discussion to arrive at a set of weights for individual performance (self-rating) and team performance (members' contributions to the success of their team). (Sources: Cameron, 1999; Cheng and Warren, 2000; Freeman and McKenzie, 2002; Johnson et al., 1991; Johnston and Miles, 2004; Millis and Cottell, 1998; Sharp, 2006; Stein and Hurd, 2000)

Addressing Student and Faculty Concerns about Group Work

"I paid tuition to learn from a professor, not to work with classmates who don't know as much." Let students know at the beginning of the term that you will be using some group techniques. Inform students about the research studies on the effectiveness of collaborative learning and describe the role it will play in your course. (Source: Millis and Cottell, 1998)

"Our group just isn't working out." Encourage students to stick with it, and help them learn how to be effective group members by offering them some of the advice in Chapter 9, "Leading a Discussion," and Chapter 10, "Encouraging Student Participation in Discussion." Agree to changing group membership only as a last resort.

"Students won't want to work in groups." Some students may object, in part because most of their education has been based on individual effort, and they may feel uncomfortable helping others or seeking help. Or they may fear that some group members won't pull their weight. The best advice is to explain your rationale, design meaningful tasks, give students clear directions, set expectations for how team members are to contribute and interact, and invite students to try it.

"Students won't work well in groups." Most students can work well in groups if instructors set strong expectations at the beginning of the term, informally check in with groups to see how things are going, offer assistance as needed, and provide time for groups to assess their own effectiveness. See Chapter 10, "Encouraging Student Participation in Discussion," for suggestions on how to

minimize monopolizers, draw out quiet students, and generally engage all students in active participation.

"If I do group work, I won't be able to cover as much material during the semester." Adding group work may mean covering fewer topics. But research shows that students who work in groups develop better problem-solving skills and demonstrate better understanding of the material. Some instructors assign additional homework or readings and distribute lecture notes to compensate for the reduction in lecturing. (Sources: Cooper et al., 2003; Millis and Cottell, 1998)

Setting Up Study Groups

Tell students about the benefits of study groups. Study groups meet regularly outside of class to study together, read and review course material, complete course assignments, comment on each other's written work, and prepare for tests and exams. Research has shown that students of all ability levels can benefit from peer teaching and from explanations, comments, and instruction offered by classmates. Some faculty share with their students the results of studies (such as Laughlin et al., 2006) that show groups can come up with more efficient solutions than the best individuals working alone.

Explain how study groups work. In one model, all students in the study group read the same assignments and each member agrees to become an expert on one portion of the material, providing in-depth coverage and answering other members' questions. In another model, the group's activities vary from meeting to meeting and might include reviewing class notes to determine the most important points, going over a test to ensure that everyone understands all the answers, reviewing problem sets, and exchanging drafts of papers for peer editing. In a third model, each session is devoted to a set of study questions provided by the professor. After three or four weeks, each member must bring a study question related to the week's lecture, and these questions structure the discussion. At the end of each study session, the group selects the most valuable study questions and submits that set for review by the instructor. (Sources: Guskey, 1988; Johnson et al., 1991; Light, 1992)

If study groups are optional, offer students extra credit for participation. For example, students who are members of an official study group might get bonus points for each assignment, based on the average grade received by the individual group members.

Enumerate students' responsibilities. In formal study groups, students make agreements such as these:

- Attend all meetings, arrive on time, and arrive prepared
- Complete any tasks that the group assigns to its members
- Participate constructively during the sessions
- Promote other group members' learning and success
- Provide assistance, support, and encouragement to group members
- Limit gossip, socializing, and other nonproductive activities
- Be involved in periodic self-assessments to determine whether the study group is working successfully (Is too much work being required? Is the time in study group meetings well spent?)

In addition, advise students about the value of a clearly articulated agenda and purpose for each session. Study groups also work more efficiently if all logistical arrangements are set for the entire semester: meeting time, length, and location.

Help students locate meeting rooms. Arrange with your department or campus room scheduler to make available small meeting rooms for study groups. If appropriate, consider using group rooms in the residence halls.

Limit groups to five or six students. Groups larger than six have several drawbacks: students can easily become passive observers, students may not get the opportunity to speak frequently, and students' sense of community and responsibility may become tenuous.

In a large-enrollment class, have students sign up for groups scheduled to meet at different times. In large classes, have students form groups based solely on when they can regularly attend a study group meeting. Try to form the groups by section, since students in the same section are more likely to feel a sense of responsibility for one another.

In other classes, let students select their own study groups. If students will be selecting their own groups, schedule several group activities during the early weeks of class and rotate the membership of these ad hoc groups so that students can get to know one another's interests and capabilities. Arrange one or two open groups for students who do not know others in the class.

Use a portion of class time to establish study groups. Announce that study groups will be set up during the second or third week of the course. At that time, hand out a description of students' responsibilities, and let students form groups or sign up for scheduled time slots. Suggest that all members of the study group exchange contact information and select one person as the convener, who will let all members know where the group will meet.

Have the study groups meet during one class session. Ask students to meet in their study groups to review course material or prepare for an exam or assignment. Use the time to check in with the groups to see how well they are operating. Some faculty regularly substitute study group meetings for lectures. To the extent possible, at least once during the semester, review a status report from each study group or meet briefly with each study group.

References

Astin, A. W. *What Matters in College? Four Critical Years Revisited*. San Francisco: Jossey-Bass, 1993.

Bacon, D. R., Stewart, K. A., and Silver, W. S. "Lessons from the Best and Worst Student Team Experiences: How a Teacher Can Make the Difference." *Journal of Management Education*, 1999, *23*(5), 467–488.

Barkley, E. F., Cross, K. P., and Major, C. H. *Collaborative Learning Techniques: A Handbook for College Faculty*. San Francisco: Jossey-Bass, 2004.

Bean, J. C. *Engaging Ideas: The Professor's Guide to Integrating Writing, Critical Thinking and Active Learning in the Classroom*. San Francisco: Jossey-Bass, 1996.

Blowers, P. "Using Student Skill Self-Assessments to Get Balanced Groups for Group Projects." *College Teaching*, 2003, *51*(3), 106–110.

Bonwell, C. C., and Eison, J. A. *Active Learning: Creating Excitement in the Classroom*. Washington, DC: ASHE and George Washington University, 1991.

Brufee, K. A. *Collaborative Learning: Higher Education, Interdependence, and the Authority of Knowledge*. (2nd ed.) Baltimore, MD: Johns Hopkins University Press, 1999.

Cameron, B. J. *Active Learning*. Halifax, Canada: Society for Teaching and Learning in Higher Education, 1999.

Cheng, W., and Warren, M. "Making a Difference: Using Peers to Assess Individual Students' Contributions to a Group Project." *Teaching in Higher Education*, 2000, *5*(2), 243–256.

Clyde, W., and Delohery, A. *Using Technology in Teaching*. New Haven, CT: Yale University Press, 2005.

Cooper, J. L., Robinson, P., and Ball, D. (Eds.). *Small Group Instruction in Higher Education: Lessons from the Past, Visions of the Future*. Stillwater, OK: New Forums Press, 2003.

Cottell, P. G. "Let Your Students Set the Curve with a Cooperative Exam Critique." *Journal of Cooperation and Collaboration in College Teaching*, 2000, *10*(1), 5–8.

Deeter-Schmelz, D. R., Kennedy, K. N., and Ramsey, R. P. "Enriching Our Understanding of Student Team Effectiveness." *Journal of Marketing Education*, 2002, *24*(2), 114–124.

Duarte, D. L., and Snyder, N. T. *Mastering Virtual Teams: Strategies, Tools and Techniques That Succeed.* San Francisco: Jossey-Bass, 1999.

Engle, R. A., and Conant, F. R. "Guiding Principles for Fostering Productive Disciplinary Engagement: Explaining an Emergent Argument in a Community of Learners Classroom." *Cognition and Instruction,* 2002, *20*(4), 399–483.

Freeman, M., and McKenzie, J. "SPARK, A Confidential Web-Based Template for Self and Peer Assessment of Student Teamwork: Benefits of Evaluating across Different Subjects." *British Journal of Educational Technology,* 2002, *33*(5), 551–569.

Gueldenzoph, L. E., and May, G. L. "Collaborative Peer Evaluation: Best Practices for Group Member Assessments." *Business Communication Quarterly,* 2002, *65*(1), 9–20.

Guskey, T. R. *Improving Student Learning in College Classrooms.* Springfield, IL: Thomas, 1988.

Jaques, D., and Salmon, G. *Learning in Groups.* (4th ed.) New York: Routledge, 2007.

Johnson, D. W., Johnson, R. T., and Smith, K. A. "Cooperative Learning: Increasing College Faculty Instructional Productivity." *ASHE-ERIC Higher Education Report,* 1991, no.4. (Publication of the School of Education and Human Development, George Washington University, Washington, DC)

Johnston, L., and Miles, L. "Assessing Contributions to Group Assignments." *Assessment and Evaluation in Higher Education,* 2004, *29*(6), 751–768.

Laughlin, P. R., Hatch, E. C., Silver, J. S., and Boh, L. "Groups Perform Better Than the Best Individuals on Letters-to-Numbers Problems: Effects of Group Size." *Journal of Personality and Social Psychology,* 2006, *90*(4), 644–651.

Light, R. J. *The Harvard Assessment Seminars: Second Report.* Cambridge, MA: Harvard University, 1992.

Lyons, R. E., McIntosh, M., and Kysilka, M. L. *Teaching College in an Age of Accountability.* Boston: Allyn and Bacon, 2003.

Meyers, C., and Jones, T. B. *Promoting Active Learning: Strategies for the College Classroom.* San Francisco: Jossey-Bass, 1993.

Michaelsen, L. K., Knight, A. B., and Fink, L. D. (Eds.). *Team-Based Learning: A Transformative Use of Small Groups in College Teaching.* Sterling, VA: Stylus, 2004.

Millis. B. J., and Cottell, P. G. *Cooperative Learning for Higher Education Faculty.* Westport, CT: American Council on Education and Oryx Press, 1998.

Oakley, B. "It Takes Two to Tango: How 'Good' Students Enable Problematic Behavior in Teams." *Journal of Student Centered Learning,* 2002, *1*(1), 19–27.

Page, S. E. *The Difference: How the Power of Diversity Creates Better Groups, Firms, Schools and Societies.* Princeton, NJ: Princeton University Press, 2007.

Pascarella, E. T., and Terenzini, P. T. *How College Affects Students: A Third Decade of Research.* Vol. 2. San Francisco: Jossey-Bass, 2005.

POD Listserv: An unmoderated online community for instructors and administrators with interests in teaching and learning in higher education; see http://podnetwork.org.

Prichard, J. S., Stratford, R. J., and Bizo, L. A. "Team-Skills Training Enhances Collaborative Learning." *Learning and Instruction,* 2006, *16*(3), 256–265.

Prichard, J. S., Stratford, R. J., and Hardy, C. *Training Students to Work in Teams: Why and How?* York, UK: Learning and Teaching Support Network in Psychology (LTSN), 2004.

Prince, M. "Does Active Learning Work? A Review of the Research." *Journal of Engineering Education,* 2004, *93*(3), 223–231.

Race, P. *500 Tips on Group Learning.* Sterling, VA: Stylus, 2000.

Sharp, S. "Deriving Individual Student Marks from a Tutor's Assessment of Group Work." *Assessment and Evaluation in Higher Education*, 2006, *31*(3), 329–343.

Slavin, R. E. "Research on Cooperative Learning and Achievement: What We Know, What We Need to Know." *Contemporary Educational Psychology*, 1996, *21*(1), 43–69.

Springer, L., Stanne, M. E., and Donovan, S. S. "Effects of Small-Group Learning on Undergraduates in Science, Mathematics, Engineering, and Technology: A Meta-Analysis." *Review of Educational Research*, 1999, *69*(1), 21–51.

Stein, R. F., and Hurd, S. *Using Student Teams in the Classroom: A Faculty Guide*. Bolton, MA: Anker, 2000.

Tiberius, R. G. *Small Group Teaching: A Trouble-Shooting Guide*. London: Kogan Page, 1999.

Toppins, A. D. "Teaching by Testing: A Group Consensus Approach." *College Teaching*, 1989, *37*(3), 96–99.

Walvoord, B. F *Helping Students Write Well: A Guide for Teachers in All Disciplines*. (2nd ed.) New York: Modern Language Association, 1986.

22

Informal Group Learning Activities

Instructors can encourage learning and student interaction by incorporating informal group activities into their teaching repertoire. The following activities can be carried out in classes of any size in almost any discipline, to reinforce concepts, check on students' understanding, or offer a change of pace. Some of these activities require planning and preparation, and some require that students work in pairs or groups outside the classroom.

If you are teaching a lecture course, you might want to select one or two activities that suit your course objectives and see how your students respond. For best results, avoid introducing too many new activities in any one course and try to avoid overusing any one activity.

General Strategies

Form ad hoc groups or pairs during a class session. To increase student participation and interaction, divide your class into small groups for an in-class exercise. Ask students to form groups with two, three, or four people sitting nearby. Have students turn to people behind (or in front of) them since students may sit next to people they know. Or ask them to form small groups with students they don't already know and to introduce themselves before working on the task. Another method is to have students count off (1, 2, 3, up to the number of groups you need), and have students gather by number (1s, 2s, and so on) to work on the task.

Give clear instructions. Explain to students the nature of the activity, your expectations, what they are to accomplish, and the amount of time they are to spend on the activity. Identify a signal for groups to stop working; for example, a raised hand, a timer, or a whistle.

Get feedback from students during the term. Ask students to give you informal feedback immediately after an activity, or conduct a midsemester evaluation to help you understand what is working and what needs to be improved. See Chapter 52, "Early Feedback to Improve Teaching and Learning."

Consult books and Web sites for ideas for activities. Search for Web sites devoted to "active learning" and review books that have compiled and catalogued hundreds of informal learning activities, such as Barkley, Cross, and Major (2004); Bean (1996); Jaques and Salmon (2007); Silberman (2006); and Staley (2003). The examples below are a sample of what you might do in your classroom.

Examples of Activities

Turn to your neighbor. Pose a problem or a question and ask students to think about it for a minute. Then ask them to turn to the person next to them and share their thoughts. After a few minutes, ask several pairs of students to share their thoughts with the entire class. This technique encourages the exchange of ideas, and it helps students clarify points or apply concepts to a problem or situation. (Sources: Cameron, 1999; Lyman, 1992)

ConcepTests. During a lecture, challenge students with a moderately difficult question—one that only 35–70 percent of students will be able to answer correctly. Give them a few moments to compose their thoughts and then have them discuss their answers with a partner or a small group. When students disagree, each should try to persuade the others by explaining their reasoning. Studies show that students in introductory physics lecture classes did better on exams when ConcepTests were used as part of a traditional lecture format. Questions can be drawn from points that are difficult or frequently misunderstood, or from past exam questions missed by half the class. (Source: Mazur, 1997)

Buzz groups. Buzz groups are teams of four or five students that form extemporaneously to respond to one or more questions; the groups can discuss the same question or different questions. Discussion is informal and students do not need to arrive at consensus—they simply exchange ideas. In a variation called *Snowball*, the size of the groups doubles with every round, and the tasks become more difficult. For example, during the first round, group members share their ideas; during the second round, the larger groups identify common patterns among the ideas; and during the third round, the still-larger groups develop guidelines, principles, or action plans. Buzz groups are typically used as a warm-up for class discussion. (Sources: Barkley et al., 2004; Jaques and Salmon, 2007)

Learning cells. For homework, students are given reading assignments and asked to prepare two questions about the reading. During class, students pair off and ask and answer each other's questions. In one variation, students have read the same assignment, and they compare their comprehension and recall, and clarify their understanding of the material. In another variation, students are assigned different readings and they pool their information and perspectives. (Source: Goldschmid, 1971)

Concept mapping. A concept map illustrates the connections between terms, ideas, or concepts. Students working alone or in groups construct a concept map by connecting individual terms with lines whose labels indicate the relationship between the terms. Developing a concept map requires students to identify and organize information and to establish relationships between pieces of information. Students create nodes which identify concepts, and the nodes are connected by lines labeled to indicate the relationship between the concepts. As appropriate, instructors can give clues about the connections. For examples of concept maps, see the references cited below and use your Web browser to search for "concept map tutorials." Some studies show that students using concept maps achieve at higher levels and retain information longer. Although students may understand and appreciate the value of concept mapping, they tend not to adopt it in their own studying. (Source: Fox and Morrison, 2005; Nakhleh and Saglam, 2005; Romance and Vitale, 1999; Santhanam et al., 1998)

Mind maps. As Budd (2004) notes, a mind map is an outline in which the major categories radiate from a central image, and lesser categories are portrayed as branches of larger branches. Students use graphics, images, and color to identify themes, subthemes, and supporting examples. For example, instructors have asked students to construct mind maps for the concept of supply and demand in housing prices. Students draw a house in the middle of a page and on one side draw pictures of supply (for example, land, construction, regulations). On the other side of the house, students draw pictures of demand (for example, location, features, affordability). Mind maps can be used during class to help students, individually or in groups, explore a concept or issue. (Source: Budd, 2004)

Jigsaw. In jigsaw projects, each member of a group completes a discrete part of an assignment. When members have completed their tasks, they report their findings to the rest of the group, and the group joins the pieces to form a finished project. For example, in a chemistry course each student in a six-person group could be assigned to research a different form of power generation (nuclear, fossil fuel, hydroelectric, and so on) and then to teach the key concepts to other members of the group. The group then comes together to prepare a comprehensive report. When all groups are working on the same topic, members of different groups who are working on the same subtopic can meet to develop strategies for teaching the material to their home group.

The jigsaw principle is commonly used to structure discussions. Students work in small groups, each of which develops expertise on a topic and formulates ways to teach their topic. These expert groups then break up, and students move to a new group, which consists of students who have developed expertise in different subtopics. In these second-round groups, students teach the material and lead the discussion on their particular subtopic. For example, in an English class, each group is assigned an author who incorporated autobiographical elements in their short stories. During the second round, students take turns leading the discussion, as the groups talk about each of the authors. The instructor then reconvenes the entire class for a discussion comparing the different authors' uses of autobiographical material. Resources and guidelines for using jigsaws can be found at www.jigsaw.org. (Sources: Barkley et al., 2004; Jaques and Salmon, 2007; Lai and Wu, 2006)

WebQuests. Students engaged in a WebQuest undertake a structured inquiry in which the information comes from online resources. The instructor provides the students with most or all of the following elements: descriptive background information, a statement of a specific task, a list of Web-based information resources, a description of the research process to accomplish the task, and suggestions for organizing the information and reflecting on the process and results. This design enables students to focus on interpreting information rather than searching for it. Collections of WebQuests and instructional resources can be found at webquest.org. Professors have used WebQuests on topics as diverse as human cloning, reducing whale mortality from collisions with ships or entanglement in fishing gear, differentiating satire and parody, and deciding whether to choose paper or plastic. (Sources: Dodge, 1995; Lamb and Teclehaimanot, 2005; Zheng et al., 2005)

Two-column lists. Students are asked to create a two-column list that compares views or presents the pros and cons of a position, and they are told to list every relevant point they can think of for each column. These lists are used to launch a discussion. The requirement to jot down items in both columns generally results in a more thorough and thoughtful discussion of the topic.

KWL. *KWL* stands for "what I know," "what I want to know," and "what I learned." To introduce a new topic, the instructor asks students to list what they know and what they want to know about that topic. The instructor collects these lists and uses them to correct erroneous preconceptions and to adjust the course content to reflect students' knowledge and interests. At the end of the unit, students list what they have learned. The instructor collects and reads all the lists but does not grade them. (Source: Fritz, 2002)

Send-a-problem. Each group of students is given a problem, tries to solve it, and then passes the problem and solution to a nearby group. Without looking at the previous group's solution, the next group works to solve the problem. After several passes, the groups analyze, evaluate, and synthesize the responses to the problem they received in the final pass and report the best solution to the class. This strategy works best when the problems are complex and do not have a single right answer. For example, an instructor in urban planning asked student groups to work on a residential rezoning problem. During the last round, the groups evaluated the solutions they had received and selected the best one. (Source: Barkley et al., 2004)

Challenging questions. Give a challenging question for groups or pairs to resolve or, better yet, ask students to pose and answer an interesting question based on the principles discussed in the course. Here are examples from an economics course: Why are child seats required in cars but not in airplanes? Why are brown eggs more expensive than white ones even though they taste the same and have identical nutritional value? Why do brides spend so much money on a wedding dress they will never wear again, while grooms often rent cheap tuxedos though they may have many future occasions that call for them?

These intriguing questions (and the economic explanations) are among those described in Frank (2007).

Debates. Debates provide an efficient structure for class presentations when the subject matter easily divides into opposing views or pro and con positions. For formal debates, students are assigned to teams, given a position to defend, and asked to present arguments in support of their position and to rebut the arguments presented by the opposing team. The assignment for a formal debate states a clear, unambiguous positive proposition, specifies the time allotments for each speaker (usually five minutes or less), and explains the responsibilities of each speaker. In traditional debates, for example, the first affirmative speaker defines the main terms and outlines the affirmative case; the first negative speaker contests poorly defined terms and outlines the negative case; the second affirmative and negative speakers complete the case for their side by providing evidence; and the rebuttal speakers focus on the weaknesses in the most important arguments of the opposing case. Students who are not debating can serve as judges and keep a record of the arguments. As a follow-up, each student writes a brief summary of either the affirmative or negative side of the debate that includes the thesis, reasons, and evidence.

For informal debates, you can pose a proposition and ask those who agree to sit in one section of the room and those who disagree to sit in the other. You may also want to create a third section for those who are undecided. Ask students from one section, then the other, to support their position. At set intervals (ten or fifteen minutes), ask students to move to another section if they have changed their minds. A variant approach is to rename the sections after students have chosen sides and have students argue for the opposite of their original position. This technique may help students move beyond a "right versus wrong" understanding of an issue to a more tolerant and nuanced view.

For examples of debate questions and supporting materials, see the series *Taking Sides: Clashing Views in . . . .* The series comes with an instructor's guide, and the more than two dozen books include debate questions and relevant readings in fields such as history, bioethics, psychology, political science, criminal justice, business, and anthropology. For example, *Taking Sides: Clashing Views on Educational Issues* poses debate questions (Is privatization the hope of the future? Can federal initiatives rescue failing schools?) and presents primary source articles to support each position. (Sources: Bean, 1996; Crone, 1997; Goodwin, 2003)

Panel discussions. Students divide into panels and each panel is assigned a topic to research. On presentation day, each panelist makes a very short presentation before the floor is opened to questions from the class. Panel discussions are most successful when instructors offer students sufficient direction on how to prepare their presentations and prepare for the question-and-answer follow-up.

References

Barkley, E. F., Cross, K. P., and Major, C. H. *Collaborative Learning Techniques: A Handbook for College Faculty*. San Francisco: Jossey-Bass, 2004.

Bean, J. C. *Engaging Ideas: The Professor's Guide to Integrating Writing, Critical Thinking, and Active Learning in the Classroom*. San Francisco: Jossey-Bass, 1996.

Budd, J. W. "Mind Maps as Classroom Exercises." *Journal of Economic Education*, 2004, *35*(1), 35–46.

Cameron, B. J. *Active Learning*. Halifax, Canada: Society for Teaching and Learning in Higher Education, 1999.

Crone, J. A. "Using Panel Debates to Increase Student Involvement in the Introductory Sociology Class." *Teaching Sociology*, 1997, *25*(3), 214–218.

Dodge, B. "WebQuests: A Technique for Internet-Based Learning." *Distance Educator*, 1995, *1*(2), 10–13.

Fox, J., and Morrison, D. Using Concept Maps in Learning and Teaching. In P. Hartley, A. Woods, and M. Pill (Eds.), *Enhancing Teaching in Higher Education: New Approaches for Improving Student Learning*. New York: Routledge, 2005.

Frank, R. H. *The Economic Naturalist: In Search of Explanations for Everyday Enigmas*. New York: Basic Books, 2007.

Fritz, M. "Using a Reading Strategy to Foster Active Learning in Content Area Courses." *Journal of College Reading and Learning*, 2002, *32*(2), 189–194.

Goldschmid, M. L. "The Learning Cell: An Instructional Innovation." *Learning and Development*, 1971, *2*(5), 1–6.

Goodwin, J. "Students' Perspectives on Debate Exercises in Content Areas Classes." *Communication Education*, 2003, *52*(2), 157–163.

Jaques, D., and Salmon, G. *Learning in Groups*. (4th ed.) New York: Routledge, 2007.

Lai, C-Y., and Wu, C-C. "Using Handhelds in a Jigsaw Cooperative Learning Environment." *Journal of Computer Assisted Learning*, 2006, *22*(4), 284–297.

Lamb, A., and Teclehaimanot, B. A Decade of WebQuests: A Retrospective. In M. Orey, J. McClendon, and R. M. Branch, (Eds.), *Educational Media and Technology Yearbook*. Vol. 30. Englewood, CO: Libraries Unlimited, 2005.

Lyman, F. T. Think-Pair-Share, Thinktrix, Thinklinks, and Weird Facts: An Interactive System for Cooperative Learning. In N. Davidson and T. Worsham (Eds.), *Enhancing Thinking through Cooperative Learning*. New York: Teachers College Press, 1992.

Mazur, E. *Peer Instruction: A User's Manual*. Upper Saddle River, NJ: Prentice Hall, 1997.

Nakhleh, M. B., and Saglam, Y. Using Concept Maps to Figure Out What Your Students Are Really Learning. In N. J. Pienta, M. M. Cooper, and T. J. Greenbowe (Eds.), *Chemists' Guide to Effective Teaching*. Upper Saddle River, NJ: Prentice Hall, 2005.

Romance, N. R., and Vitale, M. R. "Concept Mapping as a Tool for Learning: Broadening the Framework for Student-Centered Instruction." *College Teaching*, 1999, *47*(2), 74–79.

Santhanam, E., Leach, C., and Dawson, C. "Concept Mapping: How Should It Be Introduced, and Is There Evidence for Long Term Benefit?" *Higher Education*, 1998, *35*(3), 317–328.

Silberman, M. *Teaching Actively*. Boston, MA: Pearson Education, 2006.

Staley, C. *Fifty Ways to Leave Your Lectern*. Belmont, CA: Wadsworth/Thomson, 2003.

"Taking Sides: Clashing Views in . . . ." A series of books from McGraw-Hill, various dates.

Zheng, R., Stucky, B., McAlack, M., Menchana, M., and Stoddart, S. "WebQuest Learning as Perceived by Higher-Education Learners." *TechTrends*, 2005, *49*(4), 41–49.

23

Formal Group Learning Activities

Students who ask questions, solve problems, create solutions, propose alternatives, engage in hands-on activities, and participate in learning groups are likely to learn more and retain information and skills longer than students who sit passively listening to a lecture (Astin, 1993; Pascarella and Terenzini, 2005; Prince, 2004).

This chapter surveys various approaches to structured group activities that will engage students. Some can easily be incorporated into a traditional lecture or discussion course, while several represent more complex and ambitious approaches to class format and structure. See also Chapter 24, "Case Studies" and Chapter 25, "Simulations: Role Playing, Games, and Virtual Worlds."

General Strategies

Select approaches that suit your style and educational objectives. Choose activities that feel comfortable. Begin by using one strategy during one or two class periods or for one segment of a course.

Teach students how to work with new approaches. Students may need some advice or help in taking a more active role in the classroom. Establish expectations for student engagement at the beginning of the course and reinforce your expectations throughout the term. Help students understand that they can learn more by doing rather than by listening, and by working with others rather than by working alone. (Sources: Felder and Brent, 1996; Leeds et al., 1998)

Get feedback from students during the term. A midsemester evaluation will help you see what is working and what needs to be improved. See Chapter 52, "Early Feedback to Improve Teaching and Learning."

Examples of Activities

Discovery learning. In a discovery format, the instructor presents a novel situation, an interesting puzzle, a set of observations to explain, or an open-ended question that students explore in a largely self-directed manner. Students may be asked to speculate, based on partial information, about what materials were used in ancient artifacts, or they may be asked to make hypotheses about the conductivity of various liquids. In the purest form of discovery learning, an instructor sets the problems and provides feedback on students' efforts but does not direct or guide those efforts. This pure form is rarely used in higher education because it can be very time consuming. More often, the instructor provides guidance throughout the process, in the form of identifying problem-solving activities, facilitating those activities during the discovery process, helping students stay on task, and pointing students toward appropriate resources. Studies show that guided discovery (a mix of instructor guidance and some free exploration) is more effective than pure discovery (where students receive little or no guidance). (Sources: Kirschner et al., 2006; Mayer, 2004; Prince and Felder, 2006)

Guided design. In guided design, which was developed in the field of engineering, students work in groups of four or five, and they are led through a complex sequence of steps to solve real-world problems, with the instructor providing feedback at each step. These steps might include defining the situation, stating the problem and goal to be achieved, generating ideas and selecting the best one, defining the new situation that would result when the selected idea is implemented, preparing a detailed plan to implement the idea, implementing the plan, and evaluating and learning from the success or failure of the process and the plan. Guided design serves as a bridge from single-solution textbook problems to applied open-ended problems. For example, in a course on the mechanics of materials, an instructor used this process to have students redesign a gate at a parking garage so that the gate would deflect on impact from a car, avoiding structural damage to the car. (Sources: Wales and Stager, 1982; Wankat, 2002)

Team-based learning. In team-based learning, a course unit begins with students completing an initial set of tasks, which may include reading or lab assignments. Students then take a short multiple-choice readiness assessment test that measures their understanding of the basic concepts. After students take the test individually, they meet in their assigned groups to discuss the questions and reach consensus on the answers. Both the students' individual scores and their team scores are recorded and will be used in the calculation of their grade in the course. The instructor offers a short lecture to clarify any problems that surfaced during the assessment test. Next, the groups undertake a challenging assignment; for example, in a psychology course, groups were asked to determine which psychological phenomena explain people's failure to exercise regularly, floss daily, and eat more fruits and vegetables. Hosted by the University of Oklahoma, www.teambasedlearning.org offers guidelines, resources, examples, and implementation tips. (Source: Michaelsen et al., 2004)

Authentic learning. Authentic learning focuses on complex real-world problems and their solutions. The instructor selects a problem that is ill-defined and that requires sustained investigation and collaboration. Students are not given a list of resources but must conduct their own searches and distinguish relevant from irrelevant information. Authentic activities engage students in making choices, evaluating competing solutions, and creating a finished product. One instructor used authentic learning to have students assume the identities of stakeholders in the Mekong River Basin of Southeast Asia and debate the merits of a proposed development project using Mekong e-Sim, an online learning environment. Another used the technique to have students investigate the arsenic contamination of the water supply. Building a three-dimensional virtual reconstruction of an ancient Athenian marketplace was the goal of another effort. (Source: Lombardi, 2007)

Inquiry-based instruction. In *structured inquiry* learning, students are given a problem to solve, a method for solving the problem, and the necessary materials, but not the expected outcome. In *guided inquiry* or *inquiry-guided* learning, students must also figure out a method for solving the problem. Students thus develop their abilities to formulate good questions, identify and collect appropriate evidence, present results systematically, analyze and interpret results, formulate conclusions, and evaluate the worth and importance of those conclusions. Teaching methods, used singly or in combination, may include interactive lectures, discussion, group work, case studies, problem-based learning, simulations, fieldwork, and labs.

Guided-inquiry approaches can be most effective for small classes and also for first-year students who are forming habits of learning. In contrast, *open inquiry* learning requires students to also formulate the problem they will investigate. Like independent research, open inquiry is most appropriate for advanced students.

In *process-oriented guided inquiry learning (POGIL)*, developed by faculty in chemistry, students working in small groups are given data or information and a set of leading questions designed to guide them to formulate their own conclusions. The learning cycle consists of exploration, concept invention or formation, and application, under the guidance of the instructor. The POGIL Web site (www.pogil.org) offers descriptions of the method and instructional materials.

Studies show that, compared with other forms of instruction, inquiry-based instruction yields equal or higher scores on achievement tests, less student attrition, and greater student satisfaction with the method of instruction. Inquiry-based methods are used extensively in the sciences; guided inquiry is particularly popular in chemistry. (Sources: Cooper, 2005; Lee, 2004; Prince and Felder, 2006)

Problem-based learning. PBL, developed in the field of medicine, is an instructional method in which carefully crafted open-ended problems are introduced at the beginning of the instructional cycle and used to provide the context and motivation for the learning that follows. Instead of teaching students what they need to know and then posing problems, PBL begins with a problem that determines what students study. The problems derive from observable phenomena or events, which students come to understand as they learn about the underlying explanatory theories. Students engage in self-directed learning, most often in groups.

For example, students are presented with an open-ended, real-world problem, which they are asked to analyze and then to generate hypotheses that explain the data or phenomena, request additional data to support or challenge the hypotheses, identify questions for additional independent study, and determine how to proceed. The emphasis is on learning a subject by tackling a problem, rather than on problem solving per se; indeed, the problem may not be solvable. The simplest problems may require a few days of work, but the method is also used on complicated problems that take an entire semester.

Courses using PBL may incorporate a variety of formats:

- *Small-group discussion with an instructor.* Students meet as a group with a faculty member who serves as facilitator and occasional expert as students discuss a problem.
- *Collaborative learning groups.* Students meet in groups, usually during part of a class session, to solve a problem, with the instructor available to all groups as a consultant.
- *Case method.* Developed in business and law education, the case method involves a large group of students in the discussion of a problem that has been carefully analyzed by students prior to the class session. The instructor leads the class discussion, which focuses on critical analysis, exploration of multiple perspectives, application of ideas and principles, and decision making.
- *Lectures.* The instructor begins a lecture by presenting a problem for class discussion.

For instructors using this method, a critical task is developing a good problem, a problem that raises a compelling issue and that is tied to course objectives.

The University of Delaware (www.udel.edu/pbl) and Samford University (www .samford.edu/ctls/problem_based_learning.html) host Web sites on PBL with descriptive information, examples, syllabi, and other resources. PBL also requires considerable subject matter expertise and flexibility on the part of instructors, who must be able to guide students to the relevant facts, laws, principles, and theories. Instructors also need skills and patience in working with students who are unaccustomed to handling project management and interpersonal conflicts.

Studies have shown the positive effects of PBL on students' skill development, intrinsic motivation, ability to work in teams, and retention of knowledge over long periods of time. However, some research shows that compared to conventionally taught students, PBL students have gaps in their cognitive knowledge and may see themselves as less well prepared in the discipline. (Sources: Albanese and Mitchell, 1993; Duch et al., 2001; Gijbels et al., 2005; Hativa, 2000; Hmelo-Silver, 2004; Knowlton and Sharp, 2003; Prince, 2004; Prince and Felder, 2006; Savin-Baden, 2003; Schwartz et al., 2001)

Project-based learning. Project-based learning begins with the assignment of one or more tasks that will lead to the creation of a final product (for example, a design, model, device, or computer simulation). Different types of project-based learning offer students different degrees of autonomy:

- On task projects, student teams work on projects that have been defined by the instructor and they rely heavily on methods prescribed by the instructor.
- On discipline projects, the instructor defines the subject area and the general approaches to be used, but the students identify the specific project and select the particular approach.
- On problem projects, students are almost completely free to choose their project and their approach.

Project-based learning is common in engineering; resources for engineering courses are available at www.pble.ac.uk (a consortium of universities in the United Kingdom). More general information on project-based learning is available at Boise State's Web site (www.pbl-online.org).

Project-based learning is similar to problem-based learning in that teams of students work on open-ended assignments, formulate solution strategies, and continually reevaluate their approach in response to the outcomes of their efforts. But project-based learning typically has a broader scope and may encompass several problems. Moreover, in project-based learning the end product is a central focus of the assignment, and the completion of the project relies heavily on the application of previously acquired knowledge. In problem-based learning, in contrast, the emphasis falls on acquiring new knowledge, and the solution is less important than the knowledge gained in pursuing it.

Studies show that relative to traditionally taught students, students who participate in project-based learning are more motivated, demonstrate better communication and teamwork skills, and have a better understanding of issues and how to apply their learning to realistic problems. However, they may acquire a less complete mastery of content fundamentals. In addition, some students are unhappy about the time and effort required by projects and about the interpersonal conflicts caused by teammates who slack off. They may also feel they work harder than students who are traditionally taught, and some dislike being tested individually after doing most of their work in groups (a common complaint of students working in teams). (Sources: Bacon, 2005; Donnelly and Fitzmaurice, 2005; Prince and Felder, 2006)

Addressing Student and Faculty Concerns

"Students don't like these kinds of activities; they prefer that I lecture." Students who are accustomed to being passive may need time to adjust to being active, and in the end some will still prefer traditional lectures. Explain the value of non-lecture activities at the beginning of the course, and reinforce your expectations throughout the term. Try as best as you can to avoid such pitfalls as assigning frustrating, unclear tasks and posing unrealistic timeframes. (Sources: Felder and Brent, 1996; Leeds et al., 1998)

"These kinds of strategies take too much class time." Formal group learning activities can take more class time than lecturing, but many instructors believe that engaging and challenging students is worth the cost of modestly pruning the curriculum and course objectives.

"I teach large-enrollment courses and it would be chaos to do anything but lecture." Faculty have had students in large classes inflate balloons to understand how the universe expands, or dunk plastic bottles into ice-filled plastic bags to explore the relationship of temperature to pressure. During these activities, the instructor is still in control, but the control is more subtle, as the instructor guides the students through the experiment. These activities are used to supplement, not to replace, the lectures. (Source: Caprio and Micikas, 1997–98)

"It takes too much time to prepare for this." You will probably need more preparation time at first, but only until you become familiar with a strategy.

On the other hand, you may find you feel energized by undertaking new instructional approaches.

"These kinds of activities are about entertainment and not about learning." Learning can be both fun and worthwhile. These strategies challenge students and require concentrated effort—they are not easy games or empty pastimes.

References

Albanese, M. A., and Mitchell, S. "Problem-Based Learning: A Review of the Literature on Its Outcomes and Implementation Issues." *Academic Medicine,* 1993, *68*(1), 52–81.

Astin, A. W. *What Matters in College? Four Critical Years Revisited.* San Francisco: Jossey-Bass, 1993.

Bacon, D. R. "The Effect of Group Projects on Content-Related Learning." *Journal of Management Education,* 2005, *29*(2), 248–267.

Caprio, M. W., and Micikas, L. B. "Getting There from Here." *Journal of College Science Teaching,* Dec. 1997–Jan. 1998, *27*(3), 217–221.

Cooper, M. M. An Introduction to Small-Group Learning. In N. J. Pienta, M. M. Cooper, and T. J. Greenbowe (Eds.), *Chemists' Guide to Effective Teaching.* Upper Saddle River, NJ: Pearson Prentice Hall, 2005.

Donnelly, R., and Fitzmaurice, M. Collaborative Project-Based Learning and Problem-Based Learning in Higher Education: A Consideration of Tutor and Student Roles in Learner-Focused Strategies. In G. O'Neill, S. Moore, and B. McMullin (Eds.), *Emerging Issues in the Practice of University Learning and Teaching.* Dublin: All Ireland Society for Higher Education (AISHE), 2005.

Duch, B. J., Groh, S. E., and Allen, D. E. *The Power of Problem-Based Learning.* Sterling, VA: Stylus, 2001.

Felder, R. M., and Brent, R. "Navigating the Bumpy Road to Student-Centered Instruction." *College Teaching,* 1996, *44*(2), 43–47.

Gijbels, D., Dochy, F., Van den Bossche, P., and Segers, M. "Effects of Problem-Based Learning: A Meta-Analysis from the Angle of Assessment." *Review of Educational Research,* 2005, *75*(1), 27–61.

Hativa, N. *Teaching for Effective Learning in Higher Education.* Norwell, MA: Kluwer Academic Publishers, 2000.

Hmelo-Silver, C. E. "Problem-Based Learning: What and How Do Students Learn?" *Educational Psychology Review,* 2004, *16*(3), 235–266.

Kirschner, P. A., Sweller, J., and Clark, R. E. "Why Minimal Guidance during Instruction Does Not Work: An Analysis of the Failure of Constructivist, Discovery, Problem-Based, Experiential, and Inquiry-Based Teaching." *Educational Psychologist,* 2006, *41*(2), 75–86.

Knowlton, D. S., and Sharp, D. C. (Eds.). *Problem-Based Learning in the Information Age.* New Directions for Teaching and Learning, no. 95. San Francisco: Jossy-Bass, 2003,

Lee, V. S. *Teaching and Learning through Inquiry: A Guidebook for Institutions and Instructors.* Sterling, VA: Stylus, 2004.

Leeds, M., Stull, W., and Westbrook, J. "Do Changes in Classroom Techniques Matter? Teaching Strategies and Their Effects on Teaching Evaluations." *Journal of Education for Business*, 1998, *74*(2), 75–78.

Lombardi, M. M. "Authentic Learning for the 21st Century: An Overview." *Educause Learning Initiative*, May 2007. http://connect.educause. edu/Library/ELI/AuthenticLearningforthe21/39343

Mayer, R. E. "Should There Be a Three-Strikes Rule against Pure Discovery Learning?" *American Psychologist*, 2004, *59*(1), 14–19.

Michaelsen, L. K., Knight, A. B., and Fink, L. D. (Eds.). *Team-Based Learning: A Transformative Use of Small Groups in College Teaching.* Sterling, VA: Stylus, 2004.

Pascarella, E. T., and Terenzini, P. T. *How College Affects Students: A Third Decade of Research.* Vol. 2. San Francisco: Jossey-Bass, 2005.

Prince, M. J. "Does Active Learning Work? A Review of the Research." *Journal of Engineering Education*, 2004, *93*(3), 223–231.

Prince, M. J., and Felder, R. M. "Inductive Teaching and Learning Methods: Definitions, Comparisons, and Research Bases." *Journal of Engineering Education*, 2006, *95*(2), 123–137.

Savin-Baden, M. *Facilitating Problem-Based Learning.* Berkshire, England: Society for Research in Higher Education and Open University Press, 2003.

Schwartz, P., Mennin, S., and Webb, G. *Problem-Based Learning: Case Studies Experience and Practice.* London: Kogan Page, 2001.

Wales, C. E., and Stager, R. A. "Teaching Decision Making with Guided Design." *Journal of College Science Teaching*, 1982, *12*(1), 24.

Wankat. P. C. *The Effective, Efficient Professor: Teaching, Scholarship and Service.* Boston: Allyn and Bacon, 2002.

24

Case Studies

The case method originated in the teaching of law and medicine (Boehrer and Linsky, 1990), was extended to business, and is now used in a wide range of disciplines in the humanities, social sciences, and physical and biological sciences (Dinan, 2005).

A case is a story or situation that illustrates a general problem or particular principle. A good case presents a realistic situation (factual or invented) and includes the relevant background, facts, conflicts, dilemmas, and sequences of events—up to the point requiring a decision or action. As students analyze and discuss the case, they retrace and critique the characters' actions, propose solutions, and try to deduce the outcome. Good cases often lend themselves to alternative actions and more than one solution.

General Strategies

Identify your teaching goals. Case studies may be incorporated into a course or serve as the central method for the course. Cases allow students to analyze, synthesize, and integrate information; to develop reasoning and problem-solving skills; to learn how to collaborate with peers; and to form judgments, weigh pros and cons, and critically evaluate solutions. (Sources: Boehrer, 1994; Grant, 1997; Smith and Murphy, 1998; Wilcox, 1999)

Determine how students will work on the case. Students can work individually, in pairs, in small groups, or as a whole class. Case studies particularly lend themselves to small groups, where multiple perspectives can support critical appraisal and broader understanding. Research has shown that students feel they learn more and like it better when they work on cases in groups than when they work alone. (Sources: Flynn and Klein, 2001; Fry et al., 2003)

Use more than one case in a course. Start out with a short case that will familiarize students with the method and process of working out a case. Build on their new skills and confidence by presenting increasingly more complex cases.

Your students' ability to learn from cases—and your facility in teaching cases—will improve with practice. (Sources: Bilica, 2004; Herreid, 2001)

Selecting a Case

Begin by using existing case studies. Before you create your own cases, use cases developed by others. The National Center for Case Study Teaching in Science at the State University of New York at Buffalo has a collection of cases in the physical, biological, and social sciences; the center also offers advice and resources on the case method and links to collections of cases in business, law, public policy, management, and international affairs. Some cases are entirely or mostly text-based; others include video reenactments and documentary accounts.

Select cases that exemplify major principles or key points. Choose cases with the following characteristics (adapted from Barnes et al., 1994; Lynn, 1999; Schullery, 1999):

- applicable to all the students in your class, despite their differences in academic focus or background
- complex enough to raise interesting questions and alternatives
- simple enough to prevent students from becoming lost in extraneous details
- amenable to more than one solution
- rich in characterizations, to allow for competing interpretations of motives
- manageable within the allotted class time
- manageable in terms of student preparation (for a case to be analyzed in a single class session, limit the advance reading to about three textbook pages)

Look for emotional as well as intellectual engagement. In the best case studies, students identify with the characters and the problems that befall them. If part of the appeal of the case is that it represents "current events," try to select a situation that is no more than five years old. (Source: Herreid, 2001)

Create a list of discussion questions. A case study should conclude with a short set of questions to stimulate thinking and discussion. The simplest of these questions may tap recall and comprehension (What are the facts of this case?). Subsequent questions should call for analysis, synthesis, and evaluation (What is the key problem? What issues need to be addressed?). Adjust the number and complexity of the questions to fit the skills and experience of your students. Students who are new to case-based learning will need more guidance. (Source: Leonard et al., 2002)

Preparing for a Case

Give students advice on how to prepare. Stress the importance of preparation. Outline the principal cognitive tasks: understanding all the facts, distinguishing facts from assumptions, distinguishing important from unimportant information, examining how people's motives shape their statements, identifying when more information is needed, and so on. Penn State University's Teaching and Learning with Technology Web site provides tips for students on how to read and understand case studies (tlt.its.psu.edu/suggestions/cases/). (Sources: Bilica, 2004; Honan and Rule, 2002)

Provide a structure that motivates students to come prepared. Students are more likely to be well prepared if you adopt one or more of the following strategies:

- Divide the class into small groups and ask them to review the case before the next session.
- Ask students or groups to submit a brief memo, due at the start of class, outlining recommendations for action.
- Assign each student to be prepared to either present the facts of the case or to critique the actions in the case.
- Assign students to be responsible for taking the part of specific characters or interests in the case.
- Select cases that can be completed within a single class session.

Prepare yourself to lead the discussion. Decide how you will start the discussion, and draw up a set of questions that highlight key points. Estimate how much time to spend on each question so that you can work through the case within the allotted time. Try to anticipate spots where students might get sidetracked or confused, and decide how you will respond. (Sources: Grant, 1997; Meyers and Jones, 1993)

Pay attention to the environment. If students don't know each other, have them wear name tags or place signs on their desks or tables. A circular or U-shaped arrangement of chairs is more conducive to discussion than long rows.

Conducting the Case

Begin by situating the case in the context of the course. Explain why you are presenting the case and how it relates to course content and learning goals. (Source: Grant, 1997)

Introduce the case, or have a student introduce it. The introduction should briefly summarize the situation and the protagonist's dilemma. You could also ask your students to write a one-sentence summary of the case, or have pairs of students collaborate on a summary. (Sources: Lynn, 1999; Wilcox, 1999)

Start the discussion by asking a general question. Ask students to identify one or two issues raised by the case or to answer previously assigned case questions. Or open by asking, "Whose viewpoint do you find most compelling?" (Sources: Cliff and Nesbitt-Curtin, 2000; Herreid, 2001)

Adopt a nondirective, facilitative role. Encourage and challenge, but let students do most of the talking. Direct your efforts toward helping students analyze the case, take a position, and defend their position. Keep the discussion going by asking questions like these (adapted from Grant, 1997):

> What possibilities for action are there?
> What are the consequences of each?
> What should Norma do at the first decision point?
> How did Norma get into this predicament?
> If you were a friend of Norma's, what advice might you have given?
> What actions should be taken?
> What concepts, principles, or theories seem to follow from this analysis?

Steer the discussion away from emotional material until the students have analyzed all the facts. Withhold your own opinions long enough for students to develop their own. (Sources: Boehrer, 1994; Herreid, 2001; Lynn, 1999)

Have a team of students lead the discussion. Assign all students to submit a recommendation for action, due a few days before the discussion. The team reviews the submissions, decides which of them to include in the discussion, and decides the order in which they will be discussed (for example, by placing the most controversial item first). The team follows that order in requesting students to justify their recommendations. At the end of the discussion, the instructor gives immediate feedback. (Source: Desiraju and Gopinath, 2001)

Concluding the Case Session

Summarize key points and help students understand what they have learned. Highlight key points and explain how the case relates to earlier or future topics in the course. Itemize which issues raised by the case were addressed, which issues were ignored, and what key questions remain.

For a real-life case, reveal the real-life conclusion. Present and discuss the conclusion, or assign students to research the events and find out what happened. Compare the actual conclusion with the recommendations made during the discussion.

Have students write about the case. Assign a short in-class writing exercise or a longer analysis for homework. If you grade students' written case analyses, distribute in advance the criteria you will be using. (Source: Gopinath, 2004)

Ask students to evaluate the discussion. For example, ask for a "one-word essay"—a single word from each student that best captures his or her experience of the discussion. (Source: Foran, 2001)

Creating Your Own Cases

Start by writing a few short cases. Lynn (1999) offers good advice on how to write a case study, and Liedtka (2001) discusses creating a case study based on a video. Cases for undergraduate courses may run ten to twenty pages with supporting documentation, but shorter cases are likely to be more effective. For a case focused on a specific problem, a few paragraphs may be sufficient.

Be on the lookout for ideas for cases. A good case poses a challenging problem. You may find the germ of a case in a news Web site, feature article, or a journal report, or in the experiences of professionals and practitioners in your field. True stories have an inherent appeal ("This really happened") and may offer closure ("This is how events resolved themselves"), but invented cases can also capture students' imagination and interest.

Write engagingly. Incorporate conflict and use quotations, as appropriate. Write in a way that forces the reader to a point of decision, but do not reveal the outcome.

Try out, revise, and try again. As you become comfortable with it, take note of which aspects the students latch onto. Sort out the obvious issues from the subtler ones, and listen for new ideas and perspectives that you may want to elicit in a future class. It often takes several trial runs and revisions to polish a case study. (Source: Forbes and Isabella, 1998)

References

Barnes, L. B., Christensen, C. R., and Hansen, A. J. *Teaching and the Case Method: Text, Cases, and Readings.* Boston: Harvard Business School Press, 1994.

Bilica, K. "Lessons from Experts: Improving College Science Instruction through Case Teaching." *School Science and Mathematics,* 2004, *104*(6), 273–278.

Boehrer, J. "On Teaching a Case" *International Studies Notes,* 1994, *19*(2), 14–20.

Boehrer, J., and Linsky, M. "Teaching with Cases: Learning to Question." In M. D. Svinicki (Ed.), *The Changing Face of College Teaching.* New Directions for Teaching and Learning, no. 42. San Francisco: Jossey-Bass, 1990.

Cliff, W. H., and Nesbitt-Curtin, L. "The Directed Case Method: Teaching Concept and Process in a Content-Rich Course." *Journal of College Science Teaching,* 2000, *30*(1), 64–66.

Desiraju, R., and Gopinath, C. "Encouraging Participation in Case Discussions: A Comparison of the MICA and the Harvard Case Methods." *Journal of Management Education,* 2001, *25*(4), 394–408.

Dinan, F. J. "Laboratory Base Case Studies: Closer to the Real World." *Journal of College Science Teaching,* 2005, *35*(2), 27–29.

Flynn, A. E., and Klein, J. D. "The Influence of Discussion Groups in a Case-Based Learning Environment." *Education Technology Research and Development,* 2001, *49*(3), 71–86.

Foran, J. "The Case Method and the Interactive Classroom." *Thought & Action,* 2001, *17*(1), 41–50.

Forbes, T., and Isabella, L. "One More Time: The Art of Revising Case Studies." *Management Communication Quarterly,* 1998, *11*(3), 486–492.

Fry, H., Ketteridge, S., and Marshall, S. *A Handbook for Teaching and Learning in Higher Education: Enhancing Academic Practice.* (2nd ed.) New York: RoutledgeFalmer, 2003.

Gopinath, C. "Exploring Effects of Criteria and Multiple Graders on Case Grading." *Journal of Education for Business,* 2004, *79*(6), 317–322.

Grant, R. "A Claim for the Case Method in the Teaching of Geography." *Journal of Geography in Higher Education,* 1997, *21*(2), 171–185.

Herreid, C. F. "Don't! What Not to Do When Teaching Cases." *Journal of College Science Teaching,* 2001, *30*(5), 292–294.

Honan, J. P., and Rule, C. S. *Using Cases in Higher Education: A Guide for Faculty and Administrators.* San Francisco: Jossey-Bass, 2002.

Leonard, J. A, Mitchell, K. L., Meyers, S. A., and Love, J. D. "Using Case Studies in Introductory Psychology." *Teaching of Psychology,* 2002, *29*(2), 142–144.

Liedtka, J. "The Promise and Peril of Video Cases: Reflections on Their Creation and Use." *Journal of Management Education,* 2001, *25*(4), 409–424.

Lynn, L. E., Jr. *Teaching and Learning with Cases: A Guidebook.* New York: Chatham House, 1999.

Meyers, C., and Jones, T. B. *Promoting Active Learning.* San Francisco: Jossey-Bass, 1993.

Schullery, N. "Selecting Workable Cases for Classroom Use." *Business Communication Quarterly,* 1999, *62*(4), 77–80.

Smith, R. A., and Murphy, S. K. "Using Case Studies to Increase Learning and Interest in Biology." *American Biology Teacher,* 1998, *60*(4), 265–268.

Wilcox, K. J. "The Case Method in Introductory Anatomy and Physiology: Using the News." *American Biology Teacher,* 1999, *61*(9), 668–671.

Simulations: Role Playing, Games, and Virtual Worlds

Simulations can be acted out in a classroom, played on a board, or run on a computer, and they can be incorporated into almost any course. Research suggests that well-chosen simulations can enhance student learning and motivation (DeNeve and Heppner, 1997; McCarthy and Anderson, 2000; Hertel and Millis, 2002). Some instructors have structured entire courses around such simulations as a mock trial (MacKay, 2000) or a negotiation (DeNeve and Heppner, 1997).

This chapter looks at three types of simulations (adapted from Educause Learning Initiative, 2006; Frederick, 1981; New Media Consortium and Educause Learning Initiative, 2007; Rymaszewski et al., 2006; Van Eck, 2006):

- In role playing, students are given a situation and a cast of characters, and they improvise dialogue and actions. In a literature class, students might be asked to play fictional characters and to respond to events that occur outside the novel in which they appeared. In language classes, students can enact everyday situations (ordering dinner in a restaurant, asking directions). In a city planning class, students might stage a meeting of the local landmarks commission.
- Board games and computer games have been developed to teach students about subjects as diverse as congressional redistricting and options for reform, life in a Darfur refugee camp, and the challenges of distributing food and resources to civilians caught in a war zone.
- Virtual worlds lend themselves to role playing and scenario building that allow learners to assume responsibilities without incurring real-world consequences. Students can give presentations, organize exhibits, build structures, talk with historical figures, practice crisis management, take field trips to museums and weather stations, view simulcast lectures, and connect with students, faculty, and experts around the world.

Role Playing

Begin informally. Start simple: divide the class into pairs and have all the pairs work for five or ten minutes on the same situation (buyer and seller; manager and employee; hero and villain; petition gatherer and reluctant voter). As students become comfortable with role playing, have some students observe others. If these activities are successful, move on to more complex role plays.

Create a compelling scenario. The best scenarios incorporate a compelling issue or problem that can be solved only through negotiation or analysis and action. The situation should involve choices, decisions, and conflicting motives and perspectives. Courtrooms, legislative chambers, and corporate boardrooms are traditional settings for conflict, but you can divide students into research teams that are competing to solve a problem, or assign students to play the role of cells undergoing mitosis, or have two competing groups attempt to persuade a third uncommitted group to adopt their policy. In "Reacting to the Past," developed by Barnard College, students are assigned roles and objectives informed by classic texts in the history of ideas. An instructor developed a "speed-dating" scenario in which students take on the identities of leading figures in the history of psychology. (Sources: Francis, 1999; McDaniel, 2000; Monahan, 2000; Wyn and Stegink, 2000; Zehr, 2004)

Identify the major roles. By yourself or with the class, develop statements that define the interests, capabilities, and limitations that come with each role. Inexperienced students will need more detail and structure, but give all students some latitude in how they portray the characters. Consider asking students in adversary roles to switch places midway through. (Source: Christensen et al., 1991)

Help students prepare. Give students reading assignments, data, and other materials. For one role-playing exercise in a psychology course, students kept a log of "overt displays of prejudice," and some events from the logs became part of the role play. (Sources: Plous, 2000; Smith and Boyer, 1996)

Set ground rules. Will students be allowed to do whatever pleasant or unpleasant things a real person might do? How free should students be in their language, rules of order, and movement?

Stay open to change as the action proceeds. Once the role play starts, students will have to make decisions and experience the consequences; the direction and outcome of the scene will reflect the decisions and choices they make early on. Monitor, coach, and intervene as necessary in order to keep the process going. (Source: Smith and Boyer, 1996)

Cut off the role play at a high point. If the situation does not call for consensus or a solution, stop the role playing before it languishes, even if students want to continue. This will make for livelier discussion. A short role play might last five to ten minutes.

Discuss and summarize. Begin the discussion immediately after the scene ends, when feelings and insights are freshest. You might pose general open-ended questions about what happened and why, or interview the players about their goals and actions.

Video Games and Virtual Worlds

Research commercial video games. Popular video games can be effective for learning because they have clear goals; they are immersive; they rely on problem-solving skills; they require players to make frequent decisions; and players immediately see the consequences of their actions. (Sources: Gee, 2007; Van Eck, 2006)

Explore virtual worlds. Some college and university courses meet in virtual worlds in which students engage in all sorts of activities: they analyze real-time data, model complex mathematical functions, stage dramas, build molecular models, conduct ethnographic research on residents, recreate historical events, understand schizophrenia through virtual hallucinations, practice their language skills, create videos, and respond to simulated disasters. Participants can create and use museums, labs, libraries, wikis, highly detailed three-dimensional renderings of buildings, and other educational resources. Typically virtual worlds showcase innovative educational projects and guide instructors on the best uses of virtual environments to promote student learning and higher level thinking.

Consider simulations as a course-hosting device. Some instructors now house their courses (or portions of them) on simulation Web sites, such as Second Life or the open source metaverse software Croquet. Each student in the course creates an avatar, and these courses have both real and virtual meetings. Avatars can communicate with others using text media or through VoIP (Voice over Internet Protocol) which lets users speak to one another. (Source: Educause Learning Initiative, June, 2008)

Keep in touch with rapid advances. The educational richness of this technology will likely expand. Educause.com is one good source of news about changing technologies. *Wikipedia* also provides updated resources on new technologies.

References

Christensen, C. R., Garvin, D. A., and Sweet, A. (Eds.). *Education for Judgment: The Artistry of Discussion Leadership*. Boston: Harvard Business School, 1991.

DeNeve, K. M., and Heppner, M. J. "Role Play Simulations: The Assessment of an Active Learning Technique and Comparisons with Traditional Lectures." *Innovative Higher Education*, 1997, *21*(3), 231–246.

Educause Learning Initiative. "7 Things You Should Know About Virtual Worlds." June, 2006. http://connect.educause.edu/Library/ELI/7ThingsYouShouldKnowAbout/39392

Educause Learning Initiative. "7 Things You Should Know About Second Life." June, 2008. http://connect.educause.edu/Library/ELI/7ThingsYouShouldKnowAbout/46892

Francis, P. J. "Using Role-Playing Exercises to Teach Astronomy." *The Physics Teacher*, October 1999, *37*(7), 436–437.

Frederick, P. "The Dreaded Discussion: Ten Ways to Start." *Improving College and University Teaching*, 1981, *29*(3), 109–114.

Gee, J. P. *Good Video Games and Good Learning: Collected Essays on Video Games, Learning and Literacy*. New York: Peter Lang, 2007.

Hertel, J. P., and Millis, B. J. *Using Simulations to Promote Learning in Higher Education*. Sterling, VA: Stylus, 2002.

MacKay, C. "The Trial of Napoleon, A Case Study for Using Mock Trials." *Teaching History: A Journal of Methods*, 2000, *25*(2).

McCarthy, J. P., and Anderson, L. "Active Learning Techniques versus Traditional Teaching Styles: Two Experiments from History and Political Science." *Innovative Higher Education*, 2000, *24*(4).

McDaniel, K. N. "Four Elements of Successful Historical Role-Playing in the Classroom." *History Teacher*, 2000, *33*(3), 357–362.

Monahan, W. G. "Everybody Talks: Discussion Strategies in the Classroom." *Teaching History: A Journal of Methods*, 2000, *25*(1), 6–14.

New Media Consortium and Educause Learning Initiative, *Horizon Report*, 2007. http://www.nmc.org/horizon/2007/report

Plous, S. "Responding to Overt Displays of Prejudice: A Role-Playing Exercise." *Teaching of Psychology*, 2000, *27*(3), 198–200.

Rymaszewski, M., Au, W. J., Wallace, M., and others. *Second Life: The Official Guide*. Indianapolis, IN: Wiley, 2006.

Smith, E. T., and Boyer, M. A. "Designing In-Class Simulations." *PS: Political Science and Politics*, 1996, *29*(4), 690–694.

Van Eck, R. "Digital Game-Based Learning: It's Not Just the Natives Who Are Restless." *Educause Review*, 2006, *41*(2), 17–30.

Wyn, M. A., and Stegink, S. J. "Role-Playing Mitosis." *American Biology Teacher*, 2000, *62*(5), 378–381.

Zehr, D. "Two Active Learning Exercises for a History of Psychology Class." *Teaching of Psychology*, 2004, *31*(1), 54–56.

Service Learning and Civic Engagement

Many colleges and universities offer undergraduate students opportunities to learn by doing. Variously called *civic engagement, service learning, public service, community service, public scholarship, practica, social action engagement, ongoing scholarship,* or *fieldwork,* these efforts productively engage students with the community. Community engagement can take various forms (Bringle et al., 2003; Furco, 1996; University of California at Berkeley Task Force, 2000):

- *Community service* emphasizes a service activity such as helping rebuild housing in low-income communities hit by natural disasters, volunteering at recreational centers, or restoring creeks and watersheds. These service activities are not connected to any particular course or curriculum, and students typically do not receive extensive training or any academic credit.
- *Co-curricular service learning* incorporates training and allied activities, which precede or accompany the service. For example, undergraduate participants in the California Reads program (which focuses on literacy) receive scheduled training, keep daily logs, meet regularly with team leaders, and attend monthly development sessions. Students typically do not receive academic credit for participating in these programs.
- *Academic courses with a field or service component* entail one or more field assignments or service activities. For example, a course in architecture might include an assignment that requires interviewing local youth about a shelter for runaways.
- *Academic service learning* equally emphasizes academic work and service. The service experience is fully integrated into a discipline-based academic course, and the course content determines the type of service students undertake. For example, a course in the physiology of aging might require students to work one three-hour shift a week throughout the term at a nearby senior center to apply what they are learning to real-world situations. Service learning emphasizes reciprocity between students and an outside agency and its clients—the insights, experiences, and benefits each can offer the other—and includes a series of formal reflective activities. Experts continue to debate definitions and nuances of nomenclature. This chapter adopts the term *service learning* to represent a type of pedagogy that encompasses teaching and civic engagement.

Service learning courses can (1) broaden and deepen the intellectual content of undergraduate instruction by integrating theory and practice; (2) increase students' motivation to engage in academic work through the experience of applying knowledge; (3) encourage students to develop their skills as independent scholars and researchers; and (4) contribute to students' sense of civic and social responsibility (Braskamp et al., 2006). The length and duration of the service activity will, of course, depend on the number of credits that the course carries and the other course requirements (reading, papers, exams). For most service learning courses, experienced faculty recommend a service commitment of two or three hours a week (Ozorak, 2003).

Faculty report that incorporating fieldwork into their courses has enhanced their teaching experience and the quality of their instruction (Kendall et al., 1990). Well-structured service learning has also been shown to have positive academic, cognitive, attitudinal, career, and personal effects on students (Astin et al., 2000; Evangelopoulos et al., 2003; Kezar and Rhoads, 2001; Marullo, 1998).

Service learning can play a role is almost every academic discipline (*Service-Learning in the Disciplines*, 2000), and field assignments can be added to almost any course, including foreign languages ("A Spanish Course," 2002) and writing classes (Wills, 2005).

Initiating a service learning course is time consuming for an instructor, especially if your college or university does not have a central office that can assist with site placement, student orientation and debriefing, and logistical support. The following suggestions can help you create and teach a successful service learning course. The advice given here applies to other kinds of field-work assignments as well.

General Strategies

Tailor the service component to meet course goals and student learning outcomes. As Dewey (cited in Hutchings and Wutzdorff, 1988, p. 5) points out, "mere activity does not constitute experience." Service learning is most likely to provide academically valuable experience when the service is structured to serve specific learning goals and to meet real community needs, and when it is preceded by orientation and preparation. The broad goals for service learning may include making learning more meaningful by challenging students to apply theories and principles in the real world, helping students develop leadership skills, preparing students to join the workforce, and promoting students' civic engagement. (Sources: Chapdelaine et al., 2005; Colby et al., 2003; Ehrlich, 2000; Ostrow, 2004)

Consult national resources. About one thousand colleges and universities belong to Campus Compact, a leading resource for conceiving and implementing service learning programs that seek to improve community life and educate students about civic and social responsibility. The organization's Web site (compact.org) has an extensive collection of sample syllabi, assignments for structured reflection, toolkits, and publications. The online resources of the National Service Learning Clearinghouse (servicelearning.org) include a library of service learning materials and subscriptions to service learning e-mail lists and newsletters. Two other national organizations in this field are Learn and Serve America (learnandserve.gov), a federally funded effort to support and encourage service learning, and the National Society for Experiential Education (nsee.org), which offers online access to publications and resources.

Collaborate with other campus groups to identify service learning opportunities. Most real-world problems can best be addressed by multidisciplinary teams. When seeking partners, look to academic departments other than your own, as well as to the campus student affairs office, career counseling office, and other service centers. (Sources: Engstrom, 2003; Vaz, 2005)

Establish relationships with outside agencies. Nonprofit organizations can be natural partners for service learning and field assignments. Before referring students to these groups, create your own relationships with people in the organizations. (Sources: Jacoby, 2003; Rubin, 2001)

Offer options. Some faculty offer fieldwork experience as an alternative to a library or research project. By giving students a choice, you can accommodate students who are unable to commit the hours to an agency placement or who may have transportation problems. (Source: Kretchmar, 2001)

Organizing a Service-Learning Opportunity

Become familiar with the service setting before placing or sending students. Learn enough to know what your students are likely to encounter. Establish good contacts in each setting so that your students will be welcomed. When you meet with agency representatives, discuss the following topics:

- their needs and objectives
- the products or outcomes that could result from student placement
- how the project or activities fit your students' skills, academic needs, and learning goals

- the sources of any funding that may be required
- the resources your department might need to provide (for example, photocopying)

Avoid placements that involve clerical or routine administrative tasks that have little or no bearing on students' academic coursework.

Identify a specific project or set of activities for students to undertake. In some cases, students can conduct research that serves an agency or organization. Or students can provide essential services to an agency's clients: the homeless, victims of domestic violence, or immigrants adjusting to their new country. Researchers stress the importance of having students meet real needs: a service setting should not be treated as merely a laboratory for student learning. (Sources: Corwin, 1996; Froese et al., 2003; Furco, 2001; Ozorak, 2003)

Take into account the developmental phases of a student's field experience. Researchers describe a developmental model that outlines students' needs, identifies effective supervisory strategies, and describes outcomes at each of four stages. The *induction stage* involves gaining entrée into the field setting. During the *acclimation stage*, the student becomes familiar with the site and is less dependent upon others for directions and information. The *application stage*, or the optimal working stage, occurs when the student is fully integrated into the site and knows its history, players, and politics. Finally, the *closure stage* involves taking stock of what was learned and what still needs to be learned. (Source: Winston and Creamer, 2002)

Pay attention to the school calendar. To avoid schedule conflicts, be sure that service learning activities do not extend beyond the academic term or interfere with midterm breaks or final exams.

Be aware of legal issues. Placing students in community settings raises various legal issues, including liability for acts of students at field sites and liability for injuries. The National Service Learning Clearinghouse (servicelearning.org) offers advice and resources related to risk management and liability. Questions or concerns about students' safety should be discussed with campus legal counsel. (Sources: Chapdelaine et al, 2005; Goldstein, 1990; Janosik and Hirt, 2002)

Create written agreements that clarify roles and responsibilities. Experts recommend preparing a written agreement that presents guidelines on the agency's responsibilities to the students, including requirements for supervision and evaluation, and descriptions of the kind of work students will undertake.

(Hurley et al., 2005). Rubin (2001) offers a checklist for professors and community partners to review:

- length of placement with start and end dates
- number of students who can be accommodated
- number of hours students will spend in their placement
- transportation/parking arrangements
- orientation procedures
- on-site supervision
- procedures for agency evaluation of students
- ongoing mechanisms for communication among agency staff, students, and the faculty member
- transition and closure procedures at the end of the placement
- special considerations (for example, fingerprinting, TB shots)

Anticipate the needs of students with disabilities. Ask students in your class whether they need accommodations or have concerns about accessibility.

Students' Roles

Clarify students' roles. The student, the faculty member, and the field site personnel should all have clear expectations of what the student will be doing. The course syllabus and other written guidelines might address the following questions:

- What will the student learn or be able to do as a result of the service learning activities?
- How many hours of service are required? What field-related assignments (report, journal, portfolio, oral presentation) will the student complete?
- How will the student integrate classroom learning and field service?
- How will the student be evaluated?

Prepare students for service learning. You may want to address such topics as the concept of service learning and why it is part of your course; the population that students will be working with; students' assumptions or stereotypes; the logistics of their placement (for example, appropriate attire, handling problems); and documentation required to complete the placement. (Source: Owen and Troppe, 2002)

Assess the knowledge and skills students bring to the project. In preparation, help students identify the skills that they will be bringing to their service or placement.

This self-assessment will help build students' confidence and identify weaknesses they need to work on to be effective in the field. (Source: Conrad and Hedin, 1990)

Make assessment of need a part of the student's role in service learning. As appropriate, involve students in gathering information about the needs of those to whom they are providing the service. Expect them to be able to describe the identified needs their work addresses. (Source: Gelmon, 2003)

Require students to reflect continually and critically on what they are learning. Ask students to keep a log or journal that is both a record of daily activities and a compendium of their reflections and ideas. Encourage them to write freely. Owen and Troppe (2002) describe three types of journals:

- The *double-entry journal* in which students write their thoughts and reactions on the left side and the key issues from class discussion and readings on the right side. Students then draw arrows to indicate relationships between their personal experiences and course content.
- The *key-phrase journal* in which you provide, at the beginning of the term, a list of terms and phrases from the course materials. Students are evaluated on their use and demonstrated understanding of the terms.
- The *three-part journal* in which students divide each journal entry into thirds: description, analysis, application.

Journals can also include a description or brief history of the agency, the role of different groups, the politics and economics of the situation, and other assigned topics. Arrange or encourage electronic group journaling and sharing of experience through a forum or wiki. (Sources: Bringle et al., 2003; Dunlap, 1998; Mills, 2001; Rubin, 2001)

Faculty Role

Give adequate guidance. The amount of guidance needed depends on the level of the students, the complexity of the activities, and the timetable. Give students written information that describes the scope of the project, the purpose, the activities, the expectations of the agency, your expectations, and the deadlines.

Discuss academic integrity. In the syllabus and during the first week of class, tell students about academic integrity in a service learning setting. Explain that students must not, for example, overstate their hours of service, leave before their scheduled hours, sign in for another student, or fabricate experiences in their journal entries. (Source: Owen and Troppe, 2002)

Give students incremental assignments. For example, if students are keeping a journal, ask them to focus on a particular issue, area of knowledge, or task for each week. Assignments might include observing and describing the kind of clients an agency seeks to serve, drawing a map of an agency's office layout to study how it encourages or inhibits communication, and reflecting on progress toward achieving learning goals.

Point students to the relevant literature. For example, if your students are going to write about their initial impressions of a service learning setting, direct them to the work of social scientists or novelists who have described other settings. If students are expected to conduct interviews, give them information about the methodology of interviewing and examples of effective interviews. (Source: LoCicero and Hancock, 2000)

Keep in touch with field or service supervisors. Field supervisors serve as second teachers for your students. Give them copies of the syllabus and other course materials that help clarify the teaching purpose. Keep them informed about the course by phone or e-mail, and arrange procedures for ongoing review. Schedule a site visit and, as appropriate, invite field supervisors to class sessions, either as speakers or as guests. (Source: Howard, 2000–01)

Monitor student performance. Remind students that they are representing the college at the community site and that their projects and activities may be made public. Monitoring and reviewing are essential to make sure that final products are up to classroom standards and appropriate for public distribution.

Provide time for students to discuss their service. Schedule some class time for students to share their concerns, problems, accomplishments, and insights. Ask students to present brief reports about their activities, and encourage groups of students involved in similar placements to relate field observations to course topics. (Source: Dunlap, 1998)

Develop contingency plans. Don't let performance problems drag on. If students encounter major difficulties, offer alternatives such as scaling down the tasks or scope of activities. If a student repeatedly fails to meet deadlines or offers excuses, terminate the student's involvement in the placement. (Source: Sand, 1986)

Evaluation of Students

Evaluate students' academic work, not the field experience itself. Explain to students that they will receive credit not for simply spending time in the field, but for the quality of the work they produce in response to their service learning activity. For example, if students submit journals, your evaluative criteria may include the accuracy of entries, thoroughness, originality, and range of issues addressed. Or you might focus on students' acquisition of knowledge about the community, improvement in personal skills, self-discovery, or exploration of career options. Some faculty grade these journals on a check-plus/check/check-minus scale. (Sources: Ozorak, 2003; Tai-Seale, 2001; Weisskirch, 2003; Zimmerman et al., 1990)

Emphasize self-reflection in evaluating service learning. Evaluate journals and participation in class discussions in terms of how actively and deeply students reflect on their experience. Do they think critically about their attitudes, beliefs, assumptions, and stereotypes? Do they relate their service learning experiences to course concepts, test theories in practical settings, and formulate their own theories based on their service learning experiences? Do they apply their classroom knowledge to provide more effective service? (Sources: Eyler, 2001; Eyler and Giles, 1999; Owen and Troppe, 2002)

Evaluate students' learning in more than one way. For example, write exam questions that ask students to demonstrate familiarity with a body of literature or to relate course readings to their service learning experiences. In class discussions, ask students to relate their understanding of a topic to a critical analysis of their field experience. Ask students to write a "tip sheet" for students who may be placed in the same agency next term. Or assign a report on a particular problem or issue facing the agency, or ask for a critical essay about the fieldwork. These papers can be evaluated according to conventional academic criteria: Are the essential aspects of the topic related to the existing literature? Does the student's experience lead to an informed understanding of the theory? Is the focus of the paper appropriate to the observations on which it is based? (Source: Conrad and Hedin, 1990)

Check in with supervisors after service is completed. Meet with representatives from the agency or office to discuss their responses to your students' performance. Ask for their comments on how to improve students'—and their own—experiences.

References

Astin, A. W., Vogelesang, L. J., Ikeda, E. K., and Yee, J. A. *How Service Learning Affects Students.* Los Angeles: UCLA Higher Education Research Institute, 2000.

Braskamp, L. A., Trautvetter, L. C., and Ward, K. *Putting Students First: How Colleges Develop Students Purposefully.* Bolton, MA: Anker, 2006.

Bringle, R. G., Phillips, M. A., and Hudson, M. *The Measure of Service Learning: Research Scales to Assess Student Experiences.* Washington, DC: American Psychological Association, 2003.

Chapdelaine, A., Ruiz, A., Warchal, J., and Wells, C. *Service-Learning Code of Ethics.* San Francisco: Jossey-Bass, 2005.

Colby, A., Ehrlich, T., Beaumont, E., and Stephens, J. *Educating Citizens: Preparing America's Undergraduates for Lives of Moral and Civic Responsibility.* San Francisco: Jossey-Bass, 2003.

Conrad, D., and Hedin, D. Learning from Service: Experience Is the Best Teacher, or Is It? In J. C. Kendall and associates (Eds.), *Combining Service and Learning: A Resource Book for Community and Public Service.* Vol. 1. Raleigh NC: National Society for Internships and Experiential Education, 1990.

Corwin, P. "Using the Community as a Classroom for Large Introductory Sociology Classes." *Teaching Sociology,* 1996, *24*(3), 310–315.

Dunlap, M. R. "Methods of Supporting Students' Critical Reflection in Courses Incorporating Service Learning." *Teaching of Psychology,* 1998, *25*(3), 208–210.

Ehrlich, T. (Ed.). *Civic Responsibility and Higher Education.* American Council on Education and Oryx Press, 2000.

Engstrom, C. M. Developing Collaborative Student Affairs–Academic Affairs Partnerships for Service-Learning. In B. Jacoby (Ed.), *Building Partnerships for Service-Learning.* San Francisco: Jossey-Bass, 2003.

Evangelopoulos, N., Sidorova, A., and Riolli, L. "Can Service-Learning Help Students Appreciate an Unpopular Course? A Theoretical Framework." *Michigan Journal of Community Service Learning,* 2003, *9*(2), 15–24.

Eyler, J. "Creating Your Reflection Map." In M. Canada and B. W. Speck (Eds.), *Developing and Implementing Service-Learning Programs.* New Directions for Higher Education, no. 114. San Francisco: Jossey-Bass, 2001, pp. 35–43.

Eyler, J., and Giles, D. E. *Where's the Service in Service-Learning?* San Francisco: Jossey-Bass, 1999.

Froese, A. D., Vogts-Scribner, V., Ealey, S. E., and Fairchild, J. A. "Service Data Institute: Bridging Research and Community Service." *Teaching of Psychology,* 2003, *30*(4), 319–321.

Furco, A. "Service Learning: A Balanced Approach to Experiential Education." In B. Taylor (Ed.), *Expanding Boundaries: Serving and Learning.* Washington, DC: Corporation for National Service, 1996.

Furco, A. "Advancing Service Learning at Research Universities." *New Directions for Higher Education,* no. 11. San Francisco: Jossey-Bass, Summer 2001, pp. 67–78.

Gelmon, S. B. Assessment as a Means of Building Service-Learning Partnerships. In B. Jacoby (Ed.), *Building Partnerships for Service-Learning.* San Francisco: Jossey-Bass, 2003.

Goldstein, M. B. Legal Issues in Combining Service and Learning. In J. C. Kendall and associates (Eds.), *Combining Service and Learning: A Resource Book for Community and Public Service.* Vol. 2. Raleigh, NC: National Society for Internships and Experiential Education, 1990.

Howard, J. "Academic Service-Learning: Myths, Challenges, and Recommendations." *Essays on Teaching Excellence,* 2000–01, *12*(3), 12–19.

Hurley, C., Renger, R., and Brunk, B. Learning from a Challenging Fieldwork Evaluation Experience: Perspectives of a Student and an Instructor. *American Journal of Evaluation*, 2005, *26*(4), 562–578.

Hutchings, P., and Wutzdorff, A. "Experiential Learning across the Curriculum: Assumptions and Principles." In P. Hutchings and A. Wutzdorff (Eds.), *Knowing and Doing: Learning Through Experience*. New Directions for Teaching and Learning, no. 35. San Francisco: Jossey-Bass, 1988.

Jacoby, B. Fundamentals of Service-Learning Partnerships. In B. Jacoby (Ed.), *Building Partnerships for Service-Learning*. San Francisco: Jossey-Bass, 2003.

Janosik, S. M., and Hirt, J. B. Legal and Ethical Issues. In D. L. Cooper, S. A. Saunders, R. B. Winston, J. B. Hirt, D. G. Creamer, and S. M. Janosik (Eds.), *Learning through Supervised Practice in Student Affairs*. New York: Brunner-Routledge, 2002.

Kendall, J. C., and others. "Increasing Faculty Involvement." In J. C. Kendall and associates (Eds.), *Combining Service and Learning: A Resource Book for Community and Public Service*. Vol. 2. Raleigh, NC: National Society for Internships and Experiential Education, 1990.

Kezar, A., and Rhoads, R. R. "The Dynamic Tensions of Service Learning in Higher Education: A Philosophical Perspective." *Journal of Higher Education*, 2001, *72*(2), 148–171.

Kretchmar, M. D. "Service Learning in a General Psychology Class: Description, Preliminary Evaluation and Recommendations." *Teaching of Psychology*, 2001, *28*(1), 5–10.

LoCicero, A., and Hancock, J. "Preparing Students for Success in Fieldwork." *Teaching of Psychology*, 2000, *27*(2), 117–120.

Marullo, S. "Bringing Home Diversity: A Service-Learning Approach to Teaching Race and Ethnic Relations." *Teaching Sociology*, 1998, *26*(4), 259–275.

Mills, S. D. "Electronic Journaling: Using the Web-Based Group Journal for Service-Learning Reflection." *Michigan Journal of Community Service Learning*, Fall 2001, *8*(1), 27–35.

Ostrow, J. Service-Learning and the Problem of Depth. In M. Langseth and W. M. Plater (Eds.), *Public Work and the Academy: An Academic Administrator's Guide to Civic Engagement and Service-Learning*. San Francisco: Jossey-Bass, 2004.

Owen, J., and Troppe, M. (Eds.) *Faculty Handbook for Service-Learning*. (2nd ed.) College Park: Commuter Affairs and Community Service, University of Maryland, 2002.

Ozorak, E. W. "Integrating Service-Learning into Psychology Courses." *APS Observer*, Nov. 2003, *16*(11), 21–22, 36–37.

Rubin, M. S. A Smart Start to Service-Learning. In M. Canada and B. W. Speck (eds.), *Developing and Implementing Service-Learning Programs*. New Directions for Higher Education, no. 114. San Francisco: Jossey-Bass, 2001, pp. 15–26.

Sand, P. Organizing Community Studies. In S. F. Schomberg (Ed.), *Strategies for Active Teaching and Learning in University Classrooms*. Minneapolis: Office of Educational Development Programs, University of Minnesota, 1986.

Service-Learning in the Disciplines, 18 volumes. Washington, DC: American Association for Higher Education, 1997–2000.

"A Spanish Course Blends Classroom Work with Community Service." *Chronicle of Higher Education*, March 22, 2002, A10.

Tai-Seale, T. "Liberating Service Learning and Applying the New Practice." *College Teaching*, 2001, *49*(1), 14–18.

University of California at Berkeley Task Force. *Advancing Public Service*. Berkeley: Service Learning Research and Development Center, University of California, 2000.

Vaz, R. F. "Connecting Science and Technology Education with Civic Understanding: A Model for Engagement." *AAC&U*, Winter 2005, 13–16.

Weisskirch, R. S. "Analyzing Student Journals in a Service-Learning Course." *Academic Exchange Quarterly*, Summer 2003, *7*(2), 141–145.

Wills, E. "The Course: 'Intergenerational Creative Nonfiction Writing.'" *Chronicle of Higher Education*, June 17, 2005, A6.

Winston, R. B., and Creamer, D. G. Supervision: Relationships That Support Learning. In D. L. Cooper, S. A. Saunders, R. B. Winston, J. B. Hirt, D. G. Creamer, and S. M. Janosik (Eds.), *Learning through Supervised Practice in Student Affairs*. New York: Brunner-Routledge, 2002.

Zimmerman, J., and others. Journals: Diaries for Growth. In J. C. Kendall and associates (Eds.), *Combining Service and Learning: A Resource Book for Community and Public Service*. Vol. 2. Raleigh, NC: National Society for Internships and Experiential Education, 1990.

27

Undergraduate Research

With appropriate mentoring, undergraduates can pursue scientific inquiries, artistic and creative activities, and other forms of research and scholarship in any field. These projects may be undertaken as a course requirement, as an independent study, or outside the regular curriculum (Kinkead, 2003). A student might work with one faculty member or as part of a faculty-led team of undergraduate and graduate students.

Involving undergraduates in research significantly benefits both students and faculty (Bauer and Bennett, 2003; Firestone, 1997; Jones and Draheim, 1994; Kuh et al., 2005; Landrum and Nelsen, 2002; Malachowski, 2003; Merkel and Baker, 2002; Nagda et al., 1998; Pascarella and Terenzini, 2005; Prince et al., 2007; Seymour et al., 2004; Shellito et al., 2001). Undergraduates who participate in research projects gain a richer understanding of the discipline; develop critical thinking, communication, and analytic skills; become more independent and self-confident; have a clearer focus on career options; and show higher rates of persistence and degree completion. For many students, working alongside a faculty member on a research project is the highlight of their undergraduate years.

For instructors, the fundamental or naïve questions posed by undergraduates can lead to reconsideration of preconceived notions or suggest new directions for research. The experience of working with undergraduates can also result in improved teaching effectiveness in the classroom.

The suggestions below are aimed at helping you design opportunities, and recruit and supervise undergraduates who are working on your research projects or one of their own. For ways to incorporate research assignments into your courses see Chapter 35, "Designing Effective Writing Assignments."

General Strategies

Think broadly about types of research-related work. In addition to laboratory work in science and engineering, students can assist a local organization in defining or solving a problem, conduct research on an aspect of campus life, or assist in assessing the course you are teaching. For a broad list of the kinds of research projects that engage undergraduates, see the Undergraduate Research Apprentice

Program at UC Berkeley (research.berkeley.edu/urap/) and the Undergraduate Research Opportunity Program at the University of Michigan (www.lsa.umich. edu/urop/). (Sources: Lancy, 2003; Picciotto, 1997; Strand et al., 2003)

Consider summer research projects. Summer may be a good time for students to participate in research. If your institution has an undergraduate senior project or thesis program, summer research might lead into a senior-year thesis. (Source: Merkel and Baker, 2002)

Seek funding. Take advantage of any campus programs that may provide funds to support undergraduate research. Write undergraduate research assistants into the budgets of grants you submit. Some funded niches usually occupied by graduate students can be assigned to undergraduates. (Source: Lancy, 2003)

Consult national resources on undergraduate research. Two allied national associations offer resources for faculty who are supervising undergraduates as part of a research team or as independent researchers. The Council on Undergraduate Research (www.cur.org) offers how-to books, journals, and events for those interested in supporting student-faculty collaborative research and scholarship. The National Conferences on Undergraduate Research (www.ncur.org) hosts conferences where undergraduates in a variety of fields present their findings.

Designing Worthwhile Research Experiences

Establish clear learning goals. At the start of the project, meet with the student to agree on the learning goals. These goals may include making a new discovery or synthesis, mastering a particular disciplinary or interdisciplinary methodology, learning how to narrow a topic for investigation, gaining skills in scientific processes, locating and critiquing primary source documents, sifting through data and drawing conclusions, and developing skills in the oral and written presentation of findings.

Define projects that suit students' interests and abilities. Look for opportunities that will allow students to design and complete their work in the time they have available. Be realistic in estimating the amount of time and training that undergraduate students will need to carry out the project. Also, some research projects do not necessarily end in a defined time frame and instead continue from student to student over several years. (Sources: Lancy, 2003; Shellito et al., 2001)

Help students narrow an independent topic. Students who wish to pursue an independent research project will need help in selecting and narrowing their topic. (Source: Bodi, 2002)

Recruiting Students

Identify potential participants. Some colleges and universities have central undergraduate research programs that match faculty sponsors and student participants. At other institutions, instructors recruit students on their own. Posting an announcement may elicit a few responses, but you should also extend a personal invitation to select current and former students. For some projects, a student's ability to meet deadlines and do reliable work may be crucial; for other projects, a key consideration may be a student's willingness to be honest in critiquing your work and writing. Some faculty look to students in their department's honors programs, while others seek out students who are underrepresented in their field of study and those who are preservice teachers. Actively seek qualified but potentially academically vulnerable students (for example, low income, first generation, or immigrant students); involvement in research can improve the retention of students. (Sources: Jones and Draheim, 1994; Kinkead, 2003; Lancy, 2003; Merkel, 2003; Steffes, 2004; Verity et al., 2002)

Advocate the value of doing research. Explain to students the benefits of conducting research or participating in a research project. In addition to describing the learning opportunities, discuss the advantages of working outside the classroom with a professor, graduate students, or other undergraduate students. If you are recruiting students for your project, tell them what your research environment offers that students "can't get anywhere else." (Source: Benson, 2002)

Link research to careers and graduate school. Offer career guidance as appropriate and discuss how an undergraduate research project may help prepare a student for graduate study or for specific vocational opportunities. (Sources: Merkel and Baker, 2002; Shellito et al., 2001)

Mentoring and Supervising Undergraduate Researchers

Decide on a model for supervising students. Whether students undertake their own original research or work on a project you have designed, the structure and supervision of the project will follow one of four models (adapted from Landrum and Nelsen, 2002):

- a mentor-colleague model in which students work closely and directly with faculty
- a hierarchical model in which students work with graduate students who are, in turn, supervised by faculty
- an apprentice model in which students attain more responsible tasks as their performance abilities grow
- a contractual model in which faculty spell out tasks and deadlines in advance

Clarify with students the model you will use for supervision, and remind them that your role is to guide—but not to direct—their research. Discuss mutual expectations.

Be available, approachable, and encouraging. Take the time to get to know the students you are mentoring. Set aside time every week for a question-and-answer period, and encourage students to ask the "stupid question" that they hesitate to ask. Give positive, constructive feedback and encouragement. Prepare students to cope with the inevitable frustrations of designing and conducting a research project, and remind them that all researchers experience repeated failure. (Sources: Kinkead, 2003; Merkel and Baker, 2002; Shellito et al., 2001)

Focus on the student's learning experience. Provide as clear a path as you can from grunt work to meaningful tasks that entail increasing levels of responsibility. For example, first- and second-year students who are not ready to perform statistical data analysis can collect and enter data, examine literature, and draft materials for the introductory section of a research paper. (Sources: Benson, 2002; Kuther, 2004; Lancy, 2003)

Discuss the ethics of research. Address ethical questions that arise in the conduct and reporting of research: for example, the handling and treatment of lab animals, the integrity of reporting the findings whatever the outcome, and privacy and confidentiality policies. (Source: Benson, 2002)

Respect the student's situation. Recognize and respect a student's time commitments outside the research project. Show that you value the student's time by being prepared when he or she arrives. As needed, back up a bit to explain concepts at the student's level. Be sure that students have the supplies, equipment, and access they need to do their work. (Source: Shellito et al., 2001)

Be patient. For example, it may take three to six months or more for undergraduates to familiarize themselves with key laboratory techniques, read the latest journal articles, and comprehend the scope of the project or to understand how to design and execute a series of laboratory experiments. (Sources: Firestone, 1997; Merkel and Baker, 2002)

Let students know their contributions are valued. Even undergraduates who have just joined a lab may have useful insights. Create an open atmosphere in which everyone feels invited to speak. (Sources: Benson, 2002; Kinkead, 2003)

Communicating Findings

Encourage students to publish or present their work. A class Web site (or class-linked student blog) is one place to publish and present. Also make students aware of electronic and print journals that publish articles by undergraduates, although Ferrari and Hemovich (2004) turned up some evidence that some graduate psychology admissions directors look askance at publication in journals created for student-based research. One national undergraduate research clearinghouse (clearinghouse.missouriwestern.edu) is housed at Missouri Western State College. Student research poster displays and other products are also disseminated at professional societies and associations such as the biennial Council on Undergraduate Research and the annual National Conferences on Undergraduate Research's Washington, DC–based "posters on the hill." (Source: Kinkead, 2003)

For team-based research, include the student as a co-author. Firestone (1997) reports that about a third of the papers published by his laboratory research group have at least one undergraduate as a co-author who played key roles in carrying out experiments and interpreting data.

Take undergraduates to disciplinary conferences. Socialize them into the profession or discipline. Let them experience the collective enthusiasm of the conference. (Source: Lancy, 2003)

References

Bauer, K. W., and Bennett, J. S. "Alumni Perceptions Used to Assess Undergraduate Research Experience." *Journal of Higher Education*, 2003, *74*(2), 210–230.

Benson, E. "Learning by Doing: Four Keys to Fostering Undergraduate Research in Your Laboratory." *Monitor on Psychology*, December 2002, *33*(11), 42–45.

Bodi, S. "How Do We Bridge the Gap between What We Teach and What They Do? Some Thoughts on the Place of Questions in the Process of Research." *Journal of Academic Librarianship*, 2002, *28*(3), 109–114.

Ferrari, J. R., and Hemovich, V. B. "Student-Based Psychology Journals: Perceptions by Graduate Program Directors." *Teaching of Psychology*, 2004, *31*(4), 272–275.

Firestone, G. L. "Undergraduate Research: An Integration of Discovery and Education." *Science 21*, 1997, *2*(1), 9–10.

Jones, J. L., and Draheim, M. M. "Mutual Benefits: Undergraduate Assistance in Faculty Scholarship." *Journal on Excellence in College Teaching*, 1994, *5*(2), 85–96.

Kinkead, J. "Learning through Inquiry: An Overview of Undergraduate Research." In J. Kinkead (Ed.), *Valuing and Supporting Undergraduate Research*. New Directions for Teaching and Learning, no. 93. San Francisco: Jossey-Bass, 2003, pp. 5–17.

Kuh, G. D., Kinzie, J., Schuh, J. H., Whitt, E. J., and associates. *Student Success in College: Creating Conditions That Matter*. San Francisco: Jossey-Bass, 2005.

Kuther, T. L. "Student-Faculty Collaborative Research: Why and How to Do It." *Newsletter of the Society for the Teaching of Psychology*, Division 2 of the American Psychological Association. Fall 2004, 4–5.

Lancy, D. F. "What One Faculty Member Does to Promote Undergraduate Research." *New Directions for Teaching and Learning*, no. 93. San Francisco: Jossey-Bass, 2003, pp. 87–92.

Landrum, R. E., and Nelsen, L. R. "The Undergraduate Research Assistantship: An Analysis of the Benefits." *Journal of Psychology*, 2002, *29*(1), 15–19.

Malachowski, M. R. "A Research-across-the-Curriculum Movement." In J. Kinkead (Ed.), *Valuing and Supporting Undergraduate Research*. New Directions for Teaching and Learning, no. 93. San Francisco: Jossey-Bass, 2003, pp. 55–68.

Merkel, C. A. "Undergraduate Research at the Research Universities." In J. Kinkead (Ed.), *Valuing and Supporting Undergraduate Research*. New Directions for Teaching and Learning, no. 93. San Francisco: Jossey-Bass, 2003, pp. 39–53.

Merkel, C. A., and Baker, S. M. *How to Mentor Undergraduate Researchers*. Washington, DC: Council on Undergraduate Research, 2002.

Nagda, B. A., Gregerman, S. R., Jonides, J., von Hippel, W., and Lerner, J. S. "Undergraduate Student-Faculty Research Partnerships Affect Student Retention." *Review of Higher Education*, 1998, *22*(1), 55–72.

Pascarella, E. T., and Terenzini, P. T. *How College Affects Students. A Third Decade of Research*. Vol. 2. San Francisco: Jossey-Bass, 2005.

Picciotto, M. "Investigating the College: Teaching the Research Process." *College Teaching*, 1997, *45*(1), 19–21.

Prince, M. J., Felder, R. M. and Brent, R. "Does Faculty Research Improve Undergraduate Teaching? An Analysis of Existing and Potential Synergies." *Journal of Engineering Education*, 2007, *96*(4), 283–294.

Seymour, E., Hunter, A-B., Laursen, S. L., DeAntoni, T. "Establishing the Benefits of Research Experiences for Undergraduates in the Sciences: First Findings from a Three-Year Study." *Science Education*, 2004, *88*(4), 493–534.

Shellito, C., Shea, K., Weissmann, G., Mueller-Solger, A., and Davis, W. "Successful Mentoring of Undergraduate Researchers: Tips for Creating Positive Student Research Experiences." *Journal of College Science Teaching*, 2001, *30*(7), 460–464.

Steffes, J. S. "Creating Powerful Learning Environments beyond the Classroom." *Change,*
    May/June, 2004, *36*(3), 46–50.
Strand, K., Marullo, S., Cutforth, N., Stoecker, R., and Donohue, P. *Community-Based Research
    and Higher Education: Principles and Practices.* San Francisco: Jossey-Bass, 2003.
Verity, P. G., Gilligan, M. R., Frischer, M. E., Booth, M. G., Richardson, J. P., and
    Franklin, C. "Improving Undergraduate Research Experiences: Lessons from a
    Historically Black University's Unusual Collaboration." *AAHE Bulletin,* February
    2002, 3–6.

28

Guest Speakers

Guest speakers can add interest, expertise, variety, and multiple perspectives to many types of courses. The following suggestions discuss inviting speakers, arranging for webcast presentations, and preparing to be a guest speaker.

General Strategies

Start early. Arranging for an outside speaker takes considerable time and work. Start contacting possible speakers as early as you can. Scheduling may involve a good deal of juggling of dates.

Define the purpose and value. Look for speakers who are integral to your course by addressing an issue in which the readings or your own knowledge are weak, by presenting an important point of view, or by offering an alternative perspective. Incorporate material from the speaker's presentation into assignments or tests, and let your students know how the presentation will figure in their course work. (Source: Lyons et al., 2003)

Choose effective speakers. Make sure the speaker is credible and an effective presenter. Be cautious about inviting speakers who come to you looking for an opportunity to speak. Invite speakers who will challenge your students and provoke discussion. Avoid a "packaged presentation" unless you have seen the performance and know it's exactly what you want. (Sources: Mullins, 2001; Sorenson, 2001)

Decide on an appropriate format. Check with the speaker for preferences in how the session might be structured: presentation with questions and answers; an opportunity for your class to "interview the expert"; open discussion led by the speaker; informal conversation so students can get acquainted with the speaker, and so forth. (Source: Sorenson, 2001)

Start small and expand. Begin with just one guest during the term. Consider adding a second during a succeeding term, but keep in mind that hosting too many speakers may dilute the focus and effectiveness of the course. (Source: Mullins, 2001)

Preparing the Speaker

Extend a detailed invitation. Discuss the content of your course and how the speaker would fit in. Describe your goals and what you hope to achieve by the speaker's participation in your class. Talk about the structure of the session. If you want the speaker to address specific points, provide a list or an outline, as appropriate. Send the following information in writing well before the presentation date (adapted from Mullins, 2001):

- time to arrive, length of session, length of class, location of classroom and your office, contact phone numbers
- driving instructions, directions about parking, and a guest parking pass
- class size, students' level of preparation, interests, and so forth

Ask about any special needs or requests. Ask your guest if he or she has any preferences about seating arrangements, length of the question-and-answer segment, photocopying, or equipment such as a laptop and data projector. If your class is small, ask if the guest would like the students to introduce themselves and say a word about their interests.

Give the speaker a copy of the reading list for the class. Or ask the speaker to suggest readings that students should complete before the session. (Source: Mullins, 2001)

Confirm the speaker's appearance a few days before the date. If you find out at the last minute the speaker is unable to show up, consider alternatives: engaging students in brainstorming regarding a concept or idea from a previous class; breaking students into small groups and having them develop questions that could be used on the midterm or final exam; showing a video relevant to the course content; giving students time to work in groups on an upcoming project or assignment. (Source: Lyons et al., 2003)

Preparing the Students

At the session before the speaker's appearance, remind students about the event. Remind students that a guest is coming and suggest that they think about questions they want to ask. Explain the connection between the speaker and the topics of the course. To encourage attendance, be sure that students know how the guest's material relates to the course goals and to grading. As appropriate, ask students to submit their questions before the day of the presentation; you or the students can then ask the questions during the presentation. (Source: Sorenson, 2001)

Let students know what will be expected of them. If students will have an opportunity to introduce themselves, tell them about that. Explain that they should feel free to applaud at the end of the presentation if they find it of value.

Hosting the Guest Speaker

Introduce the speaker. Use whatever biographical information the speaker has provided and introduce the topic of the presentation. Make sure that the speaker's needs are met, and provide water. Remain attentive throughout the presentation.

Be prepared to moderate. Explain any ground rules for the session and, as needed, serve as the moderator for the question-and-answer period. Watch the time, and politely intervene if the speaker exceeds the time limit. (Source: Lyons et al., 2003)

At the conclusion, publicly thank the speaker. Lead the applause. If time permits, offer a few summarizing comments or assess the value of the session.

After the guest departs, discuss the presentation. Respond to any student criticism of the speaker. Indicate how the material relates to your instructional objectives.

Follow up with a thank you note to the speaker. You might say something about how the class responded to the presentation and how you will incorporate the presentation into subsequent class sessions. As appropriate, send a copy of the note to the speaker's department chair or supervisor.

Guests Courtesy of Webcasting

Provide guest speakers via webcast. A webcast is a video presentation—either live or archived—transmitted over the Internet. Webcasts give you access to experts who would be unable to come to your classroom.

Use archived or on-demand webcasts. Using an archived webcast gives you more control of the presentation than arranging for a live webcast. Check with your campus instructional technology unit or multimedia resource collection to determine what they have available. At the University of California at Berkeley, for example, live and on-demand webcasts, of both courses and public events, are listed at webcast.berkeley.edu. For more options, you can search the Web for "webcast" and the keywords of your topic.

Decide whether to show the webcast in class or ask students to view it on their own. If you decide to show the webcast in class, experiment with viewing webcasts on your own computer before showing one to your students. Also test the classroom hardware and software. If possible, download the entire webcast before a presentation. Have backup plans in case you experience technical problems. (Source: Bell, 2003)

Explore other forms of electronically mediated guest appearances. You can invite outside experts into an online asynchronous discussion in your course. Videoconferencing (real-time two-way televised communication) has become a regular part of some college programs, especially where some students attend a satellite campus. (Sources: Medley, 2005; Educause Learning Initiative, 2006)

Being a Guest Speaker

Ask why you are being invited. Ask the instructor what topics or themes you should cover. Ask for a copy of the syllabus and a description of the students (year in school, major, enrollment, and so on). Clarify any honorarium and whether your expenses will be covered.

Highlight the place of your material in the continuum of the course. Begin your talk by sketching the context of your topic; then go for depth rather than breadth. Toward the end of your presentation, summarize key points. (Source: Cook, 2005)

If your schedule permits, let students know how to contact you. Students appreciate the opportunity to follow up with you if they have questions.

References

Bell, S. "Cyber-Guest Lecturers: Using Webcasts as a Teaching Tool." *TechTrends*, 2003, *47*(4), 10–14.

Cook, D. "When You Are the Guest Lecturer." *Teaching and Learning Exchange*, 2005, *12*(2).

Educause Learning Initiative. "7 Things You Should Know about Virtual Meetings." February 2006. http://connect.educause.edu/Library/ELI/7ThingsYouShouldKnow About/39388

Lyons, R. E., McIntosh, M., and Kysilka, M. L. *Teaching College in an Age of Accountability*. Boston: Allyn and Bacon, 2003.

Medley, R. M. "Inviting Experts to Class through Computer-Mediated Discussions." *College Teaching*, 2005, *53*(2), 71–74.

Mullins, P. A. "Using Outside Speakers in the Classroom." *APS Observer*, 2001, *14*(8).

Sorenson, L. "Guest Speakers: Agony or Ecstasy." Brigham Young University, *Focus on Faculty*, 2001, *9*(2), 4. http://fc.byu.edu/opages/reference/focusonfaculty.htm

PART VI

Enhancing Students' Learning and Motivation

29

Helping Students Learn

You can improve your students' academic performance by incorporating concepts derived from research into how learners acquire, process, integrate, retrieve, and apply information and skills. Research validates the following general principles (adapted from Bransford et al., 2000; Donovan et al., 1999):

- Students who have inaccurate or incomplete assumptions and beliefs about a topic will have difficulty grasping new concepts and information.
- Students can more easily recall what they already know and integrate new material when they are given a conceptual framework.
- Dividing new material into discrete chunks improves students' acquisition of that material.
- All learners need practice, feedback, and review.
- Social interactions and discourse facilitate learning and motivation.
- Students' motivation affects the amount of time and effort they are willing to devote to learning.
- Because learning tends to be situation-dependent, students may need help in transferring material learned in one context to other contexts.

These principles suggest the following practices (adapted from Bransford et al., 2000):

- Introduce a new topic by reviewing background and prerequisite information, taking care to dispel common misconceptions.
- Announce the learning objectives: the knowledge or skills you expect students to acquire during the class meeting or the upcoming sessions.
- Emphasize fundamental concepts and principles.
- Present material in organized, manageable chunks that include opportunities for practice.
- Ask students to demonstrate mastery by answering questions or showing what they have learned.
- Give feedback to students to reinforce their learning.
- Provide opportunities for students to generalize, apply, and transfer what they have learned.

The suggestions below are designed to help you optimize student learning for long term retention and retrieval, and flexible adaptation to new problems and settings.

Promoting Students' Intellectual Development

Become familiar with models of intellectual development. Perry (1970) has conceptualized college students' intellectual development as a series of nine stages commonly grouped into four substages. The earliest stages are dominated by either-or thinking (dualism). Students at these stages believe that there is a single right answer, that knowledge is a set of indisputable truths, and that education consists of a professor giving authoritative explanations to students. Belenky, Clinchy, Goldberger, and Tarule (1986), in examining women's epistemological development, describe this situation as "received knowledge," a dependence upon authority. As Erickson, Peters, and Strommer (2006) point out, students at these stages become uneasy when they are asked to think independently, draw their own conclusions, or state their own points of view; they are also uneasy when authorities disagree.

Over time, students begin to revise their thinking as they encounter more areas of disagreement among authorities, compare different interpretations, and realize that on some topics no one has definitive answers. In these next stages (which Perry [1970] calls *multiplicity* and Belenky et al. [1986] call *subjective knowledge*), knowledge no longer consists of right and wrong answers; knowledge becomes a matter of educated opinion. They see both faculty and students as entitled to have their opinions, and they initially treat all opinions as equally valid. This mode of thinking is dominant among college students (Kurfiss, 1998).

Students' thinking begins to change again after instructors and peers repeatedly ask them for evidence to support their points of view. As students learn to distinguish weak evidence from strong, they also come to see that knowledge is contextual and situational. What one "knows" is relative and affected by one's values, assumptions, and perspectives (relativism/procedural knowledge). Ambiguity is a part of life. Faculty are now viewed as experienced resources, who teach specialized procedures for reasoning within a discipline and who can help students learn the skillful use of analytic methods to explore and compare alternative points of view.

In the final stages of cognitive development, students begin to take their own stands on issues on the basis of their own analysis, which they view as the product of their values, experience, and knowledge. Perry (1970) calls this "commitment in relativism," reflecting the need to take a position and make a commitment. Belenky, Clinchy, Goldberger, and Tarule (1986) describe this level as "constructed knowledge," integrating knowledge learned from others with knowledge learned from self-experience and self-reflection.

Provide sufficient structure for students in introductory courses. Students in introductory courses are more likely to want yes-or-no answers, and some may have little patience for open-ended discussions. When you grade these students' papers, be explicit about your criteria so that students do not dismiss your comments as simply "your opinion." (Sources: Erickson et al., 2006; Tiberius, 1999)

Help students become more intellectually sophisticated. Encourage students to move beyond either-or thinking (adapted from Schmidt and Davidson, 1983, and cited in Tiberius, 1999):

- *Help students appreciate other points of view.* Challenge students' clichés; ask them to provide evidence in support of their opinions; reinforce the value of entertaining competing points of view; support students in their growing awareness that there is no shame in changing one's mind after weighing well-reasoned arguments.
- *Help students evaluate different points of view.* Explore why some points of view are logically stronger than others; help students understand why authorities disagree; identify criteria for judging between conflicting points of view; divide arguments into component parts; discuss the relative validity of different types of evidence.
- *Help students understand the process of making judgments.* Remind students to rethink their decisions when conditions change or when new information comes to light; discuss how to make decisions when information is uncertain; explain reasoned judgment; encourage probabilistic statements.

Include real-world experiences in your courses. Hands-on activities or fieldwork provide a bridge between abstract and concrete learning, and they can help students develop a more complex approach to learning. (Source: Kurfiss, 1998)

Be sensitive to students' struggles. Students may need guidance and empathy in coping with multiple points of view, making wrong decisions, and dealing with uncertainties. Dogmatic students may need help in seeing others' points of view; indecisive students may need help in forming judgments; complacent students may need help in thinking skeptically. (Sources: King and Kitchener, 1994; Kurfiss, 1998; Schmidt and Davidson, 1983; Tiberius, 1999)

Helping Students Contextualize New Information

Emphasize deep learning. Students engaged in "deep learning" try to understand the significance and meaning of new material, and they strive to integrate new information with what they already know. In contrast, students engaged in "surface learning" do just enough to complete the task or pass a test: they memorize information, make little effort to relate new information to old, and treat learning as an externally imposed task. Deep and surface approaches are not fixed. Students adopt an approach depending upon their view of the task. At different times, students may use deep or surface approaches. Research shows that students who acquire a deep understanding of course content retain it longer and achieve higher grades than students who learn only on the surface.

Try to provide a context that encourages deep learning:

- Help students develop a strong conceptual framework that they can use to organize information into meaningful patterns.
- State learning objectives that emphasize synthesis, evaluation, and analysis.
- Keep workloads and schedules manageable.
- Focus on issues that are most problematic for students, especially the inconsistencies or misconceptions that prevent them from understanding new material.
- Avoid assignments and tests that require the recall of trivial details.
- Encourage students to apply concepts to real-life problems and experiences.

The Biggs Study Process Questionnaire (Biggs et al., 2001) and the Lancaster Approaches to Studying (Ramsden, 2003) can be administered to students to help them explore whether they use deep or surface strategies. (Sources: Bacon and Stewart, 2006; Donovan et al., 1999; Fry et al., 2003; Ramsden, 2003; Roediger et al., 2002; Svinicki, 2004)

Work through students' erroneous preconceptions. Learners tend to place new material in the framework of what they already know about the subject. When new material conflicts with students' earlier understandings or beliefs, they may distort the new information so that it fits into their existing framework. In structuring your course and in providing feedback, ask yourself, What do my students know? What don't they know? What might they mistakenly believe they know? (Sources: American Psychological Association, 1997; Dochy et al., 1999; Donovan et al., 1999; Bransford et al., 2000; Linn, 2006; Pelligrino et al., 2001; Taber, 2001)

Assess what students know at the beginning of the term. What and how much is learned in any situation depends on a student's prior knowledge and experience.

Devise diagnostic tests or other means to identify what students know about the topic. (Sources: Dochy et al., 1999; Halpern and Hakel, 2003)

Present material in ways that are meaningful to students. Let students know what they are expected to learn, and alert them to key points ("Now, this is really critical"). Limit each course session to three or four key points. Similarly, to maximize retention and retrieval, address fewer topics in greater depth over the term rather than cover many topics superficially. Try to tailor your examples to your students' interests and backgrounds, and encourage students to relate a new topic to what they already know. (Sources: American Psychological Association, 1997; Bacon and Stewart, 2006; Donovan et al., 1999; Erickson et al., 2006; Lowman, 1995; Svinicki, 2004)

Give students a framework within which to fit new information. Use outlines, study guides, and other aids to help students see conceptual frameworks and systems. Focus on key concepts, and use a vivid story or memorable example to illuminate key concepts. Refrain from mentioning stray bits of data and details that may overwhelm or confuse students. (Sources: Bransford et al., 2000; Graesser et al., 2002)

Recognize that different students learn, think, and process information in different ways. Learning is a highly individual process. Because learning is based on personal constructions of meaning, perceptions of the learning situation, and prior experiences of learning, students vary in how they learn—and how long they take to learn. These differences are more noticeable when the new information is abstract and complex rather than simple and concrete. Moreover, learners do not make uniform progress. Sometimes students reach plateaus and their rate of learning slows down. Research also suggests that men and women may differ in "ways of knowing" and that women may respond better to certain types of learning strategies, such as small-group discussion and experiential learning activities. (Sources: American Psychological Association, 1997; Belenky et al., 1986; Hayes and Flannery, 2000; Prosser and Trigwell, 1999)

Helping Students Retain, Retrieve, and Apply Information

Emphasize the value of review. Studies suggest that within a matter of days or weeks, students may forget up to half of the new material they have encountered if they do not continue to review that material. To help students retain key concepts, encourage them to develop retrieval cues (such as mnemonics or visual images). In class, reiterate important points throughout the semester. (Sources: Bransford et al., 2000; Grasha, 1996)

Recognize that mental effort or concentration can be a limited resource.
Cognitive load theory hypothesizes that the mental effort people can devote to challenging tasks is limited. If the demands of a task exceed available mental effort, performance will suffer. A certain amount of mental effort is needed to meet the cognitive demands of a task, and additional effort or capacity is needed to reflect on and learn from that task. Students may be able to complete an activity but learn nothing from it; if they use all available mental effort to complete the task, no spare effort will be available for learning the task.

Because of cognitive load, a more complex activity may be less effective for learning than a simpler one. When information is new, complex, and challenging, cognitive capacities of learners may be overwhelmed.

Help students' mental efforts by managing cognitive load, providing sufficient learning time, discriminating among core and tangential information, and recognizing that students may fail at tasks because of overwhelming cognitive load and not because of lack of motivation or effort. (Sources: Chew, 2007; Clark et al., 2006)

Provide opportunities for active learning. Students learn by doing, writing, discussing, and other activities and situations that allow them to test what they have learned and how thoroughly they understand it. The more opportunities students have to restate or apply key concepts, the better they will be able to remember those concepts. In a phrase: Don't tell students when you can show them—and don't show them when they can show themselves. Ask students to summarize, paraphrase, or generalize about important concepts through discussions, role playing, simulations, case studies, and written assignments. (Sources: American Psychological Association, 1997; Lowman, 1995; Mentkowski and Associates, 2000)

Encourage cooperation and group work. Learning is enhanced by social interaction, as students build communities of practice, test their understanding, and repeat and review material. Collaborative teamwork and projects undertaken by heterogeneous groups encourage higher-order thinking and problem solving. (Sources: American Psychological Association, 1997; Pelligrino et al., 2001; Ybarra et al., 2008)

Vary the context and conditions for learning and testing. Learning is generally enhanced when learners encounter the same principles in a variety of contexts or formats (for example, auditory, verbal, visual, and spatial presentations). Although students may prefer solving homework problems that are exactly like those discussed in class, they are more likely to master the concepts if the problems are different. (Sources: Bransford et al., 2000; Halpern and Hakel, 2003)

Create opportunities for students to learn in the context of real-world challenges. Real-world challenges reflect how knowledge is obtained and applied in everyday situations—called situation learning. Examples of situation learning include asking students to create archives of primary source materials on a particular topic, interview an individual for an oral history, or develop a marketing campaign for a nonprofit. (Sources: Anderson et al., 1996; Lave and Wenger, 1991)

Give students specific pointers. Frequent, immediate, and specific feedback helps students learn, and most students increase their effort in response to praise and encouragement. Focus your comments on one or two items at a time, helping students see the destination, the path, and the next immediate steps. Constructive criticism and evidence of progress will sustain students' motivation to learn and to persevere. (Sources: American Psychological Association, 1997; Hattie and Timperley, 2007; Lowman, 1995; Weimer, 2002)

Give students opportunities for self-reflection. Self-beliefs ("I am terrible at math"), emotions, and anxieties can interfere with learning. So can the misconception that learning simply "happens" without effort or perseverance. To the extent possible, maximize students' passion for the content and minimize their anxieties. Some students may benefit from keeping a learning log (notes on what and how they are learning) or a learning agenda (what they need or want to learn and a plan of action). (Sources: Fink, 2003; Halpern and Hakel, 2003; Leamnson, 1999; Mentkowski and Associates, 2000)

Design tests that emphasize what you want students to learn. Studies show that studying for frequent quizzes enhances students' long-term retention. What students remember (and what they forget) is also influenced by the kind of material that appears on tests. Cumulative tests—those that touch on all the topics already covered in the course, not just the most recent ones—are extremely effective (though highly unpopular) because they require students to continually review and integrate the course material. (Sources: Bacon and Stewart, 2006; Halpern and Hakel, 2003; Roediger and Karpicke, 2006; Rohrer and Pashler, 2007)

Student Note Taking

Encourage students to take notes. Note taking increases students' attention in class and increases their performance on tests, although note taking can also interfere with students' efforts to understand the content. (Source: Piolat et al., 2005)

Researchers estimate that typical students record only about one-third of the important ideas in a lecture (Kiewra, 2002). Try these strategies to facilitate better note taking by your students (adapted from Armbruster, 2000; Chew, 2007; DeZure et al., 2001; Kiewra, 1987; Peverly et al., 2007; Titsworth, 2004):

- Pace your speech to give students time to write.
- Pause periodically to allow students time to assimilate and record information.
- Provide an outline that alerts students to the organizational pattern.
- Use cues to reinforce the organization of ideas: topics, definitions, examples, applications, and the like.
- Flag key concepts and important ideas ("Be sure to highlight this concept").

Some faculty ask students not to take notes for a segment of the class, for example, when the instructor is working through a problem on the board. After the demonstration, they give students five minutes to write down the example and the solution.

Give students opportunities to review their notes during class. "Remember when we discussed the Grand Unification Theory? You should have that in your notes. What do you have written down?" Or stop five minutes before the session ends and ask students to review their notes and highlight or underline key concepts. Some instructors tell their students which key points they should highlight. (Source: Chew, 2007)

Give students pointers on how to take notes in your class. Some faculty advise students in note-taking techniques such as these (adapted from Armbruster, 2000; Bjork, 2001; Helft, 2007; Kiewra, 1987; Peverly et al., 2007; Titsworth and Kiewra, 2004):

- Develop symbols or indents to distinguish major from minor points.
- Leave blank spaces for material or points you don't understand.
- Wait until an idea has been presented in full before writing notes about it.
- Paraphrase main ideas and concepts in your own words rather than writing things down verbatim.
- Review webcasts or podcasts of lectures to fill in blanks in your notes.

One faculty member requires each student to sign up to take notes for one class during the semester. With a large class, this provides multiple sets of notes for each day. These notes are placed online so that all the students can see how others have organized and interpreted the material.

Distribute your notes. Some instructors post their own notes on the class Web site for students to review before or after class. One effective method is to post an outline or partial set of instructor's notes before the class and encourage students to add to those notes during class. Researchers report that students who receive partial notes perform better on exams and earn higher course grades than students who receive a full set of notes. However, students report that having a full set of instructor's notes gives them a measure of confidence about succeeding in the course. (Sources: Cornelius and Owen-DeSchryver, 2008; Murphy and Cross, 2002; Vandehey et al., 2004)

Self-Regulated Learning

Help students become self-regulated learners. Self-regulated learners monitor and manage their learning resources (such as time, study space), motivation, and strategies. They set goals for increasing their knowledge, select appropriate strategies, manage their efforts, respond to external feedback, and monitor the cumulative effects of their practices. Self-regulated learners are aware of their own knowledge, beliefs, motivations, and cognitive processing. (Sources: Pintrich, 2000; Schunk, 2004)

Give students choices. For self-regulation to occur, learners must have some choice in their methods of learning, time spent studying, the setting where learning occurs, and so on. When learners have few choices, their behavior is externally regulated rather than self-regulated. (Source: Zimmerman and Schunk, 2001)

Introduce the notion of metacognitive skills. Metacognition is the process of reflecting on, regulating, and directing one's cognitive processes. Studies have shown that learners who monitor their own understanding have better recall when they are tested. Help students learn how to explain concepts to themselves, stay on task, note gaps in their comprehension, plan ahead, self-correct errors, and apportion time and effort. (Sources: Bransford et al., 2000; Donovan et al., 1999; Fink, 2003; Koriat and Helstrup, 2007; Pellegrino et al., 2001)

Provide frequent assessments and pointers. When an instructor provides frequent assessments and feedback, students can better monitor their progress, become aware of what they do not know, and determine whether their learning strategies are working. Feedback clarifies the standards for good performance, which helps students identify the strengths and weaknesses of their own work. (Sources: Bransford et al., 2000; Butler and Winne, 1995; Kruger and Dunning, 1999; Nicol and Macfarlane-Dick, 2006)

Helping Students Develop Effective Learning Strategies

Give advice on how to study and learn. Unfortunately, few students have been taught how to study (Gardiner, 1998). You can help your students become self-regulated learners by coaching them on how to improve their reading comprehension and retention, how to take notes, how to participate in class discussions, and how to study for tests. Most students can benefit from the following strategies (adapted from Bjork, 2001; Rohrer and Pashler, 2007):

- Divide up the material to be studied. Research shows that reading five to seven pages of a text each day is better than reading the entire chapter a day or two before the test.
- Organize the information. Summarizing key points or generating new examples leads to better long-term retention than reading passively.
- Generate questions about the material as a way of focusing study efforts and identifying what is known and what is not known.
- Form a study group. Students benefit from hearing other points of view and from seeing how others organize the material.
- Practice by saying ideas aloud, making mental pictures of ideas, and associating new knowledge with something familiar.
- Schedule a series of study sessions rather than cramming right before a test.
- Avoid overlearning. Time spent studying material that has already been mastered is an inefficient strategy for long-term retention. Once students have mastered the content (achieved one perfect run-through), it is more effective for long-term retention to review concepts and materials learned weeks or months earlier.
- Balance study with sleep, healthy meals, and exercise.
- Seek help from teachers, tutors, and other students.

Structure assignments to encourage realistic planning and minimize procrastination. Left to their own devices, most students do not take advantage of long deadlines: if you assign a term paper in the fifth week of a fifteen-week semester, the typical student will spend five weeks, not ten, on the project (Ackerman and Gross, 2005). In addition, students tend to greatly underestimate how long an academic task will take. Here are some strategies to discourage procrastination and facilitate realistic planning (adapted from Ackerman and Gross, 2005; Buehler et al., 2002; Wolters, 2003):

- Devise assignments that appeal to students' interests, professional aspirations, and desire to participate in real-world situations.
- Give students a choice of assignments.

- Provide clear instructions on how to get started and how to proceed. Students who are confused about what is expected are more likely to procrastinate.
- Break large tasks into parts, and set deadlines for each part. Show students how to turn assignments into manageable chunks that require about an hour's work on any given day.
- Help students set reasonable expectations about the amount of effort needed to complete a task.
- Encourage students to generate their own schedules for finishing the assignment.

References

Ackerman, D. S., and Gross, B. L. "My Instructor Made Me Do It: Task Characteristics of Procrastination." *Journal of Marketing Education*, 2005, *27*(1), 5–13.

American Psychological Association. *Learner-Centered Psychological Principles: Guidelines for School Redesign and Reform*. Washington, DC: American Psychological Association, 1997.

Anderson, J. R., Reder, L. M., and Simon, H. A. "Situated Learning and Education." *Educational Researcher*, 1996, *25*(4), 5–11.

Armbruster, B. B. Taking Notes from Lectures. In R. F. Flippo and D. C. Caverly (Eds.), *Handbook of College Reading and Study Strategy Research*. Mahwah, NJ: Erlbaum, 2000.

Bacon, D. R., and Stewart, K. A. "How Fast Do Students Forget What They Learn in Consumer Behavior? A Longitudinal Study." *Journal of Marketing Education*, 2006, *28*(3), 181–192.

Belenky, M. F., Clinchy, B. M., Goldberger, N. R., and Tarule, J. M. *Women's Ways of Knowing: The Development of Self, Body, and Mind*. New York: Basic Books, 1986.

Biggs, J. B., Kember, D., and Leung, D. Y. P. "The Revised Two-Factor Study Process Questionnaire: R-SPQ-2F." *British Journal of Educational Psychology*, 2001, *71*(1), 133–149.

Bjork, R. A. "How to Succeed in College: Learn How to Learn." APS *Observer*, March 2001, *14*(3), 9.

Bransford, J. D., Brown, A. L., and Cocking, R. R. *How People Learn: Brain, Mind, Experience, and School*. Washington, DC: National Academy Press, 2000.

Buehler, R., Griffin, D., and Ross, M. Inside the Planning Fallacy: The Causes and Consequences of Optimistic Time Predictions. In T. Gilovich, D. Griffin, and D. Kahneman (Eds.), *Heuristics and Biases: The Psychology of Intuitive Judgment*. New York: Cambridge University Press, 2002.

Butler, D., and Winne, P. "Feedback and Self-Regulated Learning: A Theoretical Synthesis." *Review of Educational Research*, 1995, *65*(3), 245–281.

Chew, S. L. Study More! Study Harder! Students' and Teachers' Faulty Beliefs about How People Learn. In S. A. Meyers and J. R. Stowell (Eds.), *Essays from Excellence in Teaching*. Vol. 7. Society for the Teaching of Psychology, 2007. http://teachpsych.org/resources/e-books/eit2007/eit2007.php

Clark, R. C., Nguyen, F., and Sweller, J. *Efficiency in Learning: Evidence-Based Guidelines to Manage Cognitive Load*. San Francisco: Pfeiffer, 2006.

Cornelius, T. L., and Owen-DeSchryver, J. "Differential Effects of Full and Partial Notes on Learning Outcomes and Attendance." *Teaching of Psychology*, 2008, *35*(1), 6–12.

DeZure, D., Kaplan, M., and Deerman, M. A. "Research on Student Notetaking: Implications for Faculty and Graduate Student Instructors." CRLT Occasional Paper, no. 16. Ann Arbor: University of Michigan, Center for Research on Learning and Teaching, 2001.

Dochy, F., Segers, M., and Buehl, M. M. "The Relation between Assessment Practices and Outcomes of Studies: The Case of Research on Prior Knowledge." *Review of Educational Research*, 1999, *69*(2), 145–186.

Donovan, M. S., Bransford, J. D., and Pellegrino, J. W. (Eds.). *How People Learn: Bridging Research and Practice*. Washington, DC: National Academy Press, 1999.

Erickson, B. L., Peters, C. B., and Strommer, D. W. *Teaching First-Year College Students*. San Francisco: Jossey-Bass, 2006.

Fink, L. D. *Creating Significant Learning Experiences: An Integrated Approach to Designing College Courses*. San Francisco: Jossey-Bass, 2003.

Fry, H., Ketteridge, S., and Marshall, S. *A Handbook for Teaching and Learning in Higher Education: Enhancing Academic Practice*. (2nd ed.) New York: RoutledgeFalmer, 2003.

Gardiner, L. F. "Why We Must Change: The Research Evidence." *Thought & Action*, Spring 1998, *14*(1), 71–88.

Graesser, A. C., Olde, B., and Klettke, B. How Does the Mind Construct and Represent Stories? In M. C. Green, J. J. Strange, and T. C. Brock (Eds.), *Narrative Impact: Social and Cognitive Foundations*. Mahwah, NJ: Erlbaum, 2002.

Grasha, A. F. *Teaching with Style: A Practical Guide to Enhancing Learning by Understanding Teaching and Learning Styles*. San Bernardino, CA: Alliance Publishers, 1996.

Halpern, D. F., and Hakel, M. D. "Applying the Science of Learning to the University and Beyond." *Change*, 2003, *35*(4), 36–41.

Hattie, J., and Timperley, H. "The Power of Feedback." *Review of Educational Research*, 2007, *77*(1), 81–112.

Hayes, E., and Flannery, D. D. *Women as Learners: The Significance of Gender in Adult Learning*. San Francisco: Jossey-Bass, 2000.

Helft, M. "Take Note: Computing Takes Up Pen, Again." *New York Times*, May 30, 2007.

Kiewra, K. A. "Notetaking and Review: The Research and Its Implications." *Instructional Science*, 1987, *16*(3), 233–249.

Kiewra, K. A. "How Classroom Teachers Can Help Students Learn and Teach Them How to Learn." *Theory into Practice*, 2002, *41*(2), 71–80.

King, P. M., and Kitchener, K. S. *Developing Reflective Judgment: Understanding and Promoting Intellectual Growth and Critical Thinking*. San Francisco: Jossey-Bass, 1994.

Koriat, A., and Helstrup, T. Metacognitive Aspects of Memory. In S. Magnussen and T. Helstrup (Eds.), *Everyday Memory*. New York: Psychology Press, 2007.

Kruger, J., and Dunning, D. "Unskilled and Unaware of It: How Difficulties in Recognizing One's Own Incompetence Lead to Inflated Self-Assessments." *Journal of Personality and Social Psychology*, 1999, *77*(6), 1121–1134.

Kurfiss, J. Intellectual, Psychosocial, and Moral Development in College: Four Major Theories. In K. A. Feldman and M. B. Paulsen (Eds.), *Teaching and Learning in the College Classroom*. (2nd ed.) Needham Heights, MA: Simon and Schuster, 1998.

Lave, J., and Wenger, E. *Situated Learning*. New York: Cambridge University Press, 1991.

Leamnson, R. *Thinking about Teaching and Learning: Developing Habits of Learning with First Year College and University Students*. Sterling, VA: Stylus, 1999.

Linn, M. C. The Knowledge Integration Perspective on Learning and Instruction. In R. K. Sawyer (Ed.), *The Cambridge Handbook of the Learning Sciences*. Cambridge, England: Cambridge University Press, 2006.

Lowman, J. *Mastering the Techniques of Teaching.* (2nd ed.) San Francisco: Jossey-Bass, 1995.

Mentkowski, M., and associates. *Learning That Lasts: Integrating Learning, Development, and Performance in College and Beyond.* San Francisco: Jossey-Bass, 2000.

Murphy, T. M., and Cross, V. "Should Students Get the Instructor's Lecture Notes?" *Journal of Biological Education*, 2002, *36*(2), 72–75.

Nicol, D. J., and Macfarlane-Dick, D. "Formative Assessment and Self-Regulated Learning: A Model and Seven Principles of Good Feedback Practice." *Studies in Higher Education*, 2006, *31*(2), 199–218.

Pellegrino, J. W., Chudowsky, N., and Glaser, R. (Eds.). *Knowing What Students Know: The Science and Design of Educational Assessment*. Washington, DC: National Academy Press, 2001.

Perry, W. G., Jr. *Forms of Intellectual and Ethical Development in the College Years: A Scheme.* New York: Holt, Rinehart & Winston, 1970. (Reprinted San Francisco: Jossey-Bass, 1998.)

Peverly, S. T., Ramaswamy, V., Brown, C., Sumowski, J., Alidoost, M., and Garner, J. "What Predicts Skill in Lecture Note Taking?" *Journal of Educational Psychology*, 2007, *99*(1), 167–180.

Pintrich, P. R. The Role of Goal Orientation in Self-Regulated Learning. In M. Boekaerts, P. R. Pintrich, and M. Zeidner (Eds.), *Handbook of Self-Regulation*. San Diego: Academic Press, 2000.

Piolat, A., Olive, T., and Kellogg, R. T. "Cognitive Effort during Note Taking." *Applied Cognitive Psychology*, 2005, *19*, 291–312.

Prosser, M., and Trigwell, K. *Understanding Learning and Teaching: The Experience in Higher Education*. Philadelphia: Society for Research into Higher Education and Open University Press, 1999.

Ramsden, P. *Learning to Teach in Higher Education.* (2nd ed.) New York: RoutledgeFalmer, 2003.

Roediger, H. L., Gallo, D. A., and Geraci, L. "Processing Approaches to Cognition: The Impetus from the Levels-of-Processing Framework." *Memory*, 2002, *10*(5–6), 319–332.

Roediger, H. L., and Karpicke, J. D. "Test-Enhanced Learning: Taking Memory Tests Improves Long-Term Retention." *Psychological Science*, 2006, *17*(3), 249–255.

Rohrer, D., and Pashler, H. "Increasing Retention without Increasing Study Time." *Current Directions in Psychological Science*, 2007, *16*(4), 183–186.

Schmidt, J. A., and Davidson, M. L. "Helping Students Think." *Personnel and Guidance Journal*, 1983, *61*(9), 563–569.

Schunk, D. H. *Learning Theories: An Educational Perspective.* (4th ed.) Upper Saddle River, NJ: Pearson Merrill Prentice Hall, 2004.

Svinicki, M. D. *Learning and Motivation in the Postsecondary Classroom*. Bolton, MA: Anker, 2004.

Taber, K. S. "The Mismatch between Assumed Prior Knowledge and the Learner's Conceptions: A Typology of Learning Impediments." *Educational Studies*, 2001, *27*(2), 159–171.

Tiberius, R. G. *Small Group Teaching: A Trouble-Shooting Guide*. London: Kogan Page, 1999.

Titsworth, B. S. "Students' Notetaking: The Effects of Teacher Immediacy and Clarity." *Communication Education*, 2004, *53*(4), 305–320.

Titsworth, B. S., and Kiewra, K. A. "Spoken Organizational Lecture Cues and Student Notetaking as Facilitators of Student Learning." *Contemporary Educational Psychology*, 2004, *29*(4), 447–461.

Vandehey, M. A., Marsh, C. M., and Diekhoff, G. M. "Providing Students with Instructors' Notes: Problems with Reading, Studying and Attendance." *Teaching of Psychology*, 2004, *32*(1), 49–52.

Weimer, M. *Learner-Centered Teaching: Five Key Changes to Practice.* San Francisco: Jossey-Bass, 2002.

Wolters, C. A. "Understanding Procrastination from a Self-Regulated Learning Perspective." *Journal of Educational Psychology*, 2003, *95*(1), 179–187.

Ybarra, O., Burnstein, E., Winkielman, P., Keller, M. C, Manis, M., Chan, E., and Rodríguez, J. "Mental Exercising through Simple Socializing: Social Interaction Promotes General Cognitive Functioning." *Personality and Social Psychology Bulletin*, 2008, *34*(2), 248–259.

Zimmerman, B. J., and Schunk, D. H. (Eds.). *Self-Regulated Learning and Academic Achievement: Theoretical Perspectives.* (2nd ed.) Mahwah, NJ: Erlbaum, 2001.

30

Learning Styles and Preferences

The concept of learning styles derives from the observation that individuals have characteristic and preferred ways of gathering, interpreting, organizing, recalling, and thinking about information. Some learners prefer to work independently, while others do better in groups. Some prefer to absorb information by reading; others like hands-on experimentation. No one style of learning has been shown to be more effective than any other.

Researchers disagree about the value and utility of the various models and theories of learning styles. Some argue that the models have little practical application (Kratzig and Arbuthnott, 2006; Leamnson, 1999); others cite data showing that educators can increase students' academic performance by focusing on learning styles (Dunn and Griggs, 2000).

For college faculty, the concept of learning styles serves as a useful reminder that both students and instructors may benefit from expanding their repertoire of cognitive strategies and processes. For example, instructors with strong analytic styles may want to also present explanations that will satisfy students whose styles are more intuitive and inductive. Instructors with predominantly intuitive styles may want to think about incorporating material that will meet their analytic students' preferences for definition and structure. Keep in mind that styles of learning do not make nearly as much difference in student achievement as do students' prior knowledge, skills and abilities, and motivation (McKeachie, 1995).

General Strategies

Vary your teaching methods, assignments, and learning activities. Experiment with different modes of presentation: lectures, discussion, reading assignments, audiovisual materials, and hands-on activities. Give students opportunities to do group work as well as to work alone. Try to provide options for assignments: written papers, oral reports, and multimedia portfolios. (Sources: American Psychological Association, 1997; Chism et al., 1989; Sarasin, 2006)

Give exams that call on different cognitive skills. For example, a midterm might include questions that ask for specific information (recall) and questions that require focused analysis (compare and contrast) as well as short-answer items that call for problem solving or the practical application of theoretical principles. (Source: Claxton and Murrell, 1987)

Encourage students to value different learning styles and orientations. Students may prefer to work with classmates whose learning styles are similar to their own, but some research suggests that students may gain useful insights from working with a variety of learners. Other research posits that learning styles may be related to cultural norms. For example, students from cultures that value the group may have a preference for collaborative learning environments. (Sources: Anderson, 1988; Bonham, 1989; Irvine and York, 1995; Nisbett, 2003; Sánchez, 2000)

Models of Learning Styles

Taxonomy of models. Cassidy (2004) summarizes attempts to simplify and categorize dozens of models of learning styles. He also critiques various self-report questionnaires that measure learning style. Four models of learning styles are briefly described here.

Kolb's learning styles. Kolb (1984) identifies four types of learners:

- *Convergers* rely on abstract conceptualization and active experimentation; they like to find concrete answers and move quickly to find solutions to problems; they are good at defining problems and making decisions.
- *Divergers* use concrete experience and reflective observation to generate a range of ideas; they excel at brainstorming and imagining alternatives.
- *Assimilators* rely on abstract conceptualization and reflective observation; they like to assimilate a wide range of information and recast it into a concise logical form; they are good at planning, developing theories, and creating models.
- *Accommodators* are best at concrete experience and active experimentation; they often use trial-and-error or intuitive strategies to solve problems; they tend to take risks and plunge into problems.

    In terms of classroom activities, convergers tend to prefer solving problems that have definite answers. Divergers may benefit more from discussion groups and working collaboratively on projects. Assimilators would feel most comfortable observing, watching role plays and simulations in class, and then generating concepts. Accommodators may prefer hands-on activities.

Visual, aural, read/write, kinesthetic (VARK). The VARK model posits four principal modalities for taking in information: visual, aural, reading and writing, and kinesthetic (hands-on manipulation). Individuals are assumed to have one predominant style for learning new information (Fleming and Mills, 1992), although styles may vary by task and situation, and preferences may blur over time. In terms of teaching strategies, an instructor might want to combine visual representations (diagrams, flow charts), auditory activities (lectures, debates), reading and writing assignments, and kinesthetic activities (role playing and field trips).

Multiple intelligences. Gardner (1999) discusses eight types of intelligence: verbal-linguistic, mathematical-logical, musical, visual-spatial, bodily-kinesthetic, interpersonal, intrapersonal, and naturalistic. Most people are stronger in one or two types of intelligence and weaker in others. Traditional college courses tend to emphasize verbal-linguistic and mathematical-logical thinking. To enhance learning, instructors are encouraged to combine strategies that tap the other intelligences, for example, by using narrative, music, role playing, free writing, and pair work.

Thinking styles. Sternberg (1997) relates thinking styles to intellectual self-government: legislative thinking is aimed at creating and formulating, executive thinking at implementation, and judicial thinking at evaluation and judgment. Sternberg's model describes four types of thinkers: monarchic thinkers prefer to do one task at a time; hierarchic thinkers like to deal with many tasks but recognize some as more important than others; oligarchic thinkers are comfortable dealing with many tasks but have trouble setting priorities; and anarchic thinkers take a random approach to tasks and dislike constraints. According to Sternberg, individuals have a preferred style but also combine different styles to meet specific situations.

Helping Students Recognize Their Learning Styles and Preferences

Explain the value of knowing about learning styles. The concept of learning styles may help your students understand their own learning processes, identify their learning needs, develop new learning behaviors, analyze what successful learners do, and learn more effectively. In this spirit, you might ask students to notice what actions they take when they are trying to learn something. For example, when trying to learn a new software application, do they read the manual? learn through trial and error? ask someone to show them? You could also ask students to think about what kinds of learning activities they find most rewarding and what kinds they most dread. (Sources: Erickson et al., 2006; Sims and Sims, 1995)

Refer interested students to self-scored surveys. Students can identify their strengths and weaknesses by using such online inventories as VARK (www .vark-learn.com), the Motivated Strategies for Learning Questionnaire (www.ulc. arizona.edu), or Kolb's Learning Style Inventory (Duff, 2004). Let students know that these questionnaires are not intelligence tests of any kind: they are intended only to help students become more aware of how they learn. Advise students to ignore any results that do not ring true to their own judgments of how they learn best.

Administer a checklist. Researchers have developed checklists that students can complete to help them understand how they have learned a specific skill or domain of knowledge. Checklist items include the amount of time spent on learning, the motivation for learning, the learning processes employed (doing, observing, practicing), and the cognitive processes used (analyzing information, using rules to guide thinking, and forming principles). (Source: Grasha, 1990)

References

American Psychological Association. *Learner-Centered Psychological Principles: Guidelines for School Redesign and Reform.* Washington, DC: American Psychological Association, 1997.

Anderson, J. A. "Cognitive Styles and Multicultural Populations." *Journal of Teacher Education,* 1988, *39*(1), 2–9.

Bonham, L. A. "Using Learning Style Information," Too. In E. Hayes (Ed.), *Effective Teaching Styles.* New Directions for Continuing Education, no. 43. San Francisco: Jossey-Bass, 1989.

Cassidy, S. "Learning Styles: An Overview of Theories, Models, and Measures." *Educational Psychology,* 2004, *24*(4), 419–444.

Chism, N. V. N., Cano, J., and Pruitt, A. S. "Teaching in a Diverse Environment: Knowledge and Skills Needed by TAs." In J. D. Nyquist, R. D. Abbott, and D. H. Wulff (Eds.), *Teaching Assistant Training in the 1990s.* New Directions for Teaching and Learning, no. 39. San Francisco: Jossey-Bass, 1989.

Claxton, C. S., and Murrell, P. H. *Learning Styles: Implications for Improving Educational Practices.* ASHE-ERIC Higher Education Report, 1987, no. 4.

Duff, A. "A Note on the Problem Solving Style Questionnaire: An Alternative to Kolb's Learning Style Inventory." *Educational Psychology,* 2004, *24*(5), 699–709.

Dunn, R., and Griggs, S. A. (Eds.). *Practical Approaches to Using Learning Styles in Higher Education.* Westport, CT: Bergin and Garvey, 2000.

Erickson, B. L., Peters, C. B., and Strommer, D. W. *Teaching First-Year College Students.* San Francisco: Jossey-Bass, 2006.

Fleming, N. D., and Mills, C. Not Another Inventory, Rather a Catalyst for Reflection. In D. Wulff and J. Nyquist (Eds.), *To Improve the Academy*, Vol. 11, San Francisco: Jossey-Bass, 1992.

Gardner, H. *Intelligence Reframed: Multiple Intelligences for the 21st Century.* New York: Basic Books, 1999.

Grasha, T. "The Naturalistic Approach to Learning Styles." *College Teaching*, 1990, *38*(3), 106–113.

Irvine, J. J., and York, D. E. Learning Styles and Culturally Diverse Students: A Literature Review. In J. A. Banks and C.A.M. Banks (Eds.), *Handbook of Research on Multicultural Education.* New York: MacMillan, 1995.

Kolb, D. A. *Experiential Learning: Experiences as a Source of Learning and Development.* Englewood Cliffs, NJ: Prentice Hall, 1984.

Kratzig, G. P., and Arbuthnott, K. D. "Perceptual Learning Style and Learning Proficiency: A Test of the Hypothesis." *Journal of Educational Psychology*, 2006, *98*(1), 238–246.

Leamnson, R. *Thinking about Teaching and Learning: Developing Habits of Learning with First Year College and University Students.* Sterling, VA: Stylus, 1999.

McKeachie. W. J. "Learning Styles Can Become Learning Strategies." *National Teaching and Learning Forum*, 1995, *4*(6), 1–3.

Nisbett, R. E. *The Geography of Thought: How Asians and Westerners Think Differently and Why.* New York: Free Press, 2003.

Sánchez, I. M. *Motivating and Maximizing Learning in Minority Classrooms.* New Directions for Community Colleges, 2000, *28*(4), 35–44.

Sarasin, L. C. *Learning Style Perspectives: Impact in the Classroom.* (2nd ed.) Madison, WI: Atwood, 2006.

Sims, S. J., and Sims, R. R. Learning and Learning Styles: A Review and Look to the Future. In S. J. Sims and R. R. Sims (Eds.), *The Importance of Learning Styles.* Westport, CT: Greenwood, 1995.

Sternberg, R. J. *Thinking Styles.* New York: Cambridge University Press., 1997.

Motivating Students

31

Some students seem naturally enthusiastic about learning, but many need—or expect—their instructors to inspire, challenge, and stimulate them. Whatever level of motivation your students bring to the classroom will be transformed, for better or worse, by what happens in that classroom.

Unfortunately, there is no single formula for motivating students. Many factors affect students' motivation to study and learn (Brophy, 2004; Svinicki, 2004; Wlodkowski, 1999): interest in the subject matter, perception of its usefulness, general desire to achieve, self-confidence and self-esteem, as well as patience and persistence. And, of course, not all students are motivated by the same values, needs, desires, or wants. Some of your students will be motivated by winning the approval of others, some by overcoming challenges, some by achieving mastery, and some by obtaining good grades.

To encourage students to become self-motivated learners, research suggests that instructors use the following strategies:

- Give frequent, early, positive feedback that supports students' beliefs that they can do well.
- Ensure opportunities for students' meaningful success by assigning tasks that are neither too easy and fail to challenge them nor too difficult and overwhelm them.
- Communicate personal interest in students by calling them by name, initiating conversations with them before or after class, asking questions during class, and referring to "our" class.
- Use teaching strategies that engage and actively involve students.
- Help students find personal meaning and value in the material.
- Create a classroom environment that welcomes the successes and accepts the stumbles and failures that accompany learning.
- Help students feel that they are valued members of a community of responsible learners.

  (Sources: Barron and Hulleman, 2006; Benson and Cohen, 2005; Bligh, 2000; Covington, 1997; Cross, 2001; Lowman, 1995; Sleigh et al., 2002; Theall, 1999; Wilson, 2006)

Good everyday teaching practices can do more to counter student apathy than special efforts to affect motivation directly. Most students respond positively to a well-organized course taught by an enthusiastic instructor who has a genuine interest in students and what they learn. Thus, activities you undertake to promote learning will also enhance students' motivation.

General Strategies

Be enthusiastic about your subject. An instructor's enthusiasm is a crucial factor in student motivation. If you seem bored or apathetic, students will lose interest and momentum. Think back to what attracted you to the field and bring those aspects of the subject to life for your students. If portions of the material seem dull to you, challenge yourself to devise the most exciting way to present that material.

Address students' basic needs and desires. Students' needs and desires include succeeding in a task or activity, perfecting skills, overcoming challenges, acquiring competency, having new experiences, feeling involved, and interacting with other people. Satisfying such needs is rewarding in itself, and such intrinsic rewards sustain learning more effectively than grades do. Design assignments, in-class activities, and discussion questions that tap these dimensions. (Source: McMillan and Forsyth, 1991)

Create opportunities for active participation. Passivity dampens students' motivation and curiosity. Students learn by doing, making, writing, designing, creating, and solving. See Chapter 9, "Leading a Discussion"; Chapter 18: "Encouraging Student Participation in the Large-Enrollment Course"; and Part V, "Alternatives and Supplements to Lectures and Discussion."

Hold high but realistic expectations for your students. Research has shown that an instructor's expectations have a powerful effect on students' performance. If you treat your students like motivated, hardworking, and independent learners, they are more likely to behave that way. Try to set standards that are high enough to motivate students to do their best but not so high that students will feel that the goals are beyond their abilities. Students need to believe that meaningful achievement is within their grasp, and they need early opportunities for success. (Sources: American Psychological Association, 1992; Bligh, 2000; Cross, 2001; Forsyth and McMillan, 1991; Lowman, 1995)

Starting the Term on a Positive Note

Tell students what they need to do to succeed in your course. Assure students that they can do well in your course, and tell them what they must do to succeed: "If you can handle the examples in the problem sets, you can pass the exam. People who have trouble with these examples can ask me for extra help." To a student who is behind, point the way forward: "Here is one way you could go about learning the material. How can I help you?" (Sources: Cashin, 1979; Tiberius, 1999)

Help students set achievable goals for themselves. Encourage students to focus on their continuing improvement, not on their grade on any one test or assignment. Help students evaluate their progress by encouraging them to critique their own work, analyze their strengths, and address their weaknesses. (Sources: Cashin, 1979; Cross, 2001; Forsyth and McMillan, 1991)

Avoid stoking competitive drives. A dash of competitive spirit may motivate some students, but strenuous competition produces anxiety, which can interfere with learning. Set a constructive tone by refraining from public criticism of students' performance and from comments or activities that pit students against each other.

Maintaining Motivation throughout the Term

Build on students' strengths and interests. Find out why students enrolled in your course and try to incorporate examples and case studies that relate to students' interests and experiences. For instance, a chemistry professor might devote some class time to examining the contributions of chemistry to resolving environmental problems. Explain how the content and objectives of your course can help students achieve their educational, professional, or personal goals.

When possible, give students choices. Give students options on term papers or assignments, let them decide between two locations for the field trip, or have them select which topics to explore in greater depth. Choosing among alternatives gives students the opportunity to develop skills in regulating their own learning: planning what to do, setting goals, monitoring their performance, and reflecting on their actions. (Sources: Cashin, 1979; Cross, 2001; Lowman, 1995; Young, 2003)

Increase the difficulty of the material as the semester progresses. Give students opportunities to succeed at the beginning of the semester and then gradually increase the level of difficulty. If assignments and exams include easier and harder questions, every student will have a chance to experience success as well as challenge. (Source: Cashin, 1979)

Vary your teaching methods. Variety reawakens students' involvement in the course and their motivation. Break the routine with a session of role playing, debating, brainstorming, field experience, demonstrations, case studies, or a guest speaker.

Ask students to explore their motivations. Suggest that students complete an online survey, such as the Motivational Strategies for Learning Questionnaire (MSLQ), developed at the University of Michigan. A short version is available on the University of Arizona Web site: www.ulc.arizona.edu/quick_mslq.php. Students receive scores on their goal orientation, beliefs about control, self-efficacy, and other items. (Source: Duncan and McKeachie, 2005)

De-emphasizing Grades

Emphasize the intrinsic rewards of learning. Research shows that motivation is undermined when students are striving for extrinsic rewards, such as grades, rather than intrinsic rewards, which include mastery, self-expression, conquering challenges, personal growth, and meaningful discovery. In addition, students who are motivated by intrinsic rewards tend to process course content at a deeper level, persist longer in learning situations, and show more interest in coursework than students who are motivated by grades. Instructors can stress the personal satisfaction that comes from mastering material and course content, help students measure their progress, and praise and reward students for making good progress. (Sources: Barron and Hulleman, 2006; Brophy, 2004; Covington, 1997; Deci and Ryan, 2002; Lowman, 1995)

Design tests that encourage the kind of learning you want students to achieve. Many students will learn whatever is necessary to get the grades they desire. If you base your tests on memorizing details, students will focus on memorizing facts. If your tests stress the synthesis and evaluation of information, students will be motivated to practice those skills when they study. (Source: McKeachie and Svinicki, 2006)

Avoid using grades as threats. The threat of low grades may prompt some students to work hard, but other students may resort to academic dishonesty, excuses for late work, and other counterproductive behavior. (Source: McKeachie and Svinicki, 2006)

Offering Feedback and Advice

Give students feedback as quickly as possible. Return tests and papers promptly, give students advice on how to improve, and reward success publicly and immediately. Rewards can be as simple as saying a student's response was good, with an indication of why it was good: "Ling-Chi's point about pollution really synthesized the ideas we had been discussing." (Source: Cashin, 1979)

Use praise judiciously. Both positive and negative comments influence motivation, but research indicates that students can be particularly affected by specific positive comments. If a student's performance is weak, offer a comment that expresses your belief in the student's capacity to improve and succeed over time. Keep your comments focused on the task at hand rather than shifting the student's attention to self, which can distract from learning. (Sources: Cashin, 1979; Cross, 2001; Shute, 2008)

Try to cushion negative comments. Criticism is a very powerful stimulus. When you identify a student's weakness, make it clear that your comments relate to a particular task or performance, not to the student as a learner or as a person. Offset negative comments with a compliment about aspects of the task in which the student succeeded. Avoid offhand or joking remarks that may hurt students' feelings. (Source: Cashin, 1979)

Give feedback to enhance student learning. A body of research has shown ways that instructors can make feedback more effective (adapted from Shute, 2008):

- Focus on the task, not the learner.
- Provide guidance in manageable chunks so as not to overwhelm students, giving only enough information to help them and no more.
- Give comments in writing rather than in person.
- Emphasize learning rather than performance by acknowledging the role mistakes play in the learning process.
- Avoid normative comparisons with other students.
- Give both immediate feedback (to fix errors in real time) and delayed feedback (to encourage transfer of learning).

Specific Tasks: Motivating Students to Do the Reading

Establish norms early in the term. On average only about one-third of your students will have completed the reading on any given day. Set expectations and hold students accountable for doing the required reading in a timely fashion. If you do not in some way monitor whether students complete the reading, some students will conclude that the reading is of little consequence. (Source: Burchfield and Sappington, 2000)

Give students guidance on how to read the assignment. Discuss appropriate reading strategies for your field: how to approach the material, the importance of distinguishing major points from minor details, and so on. Your campus probably has resources to help students develop their critical reading skills; or you can refer students to materials developed at Dartmouth ("Reading Textbooks Effectively") or Stanford ("Reading Efficacy"), available on the university Web sites by searching for the title. Bean (1996) and Erickson, Peters, and Strommer (2006) also offer tips on helping students get the most from the assigned reading.

Assign the reading and the study questions at least two sessions in advance. Give students ample time to prepare, and give them study questions that highlight the key points. Try to pique students' curiosity about the reading: "This article is one of my favorites, and I'll be interested to see what you think about it." (Source: Lowman, 1995)

Ask students to prepare questions based on the reading. As class size permits, have students turn in two index cards, each of which contains a question and their name. Randomly redistribute the cards in class and call on a student to read the question from the card, indicate who wrote it, and attempt to answer it; then open the floor to comments from others. (Source: Martin, 2000)

Give a graded assignment on the reading. Ask students to prepare written responses to questions you pose about the reading and turn in their responses for credit or for extra credit. (Source: Uskul and Eaton, 2005)

Allow students to create "survival cards" that they can use during exams. At the start of each class, a professor in the physical sciences asks students to submit a three-by-five card that contains an outline, definitions, key ideas, or other material from the day's assigned reading. After class, he checks the cards and stamps them with his name. At a class session before the midterm, he returns the cards to students and allows them to add material, but they cannot submit additional cards. The students hand in their cards, and the professor distributes them to students during the midterm. This faculty member reports that this technique encouraged 90 percent of his students to complete all the reading. Another professor uses five-by-eight cards and gives students one point of extra credit for each card they submit as well as allowing students to use the cards during the exam. This faculty member reports that about one-third of the class ended up with higher grades as a result. (Sources: Carkenord, 1994; Daniel, 1988)

Give frequent quizzes. Quizzes can prompt students to keep up with the reading and motivate students to attend class. In addition, frequent quizzes give students practice in test taking, which helps minimize anxiety and can lead to improved final exam performance. Quizzes also give you and your students a sense of how well they are learning the material and what topics are especially difficult. Students report that they are more likely to do the reading if they expect they will be quizzed. To ameliorate student anxiety about frequent testing, some instructors treat quizzes as opportunities for extra credit. (Sources: Kouyoumdjian, 2004; Marchant, 2002; Narloch et al., 2006; Thorne, 2000)

Specific Tasks: Motivating Students to Attend Class

Be realistic about student attendance. Student absenteeism is, unfortunately, common across colleges and universities. Research from the early 1990s showed that on any given day about one-third of the enrolled students do not show up for class (Romer, 1993). While there have been no comparable recent studies, faculty anecdotally report that half the class may be absent at various times during the term. Some faculty are deeply pained when students skip class, taking it personally, as a sign of disrespect to the instructor and other students. For them, classroom dynamics, climate, and intellectual exchanges are diminished when significant numbers of students are absent. Other faculty are not particularly bothered by disappearing students and teach enthusiastically to whoever shows up. How you personally feel about student attendance will affect steps you might take to address this issue.

Understand factors that affect student attendance. Researchers have surveyed students and identified the variables that appear related to attendance (Brewer and Burgess, 2005; Dolnicar, 2001; Fjortoft, 2005; Friedman et al., 2001; Gump, 2005; Moore, 2005; Rocca, 2003):

- GPA (students with better academic records attended class more regularly)
- elective versus required courses (students in elective courses attend more regularly)
- size of class (the smaller the class, the more likely students are to attend)

- type of teaching method (attendance tends to be lowest in lecture courses)
- personal qualities of the instructor (students are more likely to attend the classes of instructors they view as "friendly and approachable," "open to feedback and criticism," "respectful toward students," and "knowledgeable about students' names and interests" according to Friedman et al. (2001)

In contrast, the following factors do not appear to significantly affect attendance: student's age or year in school, student's employment status, student's residence (on or off campus), student's course load, and schedule of the class (time of day or days of the week). Popular reasons for skipping class include "I had to study for an upcoming test in another class"; "I had to run personal errands"; "I was too tired and needed to sleep"; "I didn't do the homework"; and "Class is useless."

Administer a brief survey to students about their attendance. If attendance is a concern for you, find out why students skip class by administering a brief online survey (if you administer the questionnaire in class, you will miss those who are absent). Sample questions can be found in Sleigh, Ritzer, and Casey (2002); Friedman, Rodriguez, and McComb (2001); and Woodfield, Jessop, and McMillan (2006).

Consider whether webcasting and podcasting might affect attendance. Research to date has provided little evidence that the availability of recorded lectures has any effect on learning outcomes or student performance, but some faculty believe that webcasting and podcasting contribute to student absenteeism. If students can access the same material online, they argue, doesn't that undermine their motivation to attend class? Working from that premise, some faculty limit their online posting to outlines or notes, saving details and examples for class. Others delay making webcasts or podcasts available for 24 or 48 hours. Students, however, tend to see webcasts as tools for review rather than as a replacement for attending class, although a small number of students indicate the availability of recorded lectures might make them more likely to miss class. (Sources: Deal, 2007; Grabe and Christopherson, 2008)

Explain the value of attending class. Share with students the body of research on attendance and academic performance: studies consistently show that students who regularly attend class earn higher course grades than students who regularly miss class. Appeal to students' sense of responsibility to their peers: students are part of a community of learners and by attending class regularly they can help the community flourish. Some faculty read to students Tom Wayman's wonderful poem "Did I Miss Anything?" (www.loc.gov/poetry/180/013.html). (Sources: Clump et al., 2003; Durden and Ellis, 1995; Gump, 2005; Launius, 1997; Marburger, 2001; Romer, 1993)

Do not assume that mandating attendance will solve the problem. Making attendance mandatory is unlikely to help students become self-motivated learners. More effective is the use of active learning strategies, open and engaging interpersonal interactions, and reminders throughout the term about the importance of attendance. Let students know that what happens in class can't be duplicated elsewhere. Try to make every class a unique, not entirely predictable learning experience. (Sources: Moore, 2005; St. Clair, 1999)

But take attendance. The act of taking attendance itself tends to increase the number of students who show up for each class and improves students' overall academic performance. When you take attendance, let students know that attendance records will not enter into your calculation of students' grades. (Source: Shimoff and Catania, 2001)

Experiment with specific incentives for attendance. Some faculty report success with the following techniques (adapted from POD and PsychTeacher listservs):

- Offer an extra-credit assignment to be completed outside of class on days that attendance is poor; students sign up during class to be allowed to submit the extra-credit assignment.
- Give one or two short for-credit assignments that can be done only in class.
- As class size permits, announce that at the end of the term you will ask each student to name two or three students whose class participation most contributed to their learning, and that students will receive credit for being nominated.
- Let students know the exams will contain material mentioned only in class.
- Give test hints at the end of randomly selected classes and do not let students know when that will be; give these hints after webcasting or podcasting concludes.
- Collect and return homework in class.
- Use personal response systems ("clickers") to engage students and monitor attendance.
- Ask students to complete two questions at the end of selected sessions and give two or three points of credit:
  - What was the most important thing you learned in class today?
  - What was something new you learned in class today?
  - What questions do you have as a result of today's class?

- Make some handouts available only in class and not online.
- Capitalize on the social nature of learning by undertaking activities that students cannot duplicate by viewing the webcast—for example, pair work or question-and-answer sessions.

But temper your expectations about incentives. Some studies show that certain individual traits such as conscientiousness influence student attendance more than incentives. Since conscientiousness is not amenable to external influence, incentives may have little impact on whether students attend your class. (Source: Conrad, 2004)

References

American Psychological Association. *Learner-Centered Psychological Principles: Guidelines for School Redesign and Reform.* 1992. http://www.apa.org/ed/lcp2/lcp14.html

Barron, K. E., and Hulleman, C. S. Is There a Formula to Help Understand and Improve Student Motivation? *Essays from E-xcellence in Teaching.* Vol. 6. Society for the Teaching of Psychology, 2006. http://list.kennesaw.edu/archives/psychteacher.html

Bean, J. C. *Engaging Ideas: The Professor's Guide to Integrating Writing, Critical Thinking, and Active Learning in the Classrooms.* San Francisco: Jossey-Bass, 1996.

Benson, T. A., and Cohen, A. L. "Rapport: Its Relation to Student Attitudes and Behaviors Toward Teachers and Classes." *Teaching of Psychology,* 2005, *32*(4), 237–239.

Bligh, D. A. *What's the Use of Lectures?* San Francisco: Jossey-Bass, 2000.

Brewer, E. W., and Burgess, D. N. "Professor's Role in Motivating Students to Attend Class." *Journal of Industrial Teacher Education,* 2005, *42*(3), 23–47.

Brophy, J. *Motivating Students to Learn.* (2nd ed.) Mahwah, NJ: Erlbaum, 2004.

Burchfield, C. M., and Sappington, J. "Compliance with Required Reading Assignments." *Teaching of Psychology,* 2000, *27*(1), 58–60.

Carkenord, D. M. "Motivating Students to Read Journal Articles." *Teaching of Psychology,* 1994, *21*(3), 162–164.

Cashin, W. E. "Motivating Students." *Idea Paper,* no. 1. Center for Faculty Evaluation and Development in Higher Education, Kansas State University, 1979. http://www.idea.k-state.edu/resources/index.html

Clump, M. A., Bauer, H., and Whiteleather, A. "To Attend or Not to Attend: Is That a Good Question?" *Journal of Instructional Psychology,* 2003, *30*(3), 220–224.

Conrad, M. A. "Conscientiousness Is Key: Incentives for Attendance Make Little Difference." *Teaching of Psychology,* 2004, *31*(4), 269–272.

Covington, M. V. A Motivational Analysis of Academic Life in College. In R. P. Perry and J. C. Smart (Eds.), *Effective Teaching in Higher Education: Research and Practice.* New York: Agathon Press, 1997.

Cross, K. P. "Motivation: Er . . . Will that Be on the Test?" *The Cross Papers,* no.5. Mission Viejo, CA: League for Innovation in the Community College, 2001.

Daniel, J. W. "Survival Cards in Math." *College Teaching,* 1988, *36*(3), 110.

Deal, A. "Podcasting." *A Teaching with Technology White Paper.* Carnegie Mellon University, 2007. http://www.cmu.edu/teaching/resources/PublicationsArchives/StudiesWhitepapers/Podcasting_Jun07.pdf

Deci, E. L., and Ryan, R. M. The Paradox of Achievement: The Harder You Push, the Worse It Gets. In J. Aronson (Ed.), *Improving Academic Achievement: Impact of Psychological Factors on Education.* San Diego: Academic Press, 2002.

Dolnicar, S. "Should We Still Lecture or Just Post Examination Questions on the Web? The Nature of the Shift towards Pragmatism in Undergraduate Lecture Attendance." *Quality in Higher Education*, 2005, *11*(2), 103–115.

Duncan, T. G., and McKeachie, W. J. "The Making of the Motivated Strategies for Learning Questionnaire." *Educational Psychologist*, 2005, *40*(2), 117–128.

Durden, G. C., and Ellis, L. V. "The Effects of Attendance on Student Learning in Principles of Economics." *American Economic Review*, 1995, *85*(2), 343–346.

Erickson, B. L., Peters, C. B., and Strommer, D. W. *Teaching First-Year College Students.* San Francisco: Jossey-Bass, 2006.

Fjortoft, N. "Students' Motivations for Class Attendance." *American Journal of Pharmaceutical Education*, 2005, *69*(1), 107–112.

Forsyth, D. R., and McMillan, J. H. Practical Proposals for Motivating Students. In R. J. Menges and M. D. Svinicki (Eds.), *College Teaching: From Theory to Practice.* New Directions in Teaching and Learning, no. 45. San Francisco: Jossey-Bass, 1991.

Friedman, P., Rodríguez, F., and McComb, J. "Why Students Do and Do Not Attend Classes: Myths and Realities." *College Teaching*, 2001, *49*(4), 124–133.

Grabe, M., and Christopherson, K. "Optional Student Use of Online Lecture Resources: Resource Preferences, Performance and Lecture Attendance." *Journal of Computer Assisted Learning*, 2008, *24*(1), 1–10.

Gump, S. E. "The Cost of Cutting Class: Attendance as a Predictor of Student Success." *College Teaching*, 2005, *53*(1), 21–26.

Kouyoumdjian, H. "Influence of Unannounced Quizzes and Cumulative Exam on Attendance and Study Behavior." *Teaching of Psychology*, 2004, *31*(2), 110–111.

Launius, M. H. "College Student Attendance: Attitudes and Academic Performance." *College Student Journal*, 1997, *31*(1), 86–92.

Lowman, J. *Mastering the Techniques of Teaching.* (2nd ed.) San Francisco: Jossey-Bass, 1995.

Marburger, D. R. "Absenteeism and Undergraduate Exam Performance." *Journal of Economic Education*, 2001, *32*(2), 99–109.

Marchant, G. J. "Student Reading of Assigned Articles: Will This Be on the Test?" *Teaching of Psychology*, 2002, *29*(1), 49–50.

Martin, G. I. "Peer Carding." *College Teaching*, 2000, *48*(1), 19–20.

McKeachie, W. J., and Svinicki, M. *McKeachie's Teaching Tips.* (12th ed.) Boston: Houghton Mifflin, 2006.

McMillan, J. H., and Forsyth, D. R. What Theories of Motivation Say about Why Learners Learn. In R. J. Menges and M. D. Svinicki (Eds.), *College Teaching: From Theory to Practice.* New Directions for Teaching and Learning, no. 45. San Francisco: Jossy-Bass, 1991.

Moore, R. "Attendance: Are Penalties More Effective than Rewards?" *Journal of Developmental Education*, 2005, *29*(2), 26–32.

Narloch, R., Garbin, C. P., and Turnage, K. D. "Benefits of Prelecture Quizzes." *Teaching of Psychology*, 2006, *33*(2), 109–112.

POD Listserv: An unmoderated online community for instructors and administrators with interests in teaching and learning in higher education; see http://podnetwork.org.

PsychTeacher listserv: A moderated online community for instructors involved in teaching psychology; see teachpsych.org/news/psychteacher.php

Rocca, K. A. "Student Attendance: A Comprehensive Literature Review." *Journal on Excellence in College Teaching*, 2003, *14*(1), 85–107.

Romer, D. "Do Students Go to Class? Should They?" *Journal of Economic Perspectives*, 1993, *7*(3), 167–174.

Shimoff, E., and Catania, A. C. "Effects of Recording Attendance on Grades in Introductory Psychology." *Teaching of Psychology*, 2001, *28*(3), 192–195.

Shute, V. J. "Focus on Formative Feedback." *Review of Educational Research*, 2008, *78*(1), 153–189.

Sleigh, M. J., Ritzer, D. R., and Casey, M. B. "Student versus Faculty Perceptions of Missing Class." *Teaching of Psychology*, 2002, *29*(1), 53–56.

St. Clair, K. L. "A Case against Compulsory Class Attendance Policies in Higher Education." *Innovative Higher Education*, 1999, *23*(3), 171–180.

Svinicki, M. D. *Learning and Motivation in the Postsecondary Classroom*. Bolton, MA: Anker, 2004.

Theall, M. (Ed.). *Motivation from Within: Approaches for Encouraging Faculty and Students to Excel.* New Directions for Teaching and Learning, no. 78. San Francisco: Jossey-Bass, 1999.

Thorne, B. M. "Extra Credit Exercise: A Painless Pop Quiz." *Teaching of Psychology*, 2000, *27*(3), 204–205.

Tiberius, R. G. *Small Group Teaching: A Trouble-Shooting Guide*. London: Kogan Page, 1999.

Uskul, A. K., and Eaton, J. "Using Graded Questions to Increase Timely Reading of Assigned Material." *Teaching of Psychology*, 2005, *32*(2), 116–118.

Wilson, J. H. "Predicting Student Attitudes and Grades from Perceptions of Instructors' Attitudes." *Teaching of Psychology*, 2006, *33*(2), 91–95.

Wlodkowski, R. J. *Enhancing Adult Motivation to Learn: A Comprehensive Guide for Teaching All Adults.* (rev. ed.) San Francisco: Jossey-Bass, 1999.

Woodfield, R., Jessop, D., and McMillan, L. "Gender Differences in Undergraduate Attendance Rates." *Studies in Higher Education*, 2006, *31*(1), 1–22.

Young, A. J. "The Challenge to Challenge: Shifting the Motivational Climate of the College Classroom for Enhanced Learning." *College Teaching*, 2003, *51*(4), 127–130.

32

Informally Assessing Students' Learning

Rather than waiting to see how students perform on a test, you can use informal methods to ascertain what and how well your students are learning, and you can take advantage of this information to shape further instruction. The techniques described in this chapter, also called "formative assessment" (Shepard, 2006), will help you determine the following information (adapted from National Research Council, 1997):

- what your students know about a topic
- whether students are motivated to learn the material
- whether students have understood the main points you were trying to convey
- whether students are prepared for class
- what problems your students are having with the material

A review of over 250 studies shows conclusively that using formative assessment strategies, and making adjustments in instruction as a result, can significantly improve student learning (Black and Wiliam, 1998).

As you experiment with these techniques, try to find a balance: if you use them too often, students may feel (rightly or wrongly) that these assessments are taking time away from—rather than contributing to—their learning and studying.

Checking Students' Understanding: Written Responses

Ask students to write a one-minute paper. Davis, Wood, and Wilson (1983) describe a technique developed by UC Berkeley physics professor Charles Schwartz in the late 1970s and popularized by Angelo and Cross (1993). At the end of a class period, ask your students to write for a minute or so on two questions: What is the most significant thing you learned today? and What question is uppermost in your mind at the end of today's class? These papers, submitted anonymously, will indicate how well you have conveyed the material and how you might structure your presentation for the next class meeting.

A variation used by a Harvard statistics professor asks students, "What was the muddiest point in my lecture today?" Other questions: What was most surprising or unexpected about today's session? At what point this past week were you most engaged in the class or the material? What is helping you learn in this class? What is making learning difficult?

Some faculty use the minute paper during class in order to stimulate discussion or break up a lecture. Research shows that the use of minute papers enhances students' performance on exams. (Sources: Angelo, 1991; Angelo and Cross, 1993; Chizmar and Ostrosky, 1998; Davis et al., 1983; Mosteller, 1989; Stead, 2005)

Use reaction cards. In small- or medium-sized classes, distribute index cards to students at the beginning of class and ask them to put their name on the card and to write a comment sometime during the class session. Comments may include responses to questions you pose or a student's questions or observations about any aspect of the class. Tell the students that you will collect the cards at the end of the hour, write a brief response at the bottom of each card, and return the cards at the next session. Both instructors and students report that reaction cards are useful for identifying content problems and monitoring student learning. (Source: Costello et al., 2002)

Ask students to list key concepts or ideas. At the conclusion of a series of sessions or readings on a topic, ask students to write or post online short phrases summarizing three to five key concepts or main ideas about the topic. Review these lists to verify whether your students have grasped the important ideas. You may want to initiate a class discussion that asks students to compare their entries or to define and apply the concepts. (Source: Angelo and Cross, 1993)

Ask students to give definitions or applications for difficult concepts. During the last ten minutes of class, ask students to complete the following or similar statements:

- As I understand it, the main idea [or *concept* or *point*] of today's session was . . . .
- A good example of an application of this idea is . . . .
- The main point of today's session was most closely related to the following concepts, processes, events, or things: . . . .

  (Source: Lancaster, 1974)

Ask students to write an exam question. At the end of a unit, ask students to write an exam question (in the format you specify) for extra credit. In addition to giving you a sense of how well your students understand the material, these test questions will also give you ideas for constructing your exams.

Ask students to provide a closing summary. At the end of a session, ask students, individually or in pairs, to write a very brief summary of the main ideas covered in class. Or at the beginning of class, ask students to summarize the main ideas from the previous class or the reading and to write one question they expect to be answered during class.

Ask students about the midterm. Append one or two questions to the end of the midterm or ask students to respond at the next class session to these topics:

- their readiness for the exam
- which test questions were most difficult and why
- what may have prevented them from achieving a higher score
- how well the exam helped them learn the material
- what they plan to do differently in studying for the next exam

Ask students to write a microtheme. A microtheme is a composition that can fit on a five-by-eight notecard. Some instructors grade these; others duplicate some of the best to hand out for class discussion. Some suggestions for microtheme assignments (adapted from Bean et al., 1982):

Summary microtheme. Summarizing an article in a few sentences requires students to identify the main and subordinating ideas. Summary microthemes can be particularly useful when the class is studying conflicting views.

Thesis-support microtheme. Ask students to choose one of the alternative propositions for an issue and to muster facts in support of their position. Two examples:

- Random portfolio diversification (is/is not) more reliable than selective diversification.
- Mutual fund performance (is/is not) superior to the average investor's performance.

Data-provided microtheme. Present students with a set of data and ask them to explain changes and trends. For example: Imagine an audience that has not seen this table. Explain to them the changes in birth and death rates in the United States in the twenty-first century. Be engaging, informative, and accurate.

Quandary-posing microtheme. Ask students to explain a given problem to someone who knows little or nothing about the subject. For example, answer the following letter as clearly as you can. If you use physics terms, you must define them.

Dear Dr. Science: My girlfriend and I were at a baseball game and someone hit a pop fly. My girlfriend said that when the ball stopped in midair just before it started back down, its velocity was zero, but its acceleration was not zero. I said she was wrong. If something isn't moving at all, how could it have any acceleration? Which of us is right?

Ask students to keep a dynamic list of questions. As a short homework assignment, ask students to write a list of questions that they hope to be able to answer by the end of the class period. During class, students cross off the questions that are answered and add new questions that arise. At the end of class they turn in their lists, which will give you a snapshot of students' preparation, learning during the session, and unanswered questions. (Source: George and Cowan, 1999)

Have students document how they solve a problem. As part of a homework assignment, ask students to write a short paragraph or two about the method they used a solve a problem. As needed, offer your students pointers about how to clearly explain their process.

Checking Students' Understanding: Questions and Discussion

Ask students whether they are understanding you. Instead of the generic "Any questions?" ask, "What questions do you have?" If many of your students look puzzled, ask, "Can you tell me where I lost you so that I can go back and find you?" Try to avoid posing questions that put students on the spot ("Who doesn't understand?"). (Source: National Research Council, 1997)

Hold a debriefing session. Reserve the last ten minutes of class for an analysis of the effectiveness of that day's discussion. Holding a debriefing at the next session after the midterm exam will allow you to probe students' reactions to the exam questions and the adequacy of their preparation.

Ask students to "think-pair-share." Pose a question, and ask students to think about it (and maybe jot down a few ideas), and then turn to a seat neighbor and share their thoughts. Next, the pairs report their discussion to other pairs and, as size and time permits, to the whole class. (Sources: Maier and Panitz, 1996; Millis and Cottell, 1998)

Checking Students' Understanding: Using Technology

Encourage students to record online their reaction to the day's session. Stanford University has developed the "Lecture Gauge" (http://ctl.stanford.edu/Faculty/

lecture_gauge.html), online questions that ask students to rate how challenging the lecture was, to indicate the most important point, and to identify any hard-to-follow portion of the lecture. Students' responses are anonymous. Instructors can instantaneously view aggregate data.

Using a learning management system, design a pre- and post-class assignment or quiz. Some learning management systems or collaborative and learning environments allow you to design, administer, and score online multiple-choice quizzes, with the results immediately available to you and the students. A pre-quiz on the reading will help students prepare for class. A post-quiz assures that students review what they have learned.

Conduct instant polling, using clickers. If your classroom has a wireless system that supports handheld clickers (electronic personal response systems), you can pose multiple-choice questions during class and have students vote on the answer. The votes will be instantaneously displayed, usually as a bar graph. If student opinion is divided, you can ask students to discuss their answer with their neighbors and revote, or you can call on students who gave different answers and ask them to explain their reasoning.

Because students purchase clickers and pay to register them for specific courses, faculty recommend that you use clickers regularly to make the expense worthwhile. Some systems provide a record of each student's responses throughout the term. Some faculty give class-participation credit for the percentage of polls to which a student responds (regardless of the correctness of the response).

At some universities, instant polling programs are loaded into students' mobile phones. Other faculty ask for a show of hands or a display of lettered signs (A, B, C, D) or response cards.

Faculty who use polling strategies, especially clickers, report increased student participation, attendance, learning, knowledge of the views of others, interest, and motivation. Some faculty have restructured their large-enrollment courses to be fully interactive using clickers. (Sources: Caldwell, 2007; Duncan, 2005; Kam and Sommer, 2006; Kellum et al., 2001; Marmolejo et al., 2004; Mehta, 1995; Meltzer and Manivannan, 2002; Nicol and Boyle, 2003; Robertson, 2000)

Conduct online polling. Faculty in an introductory biology course posed multiple-choice questions about key concepts on their course Web page. Students selected the best answer and rated their confidence that their answer was correct. Once they submitted their answer, they could view the results: the percentage of students who chose each response and a graph displaying the respondents' confidence level. Correct answers were not provided until the next class meeting, which served as an incentive for students to attend. The online questions were not graded, but students received credit for responding. Consider online strategies to probe students' understanding of course information, provide individualized feedback, and track student performance. (Sources: Brewer, 2004; Hunt and Pellegrino, 2002)

Implement a just-in-time approach. Just-in-time teaching allows students to tell you what they know a few hours before coming to class, so that you can structure the session accordingly. The technique requires the instructor to post several short-answer or multiple-choice questions online once a week. Students submit their responses online at least three hours before class, and the instructor uses their responses to prepare for class. During class, selected responses are displayed (correct, partially correct, incorrect) and used to illustrate various points in lecture or discussion. Students' responses are graded and returned. Researchers report that students enjoy the process and benefit from receiving immediate feedback on their level of understanding. (Sources: Benedict and Anderton, 2004; National Research Council, 2003; Novak et al., 1999)

Checking Students' Understanding: Resources

Undertake your own simple assessments to ascertain how well your students are learning. Angelo and Cross (1993) describe a variety of classroom assessment techniques (CATs) that are easy to implement and will give you feedback on how students are learning. They also describe how you can develop your own assessments. For example, the "Background Knowledge Probe" is a short questionnaire given to students at the start of a course to assess their preconceptions about the course content.

Consult compilations on the Web. Other sources of informal assessment techniques are presented by FLAG (Field-tested Learning Assessment Guide) at www.flaguide. org; this compilation of faculty-generated strategies for evaluating student learning pertains primarily to courses in science, math, engineering, and technology.

References

Angelo, T. A. Introduction and Overview: From Classroom Assessment to Classroom Research. In T. A. Angelo (Ed.), *Classroom Research: Early Lessons from Success*. New Directions for Teaching and Learning, no. 46. San Francisco: Jossey-Bass, 1991.

Angelo, T. A., and Cross, K. P. *Classroom Assessment Techniques: A Handbook for College Teachers*. (2nd ed.) San Francisco: Jossey-Bass, 1993.

Bean, J. C., Drenk, D., and Lee, F. D. "Microtheme Strategies for Developing Cognitive Skills." In C.W. Griffin (Ed.), *Teaching Writing in All Disciplines*. New Directions for Teaching and Learning, no. 12. San Francisco: Jossey-Bass, 1982.

Benedict, J. O., and Anderton, J. B. "Applying the Just-in-Time Teaching Approach to Teaching Statistics." *Teaching of Psychology*, 2004, *31*(3), 197–199.

Black, P. and Wiliam, D. "Assessment and Classroom Learning." *Assessment in Education: Principles, Policy and Practice*, 1998, *5*(1), 7–74.

Brewer, C. A. "Near Real-Time Assessment of Student Learning and Understanding in Biology Courses." *BioScience*, 2004, *54*(11), 1034–1039.

Caldwell, J. E. "Clickers in the Large Classroom: Current Research and Best-Practice Tips." *CBE-Life Sciences Education*, 2007, *6*(1), 9–20.

Chizmar, J. F., and Ostrosky, A. L. "The One Minute Paper: Some Empirical Findings." *Journal of Economic Education*, Winter 1998, *29*(1), 3–10.

Costello, M. L., Weldon, A., and Brunner, P. "Reaction Cards as a Formative Evaluation Tool: Students' Perceptions of How Their Use Impacted Classes." *Assessment and Evaluation in Higher Education*, 2002, *27*(1), 23–33.

Davis, B. G., Wood, L., and Wilson, R. *ABC's of Teaching with Excellence: A Berkeley Compendium of Suggestions for Teaching with Excellence*. Berkeley: Office of Educational Development, University of California, 1983. http://teaching.berkeley.edu/compendium/

Duncan, D. *Clickers in the Classroom*. San Francisco: Addison Wesley, 2005.

George, J. W., and Cowan, J. *A Handbook of Techniques for Formative Evaluation*. Sterling, VA: Stylus, 1999.

Hunt, E., and Pellegrino, J. W. *Issues, Examples and Challenges in Formative Assessment*. New Directions for Teaching and Learning, no. 89. San Francisco: Jossey-Bass, 2002, pp. 73–85.

Kam, C. D., and Sommer, B. "Real-Time Polling Technology in a Public Opinion Course." *PS: Political Science and Politics*, 2006, *39*(1), 113–117.

Kellum, K. K., Carr, J. E., and Dozier, C. L. "Response-Card Instruction and Student Learning in a College Classroom." *Teaching of Psychology*, 2001, *28*(2), 101–104.

Lancaster, O. E. *Effective Teaching and Learning*. New York: Gordon and Breach, 1974.

Maier, M. H., and Panitz, T. "End on a High Note: Better Endings for Classes and Courses." *College Teaching*, 1996, *44*(4), 145–148.

Marmolejo, E. K., Wilder, D. A., and Bradley, L. "A Preliminary Analysis of the Effects of Response Cards on Student Performance and Participation in an Upper Division University Course." *Journal of Applied Behavior Analysis*, 2004, *37*(3), 405–410.

Mehta, S. I. "A Method for Instant Assessment and Active Learning." *Journal of Engineering Education*, 1995, *84*(3), 295–298.

Meltzer, D. E., and Manivannan, K. "Transforming the Lecture-Hall Environment: The Fully Interactive Physics Lecture." *American Journal of Physics*, 2002, *70*(6), 639–654.

Millis, B. J., and Cottell, P. G., Jr. *Cooperative Learning for Higher Education Faculty*. American Council on Education and Oryx Press, 1998.

Mosteller, F. "The 'Muddiest Point in the Lecture' as a Feedback Device." *On Teaching and Learning*, April Vol. 3, 1989, 10–21.

National Research Council. *Science Teaching Reconsidered: A Handbook*. Washington, DC: National Academy Press, 1997.

National Research Council. *Evaluating and Improving Undergraduate Teaching in Science, Technology, Engineering, and Mathematics*. Washington, DC: National Academy Press, 2003.

Nicol, D. J., and Boyle, J. T. "Peer Instruction versus Class-Wide Discussion in Large Classes: A Comparison of Two Interaction Methods in the Wired Classroom." *Studies in Higher Education*, 2003, *28*(4), 457–473.

Novak, G. M., Patterson, E. T., Gavrin, A. D., and Christian, W. *Just-in-Time Teaching: Blending Active Learning with Web Technology*. Upper Saddle River, NJ: Prentice Hall, 1999.

Robertson, L. J. "Twelve Tips for Using a Computerized Interactive Audience Response System." *Medical Teacher*, 2000, *22*(3), 237–239.

Shepard, L. A. Classroom Assessment. In R. L. Brennan (Ed.), *Educational Measurement*. (4th ed.) Westport, CT: American Council on Education/Praeger, 2006.

Stead, D. R. "A Review of the One-Minute Paper." *Active Learning in Higher Education*, 2005, *6*(2), 118–131.

33

Mobile Learning

Mobile technologies offer a way to create dynamic, interactive learning environments inside and outside the classroom. The current generation of wireless computing and portable communication devices includes laptops/tablets, PDAs (personal digital assistants), mobile phones, digital cameras, MP3 players, iPods, iPhones, small electronic book readers, and various multiple-function devices.

Mobile devices can be used to facilitate quick feedback or reinforcement; deliver interactive demonstrations and quizzes; provide immersive experiences (for example, foreign languages); enrich learning outside the classroom (for example, data collection in the field); and share information (for example, syllabi, assignments, and calendars). Of course, these devices can also interfere with learning when students shop online, send e-mail, or play games during class. Some students may even feel sanguine about missing class if they can view the webcast at their convenience.

General Strategies

Decide how you feel about students using mobile devices in your classroom. Although you may want to banish students who shop on their laptops, send messages on their mobile phones, and engage in other electronic pastimes during class, banning the devices may not be the best solution. You can't force students to pay attention if they don't want to. And even if you forbid all electronic gadgets, students will still daydream, whisper, and pass notes. Banning mobile devices may also pose communication problems during emergencies. Nonetheless, some faculty prohibit laptops in the classroom and feel that students are more engaged and involved as a result. Others use software that allows them to see which programs are running on students' laptops, to block specific applications, and to disable specific laptops. Still other faculty ask students who bring laptops to sit where their screens can be observed. (Sources: Fried, 2008; Young, 2006)

If you permit mobile devices, establish rules of etiquette. Consider asking students at the beginning of the term to set norms for what constitutes respectful classroom use of mobile devices. Or state your policies on your syllabus, and refer to those policies on the first day of class. The following guidelines are adapted from Bloom (2007), Efaw, Hampton, Martinez, and Smith (2004), Hembrooke and Gay (2003), Lang (2001), Rubinstein, Meyer, and Evans (2001), and discussions on a UC Berkeley listserv:

- Emphasize that students' use of electronic devices for purposes not relevant to the course must be kept to an absolute minimum.
- Require students to silence their phones.
- Share research findings on task switching that show that multitasking students learn significantly less and perform on tests more poorly than students who focus solely on classwork.
- Use a simple activity to show how multitasking is less effective than single tasking: Ask students to count from one to ten, then ask them to recite the letters A through J. Either task takes about five seconds. Next, ask students to switch between the tasks: "A, 1, B, 2, C, 3 . . ." This takes much longer because of the time required to switch back and forth.
- Ask students to put their screens and devices down during portions of the class session; make exceptions, as needed, for students with disabilities.
- Point out how laptops can distract students seated nearby.
- Ask students using laptops to place them off to the side so that you can maintain eye contact.
- Establish consequences for inappropriate use.
- Design in-class assignments that use laptops or other devices for pairs or small groups; such exercises lessen the chance that students will use their devices inappropriately.
- Walk around the room during class and stand in the back of the room for a time.

Try to anticipate technical challenges. If you will be using mobile technologies in your class, ask the campus technology staff for advice on how to handle problems such as unreliable wireless connections, differences among students' devices, protection and backup of files, and the like. (Sources: Caudill, 2007; Corbeil and Valdes-Corbeil, 2007; Reeves and Ward, 2005; Rekkedal and Dye, 2007)

Examples of Mobile Learning

Laptops. Faculty have put students' laptops to work in various ways (Barak et al., 2006; Efaw et al., 2004; Felder and Brent, 2005; Nilson and Weaver, 2005):

- Ask students to share access to information or to find facts online (for example, in a psychology class on sleep deprivation, an instructor asks, "Who holds the record for most consecutive hours without sleep?" "What are five established symptoms of sleep deprivation?")

- Conduct online searches using the resources of the library or a scholarly Web site.
- Work through problems using spreadsheet software.
- Take online quizzes.
- Conduct experiments in virtual science labs.
- View online images and video clips.
- Solicit anonymous questions from students during class.
- Ask students to produce a graphic simulation of a mathematical process.
- Conduct public chats or private "back channel" text messages that comment about the lecture or demonstration.
- Have students work in small groups that take a position for or against an issue, and post their key points on an online discussion board.

Podcasts. Podcasts are digital audio or video programs (sometimes called vodcasts) that can be accessed on mobile devices at the convenience of the listener or viewer. Some campus instructional technology offices maintain directories of podcasts from which instructors can select items appropriate to their course. In addition, instructional podcasts are available at iTunes U and YouTube, where universities have their own pages listing courses, speakers, and events. Instructors with the interest, time, and skills can also create their own podcasts or help students produce podcasts on course-related topics. UCLA and Purdue University offer information on creating podcasts.

Experienced faculty offer the following tips (adapted from Bell et al., 2007; Corbeil and Valdes-Corbeil, 2007; Eisenberg, 2007; Frydenberg, 2006; Staley, 2007):

- Select or create podcasts on the assumption that many students will access the material from a mobile device while they are engaged in another activity (such as commuting, exercising, or doing chores). In other words, assume that students may not be able to follow complex material or take notes.
- Select or create podcasts that provide supplementary materials: interviews with experts, guest speakers, debates, film clips, topical news, and the like.
- Limit the content of a supplementary podcast to a few main themes. As needed, divide topics or presentations into short chunks (10–15 minutes each) and create a series of podcasts from which students may choose the topics that interest them.
- If you are going to produce your own supplementary podcasts, create a weekly summary of the questions asked during office hours, offer a quick preview of the upcoming unit, or present a pre-exam review.

- If you are going to record your entire lecture, take advantage of lecture-capture software that records both words and digital images. Such software indexes words so that students can search for a specific term or point when they replay the lecture.

Cell phones as converged devices. Multiple-function phones can be used to store and manipulate data; take pictures; download music; receive and send text messages and e-mail; access the Internet; show videos; stream live video; video conference; receive and send global-positioning signals; receive alerts about campus safety; replace clickers as classroom response devices; send round-the-clock updates; browse mobile social networks; and conduct class business (find grades, register for classes, add/drop classes, use a content management system). Faculty also use mobile phones to quiz students during class; assign students to take photos on field trips and send the instructor the images in real time; and text message students as appropriate.

No matter how often you ask students to silence their phones, you will hear an occasional ring tone during class. Some instructors impose a penalty (the offending student has to provide snacks for the class at the next session), and others use the interruption as an opportunity to review and interact with students, asking "Who can summarize the previous point?" or "What's the last thing you wrote down in your notes?" (Sources: Bloom, 2007; Campbell, 2006; Fischman, 2007)

References

Barak, M., Lipson, A., and Lerman, S. "Wireless Laptops as Means for Promoting Active Learning in Large Lecture Halls." *Journal of Research on Technology in Education*, 2006, *38*(3), 245–262.

Bell, T., Cockburn, A., Wingkvist, A., and Green, R. "Podcasts as a Supplement in Tertiary Education: An Experiment with Two Computer Science Courses." Paper presented at the conference on Mobile Learning Technologies and Applications, Massey University, Auckland, New Zealand, 2007.

Bloom, A. "Making Cell Phones in the Class a Community Builder." *Teaching Professor*, Mar. 2007, 4.

Campbell, S. "Perceptions of Mobile Phones in College Classrooms: Ringing, Cheating, and Classroom Policies." *Communication Education*, 2006, *55*(3), 280–294.

Caudill, J. G. "The Growth of m-Learning and the Growth of Mobile Computing: Parallel Developments." *International Review of Research in Open and Distance Learning*, 2007, *8*(2), 1–13.

Corbeil, J. R., and Valdes-Corbeil, M. E. "Are You Ready for Mobile Learning?" *Educause Quarterly*, 2007, *30*(2), 51–60.

Efaw, J., Hampton, S., Martinez, S., and Smith, S. "Miracle or Menace: Teaching and Learning with Laptop Computers in the Classroom." *Educause Quarterly*, 2004, *27*(3). 10–18.

Eisenberg, A. "What Did the Professor Say? Check Your iPod." *New York Times*, Dec. 9, 2007.

Felder, R. M., and Brent, R. "Screens Down Everyone: Effective Uses of Portable Computers in Lecture Classes." *Chemical Engineering Education*, 2005, *39*(3), 200–201.

Fischman, J. "The Campus in the Palm of Your Hand." *Chronicle of Higher Education*, May 11, 2007, A41–A42.

Fried, C. B. "In-Class Laptop Use and Its Effects on Student Learning." *Computers and Education*, 2008, *50*(3), 906–914.

Frydenberg, M. "Principles and Pedagogy: The Two P's of Podcasting in the Information Technology Classroom." In the Proceedings of the 23rd Annual Conference of Information Systems Educators, Dallas, TX, 2006.

Hembrooke, H., and Gay, G. "The Laptop and the Lecture: The Effects of Multitasking in Learning Environments." *Journal of Computing in Higher Education*, 2003, *15*(1), 46–64.

Lang, A. "The Limited Capacity Model of Mediated Message Processing." *Journal of Communication*, 2001, *50*(1), 46–70.

Nilson, L. B., and Weaver, B. E. (Eds). *Enhancing Learning with Laptops in the Classroom*. New Directions for Teaching and Learning, no. 101. San Francisco: Jossey-Bass, 2005.

Reeves, J., and Ward, C. R. Wireless in the Lecture. In N. J. Pienta, M. M. Cooper, and T. J. Greenbowe (Eds.), *Chemists' Guide to Effective Teaching*. Upper Saddle River, NJ: Prentice Hall, 2005.

Rekkedal, R., and Dye, A. "Mobile Distance Learning with PDAs: Development and Testing of Pedagogical and System Solutions Supporting Mobile Distance Learners." *International Review of Research in Open and Distance Learning*, 2007, *8*(2), 1–26.

Rubinstein, J. S., Meyer, D. E., and Evans, J. E. "Executive Control of Cognitive Processes in Task Switching." *Journal of Experimental Psychology: Human Perception and Performance*, 2001, *27*(4), 763–797.

Staley, L. *Blended Learning Guide*. Dublin, OH: OCLC—Online Computer Library Center, 2007.

Young, J. R. "The Fight for Classroom Attention: Professor vs. Laptop." *Chronicle of Higher Education*, June 2, 2006, *52*(39), A27.

PART VII

Strengthening Students' Writing and Problem-Solving Skills

34

Helping Students Write Better in All Courses

In every academic discipline, writing assignments can help students master new material, formulate and clarify their ideas, demonstrate creativity, and develop critical thinking skills. You don't have to be a writing specialist, or even a strong writer, to help your students improve their writing skills. The following techniques illustrate how to incorporate writing into your courses—without noticeably increasing the time you devote to grading and reviewing student work.

General Strategies

View writing as essential for learning. Require writing during the semester, in addition to exams or an end-of-term paper, and give both in-class and outside writing assignments. When students are writing to learn, you do not need to collect or read their work. Discipline-specific advice on incorporating writing in the sciences is available for courses in biology (Holyoak, 1998; Moore, 1994); chemistry (Kovac and Sherwood, 1999); physics (Becker, 1995); and mathematics (Artzt, 1994; Green, 2002; Panitz, 2001).

Discuss the general standards for good writing. Define good writing in terms of the contexts, purposes, and audiences appropriate to your course and discipline. Let students know that you value clarity, good organization, and correct usage. Don't let students fall back on the rationalization that grammar, spelling, and diction matter only in English classes.

Show students that you value their writing. Publicly and privately, praise students whose writing shows productive effort. Share good examples with the class and point out what is good about them. In the syllabus, on the first day of class, and throughout the term, remind students to make their best efforts to express themselves on paper.

Ask students about their perspectives on writing. Many students are somewhat fearful about academic writing. During office hours, in class, or on an online discussion board, you can pose the following kinds of questions (adapted from O'Farrell, 2005; "Situating Student Writers," 2003):

- What concerns do you have about the writing assignments you will complete this term?
- Writing is like . . . (ask students to write a short response).
- Describe your best writing experience and why it was so good.

Be sensitive to the needs of students with disabilities. Various disabilities may affect students' skills in organization, expression, or word choice. You can help students with disabilities, and all students, by incorporating in-class writing activities that are ungraded or minimally weighted, have clear instructions on how students can complete the exercise, and provide opportunities for self-assessment. See Chapter 6, "Students with Disabilities." (Source: Lewiecki-Wilson and Brueggemann, 2008)

Teaching the Fundamentals of Writing

Provide guidance throughout the writing process. After you have made a formal writing assignment, discuss the value of outlines and notes; how to select and narrow a topic; how to use sources appropriately; and how to review and revise. Students are more likely to learn from guidance and feedback during their drafting and revising; in contrast, most students are less interested in the comments they receive after their work has been submitted and graded.

Remind students that writing is a process that helps us clarify ideas. Explain that writing is a hard, messy, nonlinear activity filled with false starts. Encourage students to see writing as a process—not as a product—as a way of learning and discovering what they know and don't know. Discuss the main steps of the process:

- developing ideas
- finding a focus and a thesis
- composing a draft
- getting feedback and comments from others
- revising the draft by expanding ideas, clarifying meaning, reorganizing
- editing
- presenting the finished work to readers

  (Source: Elbow, 1998)

Share your own struggles in grappling with difficult topics. Undergraduate students tend to underestimate the time and effort that writing requires. Discuss your experiences: the number of drafts you have written before submitting an article for publication, the external review process, and the revisions you made after seeing the reviewers' comments. One faculty member writes a new research paper during the same time frame that students complete their research papers, following the same steps and sharing with his students his challenges and his drafts. (Source: Edwards, 2002)

Give students opportunities to talk about their work in progress. Students need to talk with peers about papers they are working on, and they benefit from hearing or reading what their peers have written. Give students time during or after class to talk about what they plan to write or to read their drafts to each other in small groups. Create an online bulletin board for students to present completed work to others.

Help students develop a writing schedule. The online Assignment Calculator developed at the University of Minnesota (www.lib.umn.edu/help/calculator/) divides the writing task into its component parts (such as writing a thesis statement, identifying sources), sets dates for each step (based on the deadline for the paper), and provides online resources for each task.

Explain thesis statements. One of the most common difficulties that beset student writers is the absence of a thesis statement or the choice of a diffuse thesis ("Health insurance is a big issue"). Define the term *thesis statement* for your students (for example, a thesis statement makes an assertion, or generalization, that the essay tries to support), and give examples of thesis statements appropriate to an assignment. A three-step method may help students understand the difference between a topic and a thesis:

> *Topic:* Career choices made by new physicians
>
> *"How" or "why" question:* Why are fewer new physicians entering general practice?
>
> *Answer to the question (= the thesis):* New physicians are turning away from general practice because the compensation system used by the health care insurance companies favors specialists over general practitioners.

Encourage specificity. Discourage students from using abstract, inflated, or overly academic-sounding language. Explain that generalizations need to be supported by specific evidence, examples, and concrete detail. Review the types of evidence most relevant to the course.

Emphasize the value of revision. Structure deadlines for phases of a writing project so that students will have time to revise. For example, ask students to submit outlines and first drafts of papers for your review or for peer critique. Provide students with a checklist for reviewing their papers, and ask that the checklist be completed and signed by an outside reviewer selected by the student. Or give students the option of revising one assignment during the term for a higher grade.

Referring Students to Resources

Distribute and recommend materials to promote good writing practices. Ask your campus's English department, composition program, or writing center for tip sheets or other materials you can post online. Unless you already have a favorite, ask these sources to recommend a short book on writing that is appropriate for your students. For example, Lanham (2000, 2006, 2007), Elbow (1998), and Fulwiler (2002) have written books that your students may find helpful. If your institution's online resources for student writers are inadequate, look at the materials on other college Web sites, including the Online Writing Lab at Purdue University, the Writing Center at Rensselaer Polytechnic Institute, Writing Tutorial Services at the University of Indiana, Bloomington, and the Center for Writing at the University of Minnesota. If your campus library doesn't have lists of discipline-specific writing guides, consult the lists of other campuses, such as the Duke University Libraries' "Style Manuals and Citation Guides" (2007).

Tell students about campus tutoring services. Most campuses offer individual or group tutoring in writing. Find out what help your campus writing center offers and urge your students to sign up for help. Post information or ask someone from the tutoring center to give a presentation in your class.

Give pointers about the limitations of computer software. Insist that students spell-check with the computer *and* proofread without the computer. Remind students that spell-checkers can't distinguish between *role* and *roll* and that grammar and style checkers are not effective tools. Also, let students know that techno spelling (B4, CU, etc.), common in instant messaging and texting, is not appropriate for college writing.

Decide whether to use blogging software. Blogging software may facilitate the sharing of written work. Note, at least one faculty member has identified the pitfalls of blogs and concluded that they are pedagogically valuable only under very specific conditions. (Sources: Dawson, 2007; Ferdig and Trammell, 2004; Martindale and Wiley, 2005)

In-Class Writing Exercises

Assign brief ungraded writing tasks. Get students in the habit of writing. Weekly practice helps students clarify their thinking and improves their learning. Researchers report that five minutes of writing per week (forty-five minutes a quarter) leads to higher test scores. Students can be asked to express their opinion about a current controversy in the field, apply a course concept to their own experience, and take a position after hearing or reading about competing viewpoints. Other informal writing activities are described in this section. Give students credit for the writing exercises without taking time to read or grade them. (Source: Drabick et al., 2007)

Ask students to write what they know about a topic before you discuss it. Ask students to write a paragraph or two of what they know about the subject or what opinions they hold. Because the purpose of this exercise is to focus students' attention, there is no reason to collect their work. (Source: Tollefson, 2002)

Ask students to respond in writing to questions you pose during class. At the beginning of a class, display two or three short-answer questions and ask students to write their responses. The questions might call for a review of material previously covered or test students' recall of the assigned readings. Asking students to write down their responses also helps generate a more lively discussion because students have had a chance to think about the material. (Source: Tollefson, 2002)

Ask students to write from a pro or con position. When an argument has been presented in class, stop for a few minutes and ask students to write down the arguments and evidence that supports one side or the other. Use these statements as the basis for discussion. (Source: Tollefson, 2002)

During class, pause for a three- or five-minute write. Ask students to write for a few minutes on a given question or topic. Tell them to write freely, without stopping and without worrying about organization or grammar. Writing experts believe that this kind of free writing helps students synthesize diverse ideas and identify points they don't understand. Do not collect these exercises. (Source: Tollefson, 2002)

Have students write a brief summary at the end of class. Give students a few minutes to jot down the key themes, major points, or general principles of the day's discussion. Research shows that students who write summaries of course material or readings learn more and earn higher grades than those who don't. (Sources: Davis and Hult, 1997; Radmacher and Latosi-Sawin, 1995)

Practice essay test writing. One history instructor has students write a four-paragraph essay (including introduction and conclusion) on a topic similar to one that may appear on a test. Students then exchange their work for peer response. (Source: Kneeshaw, 1999)

Structure small-group discussion around a writing task. For example, ask each student to pick three words of major importance to the day's session. Then ask the class to write freely for two or three minutes on one of the words. Next, give the students five to ten minutes to meet in groups of three, sharing what they have written and generating questions to ask in class. (Source: Tollefson, 2002)

Using Peer Review

Incorporate peer review into your course. Students benefit from their peers' comments and from evaluating the work of others. Schedule the peer review early enough to leave students time to revise their work before submitting it to you. UCLA has developed a Web-based instructional tool called Calibrated Peer Review that helps students critically evaluate their peers' and their own writing. (Sources: Educause, 2005; Koprowski, 1997; Marcoulides and Simkin, 1995; Topping, 1998)

Give students a procedure for peer review. Divide the class into groups of three or four students, and have them bring to the peer review session copies of their rough draft for each member of their group. Explain that the most important step for the peer reviewer is to note which part of the draft is the strongest and to describe to the writer why it works well. In addition, provide guidelines for critiquing the drafts (based on "Peer Response Sheet", n.d.): Reviewers should answer these questions after a first quick reading:

- What single feature of the paper stands out to you?
- What do you think is the writer's main point?
- What, if anything, in the paper was confusing?

After a slower reading, readers should then answer these questions:

- Underline the thesis statement. Is it clearly stated?
- Do any of the points need more support, more detail, or a better explanation?
- How well does the writer make transitions between main ideas?
- Suggest two or more ways in which the draft could be improved.
- What would you like to know more about? What questions do you still have?
- In what ways is the paper interesting, surprising, intriguing, and so forth?

Be sensitive to cultural differences. For students who are not fluent in English or whose cultural background discourages peer critique, working in pairs (rather than trios or quartets) may be easier. They may also need more explicit guidelines for reviewing work. (Source: Nelson, 1997)

Selective Review and Grading

Don't collect or read every piece of your students' writing. Students can and should be writing primarily to learn and clarify their own thinking on a subject. Short, informal writing assignments enable them to practice and improve their skills. (Source: Elbow and Sorcinelli, 2006)

Skim papers but don't fix the errors. Point out problems, ask questions, but do not spend time reorganizing, revising, or editing student work. Let students work out the problems for themselves.

Have students assess their work before they submit it. Self-critique helps students better understand evaluative criteria (Shepard, 2006). Here are some sample self-assessment questions (Elbow and Sorcinelli, 2006; Hobson, 1996; Mattenson, 2004; "Peer Response Sheet," n.d.):

- In one sentence, what is the main point you are trying to convey?
- What do you like most about your paper? What do you like least?
- What will you do differently the next time you write a paper? Why?
- What would you like me to address in my comments that would help you revise your paper?

Grade a random sample of assignments. You can collect all the assignments but grade only one in five or one in ten.

Stagger the due dates of assignments. If you teach a large-enrollment course, randomly assign students to due dates so that one-third of the class turns papers in one week, one-third turns papers in a week later, and so on. Or give students extra credit if they turn their papers in early (at a date you specify).

Work with colleagues. Arrange for colleagues to share the writing assignments they have developed and discuss how students did on the assignments. Pool ideas about ways in which writing can help students learn the subject matter. Explore ways to use technology to facilitate peer review and writing groups. (Source: Kuriloff, 2004)

References

Artzt, A. F. "Integrating Writing and Cooperative Learning in the Mathematics Class." *Mathematics Teacher*, 1994, *87*(2), 80–85.

Becker, S. F. "Guest Comment: Teaching Writing to Teach Physics." *American Journal of Physics*, 1995, *63*(7), 587.

Davis, M., and Hult, R. E. "Effects of Writing Summaries as a Generative Learning Activity During Note Taking." *Teaching of Psychology*, 1997, *24*(1), 47–49.

Dawson, K. M. "Blog Overload." *Chronicle of Higher Education*, Feb. 2, 2007, *53*(22), C2.

Drabick, D.A.G., Weisberg, R., Paul, L., and Bubier, J. L. "Keeping It Short and Sweet: Brief Ungraded Writing Assignments Facilitate Learning." *Teaching of Psychology*, 2007, *34*(3), 172–176.

Educause. *Calibrated Peer Review: A Writing and Critical Thinking Instructional Tool*, 2005. http://connect.educause.edu/library/abstract/ELIInnovationsImplem/39347

Edwards, M. E. "Writing Before Students. A Model for Teaching Sociological Writing." *Teaching Sociology*, 2002, *30*(2), 254–259.

Elbow, P. *Writing with Power: Techniques for Mastering the Writing Process*. New York: Oxford University Press, 1998.

Elbow, P., and Sorcinelli, M. D. How to Enhance Learning by Using High-Stakes and Low-Stakes Writing. In W. J. McKeachie and M. Svinicki, *McKeachie's Teaching Tips*. (12th ed.) Boston: Houghton Mifflin, 2006.

Ferdig, R. E., and Trammell, K. D. "Content Delivery in the Blogosphere." *T.H.E. Journal*, 2004, *31*(7), 12, 16–17, 20.

Fulwiler, T. *College Writing: A Personal Approach to Academic Writing*. (3rd ed.) Portsmouth, NH: Boynton/Cook/Heinemann, 2002.

Green, K. H. "Creating Successful Calculus Writing Assignments." *PRIMUS: Problems, Resources, and Issues in Mathematics Undergraduate Studies*, 2002, *12*(2), 97–121.

Hobson, E. H. "Encouraging Self-Assessment: Writing as Active Learning." *New Directions for Teaching and Learning*, no. 67, San Francisco: Jossey-Bass, 1996, pp. 45–58.

Holyoak, A. R. "A Plan for Writing throughout (Not Just across) the Biology Curriculum." *American Biology Teacher*, 1998, *60*(3), 186–190.

Kneeshaw, S. "Using Reader Response to Improve Student Writing in History." *OAH Magazine of History*, 1999, *13*(3), 62–65.

Koprowski, J. L. "Sharpening the Craft of Scientific Writing." *Journal of College Science Teaching*, 1997, *27*(2), 133–135.

Kovac, J., and Sherwood, D. W. "Writing in Chemistry: An Effective Learning Tool." *Journal of Chemical Education*, 1999, *76*(10), 1399–1403.

Kuriloff, P. C. "Rescuing Writing Instruction: How to Save Time and Money with Technology." *Liberal Education*, 2004, *90*(4), 36–41.

Lanham, R. A. *Revising Business Prose.* (4th ed.) New York: Longman, 2000.

Lanham, R. A. *The Longman Guide to Revising Prose.* New York: Pearson Longman, 2006.

Lanham, R. A. *Revising Prose.* (5th ed.) New York: Pearson Longman, 2007.

Lewiecki-Wilson, C., and Brueggemann, B. J. (Eds.) *Disability and the Teaching of Writing.* Boston: Bedford/St. Martin's, 2008.

Marcoulides, G. A., and Simkin, M.G. "The Consistency of Peer Review in Student Writing Projects." *Journal of Education for Business*, 1995, *70*(4), 220–223.

Martindale, T., and Wiley, D. A. "Using Weblogs in Scholarship and Teaching." *TechTrends*, 2005, *49*(2), 55–61.

Mattenson, L. M. "Teaching Student Writers to Be Warriors." *Chronicle of Higher Education*, August 6, 2004.

Moore, R. "Writing to Learn Biology." *Journal of College Science Teaching*, 1994, *23*(5), 289–295.

Nelson, G. L. "How Cultural Differences Affect Written and Oral Communication: The Case of Peer Response Groups." *New Directions for Teaching and Learning*, no. 70. San Francisco: Jossey-Bass, 1997.

O'Farrell, C. The Write Approach: Integrating Writing Activities into Your Teaching. In G. O'Neill, S. Moore, and B. McMullin (Eds.), *Emerging Issues in the Practice of University Learning and Teaching.* Dublin: All Ireland Society for Higher Education, 2005.

Panitz, T. *Learning Together: Keeping Teachers and Students Actively Involved in Learning by Writing Across the Curriculum: A Sourcebook of Ideas and Writing Exercises.* Stillwater, OK: New Forums Press, 2001.

"Peer Response Sheet." Available from Derek Bok Center for Teaching and Learning at: http://isites.harvard.edu/fs/html/icb.topic58474/PeerResponse.html

Radmacher, S. A., and Latosi-Sawin, E. "Summary Writing: A Tool to Improve Student Comprehension and Writing in Psychology." *Teaching of Psychology*, 1995, *22*(2), 113–115.

Shepard, L. A., Classroom Assessment. In R. L. Brennan (Ed.), *Educational Measurement.* (4th ed.) Westport, CT: American Council on Education/Praeger, 2006.

"Situating Student Writers." *Faculty Resources: Writing in Your Classroom.* The Writing Center, University of North Carolina, April 9, 2003. http://www.unc.edu/depts/wcweb/faculty_resources/classroom_writing.html

"Style Manuals and Citation Guides," Duke University Libraries Web site, 2007. http://www.lib.duke.edu/reference/style_manuals.html

Tollefson, S. K. *Encouraging Student Writing.* Berkeley: Office of Educational Development, University of California, 2002. http://teaching.berkeley.edu/publications.html

Topping, K. "Peer Assessment between Students in Colleges and Universities." *Review of Educational Research*, 1998, *68*(3), 249–276.

35

Designing Effective Writing Assignments

To do their best written work, students need clear, specific instructions regarding the topic, approach, and format for their papers. The suggestions below are designed to help you prepare assignments that challenge students without intimidating or frustrating them.

General Strategies

Assign several short papers. A short assignment early in the term will allow you to identify students whose writing skills are weak and to refer them to the campus tutoring center. Short assignments also give all students the benefit of your comments and suggestions before they tackle a long paper.

Solicit critiques of your draft copy for an assignment. Ask your graduate student instructor or a colleague to comment on the clarity of the assignment (criteria based on Speck, 2000):

- Is the purpose of the assignment clearly stated?
- Is the students' audience specified?
- Do the instructions include the due date, length, and any relevant formatting conventions?
- Does the assignment describe the grading criteria?

Consider asking your students to critique a draft of the assignment before you finalize it. (Source: Leahy, 2002)

Share copies of good papers with students. Students appreciate seeing a variety of examples of other students' work. Keep in mind that you will need students' permission to retain and share copies of their papers.

Keep notes on the success and pitfalls of each assignment. As you grade papers, keep a running list of problems. Use these notes to modify future versions of an assignment.

Shaping the Research or Term Paper Assignment

Define the task. Freshman and sophomore students will appreciate your sup-plying paper topics; otherwise some will waste a lot of time searching for a topic. Even juniors and seniors are often better served by being given a set of topics to choose from. For best results, the assignment should define a task, not simply state a topic. Here are some examples (adapted from Simon, 1988, p. 8):

> *Vague topic.* Much has been written about the use of animals in laboratory experiments. Discuss these views and the moral considerations that define this debate.
>
> *Defined task.* Animal rights activists believe that laboratory experiments on animals should be significantly curtailed and rigorously monitored. Write an essay refuting their point of view.
>
> *Defined task.* Animal rights activists, scientists, and agencies funding research are engaged in an ongoing debate on the use of animals in laboratory experiments. Define and defend your position in this debate.

Turn each step of a large assignment into a smaller assignment. For example, give separate deadlines for submitting an outline, an annotated bibliography, and a first draft. Or make a cumulative assignment: in a political science course, the stu-dents' first paper describes the basic schools of political thought; the second paper argues that one of those schools best explains historical events; the third paper uses that school of thought to analyze a current event. Students then revise their papers and combine the three into a cohesive term paper. Assigning a series of short papers during the term can save you time when it comes to grading the final longer essay. (Sources: Smith, 1994; Zeiser, 1999)

Distribute or post online a handout for each written assignment. Include all the essential information about the assignment:

- the specific task and your expectations of what should be included in the fin-ished product
- the genre of paper you expect (for example, memo, report, essay, letter, outline)
- the audience for the assignment (to help students make decisions about tone, language, and organization)
- the approximate length (number of words or pages)
- the physical format of the paper (margins, line spacing)
- how the paper will be submitted (online or hard copy)

- guidelines about types and number of sources and format for citations, footnotes, or bibliography
- a reminder to retain all drafts and notes (should issues of plagiarism arise) and a copy of the completed paper
- the criteria you will use in grading the assignment so that students are aware in advance how they will be graded
- opportunities for preliminary review by you or other students
- schedule for any options to revise papers for a higher grade
- the due date for the assignment and policies regarding late papers

Tollefson (2002) presents an example of a term paper assignment in biology that could be adapted to other disciplines. The assignment specifies clearly and in detail the task, explains how to develop a thesis statement, gives sources for research, offers tips on writing, and identifies common problems students have encountered in the past.

Involve students actively in the assignment right away. After presenting an assignment, take some class time for small-group discussion. Ask students to free associate words, facts, ideas, questions to begin to formulate theses or plan their research strategies.

Developing Students' Research Skills

Direct students toward resources for acquiring research skills. Find out what tutorials or workshops your campus library offers. Important topics include how to use the library's electronic resources, the differences between popular magazines and scholarly journals, the difference between primary and secondary materials, and how to evaluate journal articles. The University of Washington's open-access online tutorial *Research 101* (n.d.) explains how to frame a topic, develop research questions, and select, search, and evaluate information sources. Librarians at UC Berkeley, Mississippi State University, and Gustavus Adolphus, among others, have developed assignments that familiarize students with research skills. Booth, Colomb, and Williams (2003) explain to students how to conceptualize a research problem, provide evidence to substantiate an argument or claim, and communicate findings clearly.

Invite a librarian to make a presentation to your students. Most campus librarians are eager to make presentations about library skills, information literacy, resources, and search strategies. Also, encourage students to ask for assistance at the library's reference desk and to take advantage of library tours, instructional workshops, and tip sheets.

Help students gain skills to become information literate. The Association of College and Research Libraries has defined information literacy as the ability to do the following tasks (Johnson and Magusin, 2005; Rockman et al., 2004):

- determine the extent of information needed
- access needed information effectively and efficiently
- evaluate information and its sources critically
- incorporate selected information into one's own knowledge base
- use information effectively to accomplish a specific purpose
- understand the economic, legal, and social issues surrounding the use of information, and access and use information ethically and legally

Teach students about electronic library research and Internet research. Even students who consider themselves tech savvy may be unaware of the difference between using a commercial search engine (for example, Google) and using a library's subscription tools to search the "hidden Web." Assign students to compare and contrast the treatment of a topic in a popular magazine and a scholarly journal, to compare the online and hard-copy versions, and to experiment with different search options (complex, advanced, keyword). Check to see if your library has developed a Web-page evaluation checklist to help students assess the quality of Web information. Help students see the difference between scholarship and information seeking. (Sources: Harmon, 2007; Jenson, 2004; Mann, 2007)

Clarify your policy regarding sources. Specify what types of sources are and are not acceptable, how to evaluate the reliability of sources, and how to cite sources. If you want students to search the Internet, help them develop effective search terms or direct them to appropriate databases or sites. To discourage students from simply Web surfing for quotes, tell them that they must be accountable for having read a substantial part of any document that they quote from. (Source: Lim, 2001)

Arrange for peer groups. Consider using peer groups to divide up, research, and write coordinated papers. Peer groups may be useful in commenting on the type or amount of research that a student has done before writing a first draft. See the discussion of peer groups in Chapter 34, "Helping Students Write Better in All Courses." (Source: Henderson and Buising, 2000)

Specify a style manual. If the assignment calls for citations, footnotes, or a bibliography, make available a handout showing the format for these or refer students to a specific style guide or manual. Many campuses have online guides, or you might select the style of your professional association, or ask students to follow the guidelines in Turabian's *A Manual for Writers of Term Papers, Theses, and Dissertations* (1996).

Alternatives to Research and Term Paper Assignments

Reactions to readings. Ask students to submit short papers that summarize, assess, and respond to the readings. This exercise prepares students to take part in class discussion. You could also pose study questions for each reading assignment and ask students to submit written answers. (Sources: Fishman, 1997; McCoy 1999; Pernecky, 1993)

Article, abstract, or book review for a professional journal. Specifying an intended audience makes written assignments more challenging and realistic. Ask students to write as though they were going to submit their work to a professional journal. Or distribute an article with the abstract removed, and ask students to write the abstract. Then distribute the published abstract, and ask students to write a short comparison of their version and the author's. Or provide sample book reviews from journals in your field, discuss the features that make them effective, and ask students to prepare a book review suitable for publication.

Research proposal. Ask students to write a research proposal for a study or series of studies that reflect the course content.

Office report. Ask students to write a memo, briefing, or report for a professional audience unfamiliar with the field. For example, business students could write a report for bankers and other financial backers. (Source: Tollefson, 2002)

Memo recommending action. Pose a controversial issue or perplexing problem and ask students to prepare a memo outlining a course of action and stating their reasons for selecting that strategy. (Source: Tollefson, 2002)

Letters. Here are some of the kinds of letters you could assign (adapted from Cabe et al., 1999; Daughaday, 1997; Fredericksen, 2000; Greenwald, 2000; Keith, 2001; Lambert, 1996; Tollefson, 2002):

- a persuasive or argumentative letter to a public official or company officer for or against a particular policy or decision (ask students to present evidence and respond to anticipated counterarguments.)

- a critique addressed to the author of the course textbook or other book, assessing the book's strengths and weaknesses
- a letter to the editor, an op-ed piece, or a response to a published editorial
- a letter to a relative or friend in which the student explains a technical topic in a conversational voice
- a letter proposing a solution to a real-world or hypothetical problem (for example [adapted from Goma, 2001], students in an economics class could write a letter to the finance minister of a country in a deep recession recommending steps the government should take)
- a response to a letter in a newspaper advice column about personal, business, or other problems

Reader's guide. Ask students to present a conceptual overview of a given topic by writing a reader's guide that they will share with their classmates. The guide includes (1) an outline of subtopics, (2) a list of main theorists or contributors and why they are important, (3) a set of important concepts related to the topic, (4) recent hot topics that have engendered debate, and (5) a selection of the most important resources on the topic. (Source: Henderson, 2000)

Update of the readings. Ask students to select a section of the text or readings and prepare a two-page update that stresses new research that was unavailable to the original authors.

Original textbook. Using primary source documents, students create their own 10–15 page textbook chapter on a topic related to the course. (Source: Frye, 1999)

Think piece. Assign short exploratory think pieces that call for one intellectual task: compare two approaches, analyze reasons for behavior, and so on. Grade the think pieces with a check, check plus, or check minus. (Source: Elbow and Sorcinelli, 2006)

Microthemes. A microtheme is a very brief essay (about 150 to 250 words) in response to a narrowly focused question (Bean et al., 1982; Clanton, 1997; Leahy, 1994). Here are some examples (adapted from Bean et al., 1982):

- From the data in Table 1 (birthrates by ethnicity) extrapolate the significant changes that have occurred in the last twenty years and speculate on the causes of these changes.
- Suppose you put a big block of ice in a bucket and then fill the bucket with water until the water level is exactly even with the edge of the bucket. After several hours, the ice melts. Which of the following has happened? (a) The

water level in the bucket has remained the same; (b) the water level in the bucket has dropped; (c) some water has overflowed the sides of the bucket. Write a brief explanation for a classmate who doesn't understand flotation.

Obituary. Ask students to write an obituary of a noted academic figure who is still living. (Source: Foley, 2001)

Investigative article about an aspect of campus life. Have students select a campus-related topic such as the increasing cost of textbooks, oversubscribed courses, cost overruns on construction projects, or recycling and sustainability efforts; gather information through research; and prepare a briefing for a senior administrator. (Source: Picciotto, 1997)

Contribution to an online knowledge base. Ask students to pick an entry and then expand or improve the knowledge on an open-access, user-written, collaboratively edited site like *Wikipedia.* Faculty anecdotally report that students work harder on the assignment when they know their work will be subjected to outside reviewers and appear publicly. A variation is to use an internal wiki where students can practice public writing that is subject to reviews and revisions by classmates but is password protected.

Invented dialogue. Ask students to write conversations between real or imagined individuals; for example, Napoleon and Caesar could discuss the difference between the leadership skills needed to conquer an empire and those needed to maintain one. (Source: Angelo and Cross, 1993)

In-class poster session. Students prepare and present a project to their classmates in a poster session similar to those at professional and scientific conferences. Projects may include traditional papers, research studies, or artistic presentations. The process can be structured in stages: (1) a one-page proposal, (2) a preview presentation for class feedback, and (3) a final presentation at the end of the term. (Sources: Baird, 1991; Crowley-Long et al., 1997; Henderson and Buising, 2000)

Realistic scenarios. Ask students to communicate with a real audience that has a genuine need for information. For example, an architecture instructor gave the following assignment:

> What makes excellent architecture? In an attempt to recognize, reward, and publicize excellent architecture, a philanthropic patron of the arts has decided to initiate the Bucky Fuller Award for Excellence in Public Buildings. The

patron has asked you to help prepare the guidelines for the judging of this annual award.

Write a concise memo (500 words) to the patron that addresses such issues as the following:

- What is the definition of excellent architecture? What criteria will be used to judge buildings?
- What evidence is appropriate to document architectural excellence?
- Who should judge excellence?
- What procedures are best used to determine excellence?

You should propose your own definition of excellence, but you must support your views by citing published sources. For example, if you feel that social factors are important, refer the patron to several key works in the literature on social factors in architecture.

Or consider this example from a business class. To elicit a short essay describing what certified public accountants (CPAs) do, the instructor devised this assignment:

You are a CPA in a large, prestigious, and highly respected firm of accountants and business consultants. You have been called to superior court to testify as an expert witness in a divorce case. To establish a fair property settlement between husband and wife, it is necessary for the court to determine the value of their restaurant. You have examined the restaurant's accounts. But before you give your financial analysis, the judge asks you to establish your authority by explaining briefly how CPAs are trained and accredited and what domains their expertise and responsibilities encompass.

Interview. Have students interview another faculty member, a professional, or another individual related to the content of the course. Give students guidelines on how to conduct and write up interviews.

Consumers' report. Ask students to review a product, a service, or a conceptual tool that is related to the course. (Source: Hobson, 1998)

Other assignments. UCLA, through its Calibrated Peer Review project, has created a Web-based assignment library which stores instructor-developed assignments organized by discipline (cpr.molsci.ucla.edu). Your campus library may also have sample assignments. If not, consult the libraries at University of Central Florida, University of Illinois, and American River College, among others.

Using Journals or Learning Logs

Ask students to keep a journal for the course. Encourage students to make entries at least twice a week that contain ideas, questions, or comments related to the course. You could also ask them to write a weekly entry that reports on their learning. You need not collect these. (Sources: Etkina and Andre, 2002; Hirt, 1995; Longhurst and Sandage, 2004; Seshachari, 1994)

Provide guidelines for journal entries. Guidelines are useful to prevent students from writing about anything and everything or from copying class notes into their journal. You could ask students to summarize the key points of readings or lectures, or you might provide study questions. Some faculty select appropriate questions from Stock (1987) as a first assignment to get students thinking and in the habit of writing; for example, Would you be willing to have horrible nightmares every night for a year if you would be rewarded with extraordinary wealth? If you are going to collect and read students' journals, limit the word count and the number of entries submitted. (Sources: Fisher, 1996; Hirt, 1995)

Give credit, but not grades, for journals. You can give students points for having done the journal work without reading and grading their work. If you do comment on their journals, write positive comments, and present any negative remarks about quality or effort to the class as a whole. (Sources: August, 2000; Bolin et al., 2005; Brand, 1999; Chandler, 1997; Moore, 1994; Seshachari, 1994)

References

Angelo, T. A., and Cross, K. P. *Classroom Assessment Techniques: A Handbook for College Teachers.* (2nd ed.) San Francisco: Jossey-Bass, 1993.

August, A. "The Reader's Journal in Lower-Division History Courses: A Strategy to Improve Reading, Writing and Discussion." *History Teacher,* 2000, *33*(3), 343–348.

Baird, B. N. "In-Class Poster Sessions." *Teaching of Psychology,* 1991, *18*(1), 27–29.

Bean, J. C., Drenk, D., and Lee, F. D. "Microtheme Strategies for Developing Cognitive Skills." *New Directions for Teaching and Learning,* no. 12. San Francisco: Jossey-Bass, 1982, pp. 27–38.

Bolin, A. U., Khramtsova, I., and Saarnio, D. "Using Student Journals to Stimulate Authentic Learning: Balancing Bloom's Cognitive and Affective Domains." *Teaching of Psychology,* 2005, *32*(3), 154–159.

Booth, W. C., Colomb, G. G., and Williams, J. M. *The Craft of Research.* (2nd ed.) Chicago: University of Chicago Press, 2003.

Brand, J. L. "The Effective Use of Logbooks in Undergraduate Classes." *Chemical Engineering Education,* 1999, *33*(3), 222–231.

Cabe, P. A., Walker, M. H., and Williams, M. "Newspaper Advice Column Letters as Teaching Cases for Developmental Psychology." *Teaching of Psychology*, 1999, *26*(2), 128–130.

Chandler, A. "Is This for a Grade? A Personal Look at Journals." *English Journal*, 1997, *86*(1), 45–49.

Clanton, G. "A Semi-Painless Way to Improve Student Writing." *Thought & Action*, 1997, *13*(1), 21–30.

Crowley-Long, K., Powell, J. L., and Christensen, C. "Teaching Students about Research: Classroom Poster Sessions." *The Clearing House*, 1997, *70*(4).

Daughaday, L. "Postcards from the Imagination: Using Letters to Teach Sociological Concepts." *Teaching Sociology*, 1997, *25*(3), 234–238.

Elbow, P., and Sorcinelli, M. D. How to Enhance Learning by Using High-Stakes and Low-Stakes Writing. In W. J. McKeachie and M. Svinicki, *McKeachie's Teaching Tips*. (12th ed.) Boston: Houghton Mifflin, 2006.

Etkina, E., and Andre, K. "Weekly Reports: Student Reflections on Learning: An Assessment Tool Based on Student and Teacher Feedback." *Journal of College Science Teaching*, 2002, *31*(7), 476–480.

Fisher, B. J. "Using Journals in the Social Psychology Class: Helping Students Apply Course Concepts to Life Experiences." *Teaching Sociology*, 1996, *24*(2), 157–165.

Fishman, S. M. "Student Writing in Philosophy: A Sketch of Five Techniques." *New Directions for Teaching and Learning*, no. 69. San Francisco: Jossey-Bass, 1997.

Foley, J. E. "The Freshman Research Paper: A Near-Death Experience." *College Teaching*, 2001, *49*(3), 83–86.

Fredericksen, E. "Letter Writing in the College Classroom." *Teaching English in the Two-Year College*, 2000, *27*(3), 278–284.

Frye, D. "Can Students Write Their Own Textbooks? Thoughts on a New Type of Writing Assignment." *History Teacher*, 1999, *32*(4), 517–523.

Goma, O. D. "Creative Writing in Economics." *College Teaching*, 2001, *49*(4), 149–152.

Greenwald, S. J. "The Use of Letter Writing Projects in Teaching Geometry." *PRIMUS: Problems, Resources, and Issues in Mathematics Undergraduate Studies*, 2000, *10*(1), 1–14.

Harmon, J. C. "Let Them Use the Internet: Why College Instructors Should Encourage Student Internet Use." *College Teaching*, 2007, *55*(1), 2–4.

Henderson, B. B. "The Reader's Guide As an Integrative Writing Experience." *Teaching of Psychology*, 2000, *27*(2), 130–132.

Henderson, L., and Buising, C. "A Peer-Reviewed Research Assignment for Large Classes." *Journal of College Science Teaching*, 2000, *30*(2), 109–113.

Hirt, D. E. "Student Journals: Are They Beneficial in Lecture Courses?" *Chemical Engineering Education*, 1995, *29*(1), 62–64.

Hobson, E. H. "Designing and Grading Written Assignments." *New Directions for Teaching and Learning*, no. 74. San Francisco: Jossey-Bass, 1998, pp. 51–57.

Jenson, J. D. "It's the Information Age, So Where's the Information? Why Our Students Can't Find It and What We Can Do to Help." *College Teaching*, 2004, *52*(3).

Johnson, K., and Magusin, E. *Exploring the Digital Library*. San Francisco: Jossey-Bass, 2005.

Keith, K. D. "Letters Home: Writing for Understanding in Introductory Psychology." *The Psychology Teacher Network*, Jan./Feb. 2001, no. 11, 12–13.

Lambert, S. "Dear Gabby: Using the Advice-Column to Teach Logical Reasoning." *Exercise Exchange: A Journal for Teachers of English in High Schools and Colleges*, 1996, *41*(2), 18–19.

Leahy, R. "Microthemes: An Experiment with Very Short Writings." *College Teaching*, 1994, *42*(1), 15–18.

Leahy, R. "Conducting Writing Assignments." *College Teaching*, 2002, *50*(2), 50–54.

Lim, J. "Effective Internet Research." *The Clearing House*, 2001, *75*(1).

Longhurst, J., and Sandage, S. A. "Appropriate Technology and Journal Writing: Structured Dialogues That Enhance Learning." *College Teaching*, 2004, *52*(2), 69.

Mann, T. *The Peloponnesian War and the Future of Reference, Cataloging, and Scholarship in Research Libraries.* Washington, DC: AFSCME 2910, The Library of Congress Professional Guild, June 13, 2007. http://www.guild2910.org/Peloponnesian%20War%20June%2013%202007.pdf

McCoy, R. K. "Integrating Writing in the Classroom with Reader Responses." *Teaching History*, 1999, *24*(1), 28–36.

Moore, R. "Writing to Learn Biology." *Journal of College Science Teaching*, 1994, *23*(5), 289–295.

Pernecky, M. "Reaction Papers Enrich Economics Discussions." *College Teaching*, Summer 1993, *41*(3), 89–91.

Picciotto, M. "Investigating the College: Teaching the Research Process." *College Teaching*, 1997, *45*(1), 19–21.

Research 101. Online tutorial, University of Washington, n.d. http://www.lib.washington.edu/uwill/research101

Rockman, I. F., and associates (Ed.). *Integrating Information Literacy into the Higher Education Curriculum.* San Francisco: Jossey-Bass, 2004.

Seshachari, N. C. "Instructor-Mediated Journals: Raising Critical Thinking and Discourse Levels." *College Teaching*, 1994, *42*(1), 7–11.

Simon, L. "The Papers We Want to Read." *College Teaching*, 1988, *36*(1), 6–8.

Smith, R. "Sequenced MicroThemes: A Great Deal of Thinking for Your Students, and Relatively Little Grading for You." *Teaching Resources Center Newsletter*, 1994, 5(3). http://www.indiana.edu/~cwp/assgn/microseq.shtml

Speck, B. W. *Grading Students' Classroom Writing: Issues and Strategies.* ASHE-ERIC Higher Education Report, 2000, *27*(3).

Stock, G. *The Book of Questions.* New York: Workman, 1987.

Tollefson, S. K. *Encouraging Student Writing.* Berkeley: Office of Educational Development, University of California, 2002. http://teaching.berkeley.edu/publications.html

Turabian, K. L. *A Manual for Writers of Term Papers, Theses, and Dissertations.* (6th ed.) Chicago: University of Chicago Press, 1996.

Zeiser, P. A. "Teaching Process and Product: Crafting and Responding to Student Writing Assignments." *PS: Political Science and Politics*, 1999, *32*(3).

36

Evaluating Students' Written Work

Evaluating and grading papers is as an opportunity to reinforce a student's strengths and identify areas needing improvement. Make your suggestions as tactful and specific as you can—no one benefits from sharp remarks or vague hints. At least one study suggests that, even outside composition classes, students value and will use feedback for revision (Beason, 1993). The following pointers will help you evaluate and grade papers efficiently, fairly, and constructively.

General Strategies

Give yourself time to read the papers. Although you will want to return papers promptly, try to avoid reading a large number of papers in a single sitting. You will be better able to maintain your concentration and apply your standards consistently if you read a few papers at a time. After each break, some instructors start by reviewing the last paper or two to make sure that fatigue didn't result in an overly generous or overly harsh evaluation.

Begin by getting a general sense of the entire set of papers. Some faculty read through all the papers quickly, sorting them into three or four piles according to a quick assessment of their quality. Once you have a general sense of how well students handled the assignment, you are less likely to overestimate an average paper or to wait expectantly for an outstanding one.

Write legibly. If you grade on hard copy, avoid felt marking pens that are too thick to be legible, and use a color that is easy to read (green, orange, purple, red). Writing the grade in pencil allows you to go back and check for consistency among the set of papers before finalizing the grades.

Type or speak your comments. Some instructors type their final comments so that they are legible and also on file. Others require electronic submissions and use the comment and editing features of word-processing software to customize and automate comments for the most common student writing problems. For more detailed responses, experiment with embedding voice comments, which some research shows that students prefer. (Sources: Bell, 2002; Still, 2006)

Get feedback on your feedback. During the term ask students to comment on the helpfulness of your responses to their written work. Research shows that students value feedback that is specific, gives suggestions for improvement, and is related to assessment criteria that have been previously distributed. See Chapter 52, "Early Feedback to Improve Teaching and Learning" for advice on how to solicit students' comments. (Source: Weaver, 2006)

Scoring Guides

Use rubrics or other scoring guides to save time and improve consistency in grading. A rubric is a set of components of an assignment—for example, Purpose, Organization, Evidence, Style, and Mechanics—accompanied by definitions of performance levels for each component. Rubrics are often formatted as a table, with the components listed in the leftmost column and the levels of performance listed across the top (adapted from Stevens and Levi, 2005):

	Performance Level		
Component	**Developing**	**Competent**	**Exemplary**
Provides supporting evidence	Gives some support for main assertions, but sources are not authoritative (e.g., popular magazines, commercial Web sites)	Generally supports main assertions with primary and secondary sources but does not provide evidence for subsidiary points or relies too heavily on a few sources or on sources that are not current	Provides strong supporting evidence for main and subsidiary assertions with multiple authoritative sources (e.g., journal articles and primary documents)

When using rubrics, you simply circle or check the comments that apply to each paper, which saves you time and gives your students detailed feedback on their work. (Of course, you can always add individual comments.) Because students can review the criteria that define each performance level, they are less likely to quibble about their grades or complain that they didn't know what you expected for the assignment.

A related approach, called "primary trait analysis" (Walvoord and Anderson, 1998), identifies the factors or traits that will count in the scoring and defines a scale for scoring student performance on each trait.

Checklists consist of rating scales (for example, a 5-point scale, with 1 = low) on selected aspects of the assignment; for example, clarity of expression, logical development, and persuasiveness.

(Sources: Andrade, 2005; Bednarski, 2003; Stevens and Levi, 2005; Walvoord and Anderson, 1998)

Adapt existing rubrics. Rubrics have been created for a wide range of assignments and projects. Online searching (for keywords "resources about rubrics" or "sample rubrics" plus "university" or "college") will yield links to collections of rubrics at Auburn University, Winona State University, Scottsdale Community College, Indiana University Kokomo, and College of St. Scholastica, among others. You can download these grids and modify them to suit your needs.

Create your own rubrics. After reviewing rubrics created by others, you may wish to create your own. For detailed advice on constructing rubrics, see Arter and McTighe (2001), Stevens and Levi (2005), and the RubiStar Web site (rubistar.4teachers.org/index.php), an online tool to help teachers create rubrics.

Share the rubrics or criteria with your students. When you assign a paper, explain your expectations and criteria to students so that they know how they will be graded. Some faculty report eye-opening experiences when they discovered how their students thought they should be evaluated. (Sources: Stevens and Levi, 2005)

Responding to Students' Writing

Read a paper quickly to form an overall impression. Identify the paper's strengths and note, but do not address or correct, problem areas. Identify the paper's main points and those features that interfere with your ability to follow the train of thought. This quick read-through will help you decide the key issues to address in your comments.

Respond to the paper as an interested reader or reviewer would. Look for things the student has done well, note errors and weaknesses that need correction, and think about ways the student can improve. Focus on the development of ideas, the construction of an argument, analysis, flow, and use of sources. Compliment the strengths and point out the weaknesses in grammar, style, and usage. If you write your comments on a separate piece of paper, you will be less inclined to spend time editing the student's work. (Sources: Elbow and Sorcinelli, 2006; Tollefson, 2002)

Balance facilitative and directive comments. Facilitative comments help students rethink their paper by posing questions: "What do you hope your reader will understand your thesis to be?" Directive comments make suggestions in an authoritative manner: "State your thesis more clearly." Use facilitative comments to call a student's attention to a paper's lack of purpose, direction, analysis, or logical structure; directive comments may be appropriate for problems of usage and style. (Sources: Ransdell, 1999; Straub, 2000)

Use constructive language. Students value both global comments (organization, content) and specific comments (word choice, sentence structure), and they are especially interested in suggestions for improvement. Students are more likely to learn from comments that focus on learning goals or established criteria. Here are some tips (adapted from Dornsife, 1993; Elbow and Sorcinelli, 2006; Kluger and DeNisi, 1996; Light, 1992; Pitts, 2005; Shepard, 2006; Smith, 1997; Speck, 2000; Straub, 1997; Tollefson, 2002):

- Balance positive and negative comments. Make some positive comments on every paper, both to encourage students and to reinforce what they are doing well. Avoid following a positive comment directly with a *but*. Direct positive comments to the student ("You did a great job clearly stating your thesis") and negative comments to the paper itself ("The opening paragraph is confusing").
- Avoid sarcastic, impatient, or punitive comments.
- Phrase criticisms as questions: Ask "I wonder what you gain by including this paragraph" rather than "Delete this paragraph."
- Provide suggestions for improvement. Instead of writing "This point was not explained fully enough," write "Explain in more detail why prices rose."
- Help students spot ambiguities or passages open to misunderstanding. You might write, "I take this sentence to mean X. If this is different from what you intended, what can you do to help the reader see what you mean?"
- Try to be concrete and specific. A student may not be able to decide whether comments such as "awkward," "unclear," or "vague" refer to organization, content, or mechanics. More helpful are comments like "How else would you describe this?" "Why is this so?" "Are you saying that X is necessary?" Don't hesitate to write, "I don't understand this sentence."
- Conclude with a brief description of what a successful or "A" paper looks like. This helps students focus on the criteria they can use to assess their own learning efforts.
- Don't rewrite students' papers. Indicate the major problems, but leave the revising to your students. If you do the rewriting for them, the main thing they will learn is that you are a better writer than they are.

Avoid overmarking. If you mark every grammatical error, respond to every idea, or propose alternatives for each section, you risk overwhelming students and diverting their attention from key problems. Try to focus on one or two major problems and on patterns of errors. Some faculty highlight all misspellings and grammatical errors, but others indicate these on the first few pages only and write a general note at the end of the paper: "Try to pay more attention to punctuation; your errors detract from your good ideas." (Source: Zeiser, 1999)

Avoid undermarking. Placing only one or two general comments on a paper and then assigning a grade, even an A, is not very helpful to students. Students want to know what you thought about their work. Praise the paper's strengths and offer constructive criticism on its weaknesses.

Respond appropriately to students who are not fluent in English. As you read papers, focus on those errors that seriously impede understanding. You may also want to correct common problems, such as dropped verb endings, problems with verb tense, subject-verb agreement, and use of articles and prepositions. Check your campus's resources for tutorial help for students who learned English as a second language. Online resources are available at the Web sites of the Purdue University Online Writing Lab, University of Minnesota, Ohio University, University of Washington, and Utah Valley State College, among others. (Sources: Holt, 1997; Tollefson, 2002)

Use marking symbols or codes. You can save time by using symbols or abbreviations for common errors (for example, AGR for an error in subject-verb agreement). Adopt the symbols from a standard composition textbook or from your campus English department or writing center. Or develop your own symbols. One faculty member gives students a code sheet of twelve items (#2 = Pay more attention to mechanics such as punctuation; #9 = Very well written; your points are clear and concise) and uses those codes when grading papers. (Source: O'Keefe, 1996)

Focus on errors that indicate cognitive confusion. Call students' attention to errors that reflect fuzzy or illogical thinking as well as to errors that are likely to confuse the reader: pronouns whose antecedents are missing or incorrect; confusing switches between past, present, and future tenses; and illogical pairings of subjects and verbs.

Grading

Keep it simple. One instructor saves time and avoids student quibbling by using a three-grade system: 0 = unacceptable, 1 = acceptable, and 2 = excellent. These levels are defined as follows: *excellent* = requires no revision, follows all assignment requirements, has no mechanical errors, attends to audience's needs, uses an appropriate tone, is written with flair; *acceptable* = requires some revision, follows all assignment requirements, has some noticeable mechanical errors, may inaccurately estimate the audience, may include negative terminology; and *unacceptable* = requires major revision, does not follow assignment requirements, has noticeable mechanical errors, ignores the reader, uses inappropriate tone, has negative terminology. (Source: Dyrud, 2003)

Use your rubrics or checklists as a general guide, but grade the assignment holistically. As you are commenting on submitted papers, phrase your remarks in terms of these criteria. But refrain from assigning a certain number of points for each criterion. Grade according to your judgment of overall quality. (Sources: Dyrud, 2003; Holt, 1993; Rodgers, 1995; Stevens and Levi, 2005; Tollefson, 2002)

Resist the temptation to assign split grades (one for content, one for writing). Split grades tend to reinforce the false notion that content can be divorced from the clarity and precision with which the ideas are expressed. (Source: Tollefson, 2002)

Give students definitions of the criteria for each grade. Some students believe that grading is purely subjective. You may want to explain what your grades mean (adapted from Crews, 1983, p. 14, and Tollefson, 2002, p. 14):

> A: Excellent in all or nearly all aspects. The interest of the reader is engaged by the ideas and presentation. Style and organization seem natural and easy. Paper marked by originality of ideas and free of minor and major errors.

> B: Technically competent, with a lapse here and there. The thesis is clear, properly limited, and reasonable, and the prose is generally effective without rising to sustained distinction.

> C: A competent piece of work but not yet "good." Writing is still an effort for the author. C papers are more or less adequately organized along obvious lines, and the thesis tends to be overly simple or imprudent without being wildly implausible. Monotony of sentence structure is apparent, and errors are sprinkled throughout. In some C papers, excellent ideas are marred by poor presentation—either development, organization, or technical errors. In other C papers, the organization, structure, and grammar are not flawed, but the ideas and how they are developed need work. In yet other C papers, there are only a few technical errors and the organization and ideas are adequate but not noteworthy. In college a C paper is fine.

D: A piece of work that demonstrates some effort on the author's part but that is too marred by technical problems or flaws in thinking and development of ideas to be considered competent work.

F: This is a failing grade, usually reserved for pieces of work that demonstrate minimal effort on the author's part. The writer has drastically misinterpreted the assignment and written half as many words as requested. Paragraph breaks are random; subjects and verbs, pronouns and antecedents turn against one another in wild discord. Plagiarism falls into this category. Most instructors consider it unproductive to give an F to a student who has made a sincere attempt; a D is a more appropriate grade in such a case.

Watch out for extraneous factors that may affect your grading. Try not to let the length of the paper or its appearance unfairly influence the grade. Make sure you're not being overly harsh on a paper solely because the student's point of view disagrees with yours. Avoid being overly generous by reading into the paper ideas that are not on the page. Separate your sympathy for a student from your assessment of the student's paper. (Source: Culham and Spandell, 1993)

Returning Assignments

Return papers at the end of class. If you return papers at the beginning of class, students will read your comments rather than pay attention to what is happening in class. Before returning papers, let students know when your next office hours are scheduled. If a student has a strong objection to the grade you gave, suggest that he or she wait a day before seeing you and take time to compose complaints or questions.

Give students an overall sense of the class's performance. When you hand back papers, comment on the set as a whole. If several students made the same kinds of errors, share information about the problem with the entire class. Tell students what you would like to see in future assignments, and reinforce the importance of writing as a way of learning the subject matter. It is also helpful to take time to read a particularly strong paper to the class.

Ask students to comment on the assignment. Inquire about the difficulties students had with the assignment and their suggestions for improving it.

Allow some rewrites. Allowing students to rewrite a paper and have it regraded can make the evaluation process more instructive. Students will tend to pay more attention to your comments when they have a chance to revise. Set a firm deadline for revisions and establish guidelines on what constitutes a rewrite. Ask that students submit both the original paper and their revision.

Portfolios

In courses with multiple writing assignments, ask students to submit portfolios. A portfolio is a student-selected collection of written assignments and exams that allows others to make judgments about the student's abilities (Annis and Jones, 1995). Portfolios can show growth or change over time, highlight strengths and weaknesses, or showcase best work. The most important component of a portfolio is the reflective essay that students prepare to accompany the work. This essay encourages students to assess on their progress as learners by discussing the following kinds of questions (adapted from Zubizarreta, 2004, p. 8):

- What did I learn?
- Is this what I thought I would learn?
- What have I learned that I didn't expect?
- Will what I learned affect my study habits or educational goals?
- What have I discovered about the way I learn or about my strengths and areas for improvement?

A less time-consuming process would call for students to identify their two best pieces of writing and fill out a short reflective questionnaire.

Decide whether to grade the portfolio. You do not need to grade portfolios that contain assignments that have already been graded. If you decide you want to give a grade, let students know what criteria you will use.

For nontext assignments, create e-portfolios. Electronic portfolios allow students to collect text, video, photographs, audio, and other multimedia materials. E-portfolios also make it easier to organize and share work for purposes beyond a single course. The Conference on College Composition and Communication (2007) has issued guidelines on e-portfolios.

References

Andrade, H. G. "Teaching with Rubrics: The Good, the Bad, and the Ugly." *College Teaching*, 2005, *53*(1), 27–30.

Annis, L., and Jones, C. Student Portfolios: Their Objectives, Development and Use. In P. Seldin (Ed.), *Improving College Teaching*. San Francisco: Jossey-Bass, 1995.

Arter, J., and McTighe, J. *Scoring Rubrics in the Classroom*. Thousand Oaks, CA: Corwin Press, 2001.

Beason, L. "Feedback and Revision in Writing across the Curriculum Classes." *Research in the Teaching of English*, 1993, *27*(4), 395–422.

Bednarski, M. "Assessing Performance Tasks: Guidelines for Developing Objective Scoring Rubrics." *The Science Teacher*, 2003, *70*(4), 34–37.

Bell, S. "Grading Papers Online." *Teaching English in the Two-Year College*, 2002, *30*(2), 198–199.

Conference on College Composition and Communication. "Principles and Practices in Electronic Portfolios." Nov. 2007. http://www.ncte.org/cccc/announcements/128846.htm

Crews, F. *English 1A-1B Instructor's Manual*. Berkeley: Department of English, University of California, 1983.

Culham, R., and Spandel, V. *Problems and Pitfalls Encountered by Raters*. Portland, OR: Northwest Regional Educational Laboratory, 1993. http://research.cps.k12.il.us/cps/accountweb/Assessment/IdeasandRubrics/Introduction/Using.html

Dornsife, R. S. "Five Ways to Improve Written Responses to Student Work." *The National Teaching and Learning Forum*, 1993, *2*(5), 4–5.

Dyrud, M. A. "Preserving Sanity by Simplifying Grading." *Business Communication Quarterly*, 2003, *66*(1), 78–85.

Elbow, P., and Sorcinelli, M. D. How to Enhance Learning by Using High-Stakes and Low-Stakes Writing. In W. J. McKeachie and M. Svinicki, *McKeachie's Teaching Tips*. (12th ed.) Boston: Houghton Mifflin, 2006.

Holt, D. "Holistic Scoring in Many Disciplines." *College Teaching*, 1993, *41*(2), 71–74.

Holt, S. L. "Responding to Grammar Errors." *New Directions for Teaching and Learning*, no. 70. San Francisco: Jossey-Bass, 1997.

Kluger, A. N., and DeNisi, A. "The Effect of Feedback Interventions on Performance: A Historical Review, a Meta-Analysis, and a Preliminary Feedback Intervention Theory." *Psychological Bulletin*, 1996, *119*(2), 254–284.

Light, R. J. *The Harvard Assessment Seminars, Second Report*. Cambridge, MA: School of Education, Harvard University, 1992.

O'Keefe, R. D. "Comment Codes: Improving Turnaround Time for Student Reports." *College Teaching*, Fall 1996, *44*(4), 137–138.

Pitts, S. E. "'Testing, Testing . . .' How Do Students Use Written Feedback?" *Active Learning in Higher Education*, 2005, *6*(3), 218–229.

Ransdell, D. R. "Directive versus Facilitative Commentary." *Teaching English in the Two-Year College*, 1999, *26*(3), 269–276.

Rodgers, M. L. "How Holistic Scoring Kept Writing Alive in Chemistry." *College Teaching*, 1995, *43*(1), 19–22.

Shepard, L. A. Classroom Assessment. In R. L. Brennan (Ed.), *Educational Measurement*. (4th ed.) Westport, CT: American Council on Education/Praeger, 2006.

Smith, S. "The Genre of the End Comment: Conventions in Teacher Responses to Student Writing." *College Composition and Communication*, 1997, *48*(2), 249–268.

Speck, B. W. *Grading Students' Classroom Writing: Issues and Strategies*. ASHE-ERIC Higher Education Report, 2000, *27*(3), 2000.

Stevens, D. D., and Levi, A. J. *Introduction to Rubrics: An Assessment Tool to Save Grading Time, Convey Effective Feedback and Promote Student Learning*. Sterling, VA: Stylus, 2005.

Still, B. "Talking to Students: Embedded Voice Commenting as a Tool for Critiquing Student Writing." *Journal of Business and Technical Communication*, 2006, *20*(4), 460–475.

Straub, R. "Students' Reactions to Teacher Comments: An Exploratory Study." *Research in the Teaching of English*, 1997, *31*(1), 91–119.

Straub, R. *The Practice of Response: Strategies for Commenting on Student Writing.* Cresskill, NJ: Hampton Press, 2000.

Tollefson, S. K. *Encouraging Student Writing.* Berkeley: Office of Educational Development, University of California, 2002. http://teaching.berkeley.edu/publications.html

Walvoord, B. E., and Anderson, V. J. *Effective Grading: A Tool for Learning and Assessment.* San Francisco: Jossey-Bass, 1998.

Weaver, M. "Do Students Value Feedback? Student Perceptions of Tutors' Written Responses." *Assessment and Evaluation in Higher Education*, 2006, *31*(3), 379–394.

Zeiser, P. A. "Teaching Process and Product: Crafting and Responding to Student Writing Assignments." *PS: Political Science and Politics*, 1999, *32*(3), 593–595.

Zubizarreta, J. *The Learning Portfolio: Reflective Practice for Improving Student Learning.* San Francisco: Jossey-Bass, 2004.

37

Homework: Problem Sets

There are several advantages to having students turn in problem sets or short homework assignments throughout the term:

- Students become accustomed to regular, systematic study and tend to procrastinate less.
- Students come to understand the kinds of problems they should be able to solve.
- The assignments give you continual opportunities to see how your students are doing.

If you assign homework, Wankat and Oreovicz (2003) advise that the homework assignments account for 10 to 15 percent of a student's course grade. If homework counts for less, some students will ignore the assignments. If it counts for more, some students may be tempted to cheat.

You will also want to ask students how long the homework is taking them. Depending on their answers, you may want to adjust the amount of homework you assign or discuss more effective study habits and problem-solving techniques.

General Strategies

Distribute the work load evenly throughout the term. Try to pace assignments so that students do not have massive amounts of homework during the last weeks of the term or immediately before or after a midterm.

Decide when you want to announce homework assignments. Some faculty distribute the entire set of assignments for the term on the first day of class so that students can plan their schedules. Other faculty announce one assignment at a time, which allows them to modify assignments to suit the pace and ability of the class. Still others list the due dates for assignments in the syllabus but make the specific assignments as the term proceeds. You should also decide whether you prefer making assignments at the beginning of the class meetings or close to the end. Whatever you decide, make it clear to students when assignments will be available, when they will be due, and what they will entail.

Convey the goal of each assignment. Students will be more motivated to work hard on the assignments if you explain the purpose of homework and its relation to the goals of the course. What will students learn by completing the problem sets? How do the problem sets reinforce other aspects of the course? How do the problem sets relate to midterms and the final exam?

Limit the amount of class time devoted to reviewing homework. An instructor going over homework problems may discourage students from doing difficult problems on their own. Moreover, students who are shown a solution and then asked to solve a similar problem sometimes still cannot solve the problem on their own. If you do review homework during class, ask students to step up to the board and demonstrate how they have solved a problem. (Source: Dominowksi, 2002)

Preparing Problem Sets

Make the first assignment a review. In the first assignment, include material that students should have learned in prerequisite courses. Use the assignment to determine whether each student is adequately prepared to succeed in your course. Ask inadequately prepared students to delay entry into your course or direct them to resources to address gaps in their knowledge.

Coordinate problem sets with course topics. Do not confuse or frustrate your students by making assignments that require information, skills, or techniques they have not yet acquired in class. If the course topics and homework diverge, explain your rationale to the class.

Try to create meaningful assignments. Students approach homework with more interest if they can see the assignment's applicability and relevance.

Be selective in your choice of problems. Include a reasonable mix of routine exercises and more challenging problems, but avoid excessively tricky problems. Try not to assign difficult problems too early in the term; early failure or frustration may reduce students' motivation to work hard on later problems. Reinforce students' learning by covering a concept or topic in at least two assignments.

Cull problem sets from a variety of sources. Look for items online and in instructor's copies of textbooks in the subject area. You could also exchange problem sets with colleagues at other institutions. Some faculty members ask students to submit problems for future assignments.

Vary the type of homework you assign. For example, two or three times during the term give students the assignment of summarizing the key concepts, principles, or formulas in the course up to that point. Summarizing helps students synthesize course material, focus on the larger context of the course, and distinguish between important and less important material.

Divide homework into "hand-in" and "also-do" problems. Collect the "hand-in" problems, but let students know that the "also-do" problems might appear on the midterm or the final exam. (Source: Reznick, 1985)

If possible, do all the problems yourself before giving them to students. By doing the assignment yourself, you can see what is required to complete the problem sets and what difficulties students might have. You will also be able to catch any errors in the instructions, problems, and data. Try to work on the problem sets a week or two before your students do. If you complete all the assignments before the course starts, you may not remember the problems well enough to advise students.

Helping Students Learn How to Solve Problems

Have students work collaboratively on sample problems in class. Students can learn from each other by working together, and group work can benefit students of differing dispositions and abilities. See Chapter 21, "Learning in Groups." (Sources: Baker and Campbell, 2005; Wieschenberg, 1994)

Let students do homework in groups outside class. Some faculty try to minimize dishonest copying by forbidding collaborative work, but such policies deprive students of the benefits of peer learning. Some faculty encourage students to discuss the problem sets but require students to write up their work independently. (Source: Wankat and Oreovicz, 2003)

Tell your students about your own problem-solving process and techniques. Discuss how you think about a problem before you decide on an approach to solving it, how you classify problems in terms of underlying principles, how you separate important from unimportant information, and how you monitor your performance and progress. Try to direct students' attention to the process rather than the solution, including how you proceed when you feel stuck—and how you decide whether you are stuck. (Sources: Anderson, 1993; Bransford et al., 2000)

Be sensitive to the differences between expert and novice problem solvers. As an instructor, by definition, you have developed expertise that your students may lack.

Research shows that compared to novices, experts have more extensive content knowledge; can flexibly retrieve important aspects of their knowledge effortlessly, with little conscious attention; have greater access to a wide repertory of skills; spend more time planning and analyzing the problem; can more easily recognize features and patterns in information; can reduce complex problems to manageable sizes by separating relevant from irrelevant information; classify problems according to an underlying structure or conceptualization; know when additional information is needed; consider an array of alternatives before deciding on a course of action; and more carefully self-monitor their own understanding and performance.

Students move from novice toward developing competency through a series of learning processes. Help students accomplish the following (adapted from Bransford et al., 2000, pp. 237–238):

- relate the knowledge they possess to new knowledge
- organize information in ways that support their abilities to remember
- go beyond the information that is given to draw inferences and conclusions
- understand under what conditions knowledge applies
- make estimates and "educated guesses"
- regulate their own processes and change strategies as necessary

Teach students how to solve problems. First published in 1945 and continuously in print, Polya's classic *How to Solve It* (2004) is the starting point for most advice on problem solving. Polya discusses problem-solving options at each of four basic steps: understanding the problem, making a plan, carrying out the plan, and looking back. The following suggestions for problem solving are adapted from Bransford, Brown, and Cocking (2000); Brown and Atkins (1988); Davidson and Ambrose (1994); Dominowski (2002); Freisem, Messemer, and Jacobson (2005); and Polya (2004):

- Read and carefully reread the problem description.
- Write out the information specifically requested by the problem.
- Restate the problem in your own words.
- List all the givens, both explicit and implicit.
- Look twice at words that might be misinterpreted.
- Distinguish the key points; identify what is important and what is unimportant.
- Try to explain the problem to someone else.
- Examine similar kinds of problems worked out by others or similar problems you have solved successfully.

- Brainstorm; there may be more than one way to solve a problem.
- Study the problem; then leave it and come back to it later.
- Make a flowchart with yes/no options, draw a diagram, or represent the problem graphically or mathematically.
- Break the problem into smaller parts.
- Do the easiest parts or steps first.
- Make a rough approximation of what the solution should look like.
- Systematically use trial and error.
- Think about your problem-solving strategy (metacognition) instead of thinking about the problem.
- Verbalize as you solve the problem.
- Be persistent in the face of frustration; few problems are easily solved.
- Keep a relaxed, calm, but alert mental state. Don't let frustration, anger, or negative feelings cloud your thinking.
- After you have solved the problem, review your solution:
  - Verbally summarize the solution to reinforce what you have learned.
  - Check to see whether there is a simpler or alternative method.
  - Identify what class of problems you now can solve.

Ask students to go beyond the solution. A mathematics professor gives students the following assignment: "Choose any one of the problems you have already solved, and explain in complete sentences, step-by-step, exactly how you solved the problem." You can use these explanations to better understand your students' thinking processes and problem-solving strategies. You could also assign students to serve, on a rotating basis, as "resident experts" for each week's homework problems. Or you can ask them to discuss or write about strategies they use to become unstuck. (Sources: Angelo, 1991; Tripp, 1998)

Collecting Homework

Set clear policies for assignments. Some faculty penalize late work by a fixed number of points for each day that the work is late unless the student has a compelling reason for missing a deadline. Other faculty announce that a student's one or two worst homework grades will not be counted. Some faculty give students two days' grace during the term, which students can use to turn in one assignment two days late or two assignments each a day late.

If you are collecting hard copy, make the assignment due at the beginning of class. If you accept homework up to the end of the period, students may come late to class.

Grading

Grade only a sample of the homework. You could collect all the homework but grade only one or two problems per set, or collect two or three problems a week for grading, or give a short quiz on selected problems and grade those. Some faculty ask their students to place all their homework in a notebook or an online file, which is called in for checking every few weeks. For assignments you do not grade, post an answer sheet after the homework is due so that students can check their work.

Check a student's method as well as the answer. When you grade students' homework, write a brief comment to praise something that is especially good. If the solution is incorrect, identify the error or suggest a better approach. If a student solves a problem with a method different from the one you would have chosen, make sure that a correct answer does not conceal conceptual or logical errors. Some students may come up with creative or inventive solutions. Even when a student's method is acceptable, you might mention simpler or more powerful methods.

Reward progress. Decide how to score answers that are partially correct. Try to reward students who chose the correct concepts or methods, even if they committed errors in their calculation. One faculty member assigns a "0" if the problem is less than one-third complete; a "1" if it is one-third to two-thirds complete; and a "2" if it is more than two-thirds finished. (Source: Wieschenberg, 1994)

Return homework promptly. Try to return homework or post the answers by the next class session so that students will have a current sense of what they have not yet mastered.

References

Anderson, J. R. "Problem Solving and Learning." *American Psychologist*, 1993, *48*(1), 35–44.

Angelo, T. A. Ten Easy Pieces: Assessing Higher Learning in Four Dimensions. In T. A. Angelo (Ed.), *Classroom Research: Early Lessons from Success*. New Directions for Teaching and Learning, no. 46. San Francisco: Jossey-Bass, 1991.

Baker, D. F., and Campbell, C. M. "When Is There Strength in Numbers? A Study of Undergraduate Task Groups." *College Teaching*, 2005, *53*(1), 14–18.

Bransford, J. D., Brown, A. L., and Cocking, R. R. (Eds.). *How People Learn: Brain, Mind, Experience, and School*. Washington, DC: National Academy Press, 2000.

Brown, G., and Atkins, M. *Effective Teaching in Higher Education*. London: Methuen, 1998.

Davidson, C. I., and Ambrose, S. A. *The New Professor's Handbook: A Guide to Teaching and Research in Engineering and Science.* San Francisco: Jossey-Bass, 1994.

Dominowski, R. L. *Teaching Undergraduates.* Mahwah, NJ: Erlbaum, 2002.

Freisem, K., Messemer, C., and Jacobson, W. H. Aligning in Math, Science and Engineering Courses. In D. H. Wulff (Ed.), *Aligning for Learning: Strategies for Teaching Effectiveness.* San Francisco: Jossey-Bass, 2005.

Polya, G. *How to Solve It: A New Aspect of Mathematical Method.* Princeton, NJ: Princeton University Press, 2004.

Reznick, B. A. *Chalking It Up: Advice to a New TA.* New York: Random House, 1985.

Tripp, J. S. "Getting Students to Do Homework." *The Mathematics Teacher*, 1998, *91*(6), 478–479.

Wankat, P., and Oreovicz, F. "Teaching: Getting Homework to Work." *ASEE PRISM*, 2003, *12*(6).

Wieschenberg, A. A. "Overcoming Conditioned Helplessness in Mathematics." *College Teaching*, 1994, *42*(2).

Part VIII

Testing and Grading

38

Promoting Academic Honesty

In surveys, one-half to nearly three-quarters of college students admit to having cheated at least once during their academic career (Cizek, 1999; Lang, 2008; Maramark and Maline, 1993; McCabe and Trevino, 1996). Students explain their dishonest behavior in various ways: they cheat in response to pressures to get good grades, or in an effort to cope with classes that seem unfair or too demanding, or because they are uncertain about the line between acceptable and unacceptable conduct, or when they feel that their instructors are uncaring or indifferent to their own teaching or students' learning. Procrastination, carelessness, panic in the face of deadlines, peer pressure to support a friend, or belief that everyone does it are other reasons students may cheat.

Some of these factors are beyond an instructor's control, but you can take several steps to promote academic honesty (adapted from Aiken, 1991; Davis et al., 1992; Roberts and Rabinowitz, 1992; Whitley, 1998):

- State the standards for scholarship and conduct. Put these standards in the syllabus and discuss them in class.
- Explain how cheating harms students and describe campus sanctions for dishonesty.
- Structure your course so that students will not be tempted to lie (for example, allow students to miss one quiz without penalty).
- Take visible precautions to detect cheating; let students see that you will not tolerate unethical conduct.
- If cheating occurs, respond swiftly.

General Strategies

Discuss standards of academic honesty at the beginning of the term. General admonitions to "avoid cheating" are relatively ineffective. Help students distinguish between acceptable and unacceptable behavior by giving examples of plagiarism, impermissible collaboration, and other practices. For example, is it plagiarism if students incorporate ideas from peers or tutors at the student learning center? Is it okay for students to work with friends on homework assignments? Discuss university policies, procedures, and penalties for academic violations. Explain the rationale for proper citations of others' work. Ask students to think about how cheating "takes the place of and prevents learning" (Isserman, 2003). Open the floor to a discussion on questions such as Why should each of us care about academic integrity? or What type of academic environment inspires ethical conduct? (Sources: Landau et al., 2002; Lipson and Reindl, 2003)

Distribute institutional policies. Some colleges and departments produce handouts that include definitions of honest and dishonest conduct, and they require students to sign a statement that they have understood the material. Here are sample definitions from one department at the University of California at Berkeley:

> *Cheating* means getting unauthorized help on an assignment, quiz, or examination. (1) You must not receive from any other student or give to any other student any information, answers, or help during an exam. (2) You must not use unauthorized sources for answers during an exam. You must not take notes, books, cell phones, PDAs, calculators, laptops, or other technological devices to the exam when such aids are forbidden, and you must not refer to any book, notes, or aids while you are taking the exam unless the instructor indicates it is an "open book" exam. (3) You must not obtain exam questions illegally before an exam or tamper with an exam after it has been corrected.
>
> *Plagiarism* means submitting work as your own that is someone else's. For example, copying material from a book, the web, or other sources without acknowledging that the words or ideas are someone else's and not your own is plagiarism. If you copy an author's words exactly, treat the passage as a direct quotation and supply the appropriate citation. If you use someone else's ideas, even if you paraphrase the wording, appropriate credit should be given. You have committed plagiarism if you purchase a term paper online or from another student, copy a paper from someone who has previously taken the course, download a paper from the web, or submit a paper as your own that you did not write.

Include information about academic integrity in your syllabus. Some faculty distribute a brief statement about the importance of academic integrity, excerpts from their institution's policy on academic dishonesty, definitions of permissible and impermissible collaboration, and information about sanctions ("If you are found to have cheated on homework or an exam, you will receive an F on that assignment"). Sample statements are posted on the Web site of the Center for Advancement of Teaching at Rutgers University.

You may also wish to include the following information (adapted from Whitley and Keith-Spiegel, 2002):

- a list of campus resources for students (counseling center, student learning center, library workshops, tutoring programs)
- recommendations for resources that discuss how to cite reference works
- an invitation to report concerns about academic dishonesty: "Please come to me with any concerns you have about the conduct of other students. You will be helping me and everyone else in this class, and I will hold your comments in complete confidence."
- An invitation to discuss any questions about an assignment: "If you are having trouble with an assignment or if you are uncertain about permissible and impermissible conduct, please come to me with your questions."

Develop a classroom climate and group norms that support honesty. Students are less apt to cheat when they feel that their instructor treats students fairly, grades consistently, encourages and praises students' contributions, promotes group work, is accessible to students, and has good relationships with students. You might also ask your class to vote to conduct exams under the honor system (without proctors). Research shows lower levels of cheating on campuses that have honor codes or modified honor codes and strong cultures of academic integrity. (Sources: McCabe and Pavela, 2000; McCabe et al., 2001; McKeachie and Svinicki, 2006; Pulvers and Diekhoff, 1999; Whitley and Keith-Spiegel, 2002)

Ensure equal access to study materials. Establish a file (in the library or department office or on the course Web site) for old homework assignments and exam questions. Or attach a sample of past exam questions to the syllabus. (Source: Singhal and Johnson, 1983)

Before exams, revisit the topic of academic integrity. Let students know your expectations and the criteria you will use in evaluating their performance. Give them information about campus resources for help in studying and managing stress. Because students are less likely to cheat if they know they can succeed without resorting to dishonesty, give more rather than fewer tests and encourage students to discuss their difficulties with you (see Chapter 40, "Allaying Students' Anxieties about Tests," and Chapter 43, "Grading Practices"). Review students' work throughout the term so that they know that you know their abilities and achievement levels. (Sources: Eble, 1988; Malehorn, 1983)

Distinguish between fraudulent, legitimate, and unacceptable excuses.
A legitimate excuse is based on events beyond a student's control; a fraudulent excuse is one fabricated to avoid an academic responsibility; an unacceptable excuse, such as forgetting when a paper was due, may be truthful but is not a justifiable reason for failure to do the assigned task. Let students know what you consider to be acceptable and unacceptable excuses, and tell them that you may request proof. But try not to become so cynical that you assume every excuse is an invention. Some faculty who give multiple exams allow students to drop the lowest score. Students who miss a test for any reason receive a zero and can just eliminate that score. Other faculty give a single makeup test that any student can take and substitute that score for an earlier exam. (Sources: Caron et al., 1992; Segal, 2000)

Assessing Students' Understanding of Academic Norms

Give a quiz or exercise on academic conduct. The simplest quiz asks students to indicate whether certain actions are acceptable or not (for example, collaborating with others on an assignment, using the views of another without proper attribution, hiding library books). Iowa State, Indiana University, Penn State, and the University of Southern California, among others, have developed formal online tests, and Roig's survey (1997) assesses students' understanding of plagiarism (reprinted in Cizek, 2003, pp. 98–99). Researchers (Landau et al., 2002) report that students who receive feedback about their performance on the survey are better able to detect plagiarism than students who don't complete the survey.

An online tutorial developed at Dalhousie University discusses plagiarism and how to avoid it. Georgetown University's online tutorial "Scholarly Research and Academic Integrity Tutorial" is required for new students. A Web search for "plagiarism tutorial" will yield other citations.

One faculty member gives students a for-credit assignment to define plagiarism. Unsigned excerpts from the responses are distributed in class, and a short class discussion focuses on discrepancies among the definitions.

Give a homework assignment on plagiarism. One faculty member gives assignments in which students are presented with a redacted page of text from a draft manuscript of a journal article (usually the first page) and asked to indicate where citations are needed, for example, "Previous research has indicated . . . ." Students who completed the citation homework assignments reported a better understanding of plagiarism and had fewer citation problems than a control group. (Source: Schuetze, 2004)

Hold a class discussion on cheating. In a sociology course, a faculty member asks students to write unsigned responses to the following questions: Have you ever cheated in school or college? If yes, how would you explain your behavior? Why did you cheat? What were the circumstances? Did you believe it was wrong at the time? Students also indicate whether their responses can be shared with the class. From those granting permission, the instructor reads a few responses aloud as part of a class discussion. (Source: Brezina, 2000)

Gauge any special needs of international students. International students who are new to your institution may be unaware of American academic norms. They may have grown up with different beliefs about, for example, permissible collaboration or the value of copying or paraphrasing the words of respected authorities (for example, copying—without attribution—may be viewed as a sign of respect for and understanding of the work of an established scholar). You may need to make a special effort to help these students. Researchers recommend giving international students tips about the American classroom and the values placed on individual effort, authorship, independent thought, and achievement. (Sources: MacDonald, 2003; Whitley and Keith-Spiegel, 2002)

Defining Plagiarism

Clarify the distinctions between plagiarism, paraphrasing, and direct citation. Give students examples of correct and incorrect ways to use others' ideas and words. You might request permission to distribute the following example from *The Random House Handbook*, 6th ed., by Frederick Crews (New York: McGraw-Hill, 1992, pp. 181–183):

Consider the following source and three ways that a student might be tempted to make use of it:

> *Source*: The joker in the European pack was Italy. For a time hopes were entertained of her as a force against Germany, but these disappeared under Mussolini. In 1935 Italy made a belated attempt to participate in the scramble for Africa by invading Ethiopia. It was clearly a breach of the covenant of the League of Nations for one of its members to attack another. France and Great Britain, as great powers, Mediterranean powers, and African colonial powers, were bound to take the lead against Italy at the league. But they did so feebly and half-heartedly because they did not want to alienate a possible ally against Germany. The result was the worst possible: the league failed to check aggression, Ethiopia lost her independence, and Italy was alienated after all. (J. M. Roberts, *History of the World* [New York: Knopf, 1976], p. 845.)

Version A: Italy, one might say, was the joker in the European deck. When she invaded Ethiopia, it was clearly a breach of the covenant of the League of Nations; yet the efforts of England and France to take the lead against her were feeble and half-hearted. It appears that those great powers had no wish to alienate a possible ally against Hitler's rearmed Germany.

Comment: Clearly plagiarism. Though the facts cited are public knowledge, the stolen phrases aren't. Note that the writer's interweaving of his own words with the source's does not render him innocent of plagiarism.

Version B: Italy was the joker in the European deck. Under Mussolini in 1935, she made a belated attempt to participate in the scramble for Africa by invading Ethiopia. As J. M. Roberts points out, this violated the covenant of the League of Nations. (J. M. Roberts, *History of the World* [New York: Knopf, 1976], p. 845.) But France and Britain, not wanting to alienate a possible ally against Germany, put up only feeble and half-hearted opposition to the Ethiopian adventure. The outcome, as Roberts observes, was "the worst possible: the league failed to check aggression, Ethiopia lost her independence, and Italy was alienated after all." (Roberts, p. 845.)

Comment: Still plagiarism. The two correct citations of Roberts serve as a kind of alibi for the appropriating of other, unacknowledged phrases. But the alibi has no force: some of Roberts' words are again being presented as the writer's.

Version C: Much has been written about German rearmament and militarism in the period 1933–1939. But Germany's dominance in Europe was by no means a foregone conclusion. The fact is that the balance of power might have been tipped against Hitler if one or two things had turned out differently. Take Italy's gravitation toward an alliance with Germany, for example. That alliance seemed so very far from inevitable that Britain and France actually muted their criticism of the Ethiopian invasion in the hope of remaining friends with Italy. They opposed the Italians in the League of Nations, as J. M. Roberts observes, "feebly and half-heartedly because they did not want to alienate a possible ally against Germany." (J. M. Roberts, *History of the World* [New York: Knopf, 1976], p. 845.) Suppose Italy, France, and Britain had retained a certain common interest. Would Hitler have been able to get away with his remarkable bluffing and bullying in the later thirties?

Comment: No plagiarism. The writer has been influenced by the public facts mentioned by Roberts, but he hasn't tried to pass off Roberts' conclusions as his own. The one clear borrowing is properly acknowledged.

Discuss "recycling" and self-plagiarism. Remind students that they cannot resubmit an old paper of theirs as a new product for your course. Ask students to check with you if they have a paper or project that they want to use as the basis for new work. Permissible activities might include reanalyzing old data using a different method or taking the conclusions of an old paper as the springboard for a new one.

As appropriate, distribute a paper from a term-paper mill. Hundreds of Web sites exist selling thousands of papers. Consider purchasing one related to the content of your course. Have students write a critique of the paper or share with them your criteria on why the paper is not very good. Or distribute and discuss Hansen's essay (2004) that shows how poorly written downloaded papers can be. You might also warn students about term-paper mills overcharging students. If students complain, the service threatens to report them to school authorities. (Source: Campbell et al., 2000)

Assigning Papers and Written Work

Assign specific topics. Create topics that are likely to require new research, that stress thought and analysis more than recall of facts, and that are challenging but not overwhelming. Topics that are too difficult invite cheating, as do boring, trivial, and uninteresting topics (see Chapter 35, "Designing Effective Writing Assignments"). Your choice of topics will not prevent dishonest students from paying someone to write a paper, but you can make it hard for students to use a paper mill or to resubmit their own or someone else's paper if you, as appropriate, frame topics in the context of current events, local issues, or conferences or symposia held on campus. You can also discourage cheating by assigning topics that require students to conduct interviews, undertake field research, solve a problem, or compare the strengths and weaknesses of two related research papers. Consider assignments that take the form of letters to authors, fictional conversations between two authors or characters, or explanations of concepts for a specific audience, such as a friend who knows nothing about the subject or elementary school children. (Sources: Anson, 2003–04; Eble, 1988; Singhal and Johnson, 1983; Sterngold, 2004)

Change the assignments for each offering of a course. Changing the topics prevents students from resubmitting work done by former students.

Require specific references. If you require students to use particular sources (for example, certain databases) or to cite at least one source that is no more than a year old, students are unlikely to be able to meet your conditions with a purchased or cut-and-paste paper.

Give a short lecture on how to research and write a paper. Teach students the skills they need to avoid plagiarism, and help them understand that writing is a difficult process and that struggling is natural. Remind students about the materials and consultation services offered by the campus library and student learning center.

Assign one or more short papers. Short assignments—written in class or at home—help students develop their writing skills and help you assess their abilities. Also, if you assign a short paper early in the term, you will have a sample of each student's writing, which may help you spot a term paper that isn't the student's own work. See Chapter 34, "Helping Students Write Better in All Courses."

Break a major assignment into parts. Give students deadlines for each of five steps: (1) stating a topic or a preliminary thesis, (2) compiling an annotated bibliography, (3) producing research notes, (4) submitting an outline of the paper, and (5) submitting a first draft. This approach helps students write better papers and prevents them from procrastinating—or from downloading a paper. In some courses, you might ask students to share their outlines and first drafts with you, with the teaching assistant, or with each other.

Require submitted papers to be accompanied by selected cited sources. As appropriate, ask students to submit photocopies of cited sources—the first page of an article, book, or Web site—as well as copies of all pages containing passages that they quote in their paper. Or tell students that you will select one bibliographic entry and ask them to produce that item.

Have students keep a research journal or log. Ask students to list the Web searches they conducted (giving the keywords for each search), the journal databases they searched, the librarians they met with, and so on. For each entry, students indicate whether the effort was helpful or not. Or ask students to submit a log of all the people—librarians, tutors at the learning center, graduate student instructors, fellow students—who have commented on their work or drafts.

Have students write a short reflective essay about their experience in writing the paper. Ask students to describe the most important thing they learned, how they located sources, the dead ends they encountered, the sources that were most or least helpful, how their ideas evolved, or how they developed the organizational structure of the paper.

Ask students to sign a statement of authorship. Some faculty ask for a one-sentence statement of authorship, and others use a checklist for each step of the process. Some faculty, finding such statements off-putting, use a portion of class time to develop a statement of authorship that reflects students' shared standards and common understandings.

Collect papers from students during class or have students turn in papers online. If papers are turned in to a department or faculty office, consider using locked mailboxes with slots for collection. If you ask students to submit papers online, you have the potential of checking students' work against the Web or plagiarism databases.

Detecting Plagiarism

Be alert to telltale signs of plagiarism. A plagiarized paper may have formatting inconsistent with what you requested, may contain odd sentences intermixed in an otherwise coherent passage (the result of a student's effort to customize the paper), may include out-of-date references or citations to material not available in your library, and may differ in writing style or quality from a student's past work. (Source: Lathrop and Foss, 2000)

Use a Web search to find plagiarized material. By copying a sentence or string of words into a search field, you can see if the phrase appears elsewhere. For instructions on how to use Web search engines or library databases of journal articles to detect plagiarism, consult with your librarian.

Learn about campus policies, if any, on text-matching software. Text-comparison for the detection of plagiarism is offered by commercial vendors (for example, Turnitin.com, which uses third-party servers) and packaged as part of learning management systems. Some campuses have site licenses for software; other colleges rely on the decisions of departments and individual faculty. Faculty who decide to use the software should inform their students of their intentions. McGill University offers advice on what to say to students (www.mcgill .ca/integrity/textmatching/). At some universities, students are encouraged to submit their papers through the software on their own before turning their paper in for a grade. *Caution:* Do not use free plagiarism-detection services that advertise on the Web. Some of these sites purloin the papers you submit and sell them.

Text-matching software may have a strong deterrent effect, and it can save instructors from having to do individual online searches to check for plagiarized material. However, the vendors' storage of student papers on non-university servers (for future comparisons) raises concerns about intellectual property, copyright, and student privacy. Some faculty also believe that the use of the software introduces mistrust into the student-faculty relationship. And, of course, the software cannot detect custom-written papers. (Sources: Hansen, 2003; Johnson et al., 2004; Scanlon, 2003)

Developing and Administering Exams

Change exam questions as often as is practical. Ask students (and graduate student instructors, if you have them) to submit questions, which you can then adapt for future exams (see Chapter 39, "Quizzes, Tests, and Exams"). Be aware of online test collection Web sites where students post and can read past exams and answers. Some faculty argue that these sites could be used to cheat. Other faculty are less concerned because students have always redistributed exams. The best strategy is to make up new tests and keep your items fresh. (Source: Young, 2008)

For multiple-choice exams, use multiple forms. Scramble the order of the pages of the exam (for example, page 2 before page 1 for some copies), or scramble the order of the questions. To signify different test versions, print the first page with just the course title and date on different colored paper. However, avoid using vividly colored paper for the full exam since research shows that students perform best when tests are printed on white paper or light pastels. (Sources: Skinner, 2004; Tal et al., 2008)

Safeguard your exams. Store electronic versions on a CD that is then kept in a secure location. Never send an exam through e-mail. Keep hard copies in a locked drawer or cabinet, and destroy extra copies.

Proctor the exam. Unless your institution or class is on an honor system, monitor the test yourself or arrange for a proctor. During the exam, a proctor should walk up and down the aisles and be alert for unusual behavior: sequences of hand and feet positions or of tapping (to represent responses to multiple-choice questions), surreptitious opening of books or trading of papers, or the use of electronic devices. Cizek's examples (1999) of student misconduct include a system of color-coded M&Ms for signaling answers and the use of a gum wrapper as a crib sheet. YouTube has clips giving students advice on ways to cheat.

Proctors should spend some time in the back of the room, so that students who are thinking about cheating will have to turn around to see where the proctors are. Students are more likely to cheat when teaching assistants monitor exams than when faculty are in the room. In large classes, cheating declines as the number of proctors increases. (Sources: Davis et al., 1992; Kerkvliet and Sigmund, 1999; Singhal and Johnson, 1983)

Seat students randomly. Impose a seating scheme that will separate friends and place students in alternate seats. Before the period begins, put the seating chart on a data projector or overhead, so that students can find their assigned seat. Have students place personal belongings on the floor rather than in empty seats. If needed, requisition a second classroom.

In large classes, check student photo IDs. Let students know in advance (in the syllabus and before the test) that you may check photo IDs against class lists to be certain that each student takes his or her own exam. Students can place their IDs on their desks while they take the exam or they can show it to the instructor when they turn in their exam. If you don't want to use photo IDs, seat students by section so that graduate student instructors can determine whether all their students are in attendance and that "ringers" are not taking tests. (Source: Whitley and Keith-Spiegel, 2002)

Keep a seating chart. Hand out blue books or exams with prerecorded seat numbers. In rooms without seat numbers, pick up the exams in the sequence of rows. (Source: Singhal and Johnson, 1983)

Ban all electronic devices, except those required for the exam. Mobile phones, PDAs, and programmable watches and pens can be used to hold, access, communicate, or disseminate information. Some faculty bring a large clock to class or write "time remaining" on the board and ask students to remove their watches and put them in their pockets. If students are allowed to use calculators, try to make certain that the memories are cleared before students begin the exam. Some faculty require students to buy a specific type of calculator so that students using unapproved devices are easy to spot. Do not post any answer keys or explanations on the Web until after the exam—dishonest students have used mobile phones to ask friends to download answers from the Web and text message them during the exam. (Source: Whitley and Keith-Spiegel, 2002)

Supply scratch paper. Some faculty do not allow students to use their own paper or pages of their blue books.

Take action if you observe inappropriate behavior. Don't let it go unchecked. If you notice "wandering eyes," whisper a warning to the student ("You may not realize this, but your behavior makes it appear as if you are looking at another person's test"), or direct the student to another seat. If you observe cheating, position yourself near the offenders to discourage them. Or make a general public announcement: "Please do your own work." If you have suspicions about students, allow them to complete the exam, take notes on what you observe, and flag the exam for close review. (Sources: Cizek, 1999; McKeachie and Svinicki, 2006)

Ask students to sign their exams indicating that the work is their own. Some faculty have students write, sign, and date the following statement: "I have neither given nor received help on this exam."

Maintain order when students turn in their exams at the end of the period. Require students to sign an attendance sheet when they turn in their exams, or collect exams from students row by row. Count those present and make certain that the number of examinees matches the number of exams—this will prevent students who did not submit an exam from claiming that they did and that the exam was later lost or misplaced.

Using Blue Books

Have students turn in blue books before the exam. Collect blue books at a pre-exam class meeting, check them, mark them with a code, and redistribute the blue books at random on exam day. (Source: Whitley and Keith-Spiegel, 2002)

Require students to write only on one side of the blue book (left or right). Or ask students to leave a certain number of pages blank at the beginning of their blue books. This prevents students from filling the blue book with notes in advance of the exam.

Examine all the blue books before leaving the classroom. In one scam, a student pretended to take the test but submitted a blank blue book without a name on the cover. The student then completed the test at home and dropped the completed blue book in the hallway near the classroom or the professor's office. When the blue book was returned to the faculty member, he or she was supposed to assume that it slipped out from the pile.

Scoring and Returning Exams

Clearly mark incorrect answers. Use a bold X or slash mark to indicate wrong answers or blank spaces. The goal is to prevent students from changing answers and claiming scoring errors. If you permit the regrading of exams, photocopy the exams or quizzes of students who have previously asked for regrading before returning their current test. (Source: Whitley and Keith-Spiegel, 2002)

Warn students about software that detects cheating on multiple-choice tests. Error-analysis programs compare two students' responses to determine the probability that their answers are likely to be the result of chance and not copying. This procedure, however, is not absolutely reliable; some faculty rely solely on the deterrent value of telling students that they may use the software. (Sources: Bellezza and Bellezza, 1995; Cizek, 2003; Dwyer and Hecht, 1996; Whitley and Keith-Spiegel, 2002)

Return exams and assignments in person. Maintain the security of graded exams: do not leave them in the department office or on your desk for students to pick up. For large-enrollment courses with graduate student instructors, return exams in section sessions. For large courses without graduate student instructors, use techniques described in Chapter 14, "Preparing to Teach the Large-Enrollment Course."

Handling Suspected Cases of Academic Dishonesty

Deal with the problem immediately. Addressing cases of academic dishonesty can be stressful, unpleasant, and time consuming. Some faculty hesitate to act because they fear lawsuits or retaliation, or they believe that campus policies are unsupportive of faculty or that campus policies and sanctions are too lenient, too harsh, too inflexible, or too arbitrary. But faculty who ignore cheating send the wrong message to students, and students become demoralized if they are aware of their instructors' inaction. (Sources: Cizek, 2003; Hansen, 2003; Keith-Spiegel et al., 1998; McCabe and Pavela, 2004; Tabachnick et al., 1991)

Follow your institution's policies. Some colleges allow faculty to resolve cases informally or formally, while other institutions require all cases to be reported centrally. Informal resolutions tend to be less time consuming and stressful, and they are preferred by most students. They also lead to immediate corrective action (if the student violated standards of academic integrity), and allow for simple resolution in cases where the problems were caused by misconceptions, ignorance, or mistakes. Note even if you informally sanction a student, you may still want to report the outcome centrally to your office of student judicial affairs. They keep records and can identify chronic cheaters. (Sources: Gehring and Pavela, 1994; Whitley and Keith-Spiegel, 2002)

***When you suspect cheating or plagiarism, call the student into your
office.*** Never impose a penalty without discussing the allegations with the student. Meet with students individually, if more than one student is involved in an
incident. Talk with the student about your suspicions and listen carefully to his or
her response. Remember, of course, that a student is innocent until proven guilty.
Researchers recommend the following (adapted from Cizek, 2003; Stevens, 1996;
Whitley and Keith-Spiegel, 2002):

- If you are unsure about what to say, consult with an experienced colleague
  or your department chair, or ask the campus student conduct office for
  guidelines and procedures.
- Give the student a chance to acknowledge wrongdoing by asking, "Is there
  anything you would like to say about this assignment or exam?"
- Explain your concerns. Treat the student with respect and fairness, but communicate the seriousness of the situation.
- Avoid using incendiary words. Instead of *cheating* or *plagiarism*, discuss *copying*
  or *insufficient citation of sources.*
- Ask the student an open-ended nonaccusatory question: "Tell me about this
  paper." Listen carefully to the student's explanation without interruption. In
  many cases you will hear a mixture of pleas, excuses, and tales of hardship and
  extenuating circumstances.
- If a student denies any wrongdoing, ask questions about specific aspects
  of the paper or exam. For example, request definitions of terms, interpretations, or restatements of points made.
- If the student admits wrongdoing, explain the consequences and take whatever actions your institution prescribes.
- If the student does not admit wrongdoing, explain that the case will be
  referred to the campus judicial affairs office for investigation.
- If the student becomes distraught, show some sympathy. If appropriate,
  suggest a referral to the counseling center.
- Avoid taking notes when you meet with the student; should there be subsequent legal action, an incomplete record of what transpired is worse than no
  record at all.

Decide on appropriate sanctions if a student admits guilt. Depending upon
your institution's disciplinary procedures, you may have discretion on whether
to assign an F on the assignment or test, or to allow the student to write another
paper or take another test, or to drop the assignment or test when calculating the
student's course grade, or devise your own sanction. For example, one faculty
member, after discovering that two students had submitted identical answers to

a take-home exam, graded one of the exams and gave each student one half of the grade. Before making your decision on sanctions, you may want to ask your department chair about campus practices and options. (Source: McKeachie and Svinicki, 2006)

Do not automatically assign an F in the course. This is a severe punishment that is best made as a result of a formal hearing process. (Source: Whitley and Keith-Spiegel, 2002)

If you encounter more than one case of cheating in a course, raise your concerns in class. One instructor who found several cases of plagiarism on an assignment began class by saying, "I have read your papers. Would anyone like to talk about honesty?" During the discussion, students asked questions, confronted one another, talked about the effects of cheating on other students, and gave their opinions on sanctions (some of which were quite severe). The discussion also reinforced the notion of community standards. The instructor then returned the papers and offered the students the opportunity to revise them.

References

Aiken, L. R. "Detecting, Understanding, and Controlling for Cheating on Tests." *Research in Higher Education*, 1991, *32*(6), 725–736.

Anson, C. M. "Student Plagiarism: Are Teachers Part of the Solution or Part of the Problem?" *Teaching Excellence*, 2003–04, *15*(1).

Bellezza, F. S., and Bellezza, S. F. "Detection of Copying on Multiple-Choice Tests: An Update." *Teaching of Psychology*, 1995, *22*(3), 180–182.

Brezina, T. "Are Deviants Different than the Rest of Us? Using Student Accounts of Academic Cheating to Explore a Popular Myth." *Teaching Sociology*, 2000, *28*(1), 71–78.

Campbell, C. R., Swift, C. O., and Denton, L. "Cheating Goes Hi-Tech: Online Term Paper Mills." *Journal of Management Education* 2000, *24*(6), 726–740.

Caron, M. D., Whitbourne, S. K., and Halgin, R. P. "Fraudulent Excuse Making Among College Students." *Teaching of Psychology*, 1992, *19*(2), 90–93.

Cizek, G. J. *Cheating on Tests: How to Do It, Detect it, and Prevent It.* Mahwah, NJ: Erlbaum, 1999.

Cizek, G. J. *Detecting and Preventing Classroom Cheating: Promoting Integrity in Assessment.* Thousand Oaks, CA: Corwin Press, 2003.

Davis, S. F., Grover, C. A., Becker, A. H., and McGregor, L. N. "Academic Dishonesty: Prevalence, Determinants, Techniques, and Punishments." *Teaching of Psychology*, 1992, *19*(1), 16–20.

Dwyer, D. J., and Hecht, J. B. "Using Statistics to Catch Cheaters: Methodological and Legal Issues for Student Personnel Administrators." *NASPA Journal*, 1996, *33*(2), 125–135.

Eble, K. E. *The Craft of Teaching* (2nd ed.) San Francisco: Jossey-Bass, 1988.

Gehring, D., and Pavela, G. *Issues and Perspectives on Academic Integrity*. (2nd ed.) Washington, DC: National Association of Student Personnel Administrators, 1994.

Hansen, B. "Combating Plagiarism." *The CQ Researcher*, Sept. 19, 2003, *13*(32), 773–796.

Hansen, S. "Dear Plagiarists: You Get What You Pay For." *New York Times* Back to School section, Aug. 22, 2004, 11.

Isserman, M. "Plagiarism: A Lie of the Mind." *Chronicle of Higher Education*, May 2, 2003, *49*(34), B12.

Johnson, D., Patton, R., Bimber, B., Almeroth, K., and Michaels, G. "Technology and Plagiarism in the University: Brief Report of a Trial in Detecting Cheating." *AACE Journal*, 2004, *12*(3), 281–299.

Keith-Spiegel, P., Tabachnick, B. G., Whitley, B. E., and Washburn, J. "Why Professors Ignore Cheating: Opinions of a National Sample of Psychology Instructors." *Ethics and Behavior*, 1998, *8*(3), 215–227.

Kerkvliet, J., and Sigmund, C. L. "Can We Control Cheating in the Classroom?" *Journal of Economic Education*, 1999, *30*(4), 331–343.

Landau, J. D., Druen, P. B., and Arcuri, J. A. "Methods for Helping Students Avoid Plagiarism." *Teaching of Psychology*, 2002, *29*(2), 112–115.

Lang, J. M. *On Course: A Week-By-Week Guide to Your First Semester of College Teaching*. Cambridge, MA: Harvard University Press, 2008.

Lathrop, A., and Foss, K. *Student Cheating and Plagiarism in the Internet Era: A Wake-Up Call*. Englewood, CO: Libraries Unlimited, 2000.

Lipson, A., and Reindl, S. M. "The Responsible Plagiarist: Understanding Students Who Misuse Sources." *About Campus*, July–Aug. 2003, 7–14.

MacDonald, D. "Originality and the Paraphrasing Machine." *College Teaching*, 2003, *51*(4), 166–168.

Malehorn. H. "Term Papers for Sale and What to Do about It." *Improving College and University Teaching*, 1983, *31*(3), 107–108.

Maramark, S., and Maline, M. B. *Academic Dishonesty among College Students*. Washington, DC: Office of Research, U.S. Department of Education, 1993.

McCabe, D. L., and Pavela, G. "Some Good News about Academic Integrity." *Change*, 2000, *32*(5), 32–38.

McCabe, D. L., and Pavela, G. "Ten (Updated) Principles of Academic Integrity." *Change*, May/June 2004, *36*(3), 10–33.

McCabe, D. L., and Trevino, L. K. "What We Know About Cheating in College." *Change*, 1996, *28*(1), 29–33.

McCabe, D. L., Trevino, L. K., and Butterfield, K. D. "Dishonesty in Academic Environments: The Influence of Peer Reporting Requirements." *Journal of Higher Education*, 2001, *72*(1), 29–45.

McKeachie, W. J., and Svinicki, M. *McKeachie's Teaching Tips*. (12th ed.) Boston: Houghton Mifflin, 2006.

Pulvers, K., and Diekhoff, G. M. "The Relationship between Dishonesty and College Classroom Environment." *Research in Higher Education*, 1999, *40*(4), 487–498.

Roberts, D., and Rabinowitz, W. "An Investigation of Student Perceptions of Cheating in Academic Situations." *Review of Higher Education*, 1992, *15*(2), 179–190.

Roig, M. "Can Undergraduate Students Determine Whether Text Has Been Plagiarized?" *Psychological Record*, 1997, *47*(1), 113–122.

Scanlon, P. M. "Student Online Plagiarism: How Do We Respond?" *College Teaching,* 2003, *51*(4), 161–165.

Schuetze, P. "Evaluation of a Brief Homework Assignment Designed to Reduce Citation Problems." *Teaching of Psychology,* 2004, *31*(4), 257–259.

Segal, C. F. "The Dog Ate My Disk and Other Tales of Woe." *Chronicle of Higher Education,* Aug. 11, 2000, A64.

Singhal, A., and Johnson, P. "How to Halt Student Dishonesty." *College Student Journal,* 1983, *17*(1), 13–19.

Skinner, N. F. "Differential Test Performance from Differently Colored Paper: White Paper Works Best." *Teaching of Psychology,* 2004, *31*(2), 111–113.

Sterngold, A. "Confronting Plagiarism: How Conventional Teaching Invites Cybercheating." *Change,* May/June 2004, *36*(3), 16–21.

Stevens, E. H. "Informal Resolution of Academic Misconduct Cases: A Due Process Paradigm." *College Teaching,* 1996, *44*(4), 140–144.

Tabachnick, B. G., Keith-Spiegel, P., and Pope, K. S. "Ethics of Teaching: Beliefs and Behaviors of Psychologists as Educators." *American Psychologist,* 1991, *46*(5), 506–515.

Tal, I. R., Akers, K. G., and Hodge, G. K. "Effect of Paper Color and Question Order on Exam Performance." *Teaching of Psychology,* 2008, *35*(1), 26–28.

Whitley, B. E. "Factors Associated with Cheating among College Students: A Review." *Research in Higher Education,* 1998, *39*(3), 235–274.

Whitley, B. E., and Keith-Spiegel, P. *Academic Dishonesty: An Educator's Guide.* Mahwah, NJ: Erlbaum, 2002.

Young, J. R. "When Web Sites Post Test Answers Online, Professors Worry." *Chronicle of Higher Education,* August 1, 2008, *54*(47), A8.

39

Quizzes, Tests, and Exams

Testing is an integral part of instruction, and well-designed tests serve four principal functions. First, tests can motivate students and help them structure their academic efforts. Researchers report that students study in ways that reflect how they think they will be tested (Martínez, 1999; McKeachie and Svinicki, 2006; Wergin, 1988). If they expect an exam focused on facts, they will memorize details; if they expect a test that will require problem solving or analysis, they will practice those skills. Second, tests give students an indication of which topics or skills they have not yet mastered and should concentrate on. Third, tests help instructors identify students' errors and misconceptions and adjust instruction to improve learning. Fourth, tests help instructors document whether students are learning what they are expected to learn. The following suggestions can enhance your ability to design tests that are effective in motivating, measuring, and reinforcing learning.

A note on terminology: Most educators use *exams* to refer to midterms and finals, in contrast to *tests*, which are more limited in scope and duration, and *quizzes*, which are more limited still. In this chapter, however, *test* and *exam* are used interchangeably, because the principles in planning, constructing, and administering them are similar.

General Strategies

Begin by focusing on learning outcomes. As you prepare a test, think about the kinds of learning you want to assess: What do you want students to remember, understand, apply, analyze, evaluate, or create? These outcomes will determine the types of items, the range of difficulty of items, the length and time limits for the test, the format and layout of the exam, and the scoring procedures.

View testing as an opportunity to understand your students' intellectual progress. In addition to determining whether students have correctly understood the course content (mastery approach to testing), tests can explore how students have mentally organized their knowledge and how students think about the concepts being studied (cognitive approach to testing). See Chapter 32, "Informally Assessing Students' Learning" and Chapter 29, "Helping Students

Learn." (Sources: Bain, 2004; Black and Wiliam, 1998; Carver, 2006; Means, 2006; Ramsden, 2003)

Decide what to assess. In some ways, testing defines the curriculum. Assessment sends a message about the standards and amount of work required and about which aspects of the course are most important. A first step in creating a test is to identify the fundamental concepts and skills that define competence in the subject at different stages of progress. To link these fundamentals to assessment, some experts recommend creating a Table of Specifications, a grid that lists key knowledge or content down the side of the page and cognitive outcomes or competencies across the top (for example, remember, understand, apply, analyze, evaluate, create). The task then is to create test items for each cell. (Sources: Brookhart, 1999; Connor-Greene, 2000; Jacobs and Chase, 1992; Ory and Ryan, 1993; Payne, 2003; Ramsden, 2003)

Aim for validity and reliability. *Validity* refers to the soundness, trustworthiness, or legitimacy of the inferences, decisions, or actions made on the basis of the results of a test. Although people often speak about the "validity of a test," tests themselves are not valid or invalid. Validity concerns the adequacy and appropriateness of a specific interpretation of a test's results. For example, the scores on a writing test may have a high degree of validity for indicating the level of a student's composition skills, a moderate degree of validity for predicting success in later composition courses, and no validity for predicting success in physics. For classroom exams, a concern is whether the content of a test adequately samples the content of the course so that an instructor can draw valid inferences about a student's competence based on a test score. An exam that consists of only three relatively difficult problems, for example, will not yield valid inferences about what students know.

Reliability is the extent to which test scores are dependable and consistent. Are identical or nearly identical scores obtained, for example, when the test is scored by different people? Statewide and nationwide tests rely on technical procedures for determining reliability, but for general classroom tests, the best advice is to write unambiguous questions, offer clear directions, and use objective scoring criteria. One other consideration: very short tests are likely to be unreliable. (Sources: AERA, 1999; Miller et al., 2008; Moss et al., 2006)

Use a variety of testing formats. Students who have good learning skills and are confident in their academic abilities often prefer essay tests, while students with poor learning skills and those who are anxious prefer multiple-choice tests. To give all your students an opportunity to do their best, use several types of questions. For best results, however, do not introduce a new format on the final exam: if you have given multiple-choice quizzes and midterms, don't ask students to write an all-essay final. (Sources: Bridgeman and Morgan, 1996; Jacobs and Chase, 1992; Lowman, 1995; McKeachie and Svinicki, 2006; Birenbaum and Feldman, 1998)

Create questions that test skills other than recall. Research shows that most classroom tests rely too heavily on students' recall of information (Milton et al., 1986). To measure a range of skills, write questions that use the following verbs (adapted from Anderson et al., 2001; Fuhrmann and Grasha, 1983; Montepare, 2005):

- *To measure knowledge* (of terms, facts, principles, procedures): *define, describe, identify, label, list, match, name, outline, reproduce, select, state, tabulate.* Example: "List the steps involved in determining the potential toxicity of a new drug."
- *To measure comprehension and understanding* (explaining or interpreting the meaning of material): *classify, convert, defend, distinguish, estimate, exemplify, explain, extend, generalize, give examples, infer, interpret, predict, summarize.* Example: "Summarize the basic tenets of deconstructionism."
- *To measure application* (using a concept or principle to solve a problem; applying concepts and principles to new situations): *apply, calculate, demonstrate, execute, implement, modify, make use of, operate, prepare, produce, relate, show, solve, use.* Example: "Calculate the deflection of a beam under uniform loading."
- *To measure analysis* (understanding the interrelationship of component parts; recognizing unstated assumptions or logical fallacies; distinguishing between facts and inferences): *analyze, attribute, diagram, differentiate, dissect, distinguish, illustrate, infer, organize, point out, relate, select, separate, subdivide.* Example: "In the president's State of the Union address, which statements are based on facts and which are based on assumptions?"
- *To measure evaluation* (judging and assessing): *appraise, assess, compare, conclude, contrast, convince, criticize, decide, describe, design, discriminate, disprove, evaluate, explain, judge, justify, interpret, prove, recommend, support, theorize.* Example: "Why is Bach's Mass in B Minor acknowledged as a classic?"
- *To measure synthesis and creating* (producing something new from component parts; integrating learning from different areas; solving problems by creative thinking): *construct, create, design, devise, explain, generate, imagine, organize, plan, produce, rearrange, reconstruct, revise, tell.* Example: "How would you restructure the school day to reflect children's development needs?"

Involve your graduate student instructors (GSIs) in designing exams. At the least, ask your GSIs to read your draft of the exam and comment on it. Better still, involve them in creating the exam. Not only will they have useful suggestions, but their participation in designing an exam will help them grade the exam.

Take precautions to avoid cheating. See Chapter 38, "Promoting Academic Honesty."

Types of Tests

Multiple-choice tests. Multiple-choice items can be used to measure both simple knowledge and complex concepts. Since students can answer multiple-choice questions quickly, you can assess their mastery of many topics on a fifty-minute exam. In addition, the items can be easily and reliably scored. Good multiple-choice questions are difficult to write, however; see Chapter 41, "Multiple-Choice and Matching Tests," for guidance on how to develop and administer this type of test.

True-false tests. Because guessing will produce the correct answer half the time, true-false tests are likely to produce high scores. Place true-false items in a separate section, not interspersed with other types of items. Some faculty add an "explain" column in which students write a sentence or two justifying their response.

Matching tests. The matching format is an effective way to test students' recognition of the relationships between words and definitions, events and dates, categories and examples, and so on. See Chapter 41, "Multiple-Choice and Matching Tests," for suggestions about developing this type of test.

Essay tests. Essay tests require students to organize, integrate, and interpret material, and to express themselves. See Chapter 42, "Short-Answer and Essay Tests," for guidelines on creating this type of test. Research indicates that students study more efficiently for essay exams than for multiple-choice tests: students preparing for essay tests focus on broad issues, general concepts, and interrelationships rather than on specific details, and this approach results in somewhat better test performance on all types of exam questions. Essay tests also give instructors an opportunity to comment on students' progress, the quality of their thinking, the depth of their understanding, and the difficulties they are having. However, because essay tests pose only a few questions, their content validity may be low. In addition, the reliability of essay tests can be compromised by subjectivity or inconsistencies in grading.

A variation of an essay test asks students to correct sample essay answers. One faculty member uses the following technique: Two weeks before the exam, he distributes ten to twelve essay questions, which he discusses with students in class. For the exam, he selects four of the questions and prepares well-written but intellectually flawed answers for the students to edit, correct, expand, and refute. The sample essays contain common misunderstandings, correct but incomplete responses, and illogical inferences. (Source: McKeachie and Svinicki, 2006)

Short-answer tests. Short-answer questions can call for one or two sentences or a long paragraph. Short-answer tests are easier to write than multiple-choice tests, but they take longer to score. See Chapter 42, "Short-Answer and Essay Tests," for guidelines.

Problem sets. In mathematics and sciences courses, tests often include problem sets. As a rule of thumb, allow students ten minutes to solve a problem you can do in two minutes. See Chapter 37, "Homework: Problem Sets," for advice on creating and grading problem sets.

Oral exams. Oral exams are rarely used for undergraduates except in foreign language classes. Most instructors find oral tests too time-consuming, too anxiety-provoking for students, and too difficult to score, even when the exam is recorded. One math professor has experimented with individual thirty-minute oral tests in a small undergraduate seminar. Students receive the questions in advance and are allowed to drop one of their choosing, or they pick a question out of a hat. During the oral exam, the professor probes students' understanding of the theory and underlying principles. A statistics professor administers fifteen-minute individual oral exams. Students are told to pass on questions they cannot answer (saves time), and their grade is determined not by the number of correct responses but by the extent and level of their understanding. Instructors who give oral exams recommend taking a moment to put students at ease, arranging for informal seating, being tactful when offering feedback, and letting students do most of the talking. (Sources: O'Connor, 2004; Race et al., 2005)

Performance tests. Performance tests ask students to demonstrate proficiency in conducting an experiment, executing a series of steps, following instructions, creating drawings, manipulating materials or equipment, or reacting to real or simulated situations. Performance tests can be administered individually or in groups. They can be difficult to set up and hard to score, but performance tests are appropriate in classes that require students to demonstrate skills (for example, health fields, the sciences, education). If you use performance tests, here are some tips (adapted from Race et al., 2005):

- Specify the criteria that will be used for rating or scoring (for example, the level of accuracy in performing the steps, or the time limit for completing a task).
- State the problem so that students know exactly what they are supposed to do.
- Give students a chance to perform the task more than once or to perform several task samples.
- Include a self-assessment.

Alternative Testing Modes

Take-home tests. Take-home tests allow students to work at their own pace with access to books and materials. Take-home tests also accommodate longer and more complex questions, without sacrificing valuable class time for exams. Problem sets, short answers, and essays are the most appropriate items for take-home exams. Be wary of designing a take-home exam that is too difficult or an exam that does not include limits on the length of the response (or time spent). Also give explicit instructions on permissible and impermissible collaboration. For example, can students consult community-driven knowledge sites where users ask and answer questions of one another? A variation of a take-home test is to hand out the questions a week or more in advance but have the students write their answers in class. Some faculty hand out ten questions and announce that three of them will appear on the exam.

Open-book tests. Open-book tests simulate the workplace, where people routinely use reference books and other resources to solve problems, prepare reports, or write memos. Open-book tests are less stressful for students, but research shows that students do not necessarily perform significantly better on open-book tests. Open-book tests may reduce some students' motivation to study, and some students perform poorly because they devote more time to consulting their references than to answering the test questions. If you offer open-book tests, specify which resources are allowed and whether students will be able to use their laptops during the exam. In order to prevent the improper use of e-mail or text messaging, some faculty propose an honor code for the exam. Faculty also recommend warning students about spending too much time looking through reference materials. (Sources: Crooks, 1988; Golub, 2005; Ioannidou, 1997; Race et al., 2005; Theophilides and Koutselini, 2000; White et al., 2001)

Group exams. According to researchers, group exams offer three advantages: group work promotes deeper understanding of the material, groups outperform individuals, and group tests are less stressful.

Some faculty offer group testing as a stand-alone exam. For example, for a fifty-minute in-class exam, they administer a multiple-choice test of twenty or twenty-five items. On the first test of the semester, students are randomly divided into groups (the most effective size is three to five students). On subsequent tests, students could be assigned to groups in order to minimize differences between group scores, or to balance talkative and quiet students, or to cluster students who are performing at the same level. Each student receives the score of the group. Another variation is to give a public, oral group exam where students answer questions individually but compete for points in teams.

Other faculty have students complete a test individually and then convene as a group and submit a group exam. When the group score is higher than the individual score of any member, bonus points are added to each individual score. Or the instructor may blend the individual score (75 percent of the grade) and the group score (25 percent of the grade). A variation is to have students work on a set of test questions in groups outside of class but take the exam individually during class; in this technique, the in-class exam includes some items that appeared on the group take-home set as well as new items. Another variation is to have students take an individual exam, meet for group discussion, and then retake the exam individually. The grade might be an average of the two scores, or the first score plus bonus points based on the second score.

Faculty who use group exams offer the following tips:

- Give students practice working in groups before implementing group testing.
- Have students work individually on a problem and then compare results.
- Ask students to discuss each question fully and weigh the merits of each answer rather than simply vote on an answer.
- Take steps to minimize "social loafing," or free-riders who do not do their share of the work.
- Ask each student to sign the group exam, verifying that it accurately reflects the work of the group.
- Show students the distribution of their scores as individuals and as groups; in most cases group scores will be higher than any single individual score.

    (Sources: Hodges, 2004; Jensen et al., 2002; Morgan, 2003; Revere et al., 2008; Shindler, 2004; Slusser and Erickson, 2006; Webb, 1997; Yuretich, 2003)

Paired testing. For paired testing, two students work on and submit a single exam. Some students may be reluctant to share a grade, but good students will most likely earn the same grade they would have earned working alone. Researchers report that students who take an exam with a partner of choice do significantly better on later tests taken individually, compared to students who take all exams solo. Paired testing can also reduce anxiety and cheating and increase confidence and enjoyment of the course.

Pairs can be assigned in three ways: *Random assignment* breaks up cliques, avoids "last chosen," and prevents perceptions of instructor bias. *Purposeful assignment* pairs students based on level of achievement or other characteristics. In *self-selection*, students choose their partners, which may ease some students' anxiety as well as relieve the teacher of responsibility if students attribute poor performance to their partner. If you have an odd number of students in class, decide whether to form a triad or allow a student to work alone. For paired in-class testing, allow students enough time to confer and reach consensus. See Chapter 21, "Learning in Groups." (Sources: Muir and Tracy, 1999; Zimbardo et al., 2003)

Portfolios. A portfolio is a selection of coursework that a student assembles in order to illustrate growth and accomplishment over the term. A portfolio might include one or more papers (drafts and revisions), journal entries, essay exams, lab reports, sketches, prototypes, or problem sets. The instructions for submitting a portfolio should state the principles for selecting the pieces, the kinds of class materials and acceptable media (hard copy, electronic files, audio, video, and so on), and the minimum and maximum amount of material to submit. Some campuses encourage students to set up electronic portfolios on the institution's server. Some instructors grade portfolios pass/not pass. If you use letter grades, explain the grading criteria when you make the assignment. (Sources: Jacobs and Chase, 1992; Race et al., 2005; Shermis and Daniels, 2002)

Online testing. For the most part, students' scores on online tests are similar to their scores on paper-and-pencil tests. Some students complain that online testing prevents them from highlighting key terms and marking up the questions as they think about the topic and their response. Students also dislike online tests that do not allow them to skip items and return to them later.

When an online exam is to be graded, the test must be secure and resistant to cheating. Options include using classrooms in which computers are monitored; using software that blocks access to information on a laptop, disk drive, or network; and giving open-book exams. Keeping the online test short (ten minutes or less) also minimizes the opportunities for cheating.

An excellent use for online testing is to provide practice quizzes that students take while studying. Such quizzes are especially helpful because they provide students with immediate feedback about their performance. Some learning management systems will prepare and administer these quizzes once an instructor has taken the time to develop a bank of questions coded by topic, learning objective, and level of difficulty. That initial investment of effort is repaid when the system generates individualized online quizzes; some systems even track how much time a student spends on each question. If your learning management system does not have an online quiz feature, some commercial software packages are available. (Sources: Brooks et al., 2003; Brothen and Wambach, 2004; Daniel and Broida, 2004; Drasgow et al., 2006; LoSchiavo and Shatz, 2002; Naglieri et al., 2004)

Constructing Effective Exams

Prepare new exams each time you teach a course. Though it is time consuming to develop tests, a past exam will not reflect changes in how you presented the material and the topics you emphasized this semester. One way to make sure the exam reflects the current course is to write test questions at the end of each class session or at the end of the week. When you write a new exam, consider making copies of the old exam available to students.

Ask students to submit test questions. Faculty who solicit test questions from students limit the number of items a student can receive credit for (say, two questions per exam), specify the question format (such as multiple choice or short answer), and ask students to supply a citation from the readings or class notes for the correct answer. Tell students that their questions must involve inductive or deductive reasoning and synthesis of the material. Some faculty assemble all the student-generated questions and answers into a database and encourage students to use the database as a study tool. Others select or adapt students' items for use on exams. If you have a large-enrollment class, you can draw randomly from the pool until you have enough questions for the exam. (Sources: Carroll, 2001; Feldberg, 1999; Fellenz, 2004; Green, 1997; Hare, 1997)

Be cautious about using item banks from textbook publishers or found online. Don't take all your questions from the item bank. Some of the items may be poorly written, or focused on trivial topics or on concepts that you did not emphasize. Some test banks are filled with quickly-dashed-off items that have not been pretested. (Sources: Forsyth, 2003; Renner and Renner, 1999; Scialfa et al., 2001)

Make your tests cumulative. Cumulative tests require students to review material they have already studied, thus reinforcing what they have learned. Cumulative tests also give students a chance to integrate and synthesize course content.

See Chapter 29, "Helping Students Learn." (Sources: Bain, 2004; Halpern and Hakel, 2003)

Look at online guides on test construction. Many universities offer online guidelines for writing multiple-choice, true-false, matching, short-answer, and essay questions. If your campus does not, look at the guidelines developed by the University of Oregon or Illinois State University. The following guidelines apply to all tests (adapted from McKeachie and Svinicki, 2006; Sechrest et al., 1999):

- *Prepare clear instructions.* Test your instructions by asking a colleague or a graduate student instructor (GSI) to read them.
- *Include advice on how much time to spend on each section.*
- *Put some easy items first.* Answering easier questions helps students calm their nerves and feel more confident.
- *Challenge your best students.* Consider ending the exam with one very difficult question—but not a trick question—to challenge your best students.
- *Try out the timing.* Allow about half a minute per item for true-false questions, one minute per item for multiple-choice questions, two minutes per short-answer question requiring a few sentences, ten or fifteen minutes for a limited essay question, and about thirty minutes for a broader essay question. Allow another five or ten minutes for students to review their work, and factor in time to distribute and collect the tests. Another rule of thumb is to allow students about three or four times as long as it takes you (or a GSI) to complete the test.
- *Attend to the layout.* Use margins and line spacing that make the test easy to read. If items are worth different numbers of points, indicate the point value next to each item. Group similar types of items (such as true-false or multiple-choice questions) together. Remember that students will interpret the amount of space after a short-answer question as an indicator of the length of the answer you expect.

Responding to Subpar Test Performance by the Entire Class

Ascertain whether the exam was faulty. If all or almost all of your students performed poorly on a exam, look carefully at the exam: Were the directions clear? Were the questions thoughtfully prepared—not too tricky and not open to misinterpretation? Did the exam cover the assigned material? Did students have enough time to complete the test?

Analyze why students performed so poorly. Look carefully at students' answers. Is there evidence that they are not reading the assigned material effectively or not understanding classroom examples? What kinds of questions are students missing?

Do not automatically raise each student's score. Simply adding points to every student's score negates the meaning of the test. Students need to earn points based on what they know and can demonstrate. Instead, you might decide to drop each student's lowest test score during the semester, or you might offer a makeup test or assignment. (Source: PsychTeacher listserv)

Talk about the disappointing results with the class. Ask your students why they think the class as a whole did poorly: shaky study habits? unrealistic expectations? time pressure?

References

American Educational Research Association (AERA), American Psychological Association, and National Council on Measurement in Education. *Standards for Educational and Psychological Testing.* Washington, DC: American Educational Research Association, 1999.

Anderson, L. W., and Krathwohl, D. R. (Eds.), *A Taxonomy for Learning, Teaching and Assessing: A Revision of Bloom's Taxonomy of Educational Objectives.* New York: Addison-Wesley/Longman, 2001.

Bain, K. *What the Best College Teachers Do.* Cambridge, MA: Harvard University Press, 2004.

Birenbaum, M., and Feldman, R. A. "Relationships between Learning Patterns and Attitudes towards Two Assessment Formats." *Educational Research*, 1998, *40*(1), 90–98.

Black, P. J., and Wiliam, D. "Assessment and Classroom Learning." *Assessment in Education: Principles, Policy and Practice*, 1998, *5*(1), 7–74.

Bridgeman, B., and Morgan, R. "Success in College for Students with Discrepancies between Performance on Multiple-Choice and Essay Tests." *Journal of Educational Psychology*, 1996, *88*(2), 333–340.

Brookhart, S. M. "The Art and Science of Classroom Assessment: The Missing Part of Pedagogy." *ASHE-ERIC Higher Education Report*, 1999, *27*(1).

Brooks, D. W., Nolan, D. E., and Gallagher, S. "Automated Testing." *Journal of Science Education and Technology*, 2003, *12*(2), 183–186.

Brothen, T., and Wambach, C. "The Value of Time Limits on Internet Quizzes." *Teaching of Psychology*, 2004, *31*(1), 62–64.

Carroll, D. W. "Using Ignorance Questions to Promote Thinking Skills." *Teaching of Psychology*, 2001, *28*(2), 98–100.

Carver, S. M. Assessing for Deep Understanding. In R. K. Sawyer (Ed.), *The Cambridge Handbook of the Learning Sciences.* New York: Cambridge University Press, 2006.

Connor-Greene, P. A. "Assessing and Promoting Student Learning: Blurring the Line between Teaching and Testing." *Teaching of Psychology*, 2000, *27*(2), 84–88.

Crooks, T. J. "The Impact of Classroom Evaluation Practices on Students." *Review of Educational Research*, 1988, *58*(4), 438–481.

Daniel, D. B., and Broida, J. "Using Web-Based Quizzing to Improve Exam Performance: Lessons Learned." *Teaching of Psychology*, 2004, *31*(3), 207–208.

Drasgow, F., Luecht, R. M., and Bennett, R. E. Technology and Testing. In R. L. Brennan (Ed.), *Educational Measurement.* (4th ed.) Westport, CT: American Council on Education/Praeger, 2006.

Feldberg, R. S. "Increasing Student Involvement in Lectures: (Very) Low Tech Innovations in a Biochemistry Lecture Class." *Biochemical Education*, 1999, *27*(2), 71–73.

Fellenz, M. R. "Using Assessment to Support Higher Level Learning: The Multiple Choice Item Development Assignment." *Assessment and Evaluation in Higher Education*, 2004, *29*(6), 703–719.

Forsyth, D. R. *The Professor's Guide to Teaching: Psychological Principles and Practices.* Washington, DC: American Psychological Association, 2003.

Fuhrmann, B. S., and Grasha, A. F. *A Practical Handbook for College Teachers.* Boston: Little, Brown, 1983.

Golub, E. "PCs in the Classroom and Open Book Exams." *Ubiquity*, 2005, *6*(9), 1–4. http://portal.acm.org/citation.cfm?id=1066320

Green, D. H. "Student-Generated Exams: Testing and Learning." *Journal of Marketing Education*, 1997, *19*(2), 43–53.

Halpern, D. F., and Hakel, M. D. "Applying the Science of Learning to the University and Beyond." *Change*, 2003, *35*(4), 36–41.

Hare, A. C. "Active Learning and Assessment in Mathematics." *College Teaching*, 1997, *45*(2), 76–77.

Hodges, L. C. "Group Exams in Science Courses." *New Directions for Teaching and Learning*, no. 100. San Francisco: Jossey-Bass, 2004, pp. 89–93.

Ioannidou, M. K. "Testing and Life-Long Learning: Open-Book and Closed-Book Examination in a University Course." *Studies in Educational Evaluation*, 1997, *23*(2), 131–139.

Jacobs, L. C., and Chase, C. I. *Developing and Using Tests Effectively: A Guide for Faculty.* San Francisco: Jossey-Bass, 1992.

Jensen, M., Johnson, D. W., and Johnson, R. T. "Impact of Positive Interdependence during Electronic Quizzes on Discourse and Achievement." *Journal of Educational Research*, 2002, *95*(3), 161–166.

LoSchiavo, F. M., and Shatz, M. A. "Students' Reasons for Writing on Multiple Choice Examinations." *Teaching of Psychology*, 2002, *29*(2), 138–140.

Lowman, J. *Mastering the Techniques of Teaching.* (2nd ed.) San Francisco: Jossey-Bass, 1995.

Martínez, M. E. "Cognition and the Question of Test Item Format." *Educational Psychologist*, 1999, *34*(4), 207–218.

McKeachie, W. J., and Svinicki, M. *McKeachie's Teaching Tips.* (12th ed.) Boston: Houghton Mifflin, 2006.

Means, B. Prospects for Transforming Schools with Technology-Supported Assessment. In R. K. Sawyer (Ed.), *The Cambridge Handbook of the Learning Sciences.* New York: Cambridge University Press, 2006.

Miller, M. D., Linn, R. I., and Gronlund, N. E. *Measurement and Assessment in Teaching.* (10th ed.) Upper Saddle River, NJ: Prentice Hall, 2008.

Milton, O., Pollio, H. R., and Eison, J. A. *Making Sense of College Grades: Why the Grading System Does Not Work and What Can Be Done about It.* San Francisco: Jossey-Bass, 1986.

Montepare, J. M. "A Self-Correcting Approach to Multiple Choice Tests." *APS Observer*, Oct. 2005, *18*(10).

Morgan, B. M. "Cooperative Learning in Higher Education: Undergraduate Student Reflections on Group Examinations for Group Grades." *College Student Journal*, 2003, *37*(1), 40–49.

Moss, P. A., Girard, B. J., and Haniford, L. C. Validity in Educational Assessment. In J. Green and A. Luke (Eds.), *Review of Research in Education*, Vol. 30. Thousand Oaks, CA: Sage, 2006.

Muir, S. P., and Tracy, D. M. "Collaborative Essay Testing: Just Try It." *College Teaching*, 1999, *47*(1), 33–35.

Naglieri, J. A., Drasgow, F., Schmit, M., Handler, L., Prifitera, A., Margollis, A., and Velásquez, R. "Psychological Testing on the Internet." *American Psychologist*, 2004, *59*(3), 150–162.

O'Connor, R. J. "Using Oral Examinations in a Statistics Class." *Teaching Professor*, Jan. 2004, 5.

Ory, J. C., and Ryan, K. E. *Tips for Improving Testing and Grading.* Newbury Park, CA: Sage, 1993.

Payne, D. A. *Applied Educational Assessment.* (2nd ed.) Belmont, CA: Wadsworth Thomson, 2003.

PsychTeacher Listserv: A moderated online community for instructors involved in teaching psychology; see teachpsych.org/news/psychteacher.php

Race, P., Brown, S., and Smith, B. *500 Tips on Assessment.* (2nd ed.) London: RoutledgeFalmer, 2005.

Ramsden, P. *Learning to Teach in Higher Education.* (2nd ed.) New York: RoutledgeFalmer, 2003.

Renner, C. H., and Renner, M. J. How to Create a Good Exam. In B. Perlman, L. I. McCann, and S. H. McFadden (Eds.), *Lessons Learned: Practical Advice for the Teaching of Psychology.* Washington, DC: American Psychological Society, 1999.

Revere, L., Elden, M., and Bartsch, R. "Designing Group Examinations to Decrease Social Loafing and Increase Learning." *International Journal for the Scholarship of Teaching and Learning*, 2008, *2*(1). http://academics.georgiasouthern.edu/ijsotl/v2n1/articles/Revere-Elden-Bartsch/index.htm

Scialfa, C., Legare, C., Wenger, L., and Dingley, L. "Difficulty and Discriminability of Introductory Psychology Test Items." *Teaching of Psychology*, 2001, *28*(1), 11–15.

Sechrest, L., Kihlstrom, J. F., and Bootzin, R. How to Develop Multiple-Choice Tests. In B. Perlman, L. I. McCann, and S. H. McFadden (Eds.), *Lessons Learned: Practical Advice for the Teaching of Psychology.* Washington, DC: American Psychological Society, 1999.

Shermis, M. D., and Daniels, K. Web Applications in Assessment. In T. W. Banta (Ed.), *Building a Scholarship of Assessment.* San Francisco: Jossey-Bass, 2002, pp. 148–166.

Shindler, J. V. "'Greater than the Sum of the Parts?' Examining the Soundness of Collaborative Exams in Teacher Education Courses." *Innovative Higher Education*, 2004, *28*(4), 273–283.]

Slusser, S. R., and Erickson, R. J. "Group Quizzes: An Extension of the Collaborative Learning Process." *Teaching Sociology*, 2006, *34*(3), 249–262.

Theophilides, C., and Koutselini, M. "Study Behavior in the Closed-Book and Open-Book Examination: A Comparative Analysis." *Educational Research and Evaluation*, 2000, *6*(4), 379–393.

Webb, N. M. "Assessing Students in Small Collaborative Groups." *Theory into Practice*, 1997, *36*(4), 205–213.

Wergin, J. F. "Basic Issues and Principles in Classroom Assessment." In J. H. McMillan (Ed.), *Assessing Students' Learning.* New Directions for Teaching and Learning, no. 34. San Francisco: Jossey-Bass, 1988.

White, B., Ceglie, R., and Puopolo, D. "Note Sheets: A Reliable Predictor of Success?" *Journal of College Science Teaching*, 2001, *31*(3), 188–193.

Yuretich, R. F. "Encouraging Critical Thinking: Measuring Skills in Large Introductory Science Classes." *Journal of College Science Teaching*, 2003, *33*(3), 40–45.

Zimbardo, P. G., Butler, L. D., and Wolfe, V. A. "Cooperative College Examinations: More Gain, Less Pain When Students Share Information and Grades." *Journal of Experimental Education*, 2003, *71*(2), 101–125.

40

Allaying Students' Anxieties about Tests

Anxiety can interfere with students' performance on tests. You can reduce students' anxiety by taking care in how you prepare students for an exam, how you administer and return the test, and how you handle makeup tests. All students, but especially first-year students, can benefit from knowing what they will be asked to do on an exam and under what conditions. Students will also feel more relaxed and less intimidated if you provide reassurance and encouragement. The suggestions that follow are designed to help you prepare your students to do their best on tests.

General Strategies

Give students advice on how to study. Help students develop strategies for organizing and understanding the course material (adapted from Pressley et al., 1997; Roediger and Karpicke, 2006):

- Show students how to identify important ideas in the readings, and let students know the level of detail you expect them to remember.
- Describe the relative importance of the readings compared to the material addressed in class.
- Give pointers on how to take notes and review them.
- Remind students to relate new information to material they already know.
- Provide practice test items or old exams.
- Help students analyze and improve their study habits.

Your student learning center will have additional suggestions. See also Chapter 29, "Helping Students Learn."

Encourage students to study in groups. According to researchers, students who study in groups learn more than students who work alone; see Chapter 21, "Learning in Groups." (Sources: Millis and Cottell, 1998; Slavin, 1991)

Provide accommodations, as needed, for students with disabilities. Students with a documented disability are entitled to receive reasonable accommodations so that they can demonstrate their skills and accomplishments. Common accommodations include extended time to complete a test, oral presentation of a written test through assistive software or a personal assistant, a modified test setting (a quiet room), and assistive technology such as magnifying equipment or a voice-activated computer. See Chapter 6, "Students with Disabilities." (Source: Cohen and Wollack, 2006)

Seek advice if a student asks for an accommodation because of test anxiety. Some students may exhibit symptoms of severe test anxiety. Several courts have ruled that test anxiety does not constitute a disability, but the best course is to ask staff in your campus's disabled student services program to determine whether a student's test anxiety warrants an accommodation. See Chapter 6, "Students with Disabilities." (Sources: "Test Anxiety May Not Be . . . ," 2004; Zuriff, 1997)

Ask students how you can help them feel less anxious. Most often, students will ask you to describe the test format, to offer a review session, or to provide options for retesting or makeup testing if they perform poorly. (Source: Chapell et al., 2005)

Approaches to Testing

Make the first test relatively easy. Research on motivation indicates that early success in a course increases students' motivation and confidence. (Sources: Guskey, 1988; Lucas, 1990)

Give periodic tests and quizzes. Students learn more, remember more, and do better on the final exam when they are tested throughout the term. Periodic testing also alleviates the pressure of the Big Exam, allows students to concentrate on one chunk of material at a time, and enables students and instructors to monitor academic progress. One faculty member gives frequent quizzes and a cumulative final exam that repeats items from the quizzes but with the response options scrambled. Instructors who give short quizzes at the start of every class report that students achieve significantly higher grades and retain the material longer than students who are not tested at each class session. However, such frequent testing runs the risk of students focusing more on grades than learning. In addition, time spent on testing is time taken away from other class activities. (Sources: Forsyth, 2003; Kennedy et al., 2002; Landrum, 2007; Leeming, et al., 2002; Myers and Myers, 2007; Padilla-Walker, 2006; Roediger and Karpicke, 2006; Sporer, 2001)

Decide whether to give surprise quizzes. Research shows that surprise quizzes can improve students' performance, although they may unfairly penalize the student who picks the wrong day to come unprepared. Even though students don't like pop quizzes, they recognize that the quizzes help them keep up with their studies. One faculty member gives extra credit for good performance on surprise quizzes (called "extra credit exercises") and ignores poor scores. The offer of extra credit encourages class attendance and preparation. Quizzes also help students gauge their progress and allow them to preview the kinds of questions they will see on midterms and the final exam. Another faculty member announces that there will be weekly quizzes but then flips a coin to see whether students complete the quiz as individuals or as a group and receive a group grade. (Sources: Byrnes and Byrnes, 2007; Graham, 1999; Snooks, 2004; Thorne, 2000)

Avert typical complaints about exams. Take steps to head off the four most common student complaints about classroom tests: the tests are too difficult; they do not match the content or level of the lectures or homework assignments; they are badly written (for example, questions are unclear or cannot be answered in the time available); and the test format came as a surprise. To address these concerns, give students practice exams, develop test items that reflect the course content, tell your students what you expect them to learn or be able to do, and discuss the structure of the test (number of questions, multiple-choice or essay, open or closed book). To gauge the length of the test, take it yourself and estimate that students are likely to need triple the time it took you. (Source: Hativa, 2000)

Preparing Students for an Exam

Give a diagnostic test early in the term. An early diagnostic test alerts students to the skills and knowledge they need to succeed in your class. Some faculty give a knowledge survey in which students rate (on a three-point scale) their confidence in their ability to correctly answer the question. (Sources: Nuhfer and Knipp, 2003; Ochs, 1998)

Post old exams. Reviewing past exams gives students clues about what to study. Students can analyze old exams for format (length of test, number of points for each type of question), types of questions, and level of difficulty.

Give or distribute practice exams. Practice tests help students gauge what is expected of them. But practice tests are most effective when students take the tests, rather than read them as though they were study guides. (Source: Balch, 1998)

Hand out the final exam on the first day of class. A faculty member in the physical sciences gives students the thirty problems from which the final exam will be drawn. A faculty member in the social sciences hands out fifty essay questions. In both cases, the class discusses the items during the term, and the final exam consists of a subset of the items. Students know that if they can answer the sample items, they will do well on the final exam, and they are relieved of weeks of worrying about what will be on the final.

Schedule extra office hours before a test. Scheduling extra office hours during the week before an exam gives students a chance to ask questions and review difficult points. Some instructors especially encourage study groups to visit during these extra hours.

Schedule review sessions before the final exam. See Chapter 59, "The Last Days of Class," for advice on how to structure a review session.

Give students a dose of commonsense advice. Remind students to avoid cramming, to get a good night's sleep, to eat sensibly before the exam, and to arrive early. (Sources: Beilock et al., 2004; Flippo et al., 2000)

Ask students to share their tips. Ask students to offer study strategies and tips, and post these online for your class. In qualitative studies, top-performing students report the following behaviors:

- Regularly attend class.
- Pay attention in class.
- Read strategically (skim; focus on introductions and conclusions), paying special attention to readings mentioned in class.
- Try to spread out studying, as opposed to cramming.
- Vary study activities: rereading texts and notes, rewriting class notes, highlighting and memorizing information, and posing questions about the material while studying.
- Seek help from campus resources.
- Study in a quiet environment with few distractions and interruptions.
- Study with others who are well prepared and can help each other.
- Get enough sleep.
  (Sources: Perlman et al., 2007; Van Etten et al., 1997)

Emphasize the importance of students rigorously monitoring their own learning. Metacognitive monitoring—which experts define as the degree to which learners are aware of how well they have or have not acquired skills and knowledge—can be as important as the actual level of skills or knowledge they have attained. People typically have little insight into their limitations and tend to overestimate their expertise and talent. Students in particular have a poorly defined metacognitive sense of how well prepared they are for an exam. See Chapter 29, "Helping Students Learn." (Sources: Koriat and Bjork, 2006; Peverly et al., 2003)

Help students distinguish their academic emotions. Research shows that is okay for students to feel some anxiety before a test. In fact, anxiety is less likely to impact achievement than feelings of hopelessness and boredom. (Source: Pekrun et al., 2002)

Let students know about campus resources. Many counseling centers offer assistance to students who are feeling overwhelmed. Tell your students about the services available on your campus.

Administering Tests

Administer the test yourself. You will want to be present to announce any corrections (of typographical errors, for example) or changes in the exam. Your presence can also motivate and reassure students and signal to them the importance of the test. Arrive early on the day of the test to greet students as they enter the room and answer last-minute questions, and stay late to talk with students. (Sources: Jacobs and Chase, 1992; Lowman, 1995)

Read the instructions aloud at the beginning of class. Even if you write the clearest of instructions, it is helpful to read them aloud to the class and answer students' questions about procedures.

Plan for contingencies and emergencies. Decide how you will respond to questions such as "What if I don't finish?" or "What if I think two answers are correct?" or "What if I need to go to the restroom?"

You should also have a plan in case the exam is disrupted by a fire alarm. Obviously, everyone must leave the building. Some faculty ask students to take their exams with them and sit outside to complete them. Other faculty ask students leave their exams on their desks. Whatever you decide, share the information on the syllabus and again before the test. Here is what one instructor includes in the syllabus:

When a final exam is interrupted by a fire alarm:

- If the alarm is pulled after the exam has been underway for at least two hours (for a three-hour final), the exam will be deemed complete, and I will adjust the grading scale accordingly.
- If the alarm is pulled after the exam has been underway for less than 15 minutes, the exam will continue after the all-clear signal and our return to the classroom.
- If the alarm is pulled at any other time, I will administer a new exam (time and place to be announced).

When a midterm exam is interrupted by a fire alarm:

- The above procedures will apply except that if the evacuation lasts more than 10–15 minutes, I will reschedule the midterm.
  (Source: Listserv at UC Berkeley)

Minimize opportunities for cheating. Actively proctor exams, unless your institution is on the honor system. Be watchful, but don't hover over the class. See Chapter 38, "Promoting Academic Honesty," for advice on ways to reduce cheating during exams.

If there is no clock in the room, keep students apprised of the time. At the start of the exam write on the board the beginning time, the finishing time, and the time remaining. Update the time remaining every twenty minutes or so, and announce the last segment ("You have five minutes left"). Some faculty give prompts during the test: "If you are not yet on question 5, you need to work a little more quickly." Enforce the finishing time; it is unfair to allow some students to continue working when others must leave to go to another class.

Devote part of the session to reviewing the answers with students. One faculty member gives a thirty-minute midterm in a fifty-minute class. Students turn in their answer sheets after thirty minutes, but they keep the question sheet, and the remaining class time is devoted to discussing the correct answers. A variation on this technique is to divide the class into small groups and have them review answers and then reconvene as a class to discuss areas of disagreement or confusion. Another faculty member distributes the answer sheet to the exam as students exit the classroom.

Letting Students Show What They Know

Give students opportunities to explain their responses. Researchers report that giving students space on the test to explain their responses to multiple-choice items helps relieve students' anxiety and reduces posttest complaints. Students were directed to write a short justification for any answer they felt needed more explanation or for questions they perceived to be tricky. The researchers noted that students averaged less than one explanation per test over four tests. The instructors added a point for a "good explanation of a wrong answer" and subtracted a point for "a bad explanation of a right answer." The students' explanations, both good and bad, can also be incorporated into a class discussion on critical thinking. (Sources: Dodd and Leal, 1988; Kee, 1994; Nield and Wintre, 1986; Wallace and Williams, 2003)

Include one or more extra-credit questions. Give students the opportunity to answer additional questions for extra credit at the end of the test.

Give partial credit. For multiple-choice tests, some faculty let students know that they can select more than one answer but will have points deducted for incorrect responses. Some faculty allow students to select only one response but give partial credit for a close but incorrect choice. Another way to give partial credit is to use scratch-off technology as an alternative to optical scanning. With scratch-off forms, the correct answer is indicated by a star underneath a waxy coating. All the other alternatives are blank underneath the coating. For each question, the student picks an answer and scratches off the coating. If the student's selection is correct, a star appears and the student moves to the next question. If the student's selection is wrong, a blank space appears. The student continues scratching alternatives until the star is revealed. Students earn full credit for answering correctly on the first try. If it takes them two or three tries to find the correct answer, they earn progressively less credit. Faculty report that students seem to like scratch-off because it lets them know right away the correct answer to every question, and because it gives them partial credit. The downside is that it may take longer for students to complete the exam. (Sources: Bush, 2001; Denyer and Hancock, 2002; Di Battista et al., 2004)

Let students "buy" information during the exam. Tell students that midway through the exam they can ask you questions at the cost of losing points. For example, asking whether an answer is right or wrong might cost one point; asking for an equation or formula, two points; asking for a diagram setup, four points. A faculty member in mathematics reports that half the class usually buys information to help them "unfreeze" on difficult problems. A chemistry professor gives every student a "test insurance page" in a lottery scratch-off format; the page contains clues to answers, and each time a student scratches off a clue, points are deducted from the test score. (Sources: Ellis, 1992; Gordon, 1988)

Decide whether to allow "crib sheets." Some faculty allow students to prepare one five-by-eight index card or one sheet of paper that they can consult during the exam. Crib sheets alleviate pretest anxiety, and they force students to make decisions about which material is most important. The disadvantages are that some students may study less, and others may fail to answer exam questions appropriately because they simply transcribe what is on their crib sheet rather than read the question carefully. Research shows that crib sheets make students feel more confident but do not significantly facilitate learning or enhance exam performance. If you allow crib sheets, researchers recommend that you tell your students to treat crib sheets as a study aid, as a tool for reviewing and organizing the material—not as a substitute for careful preparation. (Sources: Dickson and Miller, 2005; Janick 1990; Vessey and Woodbury, 1992; White et al., 2001)

Ask students to write an unsigned evaluation of the exam. At the next class session, some faculty ask students to give a letter grade to the content, format, and fairness of the test, while others pose the following kinds of questions:

- Identify the questions you didn't expect to see on the test.
- Were the questions clear enough that, even though you may not have known the answer, you knew what was being asked?
- What questions confused you?

Encourage students to reflect on their test performance. Ask students to think about their preparation, study habits, readiness for the exam, and changes they will make in preparing for the next exam. For example, students can ask themselves, What did I do well on and why? What did I do poorly on and why? What can I do to improve on the next exam? (Sources: Aldrich, 2001; Kher et al., 2002)

Give students a second chance to learn. The following strategies offer students an opportunity to raise their scores on multiple-choice tests:

- After students turn in their in-class, closed-book exam, they receive a second copy to take home and complete as an open-book exam, including conferring with other students. Both exams are scored, and students receive additional points for correcting their incorrect answers.
- Several days after exams are scored and returned, students take a second test that contains equivalent items. Both scores are used, with the lower score weighted at, say, 25 percent and the higher score at 75 percent.

- Students have one week after receiving their scored exam to present a written rebuttal for a specified number of incorrect answers. The rebuttal must include citations from the readings and class notes that support the response they selected. Students earn additional points for a persuasive rebuttal.
- Students have one week after receiving their scored exam to write explanations for why the correct answer to a question is better than the incorrect option they selected. Students earn additional points for thoughtful explanations.

(Sources: Deeter, 2003; Hamilton, 2003; Hare, 1997; Kottke, 2001; Montepare, 2005)

Returning Examinations

Explain that testing and assessment are part of learning. Help students view assessment as part of the learning process, not as a reward or punishment: give timely feedback, offer suggestions for improvement, and maintain a respectful tone. (Source: Wiggins, 1998)

Return tests promptly. Most students are anxious to know how they have done, and a quick turnaround also encourages relearning or corrective learning. Most experts recommend that tests be returned within five days. Laws governing the privacy and confidentiality of student records forbid the posting of grades by name, initials, or student identification numbers, although instructors may post grades by using a unique code known only by the instructor and the student. Confidentiality and concerns about security also dictate that exams not be left in a pile in the department office or circulated in a stack in class for students to help themselves. Instead divide the tests into batches and have your graduate student instructor (GSI) or reader help distribute exams in different corners of the room by calling out names. Or prepare folders or manila envelopes with students' names and place these around the room for pick up. (Source: Lowman, 1995)

Use class time to discuss the overall results. Explain how the tests were graded and the criteria you used. Indicate how the class performed as a whole, or show the distribution of scores. Note which items were missed by many students, and correct widespread misunderstandings. For essay tests, describe the elements of a good answer and mention the most common problems. Some faculty read or distribute unsigned excerpts from outstanding essays. For multiple-choice tests, some faculty have students discuss the results in small groups. Having students review exams in groups often takes less time than an instructor's own review, and students may enjoy it more. One faculty member gives students their grades prior to going over the exam in class so that they know their overall score but not which specific items they missed. During class time, students discuss why they selected the option they did, and then the instructor lets the class know the correct answer. (Sources: McKeachie and Svinicki, 2006; Lucas, 2002; Wininger, 2005)

Give students advice on how to go over the exam on their own. Suggest they look at missed questions to determine which came from the readings and which from class notes. (Source: Weimer, 2002).

Schedule extra office hours after returning a test. Be prepared for students who are unhappy about their grade:

- Ask students who want to discuss their grade to wait twenty-four hours before coming to see you. This gives them a chance to reread the exam, cool down, and prepare specific questions.
- Let students know that if they request a review of their test, the review might result in a higher or a lower grade.
- Ask students to come with specific questions (not "Why is my grade so low?"). Some faculty request that students prepare a brief paragraph or complete a short form, which might be titled "Request to Review a Test Item," expressing their complaint and justifying the correctness of their answer with specific reference to readings or class notes.
- Listen carefully to the student's complaint. Do not interrupt to rebut each point.
- Try to shift the focus of the discussion from grades to problem solving. Ask, "What can we do to help you do better next time?" Help the student think less about blaming you or the test and more about how to learn and study more effectively.
- Don't change a grade out of sympathy or compassion. Make a change only if you made a clerical error or mistakenly evaluated a response.
- Set a one-week time limit for students to ask for a review of exam grades. (Sources: Jacobs and Chase, 1992; Kher et al., 2002; Lucas, 2002; McKeachie and Svinicki, 2006)

Arranging Makeup Tests

Decide whether to give makeup tests. The majority of students requesting a makeup exam have reasonable needs, such as illness, family emergency, religious observance, or unavoidable travel for graduate school interviews or athletic competition. Encourage students to notify you right away if they will miss the exam. Options for makeup exams include giving the same test at a mutually agreed-on time or creating a new test in the same format.

Double the weight of tests students have taken. Makeup tests can be problematic: a new test might not be comparable to the original test, but using the same test may advantage students who talked to others. Scheduling makeup tests can also be difficult. Some faculty give two midterms and double the weight of one when a student misses the other. (Source: McKeachie and Svinicki, 2006)

Decide whether to let students drop their lowest test score. Other faculty avoid makeup tests by giving multiple exams during the term and letting students drop the lowest score. Some research suggests that students may not study as diligently when they know they can drop a test score. If you do decide to do this, keep in mind that the lowest score may not be the best one for students to drop unless all tests are worth the same number of points. Kane and Kane (2006) give the following example: Leslie scores 80 out of 100 on midterm 1, 20 out of 100 on midterm 2, and 1 out of 20 on midterm 3. If midterm 3 is dropped, her mean score on midterms 1 and 2 would be $(80 + 20) / (100 + 100) = 50$. On the other hand, if midterm 2 is dropped instead, she would receive a mean score of $(80 + 1) / (100 + 20) = 67.5$. Kane and Kane have developed an efficient algorithm to maximize the resulting average grade. If you do allow students to drop their lowest test score, be sure to give a cumulative final exam so that students study all the material in the course. (Sources: Forsyth, 2003; Kane and Kane, 2006; McKeachie and Svinicki, 2006)

Give students options on the number of tests they take. Some faculty offer students three options: (1) four multiple-choice tests, (2) four multiple-choice tests and a final, or (3) three multiple-choice tests and a final. In options 1 and 3, each test is worth 25 percent of the course grade; in option 2, each test is worth 20 percent. Students who miss one of the multiple-choice tests must elect option 3, and students who miss two tests are handled on a case-by-case basis. (Source: Buchanan and Rogers, 1990)

Give an additional exam for the entire class at the end of the semester. The grade on this extra test can replace a missed exam or replace a low grade for a student who had an off day. (Source: Shea, 1995)

Hand out essay questions in advance. If you distribute a list of essay questions from which the midterm questions will be taken, you will not have to write a makeup test. (Source: Lewis, 1990)

Give a shorter final exam and use the last hour for makeup tests. By administering makeup tests during the time block reserved for the final exam, you can avoid the complexities of special scheduling.

Give an oral exam as a substitute. In small classes and advanced courses, you can offer an oral exam. Oral exams typically cover less material but in more depth than written exams. You could also include a customized follow-up writing assignment to probe more deeply into a relevant portion of the material. (Source: Listserv at the University of California, Berkeley)

Assign a paper for a missed exam. Grading a paper may take less time than designing and scoring a new exam.

References

Aldrich, H. E. "How to Hand Exams Back to Your Class." *College Teaching*, 2001, *49*(3), 82.

Balch, W. R. "Practice versus Review Exams and Final Exam Performance." *Teaching of Psychology*, 1998, *25*(3), 181–185.

Beilock, S. L., Kulp, C. A., Holt, L. E., and Carr, T. H. "More on the Fragility of Performance: Choking under Pressure in Mathematical Problem Solving." *Journal of Experimental Psychology: General*, 2004, *133*(4), 584–600.

Buchanan, R. W., and Rogers, M. "Innovative Assessment in Large Classes." *College Teaching*, 1990, *38*(2), 69–73.

Bush, M. "A Multiple Choice Test That Rewards Partial Knowledge." *Journal of Further and Higher Education*, 2001, *25*(2), 157–163.

Byrnes, M., and Byrnes, J. F. "Quizzes Are the Right Answer." *Teaching Professor*, March 2007.

Chapell, M. S., Blanding, Z. B., Silverstein, M. E., Takahashi, M., Newman, B., Gubi, A., and McCann, N. "Test Anxiety and Academic Performance in Undergraduate and Graduate Students." *Journal of Educational Psychology*, 2005, *97*(2), 268–274.

Cohen, A. S., and Wollack, J. A. Test Administration, Security, Scoring and Reporting. In R. L. Brennan (Ed.), *Educational Measurement*. (4th ed.) Westport, CT: American Council on Education/Praeger, 2006.

Deeter, L. "Incorporating Student Centered Learning Techniques into an Introductory Plant Identification Course." *North American Colleges and Teachers of Agriculture (NACTA) Journal*, June 2003, 47–52.

Denyer, G., and Hancock, D. "Graded Multiple Choice Questions: Rewarding Understanding and Preventing Plagiarism." *Journal of Chemical Education*, 2002, *79*(8), 961–964.

Di Battista, D., Mitterer, J. O., Gosse, L. "Acceptance by Undergraduates of the Immediate Feedback Assessment Technique for Multiple-Choice Testing." *Teaching in Higher Education*, 2004, *9*(1), 17–28.

Dickson, K. L., and Miller, M. D. "Authorized Crib Cards Do Not Improve Exam Performance." *Teaching of Psychology*, 2005, *32*(4), 230–233.

Dodd, D. K., and Leal, L. "Answer Justification: Removing the 'Trick' from Multi-Choice Questions." *Teaching of Psychology*, 1988, *15*(1) 37–38.

Ellis, A. "Scratching for Grades." *National Teaching and Learning Forum*, 1992, *1*(5), 4–5.

Flippo, R. F., Becker, M. J., and Wark, D. M. Preparing for and Taking Tests. In R. F. Flippo and D. C. Caverly (Eds.), *Handbook of College Reading and Study Strategy Research*. Mahwah, NJ: Erlbaum, 2000.

Forsyth, D. R. *The Professor's Guide to Teaching: Psychological Principles and Practices*. Washington, DC: American Psychological Association, 2003.

Gordon, L. "Cost-Benefit Testing." *Academic Leader*, 1988, *4*(4), 1–2.

Graham, R. B. "Unannounced Quizzes Raise Test Scores Selectively for Mid-Range Students." *Teaching of Psychology*, 1999, *26*(4), 271–273.

Guskey, T. R. *Improving Student Learning in College Classrooms*. Springfield, IL: Thomas, 1988.

Hamilton, T. M. "Everyone Deserves a Second Chance: Using the Day after the Exam as a Learning Opportunity." *College Teaching*, 2003, *51*(1), 21.

Hare, A. C. "Active Learning and Assessment in Mathematics." *College Teaching*, 1997, *45*(2), 76–77.

Hativa, N. *Teaching for Effective Learning in Higher Education*. Norwell, MA: Kluwer Academic Publishers, 2000.

Jacobs, L. C., and Chase, C. I. *Developing and Using Tests Effectively: A Guide for Faculty*. San Francisco: Jossey-Bass, 1992.

Janick, J. "Crib Sheets." *Teaching Professor*, 1990, *4*(6), 2.

Kane, D. M., and Kane, J. M. "Dropping Lowest Grades." *Mathematics Magazine*, June 2006, *79*(3), 181–189.

Kee, C. "Multiple-Choice Questions: A New Twist for an Old Standard." *Teaching Professor*, 1994, *8*(6), 6.

Kennedy, E. J., Lawton, L., and Plumlee, E. L. "Blissful Ignorance: The Problem of Unrecognized Incompetence and Academic Performance." *Journal of Marketing Education*, 2002, *24*(3), 243–252.

Kher, N., Juneau, G., and Molstad, S. "Test Feedback Class Sessions: Creating a Positive Learning Experience." *College Teaching*, 2002, *50*(4), 148–150.

Koriat, A., and Bjork, R. A. "Illusions of Competence during Study Can Be Remedied by Manipulations That Enhance Learners' Sensitivity to Retrieval Conditions at Test." *Memory and Cognition*, 2006, *34*(5), 959–972.

Kottke, J. L. "Students' Reactions to Written Test Item Rebuttals." *Journal of Instructional Psychology*, 2001, *28*(4), 256–261.

Landrum, R. E. "Introductory Psychology Student Performance: Weekly Quizzes Followed by a Cumulative Final Exam." *Teaching of Psychology*, 2007, *34*(3), 177–180.

Leeming, F. C. "The Exam-a-Day Procedure Improves Performance in Psychology Classes." *Teaching of Psychology*, 2002, *29*(3), 210–212.

Lewis, K. G. *Taming the Pedagogical Monster*. (3rd ed.) Austin: Center for Teaching Effectiveness, University of Texas, 1990.

Lowman, J. *Mastering the Techniques of Teaching*. (2nd ed.) San Francisco: Jossey-Bass, 1995.

Lucas, A. F. "Using Psychological Models to Understand Student Motivation." In M. D. Svinicki (Ed.), *The Changing Face of College Teaching*. New Directions for Teaching and Learning, no. 42. San Francisco: Jossey-Bass, 1990.

Lucas, S. G. Returning Graded Assignments Is Part of the Learning Experience. In B. Perlman, L. I. McCann, and S. H. McFadden (Eds.), *Lessons Learned: Practical Advice for the Teaching of Psychology*. Vol. 2. Washington, DC: American Psychological Society, 2002.

McKeachie, W. J., and Svinicki, M. *McKeachie's Teaching Tips*. (12th ed.) Boston: Houghton Mifflin, 2006.

Millis, B., and Cottell, P. G. *Cooperative Learning for Higher Education Faculty*. American Council on Education and Oryx Press, 1998.

Montepare, J. M. "A Self-Correcting Approach to Multiple Choice Tests." *APS Observer*, October 2005, *18*(10).

Myers, C. B., and Myers, S. M. "Assessing Assessments: The Effects of Two Exam Formats on Course Achievement and Evaluation." *Innovative Higher Education*, 2007, *31*(4), 227–236.

Nield, A. F., and Wintre, M. "Multiple Choice Questions with an Option to Comment: Students' Attitude and Use." *Teaching of Psychology*, 1986, *13*(4), 196–199.

Nuhfer, E., and Knipp, D. The Knowledge Survey: A Tool for All Reasons. In C. M. Wehlburg and S. Chadwick-Blossey (Eds.), *To Improve the Academy*. Vol. 21. San Francisco: Jossey-Bass, 2003.

Ochs, R. S. "The First-Day Quiz as a Teaching Technique." *Journal of Chemical Education*, 1998, *75*(4), 401–403.

Padilla-Walker, L. M. "The Impact of Daily Extra Credit Quizzes on Exam Performance." *Teaching of Psychology*, 2006, *33*(4), 236–239.

Pekrun, R., Goetz, T., Titz, W., and Perry, R. P. "Academic Emotions in Students' Self-Regulated Learning and Achievement: A Program of Qualitative and Quantitative Research." *Educational Psychologist*, 2002, *37*(2), 91–105.

Perlman, B., McCann, L. I., and Prust, A. "Students' Grades and Ratings of Perceived Effectiveness of Behaviors Influencing Academic Performance." *Teaching of Psychology*, 2007, *34*(4), 236–240.

Peverly, S. T., Brobst, K. E., Graham, M., and Shaw, R. "College Adults Are Not Good at Self-Regulation: A Study on the Relationship of Self-Regulation, Note Taking and Test Taking." *Journal of Educational Psychology*, 2003, *95*(2), 335–346.

Pressley, M., Yokoi, L., van Meter, P., van Etten, S., and Freebern, G. "Some of the Reasons Why Preparing for Exams Is So Hard: What Can Be Done to Make It Easier?" *Educational Psychology Review*, 1997, *9*(1), 1–38.

Roediger, H. L., and Karpicke, J. D. "Test-Enhanced Learning: Taking Memory Tests Improves Long-Term Retention." *Psychological Science*, 2006, *17*(3), 249–255.

Shea, M. A. *Compendium of Good Ideas on Teaching and Learning*. Boulder: Faculty Teaching Excellence Program, University of Colorado, 1995.

Slavin, R. E. "Synthesis of Research on Cooperative Learning. *Educational Leadership*, 1991, *48*(5), 71–82.

Snooks, M. K. "Using Practice Tests on a Regular Basis to Improve Student Learning." *New Directions for Teaching and Learning*, no. 100. San Francisco: Jossey-Bass, 2004, 109–113.

Sporer, R. "The Quick Fix: The No-Fault Quiz." *College Teaching*, 2001, *49*(2), 61.

"Test Anxiety May Not Be a Disability But It Can Impair Functioning." *Disability Compliance for Higher Education*, Aug. 2004, *10*(1), 3.

Thorne, B. M. "Extra Credit Exercise: A Painless Pop Quiz." *Teaching of Psychology*, 2000, *27*(3), 204–205.

Van Etten, S., Freebern, G., and Pressley, M. "College Students' Beliefs about Exam Preparation." *Contemporary Educational Psychology*, 1997, *22*(2), 192–212.

Vessey, J. K., and Woodbury, W. "Crib Sheets: Use with Caution." *Teaching Professor*, 1992, *6*(7), 6–7.

Wallace, M. A., and Williams, R. L. "Multiple-Choice Exams: Explanations for Student Choices." *Teaching of Psychology*, 2003, *30*(2), 136–138.

Weimer, M. *Learner-Centered Teaching: Five Key Changes to Practice.* San Francisco: Jossey-Bass, 2002.

White, B., Ceglie, R., and Puopolo, D. "Note Sheets: A Reliable Predictor of Success?" *Journal of College Science Teaching,* 2001, *31*(3), 188–193.

Wiggins, G. *Educative Assessment: Designing Assessments to Inform and Improve Student Performance.* San Francisco: Jossey-Bass, 1998.

Wininger, S. R. "Using Your Tests to Teach: Formative Summative Assessment." *Teaching of Psychology,* 2005, *32*(3), 164–166.

Zuriff, G. E. "Accommodations for Test Anxiety under ADA?" *Journal of the American Academy of Psychiatry and the Law,* 1997, *25*(2), 197–206.

41

Multiple-Choice and Matching Tests

A multiple-choice item presents a question or incomplete statement (a *stem*) and three to five suggested answers or completions, one of which is best (the *key*); the incorrect choices are called *distractors*. A matching-test item presents two columns of information (such as terms, names, or dates) and asks students to choose from the second column a response that fits the stimulus in the first column. Multiple-choice and matching tests are the two best-known forms of selected-response tests (also called *forced choice tests, constructed response tests,* or *choice-type tests*).

Selected-response items are useful for testing the breadth of students' learning (a selected-response test can cover more topics than an essay test) and for testing different levels of learning (from recall of factual information to problem solving). Compared to short-answer and essay tests (called *supply-type tests*), selected-response tests require more time to prepare but less time to score. Although selected-response tests are often criticized as measuring only rote memorization, selected-response items can also be used to assess students' mastery of complex concepts and ideas.

General Strategies

Write test items throughout the term. Good test items are difficult to create, and it is impossible to compose an effective selected-response test at the last minute. Spread out the work by writing three to five items every week. (Source: Jacobs and Chase, 1992)

Give students advice on how to take a selected-response test. The following tips will help your students do their best (adapted from McKeachie and Svinicki, 2006; Sechrest et al., 1999):

- Go through the test once and answer all the questions you can.
- When you go through the test again, spend a reasonable amount of time on each question but move on if you get stuck.

- If you are stuck, try to reason the correct answer from some general concept or principle.
- Change your answer if you wish; research shows that most students gain more than they lose on changed answers (Kruger et al., 2005).
- Save some time at the end to double-check your answers and make sure you haven't made any clerical errors.

Types of Multiple-Choice Questions

Include some items that require complex thinking. For example, write a question that requires students to predict the outcome of a situation, or ask students to select examples that illustrate an abstraction or a principle. Or give examples and ask students to select the principle or theory that the examples illustrate.

The following multiple-choice items probe a range of learning outcomes (adapted from Welsh, 1978).

Question 1 requires students to make comparative generalizations.

1. Which of the following has contributed most to long-term economic growth in the United States?
   A. Increasing personal income tax rates.
   B. Reducing hours worked per week to spread employment among more people.
   C. Increasing tariffs on imported goods that compete with domestically produced goods.
   D. Increasing levels of education and technological improvement.

Question 2 asks students to apply supply-and-demand principles to a specific situation.

2. A large city is investigating the elimination of rent controls on housing at a time when the vacancy rate is extremely low—only 1 percent. Which of the following is most likely to occur if rent controls are eliminated?
   A. An increase in the demand for housing, followed by a decrease in the supply of housing.
   B. An increase in rents, followed by an increase in the supply of housing.
   C. A decrease in rents and a decrease in the supply of housing.
   D. No change in rents because price controls are usually set where supply and demand intersect.

For question 3, students must analyze the situation, select the most appropriate policy, and predict the expected effects of the policy.

> 3. Because of rapidly rising national defense expenditures, the country of Parador will experience price inflation unless measures are taken to restrict the growth of aggregate private demand. If Parador wishes to minimize the adverse effects of anti-inflationary policies on economic growth, it should implement
>
>   A. A tight monetary policy because that would restrict consumption expenditures more than investment.
>
>   B. A tight monetary policy because that would restrict consumption expenditures.
>
>   C. An increase in personal income taxes because that would restrict consumption expenditures more than investment.
>
>   D. Either a tight monetary policy or an increase in personal income taxes because both depress investment equally.

Create "You are the teacher" questions. Some multiple-choice items require students to evaluate the response to a short-answer question (from Jensen et al., 2006, p. 69):

> Pretend you are a science teacher who is correcting the following answer on a quiz. How many scientific errors does the answer contain? *Note:* There is a maximum of one error per sentence.
>
>   During the depolarization phase of an action potential, sodium gates are open and sodium diffuses from the extra-cellular fluid to the intra-cellular fluid. At the end of the depolarization phase, sodium gates close and potassium gates open. Repolarization begins when potassium moves by active transport from the intra-cellular fluid to the extra-cellular fluid of the cell. After the action potential passes, ion gradients are maintained by the sodium/potassium pump.
>
>   A. 0 errors
>
>   B. 1 error
>
>   C. 2 errors
>
>   D. 3 errors
>
>   E. 4 errors

Jensen et al. (2006) recommend that this type of question be used only after students have done practice sets before the exam.

Experiment with assertion-reason questions (ARQs). An ARQ consists of two statements—an assertion and a reason—linked by *because*. The student selects from five response options that indicate the correctness of each statement and the validity of the reasoning. Here is an example (adapted from Williams, 2006, p. 292):

> (*Assertion*) In a small open economy, if the prevailing world price of a good is lower than the domestic price, the quantity supplied by the domestic producer will be greater than the domestic quantity demanded, increasing domestic producer surplus.
>   Because
> (*Reason*) In a small open economy any surplus in the domestic market will be absorbed by the rest of the world. This increases domestic consumer surplus.
>
> A. The assertion and reason are both correct, and the reason is valid.
>
> B. The assertion and reason are both correct, but the reason is invalid.
>
> C. The assertion is correct, but the reason is incorrect.
>
> D. The assertion is incorrect, but the reason is correct.
>
> E. Both the assertion and the reason are incorrect.

If you want to use ARQs, give your students time to become familiar with the format and offer examples and practice quizzes. ARQs pose special problems for students whose reading comprehension skills are below average. (Source: Williams, 2006)

Constructing Multiple-Choice Test Items

Instruct students to select the "best answer" rather than the "correct answer." Asking for the correct answer may invite arguments from contentious students that their selections are correct as well. If you ask for the best answer, you can acknowledge that other responses have some element of truth or accuracy but that the keyed response is the best. (Source: Jacobs and Chase, 1992)

In the instructions, state the rewards or penalties for guessing. Some instructors encourage students to make their best guess, even when they are unsure about the correct answer. Other instructors penalize students for guessing. Some faculty award partial credit for reasoned but flawed answers. (Source: Baranchik and Cherkas, 2000)

Express the full problem in the stem, typically as a question. Make sure that students can understand the problem before reading the choices. Direct questions are usually clearer than sentence completions, although incomplete statements may avoid cumbersome phrasing. The stem may also include a map, diagram, picture, or graph.

In the following pair, the stem of the poorly constructed item is so brief that it fails to state the problem.

Poor: Grading is

A. Most often used to distinguish between students.

B. A way of reporting students' progress.

C. The only reason students study.

D. Something teachers put off if they can.

Better: What is the main reason most universities use a letter-grading system?

A. Convenience in reporting students' progress.

B. Utility in keeping permanent records.

C. Ease in distinguishing among students.

D. Usefulness in motivating students to learn.

When the item concerns the definition of a term, the preferred format is to present the definition in the stem and list several terms as options, rather than placing the term in the stem and listing several definitions as options. (Source: Kehoe, 1995)

Put all relevant material in the stem. Do not repeat a phrase in the options if the phrase can be stated in the stem. In the following example, students must waste time reading the repetitions of *chosen by* (adapted from Ory and Ryan, 1993):

Poor: In national elections in the United States the president is officially

A. chosen by the people.

B. chosen by members of Congress.

C. chosen by the House of Representatives.

D. chosen by the Electoral College.

Better: In national elections in the United States, who officially chooses the president?

A. the people.

B. members of Congress.

      C. the House of Representatives.

      D. the Electoral College.

Keep the stem short. In the following example, the unnecessary information in the stem is likely to confuse students and waste their time (adapted from Frary, 1995):

> *Poor:* The presence and association of the male seems to have profound effects on female physiology in domestic animals. Research shows that in cattle the presence of a bull has the following effects:
>
> *Better:* Research shows that the presence of a bull has which of the following effects on cows?

Write the correct response (key) first, and then create appealing distractors. Clearly formulate the best or correct answer, and then draft a set of plausible distractors. If the distractors are farfetched, students will too easily guess the correct answer. Effective distractors represent errors commonly made by students: statements that include errors in logic or interpretation, statements that are too general or too specific for the requirements of the problem, statements that are accurate but do not fully meet the requirements of the problem, and incorrect statements that will seem correct to the poorly prepared student. (Sources: Clegg and Cashin, 1986; Forsyth, 2003; Sechrest et al., 1999)

Limit the number of response alternatives. Studies show that three-choice items are more effective or about as effective as four-choice items, and yet the four-choice format is the most popular. Never give students more than five choices. You need not give the same number of choices for each test item. However, if students use optical scanning sheets or need to mark their answers on a scoring sheet, use the same number of distractors for each question to minimize the chances of transposition errors. (Sources: Green, 1997; Haladyna, 2004; Landrum et al., 1993; McKeachie and Svinicki, 2006; Sechrest et al., 1999)

Make all choices roughly equal in length. Do not signal the best choice by making it longer, more detailed, or more nuanced than the alternatives. (Sources: Green, 1997; Kehoe, 1995; Sechrest et al., 1999)

Avoid negative wording. Negative wording often confuses students, for example:

> *Poor:* Which of the following is not a characteristic of Brutalism?
>
> *Better:* Which of the following best distinguishes Brutalism from other architectural movements?

If you must use negatives, emphasize them with underlining, capital letters, or bold type. (Sources: Clegg and Cashin, 1986; Kehoe, 1995)

Refrain from using words such as always, never, all, or none. Savvy students know that few statements are absolute or universally true. (Source: Clegg and Cashin, 1986)

Avoid giving "all of the above" or "none of the above" as choices. These items do not discriminate well among students with differing knowledge. Students need only compare two choices: if both are acceptable, then "all of the above" is the logical answer, even if the student is unsure about a third choice. (Sources: Haladyna, 2004; Jacobs and Chase, 1992)

Begin with a few easy items. Some research shows that students do better when the sequence of the items reflects the order in which the material was presented in the readings and in class, but placing a few easy questions first will calm nervous students. (Source: Sechrest et al., 1999)

Make the choices grammatically consistent with the stem. Read the stem and each of the choices aloud to be sure that each is correct in the use of _a_ or _an_, singular and plural, and subject-verb agreement. In the following example, choices B and C should be reworded (adapted from Welsh, 1978):

> _Poor:_ The functions of the Federal Reserve are to provide the nation with an elastic money supply and to
>
> A. help stabilize the economy.
> B. correction of national income statistics.
> C. correction of tax laws.
> D. help levy property taxes.

Vary the position of the best answer. Research shows that faculty tend to locate the best answer in the B or C position. If appropriate, list options alphabetically or in some meaningful order (for example, numerical, chronological, or conceptual). Or use a deck of cards to locate the correct responses randomly. (If the card you turn over is a heart, the correct answer goes in slot A; if it is a spade, in slot B; and so on.) For ease of reading, mark each option with a capital letter and list the options vertically. (Source: Haladyna, 2004)

Guard against overlapping items. Make test questions independent of one another so that the stem or alternative in one question doesn't give students a clue to the correct answer to another question. (Source: Haladyna, 2004)

Keep the test length manageable. Students can complete between one and two multiple-choice items per minute. (Source: Lowman, 1995)

Print the test on white paper. Though some observers recommend printing alternate forms of multiple choice exams on paper of different colors to prevent cheating, researchers report that white paper leads to better test performance. If you do scramble questions, add a cover sheet that is a different color (with just the name of the class and the date), and keep the questions themselves on white paper. (Source: Skinner, 2004)

Matching-Test Items

Write clear instructions. Let students know the basis on which items are to be paired, where to write answers, and whether a response may be used more than once. For example: "Next to each literary movement in column 1, write the letter of the work in column 2 that best exemplifies that movement. You may use each work in column 2 more than once or not at all."

Do not mix different classes of items in a column. For example, column 1 might list events and column 2 might list dates, but do not combine events, dates, and names in a single column. (Source: Fuhrmann and Grasha, 1983)

Place the responses in order. When the items in column 2 are in order (alphabetical, chronological, or conceptual), students will be able to read the series quickly and locate answers rapidly. Limit column 2 to five to ten items; longer lists require students to spend too much time searching for responses. (Source: Ory and Ryan, 1993)

Be conscious of layout and format. Do not allow the columns to break across a page; students should not have to flip back and forth. Place answer blanks to the left of each entry in column 1. Use numbers for the items in column 1, and use capital letters for the responses in column 2. Place a heading at the top of each column. (Source: Fuhrmann and Grasha, 1983)

Scoring the Test

Use machine scoring systems. Optical scanning equipment can quickly score selected-response exams. Your learning management system may also have features for online testing and scoring. Scratch-off technology can also save time.

Have students score their own exams. Self-scoring provides students with immediate feedback on their performance. To assure that the scoring is accurate and
fair, give students a separate answer sheet ("declaration sheet") along with the test.
While taking the test, students mark their answers on the exam itself and they
also mark ("declare") their answers on their signed declaration sheet. When all
students have completed the test, the declaration sheets are collected, the answers
are revealed, and students score their own tests and turn them in. Studies show that
students are accurate in scoring and reporting their scores so faculty need not spend
time marking each student's exam. (Source: Carkenord and Laws, 2005)

Item Analysis

Perform an item analysis to evaluate the test. In classes large enough to provide
statistically useful results (say, fifty students or more), you can perform an item
analysis to determine which items are too easy or too hard and how well items distinguish between students at the top and bottom. Most test scoring software and
learning management systems include options for these calculations; your campus
testing office may also have analytic tools. The results will help you in improving
future versions of the test items. (Source: Ory and Ryan, 1993)

Look at the difficulty of each item. Calculate the percentage of students who
answered each item correctly. If you are administering the test to identify the best
performers (norm-referenced testing), the ideal test will contain only a few items
that are very difficult (answered correctly by less than 30 percent of students) or
very easy (answered correctly by more than 90 percent). For norm-referenced
testing, experts recommend the following difficulty levels: 5 percent of the items
are answered correctly by 90 percent of the students (to boost confidence), 5 percent of the items are answered correctly by 10 percent of the students, and the
remainder of the items are answered correctly by an average of 50 percent of
the students.

In contrast, if you are administering the test to measure information, skills,
and competencies that all students need to have acquired (standards-referenced
testing), then the point of your item analysis is not to check the distribution
of scores but to ascertain how well the test items represented the targeted
competencies. If an item proved too difficult for many of your students, consider three possibilities: Was the item poorly written or unclear? Was the content
too challenging? Were too many students insufficiently prepared? (Sources:
Jacobs and Chase, 1992; Lowman, 1995; Scialfa et al., 2001; Sechrest et al.,
1999; Wergin, 1988)

Look at how well each item discriminates between high and low scorers. *Item discrimination* is a statistical technique for calculating how well an individual test item differentiates between the top scorers and the bottom scorers on a test. Test-scoring software can generate a discrimination ratio—a number between -1.0 and $+1.0$— for each item. The closer the ratio is to $+1.0$, the more effectively the item distinguishes students who know the material from those who don't. Ideally, each item will have a ratio of at least .30, but some items that have lower discrimination ratios are useful to ensure that a test contains a few items that everyone can answer correctly. If you have an item that few of the top-scoring students answered correctly, look for defects in the structure of the item and the distractors. (Sources: Lowman, 1995; Miller et al., 2008; Schmeiser and Welch, 2006; Sechrest et al., 1999)

Examine the reliability coefficient. If your test-scoring software calculates a reliability estimate, a coefficient of .65 or higher is desirable. Interpret a coefficient of less than .60 to mean that the test is unlikely to produce similar results on second administration. (Source: Ory and Ryan, 1993)

Use these analyses to improve your tests. Let the results of the statistical analyses suggest which items you might drop or revise for future tests. Aim for a test on which the mean percentage of correct answers is about 70 percent, with items whose difficulty level is between 30 percent and 70 percent (items within this range can be expected to have an acceptable discrimination ratio, $+.30$ or higher). When an item has a high difficulty level and a low discrimination ratio (below $+.30$), the item should be revised. Items that fall on the borderline (a discrimination ratio just under $+.30$ and a difficulty level between 30 percent and 70 percent) do not necessarily need revision. (Sources: Schmeiser and Welch, 2006; Sechrest et al., 1999)

Examine the distractors. Look at the percentage of students who selected a particular distractor, and consider replacing a distractor that few students chose. You may also want to double-check items missed by a majority of students, especially those items for which any one distractor was selected more often than the correct answer. (Source: Sechrest et al., 1999)

References

Baranchik, A., and Cherkas, B. "Correcting Grade Deflation Caused by Multiple-Choice Scoring." *International Journal of Mathematical Education in Science and Technology*, 2000, *31*(3), 371–380.

Carkenord, D. M., and Laws, E. L. "Assuring Accuracy of Student Self-Scored Quizzes." *Teaching of Psychology*, 2005, *32*(3), 175–177.

Clegg, V. L., and Cashin, W. E. "Improving Multiple-Choice Tests." *Idea Paper*, no. 16. Manhattan: Center for Faculty Evaluation and Development in Higher Education, Kansas State University, 1986.

Forsyth, D. R. *The Professor's Guide to Teaching: Psychological Principles and Practices.* Washington, DC: American Psychological Association, 2003.

Frary, R. B. "More Multiple-Choice Item Writing Do's and Don'ts." *Practical Assessment, Research and Evaluation*, 1995, *4*(11). http://pareonline.net/getvn.asp?v=4&n=11

Fuhrmann, B. S., and Grasha, A. F. *A Practical Handbook for College Teachers.* Boston: Little, Brown, 1983.

Green, D. H. "Student-Generated Exams: Testing and Learning." *Journal of Marketing Education*, 1997, *19*(2), 43–53.

Haladyna, T. M. *Developing and Validating Multiple-Choice Test Items.* (3rd ed.) Mahwah, NJ: Erlbaum, 2004.

Jacobs, L. C., and Chase, C. I. *Developing and Using Tests Effectively: A Guide for Faculty.* San Francisco: Jossey-Bass, 1992.

Jensen, M., Duranczyk, I., Staats, S., Moore, R., Hatch, J., and Somdahl, C. "Using a Reciprocal Teaching Strategy to Create Multiple Choice Exam Questions." *American Biology Teacher*, 2006, *68*(6), 67–71.

Kehoe, J. "Writing Multiple-Choice Test Items." *Practical Assessment, Research and Evaluation*, 1995, *4*(9).

Kruger, J., Wirtz, D., and Miller, D. T. "Counterfactual Thinking and First Instinct Fallacy." *Journal of Personality and Social Psychology*, 2005, *88*(5), 725–735.

Landrum, R. E., Cashin, J. R., and Theis, K. S. "More Evidence in Favor of Three-Option Multiple Choice Tests." *Educational and Psychological Measurement*, 1993, 53, 771–778.

Lowman, J. *Mastering the Techniques of Teaching.* San Francisco: Jossey-Bass, 1995.

McKeachie, W. J., and Svinicki, M. *McKeachie's Teaching Tips.* (12th ed.) Boston: Houghton Mifflin, 2006.

Miller, M. D., Linn, R. I., and Gronlund, N. E. *Measurement and Assessment in Teaching.* (10th ed.) Upper Saddle River, NJ: Prentice Hall, 2008.

Ory, J. C., and Ryan, K. E. *Tips for Improving Testing and Grading.* Newbury Park, CA: Sage, 1993.

Schmeiser, C. B., and Welch, C. J. Test Development. In R. L. Brennan (Ed.), *Educational Measurement.* (4th ed.) Westport, CT: American Council on Education/Praeger, 2006.

Scialfa, C., Legare, C., Wenger, L., and Dingley, L. "Difficulty and Discriminability of Introductory Psychology Test Items." *Teaching of Psychology*, 2001, *28*(1), 11–15.

Sechrest, L., Kihlstrom, J. F., and Bootzin, R. How to Develop Multiple-Choice Tests. In B. Perlman, L. I. McCann, S. H. and McFadden (Eds.), *Lessons Learned: Practical Advice for the Teaching of Psychology.* Washington, DC: American Psychological Society, 1999.

Skinner, N. F. "Differential Test Performance from Differently Colored Paper: White Paper Works Best." *Teaching of Psychology*, 2004, *31*(2), 111–113.

Welsh, A. L. Multiple Choice Objective Tests. In P. Saunders, A. L. Welsh, and W. L. Hansen (Eds.), *Resource Manual for Teaching Training Programs in Economics.* New York: Joint Council on Economic Education, 1978.

Wergin, J. F. "Basic Issues and Principles in Classroom Assessment." In J. H. McMillan (Ed.), *Assessing Students' Learning.* New Directions for Teaching and Learning, no. 34. San Francisco: Jossey-Bass, 1988.

Williams, J. "Assertion-Reason Multiple Choice Testing as a Tool for Deep Learning: A Qualitative Analysis." *Assessment and Evaluation in Higher Education*, 2006, *31*(3), 287–301.

42

Short-Answer and Essay Tests

Short-answer items call for answers of about fifty words or less: Define *impedance;* List three causes of concrete failure; What happens during a solar eclipse? Essay questions, in contrast, require students to demonstrate their understanding of a topic and their ability to think critically and organize their thoughts. Although short-answer and essay questions are easier to create than multiple-choice items, they are more time-consuming to score, and maintaining consistency in grading is more difficult when evaluating essays. On the other hand, essay tests are the best measure of students' skills in higher-order thinking and written expression. In addition to the suggestions below, see Chapter 35, "Designing Effective Writing Assignments," and Chapter 36, "Evaluating Students' Written Work," for other ideas about creating topics and grading essays.

General Strategies

Do not use essay questions to evaluate understanding that could be tested with multiple-choice questions. Save essay questions for assessing reasoning and thinking skills. Appropriate tasks for essays include the following (adapted from Reiner et al., 2003):

Analyzing: "Find and correct the reasoning errors in the following passage."

Applying: "Describe a situation that illustrates the principle of . . ."

Comparing: "Identify two similarities and two differences between . . ."

Defending: "Present an argument to support your recommendation for . . ."

Designing: "Create a plan to . . ."

Evaluating: "Assess the strengths and weaknesses of . . ."

Generalizing: "State a set of principles that explains the following events."

Inferring: "How would character X respond if . . . ?"

Interpreting: "Interpret the second stanza of . . ."

Justifying: "Explain why you agree or disagree with the following statement."

Predicting: "What will happen when . . . ?"

Relating cause and effect: "What are the major causes of . . . ?" "What would be the most likely effects of . . . ?"

Give students some test-taking advice. Most students will benefit from pointers like the following:

- Survey the entire test quickly, noting the directions and estimating the importance and difficulty of each question. If ideas or answers come to mind, jot them down quickly.
- Do a "brain dump"—write down anything that you fear you might forget later.
- Divide the time available among the questions. Allow more time for important or difficult questions. Allocate some time at the end to review your answers. Stick to your plan—four partially complete answers will earn a better grade than two extremely complete answers and two blanks.
- Analyze each question and its parts. The key nouns in the question should suggest the topic and subtopics, and the verbs *(compare, define, predict)* will indicate an approach to the topic. Observe any limitations (for example, "from 1900 to 1945") expressed in the question.
- If you are completely stumped by a question, jot down *anything* you can think of that might be relevant. Free association may prompt your memory.
- Outline each answer before you begin to write. Write down your main points, arrange them in a pattern, and add details under each point. A quick outline will help you write with greater purpose, clarity, completeness, and speed.
- The first paragraph of an essay response should include a thesis statement that expresses your main point or conclusion. If the test question states a topic, create a *how* or *why* question about that topic. Your answer to that question will become your thesis. For example, if the test reads "Discuss the concept of love in D. H. Lawrence's novel *Women in Love*," one *how* question is "How does Lawrence portray different types of love in this novel?" The thesis statement could be "In depicting bisexual, homosexual, and familial love in *Women in Love*, Lawrence shows that hatred and isolation are present even in the closest love relationships" (based on Walvoord, 1986, p. 11).
- Follow your outline as you write. Skip every other line to leave room for additions or changes that occur to you as you reread your response.
- Support your thesis with examples and evidence.
- Include a conclusion, even if only a sentence or two that ties together the main points and states their importance.

- Reread your exam before you turn it in. Check for omissions, repetitions, and errors. Cross out and insert words as neatly as possible.
- If you are running out of time, list your main points and examples and write, "ran out of time."

(Sources: Brooks, 1990; Forsyth, 2003; McKeachie and Svinicki, 2006; Sanders, 1966; and Walvoord, 1986)

Don't give students a choice of questions to answer. There are three drawbacks to giving students a choice. First, some students will waste time trying to decide which questions to answer. Second, you will not know whether all students are equally knowledgeable about all the topics covered on the test. Third, since some questions are likely to be harder than others, the test could be unfair. (Sources: Jacobs and Chase, 1992; Reiner et al., 2003)

Ask students to write more than one essay. Tests that ask only one question are less valid and reliable than those with a wider sampling of items. On a fifty-minute test, you could pose two or three essay questions or eight to ten short-answer questions.

Writing Effective Test Questions

State the question clearly and precisely. Avoid broad questions that invite different interpretations and that will make it hard to score the responses. Rather than asking students to "discuss" a topic, select a verb that suggests an approach to the topic. Often, adding *how* or *why* to an essay question will help students develop a thesis. The following examples illustrate ineffective and effective questions (adapted from Cashin, 1987; Jacobs and Chase, 1992; Reiner et al., 2003; Welsh, 1978):

> *Poor:* What are three types of market organization? In what ways are they different from one another?
>
> *Better:* Define *oligopoly*. How does *oligopoly* differ from both *perfect competition* and *monopoly* in terms of number of firms, control over price, conditions of entry, cost structure, and long-term profitability?
>
> *Poor:* Name the principles that determined American foreign policy after September 11.
>
> *Better:* Describe three principles on which American foreign policy has been based since September 11, 2001; illustrate each of the principles with two actions taken by the executive branch of government.

Poor: You are the president of the United States. What economic policies would you pursue?

Better: You are the president of the United States. State your goals for employment, price levels, and the rate of real economic growth. What fiscal and monetary policies would you implement to achieve your goals?

Poor: Why does an internal combustion engine work?

Better: Explain the functions of fuel, carburetor, distributor, and the operation of the cylinder's components in making an internal combustion engine run.

Poor: Was the above passage written by a classical or patristic Latin writer? Why do you think that?

Better: Decide whether the above passage was written by a classical or patristic Latin writer. Support your position by identifying specific phrases or other linguistic features of the author's style.

Specify the point value and criteria for each question. Giving the point value will help students allocate their time. Stating the criteria—for example, accuracy, completeness, relevance, clarity and strength of argument—may help students focus their efforts. (Source: Reiner et al., 2003)

Write out the correct answer yourself. Use your version to help you revise the question and to estimate how much time students will need. If you can answer the question in ten minutes, students will probably need twenty-five to thirty-five minutes. Some instructors give students advice on how much time to spend on each question.

Grading and Evaluating Exams

Create and use a scoring guide or rubric. Decide which facts or ideas a student must mention to earn full credit or partial credit. The following guide outlines the scoring of a 10-point essay question (adapted from Erickson et al., 2006, p. 173):

- *9 or 10 points.* The essay clearly states a position, provides support for the position, and raises at least one counterargument or alternative view and refutes it. Evidence is both persuasive and original. Counterargument is significant.
- *7 or 8 points.* The essay states a position, supports it, and raises a counterargument and refutes it. The essay contains one or more of the following ragged edges: evidence is not uniformly persuasive, counterargument is not a serious threat to the position, some points are extraneous or out of place.

- *6 points.* The essay states a position and raises a counterargument, but neither is well developed. The objection or counterargument seems rather trivial.
- *5 points.* The essay states a position and provides evidence supporting the position, but it does not raise possible objections or counterarguments.
- *3 or 4 points.* The essay states a position and provides some support, but the evidence is sparse, trivial, or general. The essay achieves its length largely through repetition of ideas and inclusion of irrelevant information.
- *1 or 2 points.* The essay does not state a position but simply restates the question and summarizes evidence discussed in class or in the reading.

Here is an example from an economics class (adapted from Ory and Ryan, 1993, p. 85). Students are given the following question: "Baseball is far less necessary than food and steel, yet professional ball players earn a lot more than farmers and steelworkers. Why? Take two or three sentences to summarize how an economist would explain the difference in salaries." The scoring guide might allocate a total of 7 points for this question:

> *3 points* for mentioning that salaries are based on the demand relative to the supply of a service
>
> *2 points* for mentioning that excellent ball players are rare (low supply)
>
> *2 points* for mentioning that many ball clubs want excellent players (high demand)

Read the exams without looking at the students' names. Try not to bias your grading by carrying over your perceptions about individual students. Some faculty ask students to put a number or pseudonym on the exam and to place that code on an index card that is turned in with the test. Other faculty have students write their names on the last page of the blue book or on the back of the test.

Skim all the exams quickly, without assigning any grades. Before you begin grading, try to get an overview of the general level of performance and the range of students' responses. (Source: McKeachie and Svinicki, 2006)

Grade the exams question by question rather than grading all questions for a single student. Shuffle the papers before scoring the next question to distribute your fatigue factor randomly. By shuffling the papers you also avoid ordering effects (that is, Riley's "B" work always follows Coco's "A" work and suffers from the comparison). (Sources: Fuhrmann and Grasha, 1983; Ory and Ryan, 1993)

Avoid judging exams on extraneous factors. Don't let handwriting, use of pen or pencil, or similar factors influence your judgment about the quality of the response.

Write comments on students' exams. Write brief notes on strengths and weaknesses to indicate what students have done well and where they need to improve. Writing comments will also keep your attention focused and will jog your memory if a student comes to talk to you about the exam. Some faculty ask students to write only on the odd-numbered pages of their blue book, leaving the even-numbered pages for the instructor's comments. Try to balance positive and critical comments, and focus on the organization of the response, not on whether you agree or disagree with a student's ideas. (Sources: Cashin, 1987; McKeachie and Svinicki, 2006; Sanders, 1966)

Read only a modest number of exams at a time. Set a time limit for each paper, and take regular short breaks. If possible, read all the responses to a single question in one session in order to minimize the effects of extraneous factors (time of day, temperature, and so forth) on your grading.

If time permits, read some of the papers twice. Wait a day or two and review a few randomly selected exams without looking at the grades you assigned. Rereading helps you increase your reliability as a grader.

Place the grade on the last page of the exam. Take care to protect students' privacy when you return or they pick up their tests.

Create standardized procedures for assistants who grade exams. The following process can promote consistency among graduate student assistants and readers (adapted from McKeachie and Svinicki, 2006):

- Meet as a group to discuss the answers to each question. Decide how many points will be given for what types of answers. Review the scoring criteria, rubric, and model answers prepared by the faculty member.
- Establish two- or three-person teams for each essay question. Give each team eight or ten exams and have each team member independently grade the team's question on each exam. Compare the grades that team members assigned and discuss the discrepancies until consensus is reached.

- If needed, have the teams grade and discuss a second batch of exams so that teams feel confident that they have arrived at common criteria.
- From this point on, each member grades independently. If any team member is unsure about a particular exam, it is passed to another team member for an opinion.

Returning Essay Exams

Return exams promptly. A quick turnaround reinforces learning and capitalizes on students' interest in the results. Try to return tests within a week or so.

Review the exam in class. Give students a copy of the scoring guide, rubric, or grading criteria. Let students know the features of a good answer and the most common errors the class made. If time permits, read examples of good and bad answers that you have created. Give students information on the distribution of scores so they know where they stand. (Source: McKeachie and Svinicki, 2006)

Convene groups to discuss test questions. Some faculty break the class into small groups to discuss answers to the test. Unresolved questions are brought up to the class as a whole. (Source: McKeachie and Svinicki, 2006)

Asks students for their opinions of the test. Ask students to tell you what was particularly difficult or unexpected. Find out how they prepared for the exam and what they wish they had done differently. Pass along the best tips to next year's class. (Source: Walvoord, 1986)

Keep a file of essay questions. Include a copy of the test with your annotations on ways to improve it, the mistakes students made in responding to various questions, the distribution of students' performance, and any comments that students made about the exam. Keep copies of good and poor exams. (Source: Cashin, 1987)

References

Brooks, P. *Working in Subject A Courses*. Berkeley: Subject A Program, University of California, 1990.

Cashin, W. E. "Improving Essay Tests." *Idea Paper*, no. 17. Manhattan: Center for Faculty Evaluation and Development in Higher Education, Kansas State University, 1987.

Erickson, B. L., Peters, C. B., and Strommer, D. W. *Teaching First-Year College Students.* San Francisco: Jossey-Bass, 2006.

Forsyth, D. R. *The Professor's Guide to Teaching: Psychological Principles and Practices.* Washington, DC: American Psychological Association, 2003.

Fuhrmann, B. S., and Grasha, A. F. *A Practical Handbook for College Teachers.* Boston: Little, Brown, 1983.

Jacobs, L. C., and Chase, C. I. *Developing and Using Tests Effectively: A Guide for Faculty.* San Francisco: Jossey-Bass, 1992.

McKeachie, W. J., and Svinicki, M. *McKeachie's Teaching Tips.* (12th ed.) Boston: Houghton Mifflin, 2006.

Ory, J. C., and Ryan, K. E. *Tips for Improving Testing and Grading.* Newbury Park, CA: Sage, 1993.

Reiner, C. M., Bothell, T. W., and Sudweeks, R. R. *Preparing Effective Essay Questions.* Stillwater, OK: New Forums Press, 2003.

Sanders, N. M. *Classroom Questions: What Kinds?* New York: Harper & Row, 1966.

Walvoord, B. F. *Helping Students Write Well: A Guide for Teachers in All Disciplines.* (2nd ed.) New York: Modern Language Association, 1986.

Welsh, A. L. Essay Questions and Tests. In P. Saunders, A. L. Welsh, and W. L. Hansen (Eds.), *Resource Manual for Teacher Training Programs in Economics.* New York: Joint Council on Economic Education, 1978.

43

Grading Practices

As Erickson, Peters, and Strommer (2006) point out, decisions about grading practices depend a great deal on an instructor's values, assumptions, and educational philosophy. For example, faculty who view introductory courses as "weeder" classes (courses that separate out students who seem unlikely to succeed in the field) will take a different approach to grading than faculty who view introductory courses as teaching important skills that all students need to master.

In addition to providing information on how well students are learning, grades are often used for other purposes (Scriven, 1974):

- to describe the worth, merit, or value of a piece of work
- to stimulate and encourage good work by students
- to communicate the instructor's judgment of the student's progress
- to inform the instructor about what students have and haven't learned
- to select people for rewards or continued education
- to improve students' ability to identify good work, to improve their self-evaluation or discrimination skills

The suggestions below are designed to help you develop clear and fair grading policies that emphasize learning. For tips on calculating final grades, see Chapter 44, "Calculating and Assigning Grades."

General Strategies

Grade students on their mastery of knowledge and skills. Restrict your evaluations to academic performance. Eliminate nonacademic considerations, such as classroom behavior, punctuality, attitude, personality, need, or interest in the course material. Some faculty grade students' work without looking at the students' names to increase objectivity and guard against bias. (Sources: Guskey and Bailey, 2001; Jacobs and Chase, 1992; Scott, 1995)

Try not to overemphasize grades. Explain your grading policies at the beginning of the term, but do not repeatedly revisit the topic. Dwelling on grades is likely to increase students' anxieties, decrease their motivation to learn for the sake of learning, and foster unhealthy, unproductive competitiveness. (Sources: Church et al., 2001; Fuhrmann and Grasha, 1983; Weimer, 2002)

Keep students informed of their progress throughout the term. For each paper, assignment, midterm, or project that you grade, give students a sense of what their score indicates about how well they are learning the material. Brief progress reports help students improve their study strategies and avoid unpleasant surprises at the end of the term. One faculty member gives each student midsemester ratings (*strong, OK,* or *needs improvement*) on the following dimensions: writes effectively; asks constructive questions during discussion; builds on others' ideas during discussion; takes responsibility for self and learning; displays wonder and curiosity; tolerates ambiguity; sees thinking as a way of life. (Source: Kloss, 1997)

Minimizing Students' Complaints about Grades

State your grading procedures in the course syllabus, and review this information in class. Students want to know how grades will be determined, the weights of various tests and assignments, and whether the class will be graded on a curve or by another system. Explain your policies regarding extra credit, late assignments, and revision of papers, and consistently enforce these policies throughout the semester. Because midcourse changes in policy may erode students' confidence in your impartiality, offer students a full explanation for any such changes.

Provide many opportunities for students to demonstrate what they know. By giving students many chances to show what they have learned, you can obtain a more accurate picture of their abilities and avoid penalizing a student who has an off day at the time of a test. In addition to a final exam, give several midterms and one or two short papers. For freshman and sophomore courses, Erickson, Peters, and Strommer (2006) recommend giving a quiz, short test, or written assignment every two or three weeks.

When possible, distribute grading criteria along with the assignment. For example, accompany a writing assignment with a description of the characteristics of an A or B paper; see Chapter 36, "Evaluating Students' Written Work." (Source: Walvoord and Anderson, 1998)

Remind students that grades are not judgments about people. Some students take grades as a sign of an instructor's approval or disapproval, or as a measure of their self-worth. Remind these students that instructors grade only a piece of paper, not a person. For students who see a low grade as dooming their professional aspirations, you might mention that research studies disagree about the relationship between grades and eventual career success. (Sources: Roth et al., 1996; Waldman and Korbar, 2004)

Give encouragement to students who are performing poorly. Students receiving poor grades on exams or papers may need help in recalibrating their overly optimistic expectations; researchers report that most students overestimate the grade they will achieve in a course by an average of one full grade. Offer these students advice on how to improve their study habits and performance; don't let them blame such factors as a lack of talent ("I just don't have the knack for this"). (Sources: Forsyth, 2003; Lowman, 1995; Svanum and Bigatti, 2006; Weimer, 2002; Wendorf, 2002)

Talk to students who are angry or upset about their grade. Ask an upset student to take a day or two to reflect and to put something on paper. Some faculty have students complete a short grade-appeals form that requires citations from the course materials in support of their case. When you meet with the student in your office, have at hand a copy of the test questions, the answer key or criteria, and examples of good answers. Let the student speak first, listen with an open mind, and avoid interrupting. Try to determine which of the following reflects the student's intent (adapted from Sabee and Wilson, 2005):

- To learn more about the source of poor performance in order to be able to improve future performance. (The conversation is about instruction.)
- To persuade you to change a lower grade to a higher grade. (The conversation is about negotiation.)
- To vent anger and frustration over a lower-than-expected grade. (The conversation is about vindicating or justifying the student's feelings.)
- To impress you and repair the student's image in your eyes. (The conversation is about your opinion of the student and the student's self-image.)

Respond in a calm manner: don't allow yourself to become antagonized, and don't antagonize the student. Describe the key elements of a good answer, and point out how the student's response was incomplete or incorrect. Help the student understand your reasons for the grade you assigned. Take time to think about the student's request or to reread the exam if you need to, but resist pressures to change a grade because of a student's situation (such as the desire to maintain a high grade-point average or to avoid academic probation). If appropriate, for final course grades, offer to write a letter to the student's adviser or to others describing the student's work and any extenuating circumstances. (Sources: Hampton, 2002; McKeachie and Svinicki, 2006; Sabee and Wilson, 2005)

Be aware of cultural variations in grading. In some countries, students are graded only on a comprehensive final examination, not on assignments and other course requirements during the semester. International students may appreciate a conversation about cultural differences and the effects of unrealistic pressures—coming either from families or from financial sponsors—to earn the highest grades. (Source: Eberly Center for Teaching Excellence and Intercultural Communication Center, n.d.)

Keep accurate records. Most departments keep copies of final grade reports, but you will want to keep a record of all grades assigned throughout the semester in case a student wishes to contest a grade, finish an incomplete, or ask for a letter of recommendation.

Minimizing Intradepartmental Complaints about Grades

Ask about your department's policies on grade distributions. Some departments have formal or informal agreements about how many high grades are desirable in an undergraduate course. Try to understand what the norms and constraints are in your department, or propose that a discussion of grading be added to the agenda of an upcoming department meeting. Are there concerns about limiting the number of As, but not the number of Bs? Or is your department more worried about courses with high failure rates (Ds and Fs)? (Source: Walvoord and Anderson, 1998)

Be prepared to show colleagues and administrators your syllabus, assignments, tests, criteria, and standards. Compile samples of student work at each grade level so that your colleagues can examine your standards. (Source: Walvoord and Anderson, 1998)

Try to dispel common misperceptions about grading practices. According to Lowman (1995), research studies contradict some common beliefs about grading:

• It is not true that the quality of education students receive is related to the difficulty of earning high grades. The quality of a college education is more a function of the quality of the faculty, the teaching, and the overall student population.

- It is not true that hard grading leads to student dissatisfaction. Students like hard graders and easy graders equally, and the majority of students seek out difficult courses rated positively over easier courses rated poorly.
- It is not true that strict grading motivates students to study. Students are more motivated by relationships (caring faculty, classmates, and friends) and by a desire for competence.

Grade Inflation

Be aware of broad national trends in grading. Grade-point averages have been rising for several decades, especially at research universities and highly selective colleges. This increase may reflect better preparation by entering students, improvements in teaching, wider use of standards-referenced grading, increased opportunities for students to revise and resubmit their work or to be retested, greater institutional attention to undergraduate teaching, and more lenient policies that allow low-achieving students to drop courses. Some campuses and departments also worry that some part of the increase is due to grade inflation—the gradual dilution of standards for A and B work. (Sources: Basinger, 1997; Boretz, 2004; Kuh and Hu, 1999; Kwon et al., 1997; Rosovsky and Hartley, 2002)

Be aware of some of the myths around grade inflation. Some people believe that grade inflation is caused by instructors watering down their courses and upping the grades they assign to secure higher ratings on students' end-of-course evaluations. The research does not bear this out (Marsh and Roche, 2000). Faculty do not get higher-than-average student ratings by offering easier courses and by giving students higher grades than they deserve. Some observers do point to a correlational (not a causal) relationship between grades and student ratings (Eiszler, 2002; Johnson, 2003), but there are competing explanations for these findings. See Chapter 60, "Student Rating Forms."

While some people believe that the biggest problem associated with grading is grade inflation, a more serious problem on some campuses is a grading disparity among different courses. This disparity, especially when it affects students' choices of courses, can cause institutional grade-point averages to rise and look like grade inflation (Hu, 2005).

Discuss the topic of grade inflation with your colleagues. Campuses and departments are experimenting with techniques for limiting or reversing the trend toward higher grades. These techniques include urging faculty to limit the number of high grades; recommending that faculty use a formula to index grades; adding supplementary information next to each grade on students' transcripts—either a rank in class or the average course grade; and publicizing each faculty member's grade distributions. Web sites, such as pickaprof.com, routinely post grade distributions for individual courses. To date, there is no published research on the effects of the public dissemination of grade distributions. (Sources: French, 2005; Kuh and Hu, 1999; Rosovsky and Hartley, 2002)

Maintain appropriate academic standards. Campus and departmental concerns about grade inflation may be minimized if all instructors make sure that their grading reflects a considered judgment of students' achievement and performance in reference to clearly articulated learning goals or standards. (Sources: Guskey and Bailey, 2001; Kwon et al., 1997; Walvoord and Anderson, 1998)

Tactics and Policies

Return the first graded assignment or test before the add/drop deadline. An early assignment can help students decide whether they are prepared to take the class. Some faculty members give students the option of throwing out the score on the first test. Students may receive a low score because they did not know what the instructor required or because they underestimated the level of preparation needed to succeed.

Select a grading system appropriate to the assignment or test. The traditional letter grade system with pluses and minuses consists of thirteen levels (A+ through F). Other grade systems have fewer levels:

> *Five levels*: A, B, C, D, F
>
> *Four levels*: Check plus, check, check minus, no check; 4, 3, 2, 1
>
> *Three levels*: Outstanding, competent, unacceptable; Exemplary, satisfactory, needs improvement; Excellent, acceptable, unacceptable; 2, 1, 0 (or 4, 2, 1)
>
> *Two levels*: Pass, not pass; Credit, no credit; Satisfactory, unsatisfactory

Experts recommend using the fewest grading levels needed to suit the task and promote effective student learning. In general, the fewer categories you use, the more reliable and valid the grades will be. And the fewer the levels, the faster you can grade. Even if your campus uses a thirteen-level system for final course grades, you can use a simpler system for at least some tests and assignments and then convert to a common metric before calculating final grades. (Sources: Baker and Bates, 1999; Bressette, 2002; Chang, 1994; Guskey and Bailey, 2001; Landrum and Dietz, 2006; McClure and Spector, 2005; Walvoord and Anderson, 1998)

Set policies on extra credit. Students appreciate opportunities to earn extra credit, but some faculty worry that students might neglect required aspects of the course in pursuit of extra-credit points. Studies, however, show that the students most likely to undertake extra-credit work are those doing well in the course; struggling students are less likely to pursue extra credit. If you allow extra credit, the following are useful policies (adapted from Forsyth, 2003; Palladino et al., 1999):

- Make extra credit available to all students in the class, not just those doing poorly, with the exception of those who failed to complete key assignments or participate adequately in class.
- Announce options for extra credit at the beginning of the term, and explain your rationale and intent.
- Select extra-credit assignments that are pedagogically sound and relevant to the course content.
- Provide several choices for extra-credit opportunities.
- Limit the amount of extra credit that a student can earn.

(Sources: Forsyth, 2003; Hardy, 2002; Moore, 2005; Palladino et al., 1999)

Set policies on late assignments. Will you refuse to accept any late work? Deduct points according to how late the work is submitted? Handle late work on a case-by-case basis? Whatever policies you adopt, state them in your syllabus, and on your course Web site, and refer to these policies in class.

Some faculty refuse to accept late work and give students an F on the assignment. Other faculty argue that too much emphasis is put on penalizing late work. Other faculty impose various kinds of markdown penalties:

- a set fraction of a letter grade (from B to B-, for example) or a certain number of points
- a sliding penalty (for example, 5 points for one day late, an additional 1 point for each subsequent day late) with a cutoff date (assignments more than a week late receive a failing score)
- a grade penalty plus one of the following additional conditions:
  - New assignments cannot be submitted until the late work has been submitted.
  - Late work will not be graded until the end of the semester.
  - Late work will be returned without any comments or feedback.

Some faculty offer a small number of bonus points for assignments submitted on time (a decorum bonus). Late assignments do not receive the decorum bonus and are subject to markdown penalties.

Set policies on incompletes. Check with your department for policies on assigning Incompletes. On some campuses, incompletes are allowed only in case of situational hardship such as health issues or family emergencies. On other campuses, incompletes may be given if the students' work to date is of passing quality and the missing work is "minor." In no cases should an incomplete be given to students who want the additional time to be able to do extra work to raise their grades.

Grade fairly. Fairness is a major concern among students, and perceptions of unfairness are a source of many complaints. Fairness in grading is fostered by the following practices (adapted from Glenn, 1998):

- setting clear standards and announcing them at the beginning of the term and throughout the course
- applying the same standards consistently to all students
- resisting students' pressure to change a grade when you are in the right
- admitting when you made a mistake and correcting it
- taking your students' work seriously
- treating students impartially and respectfully

   (Sources: Forsyth, 2003; Glenn, 1998; Holmes and Smith, 2003; Walvoord and Anderson, 1998)

Evaluating Your Grading Policies

Compare your grade distributions with those for similar courses in your department. Differences between your grade distributions and those of your colleagues do not necessarily mean that your methods are faulty. But glaring discrepancies should prompt you to reexamine your practices. (Source: Frisbie et al., 1979)

Include questions about grading policies on the end-of-course evaluation. On the evaluation form, ask your students questions like these (adapted from Frisbie et al., 1979, p. 22):

- Were the grading procedures for the course fair?
- Were the grading procedures for the course clearly explained?
- Did you receive adequate feedback on your performance?
- Were requests for regrading or review handled fairly?
- Did the instructor evaluate your work in a meaningful and conscientious manner?

References

Baker, H. E., and Bates, H. L. "Student and Faculty Perceptions of the Impact of Plus/Minus Grading: A Management Department Perspective." *Journal of Excellence in College Teaching*, 1999, *10*(1), 23–33.

Basinger, D. "Fighting Grade Inflation: A Misguided Effort?" *College Teaching*, 1997, *45*(3), 88–91.

Boretz, E. "Grade Inflation and the Myth of Student Consumerism." *College Teaching*, 2004, *52*(2), 42–46.

Bressette, A. "Arguments for Plus/Minus Grading: A Case Study." *Educational Research Quarterly*, 2002, *25*(3), 29–41.

Chang, L. "A Psychometric Evaluation of 4-Point and 6-Point Likert-Type Scales in Relation to Reliability and Validity." *Applied Psychological Measurement*, 1994, *18*(3), 205–215.

Church, M. A., Elliot, A. J., and Gable, S. L. "Perceptions of Classroom Environment, Achievement Goals and Achievement Outcomes." *Journal of Educational Psychology*, 2001, *93*(1), 43–54.

Eberly Center for Teaching Excellence and Intercultural Communication Center. "Recognizing and Addressing Cultural Variations in the Classroom." Carnegie Mellon University, n.d. / http://www.cmu.edu/teaching/resources/PublicationsArchives/InternalReports/culturalvariations.pdf

Eiszler, C. F. "College Students' Evaluations of Teaching and Grade Inflation." *Research in Higher Education*, 2002, *43*(4), 483–501.

Erickson, B. L., Peters, C. B., and Strommer, D. W. *Teaching First-Year College Students.* San Francisco: Jossey-Bass, 2006.

Forsyth, D. R. *The Professor's Guide to Teaching: Psychological Principles and Practices.* Washington, DC: American Psychological Association, 2003.

French, D. P. "Grade Inflation: Is Ranking Students the Answer?" *Journal of College Science Teaching*, 2005, *34*(6), 66–67.

Frisbie, D. A., Diamond, N. A., and Ory, J. C. *Assigning Course Grades.* Urbana: Office of Instructional Resources, University of Illinois, 1979.

Fuhrmann, B. S., and Grasha, A. F. *A Practical Handbook for College Teachers.* Boston: Little, Brown, 1983.

Glenn, B. J. "The Golden Rule of Grading: Be Fair." *PS: Political Science and Politics.* 1998, *31*(4), 787–788.

Guskey, T. R., and Bailey, J. M. *Developing Grading and Reporting Systems for Student Learning.* Thousand Oaks, CA: Corwin Press, 2001.

Hampton, D. R. "The Quick Fix: Making Complaining Appealing." *College Teaching*, 2002, *50*(2), 62.

Hardy, M. S. "Extra Credit: Gifts for the Gifted?" *Teaching of Psychology*, 2002, *29*(3), 233–234.

Holmes, L. E., and Smith, L. J. "Student Evaluations of Faculty Grading Methods." *Journal of Education for Business*, 2003, *78*(6), 318–323.

Hu, S. "Beyond Grade Inflation: Grading Problems in Higher Education." *ASHE-ERIC Higher Education Report*, 2005, *30*(6).

Jacobs, L. C., and Chase, C. I. *Developing and Using Tests Effectively: A Guide for Faculty.* San Francisco: Jossey-Bass, 1992.

Johnson, V. E. *Grade Inflation: A Crisis in College Education.* New York: Springer, 2003.

Kloss, R. J. "The Way It Looks Right Now: A Simple Feedback Technique." *College Teaching*, 1997, *45*(4), 139–142.

Kuh, G. D., and Hu, S. "Unraveling the Complexity of the Increase in College Grades from the Mid-1980s to the Mid-1990s." *Educational Evaluation and Policy Analysis*, 1999, *21*(3), 297–320.

Kwon, I. G., Kendig, N. L., and Bae, M. "Grade Inflation from a Career Counselor's Perspective." *Journal of Employment Counseling*, 1997, *34*(2), 50–54.

Landrum, R. E., and Dietz, K. H. "Grading without Points: Does It Hurt Student Performance?" *College Teaching*, 2006, *54*(4), 298–301.

Lowman, J. *Mastering the Techniques of Teaching.* (2nd ed.) San Francisco: Jossey-Bass, 1995.

Marsh, H. W., and Roche, L. A. "Effects of Grading Leniency and Low Workload on Students' Evaluations of Teaching: Popular Myth, Bias, Validity, or Innocent Bystanders?" *Journal of Educational Psychology*, 2000, *92*(1), 202, 228.

McClure, J. E., and Spector, L. C. "Plus/Minus Grading and Motivation: An Empirical Study of Student Choice and Performance." *Assessment and Evaluation in Higher Education* 2005, *30*(6), 571–579.

McKeachie, W. J., and Svinicki, M. *McKeachie's Teaching Tips.* (12th ed.) Boston: Houghton Mifflin, 2006.

Moore, R. "Who Does Extra-Credit Work in Introductory Science Courses?" *Journal of College Science Teaching*, 2005, *34*(7), 12–15.

Palladino, J. J., Hill, G. W., and Norcross, J. C. Using Extra Credit. In B. Perlman, L. I. McCann, and S. H. McFadden (Eds.), *Lessons Learned: Practical Advice for the Teaching of Psychology.* Washington, DC: American Psychological Society, 1999.

Rosovsky, H., and Hartley, M. *Evaluation and the Academy: Are We Doing the Right Thing? Grade Inflation and Letters of Recommendation.* Cambridge, MA: American Academy of Arts and Sciences, 2002.

Roth, P. L., BeVier, C. A., Switzer, F. S., and Schippmann, J. S. "Meta-analyzing the Relationship between Grades and Job Performance." *Journal of Applied Psychology*, 1996, *81*(5), 548–556.

Sabee, C. M., and Wilson, S. R. "Students' Primary Goals, Attributions, and Facework during Conversations about Disappointing Grades." *Communication Education*, 2005, *54*(3), 185–204.

Scott, E. L. "Mokita—The Truth That Everybody Knows But Nobody Talks About: Bias in Grading." *Teaching English in the Two-Year College*, 1995, *22*(3), 11–16.

Scriven, M. "Evaluation of Students." Unpublished manuscript, University of California, Berkeley, 1974.

Svanum, S., and Bigatti, S. "Grade Expectations: Informed or Uninformed Optimism or Both?" *Teaching of Psychology*, 2006, *33*(1), 14–18.

Waldman, D. A., and Korbar, T. "Student Assessment Center Performance in the Prediction of Early Career Success." *Academy of Management Learning and Education*, 2004, *3*(2), 151–167.

Walvoord, B. E., and Anderson, V. J. *Effective Grading: A Tool for Learning and Assessment.* San Francisco: Jossey-Bass, 1998.

Weimer, M. *Learner-Centered Teaching: Five Key Changes to Practice.* San Francisco: Jossey-Bass, 2002.

Wendorf, C. A. "Grade Point Average and Changes in (Great) Grade Expectations." *Teaching of Psychology*, 2002, *29*(2), 136–138.

44

Calculating and Assigning Grades

Instructors' decisions about grading depend on the type of course they are teaching, their department's policies, and their views of the purpose of grades. In the broadest terms, the choice is between standards-referenced grading and norm-referencing grading.

Under standards-referenced grading (also called *criterion-referenced grading, task-based grading,* or *absolute grading*), a letter grade reflects a student's level of achievement against a specified standard or benchmark, independent of how other students in the class have performed. If all the students in a seminar give strong oral presentations, they will all receive As or Bs on that project. Conversely, if none of the students in a class scores better than 80 percent on a midterm, then no one in the class will receive higher than a B– on the exam.

Under norm-referenced grading (also called *grading on the curve, relative grading,* or *group-referenced grading*), in contrast, a letter grade reflects a student's level of achievement relative to other students in the class. Typically the proportion of students receiving each grade follows a pattern of a few As, lots of Bs and Cs, and a few Ds and Fs.

In large classes in which students' test scores are fairly well distributed, it may not matter which model an instructor chooses. But in smaller classes (forty students or fewer), it can matter a great deal: under norm-referenced grading, only a handful of the highest-scoring students will earn an A—no matter how many students did very well on an exam.

Educational measurement experts strongly recommend standards-referenced systems, especially for smaller classes, so that a grade reflects how well a student has mastered the material rather than how well a student performs compared to others (Brookhart, 1999; Dominowski, 2002; Gronlund and Waugh, 2008; Payne, 2003; Shepard, 2006).

The suggestions below are designed to help you understand the advantages and disadvantages of various grading strategies.

General Strategies

Familiarize yourself with department standards. Check to see how grading has been handled for the course in past semesters, and try to obtain grade distributions for earlier offerings. Ask colleagues who have taught the course before about their grading criteria and their classes' overall performance. (Source: Heppner, 2007)

Relate department standards to your conception of the course. Identify the objectives or goals you want your students to meet. What skills and knowledge are absolutely essential for students to pass the course? What would you wish from an A student?

Weight various course components in proportion to their importance. A three-hour final exam or a fifteen-page research paper should, obviously, count more than scores on two fifteen-minutes quizzes. Another consideration: usually the final exam should count for no more than a third of the course grade. If the final is weighted too heavily, students will cram at the end of the term rather than work at an even pace. (Source: Lowman, 1995)

Use electronic gradebooks. Most learning management systems have an e-gradebook feature, and standalone gradebook software is available. E-gradebooks simplify record keeping, make it easy to enter and tally numerical information, and offer options for generating statistical data (such as mean scores and standard deviations).

Standards-Referenced Approaches

Grading according to absolute standards. *Absolute standards* refers to performance levels that an instructor sets at the beginning of the term. (Some faculty occasionally grade more generously than the announced standards.) For example, an instructor might decide on the following scale for a test worth 100 points: 93 or higher = A; 90–92 = A-; 86–89 = B+, and so on. The segments for each grade do not have to be of equal size.

This is the most commonly used standards-referenced model. An advantage of this approach is that it imposes no limit on how many students may earn As and Bs. Also, students know in advance how well they have to perform to earn the grade they want.

One difficulty arises in how to set rational standards. Experienced faculty can set cutoffs based on how students typically perform (a norm-referenced perspective), but new instructors may need guidance. Dominowski (2002, p. 137) proposes the following guidelines: A = 90 percent and above; B = 82–89; C = 63–81 (that is, the center of the C range is 72 percent); D = 48–62; F = 47 or below.

If many students perform very poorly, some instructors reset the standards to reflect students' performance, but such adjustments defeat the premise of creating absolute standards; see Chapter 39, "Quizzes, Tests, and Exams," for a discussion of how to respond when the entire class performs poorly. (Sources: Dominowski, 2002; McKeachie and Svinicki, 2006; Sadler, 2005)

Grading according to achievement of course objectives. This standards-referenced approach requires instructors to prepare a list of detailed objectives or learning outcomes, the measurable skills and knowledge students are expected to attain. The instructor then evaluates whether a student has or has not attained those outcomes. Under this model, most students who work hard enough and receive good instruction will obtain good grades. The difficulty is that the instructor must be able to clearly define the knowledge and skills that each grade represents as well as determine the minimum level of performance necessary to attain each grade and the best ways to measure achievement. In many college courses, the content is so extensive that an instructor cannot specify the requisite knowledge and skills with precision. (Sources: Frisbie et al., 1979; Hanna and Cashin, 1988; Ory and Ryan, 1993; Sadler, 2005)

Grading according to specified patterns of achievement. Under this model, an instructor specifies various levels of performance for each grade; for example, a student will receive an A if he or she performs at the A level on at least two-thirds of the assessment tasks and at the B level on the other third. The advantage of this approach is that different "formulas" and relative weights allow students to compensate for weak performance in some areas by superior performance in others. The disadvantages include complexity (the instructor must devise clear specifications and track performance levels for each component) and the need to familiarize students with this unusual method. (Source: Sadler, 2005)

Challenges in setting standards. All these methods require instructors to grapple with how to set standards. Numerical cutoffs seem arbitrary, but reliance on professional intuition—the expertise and "feel" that an instructor develops over time—is not transparent or objective. Describing exemplars (listing the characteristics of typical performance at designated levels of quality or competence) is not realistic or suitable for all courses and all instructors. (Source: Sadler, 2005)

Norm-Referenced Approaches

Grading on a curve. In this approach, grades are determined by comparing a student's performance with that of other students. All the scores in a class are listed from highest to lowest, and grades are assigned according to cutoff points. Some instructors rely on a preset allocation; for example, Gronlund and Waugh (2008) recommend the following guidelines: 10 to 20 percent As, 20 to 30 percent Bs, 40 to 50 percent Cs, 10 to 20 percent Ds, 0 to 10 percent Fs. Other faculty use software to calculate the mean score and standard deviation, convert each student's score into a standard score and then convert the standard scores into a percentile based on a normal curve. A student's score is indicated as being in the 80th percentile or the 60th percentile, with the instructor determining in advance percentiles that represent letter grades.

Grading on the curve is a flexible approach that rewards students whose academic performance is outstanding in comparison to their peers. It also capitalizes on students' competitive tendencies. But it has many drawbacks:

- The grades do not indicate how much or how little students have learned— only where they stand in relationship to others.
- No matter how strong the class is, some students will receive low grades; no matter how weak the class is, some students will receive high grades. Some faculty compensate for inequities by adjusting the cutoff scores or by assigning a higher percentage of As when a class is unusually good.
- Grading standards may fluctuate from term to term. A student who earns a C+ might have received a B– a term earlier.
- Researchers note that grading on the curve may encourage exclusion, isolation, and competitiveness. It also may threaten students' sense of autonomy and fairness—their belief that their grade should depend on their efforts, not on how others perform.
- Grading on a curve assumes that every class is large enough and diverse enough to generate a full range of grades. But a small class of highly motivated students might not contain any subpar students. In difficult courses, the enrollment may be unrepresentative because struggling students dropped the course after doing poorly on the first quiz.
- Grading on the curve obscures the effects of course design and teaching (whether excellent or poor) because those factors are not scrutinized in analyzing student performance.

- Grading on the curve makes it difficult for an instructor to tell students at the beginning of the term what they must know or be able to do in order to earn an A or B.

   (Sources: Dominowski, 2002; Forsyth, 2003; Guskey and Bailey, 2001; Hanna and Cashin, 1988; Sadler, 2005)

Grading according to department practices or faculty consensus. Some faculty try to have their grade distributions reflect the averages reported in their department. All faculty who teach the same course might develop a consensus on the distribution of grades suitable for a typical class (say, 20 percent As, 25 percent Bs, 30 percent Cs, 20 percent Ds, and 5 percent Fs), with adjustments for an unusually strong or unusually weak class. (Source: Hanna and Cashin, 1988)

Grading according to breaks in the distribution. In this model, the instructor lists students' scores from highest to lowest and looks for natural gaps or breaks in the distribution. For example, if six students score 80 or higher, and no one scores between 73 and 79, and two students score 72, the instructor might assign As to students who scored 80 and above, and start the Bs at 72. Significant gaps, however, are rare in large classes. Even a gap that looks meaningful might not represent a true difference in achievement as much as the vagaries of an unreliable test, good guessing, or poorly written items. Further, the grade distribution depends on judgments made after students have taken the test rather than on preestablished guidelines that can be stated prior to testing. (Sources: Forsyth, 2003; Jacobs and Chase, 1992; Ory and Ryan, 1993; Payne, 2003)

Grading on a bell curve. A bell curve is a symmetrical statistical model that is inappropriate for grading coursework. The classic bell curve results from the following distribution of grades: 7 percent As, 24 percent Bs, 38 percent Cs, 24 percent Ds, 7 percent Fs. Bell curves have their uses, but student performance is not distributed normally within a class, nor are teacher-made tests so well designed as to yield bell-shaped distributions. Even proponents of grading on the curve do not recommend using the bell curve. (Source: Gronlund and Waugh, 2008)

Hybrid Models

Grading according to highest scores earned and percentages thereof. This hybrid model (developed by Carter as reported in Fuhrmann and Grasha, 1983, p. 184) combines the advantages of standards-referenced and norm-referenced approaches. Grades are assigned by comparing each student's score with the highest scores earned in the class:

- Compute a score for each student.
- Compute the mean score of the best-performing portion of the class:
  - For an average class, use the scores of the top 10 percent; for a superior class, the scores of the upper 15 or 20 percent; for a weak class, the upper 5 to 8 percent.
  - Add all the scores in this best-performing sample and divide by the number of scores in the sample. The result is the mean for the best performers.
- Assign grades according to a predetermined scale; for example: A = 95 percent of the mean of the best-performing sample, B = 85 percent of the mean, C = 75 percent of the mean, D = 65 percent of the mean.

In this model, class performance affects the score needed for each grade, but the number of students who can earn As and Bs is not limited. Some faculty take a shortcut by using the highest score (rather than the mean of the highest scores), but this shortcut is far too dependent on a single student's score.

Grading according to core and developmental objectives. In this model, the instructor identifies the *core objectives*, or essential content that all students must master to a satisfactory degree to receive a passing grade. The instructor also identifies those aspects of the content that students may never fully master but to which they can aspire (called *developmental objectives*). In Chemistry 1A, for example, core objectives would include the concepts, skills, and knowledge that students will need in order to be prepared for Chemistry 1B; developmental objectives might include "thinking like a scientist." The core objectives are graded against an absolute standard (students either know or do not know the core), but developmental objectives are graded by comparisons among students. (Source: Gronlund and Waugh, 2008)

Other Approaches

Self-grading and peer grading. Some faculty let students grade themselves. The grade must be accompanied by a detailed justification that takes into account the extent and level of their learning, their performance on exams and assignments, their perceived grasp of the material, the amount of time spent on the course, and the amount of reading completed. This approach has the advantage of fostering students' abilities to evaluate their work, but it abrogates one of the faculty's chief responsibilities, the rendering of professional judgments about students' learning and performance. Self-grading, however, can be used formatively to give students the skills they need to assess their own learning. Peer grading, where students grade one another's work, works best in classes that feature a lot of small-group work; see Chapter 21, "Learning in Groups," for suggestions. (Sources: Adams and King, 1995; Dochy et al., 1999; Jacobs and Chase, 1992; MacGregor, 1993; Strong et al., 2004)

Contract grading. In contract grading, instructors create a menu of required and elective assignments, and each student decides which assignments to do and how much weight each assignment will carry. For example, the following menu requires a student to make choices that total 200 points:

> Complete two required assignments:
>> Two exams (worth 20 to 35 points each)
>> Group project (50 to 70 points)
> In addition, complete two of these elective assignments:
>> Prepare an annotated bibliography (15 to 35 points)
>> Review a journal article (15 to 35 points)
>> Write the abstract of an unpublished manuscript (15 to 35 points)
>> Keep a weekly learning log (15 to 35 points)

Contract grading gives students choices in their learning goals and how they are evaluated, which may increase motivation and interest in learning. The drawback is the increased administrative burden, as instructors must develop grading alternatives, negotiate and renegotiate contracts, and keep track of each student's progress which quickly becomes impractical in medium- or large-enrollment courses. (Source: Hiller and Hietapelto, 2001)

Calculation of Final Grades for the Course

Become familiar with various methods. There are many different ways to calculate course grades, using weighted letter grades, accumulated points, median grading, and holistic grading or mastery of key elements; see Brookhart (1999), Ory and Ryan (1993), Walvoord and Anderson (1998), or Zlokovich (2004). One commonly used strategy is described below.

Convert the grades on all course components to numerical scores. Calculating final grades is usually easiest if the grades on all assignments are converted to numerical scores. For this purpose, many faculty use A = 95, A- = 90, B+ = 87, and so on. (Source: Brookhart, 1999; Forsyth, 2003)

Decide how to handle missing scores. Some instructors ignore the missing work and base their calculations on a student's other scores; other instructors take into account the reason for the missing work. If you want to assign a number for a missed assignment or test, your choices include (1) assigning a zero—but this is likely to overpenalize the student and is not recommended; (2) assigning a score at the bottom of the F range; (3) assigning a score somewhat lower than the lowest score earned by a classmate on the assignment; (4) assigning the lowest score earned by a classmate. (Sources: Brookhart, 1999; Forsyth, 2003)

Weight each course component. Use the weights that you announced at the beginning of the semester. In general, weights should reflect a component's importance to the course goals and its complexity and difficulty; in addition, most faculty assign greater weight to tests later in the term. One professor adjusts the weighting to reflect a student's performance: in a course with two midterms and a final, the student's highest test score is weighted 50 percent, the middle score 30 percent, and the lowest 20 percent. Students appreciate having their best work weighted so heavily in their course grade, but the disadvantage is that students do not know until after the final exam how much weight each component carries. (Sources: Brookhart, 1999; Dominowksi, 2002; Forsyth, 2003; Guskey and Bailey, 2001)

Create a composite score. Your grading software will adjust the numerical scores on each component by the weights you indicate and provide a composite score for each student. (If you are doing these calculations by hand, consult with your campus testing office.) You would then assign final grades using preset cutoff points (standards referenced) or relative standing in the class (norm referenced) or a hybrid method.

If you use a standards-referenced model, you can simplify the calculations by using a total-points method of grading as described by Forsyth (2003): at the beginning of the term, state the maximum number of points students can earn for each assignment and test, with these points reflecting the importance of each component. For example, each of two tests might be worth 100 points, the homework 150, and the final exam 150—for a total of 500 points. In order to earn an A, a student would need to accumulate 450 points (90 percent of 500 points).

If you use a norm-referenced model, you may need to take the additional step of equalizing the variances—otherwise a test with a wide range of scores will more heavily influence the final grades than a test with a narrower spread. Most testing and grading software perform these conversions; consult with your testing office for more information.

Review borderline cases. Because graders are fallible and grading is imprecise, take a careful look at students who fall right below the cutoff for a higher grade. Consider the full range of the student's achievement and trajectory of improved performance. Would dropping the first test score or the lowest test score bump up the final grade? If the final exam were cumulative, an instructor might give the higher grade if the student did particularly well.

One faculty member allows students to "purchase" grade "insurance" by completing a small number of problems any time before the final exam. If a student's course grade is not on the borderline, the insurance problems are not graded. But students within one percentage point of the cutoff will receive the higher grade if they answered the insurance problems correctly. Another faculty member includes an optional question on the final exam. The optional question is read only if a student is within five points of the next highest grade, and it is scored 0 through 5. (Sources: Brookhart, 1999; Dominowski, 2002; Peploski, 2004)

Decide how to handle improvement. Some faculty believe that course grades should take into account a measure of a student's growth and development over the semester. Otherwise, these faculty argue, a student who enters the course fairly knowledgeable will receive an A even if he or she learns very little or demonstrates little effort. But an overemphasis on improvement can also produce inequities: a student who scores 55 percent on the first two quizzes and 70 on the final has made substantial progress but knows less about the subject than the student who scored 85 on the first two quizzes and 88 on the final. And only the second student deserves a grade high enough to proceed to a more challenging upper-level course. Grading on the basis of improvement also makes it difficult for students to interpret what their grades mean: does a B mean that their work is above average or that their improvement is above average? Experts recommend that any bonus for improvement be quite modest: a few extra points for steady, significant improvement throughout the semester.

One math professor quantifies students' improvement over the semester. Say a class has two midterms worth 100 points each and a final worth 200 points. Ole's scores are 50 out of 100 on the first midterm, 80 out of 100 on the second midterm, and 190 out of 200 on the final. His unadjusted total score for the course is 320. To take into account Ole's steady improvement, the professor weights Ole's scores for the second midterm and final more heavily. The weight of the second midterm is calculated by subtracting Ole's score on the first midterm from the total points available for both first and second midterms, or $200 - 50 = 150$. His actual score on the second midterm is then multiplied by this weighting factor. Thus his adjusted score for the second midterm is $(200 - 50)(80/100) = 120$. His first score and his second, adjusted score are then added together, $50 + 120 = 170$. His adjusted score on the final is calculated using the same process. Ole's cumulative total score (170) is subtracted from the total points available for both midterms and the final (400). His actual score on the final is then multiplied by this new weighting factor, or $(400 - 170)(190/200) = 218.5$. To calculate the total adjusted score, add his adjusted score on the midterms (170) to his adjusted score on the final (218.5) for a total of 388.5. (Sources: McKeachie and Svinicki, 2006; Ory and Ryan, 1993)

Decide how to handle effort. Studies show that undergraduate students believe that if they work hard, they should receive at least a C in the course even if they cannot demonstrate that they have met the academic goals of the course. Most faculty, however, do not believe that effort (however measured) trumps learning in the assignment of grades. Experts recommend that instructors clarify this issue at the beginning of the term. (Sources: Adams, 2005; Gaultney and Cann, 2001; Miley and Gonsalves, 2004)

References

Adams, J. B. "What Makes the Grade? Faculty and Student Perceptions." *Teaching of Psychology*, 2005, *32*(1), 21–24.

Adams, C., and King, K. "Towards a Framework for Student Self-Assessment." *Innovations in Education and Training International*, 1995, *32*(4), 336–343.

Brookhart, S. M. "Art and Science of Classroom Assessment: The Missing Part of Pedagogy." *ASHE-ERIC Higher Education Report*, 1999, *27*(1). Washington, DC: George Washington University, Graduate School of Education and Human Development.

Dochy, F., Segers, M., and Sluijsmans, D. "The Use of Self-, Peer and Co-Assessments in Higher Education: A Review." *Studies in Higher Education*, 1999, *24*(3), 331–350.

Dominowski, R. L. *Teaching Undergraduates*. Mahwah, NJ: Erlbaum, 2002.

Forsyth, D. R. *The Professor's Guide to Teaching: Psychological Principles and Practices*. Washington, DC: American Psychological Association, 2003.

Frisbie, D. A., Diamond, N. A., and Ory, J. C. *Assigning Course Grades*. Urbana: Office of Instructional Resources, University of Illinois, 1979.

Fuhrmann, B. S., and Grasha, A. F. *A Practical Handbook for College Teachers*. Boston: Little, Brown, 1983.

Gaultney, J. F., and Cann, A. "Grade Expectations." *Teaching of Psychology*, 2001, *28*(2), 84–87.

Gronlund, N. E., and Waugh, C. K. *Assessment of Student Achievement*. (9th ed.) Boston: Allyn and Bacon, 2008.

Guskey, T. R., and Bailey, J. M. *Developing Grading and Reporting Systems for Student Learning.* Thousand Oaks, CA: Corwin Press, 2001.

Hanna, G. S., and Cashin, W. E. "Improving College Grading." *Idea Paper*, no. 19. Manhattan: Center for Faculty Evaluation and Development, Kansas State University, 1988.

Heppner, F. *Teaching the Large College Class: A Guidebook for Instructors with Multitudes.* San Francisco: Jossey-Bass, 2007.

Hiller, T. B., and Hietapelto, A. B. "Contract Grading: Encouraging Commitment to the Learning Process through Voice in the Evaluation Process." *Journal of Management Education*, 2001, *25*(6), 660–684.

Jacobs, L. C., and Chase, C. I. *Developing and Using Tests Effectively: A Guide for Faculty.* San Francisco: Jossey-Bass, 1992.

Lowman, J. *Mastering the Techniques of Teaching.* (2nd ed.) San Francisco: Jossey-Bass, 1995.

MacGregor, J. (Ed.). "Student Self-Evaluation: Fostering Reflective Learning." *New Directions in Teaching and Learning*, no. 56. San Francisco: Jossey-Bass, 1993.

McKeachie, W. J., and Svinicki, M. *McKeachie's Teaching Tips.* (12th ed.) Boston: Houghton Mifflin, 2006.

Miley, W. M., and Gonsalves, S. "Grade Expectations: Redux." *College Student Journal*, 2004, *38*(3), 327–332.

Ory, J. C., and Ryan, K. E. *Tips for Testing and Grading.* Newbury Park, CA: Sage, 1993.

Payne, D. A. *Applied Educational Assessment.* (2nd ed.) Belmont, CA: Wadsworth/Thomson, 2003.

Peploski, J. "Grade 'Insurance' in Large Enrollment Courses." *Teaching Professor*, October 2004, *18*(8), 6.

Sadler, R. "Interpretations of Criteria-Based Assessment and Grading in Higher Education." *Assessment and Evaluation in Higher Education*, April 2005, *30*(2), 175–194.

Shepard, L. A. Classroom Assessment. In R. L. Brennan (Ed.), *Educational Measurement.* (4th ed.) Westport, CT: American Council on Education/Praeger, 2006.

Strong, B., Davis, M., and Hawks, V. "Self-Grading in Large General Education Classes: A Case Study." *College Teaching*, 2004, *52*(2), 52–57.

Walvoord, B. E., and Anderson, V. J. *Effective Grading: A Tool for Learning and Assessment.* San Francisco: Jossey-Bass, 1998.

Zlokovich, M. S. Grading for Optimal Student Learning. In B. Perlman, L. I. McCann, and S. H. McFadden (Eds.), *Lessons Learned: Practical Advice for the Teaching of Psychology.* Vol. 2. Washington, DC: American Psychological Society, 2004.

PART IX

Presentation Technologies

45

Flipcharts

Like a chalkboard, a flipchart—a large pad of newsprint paper that sits on an easel or display stand—can be used for prepared material or for impromptu jottings. The advantages of flipcharts include portability (important for instructors conducting an outdoor field class) and ease of preparation. Select a pad that is at least 22 inches by 32 inches. Flipcharts are best used with small groups; for larger groups, consider using overhead projection (see Chapter 48).

General Strategies

Use flipcharts to highlight the organization of your presentation, to emphasize its main points, and to stimulate students' interest. Whether you prepare a flipchart before class or write on it during class, you can use it to visually reinforce your presentation. For example, you can use it for the following purposes:

- Outline the day's topics or schedule.
- Write difficult names, terminology, or unfamiliar vocabulary.
- Show diagrams, charts, graphs, drawings, or illustrations.
- List important dates.
- Work through formulas, proofs, or theorems.
- Summarize major points.
- Capture students' ideas.

Write legibly. In small rooms, two-inch-high lettering should suffice; in larger rooms, use four-inch-high lettering. Be sure to print. Limit the amount of material on each sheet to a few key words or main points. Highlight important points by underlining, boxing, or using color. Bold colors such as red, dark blue, and black work best. Graphs or pie charts are preferable to tables for representing numerical data.

Don't turn your back to the class to look at the flipchart. With practice you can flip the pages without breaking eye contact. If you use a pointer and stand off to the side, you will be able to face the class without obstructing your students' view of the chart.

Bring extra pens. Keep a fresh set of spares handy.

Using a Flipchart as a Chalkboard

Organize your work. Start at the top left-hand corner and work across and then down to the next line, as you would on a blank piece of paper. Place important material at the top of the page, the most visible portion of the flipchart. Alternate colors for each new point or idea to make the text easier to read.

Use the same principles for writing on flipcharts as you would for the chalkboard. For example, use titles and headings to structure your work, underline or box off key statements, give students time to copy what you have written, distribute complex diagrams or drawings online or on hard copy rather than have students try to copy them.

Give your students experience using flipcharts. Flipcharts are common in industry, and students can benefit from using them in small-group work. Ask your students to use flipcharts to brainstorm ideas, develop options, and solve problems. (Source: Wankat and Oreovicz, 2001)

Using Prepared Flipcharts

Place the sheets in order. If you will be referring to a particular chart or diagram at several points during your presentation, it may be easier to include a copy of that page at each point rather than having to flip back and forth to find it. If you do plan to flip through the pad, tab key pages with large sticky notes to help you find important material quickly.

Don't spend too long on each page. Plan each sheet so that you change pages within a few minutes. If you want to spend more time on one point, devote more than one page to it.

Follow the practices for making PowerPoint presentations. After revealing a flipchart, hesitate briefly before speaking to give students time to scan the material you are showing; don't read material on the flipchart that students can read for themselves. (See Chapter 51, "PowerPoint Presentations.")

Reference

Wankat, P., and Oreovicz, F. "Turning Back the Clock: Simple Aids Make Teaching Effective without Denting Your Budget." *ASEE PRISM*, 2001, *11*(4). http://www.prism-magazine .org/dec01/teaching.cfm

46

Chalkboards and Whiteboards

Chalkboards and large wipe-off whiteboards are dependable and useful tools for displaying text and diagrams. These kinds of boards provide much more display area than electronic displays, and they do not need plugs or connections, do not crash, and allow content to be changed on the fly (Forsyth, 2003; O'Hare, 1993). The disadvantage of chalk and whiteboards is the ephemeral nature of their contents. Board work also requires the instructor to write legibly and to organize arrays of terms, examples, and diagrams (Forsyth, 2003).

Some instructors arrive well before the start of class and write detailed outlines and diagrams on the board. Others use the board only during class, writing a key term or critical diagram as it comes up or listing students' responses to a question. Because most students copy or photograph using their cell phones exactly what appears on the board, it is worthwhile to take some care in planning your board work.

General Strategies

Analyze your current use of the board. O'Hare (1993) characterizes different types of use of the board as "slides" (notes prepared in advance and written on the board before class starts); "lecture notes" (putting up key terms or points as you present them during class); and "public notes" (putting up key terms or points as raised by students). The "slide" approach tends to transmit to students that what you are going to say is fixed, and their participation will not change the discourse. "Lecture notes" invite more interaction. With "public notes," student input affects what gets written on the board.

Use the board to provide visual reinforcement, to highlight the organization of your presentation, and to emphasize your main points. You can use the board in the following ways:

- Outline the session's topics or main points. If you write the complete outline in advance, students can see where you are headed and find their place when their attention drifts. Or you can generate the outline as you go, adding each new item as you begin to talk about it (Waksler, 1996).

- Summarize ideas raised during class discussion.
- Write out proper names, unfamiliar vocabulary, and new terminology.
- Present diagrams, graphs, and time lines.
- Show formulas, computations, or steps in a proof.

   If possible, arrange your board work so that you can erase details and leave the key points as a summary.

Give students time to take notes. Students tend to copy everything an instructor writes on the board, but they cannot copy and listen to new information at the same time. Let them catch up with you before you resume lecturing or continue a discussion. One instructor received a good suggestion from her class about how to reduce her tendency to erase too quickly: park her eraser on a nearby table, rather than on the chalk tray. Sometimes students will photograph or take a video of the board rather than take notes. Let students know that the act of writing can help reinforce their learning. (Sources: Lowman, 1995; White et al., 1978)

If class size permits, invite students to work at the board. In language, quantitative, and other courses, you can have several students working independently at the board at the same time. You can use student board work to gain insights into students' thinking, problem-solving, and writing processes. Some instructors encourage students to experiment by erasing and revising as they go, or to ask and respond to questions from others at the board. You may want to precede student work at the board with individual or pair work in their seats, then bring good examples to the board for "publication." Dobbs (1997) offers tips on making the board "part of the student's domain." Jones (1993) and Black (1993) describe different ways to have small groups of students each tackle a chemistry problem at the board, followed by class discussion of the results.

Visual Reinforcement

Create a public record. Use the board to annotate the steps or phases of a discussion. This kind of record can help students in thinking through a problem, and it also helps to preserve remarks or questions that might otherwise get lost. Leave competing analyses or points of view on the board until all are explained or resolved. (Sources: O'Hare, 1993; Waksler, 1996)

Record students' comments verbatim. When using the board to summarize a discussion, write exactly what the student says. If the comment is dubious, put it in the form of a question, with the speaker's okay. (Source: O'Hare, 1993)

Take special care with diagrams. Practice drawing your diagrams before class. If a diagram will grow larger as the lecture progresses, let students know how much room to leave in their notes. If you are modifying a drawing, use dotted lines or colored chalk or colored markers to show the changes, and give students enough time to copy the modified diagram. (Source: White et al., 1978)

In quantitative classes, write complete statements of what you propose to prove. When writing out proofs, define any special notation. Include all important steps. Do not simplify steps by erasing them; instead, use a single strikethrough.

Be selective. Write down only the basic principles and indicate the omission of details ("Computation omitted"). If your board work involves complex diagrams or detailed derivations, make available an online or hard-copy handout so that students will have an accurate rendering of what is on the board.

Explain any mistakes you have made in your board work before correcting them. If you make an error, make sure your students know exactly where the error lies before you erase and correct it.

Visually highlight important points. Before you leave a topic, emphasize the major points, assumptions, or conclusions by underlining, circling, or otherwise marking key words on the board.

Hands-on Tips

For chalkboards, use large railroad chalk. It is easier to print legibly with large chalk. Stick with yellow or white chalk. Red, blue, and green chalk are difficult to see.

Avoid squeaking chalk. To avoid spine-tingling screeches, hold the chalk at a 45-degree angle and press it firmly against the board. Breaking the chalk in half will also stop an annoying squeak.

For whiteboards, use different colored markers. Black and blue are easiest to read. Avoid yellow and orange.

Write clearly. Check a sample of your board writing from the back of the room before class. Bold block letters about 3 inches high should be readable from about 30 feet away. Arrange the window shades so that there is no glare on the board. After you write something, stand to the side so that the board is visible to everyone. (Sources: Svinicki and Lewis, 2002; White et al., 1978)

Read aloud while you write. Reading aloud is especially important for math and science instructors who write formulas on the board, and this will also help students with visual disabilities. This technique allows students to write while you do, helping them keep up with the presentation. Avoid discussing other points while you are at the board with your back turned to your students.

Name the items you are pointing to. When talking about terms on the board, instead of saying "this" or "there," name the thing you are pointing to ("the concept of freedom," "the head of the party"). This way, students who are taking notes will not miss your reference, and audio-recorded notes or podcasts will be more comprehensible. (Source: Waksler, 1996)

Erase old work. Erase other instructors' board work before your class begins, and erase your board work throughout class after students have had a chance to copy it and before you move on to a new topic. Students will use the moment to catch up with you and refocus their attention. At the end of class, as a courtesy, erase the board for the next instructor.

Structure your board work. Use titles, headings, underlining, circling, boxing, and capital letters to differentiate and emphasize items. You can also organize your work by dividing the board into sections; for example, work out proofs and computations on the right-hand panel, and list major theorems on the left. Or list students' arguments on the right, and summarize the conclusions on the left.

Use the most visible parts of the board for the most important points. The upper left-hand corner of the board is the most prominent spot. Notice whether students are craning their necks or shifting positions as they write—a sure sign that your board work is hard to see. Be sure that materials on your desk or lectern do not obstruct the view. (Source: White et al., 1978).

With sliding three-layer chalkboards, fill the middle panel first. After the middle panel is full, push it up and pull down the front board—this keeps what you have written in sight. Finally, push up the front board and use the back board. (Source: White et al., 1978)

Take spare chalk or markers and erasers to class. If the chalk is in small pieces or the markers dried out, you will have your own set.

Evaluating Your Board Work

Ask students to let you know whether your board work is clear. You can also take a moment after class to walk to the back of the room and critique your board work before erasing it. (Source: Svinicki and Lewis, 2002)

Ask one or two students to lend you their notes. Explain that you want to get a sense of how well you are doing. Note how much the students are copying from the board and what they are copying. Are the essential points clear? (Source: White et al., 1978)

References

Black, K. A. "What to Do When You Stop Lecturing: Become a Guide and a Resource." *Journal of Chemical Education*, 1993, *70*(2), 140–144.

Dobbs, J. "The Blackboard as an Active/Interactive Language Teaching Tool." *College ESL*, 1997, *7*(2).

Forsyth, D. R. *The Professor's Guide to Teaching: Psychological Principles and Practices*. Washington, DC: American Psychological Association, 2003.

Jones, M. B. "A Day at the Blackboard." *Journal of College Science Teaching*, 1993, *22*(5), 308.

Lowman, J. *Mastering the Techniques of Teaching*. (2nd ed.) San Francisco: Jossey-Bass, 1995.

O'Hare, M. "Talk and Chalk: the Blackboard as an Intellectual Tool." *Journal of Policy Analysis and Management*, 1993, *12*(1).

Svinicki, M. D., and Lewis, K. G. "Media Aids for the Classroom." Center for Teaching Effectiveness, University of Texas at Austin, October 3, 2002. http://www.utexas.edu/academic/cte/sourcebook/media.pdf

Waksler, R. "Teaching Strategies for a Barrier Free Classroom." *Journal on Excellence in College Teaching*, 1996, *7*(2), 99–111.

White, S., Hennessey, R., and Napell, S. "Blackboardsmanship for Neophytes." *Journal of College Science Teaching*, 1978, *7*(3), 178–179.

47

Interactive Whiteboards

Interactive whiteboards (also called *electronic whiteboards* or *smart boards*) are oversized projection screens that are hooked up to laptops and to the Internet. Interactive whiteboards can display notes that are placed on the board, files that are stored on the computer, and pages downloaded from the Internet. Some interactive whiteboards accept both text that an instructor types on the computer and notes handwritten directly on the board with a stylus. All the typed or written notes are easily saved as computer files; they can then be sent by e-mail, posted to a Web page, incorporated into a blog, or printed out and distributed to students. Instructors can also record an accompanying audio track.

The primary advantage of using an interactive whiteboard is that the presentation can include a range of prepared text, graphics, video, and sound. In addition, students' attention is on the course material rather than on their individual laptops or mobile learning devices, where the lure of online shopping or gaming might distract them (Smith et al., 2005). The principal disadvantages are the preparation time, the time needed to master the equipment, and the need for tech support to troubleshoot problems (Glover et al., 2005).

General Strategies

Exploit the multimedia capabilities. An electronic board is not simply a replacement for a conventional board. Experiment with multimedia presentations and webstreaming, for example, to show cells as they change during an experiment or to present maps, artwork, and audio accompanying a lecture on a battle during the Civil War.

Emphasize the interactivity. Invite students up to the board for problem solving, collaborative learning, and other activities. Beauchamp and Parkinson (2005) describe how a science instructor uses interactive whiteboards to engage students in discussion and generate hypotheses: On the board, the instructor displays a video of a solid being heated as well as a table and graph that plot temperature against time. Groups of students are asked to explain what happens to the particles as the temperature increases, and the students write their explanation on the board. The instructor then uses simulation software to explain particle movement at various temperatures and to compare the results with the students' hypotheses.

Hands-on Tips

Use a wireless keyboard. A wireless keyboard allows you to move to the back or side of the room and see the board from the students' perspective. Students can then focus their attention on the screen instead of on you.

Select materials judiciously. Resist the temptation to present extensive amounts of material. Overloading students with information can overwhelm or frustrate them. Edit carefully what you present to make certain it matches your learning goals.

Double-check any links you plan to use. Bookmark the sites and check them right before class. Students will quickly tune out if they have to watch you struggle to find the right Web page.

Use the screen to focus students' attention. As students walk into class, post reminders or the outline for the day or a starter activity for students to do in their seats.

References

Beauchamp, G., and Parkinson, J. "Beyond the Wow Factor: Developing Interactivity with the Interactive Whiteboard." *School Science Review*, 2005, *86*(316), 97–103.

Glover, D., Miller, D., Averis, D., and Door, V. "The Interactive Whiteboard: A Literature Survey." *Technology, Pedagogy and Education*, 2005, *14*(2), 155–170.

Smith, H. J., Higgins, S., Wall, K., and Miller, J. "Interactive Whiteboards: Boon or Bandwagon? A Critical Review of the Literature." *Journal of Computer Assisted Learning*, 2005, *21*(2), 91–101.

48

Overhead Projection

Most campuses have several types of projectors available for classroom use:

- Overhead transparency projectors cast onto a screen the text or image that appears on a transparent plastic sheet. Tabletop overhead projectors are easy to operate and can be used in well-lighted or partially darkened rooms. Speakers can prepare transparencies in advance or write on a blank transparency during their presentation.
- Digital document cameras project onto a large screen both two-dimensional objects (including detailed drawings, photographs, and newspaper articles) and three-dimensional objects (such as a live experiment in real time with vials of fruit flies). In effect, the document camera is an overhead projector that has the capabilities of a scanner, microscope, and computer; for example, it can zoom, freeze-frame, and display an object from different angles.
- LCD (liquid crystal display) projectors and DLP (digital light processing) projectors are hooked up to a computer and display video, data, and text files onto a screen or other flat surface.

In the classroom, all three types of projectors have advantages over chalkboards and whiteboards (adapted from O'Hare, 1993; Paldy, 1997):

- Instructors can easily prepare good-looking transparencies and digital images using commercial software, and they can reuse these materials as desired.
- Instructors can write on transparencies or use the computer while facing their students.
- Projected images are clearer and easier to view than images on chalkboards.
- The projector can be dimmed or turned off during the presentation to focus students' attention on the instructor or on other materials.

However, overhead projection entails some inconveniences (O'Hare, 1993; Paldy, 1997):

- The screen is typically smaller than a chalkboard or interactive whiteboard.
- The noise from the equipment or cooling fan may be distracting.

- The instructor may have to remain near the equipment when using it.
- Arrangements to reserve, borrow, and return shared equipment can be bothersome.

The following sections discuss the use of transparency projectors; many of the tips are applicable to other types of projection.

General Strategies

Use transparencies to track your presentation. You can highlight the organization of your presentation, emphasize your main points, stimulate students' interests, and record and synthesize the discussion. Limit yourself to no more than a dozen transparencies in a fifty-minute lecture. (Source: Cook, 1995)

Make certain that students can view the screen and the image. Focus the projector before class and make sure the classroom lighting does not interfere with the image. Placing the projector slightly at the side of the room, rather than the center, offers better sight lines. Experts recommend the projector be about six feet or so from the screen. Keep an extra lamp handy, and know how to replace a burned-out bulb. Slightly dimming the lights in the room will improve visibility. (Source: Cook, 1995)

Maintain eye contact with your students. Stand to the side of the projector so that you don't block the screen. Don't turn your back to the class to look at the screen; glance at the screen only to check the focus or visibility. Move away from the projector when you don't need to tend it. (Source: Cook, 1995)

Get students' feedback. One instructor, very proud of his overheads, apologized to the class one day when he had mislaid them. The class rose and applauded. The instructor analyzed and improved his technique. (Source: Cook, 1995)

Using an Overhead Projector as a Chalkboard

Write on transparencies just as you would write on a chalkboard. Start writing at the top left-hand corner and work across and then down to the next line; use titles, headings, and underlining or colors to emphasize key statements; give students time to copy what you have written; distribute copies of complex diagrams or drawings. If you make a mistake or want to reuse the sheet, erase the material with a damp tissue or cloth.

Limit the amount of material on a single transparency. Print in capital and lowercase letters. Write no more than seven lines of text per transparency and no more than seven words per line. One-inch-high letters should be legible at a distance of thirty-two feet; in a smaller room, use smaller lettering. Test out various sizes of lettering in your classroom under typical viewing conditions. (Sources: Cook, 1995; Svinicki and Lewis, 2002)

Use color. Use blue or black ink; red or green may be hard to read. Highlight important points as you go by underlining and boxing with colored pens intended for use on transparencies. (The ink in regular felt-tip pens does not adhere to the plastic.)

Use a small pointer. Have a pointer that will rest in place on the transparency (Cook, 1995, recommends small plastic cocktail stirrers). Because any pointer movement will be magnified by projection, you need to move the pointer slowly and steadily over the transparency. Rapid movements will be startling, and small shakes can look like major tremors on the screen.

Place a piece of non-transparent paper on the projector to signal a pause. When you are talking but no longer referring to a transparency, darken the screen by placing a piece of semiopaque paper on the projector. (A blank lighted screen can be distracting, but turning off the machine can make the room seem too dark, and some projectors will lock up if switched off and then switched on too soon).

Creating Sets of Transparencies

Use word processing, presentation, or graphing software. It's easy to produce nice-looking transparencies on a computer, and you can also print out hard copies or post the transparencies online. Pick a sans serif font (like Helvetica), and use uppercase and lowercase letters of at least 30–40 points. Format your page in landscape (using the width of the page, not the length) so text is not cut off by heads in the audience. If your printer doesn't handle transparency sheets, check with your institution's media center or go to a commercial copy shop. (Sources: Cook, 1995; Gribas et al., 1996)

Take care in preparing handwritten transparencies. Use permanent ink if you intend to reuse the transparency; otherwise use water-soluble ink or a grease pencil. The best colors are black, blue, and green. Letters approximately one-quarter to one-half inch tall will project well in a small classroom. Place a sheet of lined paper underneath the transparency to serve as a guide as you write on the sheet. To prevent smudging, place a clean sheet of paper under your hand.

Showing Prepared Transparencies

Arrange your transparencies in the order you will show them. Make sure that your notes match the same sequence. Flag the margins of your notes to show when to put up the next transparency. To avoid exposing the light when you change transparencies, hold the new one above and drop it as you remove the old one.

After displaying a transparency, wait briefly before speaking. Give students time to scan the material; don't read it for them. Leave the transparency up long enough for students to take notes or photograph the material; let them know if you are going to post the image online.

Place a clear plastic sheet on top of transparencies you will use repeatedly. On the plastic overlay, you can highlight or emphasize key parts of the permanent transparency or add details to it.

Bring at least one blank transparency to class. Use the blank transparency to record students' ideas, expand a concept briefly mentioned, or clarify issues raised during class.

References

Cook, D. "Use and Abuse of Overhead Transparencies." University of Alberta, *Teaching and Learning Exchange*, 1995, *2*(3).

Gribas, C., Sykes, L., and Dorochoff, N. "Creating Great Overheads with Computers." *College Teaching*, 1996, *44*(2).

O'Hare, M. "Talk and Chalk: The Blackboard as an Intellectual Tool." *Journal of Policy Analysis and Management*, 1993, *12*(1).

Paldy, L. G. "Graphics in the Lecture Hall." *Journal of College Science Teaching*, 1997, *27*(1), 4–5.

Svinicki, M. D., and Lewis, K. G. "Media Aids for the Classroom." Center for Teaching Effectiveness, University of Texas at Austin, October 3, 2002. http://www.utexas.edu/academic/cte/sourcebook/media.pdf

49

Slide Shows

In some courses—in art history, architecture, and plant biology, for example—a considerable portion of class time may be devoted to the showing of digital slides. But images can add interest, variety, and instructional value to presentations in any field. One image can engage students in ways that verbal or written descriptions cannot. The chief disadvantage of projecting images on a screen is that the room must be darkened, which may make it hard for students who are taking notes on paper (but not on laptops).

Because photographic slides degrade over time, some experts recommend converting photographic slides to digital files (Pitt et al., 2002). Many inexpensive scanners can do these conversions, with varying results and speed. More sophisticated equipment is needed to ensure the faithful reproduction of colors or to make other adjustments to the images (Carlson, 2005; Lancy, 1999). While photographic images are sharper and can be more beautiful, digital images are more expedient, easier to store, and offer the option of adding text or diagrams to the original image. Some campuses provide digital conversion services.

General Strategies

Use images to reinforce concepts, illustrate ideas, or stimulate students' interest. You can use images to illustrate the steps of a process, to clarify spatial or visual relationships, and to show objects or source documents. (Source: Pitt et al., 2002)

Design your presentation around your images. Your images and lecture should complement each other. If you have only six or seven images, you may want to group them all together rather than dispersing them throughout a fifty-minute class. Or you may want to create several small content units around each slide.

Be aware of copyright law. Under the fair-use provisions of U.S. copyright law, instructors may make one copy for educational purposes of a copyrighted image from a book or periodical without asking permission from the copyright holder.

But copyright law is evolving, and provisions for copying images from the Internet are, in particular, likely to change. To prepare for future contingencies, keep notes on the source of each image. These source notes will also be important if you later want to use an image to illustrate an article, essay, or monograph. (Source: Lancy, 1999)

Locating and Creating Slides

Take advantage of existing collections. Examine on-campus collections of photographic slides and digital images. Network with other faculty to share and explore resources. Research online providers of images in your field such as ARTstor or Getty Images. (Source: Rockenbach and Marmor, 2005)

Create your own images. Using a computer, a scanner, a photocopier, and a camera, you can copy and modify almost any print or online image. Most textbook illustrations and detailed maps, however, reproduce poorly; look for simpler maps that emphasize the most important locations or routes. Use word processing, graphics, and spreadsheet software to create diagrams, graphs, and charts. For those images that will not be on the screen for long, don't spend too much time on production values. Strive for well-lighted images that have good contrast and little or no distracting or extraneous information. (Source: Svinicki and Lewis, 2002)

Choose software that suits your needs and skills. If you have not used image-editing software before, ask colleagues and students for suggestions about what program might suit your needs. Sophisticated programs such as Photoshop can create wonderful, complex images, but these programs take time and patience to learn. If your goal is to produce simple flowcharts, you may well prefer to work with simpler tools.

Hands-on Tips

Arrange for a small light for your notes. If the podium in your classroom is not equipped with a light, bring a flashlight.

Use a laser pointer. A manual pointer or hand gesture may get lost in the projected image.

Use an LCD projector with a wireless remote control. For maximum mobility, select a projector that has a wireless remote control. Most remote devices have three buttons (forward, reverse, focus) and are easy to operate.

Show an image for about one to three minutes. You want to give students time to study the image and listen to what you are saying about it. Experienced faculty show no more than forty images in a fifty-minute talk, and more typically twenty to thirty. Show fewer, better slides rather than rush through many unless your point is to run through a lot of quick images. As appropriate, pan, zoom in, and zoom out on the image and details. Present images side by side for comparisons or perspectives.

As appropriate, ask students to sketch the images in their notes. Drawing the images will reinforce students' comprehension and retention. In addition to posting the images on the course Web site, you can also post them outside your office and invite students to come by and improve their sketches. Don't be surprised if some of the sketchers form spontaneous discussion groups.

In large classes, show images while students are arriving. By showing images while students are settling in, you can direct their attention to the front of the room, which may make it easier to call the class to order. When the room lights are on, only stark, simple images will be viewable. (Source: McKeachie and Svinicki, 2006)

References

Carlson, S. "Ditch the Slide Projector: An Art Professor Brings Paintings to Life with Software." *Chronicle of Higher Education,* June 24, 2005.

Lancy, D. F. "Teaching with Technology—Digital Slides." *College Teaching,* 1999, *47*(3), 82–83.

McKeachie, W. J., and Svinicki, M. *McKeachie's Teaching Tips.* (12th ed.) Boston: Houghton Mifflin, 2006.

Pitt, S. P., Updike, C. B., and Guthrie, M. E. "Integrating Digital Images into the Art and Art History Curriculum." *Educause Quarterly,* 2002, *25*(2), 38–44.

Rockenbach, B., and Marmor, M. "ARTstor's Digital Landscape." *Library Journal,* 2005, *130*(12), 34–37.

Svinicki, M. D., and Lewis, K. G. "Media Aids for the Classroom." Center for Teaching Effectiveness, University of Texas at Austin, October 3, 2002. http://www.utexas.edu/academic/cte/sourcebook/media.pdf

50

Video Recordings and Clips

On most campuses, equipment for viewing and producing video is available through a media center or library, and many campuses have extensive collections of video content. Videos of various types may also be downloaded from the Internet; sites like YouTube, Video Google, and Video Yahoo offer thousands of short clips and, increasingly, full lectures on various topics. Broadcasts of selected television documentaries, panel discussions, public affairs programs, and how-to and entertainment shows are also available online at the channel's Web site or at third-party video sites.

Some instructors and students produce their own videos of scientific experiments, interviews, performances, and guest speakers. In some classes, students submit video projects or term projects that have a video component.

If you are planning to record and present to your class material that is copyrighted by others (for example, all or a portion of a television program), ask your campus copyright officer, media staff, or librarians for help in determining whether you need written permission from the copyright holder.

General Strategies

Use "trigger" video clips. Some instructors use short video clips to trigger or stimulate classroom discussion, break up a long lecture, provoke an emotional response, or capture students' attention. For example, social psychology instructors found that showing relevant content clips generated student interest and improved their comprehension of basic concepts. (Source: Eaton and Uskul, 2004)

Match videos to learning objectives. For example, video can effectively replace some live demonstrations in science classes, saving instructors time and effort (Laroche et al., 2003). Longer video presentations should serve particular learning objectives, such as the teaching of a process or the understanding of a distant time or place. Analyze your objectives, and structure appropriate activities for before, during, and after the video presentation.

View the entire video before you show it to the class. Make sure that the content is appropriate for your students and that the video is the best way for students to learn the concepts or material you want to teach. Decide whether you want to show the video during class or assign students to view it as homework. While you prescreen the material, pause to jot down questions to raise with the class after the presentation.

Structure an Active Viewing Experience

Prepare your students to see the video. Explain why you are showing a video and what you expect students to learn from it. Does the video demonstrate examples of key concepts, review material previously covered, or pose a new problem? Relate the video to what your students already know about the subject, and introduce new terms or proper names on the board.

Provide guiding questions. Research suggests that students gain more factual knowledge from watching a video and are more successful at drawing inferences from it if they write answers to open-ended guiding questions while they watch the video. This procedure is more effective than pausing a video in order to pose comprehension questions to the class. (Sources: Kreiner, 1997; Lawson et al., 2006)

Pair a video with a reading assignment. Bassham and Nardone (1997), for example, discuss the topic of critical thinking by pairing the feature film *JFK* with relevant readings.

Break up or rearrange parts of the viewing. You can pause a video to ask students to predict what will happen next. Or stop the video to discuss their developing view of an issue before they see the outcome. Or show the ending or outcome first and challenge students to describe the earlier phase or steps.

Conduct a follow-up activity. After the presentation, engage students in assessing the meaning of what they have seen and its relationship to the course content. You could lead a discussion, ask students to write a brief analysis, or have them form small groups to resolve problems or discuss issues raised in the video.

Hands-on Tips

Have students generate their own videos. Some instructors teach by guiding students through a process of recording events or phenomena and then analyzing them. (Source: Lessie, 2001)

When you show a video in class, view it with your students. You can learn a great deal by observing your students as they watch the video. Refrain from showing videos as a way to occupy students during your absence or while you do other things.

Put students' equipment to work. Many students bring video hardware to every class: laptops, cell phones, and other display devices. You can avail yourself of this equipment by assigning small groups to analyze different videos or portions of a video and then report back to the class as part of a broader investigation.

References

Bassham, G., and Nardone, H. "Using the Film *JFK* to Teach Critical Thinking." *College Teaching*, 1997, *45*(1), 10.

Eaton, J., and Uskul, A. K. "Using *The Simpsons* to Teach Social Psychology." *Teaching of Psychology*, 2004, *31*(4), 277–278.

Kreiner, D. S. "Guided Notes and Interactive Methods for Teaching with Videotapes." *Teaching of Psychology*, 1997, *24*(3), 183–185.

Laroche, L. H., Wulfsberg, G., and Young, B. "Discovery Videos: A Safe, Tested, Time-Efficient Way to Incorporate Discovery-Laboratory Experiments into the Classroom." *Journal of Chemical Education*, 2003, *80*(8), 962–966.

Lawson, T. J., Bodle, J. H., Houlette, M. A., and Haubner, R. R. "Guiding Questions Enhance Student Learning from Educational Videos." *Teaching of Psychology*, 2006, *33*(1), 31–33.

Lessie, D. "Video Capture and Analysis: Seizing on Computer Technology to Teach the Physical Sciences." *Journal of College Science Teaching*, 2001, *30*(4).

51

PowerPoint Presentations

Various software programs can be used to create slides of formatted text and graphics, but Microsoft's PowerPoint has so dominated the market that many people use *PowerPoint* as though it were a generic term. Proponents say that PowerPoint and similar programs are quick and effective tools that save instructors time, reduce the note-taking burden on students (since they can obtain hard copy of the slides), and allow presentations to be easily modified, annotated, and archived (Doumant, 2005; Lyons et al., 2003). Critics use the slogans "PowerPointless" and "Death by PowerPoint" to describe the intellectual and pedagogical disadvantages of these slide shows: the hierarchical outline structure drives the presentation, requiring that ideas be reworked and truncated into bullet points; the click-click format serves to dilute content, oversimplify complicated ideas, discourage spontaneity, hinder serious analysis, and turn viewers into passive and uncritical thinkers (Adams, 2006; Klemm, 2007; Tufte, 2006).

Researchers who have looked at the effects of PowerPoint in the classroom report that students tend to be satisfied with the presentations, but the impact on student learning is mixed (Apperson et al., 2006; Bartsch and Cobern, 2003; Hardin, 2007; James et al., 2006; Susskind, 2005). PowerPoint appears to neither hinder nor enhance student learning (Clark, 2008; Levasseur and Sawyer, 2006; Noppe et al., 2007).

The suggestions below will help you avoid common problems with PowerPoint. For advice on the technical aspects, consult your campus technology center or read the materials developed by other universities, such as the University of Washington (catalyst.washington.edu).

General Strategies

Use PowerPoint selectively. Don't use PowerPoint at every session of class, and don't use it for the full class period. Combine short PowerPoint presentations with other media and with board work. (Source: Gallagher and Reder, 2004–05)

Never read your slides. Use the slides to highlight your talking points or headings. Reading slides aloud, as though from a teleprompter, is perhaps the single most boring thing an instructor can do in the classroom.

Do not give away the store. Research shows that PowerPoint enhances learning when students can print copies of course slides. Avoid making so much material available for downloading that students see little reason to come to class. Remind students of the important role writing notes plays in the learning process. Some faculty omit some material from the downloadable version—that material is presented only in class. If you are showing slides that accompany a textbook, add other material so that students will not feel that the class is merely a summary of the book. Some faculty prepare "talking points" that students are to download before class and come prepared to discuss. Other faculty, as course size permits, distribute skeletal notes in advance of class, with key terms, a general outline, and diagrams that students fill in during class. Note: Because not all students have access to PowerPoint software, post your notes in PDF format which is free. (Sources: Levasseur and Sawyer, 2006; Klemm, 2007; Noppe et al., 2007; Quible, 2002)

Have a contingency plan. If a technical problem arises, don't waste class time trying to fix it. Come prepared with a backup plan—a batch of hard copies of your presentation or a set of transparencies for an overhead projector. (Source: Lyons et al., 2003)

Preparing a Presentation

Design your presentation with learning principles in mind. Research on multimedia learning shows that the following characteristics make learning more effective (adapted from Mayer, 2005):

- words and images rather than words alone
- no extraneous material
- a conversational style rather than a formal style
- organization of material with clear outlines and headings
- corresponding words and images presented at the same time or next to each other on a screen
- animations presented with spoken words rather than printed text

Limit the number of slides. Some faculty suggest limiting PowerPoint presentations to fifteen minutes in an hour-long class. If you want to do a longer presentation, researchers recommend no more than thirty slides for a forty-five-minute presentation, leaving fifteen minutes for discussion at the end. (Source: Bates and Poole, 2003)

Be economical with text. When students are reading a slide, they are not listening to you. For landscape-oriented slides, follow the "one slide, one idea" principle. Text should run no more than a sentence or two headline. Use a plain, sans serif typeface (Arial, Helvetica, or Lucida Grande), capital and lowercase, in a bold font of 18 to 30 points. (Sources: Alley, 2003; Yaffe, 2008)

Limit the number of bulleted lists. Because you are limited to a few words, bulleted lists may truncate complex ideas, leave critical information unspecified, or lead to superficial generalizations. If you do use bullets, keep the list to a few items and the text parallel in structure. (Sources: Alley, 2003; Tufte, 2006)

Use graphs and diagrams instead of tables. Graphs are easier to read and comprehend than tables; if tables are needed, distribute them as a handout. Double-check each graph to make sure you have defined the variables, labeled each axis, and labeled the units.

Choose colors carefully. For most purposes, you will want to use white type on a dark background. A white screen with black type can be hard on the eyes. Avoid combinations where the background swallows the text: white text on red; white on blue; yellow on blue; blue on yellow; red on black. Select color combinations that make the text easy to read. About 8 to 10 percent of men have some degree of color-blindness (usually red-green blindness), so be sure that important colors differ in brightness as well. Unless you have a background in graphic design, limit yourself to two or three colors per slide. (Sources: Marieb and Hoehn, 2006; Yaffe, 2008)

Avoid eye-candy. Research indicates that elaborate slide constructions can actually result in less learning. Resist the temptation to add flying text, clip art, animation, and sound. Instead of trying to jazz up uninteresting content, choose interesting content. Use static images, simple backgrounds, and good contrast between them. When in doubt about an image, leave it out. Do not use sound unless it is directly related to your point. (Source: Levasseur and Sawyer, 2006)

Conduct a tech rehearsal. To make sure the text and graphics are legible, preview the slides under conditions similar to those in your classroom. Rework any slides that are too cluttered or too detailed. Use handouts, rather than slides, for complex diagrams.

Hands-on Tips

Monitor and maintain student engagement. A steady stream of slides lulls students into passivity. Direct and refocus students' attention by asking questions or including slides that pose questions. Maintain eye contact with students. (Source: Klemm, 2007)

Make certain that the slide on view corresponds to what you are saying. Temporarily blank out a slide when you are making comments unrelated to that slide or interacting with students to engage them in discussion. Otherwise students will be distracted by trying to puzzle out the relationship between your words and the slide. (Source: Klemm, 2007)

Bring spontaneity to your presentation. For example, you can use digital ink pens to annotate your slides during your presentation. Erase as needed, and save the results for later distribution to students.

Place an image on the screen as students enter the classroom. The image can set the tone for the session, pique students' interest, or be the basis of your opening question to the class. (Source: DenBeste, 2003)

References

Adams, C. "PowerPoint, Habits of Mind, and Classroom Culture." *Journal of Curriculum Studies*, 2006, *38*(4), 389–411.

Alley, M. *The Craft of Scientific Presentations: Critical Steps to Succeed and Errors to Avoid.* New York: Springer, 2003.

Apperson, J. M., Laws, E. L., and Scepansky, J. A. "The Impact of Presentation Graphics on Students' Experience in the Classroom." *Computers and Education*, 2006, *47*(1), 116–126.

Bartsch, R. A., and Cobern, K. M. "Effectiveness of PowerPoint Presentations in Lectures." *Computers and Education*, 2003, *41*(1), 77–86.

Bates, A. W., and Poole, G. *Effective Teaching with Technology in Higher Education.* San Francisco: Jossey-Bass, 2003.

Clark, J. "PowerPoint and Pedagogy: Maintaining Student Interest in University Lectures." *College Teaching*, 2008, *56*(1), 39–45.

DenBeste, M. "PowerPoint Technology and the Web: More Than Just an Overhead Projector for the New Century?" *History Teacher*, 2003, *36*(4), 491–504.

Doumant, J. L. "The Cognitive Style of PowerPoint: Slides Are Not All Evil." *Technical Communication*, 2005, *52*(1), 64–70.

Gallagher, E. V., and Reder, M. "PowerPoint: Possibilities and Problems." *Teaching Excellence*, 2004–05, *16*(3).

Hardin, E. E. "Presentation Software in the College Classroom: Don't Forget the Instructor." *Teaching of Psychology*, 2007, *34*(1), 53–56.

James, K. E., Burke, L. A., and Hutchins, H. M. "Powerful or Pointless? Faculty vs. Student Perceptions of PowerPoint Use in Business Education." *Business Communication Quarterly*, 2006, *69* (4), 374–396.

Klemm, W. R. "Computer Slide Shows: A Trap for Bad Teaching." *College Teaching*, 2007, *55*(3), 121–124.

Levasseur, D. G., and Sawyer, J. K. "Pedagogy Meets PowerPoint: A Research Review of the Effects of Computer Generated Slides in the Classroom." *Review of Communication*, 2006, *6*(1), 101–123.

Lyons, R. E., McIntosh, M., and Kysilka, M. L. *Teaching College in an Age of Accountability*. Boston: Allyn and Bacon, 2003.

Marieb, E. N., and Hoehn, K. *Human Anatomy and Physiology*. (7th ed.) San Francisco: Benjamin Cummings, 2006.

Mayer, R. E. "Introduction to Multimedia Learning." In R. E. Mayer (Ed.), *The Cambridge Handbook of Multimedia Learning*. Cambridge, England: Cambridge University Press, 2005.

Noppe, I., Achterberg, J., Duquaine, L., Huebbe, M., and Williams, C. "PowerPoint Presentation Handouts and College Student Learning Outcomes." *International Journal for the Scholarship of Teaching and Learning*, 2007, *1*(1). http://academics.georgiasouthern.edu/ijsotl/v1n1/noppe/IJ_Noppe.pdf

Quible, Z. K. "Maximizing the Effectiveness of Electronic Presentations." *Business Communication Quarterly*, 2002, *65*(2), 82–85.

Susskind, J. E. "PowerPoint's Power in the Classroom: Enhancing Students' Self-Efficacy and Attitudes." *Computers and Education*, 2005, *45*(2), 203–215.

Svinicki, M. D., and Lewis, K. G. "Media Aids for the Classroom." Center for Teaching Effectiveness, University of Texas at Austin, October 3, 2002. http://www.utexas.edu//academic/cte/sourcebook/media.pdf

Tufte, E. R. *The Cognitive Style of PowerPoint: Pitching Out Corrupts Within*. (2nd ed.) Cheshire, CT: Graphics Press, 2006.

Yaffe, P. "Why Visual Aids Need to Be Less Visual." *Ubiquity*, Mar. 25–31, 2008, *9*(12).

PART X

Evaluation to Improve Teaching

Early Feedback to Improve Teaching and Learning

The most widely used method for evaluating teaching is the end-of-course questionnaire completed by students. The questionnaires arrive too late, however, to benefit the students doing the evaluation. Nor do the questionnaires typically encourage students to give the specific comments an instructor might need either to spot weaknesses in classroom organization, pacing, and work load or to identify how well students have understood the material.

Much more effective are early feedback activities that take place during the term (sometimes called *formative evaluation* or *informative feedback*). Early feedback activities can elicit the specific comments and constructive criticism you need to improve students' understanding of the material and their subsequent performance on exams. In addition, considerable research shows that gathering feedback throughout the term allows an instructor to improve even very challenging classes, strengthen student learning, enhance student motivation, and positively alter student attitudes toward the instructor and course, as reflected in end-of-term student ratings (Cohen, 1980; Fabry et al., 1997; Hamilton et al., 2002; Hampton and Reiser, 2004; Kreutzer, 1993; L'Hommedieu et al., 1990; Marincovich, 1999; Overall and Marsh, 1979; Rando and Lenze, 1994; Svinicki, 2001).

The techniques described here require modest effort, are easy to carry out, use little class time, and focus on students' experiences of learning during instruction. See Chapter 32: "Informally Assessing Students' Learning" for additional strategies.

General Strategies

Decide what you want to assess. When you gather information on the effectiveness of your teaching, focus on items that you can change during the term—for example, the pace of the course, turnaround time on exams and assignments, or the level of difficulty of the material. Ask your students for specific comments about particular issues rather than general responses to the course or your teaching.

Schedule feedback at times appropriate to the course. If you are teaching a course for the first time or have significantly revised a course you have taught previously, you may want to canvass students as early as three or four weeks after the term begins. If you are teaching a course you have taught many times before, you may want to wait until midsemester before asking for student assessments. (If you solicit feedback immediately after a midterm, however, most of the comments will relate to the exam.)

Encourage students to give meaningful feedback. Let students know that you will use their comments to plan for the rest of the term and that you will summarize the comments for the class. As appropriate, give examples of how students' comments from previous terms led to changes in the current term. Svinicki (2001) recommends that you encourage students to:

- Give specific examples. "The teacher brought the wrong notes to class on two occasions" is a more helpful comment than "The teacher is unorganized."
- Focus on observable behaviors. "When I went during office hours, the instructor was not there" is more helpful than "This teacher doesn't care about students."
- Describe the effect of the instructor's behavior on learning. "When the instructor faces the board while talking, I have trouble following the presentation."
- State alternatives and preferences. "Please distribute the essay topics on a Friday—before the weekend—rather than on a Monday."
- Provide both positive and negative comments.

Use different techniques throughout the term. Many of the techniques described below are quite simple and take very little time; a few require planning or technical assistance. Select those techniques that fit with your teaching approach and philosophy. Of course, you won't want to use all these techniques in any one course; nor would you want to use the same one again and again. Experiment with the ones that appeal to you, modifying them if you want, and see which provide the most helpful information.

Eliciting Students' Written Opinions about the Course

Distribute index cards during the first or last five or ten minutes of class, if your class size is less than 100. Pass out three-by-five cards to students and ask them to respond anonymously to two questions, one on the front of the card, the other on the back. Explain that the purpose is for you to get feedback. You can pose general questions about what is going well in the course and what needs to be improved or changed. Other general questions include these: What do you want more of? Less of? How are you finding the course? Any suggestions for improving the course? Any problems? What do you need before the end of the term? How can I help you learn better? What is helping you learn in this course? What is making learning difficult? If you could change one thing about this course, what would it be?

Brookfield (1995) suggests these questions: At what moment in the class this past week did you feel most engaged with what was happening? Most distant? What action by the teacher or a fellow student did you find most helpful? Most puzzling or confusing? What about this class this past week surprised you the most? You may prefer to ask more specific questions about aspects of the course, such as whether the problem sets are too challenging or whether the pace of the class is causing difficulties.

Leave the room while students write their comments. Ask a student volunteer to collect the cards in a manila envelope and return them to your office.

Ask students to complete a brief questionnaire in class. During the first or last few minutes of class, distribute a short questionnaire to students or to a random sample of students in a large-enrollment class. Keep the number of items small—no more than ten or twelve (Boice, 2000). You can use relevant items from your campus's or department's end-of-term questionnaire, create your own questions, or select them from existing instruments. Murray (1987) has identified sixty items, each referring to a specific classroom teaching behavior, that are significantly correlated with teaching effectiveness. His inventory includes items about the pace of the class, clarity of explanations, student-faculty interaction, and so on.

The questions you select should be ones you can respond to during the term; otherwise your students may develop false expectations about the remainder of the course. Include questions that help students focus on their own learning (How do you know when you have learned the material?), or probe what students themselves could do in class (What is the one thing you want the other students to do to improve this course? What do *you* need to do to improve your learning in this course?). You might ask about the level of difficulty of course content, the quality and quantity of assignments, the use of class time, things the instructor does that enhance or inhibit student learning, the nature of student preparation outside of class, or the pace of the class. Svinicki (2001) recommends adding as the final item, What question should I have asked that I didn't and what would your response have been?

Ask students to write *to* you rather than about you. To assure that students respond candidly, leave the room while they complete the questionnaire anonymously, and ask a student volunteer to collect the forms in a manila envelope and return them to you or place in your department mailbox.

Ask students to complete a brief questionnaire online. Some learning management systems (such as Blackboard) and collaboration and learning environments (for example, Sakai) enable you to survey students during the term and receive a summary of the results. You can also create your own online questionnaire through commercial Web sites such as Zoomerang or SurveyMonkey or from college Web sites such as FAST (Free Assessment Summary Tool) developed at Mount Royal College in Canada. Some faculty give modest extra credit if students complete the online evaluation form. Commercial sites can report the names of students who fill out forms independent of their responses. Faculty who create their own online surveys build in a feature so that after students complete the survey, they are directed to a page to print off and hand in to the instructor to receive extra credit.

Compare students' perceptions of the course to your own. Before looking at the questionnaire that students completed, fill out the form yourself on the basis of your perceptions of your behavior or on what you expect, on average, that your students will say. In general, self-evaluations tend to be more positive than students' responses. In comparing your assessment to that of your students, look for any discrepancies and deficiencies. A variation is to ask students to complete a questionnaire that probes what they have done in class since the semester began (for example "Asked a question during class," "Contributed to the discussion," "Came to class without completing the reading") while you complete a questionnaire that identifies what students need to do to be successful (for example, "Ask a question during class," "Participate in class discussions," "Come to class prepared having done the reading"). These items are taken from CLASSE, a project of the National Survey of Student Engagement that makes available forms for students and faculty (nsse.iub.edu). In looking at the results, focus on any disparities between your expectations and student behaviors and use these as a basis for class discussion.

Ask students to send you a short message. Give each student three postcards at the start of the term and ask them to mail a card to you during the semester whenever they want to offer feedback about the course. Another variation is to have students send you a short letter or e-mail reflecting on the learning that has occurred so far in the course. (Sources: Hallett, n.d.; Rando and Lenze, 1994)

Use an old-fashioned suggestion box. Place a labeled box at the back of the classroom. Invite students to submit comments, questions, real-world applications, or suggestions. A faculty member who uses a question box asks students to write their names on their submissions. If students with four or more submissions fall between two final grades, he awards them the higher grade. (Source: Stein, 1997)

Eliciting Students' Opinions through Discussion and Interviews

Break students into small groups for Stop/Start/Continue. Ask small groups to identify teaching activities and behaviors that they wish you would stop doing, start doing, and continue doing, and to supply a reason or explanation for each request. A variation is to focus on the class instead of the instructor: "What is the class doing that frustrates or blocks your learning? What could we be doing as a class that would help you learn?" Have the groups report back to the class and share their lists. (Source: George and Cowan, 1999)

Arrange for your students to be interviewed. Invite a colleague or staff member to conduct an oral evaluation with your students during the last ten or fifteen minutes of class, called Small Group Instructional Diagnosis (SGID) or Small Group Analysis. After you leave, the evaluator asks students to cluster into groups of five or six and to take several minutes to do the following:

- Select a spokesperson who will also write down the groups' comments.
- Name something in the course that they find helpful or worthwhile and that has helped their learning.
- Name something that has hindered their learning and that they would like to see changed; identify how the change would be implemented.
- Name something that students can do themselves to improve the course.

The evaluator circulates among the groups as they work to remind them how much time they have left and to make certain that they are staying with the task. The evaluator then asks each spokesperson to report the group's findings, and the evaluator records the results on the board. After all groups have reported, the evaluator summarizes for the class the points of consensus and asks for clarification on points of disagreement. The evaluator collects the written comments from the spokespersons and prepares an oral or written summary for you. A variation of this technique is to have students select the five items on the list for each question that are most important to them and to independently rank them from 1 (most important) to 5 (least important). Results are tallied and shared with the group as well as with you.

Another variation called Bare Bones Questions considerably reduces the amount of time and training the SGID technique requires with no loss in effectiveness by streamlining the class discussion and sharing raw data instead of a summary report. Even less time consuming and labor intensive is Quick Course Diagnosis. Students jot down on an index card a word or phrase to describe the course and a ranking from 1 to 5 to indicate their level of satisfaction. Students then share their responses with others in the class. Next, students are given a sheet of blank paper and asked to identify a strength and a weakness of the class. The sheet of paper circulates from one student to another with each student adding ideas and reporting aloud what they are writing down. The strengths and weaknesses are ranked order by the group to reach consensus.

Researchers report that SGID and its variations lead to improvements in courses and a better understanding of students' needs. (Sources: Black, 1998; Clark and Redmond, 1982; Coffman, 1991; Diamond, 2002; Lenze, 1997; Lieberman, 1999; Millis, 2004; Snooks et al., 2004)

Convene focus groups. Ask for volunteers to meet with you to talk about the course and improvements in organization, structure, assignments, and the like. Begin by posing an issue, concern, or dilemma and ask the group to help you understand it. This is more effective than asking, "What improvements are needed in this course?" Faculty who use this technique report animated discussions that contain helpful suggestions. Instructors who convene focus groups also tend to receive higher student ratings at the end of the term. (Sources: Hamilton et al., 2002; Tiberius, 2001)

Name a set of "spotters" for each class session. Spotters are students who arrive in class a few minutes early and report to you on troublesome aspects or challenges in the previous assignment, readings, or class session. Plan to address the spotters' issues immediately, toward the start of class. In large courses, the spotting system will also give you the opportunity to meet more students. (Source: Fisch, 1996)

Establish a student liaison committee. Ask two to four students to meet with you periodically outside of class to discuss difficulties or dissatisfactions with the course. Membership on the committee may be rotated from a list of volunteers, as long as the entire class always knows who the liaisons are and how and why to contact them. If you teach a course with a large number of discussion sections, invite each section to select a delegate. Encourage the liaison students to circulate and seek out information formally or informally from other students. Report back to the class about your meetings with the liaison committee. (Sources: Fuhrmann and Grasha, 1983; National Research Council, 2003; Tiberius, 1997)

Form a student management team. After the first three or four weeks of class, ask for student volunteers to serve as the management or resource team for the course. The team meets regularly to identify problem areas and propose changes, and you visit their meetings to hear their suggestions. Faculty who use this strategy have found it effective for improving course quality and are enthusiastic about the results. (Sources: Kogut, 1984; Nuhfer, 1997)

Encourage students to form study groups. Invite representatives of the study groups to meet with you to discuss any difficulties with the subject matter. Study groups provide students with opportunities to learn from one another, and some students may find it easier to seek assistance as a group rather than as individuals. While this technique seems workable in small classes, it can be particularly effective in large-enrollment courses, where students may feel less connection with their peers. If you form study groups in class, it's important to help all students feel included. See Chapter 21, "Learning in Groups."

Responding to Students' Feedback

Respond quickly to students' comments. Reporting back to the students lets them know that you appreciate and value their concerns, and it also helps them understand the diversity of opinion among their classmates. When you distribute index cards, administer online questionnaires, or schedule interviews, respond to students' comments at the next appropriate class meeting. If you are working with student teams or committees, plan to report back to the class periodically.

Consider carefully what students say. Begin by looking at the positive comments your students have made. This is important because it is easy to be swayed by negative comments. Then read their statements about problems and their suggestions for improvement. Look for patterns: What are the most common problems? Are there broad agreements or disagreements? Do their comments verify your own hunches? Try not to place undue significance on any one student's comments. As you identify the major themes, group your students' suggestions into three categories:

- those you can change this term (for example, the turnaround time on homework assignments)

- those that must wait until the next time the course is offered (for example, the textbook)
- those that you either cannot or will not change (for example, the number of quizzes or tests)

When you present your findings to your class, share conflicting responses on topics in all three categories, so that students are aware of the diversity of opinion within the class. Also, you may want to ask a colleague or a teaching consultant to help you identify options for making changes. Research shows that faculty who receive expert consultation are more likely to improve their teaching. (Sources: Brinko, 1991; Cohen 1980; Marincovich, 1999)

Let students know what changes you will make in response to their feedback. Thank your students for their comments and invite their ongoing participation in helping you improve the course. Public acknowledgment of shared annoyances (for example, outside construction noise, inoperable window blinds) can lower frustration levels boost morale. Take time to clarify any misunderstandings about your goals or about their expectations. Explain which of their suggestions you will act upon this term, which must wait until the course is next offered, and which you will not act upon. Let students know what they can do as well. For example, if many students wrote that they were often confused by your board work, invite them to ask questions more often. As you discuss these matters, try to avoid sounding defensive, indignant, or unduly apologetic. (Source: Kreutzer, 1993)

Select a response method that works for you. Most faculty simply discuss the results with the class as a whole. Some faculty provide a handout of responses to all questions other than those that seem idiosyncratic (for example, a single complaint about *x* or *y*). Other faculty prepare graphs and charts of responses, or post summary responses on the course Web site. Whichever method you select, the most important thing is to respond in a thoughtful and timely manner.

Using Video and Colleague Evaluation

Video one of your classes. Watching yourself on digital video allows you to see for yourself whether you dominate the discussion, whether you allow students enough time to think through questions, whether you maintain adequate eye contact, and so on. For pointers on how to plan and use video, see Chapter 53, "Video Recordings and Classroom Observations."

Invite an observer to visit your class. Invite a colleague or a teaching consultant to observe one of your classes and make suggestions on specific aspects of your presentation; see Chapter 53, "Video Recordings and Classroom Observations." Before class, brief your observer on your specific goals for the session or on a particular technique you are trying to perfect (for example, the level and method of questioning). Meet with the observer immediately after class, while the experience is fresh in both of your minds. Consider pairing up with another instructor to observe each other's classes and to meet regularly to discuss teaching. (Sources: Braskamp and Ory, 1994; Katz and Henry, 1988)

Have a colleague review your course syllabus, assignments, exams, or other materials. Ask a colleague who teaches a comparable course or who is knowledgeable about the subject matter to look at your teaching materials and make suggestions about such topics as the amount of assigned reading, whether the exams adequately cover the subject matter, or whether the homework assignments give students the opportunity to apply concepts and demonstrate their understanding. (Source: McKeachie and Svinicki, 2006)

Encourage graduate student instructors (GSIs) to give you comments about the course. In large courses, most student complaints eventually find their way to a GSI. If you have GSIs, ask them to give you brief written reports on any problems the students are having. You can also ask the GSIs to list the one or two topics or problems sets that caused students the most difficulty in the last week.

References

Black, B. Using the SGID Model for a Variety of Purposes. In M. Kaplan (Ed.), *To Improve the Academy*. Vol. 17. Stillwater, OK: New Forums Press, 1998.

Boice, R. *Advice for New Faculty Members*. Boston: Allyn and Bacon, 2000.

Braskamp, L. A., and Ory, J. C. *Assessing Faculty Work: Enhancing Individual and Institutional Performance*. San Francisco: Jossey-Bass, 1994.

Brinko, K. T. "The Interactions of Teaching Improvement." In M. Theall and J. Franklin (eds.), *Effective Practices for Improving Teaching*. New Directions for Teaching and Learning, no. 48, San Francisco: Jossey-Bass, 1991.

Brookfield, S. D. *Becoming a Critically Reflective Teacher*. San Francisco: Jossey-Bass, 1995.

Clark, J., and Redmond, M. *Small Group Instructional Diagnosis Final Report*. (ED 217954) Seattle: Department of Biology Education, University of Washington, 1982.

Coffman, S. J. "Improving Your Teaching through Small-Group Diagnosis." *College Teaching*, 1991, *39*(2), 80–82.

Cohen, P. "Effectiveness of Student Rating Feedback for Improving College Instruction: A Meta-Analysis of Findings." *Research in Higher Education*, 1980, 13, 321–341.

Diamond, N. A. Small Group Instructional Diagnosis: Tapping Student Perceptions of Teaching. In K. H. Gillespie (Ed.), *A Guide to Faculty Development*. San Francisco: Jossey-Bass, 2002.

Fabry, V. J., Eisenbach, R., Curry, R. R., and Golich, V. L. "Thank You for Asking: Classroom Assessment Techniques and Students' Perceptions of Learning." *Journal on Excellence in College Teaching*, 1997, *8*(1), 3–21.

Fisch, L. *The Chalkdust Collection*. Stillwater, OK: New Forums Press, 1996.

Fuhrmann, B. S., and Grasha, A. F. *A Practical Handbook for College Teachers*. Boston: Little, Brown, 1983.

George, J. W., and Cowan, J. *A Handbook of Techniques for Formative Evaluation*. Sterling, VA: Stylus, 1999.

Hallett, K. "Postcards." Instructional Consulting, Indiana University, n.d. http://www.indiana.edu/~icy/assessment/postcard.html

Hamilton, D. M., Pritchard, R. E., Welsh, C. N., Potter, G. C., and Saccucci, M. S. "The Effects of Using In-Class Focus Groups on Student Course Evaluations." *Journal of Education for Business*, 2002, *77*(6), 329–333.

Hampton, S. E., and Reiser, R. A. "Effects of a Theory-Based Feedback and Consultation Process on Instruction and Learning in College Classrooms." *Research in Higher Education*, 2004, *45*(5), 497–527.

Katz, J., and Henry, M. *Turning Professors into Teachers*. New York: American Council on Education and MacMillan, 1988.

Kogut, L.S. "Quality Circles: A Japanese Management Technique for the Classroom." *Improving College and University Teaching*, 1984, *32*(3), 123–127.

Kreutzer, C. S. "Midterm Evaluation of Teaching Provides Helpful Feedback to Instructors." *Teaching of Psychology*, 1993, *20*(4), 238–240.

Lenze, L. F. Small Group Instructional Diagnosis (SGID). In K. Brinko and R. Menges (Eds.), *Practically Speaking: A Sourcebook for Instructional Consultants in Higher Education*. Stillwater, OK: New Forums Press, 1997.

L'Hommedieu, R., Menges, R., and Brinko, K. "Methodological Explanations for the Modest Effects of Feedback." *Journal of Educational Psychology*, 1990, *82*(2), 232–241.

Lieberman, D. A. Evaluating Teaching through Electronic Classroom Assessment. In P. Seldin and associates (Eds.), *Changing Practices in Evaluating Teaching*. San Francisco: Jossey-Bass, 1999.

Marincovich, M. Using Student Feedback to Improve Teaching. In P. Seldin and associates (Eds.). *Changing Practices in Evaluating Teaching*. San Francisco: Jossey-Bass, 1999.

McKeachie. W. J., and Svinicki, M. *McKeachie's Teaching Tips*. (12th ed.) New York: Houghton Mifflin, 2006.

Millis, B. J. A Versatile Interactive Focus Group Protocol for Qualitative Assessments. In C. M. Wehlburg (Ed.), *To Improve the Academy*. Vol. 22. San Francisco: Jossey-Bass, 2004.

Murray, H. G. "Acquiring Student Feedback that Improves Instruction." *New Directions for Teaching and Learning*, no. 32. San Francisco: Jossey-Bass, 1987, 85–96.

National Research Council. *Evaluating and Improving Undergraduate Teaching in Science, Technology, Engineering, and Mathematics*. Washington, DC: National Academy Press, 2003.

Nuhfer, E. B. Student Management Teams: The Heretic's Path to Teaching Success. In W. E. Campbell and K. A. Smith (Eds.), *New Paradigms for College Teaching*. Edina, MN: Interaction Book Company, 1997.

Overall, J. U., and Marsh, H. W. "Midterm Feedback from Students: Its Relationship to Instructional Improvement and Students' Cognitive and Affective Outcomes." *Journal of Educational Psychology*, 1979, *71*(6), 856–865.

Rando, W. C., and Lenze, L. F. *Learning from Students: Early Term Feedback in Higher Education.* University Park, PA: National Center on Postsecondary Teaching, Learning and Assessment Publications, Pennsylvania State University, 1994.

Snooks, M. K., Neeley, S. E., and Williamson, K. M. From SGID and GIFT to BBQ: Streamlining Midterm Student Evaluations to Improve Teaching and Learning. In C. M. Wehlburg (Ed.), *To Improve the Academy.* Vol. 22. San Francisco: Jossey-Bass, 2004.

Stein, A. "The Suggestion Box: An Old Idea Brings the Real World Back to Freshman Chemistry Students (and Professors)." *Journal of Chemical Education*, 1997, *74*(7), 788–790.

Svinicki, M. D. "Encouraging Your Students to Give Feedback." *New Directions for Teaching and Learning*, no. 87. San Francisco: Jossey-Bass, 2001, pp. 17–24.

Tiberius, R. Small Group Methods of Collecting Information from Students. In K. T. Brinko and R. J. Menges (Eds.), *Practically Speaking: A Sourcebook for Instructional Consultants in Higher Education.* Stillwater, OK: New Forums Press, 1997.

Tiberius, R. "Making Sense and Making Use of Feedback from Focus Groups." *New Directions for Teaching and Learning*, no. 87. San Francisco: Jossey-Bass, 2001, pp. 63–75.

53

Video Recordings and Classroom Observations

Watching a video recording of your teaching is a powerful and extremely valuable experience. Video allows you to see and hear yourself teach, and also to observe the overall class atmosphere and your students' responses to your teaching. By analyzing the dynamics in your classroom on video, you can check the accuracy of your perceptions of your teaching and identify those techniques that work and those that need revamping.

Another way to gain insight into your teaching is to invite a colleague to observe your class. Faculty members at all levels and in all disciplines can benefit from the opportunity for self-reflection provided by carefully planned observation by peers or a faculty development specialist (Braskamp and Ory, 1994; Millis and Kaplan, 1995; Webb and McEnerney, 1995).

The suggestions below will help you use video recordings and classroom observation to think about your teaching and develop a broader repertoire of instructional strategies.

Preparing for Video Recording

Contact your campus educational technology office. Many colleges and universities offer classroom video or webcast services to faculty members. The educational technology office can explain what services and equipment are available. On some campuses, large-enrollment courses are routinely webcast for the entire term, making it easy to access recordings of class sessions.

Select a typical class—or an innovative one. Most instructors choose a class session that typifies their teaching and that includes both lecture and discussion. But you might also want to record a session in which you are trying out a new instructional format or teaching new material for the first time.

Announce that the class will be recorded. Tell your students that the purpose of the recording is for you to review your performance—not theirs—and analyze your teaching. Assure them that the recording will not be preserved, or explain how it may be used as part of your portfolio (see Chapter 54, "The Teaching Portfolio"). Some researchers recommend setting up a "video-free zone" for students who don't wish to appear on the recording. (Source: Malmstrom et al., 2004)

Don't worry about the camera. The recording equipment is not intrusive, and no extra lighting is required. Though you may feel a bit awkward at the beginning of the session, focus on your teaching and you will soon forget about the camera. Remember that no one will see the recording except you, unless you choose to share it.

Viewing the Recording

View the video with a supportive consultant. A staff member at your campus's office of faculty development or instructional improvement can assist you in identifying your strengths and weaknesses. In addition to providing helpful suggestions, the consultant can help you temper any tendency to be hypercritical of yourself. Or ask a trusted, experienced colleague to give you constructive feedback.

View the video as soon as possible. Plan to view the video on the day it is made or the next day so that your memory of the class is fresh. Play the first ten or fifteen minutes of it just to get used to seeing yourself on video. Be prepared for a dose of "video-induced despair," a common ailment brought on by the distortions of the medium. Most people tend to cringe at their voice, appearance, gestures, and mannerisms: Do I really sound like that? Is my hair always this disheveled? Why didn't I notice that my shirt collar was askew? It is important to realize that these details are exaggerated on video and are far less noticeable and distracting in real life. In any case, a wrinkled blouse or a crooked tie has nothing to do with effective teaching. (Source: Krupnick, 1987)

Plan to spend at least two hours analyzing a one-hour recording. Once you're used to seeing yourself on video, restart the recording and begin to analyze it. The problem areas are likely to jump out at you, but don't overlook those things that you are doing well: talking to the class, not the screen; answering questions clearly; and summarizing key points. During this viewing, focus on the following questions (from Fuhrmann and Grasha, 1983, p. 214):

- What specific things did I do well?
- What things could I have done better?

- What do students seem to enjoy most?
- What do students seem not to enjoy?
- How was the overall flow of the class?
- If I could teach the session over, what three things would I change?
- How can I make those changes?

On the next viewing, focus on selected aspects. For example, you might want to pay attention to your presentation style, or to the kinds of questions you ask or the kinds of answers you give to students' questions. Identify your strengths and those areas that need improvement. Watch a portion of the video with the sound turned off so that you can focus on your nonverbal behavior. (Source: Murray, 1995)

Chart the frequencies and types of classroom interactions. For seminars and small classes, one simple method for analyzing a classroom discussion is Contracted BIAS (Brown's Interaction Analysis System). As you watch a segment of the video, stop every five seconds to make a tick mark in one of three columns: Teacher Talk, Student Talk, Silence. You can also write a "Q" each time you or a student poses a question. (Source: Brown and Atkins, 1988)

Analyze specific types of comments. Focus on specific types of questions and statements: teacher's questions, students' responses to teacher's questions, students' questions, teacher's response to students' questions, teacher's reward and praise statements, and teacher's criticism. To analyze your use of questions, for example, view the video, write down all the questions you asked, and examine the following issues:

- How many questions actually requested a response from students?
- Did all the questions require yes/no responses or short answers? Or did some questions require more complex answers? Did some questions require students to explain their reasoning?
- What kind or thinking (or level of thinking) did the questions require?
- Did you allow sufficient time between questions for students to respond?

   If you observe that you are asking too many questions or not pausing to give students time to answer, you can focus on improving those aspects of your questioning skills. (Source: Acheson and Gall, 2003)

Use checklists to focus your analysis. Create self-observation checklists that reflect your particular areas of interest, or select items relevant to your teaching style, subject matter, and class size from the following checklists (adapted from Davis, 1988, based on questionnaires from the University of California, Berkeley;

University of California, Los Angeles; University of Illinois, Urbana-Champaign; University of Texas at Austin; and Northwestern University).

Opening, Organization, and Closing

Do you

- state the purpose of the class session and its relationship to the previous class?
- briefly summarize the key concepts from the previous class?
- present a brief overview or outline of the content at the beginning of the session or state the problem to be solved or discussed?
- emphasize or restate the most important ideas?
- make smooth transitions from one topic to another?
- restate, at the end of the class, what students are expected to have gained from the session?
- summarize the main points or ask students to do so?
- relate the day's session to upcoming presentations?
- seem at ease with the material?
- begin and end class promptly?

Voice, Pace, and Eye Contact

Do you

- speak in a clear, strong, audible voice?
- speak neither too quickly nor too slowly?
- speak at a rate that allows students to take notes?
- avoid filler phrases such as "you know" or "umm?"
- use intonation to vary emphasis?
- adjust tempo when necessary?
- make appropriate eye contact and talk to the class, rather than to the board or windows?
- avoid reading from notes?

Clarity of Explanations and Student Understanding

Do you

- define new terms, concepts, and principles?
- give examples, illustrations, or applications to clarify abstract concepts?
- explicitly relate new ideas to familiar ones?
- know when the class is understanding or not understanding you? know when students are puzzled or confused?

- offer alternate explanations when students do not understand?
- slow down when discussing complex or difficult ideas?
- avoid needless digressions from the main topic?
- use technology effectively?
- write legibly and clearly?

Questioning Skills

Do you

- ask questions to determine what students know about the topic?
- periodically ask questions to gauge whether students need more or less information on a topic?
- pause sufficiently after all questions to allow students time to respond?
- ask different levels and kinds of questions to challenge and engage students?
- encourage students to answer difficult questions by providing cues or rephrasing?
- ask follow-up questions if a student's answer is incomplete or superficial?
- refocus students' "off-the-wall" questions, when possible, to help explain course concepts?
- when necessary, ask students to clarify their questions?
- request that time-consuming questions of limited interest be discussed during office hours?

Student Interest and Participation

Do you

- encourage students' questions and comments?
- listen carefully to students' comments and questions without interrupting?
- accept other points of view?
- provide opportunities for students to apply what they are learning to new examples or situations?
- engage students' intellectual curiosity?
- note and respond to nonverbal cues of puzzlement, confusion, or boredom?

Classroom Climate

Do you

- address all or some students by name?
- call on male and female students in equal or proportional numbers?

- call on students sitting in different areas of the classroom?
- give praise, encouragement, and criticism evenhandedly?
- avoid language and examples that may exclude or derogate any groups?
- offer meaningful encouragement and support?

Discussion

Do you

- encourage all students to participate in the discussion?
- draw out quiet students and prevent vocal students from monopolizing the discussion?
- refrain from monopolizing the discussion yourself?
- let students challenge what you say?
- encourage students to challenge and respond to one another?
- mediate conflicts or differences of opinion?
- bring closure to the discussion?

Physical Space and Classroom Features

Do you

- move about the room to reduce the physical distance between you and the students and keep their interest?
- engage students seated in the back of the room?
- acknowledge problems, if any, with noise level, ventilation, and lighting?
- arrange the furniture, if appropriate, to reflect your instructional strategies?

Having Colleagues Observe Your Class

Invite a faculty development consultant or a colleague to observe you teach. If your campus has an office of faculty development or instructional improvement, one of the staff members can observe you teach. Or you can ask a supportive, experienced colleague—perhaps someone with a reputation for teaching excellence—to sit in on your class. Keep this observation separate from any department process related to tenure or other rewards. There are advantages to selecting someone who is familiar with the course content, but faculty from a different field may be better able to focus on your teaching methods. If no single class is representative of your course, ask the observer to attend two sessions. For small classes, let the students know in advance that you have invited an observer to sit in. (Sources: Braskamp and Ory, 1994; Keig, 2000; Webb and McEnerney, 1995)

Arrange a collaborative peer review. In a collaborative peer review (also called *reciprocal review*), two or more teachers agree to exchange class visits and observations. The collaborators may be at the same level, or a senior colleague may provide a more experienced perspective. A variation called *teaching squares* consists of four faculty members from different disciplines who observe at least one class taught by each of the other three. Observers share their comments first in pairs and then with the entire quartet. Another variation called *video clubs* involves teachers viewing one another's digital recordings and discussing best practices. These collaborative reviews may also include examining course materials such as syllabi, handouts, and tests. (Sources: Hammersley-Fletcher and Orsmond, 2004; Keig, 2000; Keig and Waggoner, 1995; Rhem, 2003; Sherin, 2000)

Plan for the observation. Meet with the observer before the visit to discuss class goals, instructional strategies, planned activities, and students' preparedness, motivation, and engagement. Offer the observer a copy of your course syllabus and an outline of topics for the class period, and mention the particular features you would like the observer to focus on during class. You and the observer should also decide on the method of observation (for example, a checklist, a rating form, open-ended comments). Some researchers recommend using six or eight open-ended questions on topics such as the organization of the presentation, instructor-student rapport, and clarity of explanations. Others recommend a combination of checklists, open-ended questions, and open narratives. Or the observer can record what is happening at a specified interval (every two minutes) during a portion of the class. Or you can ask the observer to tally specific behaviors (for example, the gender of students who ask questions, the number of questions from a particularly dominant student, and so on). For examples of rating forms, narrative prompts, and teacher behavior systems, see Chism (2007). Regardless of the format, the observer should try to report actions without imposing opinions or making judgments. Here are examples of good feedback statements from experienced observers. Note that they all begin with *I*:

"I noticed student energy sagging when you started talking about X."

"I understood the principle best when you used the Y example."

"I could tell Herb felt affirmed when you understood what he was trying to say. I noticed that he spoke up again."

(Sources: Chism, 2007; DeZure, 1999; Kumaravadivelu, 1995; Millis, 1992)

Introduce the observer to the class, as appropriate. In small classes, where an observer might be noticed, let students know the purpose of the observation (for example, giving you feedback on your teaching) and what the observer will be doing (for example, taking notes) and not doing (for example, participating in the class).

Meet with the observer as soon as possible after the visit. The sooner you meet, the fresher your memories will be. You might begin by discussing general impressions of the class: Which aspects went well? Which did not? What was typical or atypical? Any surprises? Were your goals for the class met? Then ask the observer for specific comments about behaviors and actions. You may also want to ask the observer for any suggestions for improvement in two or three specific areas. Throughout, try to listen with an open mind and try not to respond defensively to criticism. If the observer makes negative comments, treat these as new information—not as an attack. Even if you disagree with the observer's comments, you can always benefit from knowing how others view your teaching. Keep in mind that the observer can benefit from positive reinforcement too: "Thanks for noticing that. I wasn't aware of it." (Sources: Martin and Double, 1998; Saroyan and Amundsen, 2004)

References

Acheson, K. A., and Gall, M. D. *Clinical Supervision and Teacher Development: Preservice and Inservice Applications.* (5th ed.) New York: Wiley, 2003.

Braskamp, L. A., and Ory, J. C. *Assessing Faculty Work: Enhancing Individual and Institutional Performance.* San Francisco: Jossey-Bass, 1994.

Brown, G., and Atkins, M. *Effective Teaching in Higher Education.* London: Methuen, 1998.

Chism, N.V.N. *Peer Review of Teaching: A Sourcebook.* (2nd ed.) San Francisco: Jossey-Bass, 2007.

Davis, B. G. *Sourcebook for Evaluating Teaching.* Berkeley: Office of Educational Development, University of California, 1988.

DeZure, D. Evaluating Teaching through Peer Classroom Observation. In P. Seldin and associates (Eds.) *Changing Practices in Evaluating Teaching.* San Francisco: Jossey-Bass, 1999.

Fuhrmann, B. S., and Grasha, A. E. *A Practical Handbook for College Teachers.* Boston: Little, Brown, 1983.

Hammersley-Fletcher, L., and Ormsond, P. "Evaluating Our Peers: Is Peer Observation a Meaningful Process?" *Studies in Higher Education*, 2004, *29*(4), 489–503.

Keig, L. "Formative Peer Review of Teaching: Attitudes of Faculty at Liberal Arts Colleges toward Colleague Assessment." *Journal of Personnel Evaluation in Education*, 2000, *14*(1) 67–87.

Keig, L. W., and Waggoner, M. D. "Peer Review of Teaching: Improving College Instruction through Formative Assessment." *Journal on Excellence in College Teaching*, 1995, *6*(3), 51–83.

Krupnick, C. G. The Uses of Videotape Replay. In C. R. Christensen with A. J. Hansen (Eds.), *Teaching and the Case Method.* Boston: Harvard Business School, 1987.

Kumaravadivelu, B. "A Multidimensional Model for Peer Evaluation of Teaching Effectiveness." *Journal on Excellence in College Teaching*, 1995, *6*(3), 95–113.

Malmstrom, T. K., Kennedy, E. A., and Korn, J. H. "Videotaping Teaching: Student and Teacher Viewpoints," *Teaching of Psychology*, 2004, *31*(3), 185–188.

Martin, G. A., and Double, J. M. "Developing Higher Education Teaching Skills through Peer Observation and Collaborative Reflection." *Innovations in Education and Training International*, 1998, *35*(2), 161–170.

Millis, B. J. Conducting Effective Peer Classroom Observations. In D. H. Wulff and J. D. Nyquist (Eds.), *To Improve the Academy*. Vol. 11. Stillwater, OK: New Forums Press, 1992.

Millis, B. J., and Kaplan, B. B. Enhancing Teaching through Peer Classroom Objectives. In P. Seldin and associates (Eds.), *Improving College Teaching*. San Francisco: Jossey-Bass, 1995.

Murray, J. P. "Successful Faculty Development and Evaluation: The Complete Teaching Portfolio." *ASHE-ERIC Higher Education Report*, no. 8, 1995.

Rhem, J. "Teaching Squares." *National Teaching and Learning Forum*, 2003, *13*(1).

Saroyan, A., and Amundsen, C. (Eds.) *Rethinking Teaching in Higher Education: From a Course Design Workshop to a Faculty Development Framework*. Sterling, VA: Stylus, 2004.

Sherin, M. G. "Viewing Teaching on Videotape." *Educational Leadership*, 2000, *57*(8), 36–38.

Webb, J., and McEnerney, K. "The View from the Back of the Classroom: A Faculty-Based Peer Observation Program." *Journal on Excellence in College Teaching*, 1995, *6*(3), 145–160.

54

The Teaching Portfolio

Creating a teaching portfolio, or dossier, by compiling your teaching materials and related documents gives you a chance to reflect on your accomplishments and to organize information that will be useful in subsequent revisions of the course. Portfolios created for these self-assessment purposes are called *working portfolios, developmental portfolios,* or *portfolio banks.*

More selective portfolios may be requested by committees making decisions about employment, promotion, and tenure; these portfolios, which combine materials from several courses, are called *presentation portfolios, evaluative portfolios, assessment portfolios,* or *showcase portfolios.*

There are no conventions governing the content of a portfolio; examples of portfolios are available online at the Web sites for Cornell University, University of Nebraska, and University of Massachusetts, among others. The suggestions below address the materials you might compile for yourself and then adapt for a personnel committee for making decisions about merit and promotion.

General Strategies

Prepare a concise working portfolio for each course you teach. Place copies of relevant documents in a folder as the term progresses: course syllabus, course materials, sample assignments, exams, and examples of graded student work. Jot down ideas for improving the course as they occur to you, and assemble the portfolio shortly after the end of the term, while your memory is still vivid.

Include samples of successes and failures. Careful and judicious selection of materials will help you think more critically about your teaching. Don't, however, overlook your teaching missteps. Good teachers take risks and experiment with new ideas. As you create your portfolio, reflect critically on what did and didn't work.

Keep a teaching file during the term. Writing regularly about your teaching can contribute to your growth as a teacher. Set up a "next time" file (hard copy or online) for each class you teach, and take five or ten minutes immediately after each session to jot down some comments: At what points did your students seem puzzled? What questions did they ask? How well did the activities engage them? How well did you allocate the class time? Add a test question that came to mind, and list one or two things you could do to improve this session. Review these notes when you are preparing to teach this course again. (Sources: McKeachie and Svinicki, 2006; Mues and Sorcinelli, 2000)

Components of a Working Portfolio

Describe the course. List the course title and course number. How many times have you taught this course? Is the course required or an elective? How does it fit within the department's curriculum? Were there any course activities that placed special demands on your time (for example, field trips or student projects)?

Describe your students. How many students enrolled? Did these students seem more or less engaged, inquisitive, passive, or hardworking than other students you have taught? How many students preregistered for the course but then dropped it? How steady was attendance throughout the term? Did students show up at office hours? Did you make extra efforts to work with students who were not well prepared for the course or with students facing special challenges? Did you make extra efforts to work with your best students?

Write a succinct self-assessment of your teaching in this course. Self-assessments generally include four components: (1) the goals of the course, (2) your teaching philosophy and methods, (3) the effects of your course on students' learning, and (4) your plans for improvement.

Goals. What were your goals in teaching the course? How well did the course meet these goals? What problems did you encounter in attempting to meet these goals? Here are examples of goals (adapted from materials on Web sites at Iowa State University, Carnegie Mellon University, and Indiana University/Purdue University at Indianapolis):

- helping students learn factual knowledge, fundamental principles, and ways to apply course material in new situations
- fostering critical thinking (ability to analyze ideas and information from multiple perspectives)
- facilitating the acquisition of lifelong learning skills
- developing problem-solving skills
- expanding creative capacities (inventing, designing, performing in art, music, or drama)

- strengthening writing
- helping students express themselves orally
- developing skills in interpreting or expressing concepts using visual or mathematical representations

Philosophy and methods. Write a brief statement about the values that inform your teaching. What imperatives guide your teaching? What do you do to help students learn? How are your goals translated into action? How did your choice of teaching strategies relate to your goals? How did your methods take into account the level and abilities of your students? What were your grading policies? What changes did you make in topics, readings, or assignments for a course you have taught repeatedly? How well did those changes work? (Sources: Chism, 1997–98; Coppola, 2002)

Because teaching is personal, you may want to draft your statement of philosophy before looking at the examples of others. If you are stumped, try to answer these questions (Korn, 2003): What are the characteristics of the best and worst teachers you have had? What metaphor would describe your teaching? If you decide you want to see examples, search the Web or your university's Web site (using "teaching philosophy" or "teaching statements") or see Tollefson and Davis (2002).

Effects. Describe how your teaching encouraged independent thinking, intellectual development, and students' enthusiasm for the subject matter. How did you know whether students were gaining competence and learning the material? What evidence do you have of student learning? How many students demonstrated understanding and at what levels? What misconceptions did students have and how did you address these? How well did student work meet your intellectual goals for the course? (Source: Bernstein, 2002)

Improvement. What were the strong and weak points of the course and your teaching? What would you do differently next time? What did you find most interesting about this course? Most frustrating? In addition, list any specific ideas you have for improving your teaching.

Compile selected course material. Include copies of the course syllabus, examinations and assignments, course reader, handouts, and your teaching notes. Annotate the materials to give details about how you used them and your candid assessment of their effectiveness. Look critically at the materials to identify the kinds of intellectual tasks you set for students. Do the materials reflect adequate breadth and depth? Your commentary might respond to the following kinds of questions:

- Are fundamental concepts and core principles adequately addressed so that students can understand advanced ideas and research in the field?

- Is the treatment of the subject matter consistent with the latest research and thinking in the field? Is this material valuable and worth knowing?
- Are the topics logically sequenced? Does each topic receive appropriate attention relative to other topics?
- Do the readings represent the best work in the field? Do they offer diverse, up-to-date views? Are the reading assignments appropriate in level and length?
- Are the assignments effectively coordinated with the syllabus and well integrated into the course? Are they appropriate in frequency?
- Do the tests and exams give students a fair opportunity to demonstrate their abilities? Do they adequately cover the subject matter? Do test questions assess students' abilities to apply concepts as well as the accuracy of their recall?
- Are the standards for grading clearly communicated to students? Is the grading fair and consistent? Are written comments on papers constructive and helpful?

Include representative examples of student learning. As appropriate, include the distribution of students' scores on tests; samples of students' work with your comments; successive drafts of student papers with your comments for improvement; graded work from the best and poorest students in the course; and student publications and presentations done under your auspices. Remember to obtain students' permission to keep copies of their papers, lab books, assignments, or reports.

Describe any instructional innovation or experiments you undertook. Whether your experiments were successful or not, discuss what you tried to do, and the effect on students and on your teaching. Include any efforts to get feedback from students during the term and changes you made in response; see Chapter 32, "Informally Assessing Students' Learning" and Chapter 52, "Early Feedback to Improve Teaching and Learning."

Comment on student ratings from the course. Include a copy of the student rating form and results, noting the response rate (the percentage of your students who turned in questionnaires). Respond briefly and candidly to the students' evaluations and critiques, commenting on those aspects with which you agree and will change in the next offering and those with which you disagree; see Chapter 60, "Student Rating Forms."

Assess your role with your graduate student instructors. If you worked with graduate student instructors (GSIs), review your role in guiding, supervising, and evaluating them. What did you do that was especially effective in helping them learn how to teach? What did the GSIs do that was especially helpful to students or to you? How satisfied were you with the GSIs' teaching performance? What would you do differently if you taught this course again? See Chapter 58, "Guiding, Training, Supervising, and Mentoring Graduate Student Instructors."

Add any evaluations by reviewers or observers. If colleagues or instructional consultants observed your course, interviewed your students, or reviewed your teaching materials, include their notes in your portfolio. If appropriate, add statements from faculty in your department or elsewhere on campus regarding the levels of preparation of your students for subsequent courses.

House your hard-copy portfolio in a convenient form. Store materials in labeled folders in a file drawer or box it in a way that will be easy to update the next time you teach the course. A three-ring binder may also work well. Date all materials, and create a brief table of contents.

Create an electronic portfolio. Compared to hard copies, electronic materials are easier to update, navigate, and disseminate. An electronic portfolio can also include video and audio, or links to multimedia material. With an electronic portfolio, it is even more important to limit the amount of information and to organize it. Barrett (2003) describes how to create an electronic portfolio; examples of e-portfolios, pros and cons, and tools and resources are described in Batson (2002), Heath (2005), and Lorenzo and Ittelson (2005). The Open Source Portfolio Initiative (www.osportfolio.org), designed to work with the Sakai Project (www.sakaiproject.org), offers free software and templates and tools for faculty interested in developing e-portfolios. The Knowledge Lab at the Carnegie Foundation for the Advancement of Teaching and Learning contains galleries of multimedia teaching portfolios and KEEP, a free toolkit (www.CarnegieFoundation.org/KML/KEEP/index.htm).

Presentation Portfolios

Find out what your institution requires and how portfolios are evaluated. Some observers (Burns, 1999, 2000; Pratt, 2005; Wright et al., 1999) have raised concerns about using portfolios for decisions about merit and promotion: faculty and administrators may not know how to review portfolios; there is scant research on the reliability and validity of faculty judgments with this type of data; portfolios can be time consuming to review; and reviewers' own philosophies of teaching may unduly influence their evaluations. Other observers (Braskamp and Ory, 1994; Centra, 2000; Zubizarreta, 1999) believe that portfolios can provide useful information when multiple reviewers work from clearly defined standards for evaluation. Quinlan (2002) analyzes how academics review a colleague's portfolio, noting that reviewers tend to pay the most attention to student evaluations, the self-reflective essay, and the course syllabus. Quinlan also recommends that faculty whose teaching practices are unorthodox explain their rationale for reviewers. Bernstein's guidelines (2002) for peer review of course portfolios focus on four areas for evaluation: the course's intellectual content, the quality of teaching practice, the quality of student understanding, and the quality of self-reflection and development.

Include materials that demonstrate your broad contributions. Present your teaching contributions, both inside and outside the classroom. Organize the materials in a way that exemplifies your thinking about teaching, your current responsibilities, and your efforts to improve your performance. Provide a table of contents and a brief executive summary. A presentation portfolio could include some of the following (adapted from Braskamp and Ory, 1994; Knapper and Wright, 2001; Mues and Sorcinelli, 2000; Murray, 1995; O'Neil and Wright, 1995; and Seldin, 2004):

- description of teaching responsibilities (courses taught, enrollments, frequencies, office hours and advising, efforts to involve students in research and publications)
- statement of teaching philosophy, values, and beliefs
- discussion of teaching objectives, strategies, and methodologies
- representative instructional materials (syllabi, exams, assignments, course readers, course Web sites, handouts)
- evaluation activities conducted during the term (feedback on teaching and learning)
- end-of-term evaluations of your teaching by students
- classroom observations by faculty peers or administrators
- review of teaching materials by internal or external colleagues
- evidence of students' learning (assignments with your comments, graded exams, other assessments)
- efforts to improve teaching (innovations, curricular revisions, conferences or workshops attended, grants for improving teaching and learning)
- contributions to the institution or profession (publications on teaching, participation in school partnerships to improve student learning)
- teaching recognition and awards

Strive for brevity. Keep your comments succinct, and present only those materials and documents that are accompanied by thoughtful analysis and reflection. Researchers recommend limiting text to ten pages, exclusive of appendices. (Source: Knapper and Wright, 2001)

Show self-awareness, but don't be overly self-critical. You are unlikely to be rewarded for focusing on your weaknesses. Showcase your best work, and cast it in the best light. Nonetheless, your institution is likely to welcome some degree of candor, which should be accompanied by your plans for improvement. (Source: Murray, 1995)

References

Barrett, H. C. Electronic Portfolios. In A. Kovalchick and K. Dawson (Eds.), *Education and Technology: An Encyclopedia.* Santa Barbara, CA: ABC-CLIO, 2003.

Batson, T. "The Electronic Portfolio Boom: What's It All About?" *Syllabus,* December 2002, *16*(5), 14–17.

Bernstein, D. J. Representing the Intellectual Work in Teaching through Peer-Reviewed Course Portfolios. In S. F. Davis and W. Buskist (Eds.), *The Teaching of Psychology: Essays in Honor of Wilbert J. McKeachie and Charles L. Brewer.* Mahwah, NJ: Erlbaum, 2002.

Braskamp, L. A., and Ory, J. C. *Assessing Faculty Work: Enhancing Individual and Institutional Performance.* San Francisco: Jossey-Bass, 1994.

Burns, C. W. "Teaching Portfolios and the Evaluation of Teaching in Higher Education: Confident Claims, Questionable Research Support." *Studies in Educational Evaluation,* 1999, *25*(2), 131–142.

Burns, C. W. "Teaching Portfolios: Another Perspective." *Academe,* Jan.–Feb. 2000, *86*(1), 44–47.

Centra, J. "Evaluating the Teaching Portfolio: A Role for Colleagues." *New Directions for Teaching and Learning,* no. 83. San Francisco: Jossey-Bass, 2000, pp. 87–93.

Chism, N. V. N. "Developing a Philosophy of Teaching Statement." *Essays on Teaching Excellence,* 1997–98, *9*(3), 1–2.

Coppola, B. "Writing a Statement of Teaching Philosophy." *Journal of College Science Teaching,* 2002, *31*(7), 448–453.

Heath, M. "Are You Ready to Go Digital? The Pros and Cons of Electronic Portfolio Development." *Library Media Connection,* 2005, *23*(7), 66–70.

Knapper, C., and Wright, W. A. "Using Portfolios to Document Good Teaching: Premises, Purposes, Practices." *New Directions for Teaching and Learning,* no. 88. San Francisco: Jossey-Bass, 2001, pp. 19–29.

Korn, J. H. Writing a Philosophy of Teaching. In W. Buskist, V. W. Hevern, B. K. Saville, and T. Zinn (Eds.), *Essays from Excellence in Teaching.* Vol. 3. Society for the Teaching of Psychology, 2003. http://teachpsych.lemoyne.edu/teachpsych/eit/eit2003/index.html

Lorenzo, G., and Ittelson, J. "An Overview of E-Portfolios." Boulder, CO: Educause Learning Initiative, July 2005. http://www.educause.edu/ir/library/pdf/ELI3001.pdf

McKeachie, W. J., and Svinicki, M. *McKeachie's Teaching Tips*. (12th ed.) Boston: Houghton Mifflin, 2006.

Mues, F., and Sorcinelli, M. D. *Preparing a Teaching Portfolio*. Amherst: Center for Teaching, University of Massachusetts, Amherst, 2000.

Murray, J. P. *Successful Faculty Development and Evaluation: The Complete Teaching Portfolio*. ASHE-ERIC Higher Education Report, 1995, no. 8.

O'Neil, C., and Wright, A. *Recording Teaching Accomplishment: A Dalhousie Guide to the Teaching Dossier*. Halifax, Nova Scotia: Dalhousie University Office of Instructional Development and Technology, 1995.

Pratt, D. "Personal Philosophies of Teaching: A False Promise?" *Academe*, Jan.–Feb., 2005, *91*(1), 32–36.

Quinlan, K. M. "Inside the Peer Review Process: How Academics Review a Colleague's Teaching Portfolio." *Teaching and Teacher Education*, 2002, *18*(8), 1035–1049.

Seldin, P. *The Teaching Portfolio: A Practical Guide to Improved Performance and Promotion/Tenure Decisions*. (3rd ed.) San Francisco: Jossey-Bass, 2004.

Tollefson, S. K., and Davis, B. G. "What Good Teachers Say About Teaching." University of California, Berkeley, 2002. http://teaching.berkeley.edu/publications.html/

Wright, W. A., Knight, P. T., and Pomerleau, N. "Portfolio People: Teaching and Learning Dossiers and Innovation in Higher Education." *Innovative Higher Education*, 1999, *24*(2), 89–103.

Zubizarreta, J. Evaluating Teaching through Portfolios. In P. Seldin and associates (Eds.), *Changing Practices in Evaluating Teaching*. San Francisco: Jossey-Bass, 1999.

PART XI

Teaching Outside the Classroom

55

Holding Office Hours

Office hours serve three main purposes. First, they allow you and your students time to review exams and papers, to discuss topics that were not addressed in class, to examine questions at greater length, and to explore students' academic futures and careers (see Chapter 57, "Academic Advising and Mentoring Undergraduates"). Second, they give you and your students a chance to get to know one another, which will motivate some students to work harder and learn more (Qualters and Diamond, 2004). Third, office hours provide you with an opportunity to gauge how the course is going and how well students are understanding the material. If several students ask you the same question during office hours, you know it is a point you need to address in class.

Despite these benefits, researchers (Jaasma and Koper, 1999; Nadler and Nadler, 2000) report that about half the students in a given course will never attend a faculty member's office hours.

The suggestions below are designed to increase students' motivation and make it easier for them to interact with you outside of class.

General Strategies

Follow department policies. If your department has no set policy, begin by holding two to four office hours a week. Often the best times are immediately before or after class, but it is worth varying the times to avoid conflicts with students' other classes; for example, instead of MWF 11–12, try M 11–12, Th 9–10, and F 2–3. Let students know that you are also available by appointment. If you have graduate student instructors, stagger your office hours to provide maximum coverage. Students are least likely to appear early Monday morning or late Friday afternoon. (Source: Brinkley et al., 1999)

List your office hours on the course syllabus and Web site. Include your office room number, office telephone number, e-mail address, and fax number. If your office is hard to find, provide a map. Mention your office hours on the first day of class and before major exams and deadlines for papers. Post your hours outside your office.

Explain the purpose of office hours. New students may be more comfortable and familiar with using e-mail to get information or ask questions. Tell students about the value of face-to-face interactions and informal conversation about course topics, assignments, outside reading, and their academic progress.

Always keep your office hours; post any last-minute changes. Students who make an effort to come to office hours are disappointed when an instructor leaves early, and these feelings can impair their motivation to work hard. If you won't be available as scheduled, send out an e-mail to the class and place a note on your office door. (Source: Lowman, 1995)

If students raise personal problems, refer them to counseling. Students sometimes ask for advice about personal problems. In most cases, the best course is for you to express your concern about the student's well-being and refer the student to campus counseling services. Warning signs that merit immediate referral for counseling include: intense anger, extreme hopelessness, and disturbed perceptions of reality. (Sources: Lancaster, 2006; Nilson, 2003)

Encouraging Students to Attend Office Hours

Be friendly and accessible and stay after class. Students may be intimidated by the thought of speaking directly and privately to an instructor. The more approachable you are, the more likely students are to come around: learn students' names, arrive early to class, and stay after. Invite students to visit you during office hours and repeat the invitation several times during the term. (Source: Nilson, 2003)

Require students to visit your office once early in the term. If your class is not too large, schedule each student for a ten- to twenty-minute appointment early in the course. In large classes, schedule small groups of students for a fifteen-minute slot. Use these appointments to learn something about your students (their reasons for taking the course, problems they anticipate or are having), to consult with students before they begin projects or essays, or to discuss recent quizzes or exams. Once students have come to your office, they will be more comfortable seeking you out. (Source: Nilson, 2003)

Use an office hour to orient students who missed the first day of class. When students add your course after the first session, schedule a group office hour to go over requirements, expectations, and course procedures.

Return student work with a "Please see me during office hours." Comments on returned exams and papers often motivate struggling students to come to office hours.

Have students satisfy a course requirement during office hours. For example, ask students to make a brief oral presentation or bring an outline of their paper for review, as class size permits.

To minimize the time students spend waiting around, schedule appointments. Use an online calendar or a sign-up sheet on your office door, and divide your office hours into fifteen- or twenty-minute blocks. Keep to the schedule, and keep some blocks open for drop-in and emergency requests.

Contact students who fail to show up for scheduled appointments. If a student misses an appointment, send an e-mail to find out what happened or ask the student in class. Let students know that if they schedule appointments, you expect them to appear or to advise you of any change. (Source: "Office Hours," 1989)

Leave your office door open whenever you are available to meet with students. If your door is closed, students may think you are busy. Hang a pad and pencil on or near your door so that students can leave a message. Make your office look inviting, and show something of who you are by displaying photos or other materials that reflect your interests. (Sources: Lang, 2003, 2004; Shoichet, 2002)

Hold office hours outside of your office. Consider holding office hours in the campus dining commons, study lounge, tutorial center, or computer lab, especially if your office is in a remote location that is difficult for students to visit. Or consider a walking office hour. One faculty member meets with prearranged pairs of students for a thirty-minute walk around campus to discuss course topics and other academic issues. (Source: Steinhaus, 1999)

Reach out to students who are having academic difficulties. Encourage students who are having trouble with their course work to come in to review their status and receive, as needed, referrals to campus tutoring resources. Faculty who include an explicit offer of help in their syllabus see more students than do faculty whose syllabi are silent on this issue. (Source: Perrine et al., 1995)

Consider converting some office hours into course or drop-in tutorial sessions. Arrange a one- or two-hour block of time when you and your graduate student instructors are available in an unoccupied classroom or at the student learning center, where peer tutoring is also available. Students can come in groups or individually to study, seek help with assignments, ask course-related questions, or work in small groups on homework. Research shows that students in physics and logic courses prefer such course centers over office hours as a way to get academic help, keep up on homework, and engage in a variety of productive learning activities. (Source: Chung and Hsu, 2006)

Schedule electronic office hours in addition to regular office hours. Electronic office hours can be especially useful for commuter students and quiet students. Online chat can also reduce the amount of time you spend exchanging e-mails with individual students, and it can help students form special interest groups that do not require your presence. Some professors also extend online chat invitations to "guest experts." (Sources: McKeage, 2001; Wallace and Wallace, 2001)

Set boundaries. Office hours are only one of your faculty responsibilities. Be careful about being available to students a disproportionate number of hours.

Making Office Hours Productive

Be prepared for students who drop by without a specific purpose. Students may want to meet you but not know what to say after that. They may be intimidated, shy, or reluctant to reveal the difficulties they are having in class. Ask them about themselves and other courses they are taking, and try to be patient with students who seem at a loss. (Source: Brinkley et al., 1999)

Limit the time a student spends with you when others are waiting. Let the student know at the beginning of the conversation that you have only a limited time to spend with them because others are waiting or expected. Or after a reasonable amount of time, let students know you need to speak with the next person in line. (Source: Brinkley et al., 1999)

Meet with groups of students. If a large number of students arrive, invite them in, in groups. That way you will not have to repeat information, and they can share ideas and learn from one another.

Remind students that office hours are not the time for a recap of a class lecture they missed. Encourage students to contact other members of the class for notes and assignments.

In quantitative courses, focus on problem-solving strategies rather than on answers. Ask students to make an effort to solve the problem on their own. As appropriate, jot down your answers to a student's questions so that the student can refer to those notes when studying. Solve problems aloud so that students can follow the steps you took in arriving at the solution. (Source: Qualters and Diamond, 2004)

Identify special topics for your office hours. Announce that you will devote certain office hours to reviewing particular topics. If enough students want to attend these help sessions, schedule a classroom for the hour.

Conducting Office Hours

Make students feel welcome. Ask the students their names, if you don't know them. A moment of small talk may help students relax. Students may feel less intimidated if you sit in front of or to the side of your desk rather than behind it. If a student needs prompting, ask, "What can I do for you?"

Give students your undivided attention. Some students may fear that they are wasting your time; you can dispel this concern by listening carefully. Put aside your papers or your work. Try not to let phone calls or visitors interrupt student conferences. (Source: "Office Hours," 1989)

Be familiar with campus resources for students. Students may have questions or problems regarding financial aid, housing, student employment, and the like. Refer students to the appropriate office.

When more than one student is in your office, introduce them to each other. If you have just explained something to one student and another comes in with the same question, ask the first student to explain to the second, while you listen in or help a third. If many students arrive at once, try to group those with similar questions and ask students to limit themselves to the most pressing questions. Invite students to return when you are less busy, or pass around a sign-up sheet. (Source: Brinkley et al., 1999)

If no other students are waiting, ask students about the course in general. After you have answered your students' questions, ask them their opinions of the class sessions, assignments, readings, and other aspects of the course: what aspects are challenging; what you can do to help them.

Be tactful with latecomers. If students arrive five minutes before the end of your office hour, thank them for coming but add that you can stay only a few minutes. Encourage them to return near the beginning of your next office hour.

References

Brinkley, A., Dessants, B., Flamm, M., Fleming, C., Forcey, C., and Rothschild, E. *The Chicago Handbook for Teachers: A Practical Guide to the College Classroom.* Chicago: University of Chicago Press, 1999.

Chung, C., and Hsu, L. "Encouraging Students to Seek Help: Supplementing Office Hours with a Course Center." *College Teaching*, 2006, *54*(3), 253–258.

Jaasma, M. A., and Koper, R. J. "The Relationship of Student-Faculty Out-of-Class Communication to Instructor Immediacy and Trust and to Student Motivation." *Communication Education*, 1999, *48*(1), 41–47.

Lancaster, H. "Not a Counselor: What, Exactly Should a Professor Do when Confronted by a Student with Psychological Problems?" *Chronicle of Higher Education*, February 3, 2006, *52*(22), C2.

Lang, J. M. "Putting in the Hours: You Can Tell a Lot about Faculty Members by How They Set Up Their Office Hours." *Chronicle of Higher Education*, May 16, 2003, *49*(36), C3.

Lang, J. M. "Flamboyant Features of the Academic Habitat." *Chronicle of Higher Education*, June 11, 2004, *50*(40), C1.

Lowman, J. *Mastering the Techniques of Teaching.* (2nd ed.) San Francisco: Jossey-Bass, 1995.

McKeage, K. "Office Hours as You Like Them." *College Teaching*, 2001, *49*(1), 32.

Nadler, M. K., and Nadler, L. B. "Out-of-Class Communication between Faculty and Students: A Faculty Perspective." *Communication Studies*, 2000, *51*(2), 176–188.

Nilson, L. B. *Teaching at Its Best: A Research-Based Resource for College Instructors.* (2nd ed.) Bolton, MA: Anker, 2003.

"Office Hours." *Teaching Professor*, 1989, *3*(7), 7–8.

Perrine, R. M., Lisle, J., and Tucker, D. L. "Effects of a Syllabus Offer of Help, Student Age, and Class Size on College Students' Willingness to Seek Support from Faculty." *Journal of Experimental Education*, 1995, *64*(1), 41–52.

Qualters, D. M., and Diamond, M. R. *Chalk Talk.* Stillwater, OK: New Forums Press, 2004.

Shoichet, C. E. "Professorial Pinups." *Chronicle of Higher Education*, September 13, 2002, A6.

Steinhaus, C. "Walking with Students to Increase Satisfaction and Retention." *NACADA Journal*, 1999, *19*(1), 54–58.

Wallace, F. L., and Wallace, S. R. "Electronic Office Hours: A Component of Distance Learning." *Computers and Education*, 2001, *37*(3), 195–209.

56

E-mail, Text Messages, and Instant Messages

Faculty have many choices for communicating with students outside of class: in conversation, of course, but also by letter, telephone, e-mail, texting, and instant messaging. For some purposes, only a face-to-face conversation or a letter will do. For example, expressions of condolence, formal apologies, inquiries about student misconduct, and discussions of complex, personal, or sensitive issues should not be handled electronically.

For some purposes, however, electronic communication is appropriate and effective. Each mode has its advantages and drawbacks:

- E-mail is an efficient, nonintrusive way to communicate with an individual or groups of people across campus or across continents. Both the sender and recipient will have a record of the exchange, and both can craft and read messages on their own schedule. However, e-mail can lead to time-consuming exchanges (especially if the original message is ambiguous or vague), and a recipient can easily misinterpret a sender's tone, which makes e-mail a poor choice for bad news, negotiation, or conflict resolution. The intentional or inadvertent forwarding of messages can also create problems (Shipley and Schwalbe, 2007).
- Instant messaging allows selected people (those on a "buddy list") to send and receive messages—including images, links, video, and audio—in real time. Users can also see who else is online and available to chat. IM exchanges tend to be briefer than phone calls or e-mail exchanges (Garrett and Danziger, 2007).
- At present, text messaging is the dominant form of electronic communication among college students. But typing on a mobile device limits most users to terse, often cryptic messages, peppered with acronyms for common words, such as $w8$ for "wait" and Y for "why." (For those unfamiliar with text acronyms, netlingo.com has compiled over five thousand terms.) Despite the popularity of text messaging, students prefer to receive institutional messages from instructors and administrators through e-mail—with the exception of campus emergency alerts (Caruso and Salaway, 2007; Harley et al., 2007).

At this time, digital communication technologies are blending. For example, several e-mail service providers offer features of social networking sites such as tracking friends, allow voice calls, and make it easy to send instant messages without clicking over to special software. Technologies that incorporate aspects of instant and text messaging, like Twitter, let users send short text messages from mobile phones to a list of prearranged contacts (the buddy list) who choose a medium for receiving the message: IM, mobile phone, or Web-based program (Educause Learning Initiative, 2007).

General Strategies

Establish ground rules for electronic communication in your course. Describe your policies in your syllabus:

- State your preferred mode for being contacted (e-mail, class Web site, social networking site).
- Give examples of appropriate messages (topics, kinds of questions to pose, types of messages you will answer).
- Encourage students to be thoughtful and judicious, and remind them that electronic messages are public documents.
- Mention how often you will check and respond to messages (for example, 24-hour turnaround, 48-hour turnaround, replies sent during office hours only).
- Provide a format for the subject line of course-related e-mail. Dictating the format will help you filter and sort the incoming messages. For example, the following subject lines have a "name of course: type of question" format:
  - Physics 10: test question
  - Physics 10: homework question
  - Physics 10: grade question
  - Physics 10: lecture question
  - Physics 10: administrative question
- Remind students to identify themselves by name in the body of the message (and not to assume that you know who "swimgirl90" is).
- Explain if and when students may use "urgent flags" or "notify sender" features.
- As appropriate, set limits on the length of messages or the number of messages.
- Include a reference to an online guide for college e-mail etiquette (for example, teaching.berkeley.edu/etiquette.html).

- For IM, let students know whether they should add their classmates and instructor to their buddy lists.

  (Sources: "Managing Electronic Communication," n.d.; Munter et al., 2003)

Set aside blocks of time to read and respond to students' messages. Some experts recommend scheduling thirty-minute blocks for handling e-mail. Answering batches of mail tends to be more efficient than responding to one or two messages at a time throughout the day, especially if several students raise similar questions. (Source: Song et al., 2007)

Triage and prioritize. For example, give priority to responding to messages from students who are feeling anxious if you can easily assuage their concern. (Source: Shipley and Schwalbe, 2007)

Limit the time you spend on e-mail. If you find yourself spending too much time handling e-mail, take steps to reduce the volume (adapted from Shipley and Schwalbe, 2007; Song et al., 2007):

- Send fewer messages. Experts estimate that for every five e-mails you send, you will receive three responses. So avoid sending unnecessary messages, including general informational messages (FYIs) and polite but trivial thank-yous.
- Be brief in your responses. Answer students' questions as directly and efficiently as possible.
- Discourage prolonged exchanges. Add "No reply necessary" or "No thanks needed" to your message.
- Ask students to redirect their questions to a course listserv, chat room, or bulletin board; see Chapter 11, "Online Discussions."

Sending E-mail Messages

Write an informative subject line. Instead of "Important Info" or "Quick Question," try "Assignment Due Oct 3" or "Going on Field Trip?" Be brief (long subject lines may be chopped off, especially on handhelds) and put the important words first. When an exchange takes a new direction, change the subject line to reflect the current content. (Sources: Munter et al., 2003; Shipley and Schwalbe, 2007)

For short messages, use only the subject line. Add "(EOM)" (end of message) so that the recipient knows there is no need to open the e-mail: "Speaker arrives at 2 PM (EOM)." (Source: Shipley and Schwalbe, 2007)

Accommodate readers who skim. Put the most important information at the beginning of your message; leave background information for later. Use short sentences, brief paragraphs, subheadings, and numbered lists. (Sources: Munter et al., 2003; Song et al., 2007)

Use salutations and closings. Select a salutation that matches the tone of your relationship to the recipient: "Dear Micah"; "Greetings"; "Hello"; "Hi." Standard closings include "Best"; "Regards"; "Cordially"; "Take Care." After the closing, write the name you would like the recipient to call you (first name only, full name, or title and surname) and provide a signature block (full name, title, department, contact information). (Source: Shipley and Schwalbe, 2007)

Be attentive to your tone. Researchers report that e-mail users overestimate both their ability to convey their intended tone and their ability to correctly interpret the tone of messages they receive. Read your draft aloud and consider adding a few words or exclamation points to enliven a flat portion. For example, "Terrific!" is more personable than "That is a good idea." Use "please," "thank you," and "would you" to convey respect. (Sources: Kruger et al., 2005; Munter et al., 2003; Shipley and Schwalbe, 2007)

Pause before you send. Reread your draft and ask yourself, Would I be upset if this e-mail were posted on the door of the department office or printed in the student newspaper? Put aside any draft written during a moment of anger or frustration, and wait until your mood has lifted. (Source: Munter et al., 2003)

Limit attachments. Attachments use up server space, take extra steps to read, and are hard to view on handhelds. When possible, paste text into the body of your e-mail or, if not possible, send a link to a Web page. When you do send attachments, provide a quick summary in the body of the e-mail and give the attachment a self-explanatory name. (Sources: Shipley and Schwalbe, 2007; Song et al., 2007)

Refrain from using "urgent flags" and "notify sender" features. Many people are irritated by urgent flags and notify-sender requests. Try instead to write a subject line that states a reason for a prompt response. You can also close by asking, "Please let me know you got this message, even if you can't provide the information right away." (Source: Shipley and Schwalbe, 2007)

Responding to E-mail Messages

Put your reply at the top, not the bottom, of the message. This makes it easier for the reader to find your response. In addition, keep only the relevant section of the message you are responding to. (Source: Shipley and Schwalbe, 2007)

Decide how formal or friendly you want the exchange to be. Try to begin and end with a pleasant or friendly comment: "Great seeing you at the colloquium" or "Glad you are doing well." To encourage informality, you can use the student's first name, sign off with your first name, praise the student's work and efforts, and use humor as appropriate. (Sources: Shipley and Schwalbe, 2007; Waldeck et al., 2001)

Err on the side of warmth. Some students will scrutinize what you write for clues as to how you feel about them. If you can't respond in detail to a lengthy e-mail, use phrases like "racing to class" or "more when we meet during office hours." (Source: Shipley and Schwalbe, 2007)

If you are unable to send a timely reply, send an acknowledgment. A quick "I'll get back to you next week" will prevent students from interpreting your silence as a snub or lack of interest. (Source: Munter et al., 2003)

Send a response even if you are embarrassingly late. Apologize briefly and sincerely for the tardiness of your reply.

Handle complaints in person. Do not try to resolve difficult or sensitive issues through e-mail. Instead, send a simple reply: "I read your message and it seems important. Please come to my office hours so we can discuss this."

Texting and IMing from Handheld Devices

Include a "Sent from handheld" tagline. Let recipients know that you are using a handheld, which accounts for typos and extreme brevity.

Explore texting and IM as mechanisms for academic support. Researchers report that many students like using IM in class to discuss tasks with other students, to share files, to do group work, and to comment on course content. Some faculty use texting to administer short yes-no quizzes, to give students feedback on their work, and to encourage students to pose a question during class, though some students report feeling uncomfortable texting faculty. (Sources: de Bakker et al., 2007; Harley et al., 2007)

Decide whether to encourage "back channeling" in class. Back channel discussions are electronic conversations that students conduct during a lecture. Using IM, for example, students can ask each other questions about the lecture topic, comment on the lecture, circulate links that support or refute the instructor's points, or answer questions posed by the instructor. Back channeling promotes student participation, especially for students who are reluctant to speak out or ask questions, but it can also mystify students who are not proficient IMers. Some students and faculty characterize back channeling as rude and say that multitasking can lead to "continuous partial (in)attention." Further, they argue, why encourage even more students to use electronic devices where they might get distracted by reading their personal messages or shopping online. Back channeling is likely to be unnecessary in small classes and may be too confusing and overwhelming in classes larger than forty students. (Sources: Educause Learning Initiative, 2005; Yardi, 2008)

References

Caruso, J. B., and Salaway, G. "The ECAR Study of Undergraduate Students and Information Technology, 2007." *Educause Connect*, Sept. 12, 2007. http://connect .educause.edu/Library/ECAR/TheECARStudyofUndergradua/45076

de Bakker, G., Sloep, P., and Jochems, W. "Students and Instant Messaging: A Survey of Current Use and Demands for Higher Education." *Association for Learning Technology Journal: Research in Learning Technology*, 2007, *15*(2), 143–153.

Educause Learning Initiative. "7 Things You Should Know about Instant Messaging." November 2005. http://www.educause.edu/LibraryDetailPage/666?ID=ELI7008

Educause Learning Initiative. "7 Things You Should Know about Twitter." July 2007. http://connect.educause.edu/Library/ELI/7thingsyoushouldknowabout/44762

Garrett, R. K., and Danziger, J. N. "IM=Interruption Management? Instant Messaging and Disruption in the Workplace." *Journal of Computer Mediated Communication*, 2007, *13*(1), article 2.

Harley, D., Winn, S., Pemberton, S., and Wilcox, P. "Using Texting to Support Students' Transition to University." *Innovations in Education and Teaching International*, 2007, *44*(3), 229–241.

Kruger, J., Epley, N., Parker, J., and Ng, Z. "Egocentrism over E-mail: Can We Communicate as Well as We Think?" *Journal of Personality and Social Psychology*, 2005, *89*(6), 925–936.

"Managing Electronic Communication." UCLA Teaching Assistant Training Program, n.d. http://www.oid.ucla.edu/units/tatp/old/lounge/pedagogy/communication

Munter, M., Rogers, P. S., and Rymer, J. "Business E-mail: Guidelines for Users." *Business Communication Quarterly*, 2003, *66*(1), 26–40.

Shipley, D., and Schwalbe, W. *Send*. New York: Knopf, 2007.

Song, M., Halsey, V., and Burress, T. *The Hamster Revolution*. San Francisco: Berrett-Koehler, 2007.

Waldeck, J., Kearney, P., and Plax, T. "Teacher E-Mail Message Strategies and Students' Willingness to Communicate Online." *Journal of Applied Communication Research*, 2001, *29*(1), 54–70.

Yardi, S. Whispers in the Classroom. In T. McPherson (Ed.), *Digital Youth, Innovation and the Unexpected*. Cambridge, MA: MIT Press, 2008.

57

Academic Advising and Mentoring Undergraduates

Most faculty members regularly engage in several kinds of advising activities. As academic advisers, faculty offer students guidance on selecting courses and majors, help students clarify their educational and professional goals, and provide referrals to support services. As career advisers, faculty help students explore career alternatives and opportunities for further education and training. Some faculty also serve as extracurricular advisers to student groups or organizations. As Nathans (1988) points out, every instructor, whether formally assigned advising responsibilities or not, is also an adviser.

Although some faculty and departments may view advising casually (Habley, 2003; Wankat, 2002), research has found that the frequency of informal interaction, outside of class, between students and supportive faculty is a potent predictor of student retention, student satisfaction, and student achievement (Alexitch, 2002; Chickering and Gamson, 1991; Pascarella and Terenzini, 2005). According to Light (2001), good advising may be the single most underestimated ingredient of a successful undergraduate experience.

Effective advising relies on the same skills as effective teaching (Appleby, 2002): demonstrated concern for and interest in students; availability and accessibility; ability to listen nonjudgmentally; ability to ask good questions; willingness to take an active role in helping students learn, balance options, and make decisions; ability to create an open and accepting climate; and respectfulness for students from diverse backgrounds and with diverse goals.

Mentoring is similar to academic advising, but with more frequent and regular interactions and with greater involvement in a student's overall academic and professional goals. A mentor helps students acculturate to academic values, provides support and vision, and serves as a role model (Daloz, 1999).

The following suggestions will help you advise and mentor undergraduates and advise student organizations with confidence and purpose. See also Chapter 55, "Holding Office Hours," for ideas about informal advising.

General Strategies

Learn how advising is handled in your department. Institutions vary in their expectations of advisers. In some departments, each faculty member is assigned a number of students, and students are required to obtain their advisers' approval each term for the courses they intend to take. Other departments may require meetings at only three key checkup points: (a) before freshman or transfer entry, when students need help making the transition to college life, (b) end of the second year, when students begin to select a major, and (c) beginning of fourth year, when students need checks that all requirements have been met and guidance on post-baccalaureate plans. (Sources: Halgin and Halgin, 1984; Vowell and Farren, 2003)

Clarify roles and responsibilities. Students may need to be reminded that they are responsible for making their own decisions, based on their best judgment and informed by advice from their faculty adviser. Let students know they must take the lead in scheduling advising appointments, preparing for the advising meeting, seeking out contacts and information related to planning their academic programs, and understanding degree and program requirements. Let students know that you will help them plan their academic program, monitor their academic progress, and make appropriate referrals to other campus offices. (Source: Wankat, 2002)

Help your advisees meet one another. Consider inviting a small group to your office or for lunch or coffee. Meeting in a group may encourage shy students to arrange for individual appointments, and it can also help students network with each other. You can form online groups using e-mail lists, social networking sites, and discussion boards to share information with your advisees and to facilitate their ability to assist each other. (Source: White and Leonard, 2003)

Becoming Prepared and Informed

Know your campus confidentiality policies regarding student records. Release of student records to third parties is limited by federal law and in most cases requires a written release signed by the student. With some exceptions, you need a student's written consent before sharing information about the student's academic progress with a member of a student's family. Note that students are entitled to see their own records. (Source: Becker, 2000)

Familiarize yourself with campus handbooks and Web sites. Most campuses have handbooks and Web sites packed with information about degree requirements, prerequisites for majors, pre-professional courses of study, procedures for changing majors, probation and suspension, adding and dropping courses, and so on. You may also want to keep a folder of printed materials that address common student questions, such as college or major requirements.

Anticipate students' needs. Habley (2000) and Alexitch (2006) list these common student needs and goals:

- developing an educational plan
- developing a career plan
- strengthening academic skills
- learning decision-making skills
- relating skills, interests, and life goals to available academic opportunities and resources
- receiving accurate information about institutional programs and resources
- obtaining referrals to institutional or community support resources

Students who are academically vulnerable, the first in their family to attend college, work off campus, or have family obligations may have special advising needs and will appreciate strategies for strengthening their sense of belonging to the campus. (Sources: Ender and Wilkie, 2000; Priest and McPhee, 2000)

Be alert to students' mental health. If you think a student may be seriously depressed or otherwise in need of psychological counseling, suggest an appointment with campus counselors or other mental health professionals and have the student make an appointment by phone from your office. If a student shows suicidal or other serious signs, walk the student to the counseling center. Do not assume that the student's privacy rights prevent the college from contacting family members or soliciting medical assistance. If your campus counseling center does not have a Web site with advice on spotting and responding to mental health issues, check the Web sites at Virginia Tech, University of California at Berkeley, and University of Texas at Austin, among others. (Sources: Angelo, 2004; Glenn, 2005)

Take the first step as needed. Effective advisers make themselves accessible to students and take the initiative when necessary to connect. Students need (and profess to want) good advising, yet in practice few visit their advisers other than to seek signatures on required forms. Contact students when necessary. Never miss an appointment if you can help it, and be sure to have a note posted if you do.

Use e-mail, texting, or the phone to keep in touch with students between face-to-face visits, as appropriate. Actively encourage students to see you for follow-up advising meetings. (Source: Alexitch, 2006)

Practice good communications and listening skills. Effective advisers listen nonjudgmentally and take an active role in helping students make decisions. They avoid suggesting solutions before a student has fully explained a problem and identified some options. As appropriate, they point out mistakes and explore how the student might avoid similar problems. (Sources: Creamer and Scott, 2000; Nutt, 2000)

Structure the session. You might begin by asking about the student's general well-being and how the term is going, or refer to the previous advising session and ask what the student has done since then. Discuss the purpose of the current meeting, starting with the student's agenda and proceeding to other issues you want to address. As needed, make referrals. Conclude by summarizing what the session accomplished and listing the tasks the student will undertake before the next meeting. (Source: Nutt, 2000)

Keep notes on your sessions. There are ethical, professional, legal, and practical reasons to keep notes on your advising sessions. In addition to basic information (student's class level, major), keep track of dates, topics of discussions, and any decisions or special issues. Refresh your memory by glancing at your notes before a student conference, and follow up on outstanding questions or issues. (Source: White and Leonard, 2003)

Use online advising systems. Many colleges have computerized "degree audits" that track each student's progress toward meeting degree requirements. Some of these systems also host a calendar on which students can schedule advising appointments and indicate why they want to meet with you. (Source: McCauley, 2000)

Evaluate your effectiveness as an adviser. If you have the time and inclination, ask students to complete a brief online or hard-copy questionnaire anonymously to help you identify your strengths and areas for improvement. You can ask students to evaluate the following points about your advising:

- your knowledge (familiarity with university policies, procedures, requirements, online advising systems, campus support services)
- your availability (allocation of enough time for discussion; minimal waits for scheduled appointments)

- rapport (putting students at ease; understanding challenges students face)
- your interest in the students' academic progress and graduate school or career plans (helping students reach their goals; facilitating decision making)
- methods (clear communication; effective use of conference time)

Advising First-Year and Undeclared Students

Identify campus resources for advising first-year and undeclared students. Many schools incorporate advising into courses focused on first-year student retention and academic success. Some large universities have professional advisers who are familiar with the campus rules, regulations, and procedures and provide students with technical and academic advice. Other schools have peer advising programs that pair an upper-division and a lower-division student; research shows that these programs may encourage retention and students' connection to the campus. (Sources: Crockett, 1985; Halgin and Halgin, 1984; Wilbur, 2003)

Consider group advising. You can use a group setting to deliver basic information and help students meet other students with whom they share academic interests and concerns. Informal student networks can also help undeclared students work through the problems of selecting courses, majors, and career paths. (Sources: Glennen, 2003; King, 2000; Strommer, 1995)

Be prepared for first-year students' special needs. First-year students are more likely than upper-division students to view the advising process as a forum to discuss personal problems. First-year students are also more likely to need direction, structured interviews, and frequent advising contacts. You may also find that first-year students appreciate advice on effective study strategies and habits. (Source: Kramer, 2000)

Help new students make the transition to college life. Help new students assess their academic needs and find out about academic support services, campus student groups, and activities. New students may also benefit from advice on how to manage their time and how to estimate how much time and effort their courses will require.

Encourage students to participate in campus life. Tell students about your department's student associations, campuswide student groups, opportunities for undergraduate research projects, study groups, and career-exploration activities. Encourage students to participate in at least one activity. Personal involvement is a prime motivator for learning and a sense of belonging. (Sources: Frost, 1991; Kramer and Spencer, 1989; Light, 2001)

Explain the value of becoming personally engaged. Students are most prone to abandon college during freshman year and before the beginning of the second term. You can promote persistence by suggesting that students take at least one course that truly excites them and that they take small classes and seminars—where they will get to know the instructor and other students. You might also propose that students make an effort to converse with at least one new faculty member each term. (Sources: Light, 2001; Tinto, 1993)

Provide a structure for undecided students to explore their options. Some undeclared students may find it useful to examine four areas of knowledge: the self, educational programs and majors, occupations and modes of entry, and decision making. A short questionnaire and checklist of interests may help students determine the source of their indecision and where their interests lie. Your counseling center or career services may administer and interpret such questionnaires. (Sources: Gordon, 1995; Strommer, 1995)

Candidly acknowledge ethnic or cultural differences between you and your advisees, as appropriate. For example, white faculty who candidly acknowledged ethnic/cultural differences and the obstacles they produce, instead of projecting an image of color-blindness, were perceived as credible sources of help by African American male students. Regardless of your ethnicity or that of your advisees, stress high and consistent standards of performance and a belief in students' capacity to reach these standards. For suggestions on responding to racial, ethnic, and cultural differences see Chapter 5, "Diversity and Inclusion in the Classroom." (Sources: Cohen et al., 1999; Grant-Thompson and Atkinson, 1997)

Advising Departmental Majors

Review your department's requirements for the major. If your department's requirements are complicated, help your advisees diagram alternative ways of fulfilling each requirement. Help students avoid the pitfalls of taking courses out of sequence, postponing required courses, and ignoring prerequisites. (Source: Halgin and Halgin, 1984)

Inform students about career opportunities in your field or related areas. At many campuses, the career center provides career counseling, but third- and fourth-year students are likely to ask you about jobs and opportunities for graduate study. Encourage students to participate in independent study experiences, such as an internship or research activity, to learn in depth about career possibilities. Try to connect students with alumni who are working in the field.

Use group advising to supplement individual meetings. Group advising fosters friendships among students who share similar academic interests and may encourage deeper exploration of career and academic issues. Possible discussion topics include what courses to take next term (and why), tips for studying for a midterm, and ways that students solve their problems with the bureaucracy. (Source: Glennen, 2003)

Anticipatory Advising

Provide anticipatory advising for students who may need it. Anticipatory advising (a less off-putting term than "intrusive advising" coined by Glennen and Baxley, 1985) consists of structured intervention strategies for new students and students who are on probation or who have academic problems. Here, the adviser takes the initiative in scheduling regular appointments to discuss a student's progress and to head off potential difficulties. Researchers report the success of "intrusive" advising in retaining students on probation and students who are members of historically underrepresented groups. To identify students who could benefit from this type of advising, look at indicators like SAT or ACT scores (if available), results of campus placement tests, whether the student is the first in the family to attend college, outside work commitments, financial issues, projected study hours, and self-assessments of academic strengths, weaknesses, and doubts. (Sources: Heisserer and Parette, 2002; Stokes, 2003; Voorhees, 1990)

Insist on regular contact. Students who are on probation or academically vulnerable may be hesitant to voluntarily meet with an adviser. Frequent contact can lead to stronger rapport and a sense of trust, which help students see you as a supportive ally in addressing academic and personal concerns. If your time is limited, meeting students in small groups can be efficient, especially for conveying basic time management and study strategies and providing a structure where students can learn from and support each other. Take care, however, not to bring together a group of students on probation without getting their permission first, since that may violate students' right to privacy. (Source: Upcraft and Kramer, 1995)

Be directive and prescriptive. Consider drawing up a contract that spells out what the student will attempt or accomplish. (Source: Heisserer and Parette, 2002)

Mentoring

Consider being a mentor. As Eble (1988) put it, a mentor does not so much tell students what to do as give them the courage to do it. There are three general components of a mentoring relationship: emotional and psychological support, direct assistance with career and professional development, and role modeling. As a mentor you will be expected to meet with students regularly, provide constructive and supportive feedback, encourage students to take risks, watch out for students' interests, challenge students to pursue educational opportunities and experiences, and help students achieve recognition, for example, through campus awards. (Sources: Jacobi, 1991; Zachary; 2000)

Contact mentored students outside the classroom. Opportunities for meeting informally with students include lunch or coffee, a meal at a residence hall, or an activity in which the student is participating (for example, a play, recital, or soccer game). You can also stay in touch by sending notes of encouragement before final exams and letters of congratulations for noteworthy achievements.

Teach students about academic values and perspectives. Students need to learn how academics think about and solve problems. Mentors can provide encouragement and support by inviting students to attend local professional meetings, involving students in research projects, encouraging collegial work, and nominating students for academic prizes and awards. (Sources: Lagowski and Vick, 1995; Light, 2001)

Advising Student Organizations

Be active and aware. Meet with the group's executive board and clarify the scope of your responsibilities. Be aware of your legal liabilities as the group's adviser—including your responsibilities to prevent misconduct. If the group is not registered with your institution, help students become an official group. Official groups are more likely to have the institution's support in legal and other respects. Attend meetings and activities, especially those that carry potential legal or financial liability. (Sources: Dunkel and Schuh, 1998; Tribbensee, 2004)

Serve as an information resource. Student leaders may look to you for an interpretation of the policies and rules of your institution. They may also ask you how to reserve a vehicle or a conference room or how to find a guest speaker. As appropriate, refer these students to the staff in the student activities or dean of students office. (Source: Dunkel and Schuh, 1998)

Gear your role to the needs of the organization. Groups that are just starting out may need an adviser to help them formulate their mission and methods; groups that have a defined purpose and identified activities may need a supportive resource and teacher; mature groups may need a facilitator and problem solver. In all cases, your task is to give students the benefit of your advice but to let them make their own decisions. Good advisers know when to allow events to fail because of students' faulty planning or lack of follow-through. (Source: Banks and Combs, 1989)

Professional Conduct

Maintain appropriate decorum. No matter how informal the setting, avoid suggestive behavior: comments or teasing remarks about a student's clothing, gender, or sexual activities; off-color stories or jokes; and unnecessary touching or physical contact. Ask yourself the following kinds of questions (based on Elliott and Lester, 2001):

- When you extend a social invitation, do you make it easy for students to decline, or might they feel under pressure to attend?
- Are some students asking you for special privileges or favors?
- Are you being inclusive, or are you leaving some students out of the social loop?
- Can you talk openly with your colleagues about your relationship with students, or do you feel you have something to hide?

Obtain a copy of campus policies on sexual harassment and complaint resolution procedures. Check your campus Web site or ask your campus ombudsman or Title IX office about campus policies on sexual harassment and on romantic relationships with students. In general, unwelcome sexual advances, requests for sexual favors, and other verbal or physical conduct of a sexual nature constitute sexual harassment (1) when submission to such conduct is made either explicitly or implicitly a term or condition of instruction, employment, or participation in other campus activity; (2) when submission to or rejection of such conduct by an individual is used as a basis for making academic or personnel decisions affecting an individual; or (3) when such conduct has the purpose or effect of unreasonably interfering with an individual's performance or creating an intimidating, hostile, or offensive campus environment. Note that the preceding types of conduct are deemed to have the *effect* of creating a hostile climate even if that was not the intent.

Avoid mixing professional and romantic relationships. Since the 1990s, there has been a controversial movement in U.S. colleges and universities to formally ban romantic or sexual relationships between teachers and students. This movement is based on the premise that such relationships are not consensual—even when the parties regard it as consensual and there is no overt exploitation—because of the power differential. If you have an interest in a student for whom you are or may be academically responsible, postpone any romantic actions until after those responsibilities end. If you are in a consensual relationship with someone over whom you have supervisory, decision-making, oversight, evaluative, or advisory responsibilities, take steps to remove yourself from any professional decisions concerning that individual. (Sources: Bargh and Raymond, 1995; Gray, 1994; Lane, 2006; Stamler and Stone, 1998)

Take steps to prevent misunderstandings. Enthusiastic behavior on your part might be misperceived by a student as sexual harassment. For example, suggesting that a student take an independent study under your direction could be misread as an expression of personal rather than professional interest. Minimize the chances for misinterpretation by leaving your office door open during student conferences, meeting with students outside of class in small groups rather than one-on-one, and avoiding physical contact with students.

If you feel a student is making advances, speak up immediately. Shrugging off the behavior or remaining silent may be misconstrued as tacit approval. Instead respond, "It is inappropriate for me to discuss these personal issues with you." If a student leans on you or gets too close, move or stand up. If the student persists, keep a record of the incident, including the date, time, place, people involved, and what was said and done. Speak with your department chairperson or ombudsman.

References

Alexitch, L. R. "The Role of Help-Seeking Attitudes and Tendencies in Students' Preferences for Academic Advising." *Journal of College Student Development*, 2002, *43*(1), 5–14.

Alexitch, L. R. Help Seeking and the Role of Academic Advising in Higher Education. In S. A. Karabenick and R. S. Newman (Eds.), *Help Seeking in Academic Settings: Goals, Groups, and Context*. Mahwah, NJ: Erlbaum, 2006.

Angelo, J. M. "Privacy, or Peril? Where, Many Are Asking, Is the Line between the Parents' Right to Know about Their Child's Mental State and the Student's Right to Privacy?" *University Business*, January 2004, *7*(10), 39–42.

Appleby, D. C. The Teaching-Advising Connection. In S. F. Davis and W. Buskist (Eds.), *The Teaching of Psychology: Essays in Honor of Wilbert J. McKeachie and Charles L. Brewer*. Mahwah, NJ: Erlbaum, 2002.

Banks, M. C., and Combs, H. W. "The Evolving Leadership Role of the Faculty Advisor in Building a Successful Student Organization." *Journal of Education for Business*, 1989, *65*(2), 60–63.

Bargh, J. A., and Raymond, P. "The Naïve Misuse of Power: Nonconscious Sources of Sexual Harassment." *Journal of Social Issues*, 1995, *51*(1), 85–96.

Becker, B. A. Legal Issues in Academic Advising. In V. N. Gordon, W. R. Habley, and associates, *Academic Advising: A Comprehensive Handbook*. San Francisco: Jossey-Bass, 2000.

Chickering, A. W., and Gamson, Z. F. (Eds.). *Applying the Seven Principles for Good Practice in Undergraduate Education*. New Directions for Teaching and Learning, no. 47. San Francisco: Jossey-Bass, 1991.

Cohen, G. L., Steele, C. M., and Ross, L. D. "The Mentor's Dilemma: Providing Critical Feedback across the Racial Divide." *Personality and Social Psychology Bulletin*, 1999, *25*(10), 1302–1318.

Creamer, E. C., and Scott, D. W. Assessing Individual Advisor Effectiveness. In V. N. Gordon, W. R. Habley, and associates, *Academic Advising: A Comprehensive Handbook*. San Francisco: Jossey-Bass, 2000.

Crockett, D. S. Academic Advising. In L. Noel, R. Levitz, D. Saluri, and associates (Eds.), *Increasing Student Retention*. San Francisco: Jossey-Bass, 1985.

Daloz, L. A. *Mentor: Guiding the Journey of Adult Learners*. San Francisco: Jossey-Bass, 1999.

Dunkel, N. W., and Schuh, J. H. *Advising Student Groups and Organizations*. San Francisco: Jossey-Bass, 1998.

Eble, K. E. *The Craft of Teaching*. (2nd ed.) San Francisco: Jossey-Bass, 1988.

Elliott, D., and Lester, P. M. "When Is It OK to Invite a Student to Dinner?" *Chronicle of Higher Education*, October 8, 2001.

Ender, S. C., and Wilkie, C. J. Advising Students with Special Needs. In V. N. Gordon, W. R. Habley, and associates. *Academic Advising: A Comprehensive Handbook*. San Francisco: Jossey-Bass, 2000.

Frost, S. H. *Academic Advising for Student Success: A System of Shared Responsibility*. ASHE-ERIC Higher Education Report, no. 3. Washington, DC: School of Education and Human Development, George Washington University, 1991.

Glenn, D. "College Instructors Should Be Prepared for Students' Mental-Health Crises, Experts Say." *Chronicle of Higher Education*, August 19, 2005. http://chronicle.com/daily/2005/08/2005081906n.htm

Glennen, R. E. The Importance of Faculty Advising: A CEO and CAO Perspective. In G. L. Kramer (Ed.), *Faculty Advising Examined: Enhancing the Potential of College Faculty as Advisers*. San Francisco: Jossey-Bass, 2003.

Glennen, R. E., and Baxley, D. M. "Reduction of Attrition through Intrusive Advising." *NASPA Journal*, 1985, *22*(3), 10–14.

Gordon, V. N. *The Undecided College Student: An Academic and Career Advising Challenge*. (2nd ed.) Springfield, IL: Charles C. Thomas, 1995.

Grant-Thompson, S. K., and Atkinson, D. R. "Cross-Cultural Mentor Effectiveness and African American Male Students." *Journal of Black Psychology*, 1997, *23*(2), 120–134.

Gray, M. W. "It's Power, Stupid!" *New Directions for Higher Education*, no. 88. San Francisco: Jossey-Bass, 1994, pp. 21–31.

Habley, W. R. Current Practices in Academic Advising. In V. N. Gordon, W. R. Habley, and associates. *Academic Advising: A Comprehensive Handbook*. San Francisco: Jossey-Bass, 2000.

Habley, W. R. Faculty Advising: Practice and Promise. In G. L. Kramer (Ed.), *Faculty Advising Examined: Enhancing the Potential of College Faculty as Advisers*. San Francisco: Jossey-Bass, 2003.

Halgin, R. P., and Halgin, L. F. "An Advising System for a Large Psychology Department." *Teaching of Psychology*, 1984, *11*(2), 67–70.

Heisserer, D. L., and Parette, P. "Advising At-Risk Students in College and University Settings." *College Student Journal*, 2002, *36*(1), 69–84.

Jacobi, M. "Mentoring and Undergraduate Academic Success: A Literature Review." *Review of Educational Research*, 1991, *61*(4), 505–532.

King, N. S. Advising Students in Groups. In V. N. Gordon, W. R. Habley, and associates. *Academic Advising: A Comprehensive Handbook*. San Francisco: Jossey-Bass, 2000.

Kramer, G. L. Advising Students at Different Educational Levels. In V. N. Gordon, W. R. Habley, and associates. *Academic Advising: A Comprehensive Handbook*. San Francisco: Jossey-Bass, 2000.

Kramer, G. L., and Spencer, R. W. Academic Advising. In M. L. Upcraft, J. N. Gardner, and associates (Eds.), *The Freshman Year Experience*. San Francisco: Jossey-Bass, 1989.

Lagowski, J. M., and Vick, J. W. "Faculty as Mentors." *New Directions for Teaching and Learning*, no. 62. San Francisco: Jossey-Bass, 1995, pp. 79–85.

Lane, A. J. "Gender, Power, and Sexuality: First, Do No Harm." *Chronicle of Higher Education*, May 5, 2006.

Light, R. J. *Making the Most of College: Students Speak Their Minds*. Cambridge, MA: Harvard University Press, 2001.

McCauley, M. E. *Technological Resources That Support Advising*. In V. N. Gordon, W. R. Habley, and associates. *Academic Advising: A Comprehensive Handbook*. San Francisco: Jossey-Bass, 2000.

Nathans, E. S. *New Faculty Members and Advising*. In A. L. Deneff, C. D. Goodwin, and E. S. McCrate (Eds.), *The Academic's Handbook*. Durham, NC: Duke University Press, 1988.

Nutt, C. L. One-to-One Advising. In V. N. Gordon, W. R. Habley, and associates. *Academic Advising: A Comprehensive Handbook*. San Francisco: Jossey-Bass, 2000.

Pascarella, E. T., and Terenzini, P. T. *How College Affects Students: A Third Decade of Research*. Vol. 2. San Francisco: Jossey-Bass, 2005.

Priest, R., and McPhee, S. A. Advising Multicultural Students: The Reality of Diversity. In V. N. Gordon, W. R. Habley, and associates. *Academic Advising: A Comprehensive Handbook*. San Francisco: Jossey-Bass, 2000.

Stamler, V. L., and Stone, G. L. *Faculty-Student Sexual Involvement: Issues and Interventions*. Thousand Oaks, CA: Sage, 1998.

Stokes, M. "Preparing for the First Advising Contact." *The Mentor: An Academic Advising Journal*, June 16, 2003. http://www.psu.edu/dus/mentor/

Strommer, D. W. Advising Special Populations of Students. In A. G. Reinarz and E. R. White, *Teaching through Academic Advising: A Faculty Perspective*. San Francisco: Jossey-Bass, 1995.

Tinto, V. *Leaving College: Rethinking the Causes and Cures of Student Attrition.* (2nd ed.) Chicago: University of Chicago Press, 1993.

Tribbensee, N. E. "Faculty Adviser, Beware: You May Be Liable." *Chronicle of Higher Education,* June 25, 2004.

Upcraft, M. L., and Kramer, G. (Eds.). *First-Year Academic Advising: Patterns in the Present, Pathways to the Future.* Columbia: National Resource Center for the Freshman Year Experience and Students in Transition, University of South Carolina, 1995.

Voorhees, R. A. A Survey of Academic Advising as an Area of Inquiry. In J. C. Smart (Ed.), *Higher Education: Handbook of Theory and Research.* Vol. 6. New York: Agathon Press, 1990.

Vowell, F., and Farren, P. J. Expectations and Training of Faculty Advisors. In G. L. Kramer (Ed.), *Faculty Advising Examined: Enhancing the Potential of College Faculty as Advisers.* San Francisco: Jossey-Bass, 2003.

Wankat, P. C. *The Effective, Efficient Professor: Teaching, Scholarship and Service.* Boston: Allyn and Bacon. 2002.

White, E. R., and Leonard, M. J. Faculty Advising and Technology. In G. L. Kramer (Ed.), *Faculty Advising Examined: Enhancing the Potential of College Faculty as Advisers.* San Francisco: Jossey-Bass, 2003.

Wilbur, F. P. Outstanding Faculty Advising Programs: Strategies That Work. In G. L. Kramer (Ed.), *Faculty Advising Examined: Enhancing the Potential of College Faculty as Advisers.* San Francisco: Jossey-Bass, 2003.

Zachary, L. J. *The Mentor's Guide.* San Francisco: Jossey-Bass, 2000.

58

Guiding, Training, Supervising, and Mentoring Graduate Student Instructors

The teaching of undergraduate courses with graduate student instructors (GSIs), also called teaching assistants or TAs, is a special form of team teaching. As in any team-teaching effort, success depends on the quality of team communication in both the planning and the conduct of the course.

In many departments, GSIs lead weekly discussion or recitation sections of large-enrollment courses; sessions may include working on problem sets or case studies, discussing new material, applying course material to new problems or contexts, analyzing and evaluating arguments and evidence, or reviewing topics covered in lecture. In foreign language and composition programs, GSIs often teach a section of an introductory course. In performance-based courses, GSIs provide critiques and guidance. In science courses, GSIs may teach a laboratory section, with duties that include setting up the lab, teaching proper techniques and use of equipment, explaining experiments, grading lab reports and quizzes, and discussing lecture material.

GSIs often complain that they do not receive sufficient training, guidance, and support from faculty members (Branstetter and Handelsman, 2000; Duba-Biederman, 1994; Prieto and Meyers, 1999). By serving as a mentor, meeting with your GSIs before and during the term, and setting up procedures for evaluation, you can enhance the instruction your undergraduate students receive and also contribute to the development of future college and university teachers.

Preparing to Teach

Select your GSIs as early as possible. The more notice your GSIs receive, the better they will be able to prepare for their teaching assignments. Appoint and reappoint GSIs on the basis of their communication skills, command of the subject matter, and potential or demonstrated teaching ability. However, on some campuses instructors do not select their own GSIs who are assigned to courses by the department chair. Check with your chair regarding policies.

For a course with many sections, designate a senior or head GSI. Ask the senior GSI to coordinate other GSIs' activities, offer orientations or serve as mentors for new GSIs, conduct demonstration classes, and observe and monitor GSI performance. (Source: Nyquist and Wulff, 1996)

Hold at least one orientation meeting with your GSIs before the term begins. As soon as you select your GSIs, meet to discuss course content, policies, procedures, activities, and responsibilities. Distribute the course textbook and reading list so that GSIs can become familiar with the material.

Introduce yourself to new GSIs. If you don't know your GSIs, tell them something about yourself, your academic interests, and the place of the course in the curriculum. Ask GSIs about their backgrounds. Some will have extensive teaching experience. For first-time GSIs, discuss concerns they may have about their abilities or about the need to juggle their various responsibilities.

Setting a Collegial Tone with GSIs

Mentor as well as train. Some GSIs value personal guidance and mentoring more than formal workshops on teaching skills because of the opportunities for informal interactions and tailored support. In addition to talking with your GSIs about the particulars of the course, discuss topics related to teaching and professional development, be open about your own successes and failures, and allow time for conversations that promote collegial relationships. Ask GSIs about their academic interests and professional goals, especially for GSIs outside your home department. (Sources: Boyle and Boice, 1998; Celeste et al., 2003; Meyers, 1995; von Hoene and Mintz, 2002)

Ensure ongoing, open communication between you and your GSIs. To develop and maintain good relations, listen carefully to what GSIs say about the course and student problems, and give them responsibilities commensurate with their experience.

Share anecdotes about your own teaching experiences. For example, tell GSIs about the kinds of problems you experienced when you began to teach, and talk about how you currently manage your time to balance teaching and research. (Sources: Boyle and Boice, 1998; Nyquist and Wulff, 1996)

Regard GSI training as part of graduate students' professional development. Treat GSIs with respect and be sensitive to them as individuals and as members of an instructional team. Ask GSIs to give you constructive suggestions on ways to improve your classroom presentation. By encouraging GSIs to articulate their ideas about the course, you increase their involvement and investment in teaching. (Source: Seymour et al., 2005)

Specifying GSIs' Roles and Responsibilities

Discuss the amount of time GSIs are expected to devote to their teaching responsibilities. Give your GSIs an estimate of the time demands, and remind them that their teaching—although very important—should not overshadow their own academic work. Suggest priorities for how they allocate their time among preparation and other course duties.

Distribute guidelines about the roles and responsibilities of GSIs and supervising faculty. GSIs may be asked to take on the following responsibilities (adapted from Davidson and Ambrose, 1994, and Lewis, 1997):

- Attend classes/lectures.
- Conduct lab, discussion, studio, or recitation sections.
- Hold office hours.
- Create homework assignments.
- Write solution sets for homework.
- Contribute exam questions.
- Conduct review sessions.
- Proctor exams.
- Grade homework, essays, papers, or exams.
- Maintain attendance records/grades for section.
- Help prepare handouts, presentations, or other course materials.
- Manage the course Web site.
- Regularly report on students' difficulties.
- Teach one session of the full course.
- Participate in GSI training offered by your department or campus.
- Attend meetings with other GSIs and the course professor.

If your GSIs belong to a union, make sure their roles and responsibilities are compatible with the labor contract.

Supervising faculty responsibilities may include the following:

- Help GSIs set priorities among class preparation, office hours, and grading of student work.
- Discuss issues of pedagogy and good teaching practices.
- Give feedback to GSIs on their teaching effectiveness.
- Meet weekly with GSIs to discuss course content and the emphasis to be given to different topics, questions to ask or points to cover, and potential problem areas.
- Provide answer keys or solution sheets for quizzes and exams as well as detailed guidelines for grading papers, problem sets, and the like. As appropriate, distribute examples of graded papers that exemplify the instructor's grading standards.
- Oversee and monitor GSI grading of student work and set standards for turnaround times.

Review relevant campus and departmental policies. Go over the job description for the GSI position, your department's policy on GSI evaluations, and procedures for GSI reappointment and promotion. Make GSIs aware of campus policies on academic integrity, sexual harassment, assigning incompletes, grade complaints, and student grievance procedures. Remind GSIs of the need to respect student confidentiality, the need to avoid physical contact with students (even in jest), and the need to treat all students fairly and respectfully. (Source: Davidson and Ambrose, 1994)

Discuss the course in detail. Go over the following topics:

- *Goals of the course.* Explain what you intend to accomplish in the course and what you hope students will learn, know, or be able to do at the conclusion of the term.
- *GSIs' role in the course.* Is the intent of the course section to review material, present new material, apply the material to new tasks and contexts, go over homework, discuss the readings, answer student questions? How much autonomy does the GSI have in choosing subject matter, setting policies on attendance, and bringing in new material? How will the section advance the goals of the course?
- *Course syllabus.* Give GSIs a copy of your syllabus and readings as early as possible and at least a month before the class begins. As needed, give GSIs

additional resources to help them refine their understanding of the course content. Let them know whether they are expected to prepare a syllabus for their own section, and if so, give them models.

- *Past exams.* Distribute copies of old exams to give GSIs an overview of the important material.
- *Logistics.* What is the maximum number of students allowed in a section? How should the GSI handle such problems as a classroom that is too small, books that have not yet arrived, or assignment of students to sections?
- *Student requests and problems.* Experienced faculty recommend that course instructors rather than GSIs handle student requests for regrading, deadline extensions, or makeup exams; suspected cases of cheating or plagiarism; and other complex problems.

Mention department support services. Will GSIs have access to administrative assistance, office supplies, copiers, and so forth? Is there a budget for course materials or grants available through campus teaching centers?

Inform GSIs about resources for learning about teaching. Tell your GSIs about campus GSI training programs, specialized courses, orientation conferences, handbooks, and other resources. If your campus has not developed training materials for GSIs, look for online information at the Web sites of other colleges and universities. For example, the University of California at Berkeley (gsi .berkeley.edu) has extensive resources for GSIs including online training modules and advice for faculty who supervise and mentor them. Let GSIs know, too, of exemplary teachers or experienced GSIs in or outside the department who can be of assistance or whom they can observe teaching. (Source: Marincovich et al., 1998)

Help GSIs can get off to a good start. To help novice GSIs prepare for the first day of class, see Chapter 3, "The First Days of Class." If possible, arrange for new GSIs to talk to experienced GSIs about typical problems. New GSIs may want suggestions on how to stimulate and lead discussion. GSIs may also need advice on how to avoid these common problems (Buskist, 2000):

- starting class abruptly or cold, rather than with suitable introductory remarks or questions
- weakly integrating or connecting major points, or asking vague questions
- relying too heavily on notes and talking while facing away from the class
- not reinforcing student participation and not repeating students' questions or comments

Inform GSIs about campus resources for students. GSIs need to know where to refer students who have emotional, personal, health, financial, or academic problems.

Set up time sheets. Ask GSIs to keep track of how many hours they are devoting to attending your class, preparing for section, leading their sections, holding office hours, participating in GSI-instructor staff meetings, and other activities. Review their time sheets to make sure they are not overworking themselves and are allocating their time effectively.

Meeting with Your GSIs during the Term

Set up regular meetings throughout the term. If you have more than one GSI, schedule group meetings—weekly or every other week—so that they can learn from each other (Austin, 2002). E-mail correspondence can also be effective. Topics may include the following (adapted from Boyle and Boice, 1998, and Davis and Huss, 2002):

- aspects of the GSIs' teaching that have gone well
- aspects of the GSIs' teaching that have been problematic and how the GSI handled it
- problems students had with the last homework assignment
- overview of the next assignment or topic and potential pitfalls
- suggestions for questions to be used on the midterm or final exam
- discussion of a teaching issue, for example, how to develop students' critical thinking skills

Review past content and new material. Review topics presented in previous classes and topics to be introduced in the coming ones, and discuss teaching strategies.

Talk about how the course is going. Ask GSIs whether their students are understanding the lectures and keeping up with the reading. GSIs are a good source of information about problems your students are having with the course.

Develop common criteria for grading students' assignments and exams. Review GSIs' comments and grades on the first set of essays, problem sets, quizzes, or lab reports and discuss the need for common criteria. Advise GSIs on ways to give students constructive comments. See Chapter 36, "Evaluating Students' Written Work," and Chapter 43, "Grading Practices."

Ask GSIs to help identify students having difficulties. You might ask your GSIs to jot down the one or two things that caused students the most difficulty in class the previous week. Find out how many and which students are having trouble, and give GSIs advice on how to help these students, including referrals to the student learning center, writing center, or tutoring center. GSIs will also appreciate suggestions on how to handle students who are causing difficulties, such as ways to prevent students from dominating the discussion or ways to encourage shy students.

Encourage creative use of office hours. Some GSIs have more success with "study tables" than with one-on-one drop-in hours. Groups of GSIs can collaborate to offer "super office hours" in which students can also help each other with homework and problem sets. See Chapter 55, "Holding Office Hours." (Source: Lee, 2003)

Evaluating and Improving GSI Performance

Give ongoing feedback, including positive feedback. GSIs often feel that the only time they get feedback is when they have done something wrong. Be sure to comment on the good things they are doing. Like all learners, GSIs will learn the most if feedback is timely. (Source: Duba-Biederman, 1994)

Encourage GSIs to keep a teaching journal. Suggest that GSIs use their journal to reflect on what works and what doesn't, what difficulties students have with the course, what could be changed the next time they teach. Or give GSIs a specific writing assignment for the week such as describing an example of inappropriate student behavior and how they handled it. Provide ways for GSIs to share their journal observations.

Arrange for GSIs to be evaluated by their students at the middle and end of the term. All instructors can benefit from student evaluations, especially first-time GSIs. Encourage GSIs to solicit informal written comments from their students partway through the term. Review these comments and give the GSI specific suggestions for improving. See Chapter 52, "Early Feedback to Improve Teaching and Learning" and Chapter 32, "Informally Assessing Students' Learning."

Arrange for GSIs to be observed. Plan to observe at least one section led by each of your GSIs. Schedule the visits in advance, and set aside time immediately afterward to discuss your observations. If you have several GSIs, ask them to visit one another's sections. See Chapter 53, "Video Recordings and Classroom Observations," for suggestions on how to conduct observations.

Arrange for GSIs to be video-recorded. If your campus has a classroom recording or webcasting service, suggest that GSIs be recorded at the beginning of the term and again near the end. Offer to review the video with your GSIs, if they wish. See Chapter 53, "Video Recordings and Classroom Observations."

If appropriate, invite GSIs to deliver a lecture to the entire class. Give GSIs comments on key aspects of their presentation: organization, explanations or examples, speed and tone of voice, use of technology, and handling of questions.

At the end of the term, prepare a written evaluation of each GSI's performance. Write a brief review that highlights the GSI's strengths and shortcomings, and offer suggestions for improvement.

Special Considerations in Working with International GSIs

Be sensitive to the needs of international GSIs. Help your international GSIs, as needed, by giving them an overview of the American educational system, teaching methods, and classroom behavior. Let them know about the wide range of abilities and motivation levels they are likely to encounter among their students. Mention how American students tend to freely express their opinions and even contradict their instructor's interpretation or problem-solving strategy. Describe the expectations American students have of their GSIs and students' preferences for relaxed, interactive learning environments. Explain the balance between lecturing and class discussion that you want the GSI to maintain. If your campus does not have resources for international GSIs, check the Web sites of other universities; the University of California at Santa Barbara has materials designed for international GSIs, including the International Teaching Assistant Handbook (1999). (Sources: Sarkisian, 2006; Twale et al., 1997)

If needed, identify resources for GSIs who need to improve their spoken English. If any of your GSIs speak with a heavy accent, suggest that they begin the term by inviting students to speak up if they don't understand what the GSI is saying. You might also advise the GSI to slowly repeat important words and phrases and use handouts, slides, overheads, or board work to supplement their oral presentations.

Pair GSIs. Assign "buddies" and promote collaboration among GSIs in your department to build friendships and provide sources of support, acculturation, and exchange of information about teaching practices.

Discuss in class the importance of international students on campus. Some undergraduates may be quick to stereotype GSIs whose first language is not English and blame the GSI's communication skills for problems the students encounter in the course. Research shows that students are more likely to learn from an international GSI if they are aware of and sensitive to differences in cultural communication and style. You may need to remind your students about the value and benefits of having international GSIs and suggest the steps students can take to make their learning easier and more efficient, such as asking clarification questions and attending their GSI's office hours. (Sources: Damron, 2003; Jenkins, 2000; Tang and Sandell, 2000)

References

Austin, A. E. "Preparing the Next Generation of Faculty: Graduate School as Socialization to the Academic Career." *Journal of Higher Education*, 2002, *73*(1), 94–122.

Boyle, P., and Boice, B. "Systematic Mentoring for New Faculty Teachers and Graduate Teaching Assistants." *Innovative Higher Education*, 1998, *22*(3), 157–179.

Branstetter, S. A., and Handelsman, M. M. "Graduate Teaching Assistants: Ethical Training, Beliefs, and Practices." *Ethics and Behavior*, 2000, *10*(1), 27–50.

Buskist, W. "Common Mistakes Made by Graduate Teaching Assistants and Suggestions for Correcting Them." *Teaching of Psychology*, 2000, *27*(4), 280–282.

Celeste, G. A., Corts, D. P., Tatum, H. E., and Allen, J. "The GTA Mentoring Program: An Interdisciplinary Approach to Developing Future Faculty as Teacher-Scholars." *College Teaching*, 2003, *51*(2), 61–65.

Damron, J. "What's the Problem? A New Perspective on ITA Communication." *Journal of Graduate Student Teaching Assistant Development*, 2003, *9*(2), 81–88.

Davidson, C. I., and Ambrose, S. A. *The New Professor's Handbook: A Guide to Teaching and Research in Engineering and Science.* San Francisco: Jossey-Bass, 1994.

Davis, S. F., and Huss, M. T. Training Graduate Teaching Assistants. In S. F. Davis and W. Buskist (Eds.), *The Teaching of Psychology: Essays in Honor of Wilbert J. McKeachie and Charles L. Brewer.* Mahwah, NJ: Erlbaum, 2002.

Duba-Biederman, L. "Graduate Assistant Development: Problems of Role Ambiguity and Faculty Supervision." *Journal of Graduate Teaching Assistant Development*, 1994, *1*(3), 119–125.

International Teaching Assistant Handbook. University of California at Santa Barbara, 1999. http://www.oic.id.ucsb.edu/ta/ITA/title.html

Jenkins, S. "Cultural and Linguistic Miscues: A Case Study of International Teaching Assistant and Academic Faculty Miscommunication." *International Journal of Intercultural Relations*, 2000, *24*(4), 477–501.

Lee, J. "Students Rave about Office Hour Alternative." *Daily Californian*, April 2, 2003.

Lewis, K. G. "Training Focused on Postgraduate Teaching Assistants: The North American Model." *National Teaching and Learning Forum*, 1997. http://www.ntlf.com/html/lib/bib/lewis.htm

Marincovich, M., Prostko, J., and Stout, F. (Eds.). *The Professional Development of Graduate Teaching Assistants*. San Francisco: Jossey-Bass, 1998.

Meyers, S. A. "Enhancing Relationships between Instructors and Teaching Assistants." *Journal of Graduate Teaching Assistant Development*, 1995, *2*(3), 107–112.

Nyquist, J. D., and Wulff, D. H. *Working Effectively with Graduate Assistants*. Thousand Oaks, CA: Sage, 1996.

Prieto, L. R., and Meyers, S. A. "Effects of Training and Supervision on the Self-Efficacy of Psychology Graduate Teaching Assistants." *Teaching of Psychology*, 1999, *26*(4), 264–266.

Sarkisian, E. *Teaching American Students: A Guide for International Faculty and Teaching Assistants in Colleges and Universities*. (3rd ed.) Cambridge, MA: Harvard University Press, 2006.

Seymour, E., Melton, G., and Wiese, D. J. *Partners in Innovation: Teaching Assistants in College Science Courses*. Lanham, MD: Rowman and Littlefield, 2005.

Tang, L., and Sandell, K. "Going beyond Basic Communication Issues: New Pedagogical Training of International TAs in SMET Fields in Two Ohio Universities." *Journal of Graduate Teaching Assistant Development*, 2000, *7*(3), 163–172.

Twale, D. J., Shannon, D. M., and Moore, M. S. "NGTA and IGTA Training and Experience: Comparisons between Self-Ratings and Undergraduate Student Evaluations." *Innovative Higher Education*, 1997, *22*(1), 61–77.

von Hoene, L., and Mintz, J. Research on Faculty as Teaching Mentors. In D. Lieberman and C. Wehlburg (Eds.), *To Improve the Academy*. Vol. 20. San Francisco: Jossey-Bass, 2002.

PART XII

Finishing Up

59

The Last Days of Class

The end of the term is hectic for everyone: faculty are rushing to get through the last topics in the course, and students turn their attention from learning new material to thinking about finals. In addition to finishing the syllabus, there are three other tasks you may want to undertake during the last days of class: (1) hold a review session before the final exam, (2) give your students a sense of closure, and (3) administer an end-of-course evaluation. This chapter covers the first two topics. For advice on the third, see Chapter 60, "Student Rating Forms."

Well-developed review sessions can help students focus their attention on course content and reduce their exam anxiety. Review sessions can also offer students the opportunity to practice skills needed for the exam, to verify what is expected of them, and to gauge the knowledge and skills they have acquired over the term. Though empirical evidence is sketchy, faculty who offer review sessions believe that students who attend them tend to do better on the final ("Exam Review Sessions," 1988).

Most students also appreciate having time to acknowledge the end of the term through activities that help them reflect on the significance of what they have learned.

Planning a Review Session

Try to schedule the review after classes have ended. Hold a review session one or two days before the final exam. Students perform better on the final if the review is held after students have had a chance to study and prepare. (Source: Sahadeo and Davis, 1988)

But keep your students' needs in mind. Scheduling a review outside of regular class hours may make it hard for some students to attend because of work obligations, family commitments, or other conflicts. If it is difficult to schedule a review session after classes are over, conduct the review during the last week of class.

Conduct the review session yourself. Asking graduate student instructors to lead the review may cause problems if their interpretation of the material does not match yours. You don't want students to challenge low grades on the final by saying, "The GSI said something different in the review session." (Source: Sahadeo and Davis, 1988)

Conducting a Review Session

Create a relaxed atmosphere for the review. Put nervous students at ease by reassuring them that they can succeed on the final; see Chapter 40, "Allaying Students' Anxieties about Tests."

Restate logistical information. Remind students about the time and place of the exam and what they need to bring to it. Make sure they know what readings or topics the exam will cover and the number and format of the questions.

Provide for an open question-and-answer period. If your class is not too large, invite students to ask specific questions about topics or problems they want to review—as long as the questions don't take the form of "Do we have to know *x* for the exam?"

Have students brainstorm about key concepts or ideas. Ask students to identify the most important topics, themes, or points from the course. Record all the students' responses on the board, adding key issues as needed, and ask students to identify connections, convergences, or points of confusion.

Distill the essence of the course. Provide an overview that integrates the major themes or topics of the course. Or ask questions that will help students identify the key relationships. In preparing for this kind of review, you may find that your course syllabus offers a conceptual framework. (Source: Duffy and Jones, 1995)

Work through questions from a practice exam. Distribute samples of exam questions for students to complete before the review session. Use these sample questions as a jumping-off point to review the course content. For short answer and essay questions, discuss the features of acceptable and unacceptable answers. For multiple-choice questions, ask students to explain their reasoning.

Consider using a game show format or puzzles. Some faculty have had success in structuring review sessions patterned after TV game shows. For example, one instructor has students play "Jeopardy," in which contestants are given an "answer" and must come up with the correct question. Other instructors have asked students to play charades using challenging words, phrases, or concepts related to the course content that they have identified prior to the review session. Another instructor uses crossword puzzles he has created specifically for student review of the material. (Sources: Gibson, 1991; Weisskirch, 2006)

Offer advice on how to prepare for the final. As appropriate, discuss the benefits of studying in groups, the need to pace oneself, the importance of reading the instructions carefully, and the value of leaving time to reread an essay response. For detailed suggestions, see Chapter 41, "Multiple-Choice and Matching Tests"; Chapter 42, "Short-Answer and Essay Tests"; and Chapter 40, "Allaying Students' Anxieties about Tests."

Providing Closure

End on a strong note. Make a special effort to prepare a last day of class that will be invigorating, reflective, and thoughtful. One instructor ends his course with a 10- to 15-minute "farewell address" in which he analyzes, summarizes, and evaluates the course. He candidly critiques his own efforts and comments overall on student performance. Another instructor opens his last day of class with high-energy music and then launches a group discussion of achievements, disappointments, and mistakes, and the responsibilities that come with the knowledge students have gained. (Sources: Newman, 1992; Uhl, 2005)

Put the course in a broader context. Discuss the relevance of the course within the curriculum or the department's sequence of courses. Or explain how practitioners are applying the course content. For example, a faculty member in cell biology discusses potential new drugs that are based on the principles students learned in the course.

Ask students to reflect on the course. During the last day of a seminar or discussion course, pose some questions for group discussion or have students write anonymous responses (from Newman, 1992; Uhl, 2005; Wagenheim, 1994):

- What is one thing you think you will remember most about this course?
- What is one thing you know now that you didn't know before you took this course?
- As a result of this class, what is something you learned about yourself?
- As a result of this class, what is something your learned from other students?
- What would you do differently in this course if you had a chance to do it all over again?

- What new actions will you take to enhance your learning in future courses?
- How will you use the knowledge you gained in this course?

After collecting the cards, read the responses aloud. Such self-evaluations can help students think about how to improve their academic performance and can suggest ways for you to improve your class procedures.

Ask students to write a short letter of advice to future students in the course. This letter can convey information your students wished they had before they started the course: learning strategies, tips for success, advice on how to study the material, the relevance or importance of the course, or potential problem areas. You can either keep the letters or post them on the course Web site for students who enroll in the next offering. (Sources: Eggleston and Smith, 2002; Maier and Panitz, 1996)

Undertake a pre-post comparison. Some instructors distribute a short pretest at the beginning of the term and then again during the last week of the course. Students compare their two versions of the test to see how much they have learned or how their perceptions of the content have changed. A variation is to have students write anonymously on index cards on the first day of class their expectations and goals for the course and then randomly distribute those cards on the last day of class for small-group discussion. (Sources: Eggleston and Smith, 2002; Timmons and Wagner, 2007)

Ask students to stay in touch. Let students know that you are interested in their academic careers and their plans after graduation. Invite them to come to your office hours to discuss their future plans.

References

Duffy, D. K., and Jones, J. W. *Teaching within the Rhythms of the Semester*. San Francisco: Jossey-Bass, 1995.

Eggleston, T. J., and Smith, G. E. "Parting Ways: Ending Your Course." *APS Observer*, March 2002, *15*(3), 15–16, 29–30.

"Exam Review Sessions." *Teaching Professor*, 1988, *2*(9), 1–2.

Gibson, B. "Research Methods Jeopardy: A Tool for Involving Students and Organizing the Study Session." *Teaching of Psychology*, 1991, *18*(3), 176–177.

Maier, M. H., and Panitz. T. "End on a High Note: Better Endings for Classes and Courses." *College Teaching*, 1996, *44*(4), 145–148.

Newman, D. M. "Gifts: 20 Great Ideas from Teaching Sociology." *Teaching Sociology*, 1992, *20*(4), 321–325.

Sahadeo, D., and Davis, W. E. "Review—Don't Repeat." *College Teaching*, 1988, *36* (3), 111–113.

Timmons, V., and Wagner, B. D. "The Last Class: A Critical Course Component." *Teaching Professor*, Jan. 2007, *21*(1), 2.

Uhl, C. "The Last Class." *College Teaching*, 2005, *53*(4), 165–166.

Wagenheim, G., and Gemmill, G. "Feedback Exchange: Managing Group Closure." *Journal of Management Education*, 1994, *18*(2), 265–270.

Weisskirch, R. S. "An Analysis of Instructor-Created Crossword Puzzles for Student Review." *College Teaching*, 2006, *54*(1), 198–201.

60

Student Rating Forms

Student rating forms (also known as *end-of-course questionnaires* or *student evaluations of teaching*) are administered at the end of the term to survey students' opinions about a course. These forms include both summary questions and specific items, and they are used by faculty committees and administrators to make decisions about merit increases, promotion, and tenure and by instructors for their own teaching improvement.

At one time, it was considered controversial to administer student rating forms. Though there are still vocal opponents who actively dispute their validity (Trout, 2000; Williams and Ceci, 1997; Yunker and Yunker, 2003), such forms have become commonplace. A substantial body of research has concluded that administering well-crafted questionnaires to students is both valid and reliable, and it makes sense to survey students, the learners themselves, as one source of information for evaluating teaching.

Research has also shown that reviewing end-of-course questionnaires alone tends not to help instructors improve their teaching (Hampton and Reiser, 2004; Kember et al., 2002; Marincovich, 1999; Nasser and Fresko, 2002; Schmelkin et al., 1997). Improvement is more likely to come from consultations about teaching improvement and feedback given by students during the term. See Chapter 52, "Early Feedback to Improve Teaching and Learning," and Chapter 32,"Informally Assessing Students' Learning."

Consensus Opinion on Student Evaluations of Teaching

Decades of research on student rating forms have resulted in the following generally accepted conclusions:

> *Learning.* Ratings of overall teaching effectiveness are moderately correlated with independent measures of student learning and achievement. Students of highly rated teachers achieve higher final exam scores, can better apply course material, and are more inclined to pursue the subject subsequently (Abrami, 2001; Braskamp and Ory, 1994; Cohen, 1981; Feldman, 1997; Kulik, 2001; Marsh and Dunkin, 1992).

Stability. A faculty member's ratings for a given course tend to be relatively consistent over the years in the absence of some type of intervention aimed at teaching improvement; there is not much variation in student ratings for an individual instructor regardless of whether the form is administered to current students or to alumni (Braskamp and Ory, 1994; Centra, 1993; Marsh, 2007; Marsh and Dunkin, 1992; Overall and Marsh, 1980).

Retention. Students of instructors who receive high ratings are less likely to drop a course (Hoffman and Oreopoulos, 2006).

Student characteristics. There is little or no relationship between the following characteristics of students and their ratings of instruction: age, grade point average, year in college, and academic ability (Abrami, 2001; Braskamp and Ory, 1994; Centra, 2003; Marsh and Dunkin, 1992; Marsh and Roche, 2000; Ory, 2001).

Electives. Students tend to rate courses in their major field and elective courses higher than required courses outside their major (Marsh and Dunkin, 1992; Marsh and Roche, 1997; McKeachie, 1997).

Years of experience. Instructors with less than one year of experience tend to receive lower ratings, and instructors with three to twelve years of experience tend to receive the best ratings (Franklin, 2001).

Personal characteristics of instructors. The more likeable, approachable, and attractive a teacher appears to students, the more the students will report having learned from that instructor (Gurung and Vespia, 2007).

Gender of students. Some research (Centra and Gaubatz, 2000) has shown no difference in ratings by male and female students, while others report higher ratings by one gender over the other (Wachtel, 1998).

Gender of instructors. Some studies report no relationship between a professor's gender and student ratings; others show differences in how male and female instructors are rated, but neither group is consistently rated more highly (Andersen and Miller, 1997; Basow, 1995; Cramer and Alexitch, 2000; Marsh and Dunkin, 1992; Wachtel, 1998; Weinberg et al., 2007).

Sexual orientation of instructors. Sexual orientation of the instructor does not seem to impact student ratings (Liddle, 1997).

Class size and discipline. Instructors of very small classes tend to receive higher ratings; ratings tend to be lower in classes of forty to sixty students. Humanities instructors tend to receive higher ratings than instructors in the physical sciences, with social and behavioral sciences in between (d'Apollonia and Abrami, 1997; Franklin, 2001; Marsh and Dunkin, 1992; Marsh and Roche, 1997; Ory, 2001).

Innovation. New or revised courses frequently get lower-than-expected ratings the first time out (Franklin, 2001).

Workload. On average, students give more difficult courses higher ratings than easier courses in which they do not learn as much. But exceptionally difficult courses that do not provide students with sufficient assistance receive lower ratings (Bain, 2004; Dee, 2007; Marsh, 2001; McKeachie and Svinicki, 2006). Students tend to prefer challenging courses over less challenging courses (Jacobson and Lawrence, 2005).

Expectations. Students' expectations may affect their ratings: students who expect a course or teacher to be good generally find their expectations confirmed (Marsh and Roche, 1997).

Grades. The relationship between grades in a course and student ratings is conflicting and complex. These studies have looked at actual grades earned (course grade distributions) or have examined students' self-reported expected grades. Some research has found little relationship between liberal grading practices and student ratings of professors (d'Apollonia and Abrami, 1997). Other research has found that students give high ratings to faculty who give high grades (Greenwald and Gillmore, 1997; Weinberg et al., 2007). In general, there appears to be a small positive correlation between student grades and ratings (Emerson et al., 2000; Feldman, 1997). However, there are competing explanations for this finding besides easy graders get high evaluations:

- Students who are better taught by better teachers learn more and (appropriately) earn high grades (Emerson et al., 2000; Marsh and Roche, 1997).
- Good students are earning good grades and give credit to their professors for their learning (Blackhart et al., 2006; McKeachie, 1997).
- Good teachers have successful students who rate their teachers highly (Franklin, 2001).
- More effective teaching inspires students to work harder and earn better grades (Wachtel, 1998).
- Lenient grading may motivate increased student effort which results in higher grades and higher ratings (d'Apollonia and Abrami, 1997).
- When a faculty member praises a student via high grades, the student, in return, praises the faculty member by giving high ratings (Germain and Scandura, 2005).
- Preexisting student characteristics (such as interest in the subject matter) affect both student's high grades and high ratings (Wachtel, 1998).

As Marsh and Roche (2000) conclude, instructors are most likely to earn high ratings when they provide demanding and challenging material, facilitate student efforts to master the material, and encourage students to value their learning. Because of the small correlation between ratings and grades, however, student rating forms should ask students to report not only their satisfaction with the course but also how much they have learned, which is a powerful indicator of overall teacher effectiveness (National Research Council, 2003).

Selecting or Designing the Questionnaire

Use existing forms whenever possible. Theall and Franklin (1990) caution about how difficult and time-consuming it is to create a valid and reliable form. If you need to create a form, however, the following researchers provide catalogues of questionnaire items: Abrami, d'Apollonia, and Rosenfeld (1996); Arreola (2000); Berk (2006); Kulik (1991); and Scriven, cited in Stake and Cisneros-Cohernour (2000).

Include a global question about teaching effectiveness. Global items (for example, "Overall how would you rate the effectiveness of this instructor?") tend to have a higher correlation to measures of student learning than other types of questions.

However, some researchers argue that no single item adequately captures the multidimensionality of teaching (Marsh and Dunkin, 1992). Marsh and his colleagues have undertaken more than a dozen studies that support nine key dimensions that distinguish effective from ineffective teaching: learning/value, enthusiasm, organization, group interaction, individual rapport, breadth of coverage, exams/grades, assignments, and workload. (Sources: Abrami et al., 1996; Braskamp and Ory, 1994; Cashin and Downey, 1992; Centra, 1993; d'Apollonia and Abrami, 1997; Koon and Murray, 1995; McKeachie, 1997)

Include both quantitative and narrative items. Forms that include both quantitative and narrative data give the broadest picture of students' reactions. The following kinds of questions produce the most reliable results: overall rating of the course and the instructor; estimate of how much students have learned; effectiveness of the instructor in stimulating student interest in the subject matter; extent to which the course challenges students intellectually (Bain, 2004; Braskamp and Ory, 1994; Cashin, 1999). To this list might be added questions about students' own engagement and level of effort and the instructor's respect for and evenhanded treatment of students in the class.

Use items that reflect your department's criteria for effective teaching.
If your institution gives you a choice of forms or items, select those that represent your department's teaching philosophy, practices, and educational goals.

Be sure that items are within the students' range of judgment. For example, students can judge how well organized an instructor is and how effectively the instructor uses class time, explains concepts, and responds to questions. But students are not qualified to judge whether instructors are up-to-date in their field or whether a course prepares them for an advanced course in the field. (Source: Scriven, 1995)

Check the clarity of the items and response options. "The instructor routinely summarizes major points" is unambiguous, but "The instructor is well organized and available outside of class" confounds two different issues. Eliminate questions that do not correlate with teaching behavior (for example, "The classroom was uncomfortable") and those that contain skewed or unclear response categories. (Source: Tagomori and Bishop, 1995)

For at least some key items, provide a numerical rating scale. Numerical ratings are helpful because one can calculate the class's average response and the distribution of responses. Use a 5-point scale (with 1 representing the low end of the continuum and 5 representing the high end) and a "don't know or doesn't apply" option.

Here are examples of several types of scales (though you would not want to use all these scales in a single questionnaire):

- Agreement
  Item: This course challenged me intellectually.
  Response choices (from 1 to 5): Strongly Disagree, Disagree, Neither Disagree nor Agree, Agree, Strongly Agree
- Behavioral
  Item: How often was the instructor accessible to students during office hours?
  Response choices (from 1 to 5): Very Little or None of the Time, Only Some of the Time, About Half of the Time, Most of the Time, All or Almost All of the Time
- Frequency
  Item: Were exams, homework, and other graded materials returned on a timely basis?
  Response choices (from 1 to 5): Almost Never, Rarely, Sometimes, Often, Almost Always

- Quality
  Item: How would you rate the overall quality of this course?
  Response choices (from 1 to 5): Very Poor, Poor, Average, Good, Very Good
- Quantity
  Item: How much did you learn in this course?
  Response choices (from 1 to 5): Almost Nothing, A Little, Some, Quite a Bit, A Great Deal

It makes it easier for respondents and shortens the length of the questionnaire if you can use a single type of scale for most of the items. Also remember to phrase questions using *you* or *I* rather than *students*.

Include at least one item that asks students about the effects of the course on their learning. Ask students to describe or rate the knowledge, appreciation, or skills they acquired in the course or their intellectual, personal, or professional growth as a result of the instructor's teaching. The following are examples of such questions (from Lewis, 2001):

In what ways has this course developed your intellectual skills and interests?

What helped your learning the most in this class? What hindered your learning the most in this class?

What suggestions for changes do you have that would have improved your learning in this class?

Include questions about the overall effectiveness of the instructor and of the course. Questions about overall effectiveness may be formatted on a 5-point scale:

Considering both the limitations and possibilities of the subject matter and course, how would you rate the overall effectiveness of this instructor?

Not at all effective		Moderately effective		Extremely effective
1	2	3	4	5

Considering both the limitations and possibilities of the subject matter and course, how would you rate the overall effectiveness of this course?

Not at all effective		Moderately effective		Extremely effective
1	2	3	4	5

Include at least one open-ended item that asks about the overall effectiveness of the instructor. For example, "Please identify what you perceive to be the greatest strengths and weaknesses of this instructor's teaching."

Limit the number of questions about student characteristics. Student characteristics have relatively little influence on ratings of overall effectiveness. You might want to know, however, whether students are taking the course as an elective or to fulfill a requirement and what grade they expect in the course. (Source: Cashin, 1999)

Ask about students' effort and interest in the course. An item about how much of the reading or homework assignments the students completed and how many classes they attended will provide context for interpreting the results. Reviewers may wish to exclude the ratings of students who attended few classes.

Encourage students to give advice to prospective students. "What are the one or two tips you would give to students who enroll in this course next term?" or "How would you summarize this course for a fellow student?" Post the summaries on your course Web site for the next offering. If new students know that you have taken past students' comments seriously, they may be more inclined to provide thoughtful responses when they next complete a rating form.

Ask students to suggest questions for future rating forms. "What question do you wish had been included on this form?" may identify perspectives or concerns unaddressed by the other items.

Keep the form short. Researchers recommend asking a small number of questions focused on an instructor's overall teaching and on student learning. Forms administered to help instructors improve, however, might include ten or twelve specific items that address behaviors that are amenable to change. (Sources: Cashin, 1999; Forsyth, 2003; Lowman, 1995)

Follow best practices in questionnaire design. Though not specific to student ratings, Dillman (2007) offers detailed advice on writing good questions and constructing effective survey forms.

Administering the Questionnaire in Class

Announce the date in advance. Schedule the distribution of the rating form during the last two weeks of the term; allow ten to fifteen minutes for this activity. To reinforce the importance of the form, highlight the date on the course syllabus.

Researchers recommend that forms be completed at the beginning of the class, when students are more alert or in the middle of class as a break. Do not distribute forms at the final exam, when students are preoccupied with other matters. (Source: Dunegan and Hrivnak, 2003)

Explain the purpose of the questionnaire. Tell students that their ratings and comments will be used by you and by your department. Research (Chen and Hoshower, 2003) shows that students are motivated to complete evaluations if they know that the data will be used to improve the course. Here are some sample instructions (adapted from faculty at UCLA and UC Berkeley):

> We hope you will take the time to answer each question carefully, thoughtfully, and thoroughly. The information you provide will be part of our ongoing efforts to improve the curriculum and the teaching in this department. Over the years, students have provided us with very helpful and constructive suggestions.
>
> We hope that these questions encourage you to reflect about your learning experiences in this course and on the diverse qualities that make for good teaching. To maintain confidentiality, these forms will be collected by someone other than the instructor and will not be available to the instructor until after the course grades have been submitted.

Ask students to complete the forms anonymously. Requiring students to sign the forms inflates the ratings. In addition, anonymity can eliminate students' concerns about possible retribution. (Sources: Fries and McNinch, 2003; Marsh and Roche, 1997)

Designate a student or GSI to collect the forms. You may hand out the forms, but you should not be present while students complete the questionnaires, and you should not collect the forms. Ask the designated collector to place the forms in a large envelope, noting on the outside your name, the course number, the number of students present, the number of forms collected, and the date. The sealed envelope should be delivered to the department office. Do not look at the forms until after you have submitted your final grades.

Administering the Questionnaire Online

Consider distributing and collecting rating forms online. Researchers report that online course ratings provide quicker feedback to faculty, assure student anonymity, yield longer and more thoughtful comments about the course, allow for customized forms and reports, reduce staff time for processing, and minimize errors. Students prefer online surveys to paper-and-pencil questionnaires, and online surveys have been shown to have no bias or a slight positive bias on students' ratings of instructors. For descriptions of ratings software, both commercial and open source, see the Brigham Young University site OnSET (onset.byu.edu), which serves as a clearinghouse for resources about online student ratings. (Sources: Anderson et al., 2005; Dommeyer et al., 2002; Dommeyer et al., 2004; Gamliel and Davidovitz, 2005; Heath et al., 2007; Johnson, 2003; Layne et al., 1999; Sorenson and Johnson, 2003)

Announce the dates of the evaluation period. Online surveys can be scheduled for the seven- to ten-day period at the end of the term. To reinforce the importance of this activity, highlight the evaluation period in the course syllabus. If your institution has a mechanism that requires students to complete the ratings forms before they see their course grades, you can ask students to submit their course evaluations after they have completed their final exams.

Identify incentives for increasing response rates. One challenge in using online rating forms is attaining a high response rate. Reasons for low response rates with online forms include perceived lack of anonymity, lack of time, apathy, inconvenience, and technical problems (Clark et al., 2005). The following strategies can increase response rates to what is typical for paper-and-pencil administration on your campus (Ballantyne, 2003; Dommeyer, et al., 2004; Johnson, 2003):

- Make completing the rating form (or going to the Web site and opting out) an ungraded class requirement.
- Tell students why you are using an online form and make sure they know how to access it.
- Demonstrate in class how to complete the online form.
- Remind students about the rating form during the evaluation period, and send them an e-mail reminder a day or two before the survey period ends.
- Emphasize that you value students' opinions and that the results will be used to improve instruction.
- Offer an incentive such as extra-credit points for participation, with the proviso that 80–90 percent of the class has to complete the form for any student to receive extra credit.
- Use class time to have students complete the ratings forms on their laptops, mobile learning devices or in a computer lab.
- Give students access to the results of selected items for choosing future courses.
- Give students early access to their grades if they complete an online rating form (or opt out from completing the form at the Web site).

- Enter students in a raffle with a meaningful prize (for example, bookstore coupons, early course registration).
- Provide a positive incentive such as contributions to a charity for each form completed.
- Explain how the system preserves students' anonymity and remind them that you will not see the results until after you submit your grades.

Summarizing Responses

Complete the questionnaire that your students used. Before looking at the ratings your students submitted, complete the form yourself. In most cases, your self-evaluation will be more positive than students' ratings. In comparing students' ratings and your self-evaluation, focus on any discrepancies and on the areas in which you gave yourself the lowest scores. (Source: Centra, 1993)

Calculate the response rate. If your department does not summarize the data for you, divide the number of completed forms by the total class enrollment (for example, 80 forms divided by 110 students = .73, or 73 percent). Experts recommend that when fewer than two-thirds of the students in classes of one hundred or less or fewer than half the students in classes of more than a hundred submit forms, the data should be interpreted cautiously for personnel decisions. (Sources: Cashin, 1999; Theall and Franklin, 1990)

Decide whether to aggregate the data. Combining an instructor's ratings for different courses may obscure differences in teaching effectiveness and may raise questions about the proper weighting of the responses in each course. Aggregating data for several offerings of the same course may obscure long-term trends, both positive and negative. Whether data are kept separate or combined, for the fullest picture of your teaching, use results from at least two courses every term for at least two years for making personnel decisions. (Source: Cashin, 1999)

Do not summarize data if there are fewer than ten questionnaires. Student questionnaires from small seminars may be accumulated over several terms and summarized when their numbers are sufficiently large. (Source: Cashin, 1999)

Prepare summary statistics for the quantifiable questions. The summary should include the frequency distribution of student ratings for each item (the number and percentage of students selecting each response) and the average response, either the mean or the median. If your department uses an automated summary program, the report may also include the standard deviation (an index of agreement or disagreement among respondents).

Summarize the narrative comments. The summary should reflect both the range and the preponderance of comments. The students most likely to respond to open-ended questions are those at the extremes: very satisfied or very dissatisfied. To prepare a summary, read all the students' comments about a single question, develop categories or headings that meaningfully group most of the comments, and tally the number of comments in each category. Resist the inclination to focus on one piercing negative comment to the exclusion of the positive remarks from most of the class. (Source: Theall and Franklin, 1991)

Interpreting Responses

For quantifiable questions, determine the percentage of omitted responses. Students may have skipped items that they think do not apply to the course. Items with low response rates should be ignored or interpreted cautiously.

Look at the average ratings for the quantifiable questions. Average ratings can be interpreted on an absolute scale and in relation to the ratings of other similar courses and instructors, although it is often difficult to establish comparison groups. Perhaps the best comparative information comes from noticing changes in the ratings of a course you have taught several times. (Source: Kulik, 1991)

Look at the range of student responses for the quantifiable questions. For example, the average rating on an item may be 3.5 on a 5-point scale, but it is worth noticing whether all students rated the item as 3 or 4, or whether some 1 and 2 ratings were balanced out by some 5s. If ratings for an item cluster at the two ends of the scale, think about why that aspect of your teaching works for only one group of students and try to formulate an alternative approach. The standard deviation also provides useful information. A standard deviation of less than 1.0 (on a 5-point scale) indicates relatively good agreement among the respondents. (Source: Theall and Franklin, 1990)

Note your highest and lowest rated items. By focusing on your highest and lowest rated items, you can determine whether your strengths and weaknesses cluster in patterns. It is usually cause for concern when a third or more of the students give low ratings to some aspect of a course. (Source: Kulik, 1991)

Be prepared to read some upsetting or hurtful comments. All instructors, even the most accomplished, encounter comments that are particularly painful, stinging, or unfair. When you receive such comments, put them aside until your emotions subside. Ask yourself what might have influenced a student to write the comments, and whether the comments capture something relevant to your teaching. Some comments may contain a constructive kernel; others simply reflect a student's immaturity, frustration, and general unhappiness. A campus faculty development specialist or supportive faculty colleague can help put such comments in perspective.

Use the open-ended comments to identify specific problems. Look for specific complaints—for example, student anxiety about the difficulty of exams. If the complaint seems justified, make a plan to address the problem. Keep in mind that students are better at spotting problems than at making detailed suggestions for improvement. If you have the time or can prevail upon an experienced teaching consultant, you could analyze open-ended comments using a grid technique, a method for determining whether students who rate a course highly are saying the same things as those who rate the course lower, which can help you more effectively interpret and make use of students' comments. (Sources: Braskamp et al., 1984; Lewis, 2001)

Consider how characteristics of a course can influence ratings. Small classes, electives, and courses in the humanities tend to receive more favorable ratings. You are also likely to find that the course you most enjoy teaching and the courses you teach frequently receive better ratings than the course you taught only at the request of the department chair.

Public Availability of Results

Be aware and beware of commercial Web sites that rate faculty members. Commercial sites have no safeguards to ensure that the comments are from students who enrolled in a given course or are even enrolled at your college or university. Further, the questions they pose do not encourage thoughtful and careful responses, and they may have no relationship to research findings on effective teaching. Some faculty, however, regularly check these sites to obtain information otherwise unavailable to them. (Sources: Heyden and Henthorne, 2002; Lang, 2003)

Consider making some of your ratings available to students. Some departments and campuses make some or all ratings available to students, who use the information to select courses. Topics of particular interest to students include workload, fairness of grading, extent of learning, instructors' responsiveness to e-mails, timeliness of returning exams and homework, explicitness about course policies, and difficulty of the course.

Some believe that because faculty members may work harder at their teaching when they know the results are on view to their peers and to students, teaching is of higher quality when the rating forms are publicly available. Further, if institutions make data public, students will be less likely to rely on information from commercial sites which can mischaracterize a faculty member's teaching. In addition, some researchers argue that it is unethical to deny students the opportunity to view the results of ratings they have contributed to.

Against these advantages are faculty concerns about invasion of privacy, potential embarrassment over low ratings, and the real or perceived tendency to lower academic standards to obtain favorable evaluations. It is unknown whether public release of teaching ratings inhibits or enhances the improvement of poor teachers.

Because of legal issues, teaching evaluations cannot be made public without faculty permission. (Sources: Coladarci and Kornfield, 2007; Dunegan and Hrivnak, 2003; Howell and Symbaluk, 2001; Robinson et al., 1996; Scriven, 1981)

References

Abrami, P. C. "Improving Judgments about Teaching Effectiveness Using Teacher Rating Forms." *New Directions for Institutional Research*, no. 109. San Francisco: Jossey-Bass, 2001, pp. 59–87.

Abrami, P. C., d'Apollonia, S., and Rosenfield, S. The Dimensionality of Student Ratings of Instruction: What We Know and What We Do Not. In J. Smart (Ed.), *Higher Education Handbook of Theory and Research.* Vol. XI. New York: Agathon Press, 1996.

Andersen, H. M., Cain, J., and Bird, E. "Online Student Course Evaluations: Review of Literature and a Pilot Study." *American Journal of Pharmaceutical Education*, 2005, *69*(1), 34–43.

Andersen, K., and Miller, E. D. "Gender and Student Evaluations of Teaching." *PS: Political Science and Politics*, 1997, *30*(2), 216–219.

Arreola, R. A. *Developing a Comprehensive Faculty Evaluation System.* San Francisco: Jossey-Bass, 2000.

Bain, K. *What the Best College Teachers Do.* Cambridge, MA: Harvard University Press, 2004.

Ballantyne, C. "Online Evaluations of Teaching: An Examination of Current Practice and Considerations for the Future." *New Directions for Teaching and Learning.* no. 96. San Francisco: Jossey-Bass, 2003, pp. 103–112.

Basow, S. A. "Student Evaluations of College Professors: When Gender Matters." *Journal of Educational Psychology*, 1995, *87*(4), 656–665.

Berk, R. A. *Thirteen Strategies to Measure College Teaching.* Sterling, VA: Stylus, 2006.

Blackhart, G. C., Peruche, B. M., DeWall, C. N., and Joiner, T. E. "Factors Influencing Teaching Evaluations in Higher Education." *Teaching of Psychology*, 2006, *33*(1), 37–39.

Braskamp, L. A., Brandenburg, D. C., and Ory, J. C. *Evaluating Teaching Effectiveness: A Practical Guide.* Newbury Park, CA: Sage, 1984.

Braskamp, L. A., and Ory, J. C. *Assessing Faculty Work: Enhancing Individual and Institutional Performance.* San Francisco: Jossey-Bass, 1994.

Cashin, W. E. Student Ratings of Teaching: Uses and Misuses. In P. Seldin and associates (Eds.), *Changing Practices in Evaluating Teaching.* San Francisco: Jossey-Bass, 1999.

Cashin, W. E., and Downey, R. G. "Using Global Rating Items for Summative Evaluation." *Journal of Educational Psychology*, 1992, *84*(4), 563–572.

Centra, J. A. *Reflective Faculty Evaluation: Enhancing Teaching and Determining Faculty Effectiveness.* San Francisco: Jossey-Bass, 1993.

Centra, J. A. "Will Teachers Receive Higher Student Evaluations by Giving Higher Grades and Less Course Work?" *Research in Higher Education*, 2003, *44*(5), 495–518.

Centra. J. A., and Gaubatz, N. B. "Is There Gender Bias in Student Evaluations of Teaching?" *Journal of Higher Education*, 2000, *71*(1), 17–33.

Chen, Y., and Hoshower, L. B. "Student Evaluation of Teaching Effectiveness: An Assessment of Student Perception and Motivation." *Assessment and Evaluation in Higher Education*, 2003, *28*(1), 71–87.

Clark, S. J., Reiner, C. M., and Johnson, T. D. Online Course Ratings and the Personnel Evaluation Standards. In D. D. Williams, M. Hricko, and S. L. Howell (Eds.), *Online Assessment, Measurement, and Evaluation: Emerging Practices.* Vol. 3. Hershey, PA: Idea Group Publishing, 2005.

Cohen, P. A. "Student Ratings of Instruction and Student Achievement." *Review of Educational Research*, 1981, 51(3), 281–309.

Coladarci, T., and Kornfield, I. "Ratemyprofessors.com versus Formal In-Class Student Evaluations of Teaching." *Practical Assessment, Research and Evaluation*, 2007, *12*(6). http://pareonline.net/pdf/v12n6.pdf

Cramer, K. M., and Alexitch, L. R. "Student Evaluation of College Professors: Identifying Sources of Bias." *Canadian Journal of Higher Education*, 2000, *30*(2), 143–164.

d'Apollonia, S., and Abrami, P. C. "Navigating Student Ratings of Instruction." *American Psychologist*, 1997, *52*(11), 1198–1208.

Dee, K. C. "Student Perceptions of High Course Workloads Are Not Associated with Poor Student Evaluations of Instructor Performance." *Journal of Engineering Education*, 2007, *96*(1), 69–78.

Dillman, D. A. *Mail and Internet Surveys: The Tailored Design Method.* (2nd ed.) Hoboken, NJ: Wiley, 2007.

Dommeyer, C. J., Baum, P., Chapman, K. S., and Hanna, R. W. "Attitudes of Business Faculty towards Two Methods of Collecting Teaching Evaluations: Paper vs. Online." *Assessment and Evaluation in Higher Education*, 2002, *27*(5), 455–462.

Dommeyer, C. J., Baum, P., Hanna, R. W., and Chapman, K. S. "Gathering Faculty Teaching Evaluations by In-Class and Online Surveys: Their Effects on Response Rates and Evaluations." *Assessment and Evaluation in Higher Education*, 2004, *29*(5), 611–623.

Dunegan, K. J., and Hrivnak, M. W. "Characteristics of Mindless Teaching Evaluations and the Moderating Effects of Image Compatibility." *Journal of Management Education*, 2003, *27*(3), 280–303.

Emerson, J. D., Mosteller, F., and Youtz, C. Students Can Help Improve College Teaching: A Review and an Agenda for the Statistics Profession. In C. R. Rao and G. J. Szekely (Eds.), *Statistics for the 21st Century.* New York: Marcel Dekker, 2000.

Feldman, K. A. Identifying Exemplary Teachers and Teaching: Evidence from Student Ratings. In R. P. Perry and J. C. Smart (Eds.), *Effective Teaching in Higher Education: Research and Practice.* New York: Agathon Press, 1997.

Forsyth, D. R. *The Professor's Guide to Teaching: Psychological Principles and Practices.* Washington, DC: American Psychological Association, 2003.

Franklin, J. "Interpreting the Numbers: Using a Narrative to Help Others Read Student Evaluations of Your Teaching Accurately." *New Directions for Teaching and Learning,* no. 87. San Francisco: Jossey-Bass, 2001, pp. 85–100.

Fries, C. J., and McNinch, R. J. "Signed versus Unsigned Student Evaluations of Teaching: A Comparison." *Teaching Sociology,* 2003, *31*(3), 333–344.

Gamliel, E., and Davidovitz, L. "Online versus Traditional Teaching Evaluation." *Assessment and Evaluation in Higher Education,* 2005, *30*(6), 581–592.

Germain, M., and Scandura, T. A. "Grade Inflation and Student Individual Differences as Systematic Bias in Faculty Evaluations." *Journal of Instructional Psychology,* 2005, *32*(1), 58–67.

Greenwald, A. G., and Gillmore, G. M. "Grading Leniency is a Removable Contaminant of Student Ratings." *American Psychologist,* 1997, *52*(11) 1209–1217.

Gurung, R.A.R., and Vespia, K. M. "Looking Good, Teaching Well? Linking Liking, Looks, and Learning." *Teaching of Psychology,* 2007, *34*(1), 5–10.

Hampton, S. E., and Reiser, R. A. "Effects of a Theory-Based Feedback and Consultation Process on Instruction and Learning in College Classrooms." *Research in Higher Education,* 2004, *45*(5), 497–527.

Heath, N. M., Lawyer, S. R., and Rasmussen, E. B. "Web-Based versus Paper-and-Pencil Course Evaluations." *Teaching of Psychology,* 2007, *34*(4), 259–261.

Heyden, T., and Henthorne, T. "What a @%#": Listening to What Students Say about Their Composition Teachers Online." *Teaching English in the Two-Year College,* 2002, *30*(2), 156–161.

Hoffman, F., and Oreopoulos, P. *Professor Qualities and Student Achievement.* NBER Working Paper, no. 12596. Cambridge, MA: National Bureau of Economic Research, 2006.

Howell, A. J., and Symbaluk, D. G. "Published Student Ratings of Instruction: Revealing and Reconciling the Views of Students and Faculty." *Journal of Educational Psychology,* 2001, *93*(4), 790–796.

Jacobson, W. H., and Lawrence, M. Aligning Evaluation Practices. In D. H. Wulff (Ed.), *Aligning for Learning: Strategies for Teaching Effectiveness.* San Francisco: Jossey-Bass, 2005.

Johnson, T. D. "Online Student Ratings: Will Students Respond?" *New Directions for Teaching and Learning,* no. 96. San Francisco: Jossey-Bass, 2003, pp. 49–59.

Kember, D., Leung, D.Y.P., and Kwan, K. P. "Does the Use of Student Feedback Questionnaires Improve the Overall Quality of Teaching?" *Assessment and Evaluation in Higher Education,* 2002, *27*(5), 411–425.

Koon, J., and Murray, H. G. "Using Multiple Outcomes to Validate Student Ratings of Overall Teacher Effectiveness." *Journal of Higher Education,* 1995, *66*(1), 61–81.

Kulik, J. A. *Student Ratings of Instruction.* CRLT Occasional Paper, no. 4. Ann Arbor: Center for Research on Learning and Teaching, University of Michigan, 1991.

Kulik, J. A. "Student Ratings: Validity, Utility, and Controversy." *New Directions for Institutional Research,* no. 109. San Francisco: Jossey-Bass, Spring 2001, pp. 9–25.

Lang, J. M. "RateMyBuns.com." *Chronicle of Higher Education,* Dec. 1, 2003.

Layne, B. H., DeCristoforo, J. R., and McGinty, D. "Electronic versus Traditional Student Ratings of Instruction." *Research in Higher Education,* 1999, *40*(2), 221–232.

Lewis, K. G. "Making Sense of Student Written Comments." *New Directions for Teaching and Learning,* no. 87. San Francisco: Jossey-Bass, 2001, pp. 25–32.

Liddle, B. J. "Coming Out in Class: Disclosure of Sexual Orientation and Teaching Evaluations." *Teaching of Psychology*, 1997, *24*(1), 32–35.

Lowman, J. *Mastering the Techniques of Teaching*. (2nd ed.) San Francisco: Jossey-Bass, 1995.

Marincovich, M. Using Student Feedback to Improve Teaching. In P. Seldin and associates (Eds.), *Changing Practices in Evaluating Teaching*. San Francisco: Jossey-Bass, 1999.

Marsh, H. W. "Distinguishing between Good (Useful) and Bad Workloads on Students' Evaluation of Teaching." *American Educational Research Journal*, 2001, *38*(1), 183–212.

Marsh, H. W. "Do University Teachers Become More Effective with Experience? A Multilevel Growth Model of Students' Evaluations of Teaching over 13 Years." *Journal of Educational Psychology*, 2007, *99*(4), 775–790.

Marsh, H. W., and Dunkin, M. J. Students' Evaluations of University Teaching: A Multidimensional Perspective. In J. C. Smart (Ed.), *Higher Education: A Handbook of Theory and Research*. Vol. 8. New York: Agathon Press, 1992.

Marsh, H. W., and Roche, L. A. "Making Students' Evaluations of Teaching Effectiveness Effective." *American Psychologist*, 1997, *52*(11), 1187–1197.

Marsh, H. W., and Roche, L. A. "Effects of Grading Leniency and Low Workload on Students' Evaluations of Teaching: Popular Myth, Bias, Validity, or Innocent Bystanders?" *Journal of Educational Psychology*, 2000, *92*(1), 202–228.

McKeachie, W. J. "Student Ratings: The Validity of Use." *American Psychologist*, 1997, *52*(11), 1218–1225.

McKeachie, W. J., and Svinicki. M. *McKeachie's Teaching Tips*. (12th ed.) Boston: Houghton Mifflin, 2006.

Nasser, F., and Fresko, B. "Faculty Views of Student Evaluation of College Teaching." *Assessment and Evaluation in Higher Education*, 2002, *27*(2), 187–198.

National Research Council. *Evaluating and Improving Undergraduate Teaching in Science, Technology, Engineering, and Mathematics*. Washington, DC: National Academies Press, 2003.

Ory, J. C. "Faculty Thoughts and Concerns about Student Ratings." *New Directions for Teaching and Learning*, no. 87. San Francisco: Jossey-Bass, 2001, pp. 3–15.

Overall, J. U., and Marsh, H. W. "Students' Evaluations of Instruction: A Longitudinal Study of Their Stability." *Journal of Educational Psychology*, 1980, *72*(3), 321–325.

Robinson, R. K., Canty, A., and Fink, R. L. "Public Disclosure of Teaching Evaluations: Privacy and Liability Considerations." *Journal of Education for Business*, 1996, no. 71, 284–287.

Schmelkin, L. P., Spencer, K. J., and Gellman, E. S. "Faculty Perspectives on Course and Teacher Evaluations." *Research in Higher Education*, 1997, *38*(5), 575–592.

Scriven, M. Summative Teacher Evaluation. In J. Millman (Ed.), *Handbook of Teacher Evaluation*. Beverly Hills: Sage, 1981.

Scriven, M. "Student Ratings Offer Useful Input to Teacher Evaluations." *Practical Assessment, Research and Evaluation*, 1995, *4*(7). (Available from ERIC Digests, ED 398240, 1995)

Sorenson, D. L., and Johnson, T. D (Eds.). "Online Student Ratings of Instruction." *New Directions for Teaching and Learning*, no. 96. San Francisco: Jossey-Bass. 2003.

Stake, R. E., and Cisneros-Cohernour, E. J. "Situational Evaluation of Teaching on Campus." *New Directions for Teaching and Learning*, no. 83. San Francisco: Jossey-Bass, 2000, pp. 51–72.

Tagomori, H. T., and Bishop, L. A. "Student Evaluation of Teaching: Flaws in the Instruments." *Thought & Action*, 1995, *11*(1), 63–78.

Theall, M., and Franklin, J. (Eds.). *Student Ratings of Instruction: Issues for Improving Practice*. New Directions for Teaching and Learning, no. 43. San Francisco: Jossey-Bass. 1990.

Theall, M., and Franklin, J. "Using Student Ratings for Teaching Improvement." *New Directions for Teaching and Learning*, no. 48. San Francisco: Jossey-Bass, 1991, pp. 83–96.

Trout, P. A. "Flunking the Test: The Dismal Record of Student Evaluations." *Academe*, 2000, *86*(4), 58–61.

Wachtel, H. K. "Student Evaluations of College Teaching Effectiveness: A Brief Review." *Assessment and Evaluation in Higher Education*, 1998, *23*(2), 191–211.

Weinberg, B. A., Fleisher, B. M., and Hashimoto, M. *Evaluating Methods for Evaluating Instruction: The Case of Higher Education*. NBER Working Paper, no. 12844. Cambridge, MA: National Bureau of Economic Research, 2007.

Williams, W. M., and Ceci, S. J. "'How'm I doing?' Problems with Student Ratings of Instructors and Courses." *Change*, 1997, *29*(5), 12–23.

Yunker, P. J., and Yunker, J. A. "Are Student Evaluations of Teaching Valid? Evidence from an Analytical Business Core Course." *Journal of Education for Business*, 2003, *78*(6), 313–318.

Writing Letters of Recommendation for Students

As a faculty member, you will be asked to write letters or serve as a reference for students who are applying for fellowships, graduate school, and employment. If you do not know a student well or have a lukewarm opinion of his or her work, tell the student that you will be unable to write a persuasive letter of recommendation and ask the student to turn to someone else. If you agree to write the letter, here are some suggestions for composing an effective recommendation.

General Strategies

Let students know the general tone of what you are likely to write. Especially if your letter will include reservations, let the student know in private what you plan to say so that he or she can decide whether to use you as a reference. One faculty member tells students he doesn't know that he can write only a standard letter, describing the nature and rigor of the course, the grade the student earned, and the student's rank out of a class of two hundred. He advises students that this type of letter is not nearly as helpful as a letter from someone who can write a more personal appraisal.

Make the letter personal. The most effective recommendation conveys a well-rounded assessment of a student's performance. Use anecdotes, observations, and specific examples to give weight to your appraisal. In preparation for writing the letter, ask the student (orally or in writing) to describe his or her strengths and give examples of these, and to list areas needing improvement. Some faculty ask the student for a brief résumé, a statement of purpose, an unofficial transcript, or a list of career goals, accomplishments, or ambitions. Ask whether there are specific items that the student feels should be mentioned in the letter.

Remember that students have a right to see your letter. Federal law gives students the right to see a copy of a letter of recommendation or to sign a waiver of that right. The extent to which letters are confidential, even if a student signs a waiver, is unclear, although litigation appears rare. Some graduate school admissions officers give little weight to letters that are not accompanied by a waiver; others do not care. (Sources: Appleby, 2005; Rosovsky and Hartley, 2002)

Obtain the student's consent before you write a letter. If a third party requests a letter because you have been listed as a reference, check with the student to see if the student is still pursuing the position. Of course, courteous students let you know in advance that they are listing you as a reference. (Sources: Swensen and Keith-Spiegel, 1991)

Getting Ready to Write

Determine whether there is a specific form or format. Some graduate schools or fellowship programs request that letters be submitted on a special form. Make sure you have all the information you need, including where to send the letter and the deadline. If the student requests more than one letter from you, keep materials for each institution separate.

Ask the student to describe the job or program. To write an effective letter, you will need a description of the job or graduate program, as well as a sense of why the student decided to apply there. Ask questions like "What attracted you to this program at this graduate school?" or "Where do you see this particular job or company fitting into your career goals?"

Ask the student to provide you with copies of papers submitted for your course, preferably with your comments. Refer to these papers as you write about the student's intellectual ability, academic skills, and the like. (Have the student include a self-addressed stamped envelope so that you can return the papers.)

Review your old grade books or records. Some faculty note both good and not-so-good points about students in the their course records immediately after the conclusion of the term. (Source: Humphreys and Wickersham, 1988)

Preparing the Letter

Limit the letter to one or two pages. Anything longer than two pages imposes on the goodwill of the readers, and anything shorter than a page may convey a lack of enthusiasm for the student. Some experienced letter readers look at the signature, read the last paragraph, and then decide whether to read the rest of the letter. (Sources: Appleby, 2005; Palmer, 1983)

Explain how you know the student and your relationship. State how long you have known the student, how well, and in what capacity (for example, former student, advisee, or research assistant). Have you worked closely with the student or only observed his or her classroom performance? If the student served as a research assistant, describe the specific responsibilities that relate to the job or graduate school.

Tailor the letter to the specific job opening or academic program. Explain why you believe the student has the potential to succeed at this particular job or school. If a student is applying for a job, try to translate the student's academic skills into business skills—for example, an outstanding group project demonstrates the capacity to work as part of a team. Focus on the most relevant clusters of abilities and knowledge (adapted from Appleby, 2005; Kiernan, 2004; Office of Instructional Development, 1988; Wolke, 1988; Workman et al., 2005):

- *Intellectual ability* compared to that of other students you have taught
- *Creativity and capacity for independent, original thought*
- *Academic and analytic skills,* capacity for learning and applying information and for addressing complex or abstract matters
- *Knowledge of the field of study*
- *Attitude toward academic work,* including intellectual curiosity, attitude toward learning, class participation, and diligence in completing assignments
- *Performance in applied settings,* such as laboratories or clinical situations
- *Communication skills,* speaking, and writing
- *Leadership:* ability to direct, organize, take charge
- *Ability to work as part of a team and interpersonal skills*
- *Initiative, motivation, and persistence*
- *Responsibility and dedication*
- *Personal characteristics:* maturity, dependability, honesty, integrity, sensitivity, empathy, sincerity, responsiveness to constructive criticism, professionalism
- *Personal achievements* or activities
- *Self-awareness of strengths and weaknesses*
- *Special circumstances* that may have affected the student's performance

Be specific. Instead of saying "an excellent student," offer a comparative assessment: "the best student in a class of twenty-five" or "among the top ten students I have taught at this institution." "Good communication skills" could be sharpened to "articulate in class discussions" or "writes well-organized and forceful analyses." Illustrate your appraisal with a supporting example or anecdote. For instance, if you are writing a letter of recommendation for a graduate student seeking a teaching position, describe how the candidate draws students into the discussion, responds to students' questions, or handles tough teaching situations.

Here is another example (adapted from Swensen and Keith-Spiegel, 1991, p. 1). Rather than saying, "Rita performed well in my social psychology course and was one of the best students in the class; she will likely be a good teacher," support your observations with facts and details: "In the research project assignment, Rita developed a well-defined hypothesis and created a design that was more feasible within the time and budgetary constraints than the other students in the course. Her oral presentation of her project was clear and thoughtful. It was illustrated by several interesting and appropriate examples that held students' attention throughout the fifteen-minute period. Based on these observations, I predict she will be an outstanding instructor."

Distinguish between opinion and facts. Use facts to support your opinions and observations and strive for factual accuracy.

Present a balanced picture. Observers have noted a disturbing increase in lofty rhetoric, excessive praise, and over-inflated superlatives. Gushing letters may mar your credibility as a recommender, and thus hurt the students you want to help. A better course is to temper any tendencies to overstate strengths and to mention those areas in which the candidate can be expected to improve, grow, and develop. Honest appraisals that accurately portray a student's skills, achievements, productivity, weaknesses, and promise carry more weight. (Sources: Grote et al., 2001; Office of Instructional Development, 1988; Palmer, 1983; Rosovsky and Hartley, 2002; Smith, 1998; Workman et al., 2005)

Provide evidence for negative comments. Try to put weaknesses in context: "Addy was insecure during the first year, which may account for some low grades, but she has since gained confidence and skills and has done quite well."

Here is another example of a specific description of weaknesses (adapted from Swensen and Keith-Spiegel, 1991, p. 1). Instead of saying, "Bailey was a mediocre student, not really interested in class," say, "Bailey scored below 70 percent on the two midterms and the final exam. The class average was more than 80 percent. (Enrollment was 120.) Her research paper was not organized and omitted important components, such as a review of the literature and directions for future research."

Avoid personal remarks. Do not mention age, ethnicity, appearance, religion, citizenship status, national origin, marital or parental status, physical characteristics, or other personal attributes. If a student has successfully balanced academic work and family responsibilities, ask the student if he or she wants that information included in the letter.

Rewrite statements that admit misinterpretation. Here are some examples from Yager et al. (1984) cited in Swensen and Keith-Spiegel (1991, p. 2):

- "He worked hard to improve himself and he did." *(What was he like when he started?)*
- "She demonstrated a commitment to excellence in those areas that draw her interest." *(What about those that don't?)*
- "She showed considerable progress." *(From what to what?)*
- "He was particularly effective in . . ." *(And mediocre or poor in other aspects?)*

Conclude with an overall recommendation. Indicate how well qualified the student is for the job or graduate program. Stress his or her potential or probable performance, if you can. Comment on whether you would choose the applicant for graduate study or for a career position.

Add that you welcome requests for more information. Include your contact information. Veteran letter readers will see this as a sign that you feel strongly about the candidate. (Source: Palmer, 1983)

Carefully proofread your letter. Be sure names are spelled correctly and dates and facts are accurate.

Using Online Systems to Submit Letters

Understand the online submission process. Many graduate schools use online systems, either proprietary or commercial, and some no longer accept nonelectronic letters. After you agree to write the letter, the student submits your e-mail address to the program, which then sends you a Web page address. You are given the choice of typing comments directly into the online form or uploading a word-processing file that will be reformatted into an electronic facsimile of the paper form. The typical form contains both multiple-choice and open-ended questions. Students can check the Web site to see whether letters have been submitted, but they cannot view the letters. (Source: Kiernan, 2004)

Recognize the limitations of online systems. Paper forms allow respondents to ignore the standardized questions and substitute a narrative letter. In contrast, most online systems will not accept a recommendation if questions are left unanswered, and some systems limit the space for open-ended comments. Some faculty have concerns about security, especially in third-party vendor sites: Do the letters remain online indefinitely? Can hackers compromise the system? Can students provide bogus e-mail addresses and generate fraudulent recommendations? Vendors point out that fraudulent paper recommendations are possible and that they have instituted safeguards to detect problem submissions. (Source: Kiernan, 2004)

Following Up

Ask about the results. Ask the student to inform you about whether the application was successful.

Save copies of your letters of recommendation. Copies are useful if the recipient contacts you for further information or if the same student requests another letter. You can also use past letters as guides for writing new ones.

References

Appleby, D. C. "A Developmental Strategy to Write Effective Letters of Recommendation." *APS Observer*, May 2005, *18*(5), 35–36, 45–47.

Grote, C. L., Robiner, W. N., and Haut, A. "Disclosure of Negative Information in Letters of Recommendation: Writers' Intentions and Readers' Experiences." *Professional Psychology: Research and Practice*, 2001, *32*, 655–661.

Humphreys, L., and Wickersham, B. Letters of Recommendation. In J. Janes and D. Hauer (Eds.), *Now What?* Littleton, MA: Copley, 1988.

Kiernan, V. "If You Like This Student, Click Here." *Chronicle of Higher Education*, June 4, 2004, A23.

Office of Instructional Development. Letters of Recommendation. In J. Janes and D. Hauer (Eds.), *Now What?* Littleton, MA: Copley, 1988.

Palmer, S. E. "What to Say in a Letter of Recommendation? Sometimes What You Don't Say Matters Most." *Chronicle of Higher Education*, Sept. 7, 1983, 21–22.

Rosovsky, H., and Hartley, M. *Evaluation and the Academy: Are We Doing the Right Thing?* Cambridge, MA: American Academy of Arts and Sciences, 2002.

Smith, C. "Beware the Pitfalls of Letters of Recommendation." *Chronicle of Higher Education*, March 20, 1998, A56.

Swensen, E. V., and Keith-Spiegel, P. *Writing Letters of Recommendation for Students: How to Protect Yourself from Liability*. Washington, DC: American Psychological Association, 1991.

Wolke, R. Writing Letters of Recommendation. In J. Janes and D. Hauer (Eds.), *Now What?* Littleton, MA: Copley, 1988.

Workman, J., Oeltmann, T., and Elam, C. "Composing a Letter of Evaluation that Captures the Applicant as an Individual." *The Advisor*, Mar. 2005, *25*(1), 20–26.